HANDBOOK OF

Academic Learning

Construction of Knowledge

This is a volume in the Academic Press
EDUCATIONAL PSYCHOLOGY SERIES

Critical comprehensive reviews of research knowledge, theories, principles, and practices

Under the editorship of Gary D. Phye

HANDBOOK OF Academic Learning

Construction of Knowledge

EDITED BY

Gary D. Phye

Department of Psychology
Iowa State University
Ames, Iowa

ACADEMIC PRESS

San Diego London Boston New York Sydney Tokyo Toronto

This book is printed on acid-free paper. ∞

Academic Press, Inc.
525 B Street, Suite 1900, San Diego, California 92101-4495, USA
http://www.apnet.com

Academic Press Limited
24-28 Oval Road, London NW1 7DX, UK
http://www.hbuk.co.uk/ap/

Library of Congress Cataloging-in-Publication Data

Handbook of academic learning / edited by Gary D. Phye.
p. cm. -- (The educational psychology series)
Includes bibliographical references and index.
ISBN 0-12-554255-0 (case: alk. paper) ISBN 0-12-665256-9 (paper: alk. paper)
1. Learning, Psychology of. 2. Constructivism (Education)
3. Thought and thinking--Study and teaching. I. Phye, Gary D.
II. Series: Educational psychology.
LB1060.H3456 1996 96-8681
CIP

PRINTED IN THE UNITED STATES OF AMERICA
96 97 98 99 00 01 BC 9 8 7 6 5 4 3 2 1

Contents

I

Academic Learning

Perspectives, Theory, and Models

1. THE SOCIAL CONSTRUCTION OF LEARNING

Eric Bredo

2. LEARNING AND REMEMBERING: THE BASIS FOR PERSONAL KNOWLEDGE CONSTRUCTION

Gary D. Phye

3. SCHOOL LEARNING AND MOTIVATION

Myron H. Dembo and Martin J. Eaton

7. A COGNITIVE PERSPECTIVE ON THE ASSESSMENT, DIAGNOSIS, AND REMEDIATION OF READING SKILLS

James M. Royer

8. PSYCHOLOGICAL FOUNDATIONS OF ELEMENTARY WRITING INSTRUCTION

Stephen L. Benton

9. TEACHING COMPOSITION: CURRENT THEORIES AND PRACTICES

Rebecca E. Burnett and Lee-Ann Marie Kastman

10. DEVELOPING STUDENT UNDERSTANDING IN ELEMENTARY SCHOOL MATHEMATICS: A COGNITIVE PERSPECTIVE

Megan Loef Franke and Douglas A. Grouws

11. MATHEMATICS (GRADES 7–12)

Steven R. Williams

12. THE TEACHING AND LEARNING OF ELEMENTARY SCIENCE

Kenneth Tobin

13. MEANINGFUL LEARNING IN SCIENCE: THE HUMAN CONSTRUCTIVIST PERSPECTIVE

Joel J. Mintzes, James H. Wandersee, and Joseph D. Novak

III

Learning to Learn

14. INDUCTIVE REASONING AND PROBLEM SOLVING: THE EARLY GRADES

Gary D. Phye

15. INCORPORATING PROBLEM SOLVING INTO SECONDARY SCHOOL CURRICULA

Richard E. Mayer

16. CRITICAL THINKING: LEARNING TO TALK ABOUT TALK AND TEXT

David R. Olson

IV

Assessment of Classroom Learning

17. CLASSROOM ASSESSMENT

William D. Schafer

18. ASSESSING CLASSROOM LEARNING POTENTIAL

J. H. M. *Hamers and* A. J. J. M. *Ruijssenaars*

19. REFLECTIONS ON PORTFOLIOS

Vicki Spandel

20. EPILOGUE: CLASSROOM LEARNING, LOOKING AHEAD

Contributors

Numbers in parentheses indicate the pages on which the authors' contributions begin.

Peter Afflerbach (152), Department of Curriculum and Instruction, University of Maryland, College Park, Maryland 20742

Steven L. Benton (236), College of Education, Kansas State University, Manhattan, Kansas 66506

Eric Bredo (3), Department of Leadership, Foundations, and Policy, University of Virginia, Charlottesville, Virginia 22903

Rachel Brown (152), School of Education, SUNY Buffalo, Buffalo, New York 14260

Rebecca E. Burnett (268), Department of English, Iowa State University, Ames, Iowa 50011

Myron H. Dembo (65), Department of Education, University of Southern California, 600 Philips Hall, Los Angeles, California 90089

Martin Eaton (65), Department of Education, University of Southern California, Los Angeles, California 90089

Pamela B. El-Dinary (152), Georgetown University, Washington, DC 20057

Megan Franke (310), Graduate School of Education, University of California–Los Angeles, Los Angeles, California 90095

Douglas A. Grouws (310), Department of Curriculm and Instruction, University of Iowa, Iowa City, Iowa 52242

J. H. M. Hamers (550), Department of Educational Sciences, University of Utrecht, Utrecht 3584 CS, The Netherlands

Lee-Ann Marie Kastman (268), Department of English, Iowa State University, Ames, Iowa 50011

Richard E. Mayer (474), Department of Psychology, University of California–Santa Barbara, Santa Barbara, California 93106

Joel J. Mintzes (405), Department of Biological Science, University of North Carolina, Wilmington, North Carolina 28403

Jennifer Mistretta (152), Department of Educational Psychology, School of Education, SUNY–Albany, Albany, New York 12222

David J. Mittelholtz (128), American College Testing, Iowa City, Iowa 55243

Paul D. Nichols (128), Department of Educational Psychology, University of Wisconsin–Milwaukee, Milwaukee, Wisconsin 53201

Joseph D. Novak (405), Department of Education, Cornell University, Ithaca, New York 14853

David R. Olson (493), Centre for Applied Cognitive Science, Ontario Institute for Studies in Education, University of Toronto, Toronto, Ontario M5S 1V6, Canada

Gary D. Phye (47, 452, 593), Psychology Department, Iowa State University, Ames, Iowa 50011

Michael Pressley (152), Department of Educational Psychology and Statistics, School of Education, SUNY–Albany, Albany, New York 12222

Joan Rankin (152), Department of Special Education, University of Nebraska, Lincoln, Nebraska 68583

Rafael Risemberg (106), Department of Communication and Educational Science, Kean College, Union, New Jersey 07083

James M. Royer (200), Department of Psychology, University of Massachusetts, Amherst, Massachusetts 01003

A. J. J. M. Ruijssenaars (550), Department of Education, Leiden University, Leiden, The Netherlands

William D. Schafer (513), Department of Measurement, Statistics, and Evaluation, College of Education, University of Maryland–College Park, College Park, Maryland 20742

Vicki Spandel (573), Northwest Regional Educational Laboratory, Portland, Oregon 97204

Kenneth Tobin (370), Science Education, Florida State University, Tallahassee, Florida 32306

James H. Wandersee (405), Department of Curriculum and Instruction, Louisiana State University, Baton Rouge, Louisiana 70803

Ruth Warton-McDonald (152), Department of Educational Psychology and Statistics, School of Education, SUNY–Albany, Albany, New York 12222

Steven R. Williams (343), Department of Mathematics, Brigham Young University, Provo, Utah 84602

Linda Yokoi (152), Department of Educational Psychology and Statistics, School of Education, SUNY–Albany, Albany, New York 12222

Barry Zimmerman (106), Graduate School and University Center, CUNY–New York, New York, 10036

Preface

Academic Press has a long and successful history of publishing the *Educational Psychology* series. New to this series are both myself as editor and handbooks as a type of publication within the series. The *Handbook of Academic Learning* is an effort to bridge the communication gap between theory and practice. Chapter authors are prominent authorities in their own areas of research and theory development. These individuals have been actively involved with the transformation of *theory* into *practice*. This commitment to providing a theoretically sound but practical basis for change is evident in the cogent ideas and practices provided in the chapters that follow.

This handbook focuses on classroom learning as the process responsible for the construction of academic knowledge. The volume is divided into four parts. Part I provides a theoretical basis for considering classroom learning. Constructivism is introduced as a perspective. Since constructivism is both learner centered and process oriented, the issues of learning and remembering, motivation, self-direction, and learner aptitude are introduced. In Part II, the discussion is centered on the classroom. Here, the construction of knowledge by students (constructivism) is considered within the curriculum domains of reading, writing, mathematics, and science. Part III is devoted to a consideration of the "tools" used in knowledge construction and "learning to learn." Part IV focuses on the general topic of knowledge assessment. Since effective teaching is typically defined in terms of learner outcomes, assessment is simply the last phase of effective instruction. In addition to classroom assessment, portfolio development is discussed. The assessment of learning potential is a relatively new topic in the United States. Two prominent researchers from the Netherlands provide an introduction to the assessment of learning potential in this section.

While the perspective taken throughout the handbook is one of constructivism, the construction of knowledge is approached from a developmental point of view. This is most apparent in Parts II and III. In Part II, the topics of reading, writing, mathematics, and science are addressed developmentally. Each topic is situated in terms of instruction at the elementary grades or the middle/secondary school grades. The developmental perspective is continued in Part III, where the basic tools of knowledge construction—reasoning, problem solving, and critical thinking—are presented.

I gratefully acknowledge the efforts of two persons responsible for providing the foundation for this effort. Allan J. Edwards was the originator and Editor of the *Educational Psychology* book series for Academic Press until his recent retirement. I will strive to continue the tradition of scholarship he so successfully established. I also want to thank Nikki Levy, Senior Acquisitions Editor for Academic Press. Nikki's willingness to take a chance by publishing handbooks for a new audience (the educational professional in the field) facilitates my efforts as Series Editor.

PART I

Academic Learning

Perspectives, Theory, and Models

CHAPTER

1

The Social Construction of Learning

ERIC BREDO
University of Virginia

INTRODUCTION

Contemporary learning theory faces a number of challenges. One of these arises from the split of learning theory largely into two opposing camps, behaviorist and cognitivist (Bower & Hilgard, 1981). At their most extreme, behaviorists studied bodily movement without mind, focusing on simple learning in animals such as chickens, rats, and pigeons, while cognitivists studied mind without bodily movement, as in human symbolic problem solving modeled on computers. Many textbooks are divided down the middle between these two approaches, sometimes even using two different definitions of learning in the same book. As one scholar put it, "It can reasonably be claimed that these two psychologies of learning remain separate in contemporary psychology" (Catania, 1992, p. 353).

The polarization between behaviorist and cognitivist approaches to learning creates both theoretical and practical difficulties. Theoretically, it makes it hard to understand the relationship between learning mechanical skills and more complex symbolically mediated learning. Practically, education based on such polarized views is likely to produce one-sided specialists who act in one-sided ways. Those instructing the "learning disabled" in schools, for example, tend to be trained as behaviorists, while those teaching the "gifted" tend to be trained in cognitive theory. To the extent that these become exclusive orientations, there is the danger that students of one group

Handbook of Academic Learning

will be taught to behave without thinking, and students of the other to think without practical application.

A second difficulty facing learning theory comes from an analogous split between psychological and sociocultural aspects of learning. Psychologists and sociologists have often drawn strong boundaries between their disciplines: psychologists focusing on individuals, sociologists on groups or larger social units. Since psychologists usually study learning, learning theory has often had an strongly individualistic bias. As Jerome Bruner put it,

> Too often, human learning has been depicted in the paradigm of the lone organism pitted against nature—whether in the model of the behaviorist's organism shaping up responses to fit the geometries and probabilities of the world of stimuli, or in the Piagetian model where a lone child struggles single-handed to strike some equilibrium between assimilating the world to himself or himself to the world. (1985, p. 25)

A learning theory that focuses on the "lone organism" to the exclusion of its participation in social activities is like a theory of learning to make music by oneself. Such a theory is likely to ignore all the sharing, the mutual construction, and modulation that is the essence of musical meaning. If one thinks of language use and reflective thinking as similarly social in character, like making music, then a narrowly individualistic approach to learning is likely to shortchange understanding these processes as well. The fact that behavioristic theories have tended to ignore mind while cognitive theories have tended to posit mental processes already in place lends some credence to this suspicion.[1]

Considerations such as these have led some to question the whole concept of "learning" (Catania, 1992; Newman et al., 1989; Suchman, 1992). Others have begun developing a third approach to learning, of which current work on "situated learning" is an example (Brown, Collins, & Duguid, 1989; Clancey, 1992, 1993; Lave & Wenger, 1991). Work relating to this view has been drawn from a number of sources, such as Vygotsky's sociohistorical approach to child development (Newman et al., 1989; Rogoff, 1990; Rogoff & Lave, 1984; Wertsch, 1985a, 1985b, 1991), ethnomethodology and conversational analysis (Suchman, 1987), cybernetics (Bickhard, 1992; Clancey, 1993; Varela, Thompson, & Rosch, 1991), neo-Marxist theories of practice (Lave, 1988; Lave & Wenger, 1991), and Deweyian pragmatism (Bredo, 1994; Schön, 1983).

In what follows I discuss these three approaches to learning—behaviorist, cognitivist, and situated. The discussion considers the assumptions and implications of each approach, while relating them to the different phil-

[1] Yet another difficulty comes from the strong division between "learning" and "development" (Newman, Griffin, & Cole, 1989). In the usual definitions, learning must be separable from development because it must be the "same" organism that learns over repeated trials. An organism that "develops" is in a sense a different one than before, insofar as learning is concerned. If learning and development are not analytically and empirically separable, then learning theory must become mere "change theory."

osophical traditions from which they have derived (see Case, 1991). I will also try to place each approach in at least an abbreviated historical context so that the evolution of different conceptions of learning is highlighted. To do this I will begin with a consideration of functional psychology, which flourished at the turn of the century. It is important to begin with functional psychology because much of American psychology derived from it and because it was a sophisticated attempt to integrate divisions between thinking and behaving and individual and sociocultural aspects of change which plague learning theory today.

The principal argument of this chapter is that conceptions of learning have evolved from a transactional conception evident in functional psychology, to an environment-centered conception in behaviorism, and then to an organism-centered conception is cognitivism. The functionalists' transactional conception of learning related learning to the ongoing life of an organism in an environment that it helps to coconstruct. It was an activist view of learning in which both the organism and the environment are evolving. Behaviorism, in contrast, tended to focus on the demands of an environment whose structure is fixed, while cognitivism tended to take the organism's mental structure as given. As a result, neither has had as active or evolving a view of the learner and environment as the functionalists. In the discussion, I try to show how the splits in learning theory derive from these commitments to fixed structures. I also suggest that situated learning theory may signal a return to a transactional approach, although with a more particularistic emphasis than in functional psychology. This story of the development of learning theory from transactionalism to environmental and organismic unilaterialism, and back to a form of transactionalism is told by briefly describing the work of a number of prominent psychologists and learning theorists.

While I have a personal preference for a transactional approach, a second theme of this chapter is not that it is the best, but that each approach to learning is more useful for some purposes than for others. As William James put it, "Every way of classifying a thing is but a way of handling it for some particular purpose. Conceptions, "kinds,' are teleological instruments" (James, 1897/1956, p. 70). Choice of conception of learning is similarly loaded with purpose, however implicit. The question is, "Which purpose does one want to advance and which conceptual tools are best adapted to it?" Does one want children to learn to "think" or to "behave," for example (assuming these are distinguishable)? Despite the evident importance of purposes or values in choosing among approaches to learning, their respective merits are rarely discussed in this way. Different approaches to learning tend, rather, to be evaluated on empirical or logical grounds alone. But empirical and logical considerations do not exhaust the matter, for what is at issue is not just where one has been but where one wants to go. Depending on one's aims, different tools may be relevant. This chapter is, accordingly, concerned with the uses and side effects of these different tools, these different conceptions of learning.

FUNCTIONAL PSYCHOLOGY

At the turn of the 20th century, the dominant orientation in American psychology was neither behaviorism nor cognitivism but functionalism. Perhaps because it had a pluralistic and practical orientation, functionalism has often been seen as a quintessentially American approach to psychology. Indeed, most subsequent American psychology derived from its various themes (Sahakian, 1975; Schultz, 1969).[2] Despite this, functional psychology as a school of thought has been largely forgotten today.[3]

Functional psychology developed in close conjunction with pragmatism as a philosophical movement. A number of the originators of pragmatism, such as William James, John Dewey, and George Herbert Mead, were also contributors to functional psychology.[4] Both emerged out of controversies over evolution that tended to polarize thought between those of "tough-minded" versus "tender-minded" temperaments (James, 1907/1963, pp. 8–10). The tough minded included materialists and empiricists who adopted reductionistic explanations. They tended to explain wholes in terms of their parts, viewing mind as a mechanism and complex ideas as made up of simple ideas. Their tender-minded opponents, idealists and rationalists, adopted holistic forms of explanation. They explained parts in terms of wholes, such as viewing mechanism as a product of mind and simple ideas

[2]Common functionalist themes included the notion that evolution selects individuals according to their mental capacities, that human development progresses through successive stages mirroring those of social evolution, and that there is continuity between animal and human learning. Differential psychologists, such as Goddard, Terman, and Yerkes, later took up the first theme, comparing individuals in terms of their "mental capacity" as measured by IQ tests. Developmental psychologists, such as G. Stanley Hall and Arnold Gesell, took up the second theme of organic development and unfolding in child development. And, comparative psychologists, who contrasted learning in animals and humans, took up the third theme, which led to behaviorism and much of learning theory.

[3]In the 1966 version of Hilgard and Bower's influential *Theories of Learning*, functionalism was given a small chapter of its own. By the 1981 edition (Bower & Hilgard, 1981), learning theories were divided into two families, "behavioral–associationist" and "cognitive–organizational," with functional theory discussed as a form of behavioral–associationist theory. This is ironic, since functional psychology was initially developed in reaction to just such a split between empiricist and rationalist lines of thought.

[4]J. R. Angell, a well-known functional psychologist and student of Dewey and James, described the relation as follows: "I should not wish to commit either party by asserting that functional psychology and pragmatism are ultimately one. . . . I only hold that the two movements spring from similar logical motivation and rely for their vitality and propagation upon forces closely germane to one another" (1907, p. 68).

as formed by larger structures (like later Gestalt theorists). To the tough minded, human evolution was conceived in naturalistic Spencerian terms, with the environment eliminating unfit individuals. The tender minded, in contrast, saw human evolution in Hegelian terms as the unfolding of Reason or the enactment of a Divine plan. Both took the world to be rational and so tacitly agreed on a quiescent acceptance of things as they are (Miller, 1968).

James and his fellow functional psychologists opted for neither of these extremes. As he put it, "Few of us are tender-foot Bostonians pure and simple, and few are typical Rocky Mountain toughs. . . . Most of us have a hankering for the good things on both sides of the line" (James, 1907/1963, pp. 9–10). They sought to gain both sets of goods by considering human mental life as a factor *inside* of the process of evolution, which it helps to alter, rather than viewing evolution as mostly mindless, like the Spencerians, or as directed by an absolute Mind, like the Hegelians. Viewed as the functionalists suggested, mental life is both product and producer of evolution. Complex mental abilities are a product of natural evolution (social evolution being an important part of human evolution). And such mental abilities alter evolution, because they allow organisms to better change their environments, hence their fates. In short, the mind is part of a causal loop, rather than being only a dependent or an independent factor.

A key feature of this resolution of the conflict between tough- and tender-minded approaches was to view mind as a function rather than as a thing. Tough-minded materialists helped create conflict by reducing mind to the brain and then wondering where the minding is hidden inside. Tender-minded idealists, on the other hand, suggested that the reason minding cannot be found in the brain is that it is a spiritual entity which therefore cannot be found in the material world. But if one considers mind to be a function, rather than a thing, the problem of locating it dissolves. The brain has no "minding" inside of it, just as a car has no "driving" inside of it. Each is a mechanism that enables these functions to be performed, but the mechanism is not the same as the function. The function is neither a material entity nor an ideal spiritual entity—"it" isn't an entity at all! It is a function, a useful process or activity, a verb rather than a noun, as in acting "mindfully" or "minding" the low doorway when entering a room. Investigating the practical functions of mind in human adaptation was at the core of functional psychology's agenda.

James

In *The Principles of Psychology* (James, 1890/1950), William James used a functional approach to reinterpret and integrate most of what was then known about psychology. He considered the physiological aspects of mind, evident from knowledge of the brain and nervous system, and the subjective aspects, evident from introspection of conscious thought.[5] In each case he sought an interpretation that avoided polarization between tough-minded reductionism and tender-minded holism.

James's analysis of the brain and nervous system was built largely on the reflex arc concept, which considered the nervous system in terms of sensory input, central ideation, and motor output. James suggested that an organism so constructed is organized to sense changes in the environment and act on them to bring about new, more beneficial states. The whole structure functions to bring organism and environment into "more suitable relations with one another." After considering the functions of different levels of the nervous system, such as spinal cord and cerebral hemispheres, he concluded that "All nervous centres have then in the first instance one essential function, that of "intelligent' action. They feel, prefer one thing to another, and have "ends'" (James, 1890/1952, p. 51). In other words, all function to aid the survival of the organism by acting to alter the environment in adaptively useful ways. The difference between them is that the lower centers handle constant and predictable contingencies, while the higher centers handle more variable and novel ones (by reorganizing and modulating the operation of the lower ones; James, 1890/1952, pp. 9–12). This scheme helped relate "lower" and "higher" parts of the nervous system by seeing them in common teleological terms, while emphasizing their complementary roles in adaptation, rather than reducing mind to lower-level mechanism or elevating it to pure, disinterested ideation.

James attempted a similar synthesis of reductionistic and holistic approaches to conscious thought. He argued that thoughts are like successive waves in a stream or pond, formed by the oscillatory dynamics of the brain and nervous system (James, 1892/1961). Each moment's thought is a unique whole, since neither the brain nor the environment will ever be the same again. And each is related to the next by the dynamics of the system, just as successive waves have information about preceding and succeeding waves in their forms. This view was meant to counter those who saw thoughts as assembled out of atomistic simple ideas (empiricists) as well as those who saw them as formed by the given assumptive structure of a transcendental ego (rationalists). Against the former, James argued that the thought of a complex object is a single whole, like a complex waveform, rather than an assembly of parts. As he noted, "Our idea of a couple is not a couple of ideas"

[5]James defined *psychology* in a way that included both objective and subjective aspects. It was "the science of mental life, both of its phenomena and of their conditions" (James, 1890/1952, p. 1). Or, as a later functional psychologist put it, "The functionalist . . . finds necessary and profitable a more constant insistence upon the translation of mental process into physiological process and conversely" (Angell, 1907, p. 85). Consistent with this emphasis, James saw a role for both experimental analysis and introspection (as well as comparative research on "animals, savages, and infants").

(James, 1892/1961, p. 64). Against the latter he argued that no ego, or given structure of assumptions, is needed to bring organization into experience, because relationships are already present in successive thoughts. James went on to build an account of all the higher mental functions based on selective attention. His model gave priority to the mental *processes* of selecting parts and forming wholes, rather than presupposing the existence of given parts or wholes. It left assumptions about how things are defined up to mental process itself, rather than seeking to settle the issue ahead of time. As James pointed out, his approach was less metaphysically arbitrary than its competitors and more parsimonious than the rationalist model because it did not require an inner ego to do the discriminating. As he put it, in his model "the thoughts themselves are the thinkers" (James, 1892/1961, p. 83).

James's model focused on the practical *uses* of mind and the dynamic processes by which minding is done. This emphasis on dynamic function contrasted with approaches focusing on static entities, whether parts or wholes. It emphasized living, rather than being. Of course, even a dynamic theory must have some source of stability, but this came from habit, rather than from given entities such as elementary facts or a transcendental ego. James viewed habits fairly actively as useful ways of managing the environment (1899/1958, pp. 36, 42), although he sometimes considered them more passively as adaptations *to* the environment. Consistent with his view of the nervous system, he saw an interplay between routine, habitual action, and higher-level conscious attention which is evoked by conflict among existing habits when confronting a novel situation. The frustration and uncertainty about how to proceed in a novel situation make consciousness motivated or interested: it is not a mere spectator. While management of a novel situation requires conscious, focused attention, James saw it as desirable for a new habit to develop so that higher mental functions can be "set free for their own proper work"; that is, handling other uncertainties (James, 1892/1961, p. 12). Thus, James emphasized an interplay of habit and conscious thought rather than giving priority to one or the other. He also situated thinking in the context of interrupted or uncertain activity which it helped to resume.

The upshot of James's psychology was an active but limited view of mental life. Mind was "partial" in the sense of being interested, engaged, emotionally involved, since it was primarily for resolving uncertainties and frustrations involved in practical action. It was also "partial" in the sense of being limited, working though selective attention and emphasis. While limited, the changes in conduct that could be wrought through conscious attention were nevertheless critical. As James put it, "The knower is an actor. . . . Mental interests, hypotheses, postulates, so far as they are bases for human action—action which to a great extent transforms the world—help to *make* the truth which they declare" (Morris, 1950, pp. 15–16).

Dewey

While James highlighted the practical, adaptive importance of mind, his psychology was primarily about the dynamics of thought rather than the dynamics of action. Dewey altered this emphasis, focusing more clearly on the evolving act, while viewing thinking as a kind of acting. In so doing, he and his colleagues at the University of Chicago further developed functional psychology as a school of psychology (Sahakian, 1975).

Dewey was critical of the reflex view on which James and others had based their psychologies. The problem with this approach was that it portrayed action in linear terms. It suggested that a sensory stimulus comes first, which then triggers inner imagination and thought, which in turn causes a motor response. But this understanding of human behavior resulted in a "disjointed psychology" that "leaves us nothing but a series of jerks" (Dewey 1896, p. 360). Since many behaviorist and cognitivist theories are based on the same model today, Dewey's criticism remains relevant, as does his revised approach to psychology.

The basic problem with the reflex arc view was that it took a piece of an organism's activity and tried to understand it outside of the context of the ongoing act of which it was a part. It assumed that a given sensory input has the same effect on an organism no matter what it is doing, as though it responded in totally knee-jerk fashion. But Dewey argued that there never has been a pure sensation independent of the context of ongoing activity. Rather than thinking that sensation comes before motion, organisms are better viewed as engaged in "sensorimotor coordinations," in which the sensory and motor aspects of an act modify each other in a *cycle*.[6] In looking for something, for instance, one moves one's body, cranes one's head, focuses one's eyes, and the like, until it can be seen. Motor activity causes sensory input as much as it is caused by it. To put it differently, an organism helps cocreate its own stimulation and does not just react to events independent of its activity.

Dewey's approach emphasized the importance of organism–environment transactions, or cycles, rather than linear sensory–motor reactions. Organisms are engaged in "trying" and "undergoing," in which the environment is modified and modifies the actor, in turn, in a cycle, until some result is achieved. Rather than a reflex arc, with its linear input–process–output sequence, one has continuing cycles in which the environment completes the arc by affecting the organism in return, making a full circle. Seen in this way, organism and environment are in a sense partners in an act, making acting much like dancing in which one must work *with* the dynamics of one's partner

[6]Mechanists are likely to point out that a cycle can be broken into sequential elements, hence there is no reason to give priority to the whole cycle rather than to its parts. Dewey's point is that one does not know where to break up the whole into *functional* segments, as opposed to functionally arbitrary ones, unless their role in a wider activity is taken into account.

for coordinated action to be possible. Just as James's metaphor of the stream of consciousness had emphasized dynamic continuity in thinking, Dewey emphasized dynamic continuity in acting.

This view was helpful in criticizing those who saw the environment as affecting a passive organism. The stimulus–response psychologists of the day, for example, sought to describe behavior in purely external terms, seeing environmentally given sensory inputs as causing motor outputs. But a given sensory event, like a flash of light, plays an entirely different role when it occurs when signaling to a friend versus while trying to keep the light out of one's eyes when driving, for example. As a result, the organism's contribution to the value of the event cannot be so easily ignored. As Dewey put it,

> The fact is that stimulus and response are not distinctions of existence, but teleological distinctions, that is, distinctions of function, or part played, with reference to reaching or maintaining an end. . . . it is only the assumed common reference to an inclusive end which marks each member off as stimulus and response, that apart from such reference we have only antecedent and consequent; in other words, the distinction is one of interpretation. (1896, pp. 360, 365–366)

The mechanistic attempt to find relationships between stimulus and response without taking the organism into account fails, then because such events have no constant function: they have widely differing significance in modifying an organism's behavior depending on what it is up to.[7]

Dewey's argument also applied to those who viewed thinking as a separate stage after stimulation and before response. James often adopted this position, as do many neobehaviorists and cognitive theorists. But this approach greatly separates thinking from acting by taking it as a separate stage following an already completed sensory-input stage. A creature that behaved in this way would be bombarded by sensory input, then sit lost in passive thought, then engage in a motor response. Its behavior would also be "nothing but a series of jerks." This passive, environmentally determined view of a learner is much like the common view of pupils:

> The very word pupil has almost come to mean one who is engaged not in having fruitful experiences but in absorbing knowledge directly. Something which is called mind or consciousness is severed from the physical organs of activity. The former is then thought to be purely intellectual and cognitive; the latter to be an irrelevant and intruding physical factor. The intimate union of activity and undergoing its consequences which leads to recognition of meaning is broken; instead we have two fragments: mere bodily action on one side, and meaning directly grasped by "spiritual" activity on the other. (1916, pp. 140–141)

Of course, it is true that one often thinks about a problematic situation before overtly acting to change it, but thinking may not be so passive as the

[7]This is not true if the organism has a well-developed habit, for one may then reliably describe its behavior in external terms. But this purely external story will neglect the organism's activity that makes such a reliable result possible and the history of learning that enabled it to do so.

reflex arc view suggests, nor is sensory input so given. Consider a dog trying to get a ball on the other side of a fence, for example. It first runs one way, then the other, seeing which approach makes the ball more accessible. Its thinking is conducted *through* actions that continually alter the situation. Through such action, stimulus and response help redefine each other until a promising whole action can be found. All that running back and forth *is* the problem-solving search. Of course, human problem solving is likely to involve more reflection on the consequences of one's actions, but even reflective thinking often involves continually looking at and redefining the problematic situation and tentative trials at its solution. In this more active view, sensory input is not so static or given as in the "reflex arc" conception, and thinking and acting are more closely integrated.

Dewey's emphasis on organism–environment transactions helped give a more active view of learning, one that James had suggested but did not fully develop because he tended to omit the environment as a partner in the act. Dewey's active view of habits resulting from learning contrasts with the usual more passive view as evident in the following:

> A habit means an ability to use natural conditions as means to ends. It is an active control of the environment through control of the organs of action. . . . If we think of a habit simply as a change wrought in the organism, ignoring the fact that this change consists in ability to effect subsequent changes in the environment, we shall be led to think of "adjustment" as a conformity to environment. . . . Adaptation . . . is quite as much adaptation *of* the environment to our own activities as of our activities *to* the environment. (1916, pp. 46–47)

If both the organism and the environment are viewed as continually changing as in Dewey's more active view, then habit need not mean adaptation to a fixed environment. Since organism and environment are always changing, such a habit should, ideally, be able to do its job under varying circumstances. It should be formed under varying conditions so that it is not a rigidly stereotyped form of behavior. Consistent with this notion, Dewey emphasized learning in the context of a larger practical activity, rather than as isolated skills, so that habits perform their functions under realistically varied circumstances. He also emphasized the close involvement of thinking in forming such habits, with thinking stimulated by genuine problems emergent in activity, rather than simply addressing externally presented abstract problems. Engaged problem solving, which is attentive to the practical meaning of events, was both the means and the end of education for Dewey. It was "the reconstruction or reorganization of experience which adds to the meaning of experience, and . . . increases the ability to direct the course of subsequent experience" (Dewey, 1916, p. 76).

Mead

Dewey developed the wider social and philosophical implications of a functional view of mind more fully than James, but his friend and colleague

George Herbert Mead was more specific about the way in which reflective intelligence is learned through social interaction. Understanding how reflective intelligence is learned extends the scope of learning theory, making it unnecessary to reject mind as a fiction (like many behaviorists) or to assume that reasoning processes are given (like many cognitivists).

If one considers simple interaction, such as might occur among animals, it is evident that the interactants commonly become attuned to the beginning phases of their acts, which Mead termed *gestures* (following Wundt), and not just to the fully completed act. When a lion looks intently at a zebra, for example, the latter likely responds to the look as it would to a possible chase. It responds to this little beginning, which signals that the rest of the chase is likely to begin, and does not wait around for the full thing to occur. Of course, the lion is also likely to learn to respond to the zebra's feints or gestures in return because of the running dash that they signal is coming. If the two engaged in this interaction often they would become ever more finely attuned to each other's tentative beginnings of larger actions, so that their joint action would be a product of a subtle dance of feints and counterfeints. Their joint action—whatever drama they worked out together—would be a sort of coevolutionary production of this process of signaling and anticipatory modification, rather than a knee-jerk reaction to a completed event.

> These beginnings of acts call out responses which lead to readjustments of acts which have been commenced, and these readjustments lead to still other beginnings of response which call out still other readjustments. Thus there is a conversation of gesture, a field of palaver within the social conduct of animals. (Mead, 1910/1970, p. 342)

One can see the similarity between this analysis and Dewey's account of sensorimotor coordination, in which stimulus and response become shaped to each other as parts of a larger, unfolding act.

This analysis is important for understanding learning because the regularities that develop within such a conjoint activity form the basis for social meaning. If two organisms are engaged in a "conversation of gestures" like that just described and one responds to the other's initial gesture as it would to the whole act, then that gesture "means" the completed act. The lion's gaze "means" the chase to the zebra.

> Just as in fencing the parry is an interpretation of the thrust, so, in the social act, the adjustive response of one organism to the gesture of another is the interpretation of that gesture by that organism. Indeed, it is the meaning of that gesture. (Mead, 1934, p. 166)

For an event to have a *social* meaning, then, it must play a role in a joint activity, it must function as a signal for what is to come in the interaction. Understood in this way, "meaning" is not in the head, it is anticipatory behavior to regularities in the (inter)actions of another. Such meaning is only implicit or unconscious at this stage, however, since each organism responds without awareness of the significance of its *own* gestures, which are just the unnoticed beginnings of its own acts, like one's posture or facial expression that is invisible to oneself (Mead, 1934, pp. 163–165).

The meaning of one's gestures may become conscious when interaction produces troublesome or unexpected results (i.e., when conscious attention is aroused) in a suitably capable organism. The search for an appropriate stimulus to respond to may then result in responding to the other's gestural response to one's own gesture. Suppose, for example, that a lion were to respond to a zebra's beginning to run in response to the lion's interested gaze. In this case the lion would be responding to the meaning of its own gaze for the zebra as reflected back to it in the zebra's behavior. Mead saw responding to such reflected meaning of one's own behavior as the basis of all reflective intelligence. Such learning enables one to act toward one's own emerging actions as another would. One can try the tentative beginnings of an act and respond to this beginning as another would; that is, to its meaning, then try another beginning, and so on. If one can do this, then the "conversation of gestures" that previously took place between different organisms, can be played out in the behavior of a single organism.[8] This ability to respond to the meaning of one's own emerging action is what reflective intelligence is.

Mead's analysis suggests that mind (i.e., *reflective* intelligence) is a learned form of social interaction rather than a thing. Viewing mind as a pattern of self-interactivity clarifies James's earlier claim that in his model "the thoughts themselves are the thinkers." Mead's analysis also makes clear that, since it takes the anticipatory behavior of others to reflect the meaning of our gestures back to us, the origins of reflective intelligence are necessarily social. As he put it, "It is absurd to look at the mind simply from the standpoint of the individual human organism; for although it has its focus there, it is essentially a social phenomenon" (Mead, 1934, p. 195). If this view is correct, learning theories that ignore the social context ignore the only way in which reflective intelligence can be learned, making it clear why they are forced to either exclude or presuppose mind.

Implications

By focusing on activity as constructed through organism–environment transactions, functional psychology helped break down the barrier between thinking and acting as well as that between the individual and sociocultural aspects of change. The important thing in acting is not the boundary between organism and environment, but their functional roles in an activity (indeed, without a functional role an event is not part of the "environment"). It is how

[8]This need not mean a shift from "external" to "internal." All that is necessary is that the organism be able to play out the conversation of gestures for itself. Doing this could involve externally visible behavior or devices as elements of the interaction.

they work together rather than what they are that matters. The boundary between the individual and the social environment likewise is softened, because a group or a society becomes more like a set of dancers engaging in a series of different dances than a thing. Similarly, an "individual" is a participant in, or contributor to, varied dances whose unique contribution helps codetermine the nature of the social "dance." Since thinking is conceived of as a type of action, a form of social interaction one has with oneself, there is no radical gulf between it and more overt forms of action. All such interaction need not take place "in the head" since some may be visible in trying and searching behavior. The functionalists' focus on activity and on the process of forming an act thus dissolved the usual hard divisions plaguing learning theory.

What values are implicit in this approach to "learning"? Dewey (1938) nicely summed them up as "interaction" and "continuity." We have seen the functionalists' emphasis on interaction or, more properly, transaction.[9] They focused on organism–environment transactions. As a result, they viewed learned habits not as matters of passive adaptation to fixed environments, unlike most learning theorists, but as ways of *changing* environments. The functionalists' emphasis on interaction thus served to shift attention away from learning as adaptation to the demands of a fixed environment. In other words, it did not give sole attention to the requirements of an external experimenter or teacher as defining the changes that count as "learning." When the desirability of such interactive adaptation is translated into educational terms it implies that learning comes from solving problems that are the learner's own; that is, from his or her own experienced uncertainty, Dewey suggested this meant creating environments in which people can be stimulated to think, such as by experiencing unexpected difficulties in a routine, yet are not overwhelmed by the difficulties of the situation, which would likely lead them to act impulsively rather than thoughtfully. Thus his notion of "interaction" was much like Vygotsky's "zone of proximal development," which will be considered later (Vygotsky, 1978).

The functional psychologists also placed great emphasis on continuity. This meant an emphasis on smooth growth, whether in thought, action, individual development, social change, or biological evolution. They were concerned with understanding the links, the specific ways in which an evolutionary process gets from here to there. Normatively, they were concerned with change that leads from the present situation onward and not with dead-end adaptation. In educational terms, Dewey (1916, 1938, 1958) suggested

[9] Dewey later distinguished between "transactions," in which organism and environment are both altered in character, and "interactions," in which a structurally constant organism and environment affect one another's behavior, like interacting billiard balls or game-theoretical actors (Dewey & Bentley, 1949). Dewey's theory was transactional not interactional, in that it allowed for changes in the character of both organism and environment.

that educational experiences should lead to "growth"; that is, to enhanced ability to extract meaning from experiences, which, in turn, can be applied to new experiences. This suggests that a learner does not remain structurally fixed; he or she is growing, evolving. Dewey's two criteria of an educative experience—interaction and continuity—are interdependent. Genuine inquiry and dialogue in the present situation ("interaction") is the best way to foster longer-run growth because it makes present learning most meaningful. Thus the end and the means of education were the same for Dewey—*growing*. When related to learning theory this suggests that learning and development can and should occur together and are preferably inseparable.

When the aim of continued growth is applied to everyone, a democratic society is suggested, one that fosters the development of the unique abilities of all of its members, including their abilities to restructure the social institutions involved in just such social fostering (Dewey, 1916). Thus, individual and social growing are also intertwined. The relation between this view of education and Progressive politics seems evident.

BEHAVIORISM

Behaviorism was both the child of functionalism and a throwback to tough-minded empiricism. It grew out of the functionalists' emphasis on science and rejection of mental entities, as well as their evolutionary interest in comparing the mental life of humans and animals. These interests were exaggerated in behaviorism, which adopted a narrowly positivistic view of science, rejected any explanatory role for mental phenomena, and gave almost exclusive priority to research on lower animals. The common theme in these reactions was an emphasis on the externally observable and minimally ambiguous. In their quest for certainty the behaviorists took a turn back to Spencer, for whom the given environment was the determining factor. Needless to say, this passive emphasis on complying with environmental demands contrasted with the functionalists' emphasis on changing the environment, including its present contingencies.

Among the reasons for this shift to tough-minded empiricism was the desire to legitimize psychology as a science, independent of philosophy, at a time when the physical sciences had great credibility. Emphasis on conformity to environmental demands may also have found support in the more conservative post-World War I political atmosphere. Certainly, a number of the founders of behaviorism, such as Watson and Skinner, were more conservative than the founders of functional psychology. In what follows, I will briefly consider their versions of behaviorism and their conceptions of learning (Pavlov and Thorndike should also be mentioned as important influences but will not be discussed here).

Watson

John Watson, the principal evangelist of behaviorism, was a student of both Dewey and Mead at Chicago. He also managed the animal laboratory of another functionalist, J. R. Angell. The origins of behaviorism in empiricist philosophy are evident in his reflection on this education:

> God knows I took enough philosophy to know something about it. But it wouldn't take hold. I passed my exams but the spark was not there. I got something out of the British School of Philosophers—mainly out of Hume, a little out of Locke, a bit out of Hartley, nothing out of Kant, and strange to say, least of all out of John Dewey. I never knew what he was talking about then, and unfortunately for me, I still don't know. (Watson, 1961, p. 274)

Among other things, Watson was upset that animal experiments, like his own, played such a marginal role in psychology at the time. His conception of psychology as a natural science, with experimentation replacing introspection, and objective (physical) descriptions of stimulus and response replacing those framed in terms of mind or consciousness, was well-designed to enhance the significance of animal experimentation. These views were expressed with vigor in his early manifesto, "Psychology as the Behaviorist Views It":

> Psychology as the behaviorist views it is a purely objective experimental branch of natural science. Its theoretical goal is the prediction and control of behavior. Introspection forms no essential part of its methods, nor is the scientific value of its data dependent upon the readiness with which they lend themselves to interpretations in terms of consciousness. . . . The time seems to have come when psychology must discard all reference to consciousness; when it no longer need delude itself that it is making mental states the object of observation. . . . I believe we can write a psychology . . . and . . . never use the terms consciousness, mental states, mind, content, introspectively verifiable imagery, and the like. . . . It can be done in terms of stimulus and response, in terms of habit formation, habit integrations and the like. . . . In a system of psychology completely worked out, given the response the stimuli can be predicted; given the stimuli the response can be predicted. (Watson, 1913, pp. 507, 511–512, 514).

Watson defined *learning* in functional terms; that is, as an adjustment adequate to "meet the situation." If the same result could be achieved faster or with fewer movements when re-encountering the same situation "then we say he has *learned* or *has formed a habit*" (Watson, 1924/1930, p. 200). But Watson was concerned with the functions of *behavior* not of mind, so he did not view learning as occurring through conscious thought or insight. Rather, it occurred through a process of "conditioning," so called because learned reflexes were *conditional* on a history of environmental events. Watson also viewed learning atomistically, as involving the association of given stimuli and responses. To be more specific, learning occurred when a new stimulus is repeated before another stimulus that already evokes a given response

(Watson, 1924/1930, p. 209). He demonstrated this on a child, Alfred, who was brought to fear a rat by loudly striking an iron bar behind his head when he was playing with the animal. Little Alfred's reaction of turning away and curling up when the rat was presented involved his responding to the previously enjoyed rat as he would have to the scary noise. More complex habits were formed by chaining together existing reflexes in a suitably contingent environment (Watson, 1924/1930, p. 207). Thus complex wholes were assembled out of given parts.

Watson's environmentalism was evident in his rejection of inner explanations, particularly mental ones, and their replacement with environmental explanations. He believed that "mental" behavior is a habit, like any other, except that it involves the parts of the body used in speech, such as the larynx. This account had the value of focusing attention on what is done when thinking (like the functionalists), but it tended to reduce thought to the operation of the peripheral organs, leading the philosopher Herbert Feigl to joke that Watson "made up his windpipe that he had no mind" (Anderson, 1990, p. 340). Consistent with his environmentalist position, Watson (1924/1930, pp. 94, 97–100, 203) also rejected instinct theory, innate intelligence, and the Gesellian notion that learning can occur simply through development.

Behaviorism after Watson took a number of directions. Some, like Tolman (1951/1966), who might not be considered a behaviorist, used holistic mental concepts like purpose, consciousness, and cognitive map but insisted that they be described in terms of objective behavior. Others, like Hull (1952), retained an atomistic stimulus–response (S-R) approach but supplemented it with hypothetical constructs describing an organism's inner states, such as "drive" and "incentive motivation." In contrast to these efforts to liberalize behaviorism, Burrhus Frederick Skinner continued to develop an atomistic and environmentalist approach in the Watsonian tradition.

Skinner

From a scientific standpoint, Watson's approach was both too successful and too unsuccessful. It was too successful because any response could be explained after the fact by *some* stimulus, since virtually anything in the environment could be taken as one. And it was too unsuccessful because specific responses could rarely be predicted ahead of time, contrary to Watson's hope of a predictive science of psychology.

Skinner helped deal with these embarrassments by making three principal changes. First, he retreated to a probabilistic rather than a deterministic approach to prediction. Changes in response probabilities, or rates, were to be predicted rather than changes in individual responses.[10] Second, Skinner

[10] Skinner talked as though he was dealing with probabilities but admitted that his data are actually about response rates, which are by no means the same.

helped tighten what counted as a "stimulus" or a "response." In his experimental situations, such as the "Skinner box," easily repeatable brief events, like bar presses, disk pecks, and food-pellet releases, could be automatically recorded and related to one another. Third, Skinner gave up predicting which stimulus an organism would respond to ahead of time, focusing instead on how behavior changes as a result of the *consequences* of its past behavior. In other words, he shifted attention from the organismic generation of behavior to its selection by the environment (i.e., from "respondent" to "operant" conditioning). In short, Skinner retreated to more defensible predictive aspirations while tightening experimental controls.

"Learning," for Skinner (1950, p. 199), involved a change in response rate following reinforcement. In other words, an animal that "learns" a set of experimental contingencies is one that responds more rapidly in a manner likely to bring about reinforcement. In this view, learning is the adoption of "functional" behavior in the sense that an animal that knows what is good for it will more frequently engage in such behavior. Defining *learning* in this way had the advantage of making it easily quantifiable and directly observable. In previous approaches, for example, a rat that went through a maze rapidly on some trials and had seemingly "learned" the maze might go slowly on another trial. This meant that learning differed from observed performance, since what was observed was (presumably) a combination of the effects of learning and motivation. To get smooth learning curves without such variation, the scores of many animals had to be averaged, but then the learning of a specific animal could not be observed. Skinner avoided this problem by defining *learning* as a change in response rate using many simple, standardized responses by a single organism. The more rapidly the individual organism did the thing that counted as a "response," the more it had "learned," making learning (so defined) directly observable. Making "learning" directly observable was a brilliant move for an externally inclined behaviorist, but one could also say that Skinner defined *learning* in a way that hid all evidence of an organism's purposes other than those Skinner chose to reinforce. That is, all the other acts of the organism that might interfere with the one being reinforced were taken as part of the randomness in a response's "probability."

Skinner accepted Watson's S-R atomism and the notion that complex behaviors are taught by combining simpler stimulus discriminations and responses into more complex units. However, he tightened Watson's definitions of *stimulus* and *response*, which were highly vulnerable to Dewey's criticism of being arbitrarily pulled out of the air. In Skinner's tighter system, *stimuli* were defined as environmental events causing changes in response rates, while *responses* were behaviors that varied systematically with changes in stimuli. Reinforcing stimuli were consequences of responses that systematically varied the future rate of response (in the presence of the same discriminating stimuli). All the terms were circularly defined in terms of each other, but each could nevertheless be identified under laboratory conditions by the way it varied when one or another condition was experimentally altered (Skinner, 1935, p. 62). Thus, they were causally linked with one another and identifiable as such, rather than mere arbitrary sequences of events. Skinner argued that looser, more popular uses of *stimulus* or *response*, like Watson's, were to be rejected "until it has been defined experimentally" (Skinner, 1935, p. 62). As will be suggested shortly, one criticism of Skinner's work derives from the fact that he did not consistently follow his own advice.

Skinner not only accepted Watson's environmentalism, he sought to radicalize it. Rather than rejecting mind, as had Watson, he sought to explain all mental behavior in environmental terms (Skinner, 1974). To do so he reinterpreted any form of conduct showing thought or intention in purely external terms. Purposeful action was interpreted as an observed behavioral tendency. The apparent use of a mental rule or operation was interpreted as a description of someone conforming to a previously learned reinforcement contingency. Having a certain personality or character was interpreted as having a particular history of reinforcement. In each case Skinner tried to show that explanations in terms of environmental contingencies could replace explanations in terms of inner causes. As he put it, "It is almost literally a matter of turning the explanation of behavior inside out" (Skinner, 1974, p. 274).

Implications

The behaviorists shared a rejection of inner mental agents with the functionalists, who also thought that positing egos or minds inside pulling the strings amounted to a metaphysical illusion. However, the behaviorists tended to extend this rejection of mental *entities* to a rejection of mental *functions*. In so doing, they shifted the focus of much of psychology from the functions of mind to the functions of behavior. Consistent with this, behaviorists also shifted the focus from the way in which an organism defines a situation, as in James's consideration of selective attention, to the way in which the environment has been defined by another (e.g. the researcher). Research shifted accordingly, emphasizing animal learning under controlled conditions at the expense of human learning in everyday situations.

This shift in focus involved a fundamental shift in aim. Behaviorists like Watson and Skinner sought to predict and control behavior by manipulating the environment. As Watson put it, the behaviorist "wants to control man's reactions as physical scientists want to control and manipulate other natural phenomena" (Watson, 1924/1930, p. 11). Success in this effort would mean getting an organism to behave as one wants. The functionalists, on the other hand, wanted to foster habits of mind, or reflective thought, aiding the *organism's* adaptation. This included an active role in selecting and changing environments, including finding or creating those with favorable contingencies.

Of course, each of these aims involves elements of prediction and control but in quite different ways. Consider the difference between educating a partner and training a servant as an example. In educating a partner one wants to foster the partner's *own* abilities to predict and control the environment. The partner is being prepared for a role in which there is shared defining and goal setting, as opposed to a servant who is being prepared for a compliant role in which the situation and its goals are defined by others. The difference between a behavioristic and a functionalist approach to learning therefore could be described as the difference between training and education.[11]

What consequences, then, is a behavioristic approach likely to have for learning? Further clues may be found in the behaviorists' atomism and environmentalism. Atomism is apparent in the assumption that the parts are already defined, larger skills being constructed from combinations of these parts. Behavioristic approaches to instruction generally adopt this assumption, teaching the parts first and then the combination of these parts into larger wholes. One learns the "basic" skills first. Given this isolation of skills, present "learning" has no longer-run value to the organism beyond the context of the immediate experimental situation because it has no idea of the relation between this part and what it will be asked to learn next to make up some larger whole. This approach can be very effective for teaching a complex skill to an organism that cannot solve the larger problem itself, but it means that all of the problem-solving effort involved in defining the situation and factoring the problem into its smaller elements is done by the instructor. A person so instructed would seem unlikely to develop his or her own analytical skills. Such a person would also be more likely to segment the different steps of the problem in a rigid manner than one who had taken a role in defining these steps and was thus familiar with the considerations involved in their selection.

A similar point can be made with regard to environmentalism. An environmental account focuses on what the instructor or experimenter does to structure the situation, such as reinforcement contingencies and manipulation of the learner's situation to ensure that certain events are reinforcing (e.g., starving an animal prior to placing it in an experimental situation). This implies that the operative goals are set by the instructor rather than being approached as a shared or negotiated activity. What learning *is* is compliance with the instructor's demands—just as teachers often define learning in their own terms and think that no other learning is occurring in their classrooms. This was evident in Skinner's definition of *learning*, which is simply the rate of doing whatever *he* reinforced. (Of course, it is true that for reinforcement to

[11] Dewey (1916, 13) discussed the difference between training and education in *Democracy and Education*. A transactional conception of control is discussed in Chapter 3, "Education as Direction."

work, for it to *be* reinforcement, it has to be important to the organism. But this is in the context of an situation over which the organism has no control.) This approach therefore seems likely to teach the meta-lesson that the learner's independent goal-setting efforts are irrelevant. One would expect that students instructed in this way to become more passive in proposing or negotiating their own instructional goals.

It seems reasonable to conclude that a behavioristic approach (of the strict Watsonian or Skinnerian variety) not only rejects mental explanations but is also unlikely to teach mental abilities. Whatever skill is being taught at a given time, however complexly contingent, the defining and planning involved in the formulation of *that* skill are all done by the instructor. Thus, higher-order abilities involved in defining the situation and planning a response to it are not taught and in fact may be inhibited. The meta-lesson seems to be to "leave the thinking to us." That a skill taught at a particular time is unrelated to life before and after the experimental situation also means that it is unlikely to facilitate growth or development. It is just a random pothole in the highway of life, so to speak. The classical economist Adam Smith offered an interesting description of the likely effects of such piecework:

> The man whose life is spent in performing a few simple operations has no occasion to exert his understanding, or to exercise his invention in finding out expedients for difficulties which never occur. He naturally loses, therefore, the habit of such exertion and generally becomes as stupid and ignorant as it is possible for a human creature to become. (Schwartz, 1986, p. 246)

Needless to say, the results of this "lesson" would be invisible to the usual behavioristic analysis.[12]

COGNITIVISM

The cognitive revolution that swept over behaviorism in the 1950s and 1960s also had an ambivalent relationship with functional psychology. In one way, it was a return to the functionalists' emphasis on mind. Indeed, Jerome Bruner described it as a "revival" rather than a revolution, since it revived the Jamesian notion that higher mental processes are central to psychology (Bruner, Goodnow, & Austin, 1956, p. vii). Herbert Simon also saw it as reviving Jamesian themes (while himself adopting a version of the reflex arc view):

> On the American side of the Atlantic Ocean, there was a great gap in research on human thinking from the time of William James almost down to World War II. Ameri-

[12] In contrast to Mead's later social and processual behaviorism in which the process of *forming* the stimulus and response, through gesture and self-indication was considered a fit subject for behavioral investigation.

> can psychology was dominated by behaviorism, the stimulus–response connection, . . . the nonsense syllable, and the rat. Cognitive processes—what went on between the ears after the stimulus was received and before the response was given—were hardly mentioned, and the word *mind* was reserved for philosophers, not to be uttered by respectable psychologists. (1991, p. 190)

In other respects the cognitive revolution was not so much a return to Jamesian functionalism as a reaction against behaviorism (Bruner, 1983). It took the behaviorist's external rules of reinforcement and placed them inside the head as the rules of a symbolic problem representation. The behaviorists' focus on an organism's externally visible search behavior was similarly replaced with inner search through an symbolic problem space. One could say that the behaviorist's external experiment was now simulated "inside" the mind and called *problem solving*. This move from an external to an internal account clearly overshot the functionalists' transactional synthesis. Considered philosophically, it went from a form of empiricism to a form of rationalism, neglecting the pragmatic third alternative. As Bower and Hilgard (1981) suggest, most cognitive learning theory had such rationalist roots. Like many revolutions, the cognitive revolution retained more in common with the prior regime than might initially be suspected. It retained a positivistic emphasis, although in a more sophisticated form that allowed unobserved variables. It also retained quiescent acceptance of a given problem, since most of the problem-solving literature assumes that "the problem" is already known.

The cognitive revolution flourished at a time when new computational methods and metaphors were becoming available and there was increased demand for scientists and technicians, due to economic expansion and the political ramifications of Sputnik. The professional advance of psychology as a legitimate science and the liberal but technocratic politics of the Kennedy and Johnson eras were consistent with the cognitive approach to learning that gained favor. To more fully suggest the character of "cognitivism," I will briefly consider the work of Noam Chomsky, Jerome Bruner, and Herbert Simon, three of the principal revolutionaries. All three, it might be noted, were much more liberal than their behavioristic predecessors. Many other contributors to cognitive learning theory, such as the earlier Gestalt theorists and Piagetians, should again be noted but cannot be discussed here.

Chomsky

The work of the linguist Noam Chomsky (1959) figures principally in a discussion of learning theory by way of critique, since Chomsky's devastating review of Skinner's *Verbal Behavior* was widely viewed as hastening the demise of behaviorism and the rise of cognitivism.

Part of Chomsky's criticism of Skinner's work was similar to Dewey's criticism of earlier S-R theorists; that is, that the description of the units of behavior requires interpretation in intentional terms. Chomsky argued that the behaviorist who seeks to avoid the risks of interpretation, as behaviorists did, is caught in a rigor–relevance dilemma. What counts as a stimulus or a response can be made rigorous under controlled laboratory conditions, but then there is no way of extrapolating from these conditions to everyday situations while remaining consistent with behaviorist premises.

> If he [a behaviorist] accepts the broad definitions, characterizing any physical event impinging on the organism as a stimulus and any part of the organism's behavior as a response, he must conclude that most behavior has not been demonstrated to be lawful. . . . If we accept the narrower definitions, then behavior is lawful by definition (if it consists of responses); but this fact is of limited significance, since most of what the animal does will simply not be considered behavior. Hence the psychologist either must admit that behavior is not lawful, or must restrict his attention to those highly limited arenas in which it is lawful. . . . Skinner does not consistently adopt either course. He utilizes the experimental results as evidence for the scientific character of his system of behavior, and analogic guesses (formulated in terms of a metaphoric extension of the technical vocabulary of the laboratory) as evidence of its scope. (Chomsky, 1965, p. 30)

In short, despite warning of "popular" definitions of stimulus and response that avoid strict laboratory identification, Skinner used broad "interpretations" of verbal behavior outside the laboratory, while claiming the tight rigor of his narrower definitions. Chomsky (1959, p. 39) concluded that, when Skinner tried to apply his laboratory generalizations to language in everyday situations, his pretense of objectivity devolved into mere "play-acting at science."

Chomsky also argued that Skinner's approach was too simple, in principle, to explain language learning. When considering the behavior of a very complex organism one needs to take into account the contribution of the inner structure of the organism. Without taking this into account, one cannot understand the efficiency of language learning or the way in which people can produce a virtually infinite number of sentences they have never heard before. The process is too efficient and well-organized to rely on sheer trial and error. As an alternative Chomsky suggested that language learning is a form of implicit hypothesis testing that is constrained by innate structures (his hypothetical "language acquisition device"). To study such inner structures and processes one needs to adopt a more round-about approach than the behaviorist's. One still needed to look at "behavior," but this should include the inner structure of stimuli and responses themselves, like the nested phrases in a sentence, as well as the processes by which such structures are generated (Chomsky, 1965, p. 27). In effect, Chomsky substituted his own rationalism for Skinner's empiricism.[13] His "language

[13] It is interesting how Skinner, the clever laboratory experimenter, thought everyone learned through experimentation, while Chomsky, the brilliant rationalist philosopher, thought everyone learned through theoretical deduction.

acquisition device" can be seen as the modern equivalent of Plato's innate ideas, Kant's a priori assumptions, or the IQ tester's "native intelligence." Sneaking in invisible structures or agents to account for intelligent behavior, of course, was just what James had rejected in the rationalist approaches of his day.

Bruner

When Chomsky was giving his early lectures on language in the late 1950s, Jerome Bruner and his colleagues were doing some of the first modern research on learning viewed as a product of thinking. Bruner had been trained in modern experimental methods at Harvard but also had strong cognitive interests deriving from classes with Gestalt theorists like Kohler and Lewin (Bruner, 1983, p. 33). His ideal at the time was Edward Tolman, a psychologist who combined cognitive concepts with behavioral methods.

What made Bruner et al.'s *A Study of Thinking* (1956) distinctive was that it studied learning as an outcome of thinking, using methods that made thinking amenable to objective study. The kind of learning Bruner and his colleagues studied was "concept attainment." One can think of concept acquisition as analogous to learning a set of rules for classifying objects, like "If x has warm blood and fur, then it is a mammal." This is an important kind of learning because classifying objects is essential to thinking. Knowing that a particular animal is a mammal, for instance, allows one to infer a variety of other properties that it is likely to possess and thereby anticipate consequences relating to these properties. The notion that "learning" involves inferring a rule clearly differs from Skinner's notion of learning, since rapidity of response is not at issue. For instance, one might *slowly* classify all instances correctly, and still be said to have "learned" a concept.

Bruner and his colleagues thought of the process of learning as like hypothesis testing. A learner uses some strategy to generate possible rules defining a concept and then tests these hypotheses against actual instances until one is found that survives the tests. They studied this by presenting subjects with a series of cards with varying attributes, such as figures of varying number, type, and color, each of which was supposed to belong to an unknown category (the concept being learned). A subject might select one card, find out its category, guess at the attributes defining that category, and then test this guess by selecting a new card from the others visible on the table. By studying the sequence of cards selected, Bruner et al. could infer the thinking strategies being used. For instance, some might focus on one known card and use all of its attributes to define the category it belonged to. Others might carefully test first one attribute of all of the cards belonging to a category, then another. Different strategies affected the rate and accuracy of learning, making "inner" processes of obvious importance to learning. In general, Bruner et al. found strategies to be well-adapted to the practical difficulties of the situation, such as its complexity or risk. Thus, learning involved thinking—generating and testing hypotheses on the basis of their implications—and it depended on the particular strategy being used (rather than being determined by the environment alone).

In later work, Bruner went on to emphasize the importance of learning the cognitive structures (concepts or rules) important in various disciplines. He suggested that learning these general rules was more important than simply memorizing a set of particular facts, because the particulars could be generated from them (Bruner, 1960):

> I had set forth a strong argument favoring the idea of "models in the head" based on general understanding, from which hypotheses about particulars could be generated and the tested against experience. The great disciplines like physics or mathematics, or history, or dramatic forms in literature, were, in this view, less repositories of knowledge than of methods for the use of mind. They provided the structure that gave meaning to the particulars. That, after all, was what culture was about. The object of education was to get as swiftly as possible to that structure—to penetrate a subject, not to cover it. (Bruner, 1983, pp. 184–185)

In focusing on learning the structures of the disciplines, Bruner allied cognitive psychology with an updated version of liberal education, which included an emphasis on science alongside of the traditional liberal arts. His report on the Woods Hole conference, which helped launch the "new" math and the "new" science curricula of the 1960s, was consistent with this theme (Bruner, 1960).

Bruner's work was widely accepted, in part, because "It made the study of thinking tough-minded" (1983, p. 120). Studying the sequence of choices made when learning concepts gave a way of inferring a subject's thinking without having to ask what he or she was doing "inside" his or her head, making it relatively acceptable to experimentally inclined psychologists. But, reflecting on this work decades later, Bruner (1983, p. 127) suggested that one of the limitations was that the categories used were not "natural kinds," that is, they did not signal meaningful differences in the behavior of objects outside of the laboratory setting, "so the strategies that we found were in the end appropriate only to the world in which we forced our subjects to operate." Put another way, the concepts learned did not allow anticipation of the significant properties of objects encountered outside that situation and, in fact, were meaningless in the broader lives of their subjects. In fairness, Bruner's latest work (1986, 1990) very helpfully works with Jamesian and functionalist themes, among others.

Simon

Herbert Simon, one of the founders of the field of artificial intelligence, helped formalize models of problem solving and learning by simulating them more explicitly on the computer. Simon was influenced by the work of the functional psychologists during his education in political science and economics at Chicago, citing James and Tolman as early influences. He was also influenced by the logician Rudolf Carnap and his early ideas involved studying the "logic" of decision making (Simon, 1991, p. 190). For his dissertation, he studied public-sector decision making, finding that most of the action was in the initial assumptions adopted by a decision maker, which were largely related to their organizational roles, rather than in the finer comparison of alternatives generated within a set of assumptions (Simon, 1945). This led to later work on bounded rationality and studies of the importance of problem representations (March & Simon, 1958; Simon, 1957). In short, much of Simon's earlier work focused on what a person contributes to the situation by symbolically framing or representing it in one way rather than another.

Beginning in the later 1950s, Simon and his colleague Alan Newell more fully formalized a model of human problem solving in the form of a series of computer programs. The gist of the model, which became the prevailing convention, is that problem solving is the inner simulation of what a series of actions would do in the outer world. It is as though each of us performed a little computer simulation in our heads to figure out how to reach a goal. This model requires a simplified, inner representation of the situation, such as a set of rules or rulelike computer procedures, specifying how conditions change from one state to another when different actions are taken. It also requires a search strategy determining the order in which these rules are tried. A problem-solving model thus consists of the cognitive structure, or knowledge base, used to define the problem and a cognitive process, such as the search strategy. Simon actually characterized problem solving as much like an inward version of running through a maze, trying first one alley, then another, in an effort to reach a goal. Thus, his model was uncannily like an inward version of the behaviorists' external maze search (Simon, 1991). Simon and Langley summarize this view of thinking as follows (Langley, Simon, Bradshaw, & Zytkow, 1987):

> • The human brain is an information-processing system whose memories hold interrelated symbol structures and whose sensory and motor connections receive encoded symbols from the outside via sensory organs and send encoded symbols to motor organs. It accomplishes its thinking by copying and reorganizing symbols in memory, receiving and outputting symbols, and comparing symbol structures for identity or difference.
>
> • The brain solves problems by creating a symbolic representation of the problem (called the *problem space*) that is capable of expressing initial, intermediate, and final problem situations . . . and using the *operators* that are contained in the definition of the problem space to modify the symbol structures that describe the problem situation (thereby conducting a mental *search* for a solution through the problem space).

> • The search for a problem solution is not carried on by random trial and error, but is selective. It is guided in the direction of a *goal situation* . . . by rules of thumb, called *heuristics*. Heuristics make use of information extracted from the problem definitions and the states already explored in the problem space to identify promising paths for search.

What is important for the present is simply that this model suggests that the use of different problem representations and search strategies will result in different problem-solving behavior. As a result, one needs to take the subject's knowledge and search processes into account to predict or understand that person's behavior.

Once problem solving had been simulated on the computer in a fairly stable way, Simon and others turned to modeling learning, conceived of as a form of problem solving.[14] Learning was defined as "any process that modifies a system so as to improve, more or less irreversibly, its subsequent performance on the same task or of tasks drawn from the same population" (Langley & Simon, 1981, p. 367). (Note the use of the term *system*, making this definition relevant to a computer.) After building a number of programs that could "learn" various types of rules from examples, such as the rules defining different concepts or those involved in sequences like numerical or musical series, Simon (1979) found that all could be seen as variants of a general problem-solving program. They all involved goal-directed search through a symbolic problem space. Thus, learning and problem solving were unified in a single conception. Such learning might involve memorizing the solution to a particular problem, such as memorizing the path taken to get to a friend's home. It could also involve memorizing a more general rule applicable to a number of specific instances, like Bruner's rules defining instances of a concept. In more recent work Simon and his colleagues have also modeled the "discovery" of scientific laws, such as Boyle's gas law, (Langley et al., 1987). In this work, the correct categorization or generalization to apply to a particular instance is not known, so the computer must be guided by more general goals such as finding a *linear* law that can account for the (neatened up) data.

In short, many kinds of learning, from learning a simple fact, to learning rules, to "discovering" scientific theories, have been modeled using the same basic computational theory of problem solving. This work has made theories of problem solving and learning much more explicit so that they now specify the processes required for them to work. But this gain in specificity has also involved corresponding losses. In particular, computers were first used to *model* human problem solving but later human problem-solving came to be considered merely a form of com-

[14] I skip over Simon's earlier work on EPAM (the "elementary perceiver and memorizor") to focus on rule induction and concept learning (Simon, 1979).

putation.[15] Simon's earlier emphasis on the way in which social roles and identities affect problem solving by specifying its premises also tended to get lost as the focus of research shifted to the formal operations of a closed computer model.

Implications

The cognitive revolution turned the behavioristic view back outside in. It replaced outer reinforcement contingencies and trial and error search behavior with inner problem representations and simulated search. The structures and processes previously located in the environment were placed inside the learner's head. Mind was brought back in, although in a peculiarly detached and abstract way.

This shift in focus involved another change in implicit aim. Where the behaviorists had aimed at predicting and controlling behavior, cognitivists aimed at changing knowledge representations to improve problem-solving effectiveness. The goal of learning shifted from getting the right answer to using the right process. For behaviorists, "learning" was a matter of rapidly getting the right answer (the desired response), all actions leading up to this being considered random error. But for cognitivists, the goal of learning was to acquire "expert" rules that solve a problem with less search than "novice" rules. Since expert rules generally solve a given problem more efficiently, such learning might result in more rapid answers, but the point was to reach the answers by using the right process, for that is what expertise consists of. A student who rapidly solves a math problem using incorrect operations would not be considered to have "learned" the related math concept even if the answer was correct. Furthermore, what seemed "random" errors to the behaviorists could be accounted for in this approach by appealing to inference processes inside the organism.

This new focus had the advantage of increasing sensitivity to what a learner brings to a given problem situation. It suggested that the same data, such as the set of examples or nonexamples of a concept, will have different impact on the conclusions drawn by different learners or on those drawn by the same learner at different points in his or her learning. Hence, one needs

[15]This shift was justified by exaggerated functionalist arguments. The functionalists had insisted on distinguishing the function of thinking (mind) from the physical entities enabling it to occur (brain). This separation between functions and things was taken further by Newell and Simon, who suggested that the material substrate of thinking is irrelevant, aside from the mechanical ability to store and manipulate tokens for symbols, making it is just as legitimate to say that computers think as that people do. But this conclusion depends on what one accepts as "thinking" in the first place. By tailoring the definition of *thinking* to one that computers could meet, Newell and Simon can be seen as finessing the issue.

to be sensitive to the problem-solving process, as defined by a learner's problem representation and search strategy, to know how to lead him or her to a certain conclusion. Since the learner is responsible for doing the problem solving in this model, instruction based on it is likely to improve problem-solving skills, such as learning to factor problems into bite-sized parts, carefully test hypotheses, and so forth. Learning these meta-level skills is not part of the model itself, but it seems reasonable that its use would promote them as a side effect.

This renewed emphasis on mind was counterbalanced by increased detachment from action. If nothing else, behaviorists focused on adaptation to felt difficulties (hungry rats had good reason to press those bars!) and rapid performance. The functionalists had similarly emphasized actual, practical difficulties or uncertainties and the trial of ideas in action. In contrast, "cognitivism" has been much like the reflex arc view that Dewey criticized, in that attention is focused on thinking as a separate stage after sensory input and before motor response. If one takes this seriously, it results in a physically passive approach to learning, in which problem solving is detached from initial feelings of uncertainty and later feelings of resolution. Learning becomes symbol manipulation, rather than dealing with difficulties in acting. In short, the values tacit in a cognitivist approach seem to involve physical and emotional passivity, even while emphasizing strengthened formal problem-solving processes.

Despite this contrast between the behaviorist and cognitivist approaches, it is important to bear in mind what they have in common—a commitment to fixed structures constraining the learning process. For the behaviorist, this is the structure of reinforcement contingencies in the environment, while for the cognitivist it is the structure of the problem representation "inside" the learner's head. Such structures are necessary to define learning itself in both approaches. Learning, for the behaviorist, consists of a change in response rate as a function of repeated experience with the *same* structure of reinforcement. For the cognitivist it is improvement in performance on the *same* task or class of tasks. Both are committed to given, well-defined problems, for without repetition of the "same" problem they would not know what "learning" is (Bateson, 1972b; Newman et al., 1989). This focus on a predefined problem contrasts with the functionalists' concern for the ongoing life of the "learner" and his or her flexibility in altering, renegotiating, or redefining "the" problem. In fact, what the functionalists were most critical of were theories that presupposed a given problem definition, whether the external predefinition of the empiricists or the internal predefinition of the rationalists. The ability to shift basic definitions of what is relevant, important, or of interest during the course of the learning experience tends to be omitted in both behaviorist or cognitivist theory, giving both a compliant or passive view of a learner who takes things as initially defined. Gordon Allport summed up the contrast between James's view and the computational view as follows:

> Men no longer "reason," they behave like giant computers: they receive *inputs* and produce *outputs*, and in spite of noise and redundance, they somehow manage to *code*—and so it goes. James, on the other hand, tells us that reasoning is the "ability to deal with novel data" (which a machine does poorly if at all). He shows us how we select and combine attributes of experience, always following a course "important to our interests." Since machines lack interests it seems that James's simple scaffolding may outlast the currently fashionable computer model. James draws his design from fresh daily experience, whereas today the tendency is to tailor human capacities to fit the alleged properties of the machine. Contemporary model builders will do well to return to James to see whether in fact their mechanical formulations do justice to the subtleties of process he depicts. (James, 1892/1961, pp. xvi–xvii)

SITUATED LEARNING

Cognitivism began to face increasing criticism and decreasing commitment in the 1970s. Computer models turned out to be more brittle, or limited to definite sets of conditions, than had initially been hoped. In addition, new problems emerged in cognitive science and in the wider society for which the computational model may be ill-adapted. These included increased interest in pragmatic and social aspects of thinking and acting (Brooks, 1991; Suchman, 1987) and increased attention to educational inequities experienced by linguistic and cultural minorities (Newman et al., 1989).

Work on situated cognition and learning began to appear in the late 1970s and 1980s. Those criticizing the computational view of mind, such as the philosopher Hubert Dreyfus or the computer scientist Terry Winograd, drew on Heidegger's phenomenology which itself had origins in the work of Husserl and Hegel (Dreyfus, 1972/1979; Winograd and Flores, 1986). Other work, such as the psychology of Lev Vygotsky and his colleagues, A. R. Luria and A. N. Leontiev, derived in part from Marx, as does more recent Soviet activity theory. Both Hegel and Marx had dialectical and evolutionary views of human life. Their dialectical and evolutionary views had much in common with the transactional and evolutionary views of the functional psychologists, although the latter derived from both German and British thought (e.g., Hegel and Darwin).

The principal theme in a situated approach is the assertion that thinking and learning are fundamentally dependent for their proper functioning on the immediate situation of action (Brown, 1989). As an example, imagine being continually told how you should have acted after you have already committed yourself in a certain direction. Such "Monday morning quarterbacking" is irksome because it is of no help with the situation at hand, which has to do with what one is doing *here* and *now*. In fact, the advice can actually interfere with dealing with the present situation because it focuses attention on irrelevancies. Those advocating a situated approach to learning suggest that conventional approaches to learning (behaviorist and cognitivist) are like this because they commonly assume a fixed definition of the situation, a fixed set of relevancies when these are better seen as changing and co-created in action with the environment. As McDermott and Hood (1982, p. 234) put it;

> Experimental procedures create constraints independent of the involvements and concerns of the people under analysis, and rob them of many of the normally available resources for organizing their own behavior. . . . Whereas participants in everyday life use a wide range of procedures to simplify, alter, and negotiate tasks . . . laboratory analysts achieve purity by the single simplifying assumption that subjects are responding to tasks predefined by the experimenter.

In what follows, I briefly summarize three diverse contributions to a view of learning as situated: the philosopher Hubert Dreyfus's criticism of the computational view of cognition, the Russian psychologist Lev Vygotsky's work on the socially constructed contexts of learning, and the anthropologist Jean Lave's work on learning as an aspect of apprenticeship in "communities of practice."

Dreyfus

Beginning in the 1970s, Hubert Dreyfus launched an attack on the computational view of mind using Heidegger's phenomenological critique of modern technicism. Dreyfus suggested that the problem with the computer models of mind is that they are based on predetermined assumptions about what is relevant or important. As a result, the functioning of these systems is limited to situations whose contingencies have been built into them from the start, making them not *generalizable* across situations (Dreyfus, 1972/1979, p. 1). Of course, a clever programmer can insert rules that allow a system to cope with more and more contingencies, but such efforts ultimately bump up against a dilemma: "they are faced either with storing and accessing an infinity of facts, or with having to exclude some possibly relevant facts from the computer's range of calculations" (Dreyfus, 1972/1979, p. 258). The former is impossible, while the latter results in an unnaturally rigid system (Winograd & Flores, 1986). Either way, the computational approach fails as a robust model of human conduct.

The determined cognitivist may attempt to get around this problem by presupposing increasingly abstract sets of rules for representing problem situations. Schemes, frames, or scripts may be used to interpret other elements of a situation (Schank & Riesbeck, 1981). For instance, facts may be interpreted in terms of varying sets of laws, or texts in terms of different story grammars, until a theory or story can be found that satisfactorily accounts for the data. This approach seems to give a person, or system, flexibility, since it allows varying interpretations of a set of initial elements. However, it still presupposes a fixed way of conceiving of the situation at base, for the initial facts or sentences (or lower-level units) are given and the schemata themselves are defined in terms of certain fixed dimensions of contrast. As a result the system will be limited by its own basic assumptions, which it will be unable to modify or correct. Dreyfus acknowledges that there is no proof that one cannot eventually extend such a system to have humanlike performance, but he suggested that there will be decreasing returns to such efforts, because the whole approach is based on an inadequate understanding of human acting and thinking.

According to Dreyfus, most of Western philosophy has been a search for a set of basic rules in terms of which things may be described. Rationalists, in particular, sought the basic assumptions or conceptual frameworks used in cognition. Cognitive theorists did much the same thing, viewing thinking and learning as the product of the inner rules of a problem representation. But Dreyfus argues that human thinking is not *produced* in this way, although rules may be useful for *describing* its patterns in concise ways. Rather than being derived from rules, thinking has its origins in practical, embodied activity:

> A machine can, at best, make a specific set of hypotheses and then find out if they have been confirmed or refuted by the data. [But] The body can constantly modify its expectations in terms of a more flexible criterion: as embodied, we need not check for specific characteristics or a specific range of characteristics, but simply for whether, on the basis of our expectations, we are coping with the object. Coping need not be defined by any specific set of traits but rather by an ongoing mastery . . . (Dreyfus, 1972/1979, p. 250)

In this view, objects with certain properties and value in a situation are created by activity, not by reflective thought. Engaging in the activity in an environment that can be made to function in the way of the activity creates relevant objects. One can play checkers by drawing lines in the sand and using differently colored rocks as the pieces, for instance. For the purposes of that activity the rocks *are* checkers pieces. They really operate as such and not just in one's head, so the activity makes the "objects" what they are. In this particular case, the activity is rather tightly defined by certain rules, but many activities are much more open to varying and evolving definition, and even this one can take on varied nuances in actual practice. Like the functionalists, Dreyfus (and Heidegger) distinguished between routine action, in which the character of the objects figuring in a situation is not given much thought, and action that produces unexpected results. As one expositor of Heidegger put it,

> When we lift a hammer or drive a car we are before we know it enmeshed in a series of meaningful relationships with things. . . . Such intricate contexts of meaning—

> which are usually implicit in our activities and become visible only when something goes wrong, when the hammer breaks or the bulb burns out—constitute what Heidegger calls "world." (Krell, 1977, p. 20)

The point of Dreyfus's criticism is that the static relevancies presupposed in both behaviorist and cognitivist approaches to learning cannot possibly model how humans learn, because human beings are much more flexible in attending to shifting, practical relevancies. They are also much more able to *make* the situation what they prefer it to be, rather than sticking with a given definition. Dreyfus's analysis suggests that one needs to focus on activity, and the varied situations that arise within it, as the background for thinking and learning. Of course, this is very reminiscent of functional psychology and Dewey's point that one needs to begin by knowing what an organism is actually attempting to do, for the organism's learning will be organized by the practical relevancies of that doing.

Vygotsky

While Dreyfus has been primarily a critic of the computational approach, a more elaborated alternative to it has been developing using the work of Lev Vygotsky. Vygotsky wrote in the years following the Russian revolution, but his work has had increasing influence on culturally interested psychologists and anthropologists in the United States (Wertsch, 1985a, 1985b, 1991; Rogoff & Lave, 1984; Lave, 1988; Scribner, 1984). Therefore, it makes some sense to discuss Vygotsky after Dreyfus, even though Dreyfus wrote long after Vygotsky died (1934).

Like Dewey and Mead, Vygotsky was concerned with the social development of mind, or the "higher mental functions." He wrote at a time when the post-revolutionary government was concerned with the modernization of Soviet citizenry. Vygotsky was well acquainted with the psychologists of his time, such as the behaviorists and gestalt psychologists, as well as with the work of Piaget, but he drew on Marx for the more social notion that people's mental lives are shaped by the social activities in which they participate. The notion that mental life is formed through practical participation in social activity was also contrasted with Durkheim's sociological analysis of the origins of the basic categories of thought, which Vygotsky and his colleagues saw as too idealistic (Durkheim, 1965). Where Durkheim saw the categories of thought as coming from ritual distinctions, such as those celebrated in primitive religious ceremonies, Vygotsky adopted a more practical or materialistic approach, emphasizing the use of signs in mundane social activity (e.g., "labor").[16]

Vygotsky argued that higher mental functions develop through participation in social activities; hence, the social context of learning is critical. At an early stage children engage in instrumental thinking when manipulating

[16]This account is based on Luria's discussion in *Cognitive Development* (Luria, 1976).

physical objects. They also engage in social speech with others and learn to use signs in such talk. These two functions develop rather separately at first, but later merge, with the use of signs gained from speech serving to reorganize and greatly extend the power of instrumental thinking. "Labor," the "specifically human" form of activity, was seen as involving such an integration of instrumental and symbolically mediated activity. The use of signs was viewed as developing in a number of stages as the sign becomes an internalized tool of thought. (Vygotsky, 1978, p. 45). At first a child might simply attempt to complete an act and fail. This beginning of the act is a gesture (as for Mead) but is not treated as such by anyone. At a later stage, the attempt becomes a gesture to which someone else responds, helping to complete the child's act. At this stage, the gesture may also function similarly for the child, as in "egotistic" speech in which a child indicates or tells himself or herself what to do. Finally, in the third stage, the whole pattern of interaction, the initial gesture and its completing response, is internalized so that a child is able to covertly respond to his or her own covert gestures. Thus, the gesture shifts from being something like an external tool for completing the act by bidding another to do it to becoming an internal tool used to stimulate oneself to respond to one's own emerging actions as another would. As Vygotsky put it:

> An interpersonal process is transformed into an intrapersonal one. Every function in the child's cultural development appears twice: first, on the social level, and later, on the individual level; first, between people (interpsychological), and then inside the child (intrapsychological). This applies equally to voluntary attention, to logical memory, and to the formation of concepts. All the higher functions originate as actual relations between human individuals. (1978, p. 57)

This view, which is extremely reminiscent of Mead's, depicts mental development as fundamentally social in origin. The basic means of thought—signs—have their origin in social interaction.

Vygotsky's well-known conception of the "zone of proximal development" used the social origin of mental development to help identify a child's points of developmental readiness. A child's growing edge was identified by finding an activity that a child can complete with assistance that he or she cannot complete alone. This zone of proximal development is

> the distance between the actual development level as determined by independent problem-solving and the level of potential development as determined through problem-solving under adult guidance or in collaboration with more capable peers. . . . The zone of proximal development defines those functions that have not yet matured but are in the process of maturation, functions that will mature tomorrow but are currently in an embryonic state. These functions could be termed the "buds" or "flowers" . . . rather than the "fruits" of development. (1978, p. 86).[17]

[17]James wrote quite similarly of the "zone of formative processes," which is the "dynamic belt of quivering uncertainty, the line where past and future meet. It is the theater of all we do not take for granted, the stage of the living drama of life" (James, 1896/1956, pp. 258–259).

The concept of the zone of proximal development, or the range of activity in which growth is possible, is important here because it indicates how learning and development are related and which learning is growth enhancing. While Vygotsky was less than crystalline in the definition of learning, he seems to define it as more capably performing a current part, or role, in a joint activity. *Development* then refers to the internalization of the whole pattern of interaction in which this part is embedded. For instance, "learning" might involve improving one's forehand return in tennis, while "development" would involve being able to place elements of this act in the context of the likely reactions of one's opponent. Given this view, learning is necessary for development, since one needs to become capable of performing a given part of an activity in order to later covertly enact the whole for oneself. At the same time, development is stimulated by learning, since learning occurs in the context of the larger activity whose different parts are internalized through such meaningful participation. This view of learning places it in the context of a changing social role, rather than taking the definition of the situation for granted (as in behaviorist and cognitivist learning theories). Seeing learning in the context of a larger social activity to which the learner contributes led Vygotsky to reject learning that takes the learner's role as fixed or already in place, for this would stifle development. As he put it, "the notion of a zone of proximal development enables us to propound a new formula, namely that the only "good learning' is that which is in advance of development" (Vygotsky, 1978, p. 89).

Vygotsky's approach was *sociohistorical* because he not only situated individual learning in the context of an evolving role in a social activity but also viewed the kinds of social activities available as themselves situated in an evolving form of social life. Here, Vygotsky primarily contrasted more practical ways of thinking associated with traditional society and the more theoretical or abstract ways introduced by modern schools and other institutions. Vygotsky's work, thus, clearly was directed toward modernization and the learning of abstract "scientific" concepts. This emphasis on the social facilitation of *modern* ways of thinking is in at least some contrast with the more contemporary work of Jean Lave.

Lave

The anthropologist Jean Lave has developed an approach to learning that, while related to Vygotsky's, is distinctive enough to merit independent discussion (Chaiklin & Lave, 1993; Lave, 1988, 1990; Lave & Wenger, 1991; Rogoff & Lave, 1984). Like Vygotsky, Lave's approach also has materialist roots, as in "the work of Marx, Bourdieu, Sahlins, and Giddens, among others" (1988, p. 15). However, it also has elements of contemporary antimodernist communitarianism, in contrast to Vygotsky's modernism. Like Dreyfus, Lave has been very critical of traditional cognitivism for its assumption that a learning situation is predefined by a given set of rules, such as the norms of an experimental or classroom situation. One might call this the *passive learner assumption* common to both behaviorist and cognitivist learning theory. In contrast, Lave suggests that neither anthropology nor psychology, as traditionally conceived, is "theoretically equipped to elaborate a theory of active social actors, located in time and space, reflexively and recursively acting upon the world in which they live and which they fashion at the same time" (Lave, 1988, p. 8).

Lave approaches learning through the use of the metaphor of apprenticeship. In her study of Liberian tailors, for example, she was impressed by the way they learned their craft with little or no direct instruction. An apprentice would begin to become a tailor by doing a part of the job involving relatively little specialized skill or financial risk and, over time, move on to more specialized, risky, and centrally valued roles. Whatever "learning" occurred was more or less incidental to participating with others in different phases in the production of finished clothing, rather than the product of isolated lessons. Furthermore, because the behavior of the other community members changed to accommodate the apprentice, the location of "learning" was unclear. As Hanks suggests, "It is the community, or at least those participating in the learning context, who 'learn' under this definition" (Lave & Wenger, 1991, p. 15). Thus, learning is not located "in" an individual, since it involves changes in activity in an environment coconstructed with others. (In the same way one might say that a child does not learn to ride a bike, but to ride *with* a bike. The riding is not in the child, but in the interaction of child and bike.) This view also places learning in a wider social context, since it involves not just improvement in a predefined task, but improvement that contributes to the role performances of others (as well as to an individual's own future role performance). As Lave and Wenger put it, "We have thus situated learning in the trajectories of participation in which it takes on meaning" (1991, p. 121). "Learning" so conceived, is not an isolated or special event since it goes on all the time as an incidental by-product of participation in social activity. Put another way, "social practice is the primary, generative phenomenon, and learning is one of its characteristics" (Lave & Wenger, 1991, p. 34).

Lave's approach to learning is summarized in the expression *legitimate peripheral participation in communities of practice*. This mouthful is a way of emphasizing, first, that in learning as apprenticeship, one's social role is also changing as a part of "learning." For instance, one may begin as a peripheral participant and move toward involvement in more central aspects of the activity, changing roles as one goes. Second, one is a "participant" or cocreator of the activity. Whatever activity is going on will ultimately be a joint product, not something determined by only one party. Finally, most learning that is of any importance occurs as a result of participation in the practical activities of a *community*. Learning is about becoming a full-fledged, contributing member of a community rather than simply performing an isolated task. Lave uses this metaphor of apprenticeship, or "legitimate peripheral participation," to reconceive many traditional aspects of learning theory in more egalitarian terms. Rather than seeing knowledge as something one owns or possesses, she sees it "not in the master but in the organization of the community of practice of which the master is part" (Lave & Wenger, 1991, p. 94). And rather than drawing hierarchical distinctions between student and teacher, or novice and expert, she contrasts "newcomers" and "old-timers" in the community.

The metaphor of learning as apprenticeship can be seen both as an analytical tool for describing learning situations and a normative ideal for how learning ought to occur. As a description, the apprenticeship metaphor helps place current learning in the context of a social activity in which various roles or identities are mutually constructed. It also helps situate learning a current "task" in the context of one's likely career in the community. *Learning* thus takes on social and developmental qualities to which an isolated or static conception would be blind, just as it did for the functional psychologists. This view of learning as highly embedded also becomes something of a normative ideal in Lave's work. Formal schooling, in particular, often serves as a model for how failure is socially constructed by not properly encouraging participation in a meaningful common activity or by use of abstractions that do not function in the practical situation at hand. Some of this criticism is also familiar from the functional psychologists, who criticized the formalism of education at the turn of the century, but the more pronounced antimodernist theme in this recent work contrasts with the turn-of-century effort to humanize modernism.

Implications

Situated learning theory, which is still in its infancy, recalls many themes from functional psychology. The transactionalism of the functional psychologists and their emphasis on the social origin of mind is paralleled by the dialectical approach of the situated learning theorists and their emphasis on the social origins of symbolically mediated activity. Both approaches blur the distinction between thinking and behaving as well as that between individual and social aspects of change. They do so by beginning with social activity. Beginning with activity allows them to approach thinking as a form of acting, thereby furnishing a starting point that is less split between mindless behavior versus bodiless cognition. Beginning with social activity allows them to find concrete origins of reflective thought rather than ignoring higher-order thinking or presupposing its basic content and processes. The result is an approach which conceives of learning as collaborative and meaningfully related to the activities of others.

While many functionalist themes are replayed in situated learning theory, there may nevertheless also be a subtle shift in values from the earlier approach that is worth pointing out. The functional psychologists were as strongly individualistic as they were socialistic in orientation. They focused on whole *lives*, as well as on whole communities. Situated learning theory, at least as Lave and Wenger have developed it thus far, seems to have shifted this focus to specialized "communities of practice," such as craft or professional associations. Socialization in such communities is very important educationally. Nevertheless, an exclusive focus on a given community of practice may lose sight of the whole person, who usually has a life outside that community. The particularistic emphasis, implicit in Lave and Wenger's approach to situated learning (if not in others), may also result in an overly narrow focus on a given community. This is an understandable reaction to the excessive individualism and universalism of behaviorist and cognitivist approaches, but it may also be something of a one-sided reaction. Without a more pluralistic approach, it may not be possible to develop a robust understanding of the role of public education, which surely involves being able to participate in diverse communities as well as in interactions between communities.

CONCLUSIONS

This chapter has considered the socially constructed character of differing conceptions of learning. The history of learning theory is one in which the very conception of what learning is has changed. Differing conceptions of learning were developed and propagated at times when particular cultural assumptions were in vogue, and particular professional and national-political interests dominant. The result is a set of views of learning reflecting differing values and biases. To point this out is not to criticize them, for every conception is partial, focusing attention on some things while overlooking others. But such partiality should be acknowledged.

Differing conceptions of learning have different likely social effects as well as differing social origins. While learning theories may seem to be merely descriptive of "the way things are," they are also tools for organizing learning experiences in ways that are thought to be better in one way or another. Organizing learning based on one conception or another is likely to teach different meta-lessons about the nature of "learning." Whether one calls this "learning to learn," or "development," or "socialization," it seems evident that a given approach to learning is likely to have secondary consequences beyond the focal "learning" that it engenders. Conceptions of learning are, thus, both socially constructed and socially constructive.[18] While this chapter has been neither a social history of learning theory nor a study of the indirect

[18]Just what effects are produced by organizing learning according to differing conceptions is largely hypothetical, although every parent has practical knowledge of this. For an interesting analysis of the meta-lessons about learning likely to be taught by differing approaches to learning see Bateson (1972a).

effects of organizing "learning" in one way or another, it has attempted to discuss conceptions of learning in a way that makes their likely social causes and consequences more evident than is often the case in such discussions.

Consider the contrast between behaviorist and cognitivist approaches to learning in this light. If behaviorism meant anything it meant a focus on the effects of the structure of the environment, such as its reinforcement contingencies. It was an attempt to describe "learning" in purely environmental terms without having to know about the structure of the organism, at least for purists like Watson and Skinner. As a practical matter this meant that the relevant planning and organizing involved in learning a complex act had to come from the outside. Since the thinking involved in learning a complex act was primarily done by others, by those who structured the environment, the resulting family of theories has been useful mostly for teaching unthinking doers, such as by gaining compliance with previously defined behavioral objectives. Thus, the descriptive strategy of focusing only on the contribution of the environment has had the practical effect of emphasizing extrinsic demands on a learner. "Learning," so conceived, meant doing what someone else wanted you to do, as concretely expressed in behavioral contingencies.

Cognitivists took the opposite tack, emphasizing the effects of the structure of the organism. They saw a new act as the product of an inner problem-solving process which is constrained by the rules of a problem representation. The structure of a complex act, like the nested phrase structure of a sentence, was the result of an inner process decomposing an overall problem into various sub-problems which it solved and assembled into a larger sequence. Thus, the structuring or organizing of behavior was seen as due to the organism rather than to the environment. As a practical pedagogical tool, the resulting approach to learning has mostly been useful for teaching undoing thinkers. It attends to the problem-solving process used to get from an initial symbolic state to a goal state, the attempt being to teach "expert" procedures so that a problem can be solved correctly or with greater efficiency. In this conception, "learning" is a change in the rules or procedures used to manipulate symbolic expressions. But what is omitted are the circumstances that lead to conceiving of the problem in a certain way in the first place, as well as concern for the practical side-effects of a given conception. In other words, such learning remains very much "in the head."

Contrasting these two approaches to learning makes evident what they have in common. They share an emphasis on describing learning from a one-sided standpoint, be it that of the environment or that of the organism. And they tend to share a strong distinction between thinking and behaving, or mind and body. One does not have to be a Marxist to see a potential social class division in these contrasting approaches to learning, with a behavioristic approach being well-adapted to the education of workers, and a cognitive approach well-adapted to the education of managers.[19] The division between these two approaches to learning may be comfortable, then, because it is relatively congruent with the current social division of labor. In fact, both approaches may be so consistent with contemporary conditions that they help blind one to other forms of social organization, particularly those that do not make such a strong distinction between thinking and doing, or to distinct classes of thinkers and doers.

Because contemporary learning theory is divided in this way it seemed a good idea to reconsider the contributions of functional psychology. Functional psychology was a sophisticated attempt to avoid just this split between organism and environment, mind and body, theory and practice. At a social level it was an attempt to develop an approach to learning consistent with a democratic society, that is, one in which people are able to think about and alter their own social environments (it being understood that this would, in turn, change their forms of thinking). The key to functional psychology was its transactional approach which emphasized dynamic relations between organism and environment. Rather than fitting the organism to the demands of the environment, or the environment to the demands of the organism, it viewed adaptation as a dynamic, collaborative affair between organism and environment. Habits were then viewed actively, that is, not just as behavior that is compliant with environmental demands, but as ways of acting that change the environment so as to help accomplish organismic goals. Thinking was viewed as reflection on such patterns of interaction so that the meaning of a given act, that is the consequences it is likely to bring about, could be known. Such conscious reflection was itself seen as a collaborative affair, since it was made possible by social interaction with others. The whole approach thus began with organism-environment transactions, or relationships, rather than with organismic or environmental constraints taken by themselves. Of course, this is also true of the contemporary situated approach to learning which also adopts a relational or dialectical starting point, making it something of a return to these earlier themes, although in post-modern garb.

Considering learning in relational rather than unilateral terms not only emphasizes its collaborative aspects, but also makes it possible to consider qualities of learning that are invisible to the usual behaviorist or cognitivist approaches. Is present learning meaningful, for instance, or is it isolated or fragmented from larger wholes, and therefore meaningless? Is its function merely to please others, or is it motivated by a desire to solve a problem that one genuinely has? Is it stultifying because it occurs in a static relationship,

[19]The experience of those in different tracks in school certainly seems to fit this division, with those in lower tracks reporting that they learn to behave while those in higher tracks report they learn to think [Oakes, 1985 #210].

or is it growth-inducing because it stretches the relationship? These are the sorts of questions that Dewey and Vygotsky asked about learning. They are questions about the character of the relationship in which learning takes place which is likely to alter how learned habits will function. Will they be used flexibly in relation with other situationally relevant habits, for example, or will they operate in a rigid and isolated fashion? Since these and related qualities of learning are among the outcomes that parents and teachers commonly care about, a functional or situated approach to learning can be of immediate practical import. Adopting it requires something more like a naturalistic or anthropological approach to research, even when experiments are involved under laboratory conditions.[20] Such an approach may not convey the traditional sense of "scientific" certainty, but perhaps this is simply a loss of false pretensions.

Acknowledgments

I thank the Institute for Research on Learning in Palo Alto, California, for its generous support during the past four summers. Walter Feinberg's and Herbert Richard's, Ray McDermott's, and Gary Phye's extremely helpful comments are also much appreciated.

References

Anderson, J. R. (1990). *Cognitive psychology and its implications*. New York: W. H. Freeman and Co.

Angell, J. R. (1907). The province of functional psychology. *The psychological review*, 14(2), 61–89.

Bateson, G. (1972a). Social planning and the concept of deutero-learning. In G. Bateson (Ed.), *Steps to an ecology of mind* (pp. 159–176). New York: Ballantine Books.

Bateson, G. (1972b). *Steps to an ecology of mind*. New York: Ballantine Books.

Bickhard, M. H. (1992). How does the environment affect the person? In L. T. Winegar & J. Valsiner (Eds.), *Children's development in social context*. Hillsdale, NJ: Lawrence Erlbaum Associates.

Bower, G. H., & Hilgard, E. R. (1981). *Theories of learning*. Englewood Cliffs, NJ: Prentice-Hall.

Bredo, E. (1994). Reconstructing educational psychology: Situated cognition and Deweyian pragmatism. *Educational Psychologist*, 29(1), 23–35.

Brooks, R. A. (1991). New approaches to robotics. *Science*, 253, 1227–1232.

Brown, J. S., Collins, A., & Duguid, P. (1989). Situated cognition and the culture of learning. *Educational Researcher*, 18(1), 32–42.

Bruner, J. (1960). *The process of education*. New York: Vintage Books.

Bruner, J. (1983). *In search of mind: Essays in autobiography*. New York: Harper and Row.

[20] Some experiments may also be meta-experiments, that is explorations of the limitations induced by the experimental situation itself. Consider Newman, Griffin, and Cole's (1989) interesting approach of trying to replicate experimental results in everyday settings so as to discover how control of the experimental setting may blind researchers to the processes by which tasks are socially defined and distributed. Vygotsky's combination of experimental and naturalistic observation is also interesting, in which he made the experimental task very difficult for a subject to perform and then noted how they attempted to cope with the relatively impossible situation, such as by using "fossilized" behavior learned earlier in their development.

Bruner, J. (1985). Vygotsky: A historical and conceptual perspective. In J. V. Wertsch (Ed.), *Culture, communication, and cognition* (pp. 21–34). Cambridge, England: Cambridge University Press.

Bruner, J. (1986). *Actual minds, possible worlds*. Cambridge, MA: Harvard University Press.

Bruner, J. (1990). *Acts of meaning*. Cambridge, Mass.: Harvard University Press.

Bruner, J. S., Goodnow, J. J., & Austin, G. A. (1956). *A study of thinking*. New York: John Wiley and Sons.

Case, R. (1991). Neo-Piagetian theories of child development. In R. J. Sternberg & C. A. Berg (Eds.), *Intellectual development*. Cambridge, England: Cambridge University Press.

Catania, A. C. (1992). *Learning* (3d ed.). Englewood Cliffs, NJ: Prentice-Hall.

Chaiklin, S., & Lave, J. (1993). *Understanding practice: Perspectives on activity and context*. Cambridge, England: Cambridge University Press.

Chomsky, N. (1959). A review of B. F. Skinner's *Verbal behavior. Language*, 35(1).

Clancey, W. J. (1992). "Situated" means coordinating without deliberation. McDonnel Foundation Conference, Santa Fe, NM.

Clancey, W. J. (1993). Situated action: A neutopsychological interpretation response to Vera and Simon. *Cognitive Science*, 17(1), 87–116.

Cole, M., Gay, J., Glick, J., & Sharp, D. (1971). *The cultural context of learning and thinking*. New York: Basic Books.

Dewey, J. (1896). The reflex arc concept in psychology. *The Psychological Review*, (3), 356–370.

Dewey, J. (1916). *Democracy and education*. New York: Macmillan.

Dewey, J. (1938). *Experience and education*. New York: Collier–Macmillan.

Dewey, J. (1958). *Experience and nature*. New York: Dover Publications.

Dewey, J., & Bentley, A. (1949). *Knowing and the known*. Boston: Beacon Press.

Dreyfus, H. L. (1972/1979). *What computers can't do*. New York: Harper and Row.

Durkheim, E. (1965). *The elementary forms of the religious life*. New York: The Free Press.

Hilgard, E. R., & Bower, G. H. (1966). *Theories of learning*. New York: Appleton-Century-Crofts.

Hull, C. L. (1952). *A behavior system: An introduction to behavior theory concerning the individual organism*. New York: Russell and Russell Press.

James, W. (1890/1950). *The principles of psychology*. New York: Dover Publications.

James, W. (1890/1952). *The principles of psychology*. Chicago: Encyclopedia Brittanica.

James, W. (1892/1961). *Psychology: The briefer course*. New York: Harper and Row.

James, W. (1896/1956). *The will to believe and other essays in popular philosophy*. New York: Dover Publications.

James, W. (1897/1956). The sentiment of rationalilty. In W. James (Ed.), *The will to believe* (pp. 63–110). New York: Dover Publications.

James, W. (1899/1958). *Talks to teachers on pschology: And to students on some of life's ideals*. New York: W. W. Norton and Co.

James, W. (1907/1963). *Pragmatism and other essays*. New York: Washington Square Press.

Krell, D. F. (Ed.). (1977). *Martin Heidegger: Basic writings*. New York: Harper and Row.

Langley, P., & Simon, H. A. (1981). The central role of learning in cognition. In J. R. Anderson (Ed.), *Cognitive skills and their acquisition*. Hillsdale, NJ: Lawrence Earlbaum Associates.

Langley, P., Simon, H. A., Bradshaw, G. L., & Zytkow, J. M. (1987). *Scientific discovery: Computational explorations of the creative process*. Cambridge, MA: MIT Press.

Lave, J. (1988). *Cognition in practice: mind, mathematics and culture in everyday life*. Cambridge, England: Cambridge University Press.

Lave, J. (1990). The culture of acquisition and the practice of understanding. In J. W. Stigler, R. A. Shweder, & G. Herdt (Eds.), *Cultural psychology* (pp. 309–327). Cambridge, England: Cambridge University Press.

Lave, J., & Wenger, E. (1991). *Situated learning: Legitimate peripheral participation*. Cambridge, England: Cambridge University Press.

Luria, A. R. (1976). *Cognitive development: Its cultural and social foundations*. Cambridge, MA: Harvard University Press.

March, J. G., & Simon, H. A. (1958). *Organizations*. New York: John Wiley and Sons.

McDermott, R. P., & Hood, L. (1982). Institutionalized Psychology and the Ethnography of Schooling. In P. Gilmore & A. Gladthorn (Eds.), *Children In and Out of School*. Washington, DC: Center for Applied Linguistics.

Mead, G. H. (1910/1970). Social consciousness and the consciousness of meaning. In H. S. Thayer (Ed.), *Pragmatism: The classic writings* (pp. 341–350). New York: Mentor Books.

Mead, G. H. (1934). *Mind, self, and society: From the standpoint of a social behaviorist*. Chicago: University of Chicago Press.

Miller, P. (1968). *American thought: Civil War to World War I*. New York: Holt, Rinehart and Winston.

Morris, L. (1950). *William James*. New York: Charles Scribner's Sons.

Newman, D., Griffin, P., & Cole, M. (1989). *The construction zone: Working for cognitive change in schools*. Cambridge, England: Cambridge University Press.

Oakes, J. (1985). *Keeping track: How schools structure inequality*. New Haven, CN: Yale University Press.

Rogoff, B. (1990). *Apprenticeship in thinking: Cognitive development in social context*. Oxford, England: Oxford University Press.

Rogoff, B., & Lave, J. (Eds.). (1984). *Everyday cognition: Its development in social context*. Cambridge, MA: Harvard University Press.

Sahakian, W. S. (1975). *History and systems of psychology*. New York: John Wiley and Sons.

Schank, R. C., & Riesbeck, C. K. (1981). *Inside computer understanding*. Hillsdale, NJ: Lawrence Earlbaum Associates.

Schön, D. A. (1983). *The reflective practitioner: How professionals think in action*. New York: Basic Books.

Schultz, D. P. (1969). *A history of modern psychology*. New York: Academic Press.

Schwartz, B. (1986). *The battle for human nature*. New York: W. W. Norton and Co.

Scribner, J. (1984). Studying working intelligence. In B. Rogoff & J. Lave (Eds.), *Everyday cognition: Its development in social context* Cambridge, MA: Harvard University Press.

Simon, H. A. (1945). *Administrative behavior*. New York: The Free Press.

Simon, H. A. (1957). *Models of man*. New York: John Wiley and Sons.

Simon, H. A. (Ed.). (1979). *Models of thought*. New Haven, CN: Yale University Press.

Simon, H. A. (1982). *Models of bounded rationality: Behavioral economics and business organization*. Cambridge, MA: MIT Press.

Simon, H. A. (1991). *Models of my life*. New York: Basic Books.

Skinner, B. F. (1935). The generic nature of the concepts of stimulus and response. *The Journal of General Psychology*, 12(1), 40–65.

Skinner, B. F. (1950). Are theories of learning necessary? *The Psychological Review*, 57(4), 193–216.

Skinner, B. F. (1974). *About behaviorism*. New York: Random House.

Suchman, L. A. (1987). *Plans and situated actions: The problem of human–machine communication*. Cambridge, England: Cambridge University Press.

Suchman, L. A. (1992). Talk on situated learning. In American Educational Research Association. San Francisco:

Tolman, E. C. (1951/1966). *Behavior and psychological man*. Berkeley: University of California Press.

Varela, A. H., Thompson, E., & Rosch, E. (1991). *The embodied mind: Cognitive science and human experience*. Cambridge, MA: MIT Press.

Vygotsky, L. S. (1978). *Mind in society: The development of higher psychological processes*. Cambridge, MA: Harvard University Press.

Watson, J. B. (1913). Psychology as the behaviorist views it. In E. H. Madden (Ed.), *A source book in the history of psychology* (pp. 507–515).

Watson, J. B. (1924/1930). *Behaviorism*. New York: W. W. Norton and Co.

Watson, J. B. (1961). John Broadus Watson. In C. Murchison (Ed.), *A history of pschology in autobiography*. New York: Russell and Russell Press.

Wertsch, J. V. (Ed.). (1985a). *Culture, communication, and cognition*. Cambridge, England: Cambridge University Press.

Wertsch, J. V. (1985b). *Vygotsky and the social formation of mind*. Cambridge, MA: Harvard University Press.

Wertsch, J. V. (1991). *Voices of the mind: A sociocultural approach to mediated action*. Cambridge, MA: Harvard University Press.

Winograd, T., & Flores, F. (1986). *Understanding computers and cognition*. Reading, MA: Addison-Wesley.

CHAPTER

2

Learning and Remembering: The Basis for Personal Knowledge Construction

GARY PHYE
Iowa State University

THEORY AND PRACTICE

The constructivist movement in education has been receiving increased attention at all levels. The movement is quite popular in other disciplines as well. The emergence of the constructivist perspective, in part, is a reflection of the interdisciplinary nature of the education profession today. While the assimilation of constructivist theory has a positive impact, constructivist do not speak with a single voice. Further, as was indicated in the introductory chapter, many of the basic issues being introduced by the constructivists are not new to educational philosophy or educational psychology. This is due, in part, to the tremendous influence of John Dewey on American education and psychology.

While the overall impact of the constructivist movement has been positive, no overwhelming evidence suggests that the theoretical issues being discussed will have much impact on educational practice in the classroom. This may be due, in part, to a communication problem. For example, educational issues can be analyzed at several theoretical levels. On the one hand, curriculum issues involving such philosophical problems as defining *meaning*, seeking "truth," or defining a content area like history are a legitimate part of the constructivist movement. Here, the level of analysis is philosophical with an emphasis on understanding how the knowledge that defines a curriculum is derived.

Handbook of Academic Learning

At the psychological level of analysis, emphasis is placed on the construction of personal knowledge (how a person acquires knowledge). This level of analysis is commonly referred to as *constructivism* and has a long tradition in educational circles. In addition to Dewey, Piaget, and Vygotsky are also major figures identified with constructivism. A major defining characteristic of constructivism is the emphasis on a child-centered approach to educational practice (pedagogy). This is the basic focus taken in this chapter. The emphasis on classroom learning and remembering simply reflects a psychological level of analysis. Obviously, philosophy influences educational policy. However, the position taken throughout this chapter is that educational practice from a psychological level of analysis is a worthy endeavor.

Why bother with a chapter on learning and remembering? Basically, because the *personal knowledge construction* that is the basis for classroom learning and achievement is the result or outcome of these two processes (learning and remembering). For cognitive and educational psychologists, all learning involves memory. All knowledge involves memory. "When we say that we know something, we imply that we have experienced it or thought about it before and that we remember our experience" (Schwartz & Reisberg, 1991, p. 237). This is a reminder that, while memory may have a bad name in some educational circles, classroom learning involves acquisition, storage, and retrieval. *Acquisition* is the study of how new information is acquired. A basic question might be, "What is the maximally efficient way to learn?" However, when something is learned, we must hold that information until it is needed at a later time. This is the *storage* function of memory. Further, the information that is stored in memory must be *retrieved* and brought into active use. "Finally, we *use* the information that is in memory; that is, we remember!" (Schwartz & Reisberg, 1991, p. 252).

In this chapter I will be focusing on personal knowledge construction in the classroom. Since the level of analysis is the student (constructivism) rather than the curriculum (constructivist), classroom learning and remembering will be emphasized. Understanding the subtle but real difference between a constructivist perspective and constructivism makes the psychological analysis of classroom learning the keystone of pedagogical practice.

Following a consideration of classroom learning examples, the construction of personal knowledge will be discussed. The second part of the chapter will be devoted to remembering. This section is relevant in terms of both theory and practice. As teachers we are continually reminded that students do not remember everything (very much?) of what they are taught. This is voiced in a frequently overheard comment made by teachers, "We covered that last week, don't you remember?" The point is, there are not two separate processes (1) learning and (2) remembering. They are simply two stages of knowledge construction. The last part of the chapter is devoted to a discussion of remembering and problem solving as elements in the teaching of higher-order thinking in the classroom.

CLASSROOM LEARNING

Academic Content and Classroom Learning

Is one more important than the other or are they the same? In answering this question, I will argue that they are not the same and that importance is not an issue. At the content level, scholars and researchers have constructed and conventionalized the meaning of their discipline (a constructivist activity). Obvious examples are English grammar and syntax or algebra. These disciplines have vocabularies, rules, concepts, models, theories, and the like that have a formal meaning and formal logic. This is recognized as subject matter content and makes up the curriculum.

When analyzing classroom learning performance, we recognize that any student in the classroom has a vocabulary, knows rules, concepts, mental models, and so forth, of a personal nature as well as a limited awareness of the formal meaning and logic of academic disciplines. In some cases, the personal meanings and logic of the student is consistent with the formal meanings and logic of the discipline being taught. In other cases, this correspondence is missing. The discrepancy between personal and formal knowledge defines for us the nature of *classroom learning*. This is similar to the distinction made by Vygotsky (1934/1992) between scientific and everyday concepts. Tharp and Gallimore (1988) have made a similar distinction, substituting the term *schooled concepts* for Vygotsky's scientific concepts. Taken together, these views of constructivism define *classroom learning* as the refinement of personal knowledge into a closer correspondence with formal academic knowledge that characterizes the curriculum.

Learning Episodes

Because classroom learning has so many meanings, precision is lost when we use the term without determining exactly what we mean. Consider the following examples:

1. Jim wants to learn new study habits.
2. Sharon is practicing her flute lesson.
3. Julie is memorizing her spelling words.
4. Jack is learning how to expand a quadratic equation.
5. Jill is studying her Spanish assignment.
6. Sam is practicing free throws.
7. Betty is completing her book report.

Three features seem to characterize all of these academic learning situations. First, they are all examples of complex activities that require attention, practice, a commitment to change, are goal directed, and will result in learning outcomes. Second, while some activities reflect the development of a formal knowledge base (algebra, Spanish, spelling words, and music) others reflect a more informal knowledge base (study habits and making free throws). The most important factor to keep in mind is that each academic learning activity includes elements of both formal and informal knowledge. The relative proportions simply vary across tasks. Third, for competence to develop, there must be a permanency to what is learned. That is, long-term memory for what is learned must be demonstrated.

Remembering

Learning is not just for the moment; we not only remember past experiences but can anticipate future events based on the present and the past. *Remembering is the conscious awareness of memory processing* that involves memory search and retrieval. Hence, remembering is not an automatic process involving memory. Rather, it is the subjective feeling of familiarity we all have when trying to isolate and identify some part of our knowledge base that has been acquired in the past (Kelly & Jacoby, 1990). This issue (awareness vs. automatic memory processing) prompted the title "Classroom Learning and Remembering" rather than learning and memory.

Much learning that occurs outside the classroom or informal learning within the classroom may be overlearned to the point that memory processing is automatic. In the examples given previously, with practice, Sharon's fingering techniques and sight reading ability will become automatic in the sense of automatic memory processing. This automaticity that comes with extensive practice can also be recognized as an important ingredient in Sam becoming a skilled free throw shooter. In each of the other examples, one can identify elements of the academic tasks where automatic processing is a valuable tool for learning (skilled reading, phonics skills, use of mnemonics, use of elaboration and rehearsal techniques, and so on). On the other hand, in the classroom where higher-order thinking is an important learning outcome, automaticity plays a limited role. While higher-order thinking includes a repertoire of automatic academic skills, higher-order thinking requires effortful cognitive processing at the level of awareness. Another way of making this point is to consider the emphasis on self-regulated learning in the classroom. Self-regulation is not an automatic process. All students must make decisions and judge about "what," "how," and "when" to learn in the classroom.

PERSONAL KNOWLEDGE CONSTRUCTION

The Student–Environment Fit

From a functionalist view, classroom learning is a relatively permanent change in behavior that occurs as the result of an affordance (J. J. Gibson,

1979). *Affordance*, a term coined by J. J. Gibson (E. J. Gibson, 1994), refers to a reciprocal relationship between a person and his or her environment. The environment provides opportunities and the person either provides or does not provide an action system that takes advantage of what the environment offers. Perceiving the relationship is perceiving an affordance, a person–environment fit. In the case of classroom learning, the person is a student and the environment can include the student working alone, in a group, with a teacher, or with technology. A defining feature of this approach to classroom learning is the requirement that, given a responsive classroom environment, the learner is responsible for taking advantage of what the environment offers. As can be inferred from this definition of affordance, the spirit of functionalism places an emphasis on the *adaptiveness* of behavior (on the part of the learner).

What Is Knowledge?

A recurring theme has been the emphasis on identifying the appropriate level of analysis when pursuing answers to the questions (1) "What is knowledge?" (2) "How is knowledge processed?" and (3) "How is knowledge used?"

Several levels of analysis can be used to provide an explanation for the "what" and "how" of personal knowledge construction. At one extreme, a reductionist would suggest that learning or knowledge be investigated at the level of the central nervous system. In this case, biopsychologists and neuropsychologists would provide neurological and biochemical explanations. These explanations might be appropriate at a physiological level of explanation but have little *functional value* for a classroom teacher. One can also err in the opposite direction and seek explanations at the level of metaphysics. This level of explanation seeks to establish first principles of causality such as ultimate "meaning" and "reality." These explanations provide good cognitive exercise for philosophers and some educational psychologists (Phillips, 1994) but have little functional value for teachers. This point has also been made by Eleanor Gibson (1994).

> Meaningful explanations should be at their own level of function. Causal relations do not exist between levels only at their own. To look for correspondence between levels is most certainly a major interest of scientists; but to be meaningful, a correspondence must exist between appropriate units of each of two levels. Correspondence as such does not in itself indicate a causal relationship, but in the final analysis we may discover more general laws that cover both levels (p. 70).

In other words, questions involving classroom practice should have a correspondence with the personal knowledge construction being undertaken by the learner. This also suggests, however, that pedagogical practices should result from an analysis of the learner's perspective. This emphasis within constructivism has drawn the most attention. For example, within the context of classroom instruction, Cooper (1993) has characterized the shifts in instructional design as a movement from behaviorism through cognitivism to constructivism. The point Cooper makes is that instruction for the behaviorist is a matter of impressing an adult's perspective of the task to be learned onto a student's blank mind. The focus is on behavioral outcomes with little consideration given to cognition (thinking and problem solving) from a developmental perspective. Unfortunately, the cognitive science focus has been almost exclusively on thinking and problem solving at the expense of motivational considerations that are goal oriented. Many see constructivism as a movement that combines cognition from a developmental perspective with motivational issues such as volition and self-directed learning. For many of us, constructivism at the level of personal knowledge construction is what defines classroom learning.

Knowledge Processing

Consistent with constructivism, the construction of personal knowledge can best be interpreted from an information processing perspective. The information processing perspective has two major advantages. First, although an individual learner may have a knowledge structure that is unique, all human beings are viewed as processing information by using a common set of processing components. The basic processing components are presented in Figure 1.

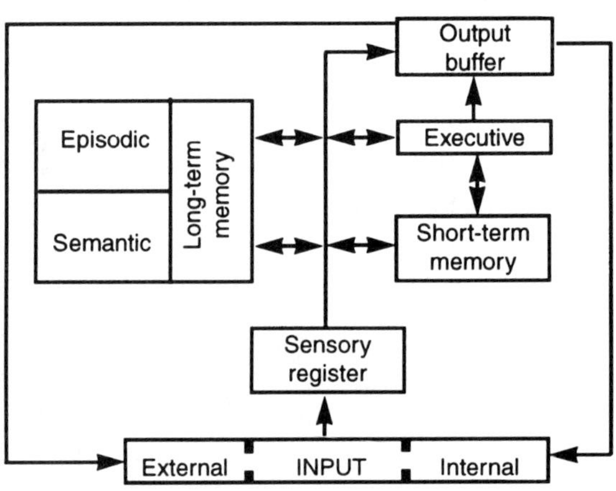

FIGURE 1
Basic information processing model.
From Cognitive classroom learning: Understanding, thinking and problem solving (p. 4), by G. D. Phye & T. Andre, 1986, Orlando, FL: Academic Press.

Second, a wealth of psychological research, based on *human performance*, provides insight into how components of the processing system function. Thousands of studies of attention, short-term memory, long-term memory, working memory, meta-cognition, and the like have been conducted with both children and adults. Both basic and applied research has studied beginning reading, skilled reading, mathematical learning, science learning, problem solving, thinking, and many other aspects of academic learning.

A particular value of the information processing perspective for the classroom teacher is the assumption that, while each student will have a unique set of prior experiences that influence entry learning level, rate of learning, style of learning, and so forth, all nondisabled students in the classroom will be approaching the learning assignment with essentially the same set of processing components. Consequently, when learning is not successful, an assessment can be quickly conducted to determine processing strengths and weaknesses. If no processing breakdown is observed, prior knowledge or cultural influences would be examined.

Interestingly, while there may be processing capacity limits, these limits can be functionally extended by the use of *cognitive tools* like chunking, mnemonic devices, concept maps, rehearsal and maintenance techniques, metacognitive monitoring, and so on. In other words, one need not rely on a neurological explanation of information processing to describe or explain personal knowledge construction.

The aforementioned *cognitive tools* have greater functional utility in some classroom learning situations than others. In Part II of this handbook, the topic of teaching "how" to learn within domains is organized around curriculum areas (e.g., subject matter content). It will become apparent that the development and use of cognitive tools within content domains has become a major focus in terms of classroom learning outcomes. These tools are viewed as essential for the construction of personal knowledge in the classroom.

What Is a Knowledge Domain?

While there is no consensus on this point, a definition offered by Alexander, Schallert, and Hare (1991) is probably most consistent with the approach taken in the following chapters. *Domain knowledge* is a "more formal subset of content knowledge; a realm of knowledge that broadly encompasses a field of study or thought" (p. 332). While the concept of a knowledge domain identifies content, what the learner can do with such knowledge must still be determined.

By defining *domain knowledge* as a formal subset of content knowledge, we have moved to the level of curriculum for our definition. To maintain a functional level of analysis, we must involve the learner. This can be accomplished at the level of personal knowledge construction by developing a functional knowledge taxonomy that is learner centered.

A Functional Knowledge Taxonomy

From a functional perspective, a distinction has been made among various types of knowledge in terms of knowing what, knowing when, and knowing how to know. This perspective gets translated in the research literature into declarative knowledge, procedural knowledge, and strategic knowledge (Phye, 1992).

Basically, *declarative knowledge* involves knowledge of facts, concepts, vocabulary, and other bits of information that are stored in memory. Information can also be stored as images and nonverbal knowledge (remember Sharon practicing her flute). For Sharon, simply learning the appropriate finger positions would constitute declarative knowledge of a nonverbal nature.

Procedural knowledge is demonstrated when a student can combine, incorporate, or assimilate (in the Piagetian sense) declarative knowledge so that it can be used procedurally (a course of action). In terms of classroom learning, this involves the incorporation of information into organized plans, strategies, ideas, schemata, and the like. Procedural knowledge would include the use of cognitive tools that are either domain specific or more widely employed (application, analysis, synthesis, evaluation, etc.).

Strategic knowledge involves knowing when and how to use declarative and procedural knowledge to construct a learning outcome. This involves such activities as problem solving in mathematics, critical thinking in social studies, or sight reading a new musical composition for the flute. The last type of knowledge, demonstrated as a learning outcome, emphasizes its self-directedness and volitional nature. This epitomizes the "active" construction of a learning outcome and places the student at the center of the teaching–learning process. In addition to reflecting a competency dimension, primary consideration is given to motivational aspects of academic learning.

Knowledge Assessment

Given a functional taxonomy that can be applied to any knowledge domain, how can it be determined that a student's knowledge within a subject matter domain is declarative, procedural, or strategic in nature? The model in Table 1 emphasizes the assessment of memory retention and transfer in determining the functional nature of knowledge a student has acquired (Mayer, 1992).

Declarative knowledge is assessed with traditional measures of memory retention (paper–pencil tasks, verbal reports, etc.). In contrast, procedural and strategic knowledge are assessed using a combination of memory retention and transfer performance. Mayer (1987) argues that competency measured in terms of understanding can be determined only when a student

TABLE 1
Model for Functional Knowledge Assessment

Type of learner	Memory retention performance	Transfer performance	Kind of knowledge
Nonlearner	Poor	Poor	None
Nonunderstander	Good	Poor	Declarative
Guided understander	Good	Good	Procedural
Self-directed understander	Good	Good	Strategic

demonstrates the ability to use previously acquired domain knowledge in a new or novel manner. This ability reflects a true comprehension or understanding of the formal or informal content that makes up the knowledge domain.

If a student can transfer procedural knowledge when told "what" and "when" to do so, procedural understanding is demonstrated. The student is relying on explicit instruction concerning "what" cognitive tools to use and "when" to use them. This is a case where the student does not demonstrate *volition* in terms of initiating, carrying out, or completing the transfer task. On the other hand, when no such instructions are provided, a student must volitionally construct an awareness of "what" cognitive tools to use plus "how" and "when" the tools should be employed. Such a student has demonstrated learning outcomes that not only meet most definitions of understanding but problem solving as well. This distinction between procedural knowledge and strategic knowledge is to be considered when using performance assessment techniques in the classroom.

Projects, performance, and other "authentic" assessment activities can be constructed to reflect either procedural or strategic knowledge performance. The critical factor that distinguishes these two types of understanding is how the task is situated. Providing students with too much direction through explicit instruction can provide an overestimate of understanding. The teacher may be assuming that the performance reflects strategic knowledge when in fact, procedural knowledge is being reflected. Strategic academic learning is the result of both the use of cognitive tools and an attitude on the part of students of self-directedness.

REMEMBERING

In terms of personal knowledge construction, the fact that memory plays a role in acquisition (the learning of new information) is obvious. As teachers, we do not credit a student with learning without some indication that the new knowledge has been encoded or stored in long-term memory. Typically in the classroom, we expect some information to be listened to but not remembered. However, the information that we think is important for future academic success is expected to become a part of the student's knowledge structure (remembered). Research findings from both learning and instructional theory tell us that this is not an automatic process.

Personal knowledge construction emphasizes the role of remembering in classroom learning. Not only does memory play a role in the acquisition, storage, and retrieval of declarative and procedural knowledge but also appears to play a critical role in problem solving (use of strategic knowledge). This point is more clearly made by referring to the recent literature in experimental psychology. "More and more evidence points to a distinction between two separate kinds of memory, two separate kinds of remembering" (Schwartz & Reisberg, 1991, p. 310). First there is the feeling of familiarity. We *may not have any knowledge of the source* of the feeling of familiarity, it simply feels familiar to us from some past experience. The second kind of remembering involves not only familiarity but *an awareness of the source* of the memory. Mandler (1980) has identified the former as generic memory and the latter as source memory.

This distinction has implications for academic learning and classroom instruction. Two frequently used classroom assessment techniques are recall and recognition. Recall tests always require source memory but recognition tests can be answered by either source memory or familiarity plus inference (Schwartz & Reisberg, 1991). Mandler, among others, has also proposed that different kinds of learning set the bases for source memory and familiarity. Two study procedures that were discussed earlier, maintenance and elaboration, are thought to produce the bases for familiarity and source memory. Maintenance as a study strategy can serve as the basis for generic memory or familiarity. However, elaboration as a study strategy, which is an attempt to place material in long-term memory and modify the knowledge structure, is necessary for source memory.

The implications are these. If a classroom teacher consistently uses only one technique to assess learning, students quickly adapt a study strategy that will produce the required results. If a teacher uses only a multiple-choice format for the development of assessment activities, students' may well adopt a maintenance study strategy that requires only familiarity plus an inference (or guess) to answer. This generic memory may reflect information gathered not only from the assignments but from other sources as well. Short answer or some form of supply-type assessment (recall) requires an elaborative study strategy to produce the source memory that is the reason for the feeling of familiarity. This type of knowledge is more reflective of what most classroom teachers think they are getting when they conduct assessments.

Is Remembering Automatic?

With reference to Figure 1, information that is being processed by the learner must be actively manipulated in short-term memory or it gets lost and is never encoded or stored in long-term memory. A student must identify information that is important and then, having made the decision that this information is worthy of study, use a maintenance strategy to hold the information so that it can be elaborated (or organized) to "fit" existing knowledge in long-term memory.

This is why we teach students to discriminate between relevant and irrelevant information when listening to a discussion or reading a text. Underlining a text or taking study notes are examples. The key to successful underlining while reading a text is the ability to maintain the "gist" of a paragraph in working memory so that we can highlight the main idea of the paragraph and critical supporting evidence. A lack of this ability can be easily identified when students make a habit of highlighting most a page for further study. While listening to a teacher explain something in class, we try to identify the important information that we do not already know and write it down (take notes).

In both examples, we use procedures that help us maintain information long enough that during study we can elaborate (organize) the maintained information so that it can be encoded in long-term memory. By successfully using maintenance and elaboration procedures to facilitate the transfer of the elaborated information into long-term memory, the student's knowledge structure has been modified. The point to make at this time is that what the student remembers and uses (e.g., maintenance and elaboration procedures) determines the successful acquisition of new information.

Using Knowledge

In the classroom, we have instructional techniques that foster maintenance and elaboration processing. Teaching note taking, the use of concept maps, or webbing are just some of the instructional activities employed by teachers to foster encoding and storage of relevant information in long-term memory. Does this ensure that students then will be able to remember (use the stored information)? Not necessarily. One must have *access* to the information in one's knowledge structure for successful remembering to occur. The inability to successfully gain access to prior knowledge has come to be referred to as the "inert knowledge" problem (Phye, 1992; Prawat, 1989; Whitehead, 1929). Here, students have the required information encoded as part of their knowledge structure but cannot successfully *search* and *retrieve* the information. Successful searching and retrieval are subprocesses necessary for access to one's knowledge. Are these subprocesses automatic in the sense that successful encoding guarantees successful searching and retrieval? No! Otherwise, there would be little or no concern for the "inert knowledge" problem just mentioned.

Should teachers be concerned with the problems associated with access to prior knowledge? Are teachers not primarily concerned with the instructional issues associated with instruction? I argue that there is a very practical reason why teachers must become sensitive to these issues of memory retrieval. The spirit of the times emphasizes the connectedness of instruction and classroom evaluation. It has been estimated that 30 to 40% of a classroom teacher's time is spent assessing classroom learning (Stiggens, 1992). In Part IV of this handbook, Bill Schafer, Johan Hamers, A. J. J. M. Ruijssenaars, and Vicki Spandal each address various aspects of classroom assessment that reflect how students remember and use prior knowledge. The point is, *from a student's perspective, assessment involves the need to successfully gain access to and use prior knowledge* that is stored in long-term memory. Once again, the question of automatic processing has been raised. If authentic classroom assessment requires thoughtful searching and retrieval of information followed by doing something with the information, what role does automatic processing play in the learning process?

Automatization

Earlier, a functional distinction was made between declarative, procedural, and strategic knowledge. From a functional perspective, declarative knowledge that consists of vocabulary, concepts, facts, and the like must be organized so that it can be used as a "tool" for problem solving (strategic knowledge). In the development of cognitive tools in the form of procedures and strategies, *automatization* occurs as a result of practice. In this sense, a skilled classroom learner has developed the ability to use cognitive tools in some learning situations without having to devote attention to the employment of the tool. The old educational psychology literature used to call this a *skill*. The advantage of automatization is obvious and has been used to explain differences in competence between novices and experts. However, this automaticity does not characterize all procedural knowledge and, in most cases, is domain specific. This view of automaticity not only has implications for classroom assessment, but the teaching of academic problem solving as well.

REMEMBERING AND ACADEMIC PROBLEM SOLVING

Before defining *problem solving* in terms of personal knowledge construction, a quick review of the problem solving process provides a context for the discussion that follows. When problem solving is being assessed in mathematics, history, foreign language, music, literature, or a vocational class, students face a common experience. The first phase of problem solving typically involves *problem identification*. This simply acknowledges that academic tasks must be identified as belonging to a particular subject matter domain before a search of prior knowledge can be initiated in long-term memory. Given that prior knowledge has been searched, the next phase is problem representation. Again, if memory search and retrieval is successful, the task may be represented in a manner consistent with the way tasks of this particular type are represented in the disciplne. This is the *problem representation* stage. Given success to this point, the student now selectively searches memory for procedural knowledge in the form of strategies, procedures, heuristics, algorithms, and the like. This phase, which ivolves planning and trying out ideas, has been referred to as the *solution selection* phase. The last phase of successful problem solving is the *solution execution* phase.

In a discussion of academic problem solving, it is assumed that strategies and procedures to be "tried out" have been a part of prior instruction and are available in long-term memory. This may or may not be the case. Although we spend a great deal of instructional time on teaching procedures and strategies, we may not observe successful problem-solving performance for several reasons. First, if problem identification does not occur, problem solving is unsuccessful. This may be because either the pertinent information was not stored in long-term memory or it may be in long-term memory but cannot be successfully retrieved. Assuming successful problem identification, the stored information that is retrieved may be a "misconception," in which case problem representation is inappropriate. If this is the case, the student does what I have found myself doing on occasion, "searching and retrieving an appropriate strategy or procedure for an incorrect representation." However, assuming an appropriate representation, I now have to retrieve procedures and strategies that may prove to be successful. Only after a successful solution execution phase have I the opportunity to confirm my hunches about the procedure or strategy that will "work." This lengthy description is meant to demonstrate that nothing is *automatic* about access to prior knowledge during problem solving.

Classroom Scenario

An academic task is presented to two students seated at the same table. The first student addresses the task by remembering having solved this problem in the past. Consequently, the student gains access to prior knowledge (search and retrieval), recalls the appropriate representation, and applies the appropriate strategy (strategy execution). This leads to a correct answer. The second student has limited prior knowledge about the task and has no access to the appropriate procedure or strategy. However, this student mindfully approaches the task of overcoming incomplete knowledge representation in long-term memory. A mindful approach might include such activities as integrating remembered strategies and procedures and trying them out. Through whatever means, the student is successful in overcoming the obstacle of limited prior knowledge and successfully arrives at a solution.

Although both students were confronted with a task that had been designed as an academic problem, did both students engage in a problem solving process? My position is no. From a personal knowledge construction perspective, *problem solving as a process can be identified only from the point of view of the learner* not the designer of the task. Hence, in the episode just described, only the second student engaged in a problem-solving process. In the past, the first student might have engaged in problem solving when initially encountering the academic problem. On the other hand, maybe the solution was initially learned by rote, having been directly supplied by the teacher. Regardless, in the situation described here, only the second student *constructed* (as contrasted with reproduced) a solution.

This approach to describing problem solving is truly learner centered and, as such, can be used in any subject matter domain with any academic task. Such a perspective emphasizes the development of a classroom environment that stresses the teaching of cognitive strategies and procedures and the development of a problem-solving attitude.

DEVELOPING A PROBLEM-SOLVING ENVIRONMENT

Training-for-Transfer

Within the context of academic problem solving, *strategic transfer* can be viewed as an ability to gain access to and use prior knowledge in the construction of solutions for complex tasks. Having defined *academic problem solving* from the perspective of personal knowledge construction, the question remains, can this ability be taught? The answer is yes (Phye, 1989, 1990; Phye & Sanders, 1992, 1994). In these studies, inductive reasoning strategies were taught to college students under various training conditions. When these students were compared on inductive problem-solving tasks with students that did not receive training, they demonstrated significantly better problem-solving performance. These students were not only better able to retrieve prior knowledge but also to use the procedural knowledge acquired during training. These results have consistently been observed when a training for transfer paradigm is employed.

A training for transfer approach to teaching problem solving takes advantage of systematic practice followed by a delayed assessment with new academic tasks from the same subject matter domain. Basic elements that characterize this paradigm are (1) multiple examples during training,

(2) multiple trials with informational feedback, (3) training problems to a high level of proficiency, and (4) a delayed transfer task requiring the application of procedures or strategies practiced during training. When the delayed transfer task is presented, no instructions about trying to remember what was taught during training are issued. This last point is important, because this is what provides insight into the motivational level of the student. This creates an opportunity for a student to demonstrate *volition* as a form of motivation. The student actively searches long-term memory trying to remember past problems successfully solved that were of the same type. This is followed up by trying out the remembered procedures and strategies to arrive at a solution. This last point is simply an acknowledgment that, while we may have an abundant knowledge structure of prior information, a problem solver must also exhibit self-regulated behavior in the form of persistence.

Training

Practice activities can take many forms. The main features of practice are a combination of test and study. During practice, the problem solver is given multiple examples with the types of academic problems to be mastered and an opportunity to try out what he or she knows. Study provides the problem solver with feedback about practice performance such that errors can be corrected and elaboration in the form of procedure or strategy development is encouraged. This should then be followed by an opportunity for the problem solver to again try out (practice), what he or she remembers from initial testing plus what has been acquired in the form of new elaborated knowledge during study. This combination of testing and informed study should continue until a high level of proficiency is demonstrated with the type of problems on which students are being trained. When training is conducted in this manner, *within task* transfer occurs, as demonstrated by increasing proficiency in problem solving from practice trial to practice trial. Also, when training is terminated because of demonstrated proficiency on problems studied, the teacher has a measure of what the problem solver has successfully stored and retrieved from long-term memory. In other words, with practice involving multiple examples and multiple study trials, both acquisition and retrieval processing is being practiced.

Delayed Transfer Task

Following the last training trial, a new set of problems that require the same types of procedures or strategies practiced during training can be used to assess strategic transfer. Instead of an immediate transfer task, an interval of several days should occur between training and the transfer task. In this latter case, successful access to prior knowledge, which translates into successful problem identification and problem translation, requires greater effort. When transfer immediately follows training, the successful retrieval of procedural knowledge requires less effort because of the continuous sequence of acquisition and problem solving. The situation remains the same and the elaboration and maintenance rehearsal can be carried out in working memory. In contrast, successfully using strategic transfer in a delayed problem solving situation requires that the acquired procedural knowledge be retrieved from long-term memory.

This difference between immediate and delayed problem solving may appear to be trivial, but there are some interesting implications for classroom practices. In the first place, regardless of when the new problems are presented, no instructions or hints for signals are provided to tell the student to remember what was practiced during training. This approach encourages the problem solver to develop an attitude of using memory as a tool for problem solving. Also, the use of delayed problem solving tasks communicates to students that they are responsible for both learning and remembering important classroom information.

Looking ahead to Part II of the handbook, one notes the focus is on teaching "how" to learn within subject matter domains. These chapters, written by some of the most prominent researchers and scholars in their respective areas, all report a common theme. Although declarative knowledge is the foundation on which procedural and strategic knowledge are constructed, we should not settle for just teaching declarative knowledge in the classroom. In every subject matter domain, the current spirit of the times is one of also teaching activities, procedures, and strategies that can be used as tools while thinking critically and solving problems.

PROMOTING PERSONAL KNOWLEDGE CONSTRUCTION

I try to communicate to my students that there is a real difference between processing information to carry out the daily tasks associated with living and processing information for learning and remembering. For example, we are all exposed to a tremendous amount of information outside the classroom every day in the form of conversations, media, and the popular press. In many of these instances, we need process the information only to the extent that we can choose to respond at the moment (conversations, locating a music station or channel, stopping at a busy intersection, etc.). Even when we want to be entertained and watch TV or a video, we process very little of the information so that we can remember it for a long period of time. Only that information we personally find interesting seems to be worth the effort involved in processing to the extent that it adds to, modifies, or changes our informal knowledge structure. So what about the classroom environment, where, for most students, less interesting information is presented for learning and remembering?

Chapter 3 addresses this question from an eclectic perspective, reviewing the research and methods that have been demonstrated to be effective in classroom settings. In chapter 4, the issue of classroom motivation is approached from a self-regulation theory point of view. Consequently, I am going to confine my suggestions to those cognitive instructional factors that directly influence learning and remembering and only indirectly promote attitudes and beliefs that are a critical part of any discussion of motivation.

The foundation for procedural and strategic knowledge is this: *do not settle for declarative knowledge*. However, absolutely no data suggest that procedural and strategic knowledge *automatically* develop without practice. We have described the use of teaching techniques that help students develop maintenance and elaboration strategies for the learning and remembering declarative knowledge. We must also develop and teach elaboration and maintenance strategies for the development of procedural and strategic knowledge.

Since procedural knowledge is identified when students demonstrate "how" they can use the declarative knowledge they have acquired and remembered, the way teachers assess classroom knowledge is important. Declarative knowledge can be assessed using traditional paper–pencil or verbal (interview or protocol techniques) methods. However, procedural knowledge also requires the employment of assessment techniques requiring the application or transfer of declarative knowledge. In the classroom, this may take the form of projects that students produce individually (an oral or written report) or collectively (lab project, skit) or some other element of performance. Problem solving where direct teacher involvement occurs in the form of "hints," "prompts," or "scaffolding" would also be included under our procedural knowledge rubric.

Cognitively, strategic knowledge is procedural knowledge used independently (volitionally) by the student to solve classroom or academic problems. Here, the student is expected to take responsibility for problem identification, problem translation, strategy selection, and problem solution. This is reflected in the functional knowledge taxonomy I proposed that is structured along two primary dimensions (higher-order thinking and self-regulation).

In closing, I reflect back on 25 years of teaching teachers as I recommend these changes for the future. I have been fortunate in that I have encountered many bright aspiring teachers. However, a widespread misconception among many of these young people is that declarative knowledge is all teachers need to know to be successful in the classroom. This attitude is reflected in the notion that all we do as teachers is translate the textbook, provide a CD-ROM, or assign supplementary materials. In fact, I would agree that this is a reasonable summary of what teachers do when promoting declarative knowledge in the classroom.

However, critical thinking and problem solving are cognitive skills, where attitude and motivation play a major role. Consequently, teachers must be knowledgeable enough to *model* critical thinking and problem solving in the subjects they teach. A teacher who can model problem solving and critical thinking in the classroom provides an *academic affordance* for his or her students. To borrow a colloquial expression "if as teachers we are going to talk the talk, we must also walk the walk."

References

Alexander, P. A., Scallert, D. L., & Hare, V. C. (1991). Coming to terms: How researchers in learning and literacy talk about knowledge. *Review of Educational Research*, 61, 315–343.

Cooper, P. A. (1993, May). Paradigm shifts in designed instruction: From behaviorism to cognitivism to constructivism. *Educational Technology*, 33(5), 12–19.

Gibson, J. J. (1979). *The ecological approach to visual perception*. Boston: Houghton-Mifflin.

Gibson, E. J. (1994). Has psychology a future? *Psychological Science*, 5, 69–76.

Kelly, C. M., & Jacoby, L. L. (1990). The construction of subjective experience: Memory attributions. *Mind and Language*, 5, 49–68.

Mandler, G. (1980). Recognizing: The judgment of previous occurrence. *Psychological Review*, 87, 252–271.

Mayer, R. E. (1987). *Educational psychology: A cognitive approach*. Boston: Little, Brown.

Mayer, R. E. (1992). *Thinking, problem solving, cognition* (2nd ed.). New York: Freeman.

Phillips, D. C. (Ed.). (1994). *Special Issue: Epistemological Perspectives on Educational Psychology*, 29(1), 1–55.

Phye, G. D. (1989). Schema training and transfer of an intellectual skill. *Journal of Educational Psychology*, 81, 347–352.

Phye, G. D. (1990). Inductive problem solving: Schema inducement and memory based transfer. *Journal of Educational Psychology*, 82, 826–831.

Phye, G. D. (1992). Strategic transfer: A tool for academic problem solving. *Educational Psychology Review*, 4, 393–420.

Phye, G. D., & Sanders, C. E. (1992). Accessing strategic memory: Individual differences in the transfer of a problem solving strategy. *Contemporary Educational Psychology*, 17, 211–223.

Phye, G. D., & Sanders, C. E. (1994). Advice and feedback: Elements of practice for problem solving. *Contemporary Educational Psychology*, 19, 286–301.

Prawat, R. S. (1989). Promoting assess to knowledge, strategy and disposition in students: A research synthesis. *Review of Educational Research*, 59, 1–42.

Schwartz, B., & Reisberg, D. (1991). *Learning and memory*. New York: Norton.

Stiggens, R. J. (1992). High quality classroom assessment: What does it really mean? *Educational Measurement: Issues and Practice*, 11(2), 35–43.

Vygotsky, L. S. (1992). *Thought and language* (E. Hanfmann & G. Vakar, Trans.) New York: Wiley (Original work published 1934).

Tharp, R. G., & Gallimore, R. (1988). *Rousing minds to life: ing, learning, and schooling in social context*. Cambridge, England: Cambridge University Press.

Whitehead, A. N. (1929). *The aims of education*, New York: Macmillan.

CHAPTER

3

School Learning and Motivation[1]

MYRON H. DEMBO AND MARTIN J. EATON
University of Southern California

Weinstein and McCombs (in press) identify three important components of academic learning—skill, will, and self-regulation. The skill component refers to the knowledge students must acquire about themselves, the subject, task, strategies for learning, and the contexts in which learning occurs. The will component refers to factors related to students' motivation to learn. Finally, the self-regulation component refers to the ability of students to monitor and control their knowledge and motivation during learning.

In the next chapter, Zimmerman and Risemberg will discuss the important self-regulatory dimension of learning and provide numerous examples of self-regulatory behavior. Information about students' knowledge and the learning process was discussed in the first two chapters by Phye and Bredo and will be expanded on in the next part of this book. This chapter focuses on the will or motivational and self-regulatory components influencing learning.

Motivation is a topic introduced early in any discussion with teachers about student learning. Teachers experience different motivational problems in the classroom. Some students are more concerned with avoiding failure than trying to learn; others believe nothing they do will lead to success; some students are so anxious that they cannot concentrate on tasks; other students limit their classroom participation because they find classroom norms and interaction different from their social or cultural experiences; some students have the ability to succeed but do not contribute in class because they lack self-confidence; other students can never find the time to complete

[1]Parts of this chapter are from Dembo (1994).

assignments; some students fail to persist when tasks become difficult; and others have difficulty paying attention during instruction. These examples are just a few of the motivational problems that teachers may encounter in a given day.

Teachers espouse hypotheses or beliefs about student motivation that influence their interaction with students and the decisions that determine how they relate to students. For example, it is not uncommon to hear teachers describe students in their classrooms who are not motivated. Yet, after learning about the behavior of these students, it is clear that they spend considerable effort avoiding doing what their teachers want them to do. They spend time in failure-avoiding activities such as avoiding being called on, providing excuses for incomplete assignments, and procrastinating. Covington (1992) believes the problem for these students is not the lack of motivation but that they are overmotivated for the wrong reasons. This example illustrates the importance of accurately diagnosing the causes or reasons for students' behavior if successful interventions are to be developed.

The purpose of this chapter is to help teachers understand the factors that influence dysfunctional student motivation so they can initiate intervention strategies to enhance positive motivation in students. These interventions emphasize *both* teacher-directed strategies during the planning and implementation of instruction and strategies that students can be taught so they can regulate their own motivation. We believe it is difficult to solve classroom motivational problems by changes in the classroom context alone without teaching students how to control and maintain their own motivation.

PERSPECTIVES ON MOTIVATION

Psychologists have different perspectives on motivation. One of the major issues is whether or not the factors determining human motivation are within or beyond human control. Motivational theorists who argue for the latter have used biological and mechanical concepts (i.e., drives, energy, tension, and forces) to explain human behavior. These perspectives view humans as passive and reactive, influenced by internal forces (needs and drives) or external forces (reinforcement and punishment). Other perspectives view individuals as rational beings that have the ability to accurately reason about their current situations and make decisions regarding their personal and social behavior (Weiner, 1991).

The following statements represent some of the different views concerning motivation:

1. If you give Susan many rewards, she will do fine.
2. The problem with Fred is that he lacks a strong desire to achieve.

3. I need to get Alice to have more confidence in her ability.
4. Juan works very well in some learning situations but poorly in others.

Statement 1 represents one of the more dominant approaches to motivation. This behavioral approach views motivation in terms of intensity and duration of behavior. The student who works harder and longer on a task is perceived to be more motivated than the student who fails to expend similar energy and persistence. Finding appropriate incentives or reinforcers to maintain task behavior is an important aspect of this approach.

Webb, Covington, and Guthrie (1993) believe that this perspective has been used unsuccessfully to develop school policy in the attempt to influence student motivation. They explain this perspective in the following amusing example:

> Donkeys are rumored to be obstinate beasts, rarely inclined to move unless tempted with a carrot at the front end or threatened with a stick at the rear. The predominant model of motivation policy in American education makes similar presumptions about school-children. Most such policies can be distinguished only by which end of the donkey they aim for. (p. 99)

They further state that some educators believe students are not naturally curious and interested in learning. Therefore, they believe students must be induced to learn by introducing positive and negative incentives to encourage learning.

The second statement represents the orientation derived from the work by Atkinson (1964) and McClelland (1965), who view motivation as an unconscious drive or need that is socialized early in a child's life. This view closely aligns motivation with the study of personality. From this perspective, responsibility for increased academic involvement rests with students. Since motivation is strongly influenced by child-rearing experiences, teachers are limited in what they can do to change achievement motivation.

The third statement represents the cognitive view of motivation (R. Ames & Ames, 1984; Pintrich & Schrauben, 1992), in which the teacher is concerned with cognitive-mediational processes, the personal explanations for success and failure and informational processing that occur in instructional settings. As a result, motivation is reflected in how students think about their goals, the task, and their feelings about completing the task. This approach seeks to understand *why* students choose to engage in academic tasks rather than what they do or how long they spend doing so. Pintrich and Garcia (1992) argue that motivational beliefs help students form an *intention to learn* while cognitive strategies are used to enact learning. This important statement emphasizes the interaction between motivation and cognition.

The final statement represents a sociocultural point of view, a relatively new perspective in motivation theory that has its roots within the sociohistorical school of psychology (Lave, 1988; Vygotsky, 1978; Wertsch, 1991). Proponents of this perspective believe that motivation does not reside in the head of the individual alone but in the interaction the individual has with others in a meaningful activity (see Rueda & Dembo, 1995; Rueda & Moll, 1994).

Whereas the cognitive perspective of motivation tends to focus primarily on classroom factors influencing students' beliefs and perceptions, the sociocultural perspective emphasizes the students' social and cultural experiences before and during the time students are in the classroom. Another difference between the two perspectives is that the cognitive perspective places primary importance on the individual student alone as a processor of information who generates the beliefs and perceptions that influence behaviors indicative of motivation. On the other hand, the sociocultural perspective emphasizes social and cultural factors as important influences on students' perceptions about learning even before they enter the classroom.

How teachers view motivation often influences their classroom behavior and interaction with students. We believe that if teachers understand how they can influence the type of motivation displayed in the classroom, they will be more likely to take steps to affect student motivation.

OVERVIEW OF THE MODEL

We will use a model adapted from Pintrich (1994) to organize our discussion of student motivation (see Figure 1). The model incorporates both cognitive and sociocultural motivational perspectives. Although it is presented in a linear format, all four variables interact simultaneously. The far left section of the model represents social and cultural contextual factors that students bring to the classroom (e.g., interaction norms, language usage, value of education). These factors can directly influence internal factors (i.e., students' beliefs and perceptions) and interact with classroom contextual factors (e.g., nature of learning tasks and peer and teacher–student interaction) to influence beliefs and perceptions.

Classroom contextual factors, the second major component in the model, are assumed to influence internal factors (i.e., students' motivational beliefs and emotions), the third component of the model. It is assumed that these beliefs and emotions mediate students' social and cultural and classroom experiences and their observable behavior.

The last component in the model is the motivated behavior that is influenced by the social and cultural, classroom context, and internal factors. We define *motivation* as an internal state that arouses, directs, and maintains behavior. As a result, our focus is on three basic questions. *What causes an individual to initiate some action? What is the level of involvement in the chosen activity? What causes a person to persist or give up?* (Pintrich, Marx, & Boyle, 1993). Motivation is manifested in the classroom by the following behaviors: choice of behavior, level of activity and involvement, and persistence of behavior and regulation of effort. Examples of these behaviors are identified in Figure 1.

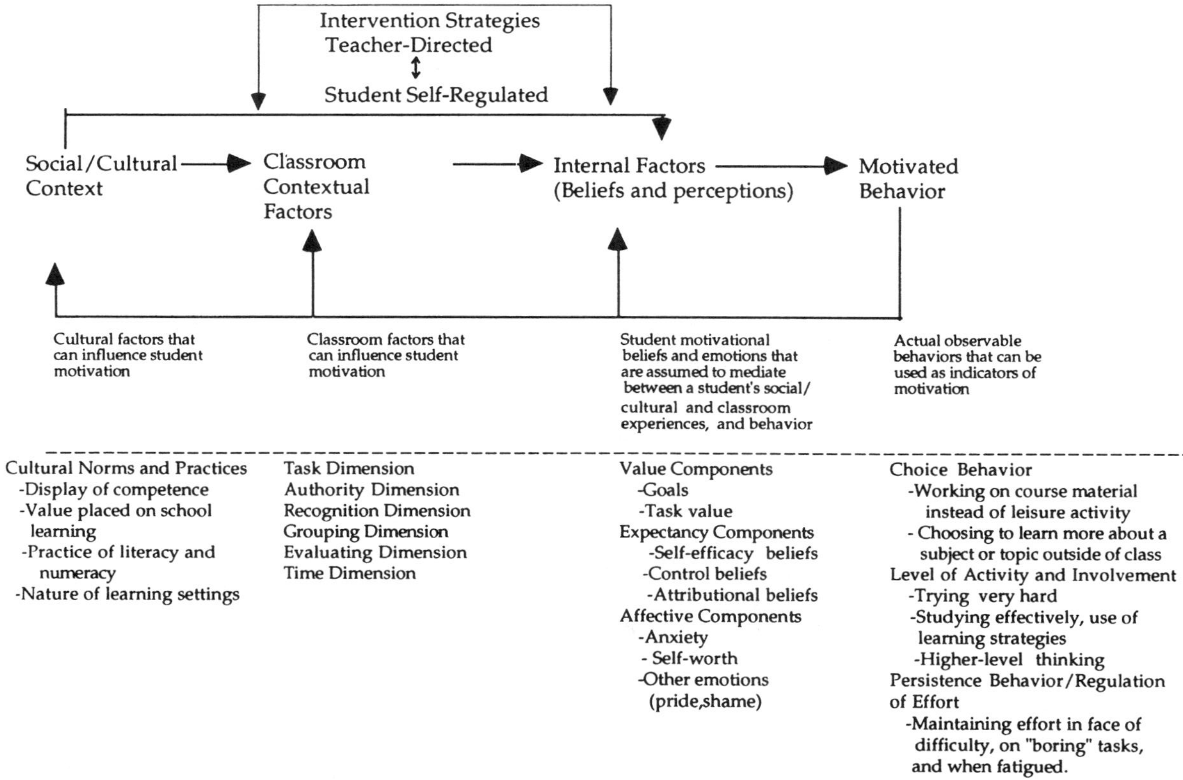

FIGURE 1

An integrated model of student motivation in the classroom. Adapted from Pintrich, 1994. Reprinted with permission.

The portion of the model identified by intervention strategies indicates that motivation can be enhanced by both the teacher (through classroom interaction) and students (through self-regulation strategies learned in the classroom). As the model in Figure 1 indicates, the two types of intervention interact with each other. That is, students are assisted by the teacher in helping them develop self-regulated behaviors, and teacher-directed interventions are influenced by the behavior of students.

Social and Cultural Factors

The motivation model in Figure 1 reminds us that students do not come to the classroom as "blank slates." They already have had many years of experience learning from peers, siblings, and parents in their homes and communities. An important issue is whether their classroom learning experiences are compatible with their prior learning experiences.

What cultural or social factors have an impact on student motivation to learn? We need to focus both on students' content knowledge (i.e., the specific information they bring to the classroom, especially information derived from their unique cultural experiences) and the cultural norms and practices that may be congruent or incongruent with classroom norms and practices. The following are some specific questions a teacher might ask about culturally different students. Does the student understand how competency is displayed in the classroom? Do students and their families believe that there is an economic, personal or social benefit to school success? How is literacy practiced and valued in the family? Is cooperation or competition emphasized in the home and community (Rueda & Moll, 1994)?

Rueda and Moll (1994) describe the sociocultural perspective in the following statement:

> A sociocultural approach suggests that motivation is (a) socially negotiated (what it is and how it is displayed), (b) socially distributed (not just in the child's head), and (c) context specific (determined by features of the activity setting). The most obvious implication of this approach is that motivation must be conceptualized as a "situated" phenomenon; located not solely within individuals, but within "systems' of activities involving other persons, environments, resources and goals. From this perspective, motivation is accomplished, it is created, it is socially and culturally relative, and it is context-specific. It is not a unitary phenomenon, a general, invariant property of the individual mind, or an abstract property of individuals; it is manifested in activities, involving most prominently, the mediation of other human beings. (pp. 131–132)

Let us analyze the three characteristics of motivation represented by this perspective (Rueda & Moll, 1994). *Socially negotiated* specifies that many rules of behavior or norms are developed by individuals in response to the needs of the environments in which they interact. Thus, cultural, historical, and institutional factors reflect and shape an individual's mental functioning. If we want to understand an individual's thinking, we have to understand where it came from. A relevant question for a teacher would be, "What shapes the thinking and motivation of a sixth grade refugee student from Cambodia or a recent immigrant from Mexico or Japan?"

The term *socially distributed* indicates that the unit of analysis in any cognitive activity is not the individual but the individual in interaction with others in a specific activity setting. The success or failure of a question and answer exchange between a teacher and student is a product of the interaction between the parties in the activity, not solely the student nor the teacher. Learning takes place first on an interpsychological (social) level and only later on an intrapsychological (personal) level. Children do things with the help of others around them long before they can do things on their own. The child who does not remember where she left an item often reconstructs memory with an adult, who asks questions that help to locate the object. The dialogue for a first grade child who cannot find her book might proceed as follows (Wertsch, 1991):

> Child: "Have you seen my book?"
> Mother: "No, when did you last see the book?"
> Child: "I had it in school."
> Mother: "Did you bring it home with you?"
> Child: "I don't know."
> Mother: "Where did you put your things when you came home from school?"

Quickly the child goes into the family room and finds her book next to her coat. This example points to the social nature of memory—neither the child nor the adult would be able to recall where the object was on her own. As the child develops, she acquires the meta-cognitive ability to ask herself the same questions initiated by her mother. Vygotsky (1978) believes that a child's thinking abilities develop from similar dialogues in the home, community, and school.

The term *context specific* specifies that learning and motivation are viewed as social activities that can be understood only within a given cultural setting. Cognition is seen as something that takes place in all cultures and in all settings, but the form it takes may vary depending on the survival needs of the group. What is considered intelligent behavior in one setting may not be viewed as intelligent in another, as it may not have the same survival value. In addition, an individual may be motivated in one setting but not in another.

Let's use student language to illustrate the dynamics of this approach to motivation. The linguistic processes in a classroom may differ from the oral discourse experienced by students from different cultural backgrounds (Ainsworth, 1984). An example of this linguistic conflict is described by Philips (1983), who studied how children's lack of responsiveness in the classroom influenced their academic achievement.

Teachers at the Warm Springs Indian Reservation in central Oregon noted that the Native American children would not talk in front of the class and participated less and less in verbal interaction as they proceeded through school. Philips points out that teachers use classroom recitation to allow students to learn from their own public mistakes; the Native American children were not familiar with this approach to learning. The children's home learning involves watching an adult perform a task or skill and practicing it alone, unsupervised. When the children are successful, they perform the skill in front of the adult who taught it. When the task or skill is fully developed, only then is it demonstrated publicly. The use of speech in the learning process from instruction to evaluation plays a minor role because verbal instruction is confined to corrections or answering questions.

This process provides some insight into the Native American children's reluctance to speak in front of their peers. The assumption by the teacher that students learn more effectively by making mistakes in front of others is inconsistent with the children's background. The Native American children have no opportunity to observe others performing successfully before they attempt a task or skill, and they lack the freedom to determine whether they know enough to demonstrate their knowledge because the teacher determines when they must respond. Finally, competence is demonstrated verbally in the classroom rather than nonverbally.

Philips found that the children's classroom participation increased when the teacher interacted privately with individual students and when students worked together in small groups. Many teachers eventually changed their methods to include the participation structures that increased the children's oral discourse.

Students and their parents' cultural backgrounds can also explain their values, attitudes, and behaviors. Ogbu (1987, 1992) explains why some minority groups have been very successful in school whereas others have not been. He differentiates between minority groups (termed *involuntary* or *caste-like*; e.g., certain Latinos, African-Americans, and Native Americans) who were incorporated into U.S. society against their will (i.e., through slavery, conquest, colonization, or forced labor) and who tend to do poorly in school; and minority groups (termed *voluntary* or *immigrant*; e.g., certain Asian-Americans) who come to the United States by their own choice because they want to better themselves economically or want greater political freedom. These minorities (Asian-Americans, say) tend to do well in school.

Ogbu (1992) believes that involuntary minorities experience difficulties in school partly because of the relationship between their cultures and the dominant white (American) culture. That is, they have more difficulty crossing cultural and language boundaries in school than voluntary minorities with similar cultural and language differences. Gibson (1987) also has made the same point. She states that involuntary minorities often equate school learning with the loss of their own cultural and ethnic identifies, while voluntary groups view school learning and acquisition of the majority culture as an additional set of skills to use when appropriate. Therefore, some minority groups see school learning and acculturation as leading to assimilation, whereas other minority groups view school learning and acculturation in a broader perspective, in which new knowledge is incorporated into their own culture, transforming but not replacing it.

Ogbu's (1992) analysis of the behavior of involuntary minorities shows that they differ significantly from the voluntary minorities. He points out that the involuntary minorities interpret culture and language as indicators of the identity that should be maintained not as barriers to be overcome. School learning is viewed as "the learning of the cultural and language frames of reference of their 'enemy' or 'oppressors'. . . . They fear that by learning the White cultural frame of reference, they will cease to act like minorities and lose their identity as minorities and their sense of community and self-worth" (p. 10). Members of these minority groups point out that, even when individuals learn the culture and language, they often are not accepted by the mainstream culture and are not given equal opportunities to advance economically.

Another important point Ogbu makes is that social pressure discourages involuntary minority students from behaving and acting in ways that enhance their school achievement (e.g., completing homework assignments, studying for examinations, asking questions in class). Peers often consider such behavior as "acting white" or being a "schoolboy" and, as a result, often criticize or isolate peers making good grades. While parents of voluntary minority students encourage school attendance and good grades, parents of involuntary minority students may not communicate the importance of education to their children. This behavior leads to less interest and involvement in formal education.

As teachers, we need to become aware of the various strategies students use to try to attain academic success without losing their cultural identities (Ogbu, 1992). A counselor expressed one strategy this way: "Do your Black thing [in the community] but know the White man thing [at school]" (p. 11). Another common strategy is *camouflage* (i.e., disguising true academic attitudes and behaviors). One approach is becoming the class clown, demonstrating lack of interest in school but studying in secret. The good grade that such students attain can be attributed to their "natural smartness" not to their effort or school behaviors.

In summary, we must understand how students' cultural and social backgrounds can influence their beliefs and perceptions and ultimately how they respond to the classroom social context. It is dangerous to assume that all students perceive classroom rules, norms, and procedures in the same manner.

Classroom Contextual Factors

Teachers structure activities, reward, and interact with students in ways that influence the students' personal learning goals or intentions for performing a task. Two different goal orientations have been identified by researchers—

mastery (or learning) and performance (C. Ames & Archer, 1988). These goals also have been referred to as task involvement versus ego involvement (Nicholls, 1984), learning versus performance goals (Dweck, 1986), and even intrinsic versus extrinsic goals. A *mastery goal* is oriented toward learning as much as possible for self-improvement, irrespective of the performance of others. A *performance goal* focuses on social comparison and competition, with the main purpose of outperforming others on the task. Different teachers establish different types of learning climates in their classrooms. Research evidence indicates that the classroom context can influence the adoption of a mastery goal orientation, which in turn can influence the nature of students' thinking and motivational beliefs (Pintrich, et al., 1993).

At different times both goals are pursued by students. However, there are times when students make choices as to which goal to pursue. An important factor influencing their choice is situation variables. For example, if evaluation is emphasized, students will be less interested in mastery and will pursue performance goals (i.e., they will select tasks to demonstrate their high ability or conceal low ability). If the value of the skill rather than evaluation is emphasized, students tend to choose the mastery goal; that is, select a task that maximizes learning, even though it may involve risks and possible confusion (Elliott & Dweck, 1981).

Different classroom environments can also affect students' use of learning strategies. C. Ames and Archer (1988) found that students who perceive their classroom as emphasizing mastery rather than performance goals were more likely to use effective learning strategies. This is an important finding for two reasons. First, students may acquire many different learning strategies but never choose to use them unless they are motivated to do so. Second, one factor determining students' motivation to use strategies is their perceptions of the classroom climate. Therefore teachers should be aware that they must establish classroom environments that support the use of the learning strategies they are teaching.

Certain teacher behaviors and classroom instructional organizational factors are more likely to encourage students to develop a mastery orientation to learning (C. Ames, 1992). The characteristics of students with a mastery orientation include an interest in improving their knowledge, willingness to take risks, enjoying academic challenges, belief that errors are part of the learning process, and belief that ability can be improved through exhibiting greater effort.

We will conceptualize the classroom environment using the dimensions first identified by Epstein (1988) and used by C. Ames (1990), Maehr (1992), and Midgley (1993). These dimensions have been identified by the acronym TARGET: task, authority, recognition, grouping, evaluation, time. Since extensive research reviews illustrating the importance of each of these dimensions have already been conducted (see C. Ames, 1990, 1992), we will limit our discussion to summarizing the impact of each dimension on student motivation.

Task

The type of academic tasks given to students can influence different types of motivation. Tasks that are interesting, meaningful, challenging, and authentic in terms of actual experiences relevant to life outside school can facilitate a mastery learning orientation (C. Ames, 1992; Meece, 1991). Tasks that emphasize drill-and-practice activities from textbook assignments and teacher handouts are less likely to have the same impact on students.

Teachers also need to think about how they present assignments and whether the assignments challenge students to become involved in the subject matter. Brophy, Rohrkemper, Rashid, and Goldberger (1983) found that students were less likely to become involved in a task when the teacher introduced it in a negative fashion (i.e., suggesting the task was boring or pointless, or that they would find it difficult or frustrating).

Authority

The authority dimension involves how much opportunity students are given to take their own initiative and responsibility for their learning. Teachers who believe that students have little inclination to learn in school and need to be encouraged to learn through external incentives are more likely to be influenced by procedures that emphasize more teacher control over learning activities. Teachers who believe that children are naturally curious and that learning is a process of self-discovery are likely to establish a different type of classroom situation. The latter teachers are more likely to support students in solving their own problems and pursuing their own interests while the former teachers are more likely to motivate students with rewards and use subtle control procedures (Deci, Nezlek, & Sheinman, 1981).

The way teachers organize the classroom environment can have considerable impact on students' motivation and their view of themselves. Research has indicated that students' motivation and perceived competence are strongly related to the orientation of their teachers. In one investigation, students who perceived their classrooms as more autonomy oriented were higher on intrinsic motivation and perceived cognitive competence and reported higher levels of self-esteem than students who perceived their classrooms as more control oriented (Ryan & Grolnick, 1984).

A number of investigations comparing elementary and middle school teachers raise concern about teachers' authority beliefs with different age students (Midgley, 1993). The studies have indicated that teachers in the middle grades believe they must control students more and trust them less than elementary teachers (Midgley, Feldlaufer, & Eccles, 1988; Sweeting, Willower, & Helsel, 1978). Furthermore, although a warm, supportive student–teacher relationship is associated with positive motivational outcomes (Fraser & Fisher, 1982), there appears to be a deterioration in student–teacher relationships after the transition to junior high school (Feldlaufer, Midgley, & Eccles, 1988).

Recognition

The recognition dimension concerns the formal and informal use of rewards, incentives, and praise in the classroom. These factors have important consequences for students' interest in learning as well as their feelings of self-worth and satisfaction with their learning (C. Ames, 1992). The problem, however, is that many classrooms are managed under the false assumption that competition motivates students to achieve. The result is a scarcity of rewards, the majority of which go to the best students in the class. Less capable students have a more difficult time being recognized for their achievement or accomplishments in these classrooms.

There are situations in which a limited amount of competition can be effective (e.g., motivating a group of bored students to complete an assignment; or motivating a group of learners of similar ability to work harder). However, competition does not motivate low-achieving or failure-avoiding students to become more involved in academic tasks (Covington, 1992). It sometimes does the opposite by causing students to withdraw from classroom activities and take fewer risks.

There is no question that teachers need to find more opportunities to recognize students for their accomplishments. However, *how* praise is given appears to be an important factor in its impact on students. Teachers need to reconsider the common strategy of finding opportunities to constantly praise students for all types of behavior and academic performance. Brophy (1981) has pointed out how the incorrect use of praise can undermine achievement behavior. When teachers try to find something good in the work of low-achieving students to encourage them, the praise is often for some irrelevant or unimportant aspect of completing the task. For example, if the task is to complete math problems, commenting on a student's neat homework paper is not likely to have the positive effect on the student that the teacher intended. What happens is that the student often discounts the praise. What is worse is that the student often interprets the praise to be unrelated to effort or performance but rather in evidence of lack of ability. The result is a negative effect on competency beliefs.

Researchers also have found that teachers can undermine intrinsic motivation and learning by too much emphasis on external rewards or incentives (see Lepper & Hodell, 1989, for a detailed discussion of this literature). It appears that, when students already enjoy an activity and receive rewards for participating in it, they will be less likely to return to the activity than students with the same interest who received no rewards for participation.

Let us look at one explanation of this phenomenon. When students receive a reward for doing something, they attribute the reward as the reason for engaging in the activity, even if, without the reward, they would have been intrinsically motivated to complete the task. Once they perceive the extrinsic reward as the reason for participating in the activity, they will engage in the activity only if the reward is given. Another way of explaining this result is that the students discount their initial interest in the task as the reason for doing the task. Instead, the more powerful extrinsic reward is perceived to be the cause (Stipek, 1988).

This research does not suggest that rewards are bad or that teachers should not reinforce students. Instructors need to differentiate between using rewards to involve students in activities they do not want to pursue (such as completing homework assignments) and using rewards in situations in which students already enjoy the assigned activity. Instructors need not worry about undermining intrinsic motivation in the former case; only when the activity may be interesting or enjoyable need you omit the use of rewards for students. Stipek (1988) suggests:

> When extrinsic rewards are used to prod students into initially engaging in a task, every effort should be made to shift students' attention away from the extrinsic reward and toward the importance of the task and the feelings of competence that derive from mastery. (p. 67)

Grouping

The grouping dimension focuses on the ability of students to work effectively with each other. There are two important aspects of this dimension. The first is assigning students to classes on the basis of their ability. Extensive research reviews have focused on the detrimental effects of this practice on student motivation and learning (e.g., Kagan, 1990; Oakes, 1987). The Carnegie Task Force on the Education of Young Adolescents calls ability grouping "one of the most divisive and damaging school practices in existence" (Carnegie Council, 1989, p. 49). The research indicates that ability grouping has little benefit for high-ability students and locks low-ability students into programs and classes where they are stereotyped as weaker students and given an inferior education.

Another approach to understanding the grouping dimension is the type of goal structure a teacher establishes for various learning activities. A goal structure determines the way in which students will relate to one another and to the teacher while working toward instructional goals (Johnson & Johnson, 1994). There are three types of goal structures:

- *Cooperative*—students work together to accomplish shared goals.
- *Competitive*—students work against each other to achieve goals that only a few students can attain.
- *Individualistic*—one student's achievement of the goal is unrelated to other students' achievement of the goal.

An example of each of these goal structures includes students working together to survey political attitudes in the community (cooperative), students completing individual projects in science that will be graded on a curve (competitive), and students working individually on specific areas of weakness in mathematics, with their grade to be based on their own progress (individualistic).

Each type of goal structure promotes a different pattern of interaction among students, thus creating a different learning climate. In addition, different types of motivation are elicited under each learning condition. A cooperative goal structure promotes positive interpersonal relations such as trust, acceptance, sharing, and helping. A competitive goal structure promotes little trust and acceptance and often generates more attempts to mislead and obstruct others. An individualistic goal structure promotes interaction with the teacher rather than with peers and minimizes positive affective outcomes.

Johnson and Johnson (1994) believe that cooperative settings are more likely to produce higher levels of motivation to learn because the interaction patterns encourage and support one's efforts to achieve. They present evidence to show more cross-ethnic and cross-handicap helping and tutoring occurs in cooperative learning situations than in competitive or individualistic learning situations.

Evaluation

The type of and frequency of evaluation in the classroom can have important implications for student motivation (C. Ames & Ames, 1991). Some teachers employ evaluation procedures that have questionable impact on student motivation. For example, many teachers use public display of students' assignments and tests as a motivational strategy. This display may be in the form of charts and graphs to show where students stand in relation to each other.

Some teachers use too much evaluation in that almost every activity and performance is related to a grade. The fear is that unless an activity is graded, the students will not complete it. If a teacher's goal is to increase intrinsic motivation, excessive grading is not the answer. Teachers must consider the extent to which their grading and evaluation procedures encourage completion of the task rather than an increase in student knowledge and motivation to learn.

Time

The time dimension concerns the appropriateness of the tasks, the pace of instruction, and the time allotted for completing learning activities and assignments. Midgley (1993) points out that the way time is structured in schools influences the type of tasks given to students and the amount of control they have over them. She further states that some learning experiences, such as projects, experiments, field trips and thematic units, require more time than traditional time periods often used in schools.

C. Ames (1992) describes how the time structure is closely related to other TARGET areas such as task (how much children are expected to accomplish in a class period), authority (whether children or the teacher determine the time and schedule of activities), grouping (whether students in all groups are given equal time to complete assignments on teacher expectation), and evaluation (time pressures on tests). Teachers need to ask, "Is the class time periods or school's class periods sufficient to complete all types of assignments? Can students handle the daily work load? Are some students more interested in quantity rather than quality of work? Do students perceive that they have some control over their work schedule?" Students' answers to these questions will affect their motivation to learn.

Internal Factors

Research has determined that students are active information processors and influence classroom events as much as they are affected by them (Pintrich, Cross, Kozma, & McKeachie, 1986). Paris and Newman (1990) believe that students actually develop different "theories of schooling" that influence their classroom behavior in terms of their motivation, study habits, learning strategies, and interests. Understanding these theories and beliefs can provide the teacher with helpful information as to why students behave as they do.

Students' beliefs are influenced by their cultural and classroom experiences. Our goal in this section of the chapter is to identify the specific motivational beliefs that emanate from these experiences to influence their behavior.

Since no one perspective represents the cognitive approach to motivation, we have selected one model that provides a comprehensive approach for understanding the relationship between students' beliefs and their behavior. This model is based on the work of Pintrich and his colleagues (Pintrich, 1994; Pintrich & DeGroot, 1990; Pintrich & Schrauben, 1992), who identified three motivational components related to self-regulated behavior: a *value component*, which includes students' goals and beliefs about the importance and interest of the task ("Why am I doing the task?"); an *expectancy component*, which includes students' beliefs about their ability to perform the task ("Can I do this task?"); and an *affective component*, which includes students' emotional reactions to the task ("How do I feel about this task?").

Value Component: "Why Am I Doing This Task?"

Two aspects of the value component include goal orientation and task value. Goal orientation pertains to students' general goals for learning in a given course, whereas task value pertains to students' perceptions of the course material in terms of their beliefs about the importance and interest of the material. Pintrich and Schrauben (1992) state: "An individual's goal orientation may guide the general direction of behavior, whereas value may influence the strength or intensity of the behavior" (p. 157). In general, individuals tend to become involved in tasks that they positively value and avoid tasks that they negatively value (Wigfield & Eccles, 1992).

We first presented the notion of goal orientation when introducing the importance of the TARGET dimensions. Research indicates that the classroom social context can influence students' goal orientations and their classroom behavior (C. Ames & Archer, 1988). There are several distinctions in the beliefs of mastery and performance goal-oriented students that can affect their achievement. Students with a mastery as compared to a performance orientation are more likely to define success as improvement, emphasize the importance of effort, and view ability as developing through effort. One of the three indicators of motivated behavior (see Figure 1) is the persistence of behavior or regulation of effort. Therefore, it would appear that students would benefit from developing a mastery orientation.

Goal Setting and Motivation. Other aspects of goals can influence learning apart from the mastery versus performance goal orientation. An important aspect is the setting of specific goals. According to Locke and Latham (1990), there are four main reasons why goal setting improves performance: goals direct our attention to the task at hand, they mobilize effort, increase persistence, and promote the development of new strategies when old strategies do not work.

Schunk (1991a, 1991b) points out some additional findings concerning goal setting and motivation. The effects of goals on behavior depend on three properties: specificity, proximity, and difficulty level. Goals that set specific performance standards are more likely to increase motivation than general goals such as, "Do your best." Specific goals help the learner determine the amount of effort required for success and lead to feelings of satisfaction when the goal is attained. As a result, learners come to believe they have the ability to successfully complete the task.

Goals also can be identified by the extent to which they extend into the future. Proximal goals are close at hand and result in greater motivation directed toward attainment than more distant goals. Pursuing proximal goals also convey reliable information about one's capabilities. When students perceive they are making progress toward a proximal goal, they are apt to feel more confident about their ability to achieve and maintain their motivation. Since it is harder to evaluate progress toward distant goals, learners have more difficulty judging their capabilities even if they perform well.

Student perceptions of the difficulty of a task influences the amount of effort they believe is necessary to attain the task. If they believe they have the ability and knowledge, learners will work harder to attain difficult goals than when the standards are lower. As they work and attain difficult goals, they develop beliefs in their competence. However, if they don't believe they have the ability to attain a goal, they are likely to have low expectations for success and not become involved in the task (Spaulding, 1992).

The best example for this discussion is to think about how student motivation is influenced by the goals established by two different teachers. The first teacher simply tells students to write a term paper and hand it in on a certain date. The second teacher breaks the assignment down into different phases: prewriting (e.g., choose a topic, find, read and take notes on three sources, use correct bibliographic notation), drafting (e.g., develop thesis statement, identify subtopics, draft subtopics), revising, editing, and submission (e.g., review and revise full document, prepare bibliography and table of contents). He provides his students with a checklist of all the activities under each phase identifying the date each activity is due. He explains the criteria for each activity and provides feedback when it is handed in. The advantage of breaking the assignment into different phases is that it makes the task more manageable. As students experience success at each phase, they are more likely to enhance their perceptions of competence. When a project is not separated into smaller tasks, the only possibility for success is the completion of the final product (Spaulding, 1992).

Task Value Beliefs. The second aspect of the value component are task value beliefs. These beliefs are assumed to be the personal characteristics that students bring with them as they engage in a task and not characteristics of the task itself (Pintrich et al., 1993). Students' interest or value for a task relates to their choice of becoming cognitively engaged in the task and their willingness to persist at it (Pokay & Blumenfeld, 1990; Renninger, 1992). J. Eccles et al. (1983) have identified three components of task value or interest that can influence achievement performance and choice: attainment value (the subjective importance of doing well on a task influenced by the impact of the task on an individual's needs), intrinsic value (the satisfaction an individual gets from doing the task), and utility value (the usefulness of a task as a means to achieve a goal that may not be directly related to it).

One of the problems educators face is dealing with the fact that children value academic tasks less as they get older. For example, junior high school students rate English and math as less important and state that they enjoy these subjects less than they did in elementary school (J. S. Eccles et al., 1989; Wigfield, Eccles, MacIver, Reuman, & Midgley, 1991). The challenge for teachers is to find ways to increase students' value of important academic tasks and courses. Teachers also need to be concerned about students who do poorly in certain school subjects and, as a result, devalue the subjects as a way to maintain a positive sense of self-worth (Harter, 1985).

Expectancy Component: "Can I Do This Task?"

Self-Efficacy Beliefs. While goals, interests and values determine a student's reasons for engaging in different tasks, self-efficacy beliefs refer to a student's evaluation that he or she has specific performance capabilities on a particular type of task (Bandura, 1982). Self-efficacy beliefs are assumed to be relatively task-specific and not related to general self-concept. For example, a person may generally feel good about succeeding in a mathematics class, but have a high or low sense of efficacy for solving quadratic equations.

Perceived efficacy can influence motivation. Students with a high sense of efficacy are more likely to choose difficult tasks, expend greater effort, persist longer, apply appropriate problem-solving strategies on tasks, and have less fear and anxiety regarding tasks than students with a low sense of efficacy for a task. Students acquire information about their sense of efficacy in a given domain from their present and past performances, observations of other students, forms of social persuasion (e.g., "I know you can do it"), and physiological indexes (e.g., heart rate, sweating) (Schunk, 1991b).

Control Beliefs. Control beliefs refer to individuals' beliefs about how much control they have over their behavior. Whereas efficacy beliefs refer to individuals' perception of their ability to *perform* a task, control beliefs refer to individuals' beliefs concerning their ability to influence outcomes. For example, an individual may believe that she has the ability to do well on her upcoming math exam (self-efficacy) but have a low outcome expectation (control belief) for her grade on the exam because of a high grading curve.

In general, research indicates that students who believe that they have internal control over their learning perform better in school than students high in external control (Pintrich et al., 1993). Students with internal beliefs are more likely to believe that attending classes, reading course material, and studying can influence academic performance, while students with external beliefs are less likely to believe that such behaviors play a major role in their academic performance.

Attribution Beliefs. Attributional theorists believe that individuals search for understanding about the causes of events. In academic settings, attributions are explanations that individuals give for the causes of their successes and failures. Common achievement attributions are ability ("I'm good/bad in math."), effort ("I studied hard for the test/I didn't study enough"), task difficulty ("The test was easy/hard"), and luck ("I guessed right/wrong") (Weiner, 1986).

Weiner (1986) argues that the specific causal attributions are less important than the underlying dimensions of the attributions in determining achievement behavior. For example, students who attribute prior success to stable factors (e.g., high ability or easy task) are likely to hold higher expectancies for success than students who attribute success to less stable factors (e.g., high effort or good luck).

Attribution beliefs can influence self-efficacy. For example, students who attribute academic problems to low ability are likely to have a low sense of efficacy and not try very hard to succeed. However, self-efficacy theorists argue that efficacy judgment, rather than attributions, are the major determiners of achievement behavior and affect (Schunk, 1991b).

Teachers need to consider some other considerations about the emphasis on effort (C. Ames, 1990). First, some students may already believe that they are working as hard as they can. If teachers convince these students that poor effort is the primary cause of their academic problems, they may decrease their sense of efficacy regarding the task. The reasoning may be as follows: if I try hard and still cannot solve the problems, then I must lack ability. Second, if teachers continually emphasize the importance of sustaining a maximal effort on tasks, some students may conclude that they do not want to work so hard to succeed.

The implication is that teachers need to know how their students attribute the causes for their successes and failures and encourage both reasonable effort attributions along with the use of appropriate learning strategies so that students can learn more effectively and efficiently.

Affective Component: "How Do I Feel about the Task?"

Anxiety. Anxiety affects a student's emotional state and can perpetuate dysfunctional thinking and behaviors (Hill & Wigfield, 1984). Researchers have indicated that for some students small amounts of anxiety can facilitate learning (Sieber, O'Neil, & Tobias, 1977). If a student feels confident and prepared for an examination, a little anxiety can serve as motivation to excel. However, if he or she has a high level of anxiety, it can be detrimental in achievement settings.

Test anxiety is a specific form of anxiety about academic and ability evaluation. Hill and Wigfield (1984) state: "Test anxiety is one of the most important aspects of negative motivation and has direct debilitating effects on school performance" (p. 106). Educators are especially concerned about this type of anxiety because it increases through the elementary grades to high school and becomes more strongly (i.e., negatively) related to indexes of intellectual and academic performance (Hembree, 1988; Wigfield & Eccles, 1989). As students proceed through school, the higher their anxiety is, the more likely it is that they will have lower achievement.

Recent research has focused on the relative independence of two dimensions of test anxiety, worry vs. emotionality. Worry reflects the cognitive aspects of anxiety—the negative beliefs, troubling thoughts, and poor decisions. Emotionality refers to the unpleasant affective reactions such as tension and nervousness. Each of the dimensions can have differential affects on students. Although both dimensions can have a debilitating effect on students, the worry dimension has a stronger negative relationship with academic performance than the emotional dimension. One reason for this finding is that emotionality tends to decrease once a student begins a test, while worrisome thoughts often continue throughout the test and may be experienced for a period of time in advance of the examination. Also, achievement suffers because attention is affected during test taking when students must remember, or retrieve, what was learned (Covington, 1992).

Covington (1992) recently proposed an interaction model of achievement anxiety, where he shows the effects of anxiety at three stages: appraisal, preparation, and test taking. Students' motivation to succeed or to avoid failure is determined in the test appraisal stage, whether they judge the upcoming test to be a challenge or a threat. In the test preparation stage, students begin studying while thinking about such things as their ability, expectation, and the futility and effectiveness of their study. Students threatened by failure may become involved in avoidance behaviors such as irrational goal setting or procrastination that will further erode their study effectiveness. Finally, in the test taking stage, students attempt to retrieve what they have learned, sometimes in the face of great physical tension and worry. Anxiety, at this stage, interferes with the retrieval of information.

Covington's Self-Worth Theory. The self-worth theory of achievement motivation (Covington, 1992) incorporates a motivational component with the causal perceptions of success and failure. According to self-worth theory, an individual learns that, in our society, one is valued because of one's accomplishments. The key factor to achievement motivation can be explained by how a person attempts to maintain positive ability perceptions that are the basis of self-worth.

If a person fails at a task, the feedback evokes the possibility of a lack of ability. In addition, failure creates feelings of unworthiness and self-rejection. As a result, when individuals are faced with the possibility of failure, they will avoid the situation or develop strategies to protect any inferences to a lack of their ability. Covington (1992) identified a number of these strategies:

- Procrastination. If an individual studies at the last minute and has too little time to properly prepare for an exam, failure cannot be attributed to lack of ability.
- Unattainable goals. If an individual selects very difficult goals, failure is often assured. However, failure in such tasks reveals little about one's ability since most individuals also would fail.
- Underachievers. If an individual avoids any test of his or her ability by just doing the minimum to get by, he or she can maintain an inflated opinion of his or her ability: "I could do it, if I really tried."

• Anxiety. If an individual argues that one's poor performance is the result of test-taking anxiety, then one can't blame the performance as the result of low ability. In other words, "It's better to appear anxious than stupid" (p. 88).

If we examine the role of effort from both the teachers' and students' perspectives, we will find that in some cases teachers and students operate at cross purposes. Although teachers value achievement highly, they often reward (or punish) some students more than others for exactly the same level of performance. Students who are perceived as having expended effort (regardless of their ability) tend to be rewarded more and punished less than students who do not try (Weiner & Kukla, 1970).

However, Covington, and Omelich (1979) found that students experienced greatest shame with a combination of high effort and failure and least shame with low effort and failure. This research helps to explain why failure-avoiding students often do not try. Expending effort and still failing poses a serious threat to one's self-esteem. The student who does not try but fails can always rationalize that success could have been achieved through proper effort, thus maintaining a reasonable level of self-esteem. Teachers, however, tend to reinforce students who demonstrate effort and punish those who do not. Understanding the perspectives of both the teacher and the student helps to see how effort can become a "double-edged sword" for many students. They must walk the tightrope between the threatening extremes of high effort and no effort at all. They must demonstrate some effort to avoid negative sanctions from their teachers, but not enough to risk shame should they try hard and fail. Some students use excuses to maintain a balance between these extremes. A popular tactic is to try hard but to use excuses (external factors) to explain why trying did not help. Such behavior avoids any inference to low ability (Covington & Omelich, 1979). Covington (1983) summarizes the safe strategy of many students: "Try, or at least appear to try, but not too energetically and with excuses always at hand" (p. 149).

TEACHER-DIRECTED INTERVENTIONS[2]

Table 1 lists a number of students' dysfunctional motivational beliefs and perceptions teachers need to help students overcome if they are to become more successful learners. These beliefs or perceptions can be linked to one or more of the three motivational components identified in the previous section—value, expectancy, and affect. For example, the beliefs "I am not interested in the task" or "I don't see any use for learning this material" are linked to the value component and the belief "I don't think I can do the task" relates to the expectancy component. However, the belief "I don't have

[2]Some of the material in this section is taken from Gorman (1974), Hudgins et al. (1983), C. Ames and Ames (1991), and C. Ames (1992).

TABLE 1
Examples of Dysfunctional Motivational Beliefs or Perceptions

"I am not interested in the task."
"I don't see any use for learning this material."
"I don't think I can do the task."
"I don't have enough time to complete the task."
"I can't make myself do the task."
"I feel anxious about completing the task."
"I can't concentrate."
"I'm not in the mood to study."

enough time to complete the task" may be related to all three of the components. The problem may be because the student doesn't value the task, or doesn't know how to establish goals to manage time, or doesn't believe that he or she has the ability to complete the task, or feels anxious about completing the task. This belief may be modified by changes in classroom instruction and teaching the student time management skills, goal setting, or anxiety reduction procedures.

We will now discuss some of the instructional changes in classrooms based on the TARGET dimensions that can help establish a mastery goal orientation and influence positive motivational beliefs. In the next section, we will focus on how students can learn to monitor and control their own motivational beliefs.

Task Dimension

Create Links between Classroom Activities and Students' Life Experiences

Spend Time Developing Ideas and Topics for Projects and Assignments. For example, conduct prewriting discussions, where students can share ideas with peers and receive assistance from the teacher in developing relevant topics they raise about events or concerns in their communities. The more students deal with personal experiences, the more likely they will want to read and write about them. This procedure emphasizes the importance of developing thematic units of instruction rather than focusing on isolated literacy skills (Rueda & Moll, 1994).

Use Project-Based Learning Activities to Increase Student Interest. These projects require a question or problem (e.g., "How can we reduce crime in our neighborhood?" "How can we reduce the dangers of acid rain?") that determines the nature of activities into the topic. These activities result in a series of artifacts or products (e.g., report or videotape) that result in a final report (see Blumenfeld et al., 1991, for more information about this type of learning).

Identify and Use Parents' Skills and Expertise in the Classroom. Moll (1992) described a successful project where he identified parents' "funds of knowledge" in a small, Latino community in the Southwest. This knowledge is acquired largely through work and daily life experiences. He points out that the knowledge that such groups possess often goes unrecognized by mainstream culture and only rarely is acknowledged within formal institutions of learning. Many teachers have little idea about the wide range of knowledge that can be tapped within a few blocks of the school, because traditional approaches to education do not allow for such exploration.

Moll provides an example of how a sixth grade teacher integrated home and school knowledge around an academic unit of instruction. She chose to develop her instructional unit on construction and building. After discussing the unit with her students, she encouraged them to visit the library and start locating information on the topic in both Spanish and English. In addition, she brought various books into the classroom on the topic. Students also built model houses for homework and wrote brief essays describing their research or their construction methods. Next, the teacher invited parents who had expertise in construction to the classroom to provide additional information to the students. The students were surprised that the teacher would want to invite their parents *as experts*, especially since many of them lacked formal education. She was especially interested in them describing their use of construction instruments and tools and their use of mathematics in their work. The visits were so successful that she invited a total of 20 different community people during the semester to contribute knowledge to other lessons she developed.

Emphasize the Teacher's Role as Mediator of Learning

Vygotsky's (1978) notion of the zone of proximal development is helpful in understanding how teachers can assist student learning. Teachers can provide assistance in many ways: modeling to guide students through a cognitive task such as when a teacher talks aloud to describe the steps taken to solve a mathematics problem; using reinforcement to communicate to students that appropriate behavior was displayed; providing feedback on tasks with specific standards; using prompting questions to encourage students to think more about the topic (e.g., "How did you reach this conclusion?" "Is there another possible solution?"); task structuring such as showing students how to use task analysis to separate a large task into smaller ones (Tharp & Gallimore, 1991). The ultimate goal in this form of instruction is to help the student eventually take over all parts of the activity with no assistance from the teacher and maintain students' interest in the task.

Provoke Curiosity

Provoke curiosity in students before stating a topic by pointing up a problem or conflict or giving a pretest to make them realize what they do not know about the topic. Arouse surprise and a feeling of contradiction in students by presenting a phenomenon that violates their expectations or runs counter to their experience and former training, such as plants that live without sunlight or chlorophyll (fungi). Arouse doubt or uncertainty by giving students a problem with no indications for its solution, such as how to find one's position (latitude and longitude) in the middle of the desert.

Arouse Attention

Arouse attention in students by starting a class with something novel, different, or unusual, such as a brainstorming demonstration or a copy of an old newspaper in history. Maintain attention and interest through variety and change; never start a class the same way day after day.

Promote Differential Goals

Provide for different levels of goals among students by encouraging them to strive for levels of performance in keeping with their abilities and by having differentiated materials, activities, and projects available for students of different ability and aspiration levels. Independent study programs are a good example of such an approach.

Allowing learners to set their own goals may encourage greater interest in attaining them. Thus, setting conferences with students to discuss individual classroom goals or establishing contracts for completing academic tasks can help students take more responsibility for their learning and develop greater self-efficacy (Schunk, 1991b).

Authority Dimension

Increase Involvement in Learning

Give students opportunities to select activities, assignments, due dates, and those with whom they want to work, as well as their own methods and pace of learning. Involve them in relating the curriculum material to their own experiences and problems. Students need to perceive choices as equally attractive and difficult so they do not select simple tasks just to succeed.

Involvement in learning also can be enhanced through games, small group teaching, cooperative learning, and class discussions.

Use Peer Models

Observing a similar peer successfully performing a task can promote a sense of efficacy in the observers. For example, if a low-achieving student observes another low-achieving students successfully completing a math problem at the blackboard, the observer is likely to believe that he or she also could learn to solve the problem. The effectiveness of the model can be enhanced if he or she describes to the class how he or she studied, persisted at the task, or overcame any difficulty learning the task (Schunk, 1991b). Using culturally different students as peer models can also be an effective way to increase their classroom status and perceived competence by other students.

Recognition Dimension

Provide Sufficient Rewards

Use praise and encouragement appropriately, particularly for average and slower students. Give personal, encouraging comments on tests and other work rather than just a grade. Inform students regularly on how they are doing in a course. Finally, reward students for setting meaningful goals and choosing moderately challenging assignments.

Promote Beliefs in Competence

On occasion, try to increase the basic achievement motivation of some students through talking with them, having them read about highly motivated persons, putting them in with a group of highly motivated students, and so forth. Make students aware of their successes and the satisfaction they bring through comments such as "You really did well in that," "Didn't it feel good to get so many right?" Try to divert students' attention away from their failures by not threatening or punishing them or dwelling on their errors.

Encourage Students' Effort Attributions

Give students individual feedback when they fail and show them concrete steps they can take to improve. Model how success is attributed to effort by describing personal experiences in which they accomplished tasks by trying hard to succeed. Students might read stories and biographies describing individuals who have accomplished goals through effort and discuss individually or in groups the reasons why people succeed or fail. The discussion should focus on how attitudes, interests, and efforts are related to succeeding. Along with emphasis on the importance of effort, teach students the necessary learning strategies so they have the competencies and skills to succeed.

Grouping Dimension

Provide Opportunities for Cooperative Learning

Use varied procedures for grouping students according to shared interest, similar ability levels, friendship patterns, and at random, for example. They should have time to talk to each other about personal affairs as well as academic tasks. Games or activities that require team effort also help students satisfy their needs for affiliation and belonging.

Evaluation Dimension

Reduce Social Comparison and Competition in the Classroom

Reduced social comparison can be achieved by having students work toward individually prescribed or group goals. Limit the use of charts, posting grades, public pronouncements of high and low scores, and other strategies that lead to excessive emphasis on comparing successful and unsuccessful students. Competition should be geared to the ability levels of the students so that all have a chance to succeed, and students should focus on their own past performance as they set new goals for themselves, rather than on what others are doing or have done.

Reduce Anxiety in Achievement Situations

Give students sufficient time to complete assignments, tests, and other work so they do not worry about them. Clearly identify what is expected in assignments and help students develop a plan to accomplish tasks. Since anxious students have trouble memorizing information as well as retrieving information that has been previously learned, the use of diagrams, outlines, and other methods for organizing information can help to reduce anxiety.

Time Dimension

Adjust Requirements

Adjust task or time requirements for students who have difficulty completing their work and allow students opportunities to plan their schedules, and progress at an optimal rate.

STUDENT SELF-REGULATION STRATEGIES

In the previous section, we discussed how changes in classroom instruction can influence students' motivational beliefs and behavior. In this section, we will describe how students can be taught to become more self-motivated so they can manage and control their own learning. We base our intervention on the dysfunctional motivation beliefs listed in Table 1 and use a social cognitive approach to self-regulation, emphasizing three interacting subprocesses: self-observation, self-judgment, and self-reaction (Zimmerman, 1989).

Corno (1994) makes an important distinction between motivation and volition: "Motivation denotes commitment, and volition denotes follow-through" (p. 230). The point is that a student may be motivated to engage in a task but have difficulty persisting because he or she easily becomes distracted while engaging in the task (Kuhl & Beckman, 1985). These distractions include off-task thoughts, irrelevant distractions from others, anxiety about the task, or physical conditions that make it difficult to complete the task. Students who have difficulty with such distracters often lack the self-management skills needed to overcome environmental distraction or competing emotional or physical needs.

Two issues need to be stressed at this time. First, self-regulation requires more than instruction. Students must believe that a strategy is worthwhile and then control its use. Therefore, it may take weeks or months of practice before a student demonstrates a new self-regulatory behavior. Second, as mentioned earlier in the chapter, the classroom environment must be conducive to the development of self-regulatory behavior. If students develop a performance rather than a mastery goal orientation, the likelihood of them developing self-regulatory behavior will be greatly reduced.

Some of the areas in which students would benefit from self-regulatory instruction is mood control (e.g., anxiety, anger, frustration), goal setting, concentration, procrastination, and time management. We begin by discussing how self-verbalization or self-talk can be used to control mood and provide an example of a classroom instruction on the topic. Next, we discuss additional areas where self-control instruction would be helpful and explain how it could be accomplished.

Mood Control (Self-Talk)

Self-verbalization, cognitive self-instruction, or self-talk (as it is often called) is an important strategy for self-control. It is used as a learning strategy to teach students to instruct themselves through verbalization while completing independent learning tasks (Manning, 1991). The theory behind self-verbalization training is that an individual's inner speech influences cognition (thinking) and emotions and ultimately guides behavior. Some individuals have inappropriate self-verbalizations and, therefore, act in an inappropriate manner. Thus, if more appropriate self-verbalizations are introduced, behavior can be changed. Meichenbaum (1977) has shown how self-verbalization can be used to modify the behavior of students who are anxious or impulsive. He trained students to replace negative self-statements like "I can't do this" or "I'm not good at it" with positive self-statements like "If I concentrate I can solve the problems" or "I just need to relax and carefully read each problem." Manning (1991), in *Cognitive Self-Instruction for Classroom Processes*, provides numerous examples of how self-instruction can be used in a variety of academic tasks.

Self-talk also has been used to control anxiety, mood, and other affective responses (see Butler, 1981; Helmstetter, 1987; Ottens, 1984). The following is an instructional plan for teaching students to use self-talk.

Teaching Students to Use Self-Talk

Develop a Rationale for the Importance of Strategy. Evidence indicates that what we say to ourselves is an important factor in determining our attitudes, feelings, emotions, and behavior. This speech or self-talk, as it is often called, is the running dialogue inside our heads. Some of our inner speech motivates us to try new tasks and persist in difficult situations; other self-talk is unproductive and inhibits our motivation to succeed. The goal of this lesson is to teach you how to use self-talk to control your own attitudes and emotions that affect your motivation to learn. The emphasis is on changing negative self-talk to positive self-talk.

A good example of the impact of self-talk is discussed by Timothy Gallwey in *The Inner Game of Tennis* (1974). Gallwey says that tennis like other sports is composed of two parts, an outer game and an inner game. The outer game consists of mastering the techniques of how to play the game, such as how to serve and use one's backhand. The inner game takes place in the mind of the player and basically is the self-talk one uses while playing. Compare the following dialogue of two different players:

> I'm hitting my forehand rotten again today. . . . Dammit, why do I keep missing those easy set ups. . . . I'm not doing anything the coach told me to do in my last lesson. You were great rallying, now you're planning worse than your grandmother . . . (p. 82)

> The last three of my backhands landed long, by about two feet. My racket seems to be hesitating, instead of following through all the way. Maybe I should observe the level of my backswing . . . yes, I thought so, it's well above my waist. . . . There, that shot got hit with more pace, yet it stayed in. (p. 83)

Explain How Self-Talk Operates. Many individuals blame others for their negative emotional reactions: "He made me mad" or "My friend's response to my question made me depressed." It is important to realize that other people or events do not directly influence your emotional reactions. Your self-talk regarding events is the primary cause of your attitudes and emotions.

The following is how Ellis (1962) believes the process operates:

A. An event occurs	A. A low score on a test.
B. Self-talk, or thoughts about the event	B1. Self-talk: "I can't learn this stuff!" "What's the use of studying."
	B2. Self-talk: "I have the ability to get these questions correct if I put forth extra effort." "I'm going to study differently next time."
C. Emotion caused primarily by the self-talk	C1. Emotion: sadness and anger
	C2. Emotion: confidence

Note the different reactions, B1 and B2, to the event (A) and the resulting emotional responses. The first response (B1) is an example of harmful self-talk leading to negative emotional responses and often inappropriate behavior in future test preparation situations. The second response (B1) us an example of positive self-talk leading to a positive emotional response and possible changes in future test preparation situations.

Most of us use more positive than negative self-talk in dealing with the events and situations in our lives. The use of positive self-talk has lead to your success in many different areas. When difficult or challenging events occur, you remind yourself that you have the ability, skill or motivation to overcome any adversity. However, occasionally negative self-talk does play a role in your emotion, attitudes, and behavior.

Identify Procedures for Changing Self-Talk. Using the procedures in Table 2 (adapted from Butler, 1981) will help you understand and change any self-talk that you believe is not productive in reaching your goals. Note how self-observation (step 1), self-evaluation (step 2), and self-reaction (steps 3 and 4) are used in instruction. The right-hand column represents the procedures for the example in Table 2.

Goal Setting

We already have discussed the relationship between motivation and performance and goal setting. In general, establishing specific goals helps to direct attention to tasks, mobilize effort, increase persistence, and promote the use of new strategies when old strategies don't work (Locke & Latham, 1990).

TABLE 2
Understanding and Changing Self-Talk

Sharon is graduating from high school and will major in biology in college because she would like to go to medical school. She decides instead to major in education because many of her friends have told her about the many years of difficult study that are necessary to achieve her goal. In addition, she doubts her ability and motivation to do well in science. During the first semester at college she becomes upset because she is not studying what she really wants to study and decides to explore her own self-talk.

Description of Steps	Questions/Example
1. Be aware: listen to your own self-talk	1. "What am I telling myself?"
You can't alter inner speech unless you understand what you are telling yourself. (*Ask students to keep track of all self-talk they experience for a week by noting the situation, time, and specific self-talk statements.*)	I'm saying to myself, "I really would like to go to medical school." Then I think, "Oh, come on, Sharon, you're being silly. Medical school is hard and you'll never be able to do the work."
2. Evaluate: decide if your inner dialogue is helpful or harmful.	2. "Is it helping?"
Examine how your inner speech affects your emotions, motivation, and behavior. If your self-talk is helping, maintain it. If your self-talk is harmful, change it.	No. it's keeping me from doing what I really want to do.
3. Support yourself: replace your harmful self-talk with positive self-talk.	3. "What permission and self-affirmation will I give myself?"
Give yourself permission to try another strategy to deal with the event or situation. Identify your positive characteristics (e.g., desire, concentration, ability) that will help deal with the event. (*Select self-talk statements from students' logs and ask students to model changing negative self-talk statements to positive self-talk.*)	I will tell myself that I need to stop listening to others and begin thinking for myself. After all, I did very well in high school and I am very motivated to succeed in college.
4. Develop a guide: decide what action to take consonant with your new supportive position.	4. "What action will I take based on my new positive position?"
If you decide that your self-talk is harmful, you want to change your behavior as well as your attitude or emotional response. Specify this new behavior.	I'm going to see my advisor and find out what courses I need to major in biology. Next semester I will enroll in two science courses and see how I do. Then I'll have a better idea of both my ability and interest.

We have taught students to write academic goals by identifying characteristics of useful goals:[3] specific (describes what you want to accomplish with as much detail as possible), measurable (describes a goal in terms that can be clearly evaluated), moderately challenging (identifies a goal that takes energy and discipline to accomplish), realistic (identifies a goal you are capable of attaining), and has a stated completion date (identifies a goal that breaks a long-term goal into a shorter-term goals and clearly specifies a completion date).

After completing exercises evaluating the elements of useful goals using the criteria identified in the previous paragraph, students practice writing goals using the following procedure:

- Identify an area in which you wish to write a goal.
- Evaluate your past and present achievement, interest, or performance in the area to consider the extent to which the goal you are considering is moderately challenging and realistic.
- State what you want to accomplish. Begin with the words, "I want to . . ." and include a specific behavior that can be measured and with a completion date.
- Evaluate your goal statement for the five components of a useful goal.
- If necessary, modify your goal statement.

Concentration and Attention

Three attentional skills appear to be most critical in school: (1) identification of important text elements, (2) comprehension monitoring, and (3) sustained attention on tasks (Krupski, 1986). In this section, we focus on the last skill, attention on tasks, since it relates to persistence, an important factor in volition. The challenge for students is to deal successfully with both internal and external distracting elements in different learning and study environments interfering with their ability to concentrate on relevant academic stimuli. External distractors refer to environmental sources of interference such as friends, noise, or a nice day. Internal distractors refer to sources within the individual such as fatigue, hunger or thirst, or worry about an upcoming event. If students are to learn to monitor and control their concentration, they must learn how to eliminate distractions and adopt strategies that encourage concentration.

Self-talk has been included in a number of interventions to help students monitor and control their concentration during learning (Corno, 1987; Ottens, 1984). Ottens (1984) developed a systematic method for students to monitor their concentration consistent with the social–cognitive perspective used in this chapter. First, students increase their awareness of their current

[3]These criteria are adapted from unpublished material developed by Claire Weinstein at the University of Texas, Austin.

level of concentration through self-observation by recording during study each time they notice attention loss or thinking unrelated to task completion. The goal is to help students understand the type of inner speech engaged in throughout the day. Second, students develop their self-evaluation skills by later identifying what type of distracters they focused on most and why these distracters are irrelevant during study time. These distracters may be objects in their room, thoughts, or concerns regarding certain events or people. Once they have increased awareness of when and why their attention drifts away, they can apply new self-instruction (through self-talk) designed to keep behavior on target. For example, certain test-taking situations can initiate anxiety followed by expressions of futility and worry. As students become aware of their thinking, they can reprogram it through conscious self-talk that returns them to task-relevant thinking that improves concentration. The goal is to develop new inner speech that assists in keeping attention and behavior on on-task issues. Students can acknowledge, as soon as possible, a lapse of attention and give themselves a simple self-reminder: "There you go again, worrying about not finishing on time. Eyes back onto the test (text) paper." The goal is to redirect attention when one realizes that one's attention has strayed. Students practice this sequence and learn that redirecting one's attention is an ongoing process.

Time Management

Much has been written about the importance of time management. Lakein (1973) points out that the problem is more than the effective use of time. He states: "Making the right choices about how you'll use your time is more important than doing efficiently whatever job happens to be around. Efficiency is fine in its place, but to my mind effectiveness is a much more important goal" (p. 11).

Time management is an factor that can predict students' study behavior (LeNy, Denhiere, & Taillanter, 1972; Zacks, 1969) and relates to many other aspects of strategic learning (Weinstein, Stone, & Hanson, 1993) and academic performance (Britton & Tesser, 1991). According to social cognitive views of time management, time is influenced by behavioral, environmental, and personal learning influences (Zimmerman, 1989; Zimmerman, Greenberg, & Weinstein, 1994). Behavioral influences relate to efforts to self-observe, self-evaluate, and self-react to academic performances. Environmental influences include the use of planning aides such as alarms and appointment books. Finally, personal influences relate to the role of goal setting, attributions, and perceptions of self-efficacy (Zimmerman et al., 1994).

Teaching students to manage their time should consider each of the three types of influences. The following is an overview of one intervention program.

Begin by teaching students to set goals and assess their use of time by keeping logs of their activities at 30 minute intervals for an entire week. Next, present strategies for managing time and reducing or eliminating time wasters and provide students practice in using the techniques in their classes. Finally, provide feedback to students and ask them to monitor and assess their success or failure with the strategies (Zimmerman et al., 1994).

Procrastination

Procrastination appears to be a universal problem negatively affecting the behavior of many individuals (Bliss, 1983; Ellis & Knaus, 1977). However, we know very little about the procrastination of elementary and secondary school students since most of the research and interventions have been conducted with college students.

Procrastination on academic tasks is especially disconcerting for instructors since it can lead to low academic performance, including poor grades and course withdrawal (Semb, Glick, & Spencer, 1979). In one investigation, Rothblum, Solomon, and Murakami (1986) found that more than 40% of the college students in their sample (N = 379) reported that they procrastinated on exams to the extent that they experienced considerable anxiety.

Ferrari, Johnson, and McCown (1995) provide the most comprehensive review of the research on procrastination presently available. We shall summarize some of the major findings from their work. First, although procrastination and task-avoidant behavior are common academic problems, little scientific investigation has focused on the etiology, prevention, or treatment of procrastination. Much of our knowledge about treatment comes primarily from self-help books written by clinicians (e.g., Bliss, 1983; Burka & Yuen, 1983; Ellis & Knaus, 1977), who have not conducted controlled studies of therapeutic outcomes. Second, definitions and causes of procrastination vary widely. Third, procrastination often is linked to a number of personality disorders such as anxiety, fear, and negative views of the self. However, researchers do not know whether procrastination causes psychological disorders or whether such disorders causes procrastination. Fourth, there are different types of academic procrastination. As a result, no one treatment can be effective with all students. In summary, procrastination is a complex problem with no simple solutions.

Although there are different reasons for procrastination, Ferrari et al. (1995) identified two dysfunctional patterns that should be considered for intervention in academic settings. The first pattern is classified as neurotic avoidance and is associated with fear, anxiety, and overarousal. The second pattern in classified as a lack of conscientiousness and is associated with such behaviors as poor time management, work discipline, self-control, responsibility, and underarousal, especially when deadlines approach. The important aspect of identifying different types of procrastination is understanding that no one intervention such as time management will be equally effective with all students.

Regardless of typology, a useful treatment involves challenging and changing cognitive distortions and misperceptions (Ferrari et al., 1995). The following cognitive misconceptions are frequent among most procrastinators:

- Overestimation of the time left to perform a task.
- Underestimation of time necessary to complete a task.
- Overestimation of future motivational states. This is typified by statements such as "I feel more like doing it later."
- Misreliance on the necessity of emotional congruence to succeed in a task. Typical is a statement such as "People should only study when they feel good about it."
- Belief that working when not in the mood is unproductive or suboptimal. Such beliefs are typically expressed by phrases such as "It doesn't do any good to work when you are not motivated." (p. 197)

A number of anxiety-reducing strategies are available for procrastinators who are anxious such as self-talk, deep-relaxation training, and visualization with relaxation (see Barlow, 1992). In addition, helping students improve their time and task management should be included with the anxiety-reducing intervention.

Finally, for academic procrastinators who exhibit a lack of conscientiousness, the treatment of choice should focus on changing irrational beliefs regarding task completion. This strategy involves getting the procrastinator to assess the amount of time necessary to complete tasks and challenge cognitions interfering with this accurate assessment (see Ellis and Knaus, 1977, for suggestions for changing beliefs and perceptions as well as behavioral strategies for dealing with task completion problems).

SUMMARY

In this chapter, we have identified a cognitive perspective of motivation whereby students' motivational beliefs and emotions are assumed to mediate between their cultural and classroom experiences and behavior. Motivation is manifested in the classroom by the following behaviors: choice behavior, level of activity and involvement, and persistence behavior or regulation of effort. Dysfunctional motivation is characterized by beliefs and perceptions that can be categorized by one or more dimensions: value, expectancy, and affective. More specifically, the following motivational beliefs or perceptions are detrimental to academic success: little value or interest for completing a task, low sense of efficacy or control over one's behavior, attributions for success and failure to ability rather than effort, the desire to protect one's sense of worth, and high anxiety.

The beliefs or perceptions that determine motivated behavior stem from students' social and cultural experiences and classroom interaction. We discussed how the nature of the classroom context, in terms of tasks, authority, recognition, grouping, evaluation, and time can influence the development of students' mastery goal orientation. This orientation influences students' cognitive engagement and motivated behavior. Finally, we identified teacher-directed classroom intervention strategies to modify goal orientation and behaviors that students need for self-regulation to sustain motivated behavior.

References

Ainsworth, N. (1984). The cultural shaping of oral discourse. *Theory into Practice*, 23, 132–137.

Ames, C. (1990). Motivation: What teachers need to know. *Teachers College Record*, 91, 409–421.

Ames, C. (1992). Achievement goals and the classroom motivational climate. In D. H. Schunk & J. L. Meece (Eds.), *Student perceptions in the classroom* (pp. 327–348). Hillsdale, NJ: Erlbaum.

Ames, C., & Ames, R. (1991). Motivation and effective teaching. In L. Idol & B. F. Jones (Eds.), *Educational values and cognitive instruction: Implications for reform* (pp. 247–271). Hillsdale, NJ: Erlbaum.

Ames, C., & Archer, J. (1988). Achievement goals in the classroom: Students' learning strategies and motivation processes. *Journal of Educational Psychology*, 80, 260–267.

Ames, R., & Ames, C. (Eds.). (1984). *Research on motivation in education: Vol. 1. Student motivation.* Orlando, FL: Academic Press.

Atkinson, J. W. (1964). *An introduction to motivation.* Princeton, NJ: Van Nostrand.

Bandura, A. (1982). Self-efficacy mechanism in human agency. *American Psychologist*, 37, 122–147.

Barlow, D. H. (1992). *Anxiety and its disorders: The nature and treatment of anxiety and panic.* New York: Guilford.

Bliss, E. C. (1983). *Doing it now: A twelve-step program for curing procrastination and achieving your goals.* New York: Scribner's.

Blumenfeld, P. C., Soloway, E., Marx, R. W., Krajcik, J. S., Guzdial, M., & Palincsar, A. (1991). Motivating project-based learning: Sustaining the doing, supporting the learning. *Educational Psychologist*, 26, 369–398.

Britton, B. K., & Tesser, A. (1991). Effects of time management practices on college grades. *Educational Psychology*, 83, 405–410.

Brophy, J. E. (1981). Teacher praise: A functional analysis. *Review of Educational Research*, 51, 5–32.

Brophy, J. E., Rohrkemper, M., Rashid, H., & Goldberger, M. (1983). Relationships between teachers' presentations of classroom tasks and students' engagement in those tasks. *Journal of Educational Psychology*, 75, 544–552.

Burka, J. B., & Yuen, L. M. (1983). *Procrastination: Why you do it and what to do about it.* Reading, MA: Addison-Wesley.

Butler, P. E. (1981). *Talking to yourself: Learning the language of self-support.* San Francisco: Harper & Row.

Carnegie Council on Adolescent Development. (1989). *Turning points: Preparing American youth for the 21st century.* Report of the Task Force on Education of Young Adolescents, New York.

Corno, L. (1987). Teaching and self-regulated learning. In D. C. Berliner & B. K. Rosenshine (Eds.), *Talks to teachers* (pp. 249–266). New York: Random House.

Corno, L. (1994). Student volition and education: Outcomes, influences, and practices. In D. H.

Schunk & B. J. Zimerman (Eds.), *Self-regulation of learning and performance: Issues and educational applications* (pp. 229–251). Hillsdale, NJ: Erlbaum.

Covington, M. V. (1983). Motivated cognitions. In S. G. Paris, G. M. Olson, & H. W. Stevenson (Eds.), *Learning and motivation in the classroom* (pp. 139–164). Hillsdale, NJ: Erlbaum.

Covington, M. V. (1992). *Making the grade: A self-worth perspective on motivation and school reform*. New York: Cambridge University Press.

Covington, M. V., & Omelich, C. (1979). Effort: The double-edged sword in school achievement. *Journal of Educational Psychology*, 71, 169–182.

Deci, E. L., Nezlek, J., & Sheinman, L. (1981). Characteristics of the rewarder and intrinsic motivation of the rewardee. *Journal of Personality and Social Psychology*, 40, 1–10.

Dembo, M. (1994). *Applying educational psychology*. White Plains, NY: Longman.

Dweck, C. S. (1986). Motivational processes affecting learning. *American Psychologist*, 41, 1040–1048.

Eccles, J. S., Adler, T. F., Futterman, R., Goff, S. B., Kaczala, C. M., Meece, J. L., & Midgley, C. (1983). Expectancies, values, and academic behaviors. In J. T. Spence (Ed.), *Achievement and achievement motivation* (pp. 75–146). San Francisco: Freeman.

Eccles, J. S., Wigfield, A., Flanagan, C., Miller, C., Reuman, D., & Yee, D. (1989). Self-concepts, domain values, and self-esteem: Relations and changes at early adolescence. *Journal of Personality*, 57, 283–310.

Elliott, E. S., & Dweck, C. S. (1981). *Children's achievement goals as determinants of learned helplessness and mastery-oriented achievement patterns: An experimental analysis*. Unpublished manuscript, Harvard University, Cambridge, MA.

Ellis, A. (1962). *Reason and emotion in psychotherapy*. New York: Lyle Stuart.

Ellis, A., & Knaus, W. J. (1977). *Overcoming procrastination*. New York: New American Library.

Epstein, J. L. (1988). Effective schools or effective students: Dealing with diversity. In R. Haskins & D. MacRae (Eds.), *Policies for America's public schools: Teacher equity indicators* (pp. 89–126). Norwood, NJ: Ablex.

Feldaufer, H., Midgley, C., & Eccles, J. S. (1988). Student, teacher, and observer perceptions of the classroom environment before and after the transition to junior high school. *Journal of Early Adolescence*, 8, 133–156.

Ferrari, J. R., Johnson, J. L., & McCown, W. G. (1995). *Procrastination and task avoidance: Theory, research, and treatment*. New York: Plenum.

Fraser, B. J., & Fisher, D. L. (1982). Predicting students' outcomes from their perceptions of classroom psychosocial environment. *American Educational Research Journal*, 19, 498–518.

Gallwey, W. T. (1974). *The inner game of tennis*. New York: Random House.

Gibson, M. A. (1987). The school performance of immigrant minorities: A comparative view. *Anthropology & Education Quarterly*, 18, 262–275.

Gorman, R. M. (1974). *The psychology of classroom learning*. Columbus, OH: Merrill.

Harter, S. (1985). Competence as a dimension of self-evaluation: Toward a comprehensive model of self-worth. In R. Keahy (Ed.), *The development of the self* (pp. 55–121). New York: Academic Press.

Helmstetter, S. (1987). *The self-talk solution*. New York: Morrow.

Hembree, R. (1988). Correlates, causes, effects, and treatment of test anxiety. *Review of Educational Research*, 58, 47–77.

Hill, K. T., & Wigfield, A. (1984). Test anxiety: A major educational problem and what can be done about it. *Elementary School Journal*, 85, 105–126.

Hudgins, B. B., Phye, G. D., Schau, C. G., Theisen, G. L., Ames, C., & Ames, R. (1983). *Educational psychology*. Itasca, IL: Peacock.

Johnson, D. W., & Johnson, R. T. (1994). *Learning together and alone: Cooperation, competition, and individualization* (4th ed.). Englewood Cliffs, NJ: Prentice-Hall.

Kagan, D. (1990). How schools alienate students at risk: A model for examining proximal classroom variables. *Educational Psychologist*, 25, 105–125.

Krupski, A. (1986). Attention problems in youngsters with learning handicaps. In J. K. Torgesen & B. Y. L. Wong (Eds.), *Psychological and educational perspectives on learning disabilities* (pp. 161–192). New York: Academic Press.

Kuhl, J., & Beckman, J. (1985). Historical perspectives in the study of action control. In J. Kuhl & J. Beckman (Eds.), *Action control: From cognition to behavior* (pp. 89–100). New York: Springer-Verlag.

Lakein, A. (1973). *How to get control of your time and your life.* New York: Signet.

Lave, J. (1988). *Cognition in practice.* New York: Cambridge University Press.

Le Ny, J. F., Denhiere, G., & Le Taillanter, D. (1972). Regulation of study-time and interstimulus similarity in self-paced learning conditions. *Acta Psychologica*, 36, 280–289.

Lepper, M. R., & Hodell, M. (1989). Intrinsic motivation in the classroom. In C. Ames & R. Ames (Eds.), *Research on motivation in education: Vol. 3. Goals and cognitions* (pp. 73–105). San Diego, CA: Academic Press.

Locke, E. A., & Latham, G. P. (1990). *A theory of goal setting and task performance.* Englewood Cliffs, NJ: Prentice-Hall.

Maehr, M. L. (1992, April). *Transforming school culture to enhance motivation.* Paper presented at the annual meeting of the American Educational Research Association, San Francisco.

Manning, B. H. (1991). *Cognitive self-instruction for classroom processes.* Albany: State University of New York Press.

McClelland, D. C. (1965). Toward a theory of motive acquisition. *American Psychologist*, 20, 321–333.

Meece, J. L. (1991). The classroom context and student motivational goals. In M. Maehr & P. Pintrich (Eds.), *Advances in motivation and achievement* (Vol. 7, (pp. 261–285). Greenwich, CT: JAI Press.

Meichenbaum, D. (1977). *Cognitive behavior modification.* New York: Plenum.

Midgley, C. (1993). Motivation and middle level schools. In M. L. Maehr & P. R. Pintrich (Eds.), *Advances in motivation and achievement* (Vol. 8, pp. 217–274). Greenwich, CT: JAI Press.

Midgley, C., Feldlaufer, H., & Eccles, J. S. (1988). The transition to junior high school: Beliefs of pre- and post-transition teachers. *Journal of Youth and Adolescence*, 17 543–562.

Moll, L. C. (1992). Bilingual classroom studies and community analysis: Some recent trends. *Educational Researcher*, 21, 20–24.

Nicholls, J. G. (1984). Conceptions of ability and achievement motivation: A theory and its implications for education. In S. G. Paris, G. M. Olson, & H. W. Stevenson (Eds.), *Learning and motivation in the classroom* (pp. 211–237). Hillsdale, NJ: Erlbaum.

Oakes, J. (1987). Tracking in secondary schools: A contextual perspective. *Educational Psychologist*, 22, 129–153.

Ogbu, J. U. (1987). Variability in minority school performance: A problem in search of an explanation. *Anthropology & Education Quarterly*, 18, 312–334.

Ogbu, J. U. (1992). Understanding cultural diversity and learning. *Educational Researcher*, 21, 5–14.

Ottens, A. J. (1984). *Coping with academic anxiety.* New York: Rosen.

Paris, S. G., & Newman, R. S. (1990). Developmental aspects of self-regulated learning. *Educational Psychologist*, 25, 87–102.

Philips, S. U. (1983). *The invisible culture: Communication in classroom and community on the Warm Springs Indian Reservation.* White Plains, NY: Longman.

Pintrich, P. R. (1994). Student motivation in the college classroom. In K. W. Prichard & R. M. Sawyer (Eds.), *Handbook of college teaching: Theory and applications* (pp. 23–43). Westport, CT: Greenwood.

Pintrich, P. R., Cross, D. R., Kozma, R. B., & McKeachie, W. J. (1986). Instructional psychology. *Annual Review of Psychology*, 37, 611–651.

Pintrich, P. R., & DeGroot, E. V. (1990). Motivational and self-regulated learning components of classroom academic performance. *Journal of Educational Psychology*, 82, 33–40.

Pintrich, P. R., & Garcia, T. (1992, April). *An integrated model of motivation and self-regulated learning.* Paper presented at the annual meeting of the American Educational Research Association, San Francisco.

Pintrich, P. R., Marx, R. W., & Boyle, R. A. (1993). Beyond cold conceptual change: The role of motivational beliefs and classroom contextual factors in the process of conceptual change. *Review of Educational Research, 63,* 167–199.

Pintrich, P. R., & Schrauben, B. (1992). Students' motivational beliefs and their cognitive engagement in classroom academic tasks. In D. Schunk & J. L. Meece (Eds.), *Student perceptions in the classroom* (pp. 149–183). Hillsdale, NJ: Erlbaum.

Pokay, P., & Blumenfeld, P. C. (1990). Predicting achievement early and late in the semester: The role of motivation and use of learning strategies. *Journal of Educational Psychology, 82,* 41–50.

Renninger, K. A. (1992). Individual interest and development: Implications for theory and practice. In K. A. Renninger, S. Hidi, & A. Krapp (Eds.), *The role of interest in learning and development* (pp. 361–395). Hillsdale, NJ: Erlbaum.

Rothblum, E. D., Solomon, L. J., & Murakami, J. (1986). Affective, cognitive, and behavioral differences between high and low procrastinators. *Journal of Counseling Psychology, 33,* 387–394.

Rueda, R., & Dembo, M. H. (1995). Motivational processes in learning: A comparative analysis of cognitive and sociocultural frameworks. In P. Pintrich & M. Maehr (Eds.), *Advances in motivation and achievement* (Vol. 9, pp. 255–289). Greenwich, CT: JAI Press.

Rueda, R., & Moll, L. C. (1994). A sociocultural perspective on motivation. In H. F. O'Neill & M. Drillings (Eds.), *Motivation: Research and theory* (pp. 117–137). Hillsdale, NJ: Erlbaum.

Ryan, R. M., & Grolnick, W. (1984). *Origins and pawns in the classroom: A self-report and projective assessment of childrens' perceptions.* Unpublished manuscript, University of Rochester, Rochester, NY.

Schunk, D. H. (1991a). Goal setting and self-evaluation: A social cognitive perspective on self-regulation. In M. L. Maehr & P. R. Pintrich (Eds.), *Advances in motivation and achievement* (Vol. 7, pp. 85–113). Greenwich, CT: JAI Press.

Schunk, D. H. (1991b). Self-efficacy and academic motivation. *Educational Psychologist, 26,* 207–231.

Semb, G., Glick, D. M., & Spencer, R. E. (1979). Student withdrawals and delayed work patterns in self-paced psychology courses. *Teaching of Psychology, 6,* 23–26.

Sieber, J., O'Neil, H., & Tobias, S. (1977). *Anxiety, learning and instruction.* Hillsdale, NJ: Erlbaum.

Spaulding, C. L. (1992). *Motivation in the classroom.* New York: McGraw-Hill.

Stipek, D. J. (1988). *Motivation to learn: From theory to practice.* Englewood Cliffs, NJ: Prentice-Hall.

Sweeting, L. M., Willower, D. J., & Helsel, A. R. (1978). Teacher-pupil relationships: Black students' perceptions of actual and ideal teacher/pupil control behavior and attitudes toward teachers and school. *Urban Education, 13,* 71–81.

Tharp, R. G., & Gallimore, R. (1991). *The instructional conversation: Teaching and learning in social activity.* Washington, DC: National Center for Research on Cultural Diversity and Second Language Learning.

Vygotsky, L. S. (1978). *Mind in society: The Development of higher psychological processes.* Cambridge, MA: Harvard University Press.

Webb, F. R., Covington, M. V., & Guthrie, J. W. (1993). Carrots and sticks: Can school policy influence student motivation? In T. Tomlinson (Ed.), *Motivating students to learn: Overcoming barriers to high achievement* (pp. 94–124). Berkeley, CA: McCutchan.

Weiner, B. (1986). *An attributional theory of motivation and emotion.* New York: Springer-Verlag.

Weiner, B. (1991). Metaphors in motivation and attribution. *American Psychologist, 46,* 921–930.

Weiner, B., & Kukla, A. (1970). An attributional analysis of achievement motivation. *Journal of Personality and Social Psychology, 15,* 1–20.

Weinstein, C. E., & McCombs, B. (in press). A model of strategic learning. In C. Weinstein & B. McCombs (Eds.), *Strategic learning: Skill, will, and self-regulation.* Hillsdale, NJ: Erlbaum.

Weinstein, C. E., Stone, G., & Hanson, G. H. (1993). *The long-term effects of a strategic learning course for college students*. Unpublished manuscript, University of Texas, Austin.

Wertsch, J. V. (1991). *Voices of the mind: A socio-historical approach to mediated action*. Cambridge, MA: Harvard University Press.

Wigfield, A., & Eccles, J. S. (1989). Test anxiety in elementary and secondary students. *Educational Psychologist, 24*, 159–183.

Wigfield, A., & Eccles, J. S. (1992). The development of achievement task values: A theoretical analysis. *Developmental Review, 12*, 265–310.

Wigfield, A., Eccles, J., MacIver, D., Reuman, D., & Midgley, C. (1991). Transitions at early adolescence: Changes in children's domain-specific self-perceptions and general self-esteem across the transition to junior high school. *Developmental Psychology, 27*, 552–565.

Zacks, R. T. (1969). Invariance of total learning time under different conditions of practice. *Journal of Experimental Psychology, 82*, 441–447.

Zimmerman, B. J. (1989). A social cognitive view of self-regulated academic learning. *Journal of Educational Psychology, 81*, 329–339.

Zimmerman, B. J., Greenberg, D., & Weinstein, C. E. (1994). Self-regulating academic study time: A strategic approach. In D. H. Schunk & B. J. Zimmerman (Eds.), *Self-regulation of learning and performance: Issues and educational applications* (pp. 181–199). Hillsdale, NJ: Erlbaum.

CHAPTER

4

Self-Regulatory Dimensions of Academic Learning and Motivation

BARRY J. ZIMMERMAN
Graduate School and University Center
City University of New York

RAFAEL RISEMBERG
Department of Communication Sciences and Educational Services
Kean College of New Jersey

In recent years, educators have grown increasingly skeptical about explanations of learning and motivation that emphasize limitations of learners' abilities and social environmental backgrounds and have turned their attention to students' strategic efforts to manage their own achievement through specific beliefs and processes. These self-regulatory beliefs and processes have become the focus of systematic research (Schunk & Zimmerman, 1994; Zimmerman & Schunk, 1989). Most current efforts to define the *self-regulation of academic learning* have adopted multidimensional criteria, which stress personal meta-cognitive, motivational, behavioral, and environmental processes used to enhance academic achievement (Zimmerman, 1986). As a topic of research, self-regulated learning challenges meta-cognitive theorists to explain *why* students learn and *what* manner they perform behaviorally on their own; conversely, it challenges motivational and behavioral theorists to explain *how* students think about themselves and academic tasks in order to learn independently. This strategic view of learning is distinct from previous models of learning because it shifts the focus of educational analyses from students' learning abilities and environment at school or home as fixed en-

Handbook of Academic Learning

TABLE 1
Self-Regulatory Processes of Underachievers and Achievers

Processes	Underachievers	Achievers
Time use	Are more impulsive	Manage study time well
Goals	Set lower academic goals	Set higher specific and proximal goals
Self-monitor	Monitor less accurately	Monitor more frequently and accurately
Self-reactions	Are more self-critical	Set a higher standard for satisfaction
Self-efficacy	Are less self-efficacious	Are more self-efficacious
Motivation	Give up more readily	Persist despite obstacles

tities to their personally initiated strategies to improve learning outcomes and study environment (Zimmerman, 1989). This chapter will describe how research on self-regulatory beliefs and processes can explain extraordinary academic learning as well as underachievement of students, will offer a dimensional analysis of academic self-regulation, and finally, will discuss self-regulatory beliefs and processes of an achieving and an underachieving student on the basis of current research.

SELF-REGULATION OF ACHIEVERS AND UNDERACHIEVERS

The strategic qualities of self-regulated learners enable investigators to explain educational findings that conflict with fixed views of human functioning, such as exemplary achievement by minority students from disadvantaged backgrounds attending inner city schools as well as underachievement of youngsters from more fortunate backgrounds. For example, with regard to motivation, Wibrowski (1992) reported that academically successful minority students attending an urban high school were more willing to work late into the night and to get up early the next morning to finish assignments that were due. In comparison, their less successful classmates preferred to go to bed early and copy a peer's work before class. In other research Caplan, Choy, and Whitmore (1992) found that immigrant Asian families spent their evenings studying at the kitchen table for more than three hours each night, a figure that contrasts markedly with the one hour or less per day spent by more than 71% of American children nationwide and the complete absence of studying by 25% of American students (National Assessment of Educational Progress Report, 1990). These Asian youngsters also displayed extraordinary levels of commitment to succeed in school and a strong sense of personal efficacy. The students were the offspring of uneducated parents and attended inner city schools with few academic resources, yet they managed to achieve through their academic time management, practice, goal-directedness, and sense of self-efficacy. These personal qualities are the hallmarks of self-regulated learners (see Table 1).

Conversely, there is evidence that a major cause of underachievement is the inability of students to control themselves effectively (Krouse & Krouse, 1981). Researchers (Borkowski & Thorpe, 1994) have reported that underachievers are more impulsive, have lower academic goals, and are less accurate in assessing themselves. In addition, they are more self-critical and less self-efficacious about their academic performance and give up more easily than achievers. These self-regulatory limitations appear to exert a strong negative effect on underachievers' personality and emotional development: they are more anxious, have lower self-esteem, higher need for approval, and are influenced more by extrinsic factors than achievers. Thus, investigation of academic self-regulation has the potential of explaining unexpected outcomes at both ends of the achievement continuum: personal accomplishment in the face of daunting odds as well as under-achievement and low self-esteem.

DIMENSIONS OF ACADEMIC SELF-REGULATION

Although research on academic self-regulation is less than a decade old, it has established that students' self-regulatory attributes are evident to their teachers and that students' self-regulatory beliefs and processes are not only measurable but highly correlated with academic achievement, whether measured using grade point average, achievement track in school, standardized tests, or task-specific measures (Zimmerman & Martinez-Pons, 1986, 1988). Self-regulation is distinct from measures of mental ability and has been found to involve sources of motivation as well as meta-cognitive skill (Zimmerman & Bandura, 1994; Zimmerman, Bandura, & Martinez-Pons, 1992). Researchers have also demonstrated that it is possible to teach self-regulated learning processes, and these processes will enhance both students' achievement and their perceptions of self-efficacy (e.g., Schunk 1995; Shapely, 1995; Zimmerman, 1995). To help explain the relationship between these learning and motivation processes as well as other aspects of academic self-regulation, a conceptual model is presented in Table 2 that highlights six key psychological dimensions. This model is an elaboration of an earlier four-dimensional formulation (Zimmerman, 1994).

In the first column of Table 2 are six essential questions to understanding all forms of human learning. Each question pertains to a key psychological dimension, such as motivation, method, and time. The question *why* addresses students' motivation to regulate their own learning. To be able to regulate his or her own motivation, a student must be able to choose whether to participate or not, and this task condition is indicated in the third

TABLE 2
Conceptual Dimensions of Academic Self-Regulation

Scientific Questions	Psychological Dimensions	Task Conditions	Self-Regulatory Attributes	Self-Regulatory Beliefs and Processes
1. Why?	Motive	Choose to participate	Intrinsically or self-motivated	Own goals, self-efficacy, values, attributions, etc.
2. How?	Method	Control method	Planned or routinized	Strategy use, relaxation, etc.
3. When?	Time	Control time limits	Timely and efficient	Time planning and management, etc.
4. What?	Performance	Control performance	Aware of own performance and outcomes	Self-monitoring, self-judgment, action control, volition, etc.
5. Where?	Environmental	Control physical setting	Environmentally sensitive and resourceful	Environmental selection and structuring
6. With whom?	Social	Control social milieu	Socially sensitive and resourceful	Model selection, seeking help, etc.

Note. From "Dimensions of academic self-regulation: A conceptual framework for education" (p. 8) by B. J. Zimmerman in *Self-Regulation of Learning and Performance: Issues and Educational Applications*, D. H. Schunk and B. J. Zimmerman (Eds.). Hillsdale, NJ: Lawrence Erlbaum Associates, Inc. Copyright 1994 by Lawrence Erlbaum Associates, Inc. Adapted with permission.

column of Table 2. If researchers or educators externally compel students to participate in a learning experience, these youngsters cannot regulate their own motivation. Self-regulation researchers often include a separate research phase in their studies in which students are allowed to choose from a range of activities. For example, pupils might be taught a strategy for writing comparative essays, but if they are not given a chance to choose this activity, it is not possible to determine if they are intrinsically motivated. The fourth column of Table 2 describes this self-motivated attributes of the learners. Attributes, such as intrinsic interest or seeking challenges, are the motivational qualities most apparent to teachers and parents of self-regulated students, and there is extensive evidence that these attributes are highly associated with academic attainment (e.g., Bandura & Schunk, 1981; Zimmerman & Martinez-Pons, 1988). Researchers who are interested in enhancing students' self-motivation have uncovered the types of underlying processes or beliefs on which intrinsically motivated students depend, such as setting goals, perceptions of self-efficacy, academic values, and attributions. These processes and beliefs are listed in column 5 of Table 2. To to help a student to become more self-regulated within a particular psychological dimension, it is necessary to understand these underlying processes and beliefs, to be able to assess them, and to know how they can be taught.

Similarly, the question *how* focuses attention on the method dimension of self-regulation (column 2) and the need to allow students to choose their own ways to learn an educational task (column 3), such as using an imaginal or a verbal strategy to memorize the names of the states in the union. For a self-regulating student, this dimension will be perceived as highly planful in the way he or she approaches a learning task, such as outlining a paper before beginning to write it (column 4). As students become more adept and their planning becomes routine, they will be able to mentally organize the information without needing to create the outline on paper. A key underlying process when regulating one's own academic method is the use of learning strategies (column 5). The range and power of such strategies has been demonstrated during two decades of research, and there have been systematic efforts to incorporate them into curricular experiences (Pressley, Woloshyn, & Associates, 1995; Weinstein & Mayer, 1986).

The third question of *when* refers to the time dimension of self-regulation (column 2). There is extensive evidence that self-regulated students plan their use of time more frequently and use it more effectively (Zimmerman, Greenberg, & Weinstein, 1994). Students are given greater autonomy in their use of academic time as they advance in age and grade level (column 3). For example, kindergartners' time in school is organized and monitored very closely by their teachers, whereas college students generally are allowed to schedule their academic activities on their own. In terms of their classroom attributes, self-regulated students are prompt and consistent in their class attendance and their completion of homework (column 4). Researchers have identified several key processes associated with effective use of time—namely, time planning, management, and self-beliefs (column 5).

The fourth question *what* pertains to the overt behavioral performance of self-regulated learners (column 2). To regulate their own performance, learners must be able to choose, modify, and adapt their form of response, particularly from the feedback it produces (column 3). For example, for a written paper, students might be permitted to choose the topic and the organizational format (e.g., compare and contrast versus a descriptive account). Self-regulated students can be identified by their awareness of performance outcomes (column 4) and by their optimal adjustment of their performance to changing conditions. For example, there is evidence these students are more aware of how well they have done on a test even before getting feedback from their teacher (Zimmerman & Martinez-Pons, 1988). Some key self-regulatory processes that influence performance proficiency are self-monitoring, self-reactions, self-instruction, and volition (column 5).

The fifth question focuses on the way that students regulate their physical environment (column 2), such as the places *where* they study (column 1) or the use of instructional supports (e.g., computers and recording devices). Unfortunately, in most schools, students have little control over the classroom setting or little opportunity to choose where they can study. Some students may lack control of their study environment at home also because of crowding, noise, television, or lack of instructional resources (column 3). Self-regulated learners can be identified by their awareness of surrounding conditions on their academic concentration, such as the influence of distracting sounds and sights (column 4). These students achieve regulatory control over these environmental conditions through selecting and structuring activities (column 5), such as by studying at a library where reference books are readily available or by disconnecting the phone from the jack while studying at home.

The sixth scientific question *with whom* concerns the social dimension of self-regulation (column 2). Socially self-regulated students are aware of how others can help or hinder their learning (column 3) and can be identified by their sensitivity and resourcefulness in choosing studymates, coaches, or instructors (column 4). These learners can be distinguished from socially dependent classmates by the way they initiate and respond to social support: they choose their helpers and the assistance they need *selectively* and *confidently*. Research has shown the non-self-regulated learners are reluctant to ask for assistance because they are (1) unsure what to ask and (2) afraid of how they might appear (Newman, 1994). Among the key social self-regulatory processes (column 5) are model selection, seeking help from teacher and peers (Nelson-Le Gal & Jones, 1990; Newman, 1994).

RESEARCH ON SELF-REGULATORY BELIEFS AND PROCESSES

With this multidimensional model in mind, let us consider some key findings about the effectiveness and interdependence of key academic self-regulatory processes. This description of research is divided into four sections: self-motivational techniques, self-regulatory methods and time management, self-regulation of performance, and regulating one's physical and social environment. As a way of illustrating these processes in the classroom setting, we have set up the following fictional scenario. Melissa and Becky are 10th grade students in the same high school, and they share the same courses. Both are college bound. They are identical in IQ, socioeconomic status, ethnicity, family configuration, and all other background variables, except for one thing: Melissa utilizes a large number of self-regulatory techniques, while Becky rarely, if ever, regulates her own learning. Becky is a classic example of a student who would be labeled an *underachiever.*

Self-Motivational Techniques

An important mid-term trigonometry exam is two weeks away, and Melissa is more self-motivated than Becky. Sensing the difficulty of the task, Melissa sets major goals for herself, and she further breaks up these goals into smaller, attainable subgoals. Melissa's goals are to learn various forms of trigonometry, not just to do well on the test. Furthermore, she sets her own specific standards for meeting these goals: to attain at least 90% proficiency. When studying at home for the exam, she rewards herself each time she meets her goals by allowing herself an ice-cream cone or perhaps an extra half-hour of TV. Becky, in contrast, sets no goals for herself. She adopts only the vaguest standards, just telling herself she wants to "do as well as I can on the test." When studying, she gives no thought to rewarding herself for getting the job done. Underlying the motivational processes of the two young ladies is Melissa's greater self-confidence that she will perform well on the exam. In the end, Melissa receives a score of 94 on the exam while Becky gets a 79.

Goal setting is the first of the self-regulatory motivational techniques we shall examine. According to Schunk (1990), a goal is what a student is consciously aiming to accomplish, while *goal setting* refers to establishing a goal and modifying it as necessary. Zimmerman and Martinez-Pons (1986) interviewed low-achieving and high-achieving high school sophomores using their self-regulated learning interview to determine the extent to which they utilized various self-regulated learning strategies, among them goal setting. As expected, high achievers reported using goal setting significantly more frequently and more consistently across academic tasks than low achievers.

Goal setting, in and of itself, however, is not the key determinant of academic success. It is important to distinguish between the *kinds* of goals and *the way they are set*. For one thing, the goals should be set realistically in terms of task difficulty. Research on achievement motivation has revealed that students with low-achievement motivation tend to set goals that are either too easy or too difficult to be helpful (McClelland, 1985; Smith, 1969). Self-regulated learners are better able to set attainable goals. Schunk (1983b) gave math students either difficult but achievable goals or easier goals for a problem solving task. Results showed that students with the easier goals performed less well than students given the higher, attainable goals.

Another important distinction is between proximal goals, which are goals set for the immediate future, and distal goals, which are set for the long term. According to Bandura (1986), proximal goal setting is important because

> most anticipated outcomes are too far off . . . to shepherd specific actions in immediate situations that present many uncertainties and complexities. People have to

> create for themselves proximal guides and self-motivators for courses of action that lead to distal attainments. (p. 336)

Indeed, research bears this out. When low-motivated elementary school students were aided in setting proximal goals in mathematics, they achieved 95% greater math proficiency and displayed 2500% higher intrinsic interest in math when compared with students who were given either no goals or distal goals (Bandura & Schunk, 1981).

Goal specificity is another important self-motivational technique. Schunk (1983a) gave math students either a general goal (to work productively) or a specific goal (the number of problems to complete). As predicted, students given specific goals outperformed students given only general goals. Furthermore, students with specific goals demonstrated greater self-confidence in achieving them.

Goals that are set by oneself appear to result in greater student achievement and confidence than goals that are set by an outside source, such as the teacher. Schunk (1985) divided learning disabled sixth grade students in a math class into three groups: one group set their own goals, a second group was provided with comparable goals by the teacher, and the third group did not set goals. Students in the two goal conditions performed better than youngsters who did not set goals, and students who set their own goals expressed greater confidence in their math abilities than youngsters whose goals were set for them. In another study (Hom & Murphy, 1985), pupils either were instructed to select their own goals for an anagram solving task or were given comparable goals by their teacher. Results showed that for subjects with low-achievement motivation, setting their own goals significantly enhanced performance.

A final consideration for goal setting concerns whether to set learning goals (for acquiring skills) or performance goals (for doing well on the final product, such as a test) for oneself (Ames, 1992). Research has found that students who set learning goals have higher self-efficacy, exhibit greater skill, display a more appropriate task orientation, complete more work, and report greater self-satisfaction than pupils who set performance goals (Schunk, 1989, 1991, 1995).

Another self-regulatory motivational technique is self-consequencing, which is defined by Zimmerman and Martinez-Pons (1986) as arranging or imagining rewards or punishment for success or failure at an academic task. Although the research on self-consequences is not as extensive as that of goal setting, they are nevertheless no less important. Two studies indicate that students who give themselves rewards and punishment outperform students who do not. Zimmerman and Martinez-Pons (1986) found that high-achieving high school sophomores reported giving themselves consequences significantly more often and more consistently than low achievers. In a later study, they showed that gifted students at the 8th grade and 11th grade levels gave themselves more consequences than did nongifted students (Zimmerman & Martinez-Pons, 1990).

Underlying these motivational techniques is a key self-regulatory belief known as *self-efficacy* or "personal judgments of one's capabilities to organize and execute courses of action to attain designated types of educational performances" (Bandura, 1986). Self-efficacy is distinguished from other related constructs, such as self-esteem, by its specificity. Instruments constructed to measure self-efficacy are intended to gauge subjects' perceived self-confidence to do a specific task, such as spelling or math division, rather than their confidence in their global academic skills.

A plethora of studies has shown self-efficacy to be an important intermediary link between student ability and various aspects of self-regulated learning (Zimmerman, 1995), including better quality learning strategies (Kurtz & Borkowski, 1984), more self-monitoring (Diener & Dweck, 1978; Kuhl, 1985; Pearl, Bryan, & Herzog, 1983), greater task persistence (Zimmerman & Ringle, 1981), more effective studying (Thomas, Iventosch, & Rohwer, 1987), better skill acquisition (Schunk, 1984), and higher academic achievement (Thomas et al., 1987). In a recent meta-analysis of 38 studies examining the effect of self-efficacy beliefs on students' academic achievement, Multon, Brown, and Lent (1991) found a significant positive effect size for self-efficacy, showing that it accounted for 14% of the variance in academic performance. Even more interesting is the finding that students' self-efficacy beliefs are more highly related to academic outcomes for low achievers than for high achievers. Thus, self-efficacy is clearly important in students' motivational processes underlying academic performance.

In light of these findings regarding the motivational component of self-regulation, the following recommendations are offered to teachers. Provide students with specific, attainable, proximal learning goals for school tasks and gradually teach these pupils to construct appropriate goals and subgoals on their own. Teach your classes to give themselves consequences, making sure they understand that the self-imposed reward comes only after the goal has been reached. Finally, create a classroom environment in which students systematically master academic tasks so that their self-efficacy for specific subject areas improves.

Self-Regulatory Methods and Time Management

With their trigonometry exam completed just days before, Melissa and Becky now face their weekly Spanish quiz. Melissa uses far more self-regulatory methods than does Becky. Melissa's strategies are tailored to the task at hand. This week's quiz will be on vocabulary, so Melissa sets up flash cards with a Spanish word on one side and its English translation on the other. Then she uses a keyword strategy that entails making paired, unusual visual images linking the two words (e.g., for the word *lapiz*, which means pencil, she visualizes a gigantic pencil sitting on her "lap"). She not only studies the flash cards but formulates meaningful sentences using each of the vocab-

> ulary words. In addition, she tape records her teacher's pronunciation of the vocabulary words and then plays the tape again and again. In addition to using self-regulated learning strategies, Melissa utilizes effective time management. She first determines that it will take her four hours to master the content. Then, she spaces her study time so that she can study an hour of Spanish per day for four days. Becky, on the other hand, uses no specific self-regulated learning strategies. She just "sort of looks at her notes a few times." Naturally, she does not plan out her time, so she ends up cramming for four hours just before the quiz. Melissa receives a grade of 100, whereas Becky gets a 70.

According to Pressley, Borkowski, and Schneider (1987), there are several components to good self-regulated strategy use. The first is that good strategy users have a variety of general and domain-specific strategies for reaching their goals. Examples of general self-regulatory strategies are goal setting, planning, self-monitoring, and reviewing. Examples of domain-specific strategies include rehearsal, clustering, mental imagery, summarizing, underlining, brainstorming, outlining, and creating graphic organizers.

To investigate specific self-regulatory learning strategies in a school context, Zimmerman and Martinez-Pons (1986) developed the self-regulated learning interview (SRLI), consisting of six hypothetical learning situations involving in-classroom and at-home tasks. For each situation, high- and low-achieving 10th grade students were asked to name all the methods they would use to help them fulfill the task requirement. Students' responses to these open-ended questions were transcribed verbatim and then classified according to the following 14 self-regulated learning strategies: goal setting and planning; organizing and transforming (rearranging and restructuring instructional materials); rehearsing and memorizing; self-evaluating; self-consequating (arranging for rewards or punishment for success or failure); keeping records and monitoring; seeking information (from nonsocial sources, such as a reference book); environmental structuring (rearranging the physical setting to make learning easier); seeking assistance from peers, teachers, and adults; and reviewing tests, notes, and texts. The investigators found significant differences between the two achievement groups in the frequency with which students used these strategies. Indeed, reports of self-regulated learning could predict with 93% accuracy to which achievement group each student belonged. The SRLI was subsequently validated with teacher reports of student self-regulated learning behaviors (Zimmerman & Martinez-Pons, 1988).

In a later study, Zimmerman and Martinez-Pons (1990) administered the same SRLI, this time expanded to eight interview situations, to gifted and regular students from the 5th, 8th, and 11th grades. Results showed that gifted subjects reported using a greater number of self-regulated learning strategies than regular subjects. There were no strategies that regular students used significantly more often than gifted students.

With regard to domain-specific strategies, studies have shown a link between the number of strategies one possesses and academic performance (e.g., Forrest-Pressley & Waller, 1984; Paris, Cross, & Lipson, 1984). As an illustration, Paris et al. (1984) trained two third grade classes and two fifth grade classes to use several domain-specific strategies for reading, such as skimming. The training lasted for four months, and the post-test on reading skills took place one month following training. Results showed that the trained students, when compared with untrained students matched for reading ability, showed significantly better performance on reading cloze and error detection tasks. With this in mind, several researchers have successfully implemented programs in which students were taught a multitude of self-regulated learning strategies and domain-specific strategies (e.g., Shapely, 1995; Taylor & Everley, 1995). For example, Manning (1995) trained teachers to implement multiple strategies for each of the following domains: listening, spelling, writing, reading, mathematics, handwriting, and problem solving, among others. However, just possessing a multitude of strategies is not enough; a good strategy user must know how, when, and where to utilize each of these strategies (Pressley et al., 1987). Heeding this, Paris and colleagues (1984) also taught students the appropriate instances for use of each reading strategy. Other studies (e.g., O'Sullivan & Pressley, 1984) have demonstrated that teaching students how, when, and where to use a specific strategy led to significantly greater use of these strategies.

The third of Pressley et al.'s (1987) maxims is that a good strategy user realizes that optimal academic performance is also linked to effort. This has been demonstrated empirically in the work of Kurtz and Borkowski (1984), who found that students who believe their level of performance is linked to their amount of effort, in fact, utilize learned strategies more often than students who do not hold these beliefs.

As well as one's choice of strategy method, another important self-regulatory dimension is academic time planning and management. Gettinger (1985) found that when students were given the opportunity to take as many trials as they wished to master a reading passage, they utilized only 68% of the time that was necessary. Other studies have shown that better students take more time to study difficult items than easier ones (e.g., Le Ny, Denhiere, & Le Taillanter, 1972) and that poorer students do not allocate enough study time for difficult items (Nelson & Leonesio, 1988). Britton and Tesser (1991) sought to determine a link between student time management and cumulative grade point average (GPA) in college students. These researchers concluded that time attitudes (i.e., their beliefs that it is important to plan for time) and short-range planning (i.e., one week or less) were significant predictors of GPA. Another study demonstrating that time management leads to higher academic achievement was reported by Weinstein, Stone, and Hanson (1993). Using a time management scale on an inventory of study skills, these researchers identified 276 college students as having either low, middle, or high time management scores at the beginning of a course. Interestingly, 69% of the A or B final grades in the course were attained by those with high time management scores, whereas in contrast, 56% of the D or F final grades were attained by those with low time management scores.

The following instructional implications for teachers regarding self-regulatory methods and time management should be considered. Students should be taught a multitude of domain-specific learning strategies and should be made aware of when, how, and where to utilize these strategies. Also, teachers need to show students that effort and strategy use should be linked, perhaps via attribution training. Finally, students should be trained in time management techniques, such as creating a weekly time management chart, and should monitor their use of the time management plans.

Self-Regulation of Performance

No sooner had the Spanish quiz ended when our two students were faced with a chemistry test on the families of elements in the periodic table. Melissa, being the better self-regulator, used self-monitoring and self-verbalizations when studying for the test, employing them as follows. After setting well-constructed goals (as described in our first scenario) and selecting her general and domain-specific strategies (as described in the second scenario), Melissa set about studying. Frequently during her study time, she monitored herself; that is, she checked to see if she was meeting her goals. Her particular approach is to read a section of her notes, then close the notebook and recite the content from memory, and finally look back to see if there was any information that she missed or got wrong. As she recites, she does so through self-verbalizing, that is, softly saying key words aloud. She makes note of what information she either leaves out or says inaccurately, and during her second round of review, she pays particular attention to these deficiencies. Becky, never having set goals at the outset, cannot monitor herself effectively. She goes over her notes more than once but only silently, and she makes no attempt to gauge her learning progress. As expected, Melissa scored a 90 on this very difficult test, whereas Becky failed the test with a score of 55.

Carver and Scheier (1981) were the first to write about the importance of a self-monitoring feedback loop to self-regulation. In this loop, the learner first sets goals for the task at hand and then goes about achieving these goals through various strategies. Periodically, the learner checks in some way the extent to which he or she has reached the goals. The learner who detects a discrepancy between the goals and the performance corrects the learning process. If there are no discrepancies between the goals and performance, the learner continues the learning process unchanged. This cycle of steps is followed until the learner has achieved his or her goals. To be more specific, in the second step of self-monitoring, the learner must make a mental or physical recording of his or her performance based on the frequency, duration, or latency of behaviors (Mace, Belfiore, & Shea, 1989). Observations can be made continuously throughout the learning process, at intermittent points in time, or perhaps only once.

In a review of the literature on self-monitoring, Ghatala (1986) drew three important conclusions. First, self-monitoring occurs very infrequently during the early school years and gradually improves from childhood to adulthood. Second, monitoring is more likely to occur during testing than during studying for a test. Third, Ghatala concluded that even adults are often poor at monitoring themselves. For example, Markman (1977) had child and adult subjects read fact-based texts with blatantly contradictory statements and found that adults often did not detect any inconsistencies. In addition, Hallahan, Lloyd, Kneeder, and Marshall, (1982) reported self-monitoring led to better student performance than teacher monitoring of student performance.

Self-monitoring training has been found to enhance performance across a wide variety of academic measures, such as the rate of assignment completion, time on task, conversational skills, problem solving, and handwriting accuracy (Mace et al., 1989). Even more important, self-monitoring training has improved the academic performance of at-risk students, such as disabled (McCurdy & Shapiro, 1992) or remedial pupils. In an illustration of self-monitoring training, Ellis (1995) studied college students in remedial speech classes who consistently mispronounced the triple consonant cluster /skt/, as embedded in the word *asked*. Some subjects received training in self-monitoring by listening to their voices on tape and writing down the number of instances in which they made errors, whereas other subjects received no such training. Results showed that the pupils trained in self-monitoring significantly outperformed those in a control group in pronunciation of the target consonant cluster on the training task and also on a near- and far-transfer task.

Another aspect of self-regulated performance is self-verbalizing; that is, speaking aloud as one studies or performs a task. Vygotsky (1934) was perhaps the first to recognize and study self-verbalizing that occurs naturally in young children. He called it *egocentric speech* and viewed it as an important transition to children's development of private, self-directive thought. More recent research has found that self-verbalizing can be used as an effective self-regulated learning strategy with older children, adolescents, and even adults. For example, Meichenbaum (1977) developed a teaching approach using self-verbalizing that takes place in five steps: (1) the teacher speaks aloud while performing a task (e.g., long division); (2) the teacher and students all speak aloud while performing the task together; (3) the students speak aloud while performing the task individually (self-verbalizing); (4) the students whisper while performing the task individually (fading); and finally, (5) the students perform the task nonverbally. Reviews of the literature on Meichenbaum's approach (Reeve & Brown, 1985; Wong, 1985) indicate that it is effective in enhancing students' achievement, maintaining that achievement, and even generalizing from it. However, self-verbalizing is only one component of Meichenbaum's approach, which includes modeling and guided practice, as well as other processes. To date, no one has conducted a study isolating the self-verbalizing component, and so it is not certain that component by itself improves learning (Harris, 1990). Nevertheless, self-verbalizing is a central element in Meichenbaum's proven technique; and from an intuitive point of view, it would seem to be of much value in focusing concentration, encoding of information, and directing motoric imitation.

The following implications of self-monitoring research can be drawn by educators. It is important that students be taught to monitor their own work under all conditions, not just while being assessed (as during a test) but also at study while involved in reading and writing. Because self-monitoring involves detecting discrepancies between one's goals and performance, it is essential to teach goal setting as well as self-observation. Furthermore, children should be taught to monitor themselves in a variety of ways: silently, aloud, and by keeping records. Finally, self-verbalizing should be encouraged, particularly when combined with modeling, systematic encoding, and motoric practice, such as in Meichenbaum's approach.

Regulating One's Own Physical and Social Environment

The semester's major research paper in English class is looming, and Melissa is prepared to marshall every resource she can. On being given the assignment, she goes to her English teacher and asks to see samples of previous students' successful research papers, which the teacher gladly provides to her. Melissa then reviews her notes on writing research papers carefully and seeks further information in the library. When she has amassed all of her sources and is ready to begin writing, Melissa makes sure to structure her physical environment so that she will not be distracted from the task. She finds a quiet place to work, a room with no windows, friends, or family members to distract her. After writing her first draft, Melissa first seeks feedback from a high-achieving peer in her class whom she trusts and then arranges to go over this draft with her English teacher before handing it in. She is as prepared as she possibly can be. As you can expect, Becky makes no such plans. It never occurs to her to ask for models of well-written research papers, and she is reluctant to ask for help from anyone regardless of how difficult this task is. And she is certainly not going to make the extra effort of finding supplementary materials in the library. When they receive their grades, Melissa is quite pleased with her A, and Becky settles for a B−.

Self-regulated learners do not work in isolation. When faced with a complex task, they seek help from whoever is knowledgeable, whether it be their peers, family members, teachers, or written resources (Zimmerman, 1989). A strength of a self-regulated learners is that they can restructure their social and physical environment to meet their needs. Indeed, high achievers seek help from others more often than low achievers even though high achievers request only limited assistance (Karabenick & Knapp, 1991; Zimmerman & Martinez-Pons, 1986). Similar findings were reported for intrinsically motivated students. Nelson-Le Gal and Jones (1990) found that elementary school children who showed high intrinsic interest in an academic area were more likely to ask for hints than for the full answer during problem solving; in contrast, students with low intrinsic motivation were just as likely to ask for the full answer than for just hints. Clearly, self-regulated learners display a desire for independent mastery whenever possible, while at the same time being willing to seek help whenever necessary. Thus, there is a crucial distinction between dependence and overdependence when seeking social assistance self-regulatively. According to Newman (1991), learners can avoid overdependence by following four steps: (1) be aware of your lack of understanding; (2) consider whether the help is necessary or not and, if so, what and who should be asked; (3) ask for help in the most suitable way; and (4) seek help in such a way that future help seeking attempts are maximized.

Affect also plays an important mediating role in seeking help. Seeking help is often interpreted as implying that a student is inadequate in ability, even with children as young as five years of age, and therefore students must weigh the consequences of feeling embarrassed about seeking help against the benefits it might provide (Graham & Barker, 1990; Newman, 1990). This is unfortunate in view of empirical evidence that teacher modeling and personal assistance can help students become more self-regulated (e.g., Rosenthal & Downs, 1985). A teacher or parent can help remedy this dilemma by providing guidance concerning when and who it is appropriate to ask for help (Paris, Lipson, & Wixson, 1983). Furthermore, as students become able to monitor themselves more accurately, they are less likely to feel stigmatized about asking for help. Rosen (1983) found that when pupils feel their lack of knowledge is due to a specific cause rather than to a more global personal failure, they are more likely to ask for help. A way to foster students seeking help from peers is provide training in reciprocal questioning (King, 1990). Small groups of students are encouraged to read a passage and ask each other questions regarding content of the material before going on to the next passage. This peer learning method has been found to enhance the quality of students' questions and improve their reading comprehension (Webb, 1982).

In addition to seeking social support, pupils may seek information from nonsocial sources, such as a reference book. Indeed, high achievers seek information from nonsocial sources significantly more often than low achievers (Zimmerman & Martinez-Pons, 1986). Cavenagh (1989) investigated students' information search in the context of computer-assisted instruction. Two groups of college students were taught a three-part lesson by computer. One group had the option (but not the requirement) to augment the computer lessons with a computer search, and the computer recorded the amount of time each subject spent reading the augmented text. Results showed that the experimental group scored significantly higher than the control group on the post-test, which measured mastery of the lesson. Furthermore, there was a strong correlation between time spent on augmenting materials and post-test scores.

A study conducted by Risemberg (cited in Zimmerman & Risemberg, 1994) demonstrated the importance of nonsocial information seeking. In this study, college students read two source texts and then were asked to write a comparison–contrast essay based on these texts. During this task, subjects had access to three additional texts: two model comparison–contrast essays and a set of guidelines for writing good comparison–contrast essays. None of these three texts were "required" reading but were made readily available to the subjects. After controlling for reading ability, results showed that information seeking from these nonrequired texts, as measured by the amount of time spent reading them, significantly predicted writing quality outcome. In a second study with the same task, some subjects were trained in the use of a strategy for writing comparison–contrast essays known as *graphic organizers*. Unexpectedly, Risemberg found that trained subjects engaged in information seeking significantly less often than untrained subjects and that information seeking predicted writing performance for only untrained subjects. This occurred because, once the students knew an effective graphic organization strategy, they no longer needed to seek information from other written sources to organize their writing. Clearly students' use of one learning strategy can obviate the need for another strategy.

In addition to seeking assistance from social sources, students can influence their environment by altering their physical surroundings. Among various ways, one can locate places to study that are quiet and not distracting. For example, studying in a carrel in a far corner of a library is much less likely to lead to interruptions than studying at home, where phone calls, general house noise, and intrusion of other family members can interfere with learning. Zimmerman and Martinez-Pons (1986) found that high achievers reported greater use of environmental restructuring than low achieving students. In another study conducted by Marcus (1988), students were brought into a room in which a television was playing and were asked to write a paper. This researcher found that students with superior writing skills were significantly more likely to lower the volume or turn off the television set than students with poorer writing skills.

Research on self-regulation of social and physical environments has a number of important implications for teachers. Students should be encouraged to seek help from peers and adults and not regard such efforts as signs of inferior ability. Furthermore, students should be given access to examples of previous assignments and tests (which are less stigmatizing than asking for overt assistance), and they should be encouraged to choose among these models. More attention should be paid to teaching students how to find nonsocial sources of information for themselves, such as in a library. Teaching students to monitor their own learning progress more effectively will enable them to ask detailed kinds of questions, which are interpreted less pejoratively by peers. Finally, teachers should alert students about the consequences of distractors on concentration, and they should teach students ways to restructure their environment to make it more conducive for learning.

CONCLUSION

The disturbing evidence of a lack of self-regulation among underachievers and the low level of studying by American high school students (National Assessment of Educational Progress Report, 1990) indicates that relatively few students attain high levels of academic self-regulation despite the many benefits. When viewing education through the prism of a multidimensional model of self-regulation, a startling implication seems evident: students have little opportunity to exercise much control over learning in school, and they are not generally taught self-regulatory skills as part of the curriculum. Table 1 reveals the detrimental consequences of poor self-regulation not only on students' achievement but also on their motivation. Because of the interaction of multidimensional self-regulatory processes, students' failure to regulate themselves during learning not only cuts them off from the source of corrective information necessary for academic acquisition, it robs them of the perception of growing personal efficacy that can fuel their goal setting and motivation to persist in the face of even bigger challenges. Conversely, students' use of self-regulatory processes, especially the use of learning strategies and self-monitoring of academic progress, can strengthen their self-efficacy beliefs and intrinsic motivation. The question of whether this self-perpetuating cycle of learning and motivation will be self-enhancing or self-defeating depends ultimately on students' development or lack of self-regulatory beliefs and skills.

Acknowledgment

We thank Gary D. Phye and Dale H. Schunk for their helpful comments on an initial draft of this chapter.

References

Ames, C. (1992). Achievement goals and the classroom motivational climate. In D. H. Schunk & J. L. Meece (Eds.), *Student perceptions in the classroom* (pp. 327–348). Hillsdale, NJ: Erlbaum.

Bandura, A. (1986). *Social foundations of thought and action: A social cognitive theory*. Englewood Cliffs, NJ: Prentice-Hall.

Bandura, A., & Schunk, D. H. (1981). Cultivating competence, self-efficacy, and intrinsic interest through proximal self-motivation. *Journal of Personality and Social Psychology*, 41, 586–598.

Borkowski, J. G., & Thorpe, P. K. (1994). Self-regulation and motivation: A life-span perspective on underachievement. In D. H. Schunk & B. J. Zimmerman (Eds.), *Self-regulation of learning and performance: Issues and educational applications* (pp. 45–74). Hillsdale, NJ: Erlbaum.

Britton, B., & Tesser, A. (1991). Effects of time management practices on college grades. *Journal of Educational Psychology*, 83, 405–410.

Caplan, N., Choy, M. H., & Whitmore, J. K. (1992, February). Indochinese refugee families and academic achievement. *Scientific American*, 266, 36–42.

Carver, C., & Scheier, M. (1981). *Attention and self-regulation: A control theory approach to human behavior.* New York: Springer-Verlag.

Cavenagh, R. W. (1989). *Learner information-seeking behavior resulting from two modes of goal-setting interventions derived from NPI theory* (Doctoral dissertation, Indiana University). *Dissertation Abstracts International, 49,* 3692A.

Diener, C. I., & Dweck, C. S. (1978). An analysis of learned helplessness: Continuous changes in performance strategy and achievement cognitions following failure. *Journal of Personality and Social Psychology, 36,* 451–462.

Ellis, D. (1995, April). *The role of discrimination accuracy in self-monitoring of dialect acquisition.* Paper presented at the meeting of the American Educational Research Association, San Francisco.

Forrest-Pressley, D., & Waller, T. (1984). *Metacognition, cognition, and reading.* New York: Springer-Verlag.

Gettinger, M. (1985). Time allocated and time spent relative to time needed for learning as determinants of achievement. *Journal of Educational Psychology, 77,* 3–11.

Ghatala, E. (1986). Strategy monitoring training enables young learners to select effective strategies. *Educational Psychologist, 21,* 434–454.

Graham, S., & Barker, G. P. (1990). The downside of help: An attributional developmental analysis of helping behavior as a low-ability cue. *Journal of Educational Psychology, 82,* 7–14.

Hallahan, D., Lloyd, J., Kneeder, R., & Marshall, K. (1982). A comparison of the effects of self- vs. teacher assessment of on-task behavior. *Behavior Therapy, 13,* 715–723.

Harris, K. (1990). Developing self-regulated learners: The role of private speech and self-instructions. *Educational Psychologist, 25*(1), 35–49.

Hom, H. L., Jr., & Murphy, M. D. (1985). Low need achievers' performance: The positive impact of a self-determined goal. *Personality and Social Psychology Bulletin, 11,* 275–285.

Karabenick, S. A., & Knapp, J. R. (1991). Relationship of academic help seeking to the use of learning strategies and other instrumental achievement behavior in college students. *Journal of Educational Psychology, 83,* 221–230.

King, A. (1990). Enhancing peer interaction and learning in the classroom through reciprocal questioning. *American Educational Research Journal, 27,* 664–687.

Krouse, J. H., & Krouse, H. J. (1981). Toward a multimodal theory of academic achievement. *Educational Psychologist, 16,* 151–164.

Kuhl, J. (1985). Volitional mediators of cognitive behavior consistency: Self-regulatory processes and action versus state orientation. In J. Kuhl & J. Beckman (Eds.), *Action control* (pp. 101–128). New York: Springer.

Kurtz, B. E., & Borkowski, J. G. (1984). Children's metacognition: Exploring relations among knowledge, process, and motivational variables. *Journal of Experimental Child Psychology, 37,* 335–354.

Le Ny, J., Denhiere, G., & Le Taillanter, D. (1972). Regulation of study time and interstimulus similarity in self-paced learning conditions. *Acta Psychologica, 36,* 280–289.

Mace, F., Belfiore, P., & Shea, M. (1989). Operant theory and research on self-regulation. In B. J. Zimmerman & D. H. Schunk (Eds.), *Self-regulated learning and academic achievement: Theory, research, and practice* (pp. 27–50). New York: Springer-Verlag.

Manning, B. (1995, April). *Translating self-regulated learning theory and research into classroom instruction.* Paper presented at the meeting of the American Educational Research Association, San Francisco.

Marcus, M. (1988). *Self-regulation in expository writing.* Unpublished doctoral dissertation, Graduate School of the City University of New York.

Markman, E. (1977). Realizing that you don't understand: A preliminary investigation. *Child Development, 48,* 986–992.

McClelland, D. C. (1985). *Human motivation.* Glenview, IL: Scott Foresman.

McCurdy, B., & Shapiro, E. (1992). A comparison of teacher-, peer-, and self-monitoring with curriculum-based measurement in reading among students with learning disabilities. *Journal of Special Education*, 26, 162–180.

Meichenbaum, D. (1977). *Cognitive-behavior modification: An integrative approach*. New York: Plenum.

Multon, K. D., Brown, S. D., & Lent, R. W. (1991). Relations of self-efficacy beliefs to academic outcomes: A meta-analytic investigation. *Journal of Counseling Psychology*, 18, 30–38.

National Assessment of Educational Progress Report (1990). National Center for Education Statistics (ED). Washington, DC.

Nelson, T., & Leonesio, R. (1988). Allocation of self-paced study time and the labor in vain effect. *Journal of Experimental Psychology, Learning, Memory, and Cognition*, 14, 676–686.

Nelson-Le Gal, S., & Jones, E. (1990). Cognitive-motivational influences on the task-related help-seeking behavior of Black children. *Child Development*, 61, 581–589.

Newman, R. S. (1990). Children's help-seeking in the classroom: The role of motivational factors and attitudes. *Journal of Educational Psychology*, 82, 71–80.

Newman, R. S. (1991). Goals and self-regulated learning: What motivates children to seek academic help? In M. L. Maehr & P. R. Pintrich (Eds.), *Advances in motivation and achievement: Goals and self-regulatory processes* (pp. 151–183). Greenwich, CT: JAI Press.

Newman, R. S. (1994). Academic help-seeking: A strategy of self-regulated learning. In D. H. Schunk & B. J. Zimmerman (Eds.), *Self-regulation of learning and performance: Issues and educational applications* (pp. 283–301). Hillsdale, NJ: Erlbaum.

O'Sullivan, J. T., & Pressley, M. (1984). Completeness of instruction and strategy transfer. *Journal of Experimental Child Psychology*, 38(2), 275–288.

Paris, S. G., Cross, D., & Lipson, M. (1984). Informed strategies for learning: A program to improve children's reading awareness and comprehension. *Journal of Educational Psychology*, 76(6), 1239–1252.

Paris, S. G., Lipson, M. Y., & Wixson, K. K. (1983). Becoming a strategic reader. *Contemporary Educational Psychology*, 8, 293–316.

Pearl, R., Bryan, T., & Herzog, A. (1983). Learning disabled children's strategy analyses under high and low success conditions. *Learning Disability Quarterly*, 6, 67–74.

Pressley, M., Borkowski, J., & Schneider, W. (1987). Cognitive strategies: Good strategy users coordinate metacognition and knowledge. *Annals of Child Development*, 4, 89–129.

Pressley, M., Woloshyn, V., & Associates. (1995). *Cognitive strategy instruction that really improves children's academic performance* (2nd ed.). Cambridge, MA: Brookline Books.

Reeve, R., & Brown, A. (1985). Metacognition reconsidered: Implications for intervention research. *Journal of Abnormal Child Psychology*, 13, 343–356.

Rosen, S. (1983). Perceived inadequacy and help-seeking. In B. DePaulo, A. Nadler, & J. Fisher (Eds.), *New directions in helping* (Vol. 2, pp. 73–107). New York: Academic Press.

Rosenthal, T. L., & Downs, A. (1985). Cognitive aids in teaching and treating. *Advances in Behavior Research and Therapy*, 7, 1–53.

Schunk, D. H. (1983a). Developing children's self-efficacy and skills: The roles of social comparative and informational goal setting. *Contemporary Educational Psychology*, 8, 76–86.

Schunk, D. H. (1983b). Goal difficulty and attainment information: Effects on children's achievement behaviors. *Human Learning*, 2, 107–117.

Schunk, D. H. (1984). The self-efficacy perspective on achievement behavior. *Educational Psychologist*, 19, 199–218.

Schunk, D. H. (1985). Participation in goal-setting: Effects on self-efficacy and skills of learning disabled children. *Journal of Special Education*, 19, 347–369.

Schunk, D. H. (1989). Social cognitive theory and self-regulated learning. In B. J. Zimmerman & D. H. Schunk (Eds.), *Self-regulated learning and academic achievement: Theory, research, and practice* (pp. 83–110). New York: Springer-Verlag.

Schunk, D. H. (1990). Goal setting and self-efficacy during self-regulated learning. *Educational Psychologist*, 25(1), 71–86.

Schunk, D. H. (1991). Goal setting and self-evaluation: A social cognitive perspective on self-regulation. In M. L. Maehr & P. R. Pintrich (Eds.), *Advances in motivation and achievement* (Vol. 7, pp. 85–113). Greenwich, CT: JAI Press.

Schunk, D. H. (1995, April). *Self-monitoring of skill acquisition through self-evaluation of capabilities*. Paper presented at the meeting of the American Educational Research Association, San Francisco.

Schunk, D. H., & Zimmerman, B. J. (Eds.). (1994). *Self-regulation of learning and performance: Issues and educational applications*. Hillsdale, NJ: Erlbaum.

Shapely, K. (1995, April). *Developing self-regulated learners in the middle school*. Paper presented at the meeting of the American Educational Research Association, San Francisco.

Smith, C. P. (Ed.). (1969). *Achievement-related motives in children*. New York: Russell Sage Foundation.

Taylor, K., & Everley, D. (1995, April). *Teaching grade seven students to self-regulate their studying: Lessons from practice*. Paper presented at the meeting of the American Educational Research Association, San Francisco.

Thomas, J. W., Iventosch, L., & Rohwer, W. D., Jr. (1987). Relationships among student characteristics, study activities, and achievement as a function of course characteristics. *Contemporary Educational Psychology*, 12, 344–364.

Vygotsky, L. (1934). *Thought and language*. Cambridge, MA: MIT Press.

Webb, N. M. (1982). Student interaction and learning in small groups. *Review of Educational Research*, 52, 421–445.

Weinstein, C. E., & Mayer, R. E. (1986). The teaching of learning strategies. In M. C. Wittrock (Ed.), *Handbook of research on teaching* (pp. 315–327). New York: Macmillan.

Weinstein, C. E., Stone, G., & Hanson, G. (1993). *The long-term effects of a strategic learning course for college students*. Unpublished manuscript, University of Texas, Austin.

Wibrowski, C. R. (1992). *Self-regulated learning processes among inner city students*. Unpublished doctoral dissertation, Graduate School of the City University of New York.

Wong, B. (1985). Issues in cognitive-behavioral interventions in academic skill areas. *Journal of Abnormal Child Psychology*, 13, 425–442.

Zimmerman, B. J. (1986). Development of self-regulated learning: Which are the key subprocesses? *Contemporary Educational Psychology*, 16, 307–313.

Zimmerman, B. J. (1989). A social cognitive view of self-regulated academic learning. *Journal of Educational Psychology*, 81(3), 329–339.

Zimmerman, B. J. (1994). Dimensions of academic self-regulation: A conceptual framework for education. In D. H. Schunk & B. J. Zimmerman (Eds.), *Self-regulation of learning and performance: Issues and educational applications* (pp. 3–21). Hillsdale, NJ: Erlbaum.

Zimmerman, B. J. (1995). Self-efficacy and educational development. In A. Bandura (Ed.), *Self-efficacy in changing societies* (pp. 202–231). New York: Cambridge University Press.

Zimmerman, B. J., & Bandura, A. (1994). Impact of self-regulatory influences on attainment in a writing course. *American Educational Research Journal*, 29, 663–676.

Zimmerman, B. J., Bandura, A., & Martinez-Pons, M. (1992). Self-motivation for academic attainment: The role of self-efficacy beliefs and personal goal setting. *American Educational Research Journal*, 29, 663–676.

Zimmerman, B. J., Greenberg, D., & Weinstein, C. E. (1994). Self-regulating academic study time: A strategy approach. In D. H. Schunk & B. J. Zimmerman (Eds.), *Self-regulation of learning and performance: Issues and educational applications* (pp. 181–199). Hillsdale, NJ: Erlbaum.

Zimmerman, B. J., & Martinez-Pons, M. (1986). Development of a structured interview for assessing student use of self-regulated learning strategies. *American Educational Research Journal*, 23(4), 614–628.

Zimmerman, B. J., & Martinez-Pons, M. (1988). Construct validation of a strategy model of student self-regulated learning. *Journal of Educational Psychology*, 80(3), 284–290.

Zimmerman, B. J., & Martinez-Pons, M. (1990). Student differences in self-regulated learning: Relating grade, sex, and giftedness to self-efficacy and strategy use. *Journal of Educational Psychology*, 82(1), 51–59.

Zimmerman, B. J., & Ringle, J. (1981). Effects of model persistence and statements of confidence on children's efficacy and problem solving. *Journal of Educational Psychology*, 73, 485–493.

Zimmerman, B. J., & Risemberg, R. (1994). Investigating self-regulatory processes and perception of self-efficacy in writing by college students. In P. R. Pintrich, D. R. Brown, & C. E. Weinstein (Eds.), *Perspectives on student motivation, cognition, and learning* (pp. 239–256). Hillsdale, NJ: Erlbaum.

Zimmerman, B. J., & Schunk, D. E. (Eds.). (1989). *Self-regulated learning and academic achievement: Theory, research, and practice*. New York: Springer-Verlag.

CHAPTER

5

Constructing the Concept of Aptitude: Implications for the Assessment of Analogical Reasoning

PAUL D. NICHOLS
University of Wisconsin—Milwaukee

DAVID J. MITTELHOLTZ
American College Testing

A number of writers in educational measurement, echoing arguments from the philosophy of science (Knorr-Cetina, 1981; Latour, 1987; Woolgar, 1988), have argued that test developers help construct aptitude and achievement concepts rather than passively measure them (Glaser, 1981; Hanson, 1993; Madaus, 1983, 1990; Stiggins, 1991). According to this perspective, test developers generate tests to conform to the intellectual and social values of the educational community and their own personal interests. The educational community, including psychometricians, educational psychologists, school administrators, and teachers, then selects and preserves tests and the aptitude and achievement concepts they represent for a variety of reasons including rational, social, and monetary ones. Logic and the methodological rules of educational and psychological measurement are all too often post hoc rationalizations of test development rather than their determining force. The aptitude and achievement tests and the concepts they represent become part of a system of theoretical concepts, methodological prescriptions, and general aims evolving slowly toward adaptation to the needs and values of the educational community.

Handbook of Academic Learning

Most current educational tests were developed to meet the needs and values of the early 20th century educational community. At that time, resources limited the information educators could gather about each student and precluded tailoring programs to individual students' needs. Individual differences in student performance were attributed to a simple model that represented aptitude as relatively fixed (Mislevy, 1993). Educators were faced with selecting which students would be able to profit best from uniform instruction designed essentially for the majority of the population (Glaser, 1981).

The needs and values of educators today are different than they were in the early part of the 20th century. The challenge now is to design instruction that helps all individuals succeed (Glaser, 1981). Less emphasis is placed on selecting individuals for available educational opportunities and more emphasis on helping students succeed in these opportunities. The goal is to create a more equitable educational climate that helps all students be successful.

The system of psychometric concepts and methods developed in the past may not help, and may even hinder, measurement specialists designing assessments to meet the new needs and values of educators. Many writers have argued that cognitive science can help measurement specialists develop new assessments that meet the needs and values of educators today (Bejar, 1984; E. Haertel & Calfee, 1983; Linn, 1986; Messick, 1984; Nichols, 1994; Snow & Lohman, 1989). Proponents of such an approach criticize traditional testing for losing sight of the psychology of the performance being tested (Glaser, 1981; Glass, 1986). An approach that can unite psychological and psychometric theory will shift the emphasis of testing practice from selecting individuals who are likely to succeed to helping individuals succeed in opportunities they select. Significant progress has been made in developing such assessments particularly in the area of aptitude research and theory.

In this chapter, we first discuss changes in the conceptualization of aptitude that reflect changes in the needs and values of the educational community. Next, we focus on the assessment of analogical reasoning to illustrate the relationship between the conceptualization and measurement of aptitude. Finally, we propose a new approach to measuring analogical reasoning that better reflects the new conceptualization of aptitude.

CHANGING CONCEPTUALIZATION OF APTITUDE

In this section, we review the changing conceptualization of aptitude and its relationship to the needs and values of the educational community. We begin by examining the dominant conceptualization of aptitude prior to the 20th century. Next, we examine how early 20th century changes in the conceptualization of aptitude reflected social and intellectual developments of that time. Finally, we synthesize some of the current thinking about aptitude. Many writers have presented aptitude as an important concept in theories of learning and instruction (see G. D. Haertel, Walberg, & Weinstein, 1983, for a review). Our review focuses on the work of Snow and his colleagues because of their sustained program of aptitude research.

Aptitude before the 20th Century

Snow (1992) provides an interesting historical perspective on aptitude demonstrating that at least as early as the first century A.D., the Roman writer and teacher of rhetoric Quintilian was espousing the importance of not only providing educational treatment that built on the aptitudes of an individual student but also of teaching to eliminate inaptitudes where possible.

Throughout much of recorded history, aptitudes were viewed as modifiable; the learner was believed to bring a certain predisposition in terms of knowledge, skills, motivation, and other personal characteristics to a learning situation. The *interaction of person and situation* was the key element that determined the success or failure of the learning episode. If the student's personal configuration of relevant learning components matched the characteristics of the learning situation, a successful learning experience was facilitated. If not, then an instructional treatment had to be developed that could either work around the student's inaptitudes or first build up the relevant aptitudes.

Aptitude in the Early 20th Century

The original conception of aptitude persisted essentially intact into the early 20th century, at which time it fell victim to some misinterpretations and misapplications of Darwin's recently formulated theory of evolution. Most notable were the dual (mis)applications of Darwin's notions of the biological inheritance of "fixed characteristics" and of the "survival of the fittest." Many social scientists of the early 20th century, including those involved in the early mental testing movement, began to view aptitude as biologically predetermined and relatively fixed. In addition, it came to be seen as a general attribute of which a person had a particular amount or capacity. In effect, as Snow (1992) points out, aptitude became synonymous with intelligence. This shift in meaning was accompanied by a decline in investigation of person–situation reciprocity in learning situations and a focus on developing instructional strategies that taught the majority of students. To support the change in pedagogy, a host of assessment instruments were developed that ranked students on the basis of how well they were able to internalize that instruction.

This view of aptitude fit well with the behaviorist paradigm that dominated much of American psychology during the early to mid-20th century. The impact on education was to focus on group means at the expense of individual differences and on product rather than process.

Aptitude in the Late 20th Century

Within the last few decades, however, the educational climate has shifted away from the group and refocused on the individual. The increasing influence of cognitive science, with its emphasis on mental processes and individual differences has begun to be felt in the educational arena. Within this context, Snow and his associates have labored not simply to restore but to extend the original notion of aptitude. This has resulted in the development of a theory of aptitude that has major implications for both educational instruction and assessment (e.g., Snow, 1991; Snow, Federico, & Montague, 1980; Snow & Lohman, 1989).

Recent conceptions of aptitude focus on the "initial states of persons that influence later developments, given specified conditions." (Snow, 1992, p. 6). Within this general description are several important points. First, the notion of initial states covers a broad array of person characteristics including cognitive, affective, conative (i.e., conscious willingness to act or exert effort), and even, in some situations, physical characteristics (Snow, 1991).

Cronbach and Snow (1977) deliberately proposed for research purposes a broad definition of aptitude as virtually any characteristic of a person that showed a relationship with an outcome. This broad definition emphasized the need to look beyond the most common, salient person characteristics such as cognitive attributes. The goal of this definition was to set aptitude research on a wide ranging course of investigation of anything in a student's repertoire that could predict his or her response in a particular instructional setting.

Going beyond this broad conception of aptitude, Snow (1987, 1991) further proposes the notion of aptitude complexes; that is, collections of personal attributes and characteristics. Thus a learner's aptitude for success in a given educational situation is likely to be directly related to a host of cognitive, affective, and other factors that form a particular configuration with respect to a particular learning situation. Aptitude configurations have varying degrees of suitability. The more closely the aptitude configuration matches the learning situation, the more success the learner will have. Snow (1992) refers to the degree of match between learner characteristics and characteristics of the learning situation by such terms as readiness, proneness, susceptibility, and predisposition.

At the heart of these terms is the notion that an aptitude is not just a correlate of success in a learning situation, but that the aptitude is propaedeutic (i.e., *needed* to respond appropriately to the treatment). Additionally, almost an inevitability is implied in this conception: a person who displays the appropriate aptitude in response to a relevant learning situation will find it difficult, if not impossible, to be *unsuccessful* in that situation. Conversely, if the learner's aptitude or initial state is qualitatively or quantitatively lacking in some crucial part of the overall configuration, then learning will be less than optimal. Thus, incomplete or flawed mental models and schemas or naive theories are examples of cognitive-based *inaptitudes* that contribute directly to some degree of failure in the learning situation.

Aptitude in the 21st Century

The foregoing conception of aptitude is too all encompassing to be educationally useful; some restrictions, or *boundary conditions* (Snow, 1991), need to be defined to make future aptitude research and theory relevant to educational instruction and assessment. Therefore Snow has noted some parameters to be applied in the investigation and conceptualization of aptitudes.

Boundary Conditions

First, aptitude constructs must fall somewhere between the extremes on a continuum of *stability*. Easily changed characteristics (e.g., lack of knowledge of a specific fact) that can be modified with only a minor change in the situation are not likely to be very important for aptitude research. Conversely, immutable characteristics of a person or situation are also unlikely to be relevant to aptitude research, except to the degree that they indicate the need to seek other avenues of instruction (e.g., teaching the shorter basketball player to "shoot from the field" or to focus on dribbling technique and quickness).

A second, related requirement for aptitude constructs is the aforementioned requirement that they be *propaedeutic to learning*. Simply demonstrating a correlation between an aptitude construct and learning is insufficient; it needs to be demonstrated that the aptitude is a necessary part of learning in a particular situation without which the desired learning cannot take place.

Theory Orientation

Snow (1992) views aptitude theory as a linking science. The goal of aptitude theory is to describe and explain the initial states (aptitudes) of learners in ways that establish solid, pedagogically useful connections with the relevant features of treatment environments, both real and desired, to reach goals of field achievement. *Field achievement* can be viewed as successful learning by the student or as successful pedagogy on the part of the teacher or instructional program.

Much current instructional theory is still based on the assumption that individual differences can be ignored; most instructional models still conceive of students as blank slates or relatively uniform in ability, prior knowledge, and other factors. It is this situation that aptitude theory is attempting to eliminate.

In Snow's conceptualization, education needs to take the results of aptitude research and focus on building appropriate aptitudes, by either repairing faulty ones or expanding incomplete ones. If working to overcome the flaw is impractical, then educational treatment needs to work around it by building on some other strength of the learner (for example, teaching by analogy). The goal of educational assessment, then, is to facilitate this instructional process through formative evaluation and, ultimately, to assess the effectiveness of the instruction in terms of student, teacher, and instructional program success through summative evaluation.

Aptitude Network

Snow (1989) proposes a network of aptitude constructs that can be used as a framework for research on assessment that clarifies and evaluates an approach to instruction based on aptitude theory. A diagram of this network is reproduced as Figure 1.

The network is displayed as a matrix in which the columns display the educational process in terms of changes in the learner's knowledge and skills (Glaser, 1976; Snow, 1989). Moving from left to right in the matrix outlines the ideal of education in which students with accurately described initial states (aptitudes) are given appropriate instruction that produces the transition to the desired end state with respect to a particular unit of instruction. The columns of the matrix encompass much of the recent theory and research into the expert–novice differences (e.g., Glaser, 1976).

The rows of the matrix indicate various categories of psychological constructs that have been investigated in educational research in recent years. Snow views the first two rows as primarily cognitive in nature, the last two rows as principally conative, and the middle row (learning strategies) as a mixture of both cognitive and conative factors. The two primarily cognitive constructs, and to some degree the learning strategies component as well, embody several current perspectives including Anderson's (1987) model of cognitive skill acquisition, schema theory (e.g., Rumelhart & Ortony, 1977), and mental models (e.g., Johnson-Laird, 1983). Similarly, the two primarily conative constructs are aligned with much of the recent work in metacognition and motivation.

Snow cautions that the distinctions within both rows and columns are somewhat arbitrary and the categories can shift rapidly, depending on the situation. For example, desired states quickly become initial states for additional learning, and the presence of appropriate cognitive constructs in a

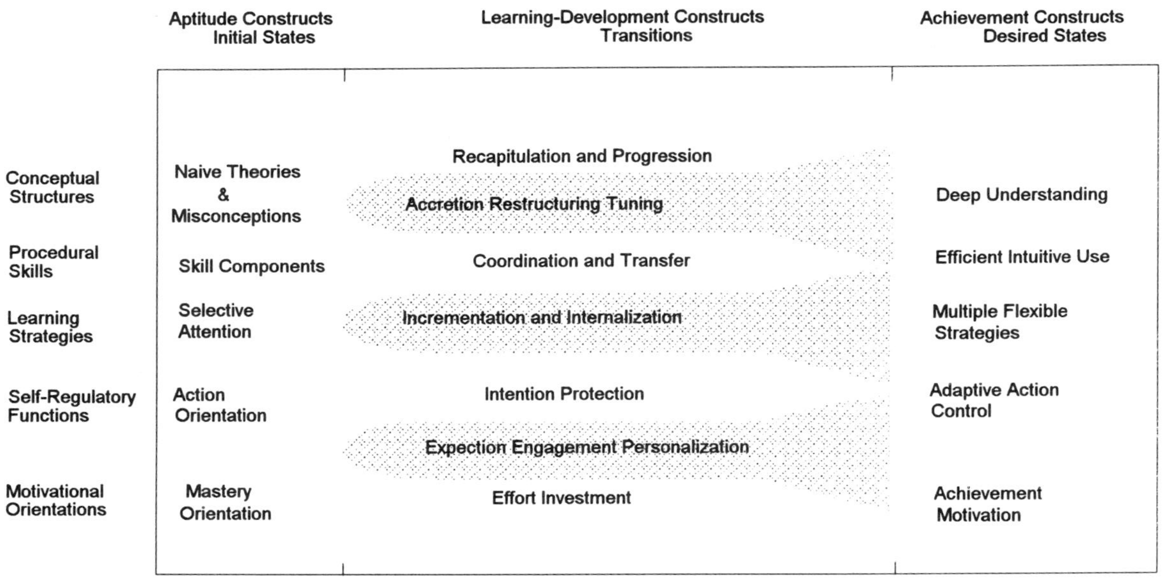

FIGURE 1

A network of psychological constructs for research on assessment in learning from instruction. Note: shading indicates presumably basic learning development processes to which other constructs relate. (From Snow, 1989, p. 9. Reprinted with permission of the author.)

particular learning situation can itself influence a learner's degree of motivation.

Snow also notes that a variety of assessment models is needed to meet various educational purposes. The matrix (Figure 1) offers a conceptual framework for developing these models. For example, if today's instruction is to be customized to help each student succeed, then it is important that teachers understand the initial states of each student. Thus, assessment instruments need to be developed that describe not only the student's current aptitudes, but also the inaptitudes: (1) the misconceptions, (2) the ineffective strategies or control processes, and (3) the motivational blocks that stand in the way of a successful transition to the desired end state. Assessments of this sort can help educators develop teaching strategies that focus on the assessed needs of individuals or groups of students.

A related educational goal is to evaluate the success of both the students and the instructional programs. Student success, as defined by the network, needs to be measured not just in terms of cognitive outcomes but also conative and motivational outcomes as well. These assessments need to occur both during and after instruction. Further, these assessments need to describe learning outcomes at a level of specificity that can be directly compared to students' initial states. For example, assessment during instruction needs to track students' evolving schemas and mental models to identify any areas in which students' understanding is breaking down. At this point, alternate teaching routes and motivational strategies based on the original and ongoing assessments need to be employed to again optimize the learning situation. After the learning session, a detailed assessment needs to be conducted to determine students' deep understanding of the information and their ability to transfer and apply the newly learned knowledge and skills to relevant new situations. Evaluation of the instructional program determines the success of the treatment(s) applied and areas where the instruction was *not* particularly effective. Ideally, alternate strategies that ultimately proved successful would be identified as well as the characteristics of situations in which those alternate strategies were effective.

At a general level, these assessment models need to be focused on diagnosis: at the heart of the new theory of aptitude is the belief that proper identification and description of a student's initial states leads to the development of effective teaching strategies and comprehensive descriptive assessments that can be used to evaluate both students and programs. Snow argues that, above all else, aptitude and instructional research needs to focus on construct validation to develop from current theory and research a comprehensive, unified system of observable constructs that can be applied to strengthen both educational instruction and assessment.

One of many areas of aptitude assessment that would likely benefit from the recent work on aptitude theory outlined previously is analogical reasoning. Most current tests of analogical reasoning were developed under the assessment philosophy that predominated during much of the early part of this century. In the remainder of this chapter, we describe current approaches to assessing analogical reasoning and outline what we see as the limitations of these approaches. Then we propose an approach that better reflects the current conception of aptitude.

CURRENT APPROACHES TO THE ASSESSMENT OF ANALOGICAL REASONING

Currently, the two major approaches to the measurement of analogical reasoning are the educational psychometric measurement (EPM) approach and the information processing (IP) approach. When reasoning using analogy, a learner uses information from a previously understood source (the base domain) such as a familiar concept or previously solved problem to understand a new concept or solve a new problem (the target domain). In this section, we examine the intellectual and social values on which each approach to the assessment of analogical reasoning appears to be based. Furthermore, we describe the limitations of each approach for designing assessments to meet the present needs and values of education.

EPM Conceptualization and Measurement of Analogical Reasoning

Current standardized assessments of analogical reasoning, such as the Differential Aptitude Test (DAT) and the Cognitive Abilities Test (CogAT), are based on what Snow and Lohman (1989) have termed the *educational psychometric measurement* (EPM) conception. The test model that dominates the EPM conception is aimed at estimating a person's location on an underlying latent variable—a true score in classical test theory (CTT) or a latent trait in item response theory (IRT). This location is typically interpreted as an amount on the latent scale. The model is judged as to how well it places people into a single sequence or aids selection into a single program (Mislevy, 1995). Either CTT or IRT may usefully inform decisions about such linearly ordered alternatives (Dawes & Corrigan, 1974).

The EPM has no explicit substantive model of the psychology of the test domain. The psychological model may be implicit in the measurement design: location on the latent scale or coverage of content domains may reflect accumulating new facts and skills. Resnick and Resnick (1992) observe that the psychology implicit in CTT reflects the assumptions of psychological theories of the early 20th century. An assumption common to both CTT and early psychological theories is that skill in a domain consists of acquiring an increasing number of knowledge elements. Students who acquired fewer elements could be said to have less competence in the domain. Assessments are designed to sample from the domain of nominally parallel and independent elements. Thus, performance on a representative sample of elements would be a valid indicator of the degree of competence or skill.

A second implicit psychological assumption common to both is that elements can be acquired and tested out of context. Thus, key elements can be selected for practice outside of the conditions in which the student normally uses the skill. Similarly, aspects of skill can be tested outside of the context in which the student uses the skill. Thus, sections of test batteries intended to assess a skill, such as mathematics, are often divided in subsections intended to test aspects of the skill.

Interestingly, Shepard (1991) reports that many measurement specialists hold views of learning similar to those early psychological theories. According to Carroll (1974; quoted in Snow & Yalow, 1982), the construction of items for at least one aptitude battery appears to be based on the test constructor's intuitive theory of learning:

> The tasks chosen for aptitude tests were those which were regarded as having *process structures* similar to, or even identical with, the process structures exemplified in actual learning tasks, even though the contents might be different. The tests were therefore measures of the individual's ability to perform the psychological functions embedded in . . . or . . . the information processing behaviors characteristic of the criterion learning tasks. The theoretical basis for assuming similarities might be of the vaguest intuitive sort; what mattered was the empirical confirmation of one's intuitions by standard test validation procedures. (p. 249)

Under EPM, differential psychologists proposed theories that described the organization of individual differences in terms of traits. The conception of individual differences in terms of static traits made impossible a better understanding of the mental processes of performers in a domain (Lohman & Ippel, 1993). As McNemar (1964) observed, "Indeed, it is difficult to see how the available individual difference data can be used even as a starting point for generating a theory as to the process nature of general intelligence" (p. 8).

IP Conceptualization and Measurement of Analogical Reasoning

Recently, researchers have developed assessments of analogical reasoning based on information processing (IP) models. The information processing approach within cognitive science provides a framework for theorizing about how test takers attempt to solve test items. Researchers following the information processing approach propose that reasoning and learning is best represented as a sequence of component processes (Sternberg, 1977). Researchers following the cognitive components approach usually cite six component processes as constituting peoples' reasoning using analogy: encoding, inference, mapping, application, comparison, and response. During encoding, the reasoner constructs an internal representation of the problem on which further mental operations can be performed. Construction of this internal representation involves identifying relevant aspects of the base domains and the target domains and retrieving relevant information from long-term memory.

Following encoding, the reasoner must infer the set of relations in the base domain that are eligible for mapping under the constraints established by the problem goals. Such an inference requires well-organized knowledge of the base domain and casual knowledge of the target domain.

In mapping, the reasoner attempts to identify the higher-order rule that relates the two domains. Next, the reasoner applies the set of relations identified in the base domain to the target domain. Reasoners are likely to produce faulty solutions if they apply irrelevant relations.

Finally, the reasoner responds in some overt manner. If the analogy task is a multiple-choice item on a test, the reasoner may execute a comparison component during which the reasoner compares the given response options to the generated solution to determine which option is closest to that solution.

The IP approach has no test model comparable to the well-developed psychological model just described. Consequently, researchers developing IP-based assessments of analogical reasoning have adopted the test model dominating the EPM conception. The IP-based tests commonly compute for each test taker the number of correct responses or the mean response time. Whitely (1981) has used a latent trait model to compute for each test taker a set of scores representing different component processes.

An analogical reasoning test that combines CTT- and IP-based models of analogical reasoning has been developed by Nichols (1991). This computer-based test consists of 96 true or false analogies of the form A:B::C:D. A new set of 96 analogies is generated for each test taker just before test administration. The analogies vary along three dimensions: number of figures in the A and C terms (two or four), symmetry of the figures (symmetrical or nonsymmetrical), and proportion of A figures transformed in B (half or all). Hence, the test has eight different analogy types. The correctness of the response and the response time are recorded. Scores for the test include the number of correct responses and the mean response time for each type of analogy.

Another computer-based analogical reasoning test that combines a CTT-based model and an IP-based model was developed by Applegate and Dattatri (1991), using Sternberg's (1977) theory of analogical reasoning. This test consists of 16 problems that vary along one or more of three dimensions: shape (rectangle, square, triangle, circle), color (red, yellow, blue), and size (small, large). On each problem, the test taker is presented with a problem in the form A:B::C:?. The test taker is instructed to respond by selecting the appropriate size and shape from the eight possible alternatives (e.g., large square) and then indicating the appropriate color. The response may be given using a joystick, keyboard, mouse, or lightpen. The correctness of the response and the response times to select the shape, select the color, and terminate the problem are recorded. Scores on the test are computed by summing the number of correct responses or the response times. In addition, Applegate and Dattatri (1991) have estimated results using a two-parameter IRT model.

Applegate (1993) has proposed extending the computer-based test, using an expert system to administer the test. The expert system would decide how many and what items to present. The proposed expert system would use an inference algorithm to decide the difficulty of the item to generate and then generate a new item. The new item would be constructed using a domain matrix of the four item terms (A, B, C, and D) and the attributes of those terms (shape, color, and size).

IP-based tests of analogical reasoning have demonstrated a number of advantages over EPM-based tests. One advantage is that item construction is more efficient because the difficulty of new, untried items can be accurately predicted. This reduces the number of items that need to be pretested by the test developer (Bejar, 1986). A second advantage is that test development can be systematically improved because of the theory-driven nature of item construction. The theory underlying the test can be modified to incorporate researchers' growing understanding of analogical reasoning. The IP approach provides a method for constructing "tests that can become vehicles of communication between the laboratory and the field" (Snow & Peterson, 1985, p. 165).

The IP-based assessments of analogical reasoning have extended the *psychological* model underlying test development but still suffer from important limitations in their design and scoring. First, the IP research on verbal and spatial analogies continues to be based primarily on tests or testlike tasks. As Sternberg (1984) has noted, component scores are used as predictors of test scores that are themselves viewed as predictors by psychometricians. The problem is that traditional verbal and spatial analogies are best characterized as *indicators* rather than *performance samples*. Indicators were designed to predict criterion performance rather than to reveal differences in the processes used by more or less competent learners. Consequently, tests tend to conceal differences in how test takers solve items rather than reveal these differences (Cronbach & Snow, 1977; Lohman & Ippel, 1993). Furthermore, perhaps as a consequence of the focus on explaining performance on tests, IP research has emphasized lower-order mappings (between the A and B terms) over higher-order mappings (between the A–B and C–D pairs). As Holyoak and Thagard (1995) noted, higher-order relations are more important in problem solving. Another limitation of most IP-based assessments is that test constructors assume that all test takers are using the same strategy. However, Bethell-Fox, Lohman, and Snow (1984) found that students adopt different strategies based on level of spatial ability and that the same student sometimes shifts strategies across different analogy items. Finally, most IP-based assessments are limited because they retain the EPM test model to score responses while revising the EPM psychological model to develop tests. As Nichols (1994) argues, the value of the information elicited through the IP-based test design is limited by the power of the EPM-based scoring model to use that information.

In the following section, we propose a new approach toward assessing analogical reasoning that addresses the limitations of current EPM- and IP-based assessments. We propose basing the assessment design on research into how learners use analogy in and out of the classroom. Furthermore, we propose that test takers' performance take place within an authentic context and be judged by teachers trained in the latest research results from cognitive science. Through this approach, we hope to construct an assessment of analogical reasoning that better meets the needs of educators to design instruction that helps all students be successful.

NEW DIRECTIONS IN ASSESSING ANALOGICAL REASONING

In this section, we propose an approach toward assessing analogical reasoning that better reflects the current conception of aptitude. First, we argue that analogical reasoning is a good candidate for a revised aptitude test because the current theory of analogical reasoning corresponds well to current conceptions of aptitude and because the current theory is not reflected in current analogical reasoning tests. Second, we describe a framework for analogical reasoning based on research describing how learners use analogy. Finally, we propose a new approach toward assessing analogical reasoning based on this theory.

New Conceptualization of Analogical Reasoning

The developing conceptualization of analogical reasoning, based on learning and problem solving research meets Snow's (1991) two criteria for a conception of aptitude that is educationally relevant. First, a conception of aptitude that is educationally relevant must emphasize that aptitude is not immutable but, conversely, is not changed with only minor changes in the learning situation. Second, a conception of aptitude that is educationally relevant must demonstrate that the aptitude is a necessary part of learning.

Analogical reasoning is not immutable but requires carefully planned interventions to modify how learners use analogy. Instruction designed to encourage analogy use in learning has produced a stable pattern of often disappointing results. Researchers have commonly found that students fail to spontaneously transfer information from a base or source domain to a target domain (e.g., Guberman & Greenfield, 1991; Novick, 1988). In contrast, through carefully designed instruction learners can be taught to search for structure across potentially analogous situations. For example, Brown and Kane (1988) found that spontaneous use of analogy could be enhanced by discussion of analogy use or by teaching others the shared solution on two previous problems.

Furthermore, analogical reasoning appears to be a central learning mechanism and the use of analogy is a critical instructional tool. Some educators have argued that if students are to become competent learners then instruction must address the use of basic thinking and reasoning skills such as analogical reasoning (Resnick & Resnick, 1992). For example, Halford (1993) has placed analogical reasoning at the core of cognitive development in his structure-mapping theory. According to Halford's model, cognitive development consists of assigning elements of one structure representing some aspect of the world to elements of another structure in a way that preserves corresponding relationships in increasingly complex ways. Similarly, Brown (1989) argues that analogy as a learning mechanism is a crucial factor in knowledge acquisition at all ages.

Analogies have been proven a useful instructional tool in a number of areas. Analogies encourage the transfer (mapping) of abstract relations from familiar base domains of knowledge to less familiar target domains. Children can use analogies as aids in both decoding and comprehension (Goswami, 1986). Analogies have been used effectively in communicating science concepts and relations (Bean, Singer, & Cowan, 1985) and computer programming techniques (Pohl & Nutter, 1985). However, analogies can be misleading if learners cannot decide which relations are appropriate for mapping and map alternative relational systems that conflict with the instructional goal.

Emerging Conceptualization of Analogical Reasoning

In contrast to IP research based primarily on testlike tasks, a growing body of research has examined how students and others use analogy in more authentic learning and problem solving contexts. Research into how learners use analogy describes analogical reasoning as the transfer of structural information from a source system to a target system (Gentner, 1983; Holyoak & Thagard, 1995). A system includes a concept, figure, story, or theory. Generally, the properties and concepts of the two systems are very different but the goals and constraints are similar. The use of analogy in learning and problem solving may involve the following subprocesses: (1) accessing the source, (2) performing the mapping between the source and target, (3) generating new inferences regarding the target, (4) evaluating the mapping, and

(5) storing inferences regarding the target. The defining characteristic of analogical reasoning is the similarity in underlying structure between source and target.

A source system in an analogy may be identified in different ways. A source analogy is often introduced by an instructor or a textbook author to help students grasp the complexities of a new topic. Students may independently adopt source systems that appear helpful in understanding new material. In each case, a source system is identified because it appears to have an underlying structure similar to the target system.

How does a learner map a concept or property from a familiar source system to a new target system when the relevant structure of the target system is not known? Vosniadou (1989) argues that correspondence between components and properties in the source and target are identified on the basis of some similarity in easily accessible aspects of the two systems such as shape, color, size, or names. However, easily accessible similarity can be similarity in relational, abstract, or conceptual aspects as long as these aspects are salient in learners' representations of the source and target. The relevance of the structural information mapped from the source to the target is then evaluated on the basis of what is known about the target. The judgment of similarity between the source and target also affects the certainty with which the concept or property is believed to hold for the target system.

Almost all learners over age 3 appear able to use analogy (Goswami, 1991) but *learners appear to differ in how well they use analogy*. Learners' poor use of analogy may impede understanding, especially in complex domains. For example, Spiro, Feltovich, Coulson, and Anderson (1989) report that some medical students developed misconceptions about the nature of blood pressure using an analogy that compared pressure in the cardiovascular system and household plumbing.

Learners' failure to effectively use analogical reasoning stems from at least four possible sources (Brown, 1989; Goswami, 1991; Spiro et al., 1989; Vosniadou, 1989). First, teachers and textbook authors may use a simplifying analogy to introduce a complex topic believing that a simplified account is a complete account. Second, teachers and textbook authors may use a simplifying analogy to introduce a complex topic but fail to adequately explain the limitations of the analogy. Third, learners may independently adopt misleading analogies. Fourth, learners may fail to search for shared structure across the source and target.

Poor instructional practice by teachers and textbook authors or poor analogical reasoning by students may result in an incomplete or an incorrect representation of the target system. Learners cannot see correspondences between source and target systems if one of the following conditions holds: (1) they do not search for correspondence between the source and target, (2) their representations do not include those concepts or properties, or (3) if teachers and textbook authors fail to make them salient. Consequently, learners may *overextend* mapping objects and relations from the source system to the target system or *omit* important aspects from the source system.

We have developed the following typology of problems in learners' analogical reasoning that may produce an incomplete or an incorrect representation of the target system:

1. The family of relationships and objects surrounding a salient characteristic in the source is exported incorrectly to a parallel characteristic in the target. The learner's understanding of the target is incorrectly constrained.
2. An important concept or relation in the target has no counterpart in the source and so is not incorporated in understanding the target.
3. A salient concept or relation in the source has no analogue in the target but is nevertheless exported to the target.
4. A nonsalient concept or relation in the source has a different value than the parallel aspect of the target. The target is incorrectly assigned the value of the source and this leads to an incorrect understanding of the target.
5. The representation of the source or target is at the wrong grain size to understand differences or similarities in underlying structures of the source and target. For example, the learner may focus on surface characteristics that do not correspond to underlying causal mechanisms.
6. Misleading properties derived from common terms not used in the same way in the source and target. Technical terms may be used in the target but not in the source. Nontechnical terms may be used in the source that have inaccurate connotations for understanding the target.
7. Lack of one-to-one correspondence between structural features of the source and the target (nonisomorphic problems). The goal structure, constraint, or problem space of the target does not match that of the source. Learners may fail to adapt the procedures of the target to bring them into correspondence with the base.

Revised Assessment of Analogical Reasoning

We propose a revised approach to assessing analogical reasoning informed by research on how learners use analogy, using teachers as trained observers of analogical reasoning, and empowering students to assess their own analogical reasoning. This approach borrows heavily from other classroom-based programs that closely link assessment and instruction such as Clay's (1991) reading instruction and the cognitively guided instruction for mathematics (Fennema, Franke, & Carpenter, 1993). In contrast to many thinking skills curriculums, students would improve their analogical reasoning within the context of their existing curriculum without extracurricular materials or lessons.

Our proposed approach would involve the following three steps: (1) researchers train teachers to understand analogical reasoning, (2) teachers apply their understanding to interpret students analogical reasoning, and

(3) students acquire an understanding of their own analogical reasoning. As the first step, we propose that teachers must understand the subprocesses students use in analogical reasoning and the ways these subprocesses interact with features of the analogies. In addition, teachers must be able to recognize learners' common misuses of analogical reasoning.

As part of training teachers to understand analogical reasoning, we propose to train teachers to use an interpersonal, diagnostic assessment technique (Nichols, 1994) in conjunction with their understanding of analogical reasoning to identify when, during learning and problem solving, students are using and misusing analogical reasoning. The constraint-based technique requires that the teacher compare the set of constraints on the target representation introduced by the analogy to the student's representation of the target and infer the quality of the student's analogical reasoning subprocesses. Using the constraint-based technique, teachers must probe students' analogical reasoning during the presentation of an analogy by the teacher or textbook during science, social studies, or other instruction. Within the context of the analogy, the teacher must judge if the student is *overextending* mapping objects and relations from the source system to the target system or *omitting* important aspects from the source system and identify possible sources of the poor analogical reasoning.

In the second step, teachers would be expected to use this approach on a daily basis in their classrooms. At the beginning of the school year, the assessment might be done one on one so that the teacher can assess each student's analogical reasoning. Subsequently, teachers could monitor students' analogical reasoning through questioning following a lesson or during small group activities. Based on the information gained through assessment, the teacher would model and support appropriate analogical reasoning.

Perhaps the most important element of this proposed approach is that students are expected to become evaluators of their own analogical reasoning. In the third step, we expect students to acquire an understanding of their own analogical reasoning subprocesses by observing the teacher's transparent use of analogical reasoning. Similarly, students would learn to critically evaluate their own analogical reasoning from the teacher modeling the assessment and sharing with the students the criteria for good analogical reasoning. Consequently, students would acquire strong analogical reasoning skills by practicing their reasoning in and out of the classroom and receiving frequent feedback from the teacher, their peers, and monitoring their own reasoning.

CONCLUSION

As we contemplate revising current assessments of analogical reasoning, we note strong contrasts between the view of analogical reasoning represented by our review of the literature and the view of analogical reasoning represented by traditional assessments. Analogical reasoning is traditionally viewed as an ability pervasive across contexts so that a learner reasons similarly in different contexts. In contrast, we view the learner as sensitive to context. Learners are more or less able to use analogy to learn depending on their previous experience in the source domain and target domain and the quality of their corresponding mental representations.

Similarly, analogical reasoning is traditionally viewed as fairly constant and unchanging across time as well as context. We conclude that children can solve analogies at an early age. This capability improves as a learner's understanding of the source and target systems improves.

Analogical reasoning, like aptitude more generally, is traditionally viewed as a predicter of which learners are likely to succeed in the classroom. Traditional assessments have been used to identify learners in need of great assistance at best or, at worst, to exclude learners not likely to succeed. We view analogical reasoning as an aptitude that can be modified to improve future learning. We intend our assessment as a tool to directly aid instructional decisions. Toward this goal, the assessment we propose focuses on the process of using analogies in learning rather than as the product of analogical reasoning.

Of course, the previous description of traditional assessments is necessarily oversimplified. However, the contrasts highlight differences between our view of analogical reasoning and the view of analogical reasoning represented by traditional assessments. We *do not* argue that traditional assessments failed to measure analogical reasoning. We *do* argue that the traditional view of analogical reasoning precluded remediation, and so traditional assessments provided minimal information for instructional decisions. Our view of analogical reasoning as a context-sensitive, malleable skill leads naturally to assessment that is linked closely to instruction.

References

Anderson, J. R. (1987). Skill acquisition: Compilation of weak-method problem solutions. *Psychological Review*, 94, 192–210.

Applegate, B. (1993). Construction of geometric analogy problems by young children in a computer-based test. *Journal of Educational Computing Research*, 9 (1), 61–77.

Applegate, B., & Dattatri, R. L. K. (1991; April). *Towards a linkage between conventional test theory and information processing theory in a computer based test*. Paper presented at the annual convention of the National Council on Measurement in Education, Chicago.

Bean, T. W., Singer, H., & Cowan, S. (1985). Analogical study guides: Improving comprehension in science. *Journal of Reading*, 29, 246–250.

Bejar, I. I. (1984). Educational diagnostic assessment. *Journal of Educational Measurement*, 21, 175–189.

Bejar, I. I. (1986). *Final report: Adaptive assessment of spatial abilities* (ID No. NR 150 531). Princeton, NJ: Educational Testing Service.

Bethell-Fox, C. E., Lohman, D. F., & Snow, R. E. (1984). Adaptive reasoning: Componential and eye movement analysis of geometric analogy performance. *Intelligence*, 8, 205–238.

Brown, A. L. (1989). Analogical learning and transfer: What develops? In S. Vosniadou & A. Ortony (Eds.), *Similarity and analogical reasoning* (pp. 369–412). Cambridge, England: Cambridge University Press.

Brown, A. L., & Kane, M. J. (1988). Preschool children can learn to transfer: Learning to learn and learning from example. *Cognitive Psychology*, 20, 493–523.

Carroll, J. B. (1974). The aptitude-achievement distinction. The case of foreign language aptitude and proficiency. In D. B. Green (Ed.), *The aptitude-achievement distinction* (pp. 121–146). Monterey, CA: CTB/McGraw-Hill.

Clay, M. M. (1991). *Becoming literate: The construction of inner control*. Portsmouth, NH: Heinemann.

Cronbach, L. J., & Snow, R. E. (1977). *Aptitudes and instructional methods: A handbook for research on interactions*. New York: Irvington.

Dawes, R. M., & Corrigan, B. (1974). Linear models in decision making. *Psychological Bulletin*, 81, 95–106.

Fennema, E., Franke, M. L., & Carpenter, T. P. (1993). Using children's mathematical knowledge in instruction. *American Educational Research Journal*, 30, 555–583.

Gentner, D. (1983). Structure-mapping: A theoretical framework for analogy. *Cognitive Science*, 77, 155–170.

Glaser, R. (1976). Components of a psychology of instruction: Toward a science of design. *Review of Educational Research*, 46, 1–24.

Glaser, R. (1981). The future of testing: A research agenda for cognitive psychology and psychometrics. *American Psychologist*, 36, 923–936.

Glass, G. V. (1986). Testing old. testing new: Schoolboy psychology and the allocation of intellectual resources. In B. S. Plake & J. C. Witt (Eds.), *The future of testing* (pp. 9–28). Hillsdale, NJ: Erlbaum.

Goswami, U. (1986). Children's use of analogy in learning to read: A developmental study. *Journal of Experimental Child Psychology*, 42, 73–83.

Goswami, U. (1991). Analogical reasoning: What develops? A review of research and theory. *Child Development*, 62, 1–22.

Guberman, S. R., & Greenfield, P. M. (1991). Learning and transfer in everyday cognition. *Cognitive Development*, 6, 233–260.

Haertel, E., & Calfee, R. (1983). School achievement: Thinking about what to test. *Journal of Educational Measurement*, 20, 119–132.

Haertel, G. D., Walberg, H. J., & Weinstein, T. (1983). Psychological models of educational performance: A theoretical synthesis of constructs. *Review of Educational Research*, 53, 75–91.

Halford, G. S. (1993). *Children's understanding: The development of mental models*. Hillsdale, NJ: Erlbaum.

Hanson, F. A. (1993). *Testing testing: Social consequences of the examined life*. Berkeley: University of California Press.

Holyoak, K. J., & Thagard, P. (1995). *Mental leaps: Analogy in creative thought*. Cambridge, MA: MIT Press.

Johnson-Laird, P. N. (1983). *Mental models: Towards a cognitive science of language, inference, and consciousness*. Cambridge, MA: Harvard University Press.

Knorr-Cetina, K. D. (1981). *The manufacture of knowledge: An essay on the constructivist and contextual nature of science*. Oxford, England: Pergamon.

Latour, B. (1987). *Science in action: How to follow scientists and engineers through society*. Cambridge, MA: Harvard University Press.

Linn, R. L. (1986). Educational testing and assessment: Research needs and policy issues. *American Psychologist*, 41, 1153–1160.

Lohman, D. F., & Ippel, M. J. (1993). Cognitive diagnosis: From statistically-based assessment toward theory-based assessment. In N. Fredriksen, R. J. Mislevy, & I. Bejar (Eds.), *Test theory for a new generation of tests* (pp. 41–71). Hillsdale, NJ: Erlbaum.

Madaus, G. F. (1983). Minimum competency testing for certification: The evolution and evaluation of test validity. In G. F. Madous (Ed.), *The court, validity, and minimum competency testing* (pp. 21–61). Boston: Kluwer-Nijhoff.

Madaus, G. F. (1990). *Testing as a social technology: The inaugural Boisi Lecture in Education and Public Policy*. Boston: Boston College, Center for the Study of Testing, Evaluation, and Public Policy.

McNemar, Q. (1964). Lost: Our intelligence? Why? *American Psychologist, 19*, 871–882.

Messick, S. (1984). The psychology of educational measurement. *Journal of Educational Measurement, 21*, 215–237.

Mislevy, R. J. (1993). Foundations of a new test theory. In N. Fredriksen, R. J. Mislevy, & I. Bejar (Eds.), *Test theory for a new generation of tests* (pp. 19–40). Hillsdale, NJ: Erlbaum.

Mislevy, R. J. (1995). Probability-based inference in cognitive diagnosis. In P. Nichols, S. F. Chipman, & R. L. Brennan (Eds.), *Cognitively diagnostic assessment* (pp. 43–72). Hillsdale, NJ: Erlbaum.

Nichols, P. D. (1991, April). The psychology of item construction. In D. F. Lohman (Chair), *Constructing test items and tasks using an understanding of the psychology of the domain*. Symposium conducted at the annual meeting of the American Educational Research Association, Chicago.

Nichols, P. D. (1994). A framework for developing cognitively diagnostic assessment. *Review of Educational Research, 64*, 575–603.

Novick, L. R. (1988). Analogical transfer, problem similarity, and expertise. *Journal of Experimental Psychology: Learning, Memory, and Cognition, 14*, 510–520.

Pohl, H. L., & Nutter, J. T. (1985). Use of analogy in computer language acquisition. AEDS *Journal, 18*, 254–266.

Resnick, L. B., & Resnick, D. P. (1992). Assessing the thinking curriculum: New tools for educational reform. In B. R. Gifford & M. C. O Connor (Eds.), *Changing assessments; Alternative views of aptitude, achievement and instruction* (pp. 37–75). Boston: Kluwer.

Rumelhart, D. E., & Ortony, A. (1977). The representation of nowledge in memory. In R. C. Anderson, R. J. Spiro, & W. E. Montague (Eds.), *Schooling and the acquisition of knowledge* (pp. 119–132). Hillsdale, NJ: Erlbaum.

Shepard, L. A. (1991). Psychometricians' beliefs about learning. *Educational Researcher, 20*, 2–9.

Snow, R. E. (1987). Aptitude complexes. In R. E. Snow & M. J. Farr (Eds.), *Aptitude, learning, and instruction: Vol. 3. Conative and affective process analyses*. Hillsdale, NJ: Erlbaum.

Snow, R. E. (1989). Toward assessment of cognitive and conative structures in learning. *Educational Researcher, 18*, 8–14.

Snow, R. E. (1991). The concept of aptitude. In R. E. Snow & D. F. Wiley (Eds.), *Improving inquiry in social science* (pp. 249–280), Hillsdale, NJ: Erlbaum.

Snow, R. E. (1992). Aptitude theory: Yesterday, today, and tomorrow. *Educational Psychologist, 27*, 5–32.

Snow, R. E., Federico, P.-A., & Montague, W. E. (Eds.). (1980). *Aptitude, learning, and instruction: Vol. 1. Cognitive process analyses of learning and problem-solving*. Hillsdale, NJ: Erlbaum.

Snow, R. E., & Lohman, D. F. (1989). Implications of cognitive psychology for educational measurement. In R. L. Linn (Ed.), *Educational measurement* (3rd ed., pp. 263–332). New York: Macmillan.

Snow, R. E., & Peterson, P. (1985). Cognitive analyses of tests: Implications for redesign. In S. E. Embretson (Ed.), *Test design: Developments in psychology and psychometrics* (pp. 149–166). New York: Academic Press.

Snow, R. E., & Yalow, E. (1982). Education and intelligence. In R. J. Sternberg (Ed.), *Handbook of human intelligence* (pp. 493–559). Cambridge, England: Cambridge University Press.

Spiro, R. J., Feltovich, P. J., Coulson, R. L., & Anderson, D. K. (1989). Multiple analogies for complex concepts: Antidotes for analogy-induced misconceptions in advanced knowledge acquisition. In S. Vosniadou & A. Ortony (Eds.), *Similarity and analogical reasoning* (pp. 498–531). Cambridge, England: Cambridge University Press.

Sternberg, R. J. (1977). *Intelligence, information processing, and analogical reasoning: The componential analysis of human ability*. Hillsdale, NJ: Erlbaum.

Sternberg, R. J. (1984). What psychology can (and cannot) do for test development. In B. S. Plake (Ed.), *Social and technical issues in testing: Implications for test construction and usage* (pp. 39–60). Hillsdale, NJ: Erlbaum.

Stiggins, R. J. (1991). Facing the challenges of a new era of educational assessment. *Applied Measurement in Education, 4*, 263–273.

Vosniadou, S. (1989). Analogical reasoning as a mechanism in knowledge acquisition: A developmental perspective. In S. Vosniadou & A. Ortony (Eds.), *Similarity and analogical reasoning* (pp. 413–437). Cambridge, England: Cambridge University Press.

Whitely, S. E. (1981). Measuring aptitude processes with multicomponent latent trait models. *Journal of Educational Measurement, 18*, 67–84.

Woolgar, S. (1988). *Science: The very idea*. Sussex, England: Ellis Horwood.

PART

II

Teaching "How to Learn" within Domains

CHAPTER

6

Elementary Reading Instruction

MICHAEL PRESSLEY and RUTH WHARTON-MCDONALD
University at Albany, State University of New York

JOAN RANKIN
University of Nebraska—Lincoln

PAMELA B. EL-DINARY
Georgetown University

RACHEL BROWN
University at Buffalo, State University of New York

PETER AFFLERBACH
University of Maryland

JENNIFER MISTRETTA and LINDA YOKOI
University at Albany, State University of New York

Two decades ago, a review chapter on reading and reading instruction during the elementary years could have been the definitive summary on reading instruction. The assumption was that children were ready to begin learning how to read at about six years of age and did so in six to eight years. There was little thinking about literacy as beginning before the start of elementary schooling, and little recognition of the development of literacy competencies after the elementary years. Indeed, there was little understanding of the nature of skilled reading compared to what is now known. Therefore, the chapter begins with description of exceptionally skilled reading, followed by an analysis of the information processing components that permit exceptionally skilled reading. This understanding is essential because exceptionally skilled reading is the endpoint that should set the course for reading instruction.

EXCELLENT READING AS CONSTRUCTIVELY RESPONSIVE READING

The excellent reader actively constructs meaning from text, a point elaborated in detail by M. Pressley and Afflerbach (1995) in light of the many verbal protocols of reading (i.e., think-aloud reports) generated in the past two decades in research studies conducted by a variety of scholars, from cognitive scientists to reading educators and rhetoricians. Meaning construction is directed in part by the reader's goal. Thus, the reader might want information that can inform the development of a term paper. Once relevant content is encountered in a text, the reader relates that information to what she or he already knows about the topic, so that each reader's understanding of the information encoded in a text will always be unique, a product both of what is in the text and what the reader brings to it—her or his prior knowledge, beliefs, and attitudes (e.g., Rosenblatt, 1978). As such, this is constructivist learning in its classic sense, with the mind of the reader assimilating ideas in text, understanding the ideas in text in terms of prior knowledge (Moshman, 1982). It is also responsive reading, with the reader accomodating to new ideas, resulting in new understanding that reflects the information in the text as interpreted by the reader. M. Pressley and Afflerbach (1995), therefore, referred to fully mature reading as *constructively responsive* reading as a way of reflecting its most important properties.

Good readers can and do actively search text, reflect on the meanings encoded in it, and respond to the ideas and opinions advanced by authors. The skilled reader does so largely because of an important meta-cognitive understanding built up through years of gainful interaction with texts, that texts do contain important ideas and information supporting those ideas. Another meta-cognitive insight built up over the years, that not all parts of any text are matched to one's reading goal, causes the skilled reader to process text selectively. This can begin with an overview. What follows is selective reading of information that seems centrally relevant to the reader's goals. The reader sometimes jumps back and forth to consider important points in the text carefully, with focus on important details as part of constructing reader understandings and interpretations of important ideas conveyed by the text. Good readers exert great effort comparing parts of text, holding disparate ideas in working memory while searching for related ideas throughout text, and rereading to clarify how previously encountered information is related to parts of text just covered.

Throughout the reading of text, the skilled reader makes predictions and hypotheses based on prior knowledge, ones that are revised as reading proceeds. The excellent reader makes inferences while reading, sometimes implicitly and sometimes intentionally. For example, the meta-cognitive understanding that writers write for particular purposes motivates the good reader to construct inferences about the author's overall intent in writing a particular piece, as well as to make inferences about why some conclusions are strongly favored in a text whereas others seem to be ignored by an author.

Throughout reading, excellent readers monitor their comprehension. Good readers are also aware of whether text really is providing information relevant to one's goals. If it is, reading continues and perhaps intensifies. If not, the skilled reader may stop reading or shift to a different part of the text.

After a text has been read, additional reflection and rereading are common. After completing a reading, excellent readers will be aware of whether they have comprehended it. If a reader feels that she or he has not comprehended the text's overall meaning, this can motivate additional or different processing to construct a more complete understanding of text.

Good readers respond evaluatively to what they read, often passionately so, particularly so when they have great expertise related to and interest in the topic of a text. Readers often embrace writing that is consistent with what they believe already and reject texts filled with information inconsistent with their own worldviews. Other times they adjust their views. In short, there is construction and response throughout skilled reading.

THE INFORMATION PROCESSING COMPONENTS THAT INTERACT TO PRODUCE CONSTRUCTIVELY RESPONSIVE READING

Although much of the dynamics of excellent reading can be lost by focussing on information processing components, doing so clarifies the nature of excellent reading and the competencies excellent reading instruction must promote. Like all human information processing models, constructively responsive reading begins with the biological substrate that supports reading.

Brain Mechanisms

One of the most important principles of brain functioning is that most processing is broadly distributed across the brain rather than strictly localized. Even so, certain parts of the brain are particularly implicated in reading.

Working Memory Capacity

An important biological bottleneck in reading is extremely limited-capacity working memory, sometimes thought of as short-term memory, consciousness, or attentional capacity. With respect to reading, decoding and comprehension are often thought of as competing for the limited capacity available.

The more automatic decoding, the more attentional capacity available for comprehension (LaBerge & Samuels, 1974; Perfetti & Lesgold, 1977). This explains why children often can decode, but not comprehend. When a child must expend great effort to sound out every word, there is little capacity left over to reflect on the word's meaning or integrate its meaning with the meanings of other words recently decoded.

With development, functional working memory capacity increases (Dempster, 1985). With development, people also use their capacity more efficiently, which permits functionally greater working memory than at earlier points in development. Thus, with increasing age, people process information more quickly (Kail, 1991, 1992). The more rapidly information is processed, the less capacity consumed in processing. With development, prior knowledge is greater, with stronger connections between conceptually related ideas. This expanded and more accessible prior knowledge permits efficient chunking of information. For example, for the beginning reader, each of the six letters of the word *pretty* might be a chunk of information that must be held in memory and manipulated as part of sounding out the word. For the reader who knows *pretty* by sight, it is at most one chunk of information. Eventually, recognition of *pretty* becomes so automatic that little or no attentional capacity must be expended in decoding it.

Consistently, individual differences in working memory capacity have been associated with individual differences in reading (Carpenter, Miyake, & Just, 1994; Hulme & MacKenzie, 1992; Shaywitz & Shaywitz, 1992; Siegel & Ryan, 1988; Swanson, 1992; Swanson & Cooney, 1991; Torgesen & Houck, 1980; Yuill & Oakhill, 1991, Chapter 5; Yuill, Oakhill, & Parkin, 1989). Working memory is clearly important with respect to decoding and the integration of ideas in memory to produce overall comprehension of text.

General Language and Meta-linguistic Processes

Competency in language seems essential to reading, with language problems often associated with difficulties in reading, a generalization that spans problems in basic perception of language to memory of language to development of syntax to language comprehension (see Catts, 1989; Katz, Shankweiler, & Liberman, 1981; Liberman, Mann, Shankweiler, & Werfelman, 1982; Mann, 1984; Olson, Kliegl, Davidson, & Foltz, 1985; Sawyer & Butler, 1991; Stanovich, 1986; Vellutino, 1979). Much of the individual differences in language that relate to reading difficulties are biologically determined and evident early in life (e.g., Scarborough, 1990).

In recent years, one general meta-linguistic deficiency has received much more attention as a correlate of problems in beginning reading than any other language problem. Children with reading disabilities often cannot reflect on the parts of language, analyze language into constituent parts (e.g., words into a stream of sounds), nor synthesize language constituents (e.g., produce words by consciously blending component sounds). Such children lack phonemic awareness (e.g., Adams, 1990; Pennington, Groisser, & Welsh, 1993; Stanovich, 1986, 1988). Although a complex construct that is determined in part by general intelligence, short-term memory, and speech perception ability, phoemic awareness can be thought of as the awareness that words are composed of separable sounds (i.e., phonemes) and that phonemes are combined to say words (McBride-Chang, 1995; Wagner, Torgesen, Laughon, Simmons, & Rashotte, 1993). Children who lack phonemic awareness also have a difficult time learning to spell and developing understanding of letter–sound relationships (Griffith, 1991; Juel, Griffith, & Gough, 1986). Poor phonemic awareness at four to six years of age is predictive of reading difficulties throughout the elementary years and beyond (Bruck, 1992; Bruck & Treiman, 1990; Juel, 1988; Pennington, Van Orden, Smith, Green, & Haith, 1990; Pratt & Brady, 1988; Stuart & Masterson, 1992).

A vicious cycle can be set off. Deficiencies in phonemic awareness can undermine learning to decode, which undermines reading a wide range of materials and comprehending what is read. That is, students who decode poorly read less than others and get less out of each piece of text read, with the long-term result of less practice in reading and exposure to information in text and, thus, less development of higher-order reading competencies (e.g., ability to make sense of complex syntax) and world knowledge that can mediate understanding of text. When low-level processes require a great deal of effort, relatively little capacity is left over for comprehension or use of complex strategies that might permit inferences and greater understanding and learning of text (LaBerge & Samuels, 1974; Walczyk, 1994). Stanovich (1986) referred to this as the Matthew effect because the young child who is rich in reading competence grows ever richer through more reading of advanced content (i.e., as specified by the biblical Matthew, the rich get richer; e.g., McBride-Chang, Manis, Seidenberg, Custodio, & Doi, 1993; Stanovich & Cunningham, 1993). Those children who are advantaged relative to peers now will be even more advantaged two years from now (Vauras, Kinnunen, & Kuusela, 1994).

Although brain mechanisms undoubtedly mediate phonemic awareness, such awareness is not a natural consequence of maturation, but rather requires rich language experiences, and for many children probably require language experiences that focus much more on the sounds of language than naturally occurring language experiences permit. Consistent with this, later in this chapter we will review the literature on instruction that stimulates phonemic awareness.

Indeed, the evidence is quite strong that instruction is absolutely essential for children to learn to read, a point that we emphasize because of claims made by whole language theorists, whose perspectives drove much of contemporary elementary language arts instruction in the early 1990s (Weaver, 1994). The whole language theorists were very much influenced by Chomsky's (e.g., 1965) work and arguments that language is innate and an inevitable development if a child experiences a speaking community, which except for feral children, is typically the case. The analogous argument was made that reading would develop naturally through immersion in an environment rich in print and writing experiences. This extrapolation by whole language theorists does not match any claim actually made by Chomsky or like-minded psycholinguists, however. Although a case can be made that the perceptual and neurolinguistic systems that underlie speech lay in waiting in the developing child, waiting for appropriate environmental stimuli to permit their functioning and development, no such case can be made for reading and writing competencies. The perceptual and neurolinguistic mechanisms (e.g., visual ability, visual short-term memory, visual discrimination) that permit reading and writing evolved for very different purposes than reading and writing. Biologically oriented scholars who study reading and writing competencies are convinced that the development of skilled reading and writing typically depends on more than environmental exposure to print and writing experiences; skilled reading and writing depends on instruction (e.g., Bertelson & De Gelder, 1989; Liberman & Liberman, 1990).

Left-Hemisphere Structures and Functions

With every passing year, there is additional evidence that the left hemisphere, the dominant hemisphere for language, is more involved in reading than the right hemisphere and that normal reading depends on normal functioning of the left hemisphere. In particular, a variety of procedures, from imaging studies of cerebral blood flow to autopsy, have been used to document abnormalities in structure and function of the left hemisphere of individuals with reading problems (e.g., Conners, 1971; F. H. Duffy & McAnulty, 1990; Flowers, Wood, & Naylor, 1991; Galaburda, Sherman, Rosen, Aboitiz, & Geschwind, 1985; Galin, 1989; Gross-Glenn et al., 1988; Harter, 1991; Hier, LeMay, Rosenberger, & Perlo, 1978; Johnson & Myklebust, 1967; Lyon, Newby, Recht, & Caldwell, 1991). For example, one interesting finding produced using MRI (magnetic resonance imagery) technology is that regions of the brain implicated in language processing tend to be smaller in reading disabled students than in normal learners (Hynd & Semrund-Clikeman, 1989); MRI studies have also detected abnormal brain structures at the back of the left hemisphere of dyslexics (e.g., Jernigan, Hesselink, Sowell, & Tallal, 1991; Larsen, Hoien, Lundberg, & Ødegaard, 1990).

Long-Term Memory

The skilled reader knows much, with that knowledge stored in long-term memory. Various types of knowledge—procedural knowledge (i.e., knowing how to do things), declarative knowledge (i.e., factual knowledge), meta-cognitive knowledge (i.e., knowledge of one's thinking), and motivational beliefs—combine to determine skilled reading, with each of these taken up in the remainder of this subsection.

Procedural Knowledge. The skilled reader has much knowledge of "how to" read. Some of it is implicit and used automatically. For example, the eyes of the skilled reader take in text in an efficient fashion. There are fixations and saccades (i.e., pauses of about a quarter of a second apiece and jumps accomplished in a 20th of a second), which are so automatic in the skilled reader that little or no capacity is consumed in regulating eye movements. Of course, the same is not true for the beginning reader. To the extent that capacity must be expended to regulate where the eyes move, the less capacity is available to decode and understand the words the eyes move to meet.

Good readers inspect the words they are reading completely. Studies of eye movement during skilled reading and related research have established that not only are good readers reading every single word when they are trying to learn what is in text (e.g., McConkie, Zola, Blanchard, & Wolverton, 1982; for a discussion, see Carver, 1990, Chapter 5), they are processing every single letter of every single word (e.g., Rayner, Inhoff, Morrison, Slowiaczek, & Bertera, 1981; Stanovich, 1986).

The skilled reader knows a variety of ways to decode words. According to dual-route theory (e.g., Ehri, 1992), good readers can read many words by sight, and for those words not known by sight, they can use knowledge of letter–sound associations, blending, and word parts (e.g., orthographs such as familiar prefixes, root words, and suffixes). The visual sight word route, of course, is faster and demands less capacity than the phonological–orthographic route, not requiring linear processing of the letter and sound relationships. Because learning sight words logically first requires being able to decode them—sight word knowledge is built up from repeated successful decodings.

Good readers also know a number of strategies that can be used to comprehend text. These include anticipating information in text based on prior knowledge, looking for information relevant to reading goals, moving backward or forward in text looking for particular pieces of information, rereading text when uncertain about meaning, attending closely to important information (e.g., reading important information more slowly than information not centrally relevant to reading goals), imagining the relationships described in text, paraphrasing or self-explaining what was in the text or generating examples illustrating text content, and summarizing (M. Pressley & Afflerbach, 1995).

Declarative (Conceptual) Knowledge. Good readers possess a great deal of declarative knowledge that can be used in conjunction with procedural knowledge as part of skilled reading. Some knowledge is so well known that there is no need to exert effort to access it or reflect on it in order to use it. The good reader knows all of the letter–sound relationships, the code mapping the sounds of a language (i.e., phonemes) onto the alphabet. They know variations in the pronounciation of particular letters, including the conditions determining when one pronounciation is favored over another (Venezky & Johnson, 1973). The most common examples are the vowels, which typically are long if there is a final *-e* in a syllable and short if there is no final *-e*. Another example is that *c* is pronounced differently if followed by an *e* or an *i* than if followed by an *a*, *o*, or *u* (e.g., compare the pronounciation of the *c* sounds in *celestial*, *city*, *cat*, *cot*, and *cut*).

Much linguistic knowledge is used automatically and is rarely reflected on during reading. For example, knowledge of text structures includes knowing the typical elements in narratives and expositions, permitting good readers to abstract main points and important details from text.

The good reader knows many words, ones that can be pronounced on sight. Meaning is often retrieved automatically when such words are encountered.

The good reader also has extensive knowledge of the world and a wide range of topics that permit inferences during reading, ones that elaborate on the stated meanings in the text and others that permit links between ideas in the text and between this text and other texts the reader has encountered in the past. For example, this knowledge base permits instantiation of concepts in text (i.e., more specific interpretations than explicitly stated in the text). Thus, readers instantiate the word *container* with *bottle* when they read, "The container held the cola" (R. C. Anderson & Ortony, 1975). It is also the basis of expectations and predictions about the content of upcoming text.

This extensive prior knowledge allows skilled readers to react to text and evaluate the text, including the quality of the content, the abilities and biases of the author, and the usefulness of the information in the text relative to one's purpose for reading the material. Such prior knowledge can cause affective responses, from smug laughter to disgust.

Meta-cognition. Meta-cognition is knowledge about and awareness of one's thinking (e.g., Flavell, Miller, & Miller, 1993). In particular, good readers possess long-term knowledge about when and where to use the procedural and conceptual knowledge they possess. Sometimes this knowledge is verbalizable (i.e., the person can say exactly when it is appropriate to use a particular comprehension strategy) and sometimes tacit (e.g., a person carries out the strategy on appropriate occasions, but cannot tell another person when and where the strategy works). Long-term meta-cognitive knowledge can be absolutely critical to the conscious regulation of strategies and other procedures (e.g., O'Sullivan & Pressley, 1984).

Although long-term meta-cognitive knowledge is important in the regulation of processing during reading, short-term, on-line meta-cognition that is the result of cognitive monitoring during reading plays an even larger role. That is, good readers monitor characteristics of the text (e.g., whether text content is relevant to the reading goal; difficulty of the text; when text is ambiguous or potentially so), the effectiveness of their ongoing reading processes and strategies, and problems they are experiencing, such as loss of concentration and presence of unfamiliar terms in text (M. Pressley & Afflerbach, 1995).

The awareness of reading produced by monitoring informs decision making and regulation of reading in a number of ways. It can lead to the activation of processes to accomodate text characteristics and text demands; for example, to skim or skip material, to read a section of text especially carefully, or to stop and attempt to determine the reason for lack of comprehension. Alternatively, it can lead to a decision to do nothing or to change one's reading goal to a more realistic one (e.g., entering a text with the goal of completely understanding a physical principle, continuing to read hoping to understand the principle at only a general level), or giving up on the text and quitting reading.

Motivational Beliefs. Technically, long-term motivational beliefs are a form of meta-cognition, because they are beliefs about thinking and learning. What is special about them is that they can have a pervasive effect in encouraging intellectual activity or discouraging it. Thus, knowing that you typically learn a great deal from reading can motivate future reading. Realizing that reading is sometimes demanding, even for good readers, can motivate continued reading of a difficult text. Good readers have such beliefs.

Articulating the Components of Constructive Information Processing

Much of skilled reading can be understood by understanding the interactions between biology, procedural knowledge, conceptual knowledge, meta-cognition, and motivational beliefs about reading. These components interact dynamically as part of good reading.

The good reader has a rich repertoire of strategies for decoding new words and comprehending text. Use of these strategies is well-practiced so that the execution of them is much less demanding than it once was. Although many reading procedures are carried out automatically and without an intention to do so (e.g., decoding by sounding out, generating expectations about what might be in a text based on its title), decoding and comprehension procedures can be used intentionally when the reader monitors a need to do so (e.g., senses a text is not being understood). The good reader knows which strategies to use and when to use them because of long-term meta-cognition about strategies, knowledge that has developed because of habitual monitoring when reading is going well and when it has not been proceeding smoothly. If a strategy used today to read a text works well, long-term meta-cognition of the strategy may be affected, with the reader even more convinced in the future that summarizing is a good way to remember text.

Readers are continually reacting to text in light of prior knowledge, with prior knowledge affecting reading procedures in a number of ways. It affects the portions of text receiving selective attention, coloring the reader's images of the text content and facilitating or interfering with interpretation of text, depending on whether the reader's prior knowledge is congruent or incongruent with the meanings expressed in text.

All of this activity during reading is fueled by the good reader's certain knowledge that the effort will be worth it, based on a history of success in gaining information from text. Today's success using summarization will only entrench that motivational belief more completely.

And so it goes, successful use of a procedure fuels a motivational belief and increases meta-cognitive understanding about the situational usefulness of the procedure. All procedural execution, activation of relevant prior knowledge, and monitoring occur in short-term, working memory, which then feeds into long-term memory when reading is going well. And so it continues, the biological architecture permitting reading activity, which in turn affects long-term memory in ways that permit more efficient short-term functioning in the future.

Constructively Responsive Reading as an End in the Development of Reading

Based on this review of constructively responsive reading, we conclude excellent elementary-level reading instruction should do the following:

- Promote the development of language competence.
- Promote meta-linguistic development, including the critical beginning-reading competency of phonemic awareness.
- Teach children how to decode.
- Encourage the development of a rich conceptual knowledge base, using every opportunity possible to do so.
- Teach children how to comprehend what they read, how actively to respond to text, to construct meanings and interpretations from text.
- Encourage children to understand the reading procedures they are learning, especially when and how particular reading procedures improve understanding of text, and encourage the important meta-cognitive understanding that meaning is an interaction between what the reader brings to the text and messages that authors express through writing.
- Maintain and promote children's motivation to do things literate by encouraging them to understand that they can learn how to direct their

intellectual resources so as to permit comprehension and interpretation of what is read.

• Assure massive amounts of practice of reading to automatize decoding and comprehension skills in application, so that skills eventually can be articulated relatively effortlessly, freeing capacity for inferences and reflection about what is being read.

As the chapter proceeds, return to this list, reflecting on how the experiences and instruction described and prescribed affects the development of these competencies. The practices described in this chapter work because they do what is listed here—they stimulate language, meta-linguistic development, decoding, conceptual development, development of comprehension skills, motivation, and automatic execution of articulated skills. These are the information processing competencies essential for all children learning to read English, with every indication that instruction stimulating these competencies is excellent instruction for a wide range of young readers (Fitzgerald, 1995).

EMERGENT READING DURING THE PRESCHOOL YEARS: PROMOTING THE DEVELOPMENT OF LANGUAGE COMPETENCE

A great deal of literacy development occurs before the elementary-school years. Preschoolers are active in the development of their own literacy, seeking out and initiating many behaviors that are literate and literacy fostering. The home environment can support and facilitate such literacy activities, although not all children live in homes that are as supportive as they could be. Homes that foster emergent literacy include rich interpersonal experiences with family members and others, a variety of literacy materials (e.g., plastic refrigerator letters, picture books, writing materials), and high positive regard by parents and others for literacy and its development in children (Morrow, 1989).

One especially rich type of emergent reading interaction for preschoolers is storybook reading. There are clear correlations between amount of storybook reading during the preschool years and vocabulary and language development, children's interest in reading, and success in early reading (Bus, van IJzendoorn, & Pellegrini, 1995; Scarborough & Dobrich, 1994; Sulzby & Teale, 1991). Storybook reading permits rich discussions and animated conversations between the reader and the child. The adult and child work out the meaning of text together, having fun coconstructing interpretations (Morrow, 1989). Adult and child question one another as part of rich dialogue filled with adult praise for the child's efforts to get meaning from pictures and print. As part of this constructive process, both reader and child relate what is happening in stories to their lives and the world around them (Applebee & Langer, 1983; Cochran-Smith, 1984; Flood, 1977; Pellegrini, Perlmutter, Galda, & Brody, 1990; Roser & Martinez, 1985; D. Taylor & Strickland, 1986).

With increasing age and experience, children are attentive to longer sections of text during storybook reading (Heath, 1982; Sulzby & Teale, 1991), and adults and children have more complex discussions about text (Sulzby & Teale, 1991). Preschoolers learn how to be attentive and derive benefit from storybook reading as a function of their storybook interactions (Bus & van IJzendoorn, 1988). Especially when adults are skillful at eliciting children's active involvement, children's lexical development thrives (e.g., Ninio, 1980; Sénéchal, Thomas, & Monker, 1995), as does language development more broadly conceived (Arnold, Lonigan, Whitehurst, & Epstein, 1994; Whitehurst *et al.*, 1988, 1994). Comprehension abilities improve as well (Heath, 1982). A lot is learned during storybook interactions, including both procedural knowledge, such as how to identify the main ideas in stories (Lehr, 1988), and declarative knowledge, such as cultural information incidentally conveyed in high-quality literature (e.g., Cornell, Sénéchal, & Broda, 1988). Much is learned largely because parents help a child as needed and "up the ante" when the child is ready for it (i.e., reads longer sequences to the child, urges the child to listen to longer stories).

Unfortunately, there is wide variability in the quantity and quality of storybook experiences for children, as well as other emergent literacy experiences (e.g., Feitelson, 1988). Although parents can learn to interact with their preschoolers more productively with respect to literacy-fostering activities (e.g., Whitehurst et al., 1988, 1994), as a society we lack the resources to reach the many parents that need to be reached, although it is clear that every effort should be made to extend that reach (Sulzby & Teale, 1991). The bottom line is that, the more parents interact verbally with their children, the more verbally competent their children are (e.g., Huttenlocher, Haight, Bryk, Seltzer, & Lyons, 1991). Emergent literacy is stimulated the more that preschoolers' worlds of play include paper, pencils, pens, magazines, and books, as well as the cozy corners in which to read them (e.g., Morrow, 1990; Morrow & Weinstein, 1986; Neuman & Roskos, 1992).

Not surprisingly, five-year-olds who are more emergent literate—reflected by greater competence in re-enacting stories, writing individual words, "writing" stories, and "reading"—tend to outperform less emergent literate five-year-olds in reading during the primary grades, which can be interpreted as a validation of sorts for emergent literacy experiences (Barnhart, 1991): That is, emergent literacy competence at age 5 predicts later reading competence.

Other experiences also make a difference during the preschool years. One great success at reaching preschoolers around the world is *Sesame Street*. Children learn a great deal about the alphabet and language from watching the program, much more so than from entertainment television (D. R. Anderson & Collins, 1988; S. Ball & Bogatz, 1970), with *Sesame Street* making contributions to the development of literacy over and above family interactions and other sources of stimulation (e.g., Rice, Huston, Truglio, & Wright, 1990).

PHONEMIC AWARENESS: AN IMPORTANT META-LINGUISTIC COMPETENCE THAT CAN BE DEVELOPED THROUGH INSTRUCTION DURING KINDERGARTEN AND GRADE 1

The awareness that words are composed of separable sounds and that phonemes are combined to say words (i.e., phonemic awareness) is one of the best predictors of success in early reading in school (e.g., Adams, 1990; Bond & Dykstra, 1967; Fletcher et al., 1994; Juel, 1988; Scarborough, 1989; Stuart & Masterson, 1992; Tunmer, Herriman, & Nesdale, 1988).

Full-blown phonemic awareness typically does not develop through emergent literacy experiences, even high-quality ones (e.g., Lundberg, 1991), although there can be some improvement in linguistic awareness as a function of storybook reading and other emergent literacy activities (Whitehurst et al., 1994). When phonemic awareness develops during the preschool years, it is often the result of explicit parental teaching of letters and their sounds (Crain-Thoreson & Dale, 1992). Many parents, however, do not engage in such teaching, so that education with an impact on phonemic awareness typically occurs in school.

The classic study of the instructional development of phonemic awareness was conducted by British scholars Lynette Bradley and Peter Bryant (e.g., 1983), although it was not the first (see Williams, 1980). Bradley and Bryant's (1983) teaching emphasized that the same word can be categorized in different ways on the basis of sound when it is in different sets of words. Thus, if *hen* is in a group of words that include *hat*, *hill*, *hair*, and *hand*, it would make sense to categorize all of these words together as starting with *h*, especially in contrast to other words starting with another letter (e.g., *b* words such as *bag*, *band*, and *bat*). If *hen* were on a list with *men* and *sun*, however, these three words could be categorized as ones ending in *n*. If *hen* were on a list of words that included *bed* and *leg*, it would be possible to categorize the words as ones with short *e* in the middle.

During the first 20 sessions of Bradley and Bryant's instruction, five- and six-year-olds who lacked phonemic awareness were taught to categorize words on the basis of common sounds using pictures of the objects (i.e., pictures of a *hen*, *men*, and a *leg*). Many sound identification tasks were included in the instruction. For example, odd-one-out games were played, with the child required to eliminate a word starting (or ending or containing) a sound different than other words in a set. Sound identification and discrimination exercises eventually gave way to production exercises, so that children had to recall words containing particular sounds in particular positions. In the latter half of the curriculum, children were required to spell words using plastic letters, with the teacher providing help as needed, up to and including spelling the word for the child if that was what was needed to move the lesson along. Spelling exercises included sets of words sharing common features. Thus, for a set involving *hat*, *cat*, and *rat*, an efficient strategy was simply to change the first plastic letter as each new word was requested. The saliency of many different sound patterns was illustrated with such spelling lists.

Bradley and Bryant's instruction produced substantial gains in standardized reading performance (i.e., about a year advantage) relative to a control condition in which children were trained to categorize words conceptually (e.g., *cat*, *bat*, and *rat* are all animals). The students taught sound categorization were even further ahead of control participants who had received no supplementary categorization training. Even more striking, however, were the results of a five-year followup. Even though many of the control subjects had received substantial remediation during the five-year interval following participation in the study, there were still striking reading advantages for students who had experienced the sound categorization training when they were in the primary grades (Bradley, 1989; Bradley & Bryant, 1991).

Others have also demonstrated both short- and long-term benefits of instruction that stimulates phonemic awareness (e.g., E. W. Ball & Blachman, 1988, 1991; Blachman, 1991; Byrne & Fielding-Barnsley, 1993; Lundberg, Frost, & Peterson, 1988; Tangel & Blachman, 1992; Treiman & Baron, 1981). Typically, successful instruction includes rhyming exercises, practice involving division of words into syllables, and exercises requiring identification of phonemes. More recent instructional studies have emphasized the importance of blending sounds, as readers do when they pronounce words (O'Connor, Jenkins, & Slocum, 1995).

Cunningham (1990) provided an important study of the impact of phonemic awareness instruction on primary-grade students' reading, comparing two approaches to increasing the phonemic awareness of kindergarten and grade 1 children. One was "skill and drill," with emphasis on segmentation and blending of phonemes. In the second, discussion centered on the value of decoding and phonemic awareness and how learning to segment and blend phonemes could be applied in reading. That is, this latter condition was meta-cognitively rich, providing children with a great deal of information about when, where, and why to use the knowledge of phonemes they were acquiring. Although both forms of instruction were effective, the meta-cognitively rich instruction was better at the grade-1 level.

Metacognitive embellishment of literacy instruction is important, for segmentation and blending are procedures that young readers are more likely to use appropriately if they are fully aware of when to use them. Analyzing the sounds in words and putting them together to sound out words seems to depend on understanding first that each word has a sequence of sounds that can be separated. Thus, instruction to develop phonemic awareness makes sense, followed by instruction to decode by sounding words out and blending the sounds.

EXPERIMENTAL RESEARCH ON PRIMARY-GRADES INSTRUCTION: WHOLE LANGUAGE VERSUS EXPLICIT TEACHING OF DECODING

What is the nature of excellent primary literacy instruction? The most famous set of such evaluations was the "first-grade studies" in the 1960s sponsored by the U.S. Office of Education (see Adams, 1990, Chapter 3; Barr, 1984; Bond & Dykstra, 1967). A strength of the first grade studies was that each of various approaches to reading instruction were tested in several different experiments and, typically, by several different research teams. By most accountings, however, there was no clear overall winner in the first grade studies nor in extensions of the comparisons to grade 2 (Barr, 1984; Bond & Dykstra, 1967). Although word reading sometimes was improved in programs targeted at increasing decoding skills and knowledge of letter–sound consistencies in words, vocabulary and comprehension were affected little by the various alternatives to the traditional basal approach. Given the ambiguity in the results of the first grade studies, the great debate (Chall, 1967) about the nature of the optimal beginning-reading instruction raged on.

The models in the debate have shifted since the late 1960s, however. The striking contrast that has dominated the great debates of the 1990s about beginning-reading instruction is whole language versus explicit teaching of phonemic awareness (e.g., in the fashion of Bradley & Bryant, 1983) and, then, decoding.

Whole Language

Whole language emphasizes language processes and the creation of learning environments in which children experience authentic reading and writing (Weaver, 1994). Both linguistic and cognitive development are presumed to be stimulated by experiencing excellent literature and attempting to compose new meanings (e.g., Y. M. Goodman, 1990). Skills instruction should be in the context of natural reading and only as needed by individual readers (e.g., King & K. S. Goodman, 1990). Whole language advocates believe that the development of literacy depends on immersion in high-quality literacy environments. Literacy is a natural by-product of such immersion.

Whole language sometimes is associated with positive effects on children's literacy achievement, autonomous use of literature, and attitudes toward reading (e.g., McKenna, Stratton, Grindler, & Jenkins, 1995; Morrow, 1992; Morrow, O'Connor, & Smith, 1990). Consistent experiences with high-quality literature foster growth in understanding the structure of stories, which positively affects both comprehension and writing, as well as the sophistication of children's language (e.g., Dahl & Freppon, 1995; Feitelson, Kita, & Goldstein, 1986; Morrow, 1992). Just as broad reading expands the knowledge of adults (Stanovich & Cunningham, 1993), extensive experiences with stories expand children's knowledge of the world; for example, as reflected by breadth of vocabulary (e.g., Elley, 1989; Robbins & Ehri, 1994; Shu, Anderson, & Zhang, 1995). Extensive experience in inventing spellings, an emphasis in whole language primary classrooms, in fact does improve decoding skills (e.g., Clarke, 1988; Ehri & Wilce, 1987; Richgels, 1995).

Whole language does not affect reading achievement as measured by standardized tests of decoding, vocabulary, comprehension, and writing (Graham & Harris, 1994; Stahl, McKenna, & Pagnucco, 1994; Stahl & Miller, 1989). In contrast, programs explicitly teaching phonemic awareness, phonics, and letter–sound analysis have promoted standardized performances and, in particular, have proven superior to programs emphasizing meaning making, such as whole language (see Adams, 1990; also Pflaum, Walberg, Karegianes, & Rasher, 1980).

Explicit Decoding Instruction

Other reading educators argue that learning to break the code is the most critical part of primary-level reading and most likely when students are provided explicit instruction in phonemic awareness followed by explicit instruction in decoding. For example, Adams (1990) and Foorman (1994) summarized evidence that the development of strong and complex connections between words and their components follows from explicit instruction in phonemic awareness, letter recognition, attention to the sounds of words, blending of sounds, and practice in reading and writing words to the point that they are automatically recognized and produced. Explicit decoding instruction based on teaching children to analyze and blend component sounds is effective, even for children who experience great difficulties learning to read (Lovett et al., 1994; Lovett, Ransby, Hardwick, Johns, & Donaldson, 1989).

Other approaches to explicit decoding instruction also improve student performance. The most traditional of these is teaching students phonics rules (e.g., "When two vowels go walking, the first does the talking," "When there is an *-e* at the end of a syllable . . ."; Clymer, 1963). Teaching children phonics rules does improve early reading (Adams, 1990; R. C. Anderson, Hiebert, Scott, & Wilkinson, 1985; Ehri, 1991) and children's abilities to sound out words (e.g., Barr, 1974–1975).

Goswami and Bryant (e.g., 1992; Goswami, 1986), in particular, have made the case that analogy is a strategy beginning readers can use. Thus, a child who knows how to pronounce *sail* could make a good guess at *pail* the first time it is encountered simply by analogy (i.e., "This is like *sail* only it starts with a *p*!"). That same *sail*-word knower would have a fighting chance with *fail*, *rail*, and *bail* as well using the analogy strategy.

Use of the analogy strategy, however, probably depends on phonological decoding skills. Ehri and Robbins (1992) found that only children who already had some phonological decoding skills were able to decode words by analogy. Peterson and Haines (1992) produced results complementary to the Ehri and Robbins outcome. Bruck and Treiman (1992) demonstrated that, even when young children can use analogies, they rely greatly on decoding of individual phonemes and orthographs in decoding new words they encounter. Moreover, it is not really an either–or situation with respect to teaching decoding by analogy or by analysis and blending. As a child sounds and blends sounds, letter strings that are encountered often eventually are perceived as wholes; that is, repeated co-occurrence of *i*, *n*, and *g*, in that order, results eventually in *-ing* being perceived as a unit (e.g., Adams, 1990, Chapter 9; Ehri, 1980, 1984, 1987, 1992; Stanovich & West, 1989). Prefixes and suffixes are obvious examples, but there are other recurring combinations, many of which are root words (e.g., *-take*, *mal-*, *ben-*, *rog-*, *do-*). Thus, the child who can analyze and blend will develop knowledge of orthographs that can be used to decode by analogy. Alphabetic decoding or phonics rule application or both consume a great deal of short-term memory. If all of the attentional capacity is consumed by decoding, nothing is left over for comprehension, with the result that words may be pronounced but not understood. The more orthographic chunks are recognized automatically, the less effort or attention is required to decode and, thus, more mental capacity is left over for comprehension (LaBerge & Samuels, 1974). Indeed, as experience with orthographic chunks increases, automatic connections between the chunks and their meanings develop (e.g., Baron, 1977). As children decode the same word over and over, eventually it comes to be recognized by sight with both its pronounciation and meaning automatically retrieved the insant the word is encountered. That is, through additional experiences with a word, reading increases in speed, accuracy, and ease (e.g., Horn & Manis, 1987).

In general, when children read more, their phonological decoding skills increase as their knowledge of orthographs improves (see Allen, Cipielewski, & Stanovich, 1992; R. Allington, 1977; Cipielewski & Stanovich, 1992; Cunningham & Stanovich, 1990, 1991; Juel, 1988; Stanovich, 1986; B. M. Taylor, Frye, & Maruyama, 1990). As children are being taught to decode, they should be encouraged to read, read, and read. Decoding instruction permits reading whole texts, but reading texts also improves decoding. Excellent decoding instruction is not a skills-first approach, as suggested by many whole language theorists, but rather involves explicit instruction of skills in conjunction with many reading opportunities.

The Great Debate Continues

The scientific study of beginning reading flourished in the last decade and a half. Consequently, it is understood better than during earlier great debates (Chall, 1967) that explicit decoding instruction improves reading both during the primary years and in the long term. Even so, whole language is the predominant language arts philosophy in the United States, although there is increasing recognition that it must include much more explicit teaching of skills, including decoding, than advocated by the most radical of whole language theorists. There are many calls for and attempts at more balanced instruction, instruction in which skills are taught explicitly in a context rich in authentic reading and writing experiences (McIntyre & Pressley, 1996; M. Pressley & Rankin, 1994). There are also impressive experimental analyses suggesting very positive effects of a balanced approach compared to more traditional whole language approaches (Castle, Riach, & Nicholson's, 1994; Iversen & Tunmer, 1993; Uhry & Shepherd, 1993). We will return to this issue of balance later in the chapter when the teaching of effective elementary language arts teachers is taken up in detail.

COMPREHENSION STRATEGIES INSTRUCTION

One of the most disturbing insights in the wake of the great debates about beginning reading (Chall, 1967) was that little explicit instruction was being provided to children with respect to comprehension beyond the word level. Dolores Durkin (1978–1979) observed that instead of teaching comprehension, elementary teachers seemed to be testing it all of the time, asking students lots of question about text content. That study motivated much research on reading comprehension.

Instructional Studies of Individual Comprehension Strategies

Much of the research on comprehension strategies instruction in the 1970s and early 1980s was of the following form (for detailed reviews, see Haller, Child, & Walberg, 1988; Pearson & Dole, 1987; Pearson & Fielding, 1991; M. Pressley, Johnson, Symons, McGoldrick, & Kurita, 1989). A researcher believed that if students constructed a particular type of representation (e.g., mental images representing the story told in a narrative, summaries) or reacted to texts in a particular way (e.g., relating it to prior knowledge, explicitly seeking clarifications when unsure of meaning), comprehension and, hence, long-term memory of text would be improved. The experimenters testing these strategies usually had reason to believe that students were not already engaging in such processing when reading or students were doing so less systematically and completely than they could. In these studies the reading comprehension of students receiving instruction typically was measured by some type of objective test of understanding (e.g., multiple-choice items over literal and implied messages in text). The performance of comprehension strategies-instructed subjects on such tests were compared to the performances of students not receiving strategy instruction (e.g., control subjects permitted to read as they normally would in preparation for an objective test). If the strategy-trained students outperformed the control students on the test, there was support for the conclusions that the students (1) probably were not using the trained strategy on their own or were not using it systematically, but (2) more positively, that they can be taught to do so.

A variety of individual strategies proved their worth in such studies:

- Children often do not remember the main ideas of what they have read (e.g., A. L. Brown & Day, 1983; A. L. Brown, Day, & Jones, 1983). A number of reading researchers reasoned that if children were taught to extract main ideas and summarize text, their comprehension and memory of it should improve. Summarization consistently improves children's comprehension and memory of text (e.g., Armbruster, Anderson, & Ostertag, 1987; Bean & Steenwyk, 1984; Berkowitz, 1986; B. M. Taylor, 1982; B. M. Taylor & Beach, 1984).
- At least after age 8, memory and understanding of text improves when children are instructed to create images depicting what they have read (e.g., Gambrell & Bales, 1986; Gambrell & Jawitz, 1993; Pressley, 1976). In particular, imagery instructions seem to encourage children who do not spontaneously link ideas in text to one another and to prior knowledge to do so (Oakhill & Patel, 1991).
- Teaching students to analyze stories with respect to their story grammar structures improves the understanding of stories by weaker readers (Idol, 1987; Idol & Croll, 1987; Short & Ryan, 1984). This entails teaching students to identify the characters in stories and their feelings, setting variables, the problems encountered by characters and their potential solutions, and problem resolutions.
- Prior knowledge activation (e.g., Levin & Pressley, 1981), question generation (e.g., Rosenshine & Trapman, 1992), and question generation to activate appropriate prior knowledge (Oakhill, 1993) are effective in promoting learning from text.

In short, strategies can be applied before (e.g., making predictions based on prior knowledge), during (e.g., imagery generation), and after (e.g., summarization) reading (Levin & Pressley, 1981). With the development of sophisticated models of thinking specifying that multiple strategies are articulated in making sense of the world (e.g., Baron, 1985; A. L. Brown, Bransford, Ferrara, & Campione, 1983; Levin & Pressley, 1981; Nickerson, Perkins, & Smith, 1985), a theoretical point of departure could provide for the development of comprehension strategies instruction that could promote the development of reading competence from the beginning to the end of a reading.

Instructional Studies of Repertoires of Comprehension Strategies

A great deal of progress was made in the 1980s and 1990s in determining whether and how students could be taught repertoires of comprehension strategies so that they could use them effectively in an articulated fashion. We cover here the most visible of the successful efforts.

Reciprocal Teaching

Four comprehension strategies were the heart of Palincsar and Brown's (1984) reciprocal teaching (i.e., prediction, questioning, seeking clarification when confused, and summarization). Palincsar and Brown (1984, Study 1) was their first study of the method. For each of 20 days of intervention, an adult teacher began by discussing the topic of the day's text with seventh grade students experiencing comprehension problems, who were the targets of the intervention. The teacher called for predictions about the content of the passage based on the title, if the passage was completely new, or for a review of main points covered thus far, for passages that had been begun on the previous day. The adult teacher then assigned one of the two students being taught to be the "teacher." The adult teacher and students then read the first paragraph of the day's reading silently, with the student teacher then posing a question about the paragraph, summarizing it, and either predicting upcoming content or seeking clarification if there was some confusion about the ideas in the paragraph. If the student teacher faltered, the adult teacher scaffolded these activities with prompts (e.g., "What question do you think a teacher might ask?"), instruction (e.g., "Remember, a summary is a shortened version . . ."), and modifying the activity (e.g., "If you're having a hard time thinking of a question, why don't you summarize first?"). Students were praised for their teaching and given feedback about the quality of it (e.g., "You asked that question well . . . ," "A question I would have asked would have been . . ."). Students took turns as the student teacher, with a session lasting about 30 minutes.

Throughout the intervention the students were explicitly informed that questioning, summarization, prediction, and seeking clarification were strategies that were to help them to understand better and that they should try to use the strategies when they read on their own. The students were also informed that being able to summarize passages and being able to predict the questions on upcoming tests were good ways to assess whether what was read was understood. At the end of each day, the reciprocal teaching participants read a 400–475-word assessment passage, which was followed by 10 questions over the content in the assessment passage.

Reciprocal teaching had a positive impact on all of the comprehension measures taken in the study. The instruction affected processing as it was intended to, increasing summarization skills, question-generation competencies, and monitoring, as reflected by detection of semantic anomalies (Markman, 1977). Importantly, for all six reciprocal teaching students, daily assessment performance jumped shortly after the onset of the reciprocal teaching intervention. For four of the six students in the reciprocal teaching condition, striking gains were made on a measure of standardized comprehension: 15, 17, 20, and 36 months growth for these students. In short, this study provided reason for enthusiasm about reciprocal teaching. Palincsar and Brown (1984, Study 2) also validated reciprocal teaching in a realistic classroom situation, again with middle school-age poor comprehenders.

Much more research on the method followed, summarized by Rosenshine and Meister (1994). There were consistent, striking effects on cognitive process measures, such as those tapping summarization and self-questioning skills. With respect to standardized comprehension, however, the effects were less striking, with an average effect size of 0.3 standard deviations (SDs). Reciprocal teaching was more successful when there was more direct teaching of the four comprehension strategies than when there was not, important in light of subsequent results presented in this section.

Bereiter and Bird (1985)

At the same time that Palincsar and Brown (1984) were conducting their research, Bereiter and Bird (1985) were collecting verbal protocols of reading from adults they believed to be good readers, to obtain insight about comprehension strategies that should be taught to students. Their adult, skilled readers reported a variety of comprehension strategies: restatement or rephrasing of a difficult portion of text, backtracking to seek clarification, demanding relationships (i.e., deciding to watch for causes for effects, reasons, links between topics, particular information that should be in text), formulating a problem and trying to solve it (i.e., by inference, closer examination of text, rejection of information), prediction, imagery, and recall of related information.

In a six-hour instructional study that followed the verbal protocol study, 80 seventh and eighth grade average-achieving readers benefited from being taught to use four of the strategies observed in Study 1 (restatement, backtracking, demanding relationships, and formulating a problem to solve), taught through teacher modeling and explanation. Increased use of trained strategies from pretest to post-test were clearly evidenced in verbal protocols in the modeling plus explanation condition but not in the control condition. Controls experienced a slight increase in standardized comprehension versus a 2.7 grade-equivalent increase in the modeling plus explanation condition.

G. G. Duffy et al. (1987)

Bereiter and Bird's (1985) report coincided with an important conceptualization of strategies instruction in terms of direct explanation generated by Roehler and Duffy (1984). In their model, strategies instruction begins with teacher explanations and mental modeling (i.e., showing students how to apply a strategy by thinking aloud; G. G. Duffy & Roehler, 1989). Then student practice of the strategies in the context of real reading begins. Practice is monitored by the teacher, with additional explanations and modeling provided as needed. Feedback and instruction is reduced as students become more and more independent (i.e., instruction is scaffolded). Teachers encourage transfer of strategies by going over when and where the strategies being learned might be used. Teachers cue use of the new strategies when students encountered situations where the strategies might be applied profitably, regardless of when these occasions arose during the school day (i.e., scaffolding continued throughout the school day). Cuing and prompting continues until students autonomously apply the strategies they were taught.

G. G. Duffy et al. (1987) evaluated the effects of direct explanation strategy instruction on grade 3 reading over the course of an entire academic year. All of the skills typically taught in grade 3 literacy instruction were taught as strategies. By the end of the year, students in the direct explanation condition outperformed control students on standardized measures of reading. These results had a profound effect on the reading education community, with direct explanation as G. G. Duffy et al. (1987) defined it subsequently used by many educators to implement comprehension strategies instructions in their schools.

Summary

By the late 1980s, the experimental demonstrations of strategies instructional effects on reading were well known. A main message emanating from these studies was that reading strategies could be explained and modeled to students as a beginning. If that was followed by teacher-assisted student practice of the strategies, improvement in reading, including as defined by standardized measures of reading achievement, was possible. Educators followed these research leads.

Descriptive Studies of Educator-Devised Comprehension Strategies Instruction

Beginning in 1989, Pressley and his colleagues set out to study school-based, educator-developed comprehension strategies instruction that seemed to be working (i.e., the educators could offer some evidence that their instruction was having an impact on students, such as pretest–post-test performance differences favoring strategy-instructed students compared to conventionally educated students in the same district). Their first studies were conducted at Benchmark School (Media, Pennsylvania), a school dedicated to helping elementary-age children overcome reading problems (Gaskins, Anderson, Pressley, Cunicelli, & Satlow, 1993; M. Pressley, Gaskins, Cunicelli, et al., 1991; M. Pressley, Gaskins, Wile, Cunicelli, & Sheridan, 1991). The Benchmark investigations were followed by studies in two Maryland county public school elementary-level programs dedicated to increasing the use of strategies for reading comprehension (R. Brown & Coy-Ogan, 1993; El-Dinary, Pressley, & Schuder, 1992; M. Pressley, El-Dinary, Gaskins et al., 1992; M. Pressley, El-Dinary, Stein, Marks, & Brown, 1992; M. Pressley, Schuder, SAIL Faculty and Administration, Bergman, & El-Dinary, 1992).

A variety of qualitative methods were used in this research, including ethnographies, ethnographic interviews, long-term case studies, and analyses of classroom discourse. Although the three programs studied differed in their particulars, a number of conclusions held across programs:

- Comprehension strategies instruction was long term, with teachers offering it in their classroom throughout a school year; the ideal was for it to continue across school years. Teachers recognized that the younger the children, the more that was required for students to understand the individual strategies; and the younger the children, the more that was required for them to learn how to coordinate the use strategies.
- Teachers explained and modeled effective comprehension strategies. Typically, a few, powerful strategies were emphasized; for example, prediction of upcoming information in a text, relating text content to prior knowledge, constructing internal mental images of relations described in text, use of problem-solving strategies such as rereading and analyzing context clues when meaning is unclear, and summarizing. The instruction was consistent with G. G. Duffy et al.'s (1987) conception of direct explanation, with all three of the school groups studied by the Pressley group consciously affected by the work of Duffy and his colleagues.
- The teachers coached students to use strategies, on an as-needed basis, providing hints to students about potential strategic choices they might

make. Many mini-lessons were taught about when it was appropriate to use particular strategies.

• Both teachers and students modeled use of strategies for one another, thinking aloud as they read.

• Throughout instruction, the usefulness of strategies was emphasized, with students reminded frequently about the comprehension gains that accompany strategy use. Information about when and where various strategies can be applied was discussed often. Teachers consistently modeled flexible use of strategies; students explained to one another how they used strategies to process text.

• The strategies were used as vehicles for coordinating dialogue about text (see especially Gaskins et al., 1993). In particular, when students related text to their prior knowledge, constructed summaries of text meaning, visualized relations covered in a text, and predicted what might transpire in a story, they engaged in personal interpretations of and responses to text, with these interpretations and responses varying from child to child and reading group to reading group (R. Brown & Coy-Ogan, 1993).

Such instruction came to be known as *transactional strategies instruction*, because it emphasized reader transactions with texts (Rosenblatt, 1978), interpretations constructed by readers thinking about text together (i.e., transacting; e.g., Hutchins, 1991), and teacher's and students' reactions to text affecting each other's individual thinking about it (i.e., interactions were transactional; e.g., Bell, 1968).

In a nutshell, transactional strategies instruction involves direct explanations and teacher modeling of strategies, followed by guided practice of strategies, consistent with Duffy et al.'s (1987) approach. Teacher assistance is provided on an as-needed basis (i.e., strategy instruction is "scaffolded"; Wood, Bruner, & Ross, 1976). There are lively interpretive discussions of texts, with students encouraged to interpret and respond to text as they are exposed to diverse reactions to text by their classmates.

There have been three reports of comparative studies of instruction that is transactional as defined by M. Pressley, El-Dinary, Gaskins et al. (1992): R. Brown, Pressley, Van Meter, and Schuder (1996); Collins (1991); and V. Anderson (1992; see also V. Anderson & Roit, 1993). Transactional strategies instruction produced better test scores and more interpretive readers in these studies.

Because of the prominence of reciprocal teaching in the literature, a question often posed to us is how transactional strategies instruction differs from reciprocal teaching. Both involve teaching cognitive processes for coming to terms with text. Both include modeling and explanation of strategies. Both include much discussion of what is being read as students practice strategies. Both include teacher scaffolding of instruction—the teacher monitors what is going on and offers supportive instruction on an as-needed basis. Both cultivate cooperative, supportive relations during reading. The assumption in both approaches is that participating in the instructional group and receiving the scaffolded instruction will result in long-term internalization of the cognitive processes being fostered by the group, so that the teacher is progressively less involved as instruction proceeds.

Nonetheless, there are important differences between reciprocal teaching and direct explanations-based transactional strategies instruction. The most important difference is the saliency of the teacher. Those committed to reciprocal teaching are committed to reducing quickly the adult teacher's control. The belief is that if they are to internalize decision making with respect to cognitive processes, students need to be the ones controlling the cognitive processes in the reading group. In contrast, the teacher is much more visibly in charge as part of direct explanations, although always with the goal of reducing teacher input; that is, direct explanation teaching is scaffolded, with the teacher cutting back as soon as it is possible to do so.

This difference has an important consequence in the saliency of the teacher in reciprocal teaching and direct explanation, one that, in our view, favors the direct explanation approach. Reciprocal teaching involves a rigid sequence. Each time, after a portion of text is read, the student leader of the moment poses a question for peers. The peers attempt to respond. Then, the student leader proposes a summary. Only then are the other students in the group invited into the conversation, to seek clarification by posing questions or to make predictions about upcoming text. Those who favor reciprocal teaching point out correctly that a great deal of flexible discussion of text and issues in text can occur with this framework. The flexibility of discussion certainly is greater during transactional strategies instruction, however, with the direct explanation approach in no way restricting the order of strategy execution or at any time limiting who may participate in group discussion of text. The transactional strategies instructional approach succeeds in stimulating interpretive dialogues in which strategic processes are used flexibly as interpretive vehicles, with consistently high engagement by all group members (see Gaskins et al., 1993).

Summary

Comprehension can be improved, through teaching of comprehension strategies. Hence, the experimental literature reviewed in this chapter thus far provides plenty of support for explicit teaching of decoding and comprehension. In the next section, we make the case that such teaching is what occurs in excellent elementary-level classrooms.

WHAT EXCELLENT ELEMENTARY LITERACY TEACHERS DO

In reviewing the literature on the elementary-level literacy instruction several years ago, we discovered a shocking gap in the literature. Virtually all of the opinions about effective elementary-level practice being heard in the great debates came from reading education scholars, professors of education far removed from actual classroom practice. Moreover, these professors seemed not to have conducted research aimed at determining in detail how excellent primary-level literacy teachers teach. That is, they had not systematically sought out teachers known to be excellent at beginning-literacy instruction and observed their teaching or even talked to them about it. That the voices of excellent teachers were absent from the great debates seemed strange to us because of our awareness of the literature on professional expertise (Chi, Glaser, & Farr, 1988; Ericsson & Smith, 1991; Hoffmann, 1992): Those with the most certain knowledge of what it takes to do a complex job well are the individuals who do that job well. Understanding of the nature of excellent complex competence depends greatly on detailed analysis of the knowledge and behaviors of the competent.

Thus, we set out to find out what excellent elementary teachers do to promote the literacy development of their students. Two very different methodologies are being used in this work, with all indications to date that converging outcomes are emerging from our studies. One methodology is a form of surveying. Reading supervisors from across the country nominated teachers whom they believed do an outstanding job of promoting literacy in their students. Such teachers were then asked to respond to open-ended questions about the elements of their teaching. All of the practices cited in response to these open-ended questions are then tapped on a questionnaire with several hundred quantifiable questions, such as the following:

- Which of the following concepts of print do you teach? __none, __directionality of print, __concept of a letter, __concept of a word, __punctuation, __parts of a book, __sounds are associated with print
- Do you use "big books"? (answered on a seven-point "never" to "several times a day" scale)
- After a story, do you ask students "comprehension questions"? (answered on a seven-point "not at all" to "all stories" scale)
- What percentage of the material read by your students is outstanding children's literature? . . . written at a "controlled" reading level? . . . written to provide practice in phonetic elements and/or patterns? . . . high interest, low vocabulary materials? (Respondents provided numerical estimate for each.)

The second methodology is ethnographic observation of a small sample of outstanding and more typical teachers (again, as nominated by supervisors, but in this case, also as confirmed by observation) over most of a school year. We are conducting this work both at the primary and grade 5 levels. The research is far enough along at this point to permit some conclusions with confidence.

Primary-Grades Teaching

At the primary level, the surveys were completed by 23 kindergarten, 34 grade 1 teachers, and 26 grade 2 teachers (M. Pressley, Rankin, & Yokoi, 1996). Rankin and Pressley (in preparation) also collected the responses of 34 primary-level special educators to the quantitative items answered in M. Pressley et al. (1996). The results unambiguously supported a balanced approach to primary literacy instruction for all students regardless of ability level, combining whole language elements and explicit teaching of skills, consistent with what is an increasingly common recommendation from well-informed observers of elementary schools (e.g., Adams, 1990; Delpit, 1986; G. G. Duffy, 1991; Fisher & Hiebert, 1990; McCaslin, 1989; M. Pressley, 1994; Stahl et al., 1994).

The many instructional practices reported by the 89 regular education teachers and 34 special education teacher in this study are summarized in Figure 1. The school days in these classrooms were reported to be filled with all types of reading and writing, as the whole language advocates would have it. There is also explicit teaching of letter-level and decoding skills, with these emphasized more for weaker readers than average-achieving and outstanding readers. We emphasize, however, that both the special education and regular education teachers reported, for the most part, they offered instruction to weaker readers that was very similar to the instruction offered to stronger readers.

There were many reasons for confidence in the survey data. One was the lack of variability in the opinions offered. Another was that the data were orderly in ways that would be expected (Harris & Sipay, 1990) if the teachers were being honest in their reports. Thus, teachers who claimed to be exclusively whole langauge, in fact, were less likely to endorse practices not endorsed by pure whole language theorists, such as out-of-context decoding instruction. Also, a number of instructional practices reportedly decreased that should decrease between kindergarten and grade 2 (e.g., letter-level skills), and a number of instructional practices reportedly increased that should increase between kindergarten and grade 2 (e.g., spelling).

Nonetheless, such survey data are somewhat removed from actual teaching. Therefore, Wharton-McDonald, Pressley, and Mistretta (1996) followed up the surveys with an ethnographic investigation based on observations and interviews. Nine teachers were studied over a six-month period. The participants had been nominated by their supervisors as either outstanding

General Characteristics of the Learning Environments

Teacher creates a literate environment in the classroom, including in-class library, displays of student work, chart stories/poems displayed, posting word lists

Classroom rich with stories: stories read, reread, and told; audiotaped stories

Learning centers: listening, reading, and writing centers

Teacher identifies with language experience/whole language approach, at least somewhat

General Teaching Processes

Overt teacher modeling of literacy skills and strategies as well as modeling of positive attitudes toward literacy

Daily practice of reading and writing with limited practice of skills in isolation

Repetition of unmastered skills, including of phonics, letter recognition, and spelling (often in the context of other reading and writing activities)

Limited use of workbooks and worksheets

Cooperative grouping used

Different approaches to instructional grouping used, with more whole-group than small-group instruction, more small-group than individual instruction, and more individual instruction than individual seatwork

Limited use of ability grouping and round robin reading

Monitoring of student needs, with mini-lessons as needed, reteaching as needed

Concern with individual achievement and participation: leadership opportunities, students permitted to progress at their own pace, assessment of student learning styles and adjustment of teaching according to learning style, individually guided reading instruction, individually guided writing instruction

Literacy instruction integrated with the rest of the curriculum

Extension experiences (e.g., arts and crafts, illustration, games)

Teaching of Reading

What Is Taught:

Teaching of skills prerequisite to reading (e.g., auditory and visual discrimination, attending and listening skills), both in the context of other reading and writing activities and in isolation (e.g., with games)

Teaching concepts of print (e.g., concept of a word, parts of a book)

Teaching letter recognition, both in the context of other reading and writing activities and in isolation

Songs conveying literacy knowledge (e.g., The Alphabet Song)

Teaching the alphabetic principle, both in the context of other reading and writing activities and in isolation (e.g., with games)

Activities focusing on the sounds of words

Teaching of letter–sound associations, both in the context of other reading and writing activities and in isolation

FIGURE 1

Classroom characteristics and instructional practices often reported by supervisor-nominated effective primary literacy teachers

Limited use of the letter of the day or week approach

Limited copying and tracing of letters

Teaching punctuation, mostly in the context of other reading and writing activities

Teaching decoding strategies, including using context and picture clues as well as sounding out words using letter–sound knowledge

Teaching phonics, in the context of other reading and writing activities, with respect to invented spellings, and sometimes using decontextualized approaches (e.g., worksheets, drills)

Developing new vocabulary and sight vocabulary, often in the context of other reading and writing

Invented spelling encouraged

Teaching spelling, including with spelling tests

Teaching reading as meaning making

Teaching text elements (e.g., cause–effect relations, theme–main idea, character analysis)

Teaching comprehension strategies, especially prediction and visualization

Teaching critical thinking skills, including brainstorming, categorization, and recalling details

Development of background knowledge before reading stories, especially through prereading discussion and reading of related books

Types of Reading:

Students reading along with teacher

Echo and choral reading

Sharing reading (besides big book reading)

Students reading aloud with others

Daily silent reading daily (USSR, uninterrupted sustained, silent reading; DEAR, drop everything and read)

Students rereading books, stories

Discussion of stories and literature read

Student book sharing (e.g., via book reports)

Teacher involving parents in reading instruction by sending books home and asking parents to listen to the child read

Reading homework

What Is Read:

Reading outstanding children's literature

Sharing reading of big books

At least some reading of chart poems and stories

Reading picture, patterned, and predictable books

Limited reading of basals, although highly variable depending on the teacher

Limited reading of chapter books, poems, and expository materials

Limited reading of materials at a controlled reading level

More reading of instructional level than either easy or frustration level materials

FIGURE 1 *(Continued)*

Reading aloud by students, especially stories written by them and classmates, with these readings most frequently to peers or the teacher

Author studies, with coverage of illustrators as well

Teaching Writing

Types of Writing:

Student story, book, and journal writing, with teachers responding to writing

Writing in response to pictures, wordless picture books, and stories read

Student dictations of stories (sometimes group dictations) to teacher as scribe

Shared writing

Students asked to write at home

Infrequent copying of other people's writing

Teaching of the Writing Process:

Writer's workshop in some classrooms

Teaching planning, drafting, and revising as part of writing

Publishing student writing

Use of computers during writing instruction, although not yet in the majority of classrooms

Explicitness or Extensiveness of Instruction as a Function of Reader Ability

Same elements of reading and writing instruction for good versus weaker readers

More explicit or extensive teaching of some prereading, letter-, and word-level skills with weaker readers

More guided reading and writing instruction and individualized instruction with weaker compared to good readers

Making Literacy and Literacy Instruction Motivating

Teachers attempting to motivate literacy by reducing risks for attempting literate activities, positive feedback, setting an exciting mood, encouraging students to believe they can be readers and writers, and so on.

Accountability

Checking comprehension, including questions following a reading and student retelling of stories heard or read

Using sentence strips or illustrations to reconstruct poems, stories heard or read

Frequently monitoring student progress in literacy

Writing portfolios and, to a lesser extent, reading portfolios

Holding regular conferences with parents and communications to home

FIGURE 1 (*Continued*)

in promoting literacy achievement or as consistent with typical grade 1 instruction in the district.

One important conclusion of this study was that the very best grade 1 classrooms (three of the nine) included most of the elements summarized in Figure 1. But the observations permitted a much more complete understanding of the teaching that went on. One striking contrast between the outstanding classrooms versus the typical ones (i.e., the three classrooms in which students were least engaged and made least progress) was the intensity of the literacy instruction, with school days in the outstanding classrooms definitely filled with high-quality reading and writing experiences. In contrast, more typical classrooms have large portions of time that is not nearly as intense or literacy relevant. For example, in one typical classroom, there was a great deal of copying, something almost never observed in the classrooms of outstanding teachers. In another, much of the literacy instruction was devoted to communication activities that occur in a sharing circle, with much of the discussion during this sharing not related to what the children were reading or other academic content. In general, less real reading and writing took place in the more typical compared to the outstanding classrooms.

More than that, however, the engagement of students was very high in outstanding classrooms. Wharton-McDonald et al. (1996) noted every few minutes the percentage of students who seemed to be attentive and gainfully involved. In outstanding classrooms, this was typically most or all students and never less than half of them. In contrast, inattention was much more commonly observed in the more typical classrooms.

Several characteristics of outstanding classrooms were detected through observations and face-to-face interviews that did not come through in the survey studies. A great deal of connection in the instruction was offered by the outstanding teachers, with students writing about what they had read, and the outstanding teachers often related concepts encountered in a lesson to ones encountered earlier in the year. Disjointedness was much more common in the more typical classrooms than in the outstanding classrooms. The outstanding teachers also are terrific managers. The behavior management of outstanding teachers was superb and always positively toned. Moreover, their management of resources was striking. Thus, when resource teachers were available to an outstanding teacher, the resource teacher's time was well spent. In contrast, resource teachers often were underused by the more typical teachers.

We believe that the conclusions emerging from this work, ones that converge across studies despite the use of very different methods, are important. This work has produced the most complete descriptions ever of outstanding primary instruction. In doing so, a real vote of confidence was generated for balanced primary-level literacy instruction, compared either to whole language or skills-first approaches. As this project continues at the grade 5 level, additional support for a balanced approach is emerging from the analyses.

Grade 5 Instruction

The M. Pressley, Yokoi, Rankin, Wharton-McDonald, and Mistretta (in press) group has conducted a national survey similar to the survey at the primary levels that was just discussed. A total of 62 fifth grade teachers responded to it, with each of the respondents nominated by supervisors as outstanding in promoting literacy in their students. As at the primary level, the instruction reported is complex but orderly—and extremely balanced with respect to a literature emphasis but also explicit instruction of critical skills. The elements of instruction reported by the teachers are summarized in Figure 2.

The teaching reported by this sample of nominated-outstanding grade 5 teachers is a balance of a variety of important language arts and instructional perspectives, rather than adherence to any one approach. They reported that their students learn both by doing things literate, consistent with holistic approaches, such as whole language, and through explicit instruction of the components of literacy (e.g., word-level skills), consistent more with skills-oriented approaches. Instruction and reading and writing experiences were aimed at developing many strategies and procedural competencies, diverse conceptual knowledge, and supportive motivational beliefs that are articulated during constructively responsive reading described earlier in this chapter.

The teachers claimed to instruct a long list of comprehension and critical-thinking strategies. Most of these strategies derived from and were validated in studies reviewed earlier in this chapter, although many of them can also be construed (see M. Pressley, El-Dinary, Gaskins et al., 1992) as broadly consistent with the reader response approaches favored by whole language (Beach & Hynds, 1991; Rosenblatt, 1978). The teachers in this sample reported extensive direct teaching of comprehension and critical thinking processes through modeling such strategies, consistent with the direct explanation models of strategies instruction discussed earlier (e.g., G. G. Duffy, Roehler, & Herrmann, 1988; Pearson & Dole, 1987). Nothing in these data suggests that the teachers felt such competencies would develop as a natural consequence of extensive reading and writing, a key assumption of extreme whole language advocates.

We were impressed with the rich set of social connections reported as supporting literacy acquisition. Students in these classrooms were portrayed as frequently reading with their teachers, peers, younger children, and parents. There were many small-group meetings, with the membership in these groups fluid and, thus, students regularly read and interacted with others who vary in ability. That is, readers in these classrooms often were not reading alone, but rather going solo in the context of cooperative, supportive relations that could provide help as needed. In making this point, however, we also point out that the students in these teachers' classrooms also did a good deal of independent reading—during free reading, as part of reading assigned texts, and at home. Typically, they also spent part of each day in teacher-led whole-group instruction.

An important concern in any classroom is with students experiencing difficulties. The nominated-outstanding teachers reported that classroom life was not much different for weaker readers compared to normally achiev-

General Characteristics of the Learning Environment

Classroom library

Public library books important

Learning centers

Commercially and teacher-produced taped readings

Impact of news sources on instruction (*Scholastic News*, radio/TV news, newspapers)

General Teaching Processes

Daily reading and writing

Overt teacher modeling of literacy skills and strategies

Different approaches to instructional grouping used, with whole group and cooperative grouping frequent; also small groups, changing frequently in composition; one-to-one instruction

Little decontextualized reading (e.g., of words on flashcards)

Literacy instruction integrated with the rest of the curriculum

Teaching of Reading

What Is Taught:

Teaching common decoding strategies

Developing new vocabulary (e.g., from texts students are reading, publishers' lists)

Teaching students how to determine meaning of words from context

Teaching spelling, including with spelling tests (from spelling texts, published spelling lists, content area units)

Teaching students to respond to literature

Teaching comprehension strategies: predicting upcoming content, thinking about what is known about a topic before reading a piece about the topic, thinking about the purpose for reading before beginning to read, asking questions about text, summarizing, asking an adult or peer for help when parts of a text do not make sense, analyzing stories for their story grammar elements (i.e., for character information, setting; problems and attempted solutions, resolution), relating text content to prior knowledge, finding the main idea and being able to support it with details, attempting to infer important details not in the text, mental imagery; seeking clarification when it seems that the text does not make sense, looking for and making sense of similes, metaphors, and analogies, critically evaluating text content, rereading even if the text made sense the first time

Teaching critical thinking skills: possibility of multiple answers to a question or problem, brainstorming, deciding between options, separating facts from opinions, identifying propaganda

Reviewing comprehension and critical thinking skills was reported as common, typically driven by student need

Development of background knowledge: word webs, story maps, with pictures or videos

In-class enrichment activities weekly

Types of Reading:

Daily silent reading

Many different types of oral reading, from individual reading to class to partner reading to reading in a small group

FIGURE 2

Classroom characteristics and instructional practices often reported by supervisor-nominated effective grade 5 literacy teachers

Choral reading is rare

Teachers reading to students, typically several times a week

What Is Read:

Mostly literature (children's classics, trade books, novels, short stories, nonfiction books, plays, poems)

Students largely determine for themselves what they read (45% of reading is self-selected)

Relatively little use of basals

Teaching Writing

Types of Writing:

Creative writing

Expositions

Single paragraphs

Multiple-paragraph compositions

Teaching the Writing Process:

Teaching planning, drafting, and revising as part of writing

Teaching mechanics on the basis of student need and sometimes on basis of set curriculum

Sharing student writing, through publication or read-alouds

Explicitness or Extensiveness of Instruction as a Function of Reader Ability

Same elements of reading and writing instruction for good versus weaker readers

More explicit or extensive teaching of decoding strategies

More use of audiotaped readings with weaker students

More guided reading and writing instruction and individualized instruction with weaker compared to good readers

Weaker students receive more peer tutoring

Weaker students taught more to seek help when having difficulties

Making Literacy and Literacy Instruction Motivating

Teachers attempting to stimulate these beliefs and attitudes often: curiosity, willingness to take reasonable risks, pride in persistence and trying hard, belief that some texts require hard work to make sense of them, belief that good writing requires substantial effort

Teachers praising students daily for reading and writing success

Teachers regularly reading student writing to the class

Teachers attempting to match literacy instruction to students' abilities to assure success

Using some games involving reading skills

Accountability

Less formal assessments (responding to comprehension questions, response journals) more common than formal assessments (standardized tests, district-produced tests)

Responding to literature most common of all written assessments (journal essays and comments, illustrations of texts, story maps)

Vocabulary, spelling, writing mechanics, and grammar tests

Writing and reading portfolios

FIGURE 2 (*Continued*)

ing readers. The differences reported here were generally in the direction of providing more intensive and individualized instruction, particularly with respect to lower-order skills, such as decoding. That is, the dumbed-down, slow-it-down approach often taken with students experiencing academic difficulties (e.g., R. L. Allington, 1991, 1994) is not what the teachers in this sample claimed to do.

Summary

Excellent elementary-level reading instruction is extremely complicated, which is sensible given how complicated capable reading is. We are struck at how well informed the teaching of excellent teachers is, with this instruction representing an amalgamation of the best of whole language and more research-based, direct explanation models. There is direct teaching of reading, including reading strategies, complemented by social support for reading. See Guthrie, Schafer, Wang, and Afflerbach (1995) for a complementary analysis based on a set of national data documenting that teaching, strategic competence, and social support of literacy are potent variables in children's literacy.

As we reflect on the excellent teaching, however, we also reflect not only on the more typical teaching we have observed, systematically now at grade 1 in the ethnographic study conducted by Wharton-McDonald et al. (1996) but also informally in our many interactions with elementary schools. There is a real need to think hard about how to encourage more teachers to be like outstanding teachers. In some cases, it will probably come naturally; for instance, one of our best grade 1 teachers in the ethnographic study was a second year teacher. More typically, it will take awhile; for instance, even good, experienced teachers needed a year or two of teaching within the transactional strategies instruction model to feel comfortable teaching students to read strategically. The envisionment of good teaching emerging from the work reported in the latter half of this chapter has high potential for informing the educator community about what excellent teaching looks like when it happens, and this is an important first step in developing new approaches to teacher education and development that can permit more teachers to be like the best teachers.

Consistent with reading as constructive responsivity, outstanding teachers teach students to use strategies to respond to ideas in text. They also teach problem-solving strategies, for dealing with unknown words encountered in text and challenging text. Concern that students read materials that are worthwhile should promote development of worthwhile knowledge. The development of meta-cognition about reading skills is encouraged through a great deal of teacher-supported practice of reading and discussion of reading between teachers and students as well as between students and students. Outstanding teachers consider it extremely important to motivate students to do things literate. In short, these teachers are trying to get their students off to a good start in becoming literate, but it is only a start.

POSTSCRIPT FOR THE ELEMENTARY YEARS

Enormous progress has been made in understanding reading and excellent contemporary elementary reading instruction. There is a much clearer vision of the active reading of excellent readers—how it is strategic, involves massive monitoring, depends on rich conceptual knowledge, and is highly evaluative. Much has been learned about how literacy begins early in life and how life in the preschool years can support the long-term development of literacy. The criticality of phonemic awareness and explicit decoding instruction are well understood. Detailed analyses have focused on classrooms that teach active articulation of strategies, meta-cognition, and conceptual knowledge, classrooms in which children learn to be critically interpretive readers. We understand excellent elementary literacy instruction to be a balancing act, one in which skills are taught in an environment rich in whole language experiences.

Not surprising, elementary instruction is working well for some students. By the end of the elementary years, good readers are more cognitively and meta-cognitively sophisticated than weaker readers; good readers know more; they also have more positive motivational beliefs (Ehrlich, Kurtz-Costes, & Loridant, 1993). Even so, there are very few, if any, fully constructively responsive readers in middle school or high school. Many students read slowly and with low comprehension (e.g., Rankin, 1993).

From the perspectives developed in this chapter, the best windows on reading by children and adolescents are the verbal protocols of reading conducted with elementary, middle school, and secondary students. Although the data base is not large, none of the studies involving such students has described reading that looks anything like the active reading when adult professionals are reading materials in their domains of expertise. For example, Meyers, Lytle, Palladino, Devenpeck, and Green (1990) observed that students in grades 5 and 6 signaled their understanding as they read, elaborated, and reasoned about text meaning (i.e., constructed hypotheses about meaning and tested the hypotheses, revising them as needed). Even so, Meyers et al.'s (1990) subjects rarely monitored their understanding, did not responsively evaluate what they read, nor did they analyze the structural or rhetorical characteristics of the text. Kucan (1993) used the same scoring scheme as Meyers et al. (1990). With grade 6 students, she observed a similar pattern of outcomes as Meyers et al. (1990), except that her subjects also monitored their understanding. Phillips's (1988) grade 6 good readers considered alternative interpretations of text, confirmed previous interpretations of text during subsequent reading, monitored when emerging interpretations conflicted with prior knowledge or previous interpretations, shifted focus when reading, and empathized with character perspectives in a story. In short, what was observed in these studies of elementary-level students was a small subset of the responses that maximally constructively responsive readers make when they encounter text. Much development remains.

And, what about weaker readers? One certainty at this point is that they are helped by one-to-one tutoring (Slavin, Karweit, & Wasik, 1994). Beyond that, not much progress has been made in understanding how to help the most challenged of readers. That is a discouraging state of affairs, one that we hope motivates much research.

Just as discouraging, however, is what we perceive awaiting the graduates of elementary schools when they advance to high school. Our impression, based on a reading of the literature and many experiences with secondary school personnel, is that many high school teachers continue to believe that students should have learned how to read during the elementary years, subscribe to the outdated model of literacy development described in the first paragraph of this chapter—that literacy should be a fait accompli by the end of the elementary years. This is even though very few students can comprehend and work with the types of texts grade 12 students are expected to read and understand (e.g., Williams, Reese, Campbell, Mazzeo, & Phillips, 1995).

The transformation of the elementary-level literacy curriculum will make much less difference than it might if there is no transformation of secondary schooling so that American high schools more become places where students learn how to learn from texts and think about the messages in text. Yes, the development of content knowledge is important, but it is not enough for the citizens of the 21st century, who must be lifelong learners, which includes being lifelong readers who can make sense of demanding texts.

Teaching the high school content that is important in the 1990s seems to us like serving students meals that are very good for them. No one could argue with doing that. But no one would also argue that, in the long run, students would be better off knowing how to prepare their own healthy meals. Knowing how to cook is analogous to knowing how to read well enough to get the most out of text. If students are to learn how to read like constructively responsive readers, there needs to be as much serious restructuring of secondary schools with respect to literacy teaching as has occurred at the elementary level—or maybe even more. We are struck when we visit high schools that the cafeteria is always a visibly salient facility and the kitchen completely out of sight of the students. Maybe we should open up the kitchen more, so that students see how meals are prepared. Somewhat ironic, cooking is a frequent enrichment activity related to content learning in elementary schools. Just as skillets are sizzling as part of content enrichment in elementary schools, so is literacy instruction, with the likelihood that the sizzle during reading and writing will, if anything, increase in intensity in elementary schools. It is time to get cooking in the high schools, to have high schools that are as active in the development of literacy competencies as contemporary elementary schools. Elementary literacy researchers and elementary educators are doing their part to create a nation of readers, but elementary education can be only a beginning.

References

Adams, M. J. (1990). *Beginning to read*. Cambridge, MA: Harvard University Press.

Allen, L., Cipielewski, J., & Stanovich, K. E. (1992). Multiple indicators of children's reading habits and attitudes: Construct validity and cognitive correlates. *Journal of Educational Psychology, 84*, 489–503.

Allington, R. L. (1977). If they don't read much, how they ever gonna get good? *Journal of Reading, 21*, 57–61.

Allington, R. L. (1991). The legacy of "Slow it down and make it more concrete." In J. Zutell & S. McCormick (Eds.), *Learner factors/teacher factors: Issues in literacy research and instruction: Fortieth yearbook of the National Reading Conference* (pp. 19–29). Chicago: National Reading Conference.

Allington, R. L. (1994). What's special about special programs for children who find learning to read difficult? *Journal of Reading Behavior, 26*, 95–115.

Anderson, D. R., & Collins, P. A. (1988). *The impact on children's education: Television's influence on cognitive development* (Office of Research Working Paper No. 2). Washington, DC: U.S. Department of Education, Office of Educational Research and Improvement.

Anderson, R. C., Hiebert, E. H., Scott, J. A., & Wilkinson, I. A. G. (1985). *Becoming a nation of readers*. Washington, DC: National Institute of Education.

Anderson, R. C., & Ortony, A. (1975). On putting apples into bottles: A problem of polysemy. *Cognitive Psychology, 7*, 167–180.

Anderson, V. (1992). A teacher development project in transactional strategy instruction for teachers of severely reading-disabled adolescents. *Teaching & Teacher Education, 8*, 391–403.

Anderson, V., & Roit, M. (1993). Planning and implementing collaborative strategy instruction for delayed readers in grades 6–10. *Elementary School Journal, 94*, 121–137.

Applebee, A. N., & Langer, J. A. (1983). Instructional scaffolding: Reading and writing as natural language activities. *Language Arts, 60*, 168–175.

Armbruster, B. B., Anderson, T. H., & Ostertag, J. (1987). Does text structure/summarization instruction facilitate learning from expository text? *Reading Research Quarterly, 22*, 331–346.

Arnold, D. H., Lonigan, C. J., Whitehurst, G. J., & Epstein, J. N. (1994). Accelerating language development through picture book reading: Replication and extension to a videotape training format. *Journal of Educational Psychology, 86*, 235–243.

Ball, E. W., & Blachman, B. A. (1988). Phoneme segmentation training: Effect on reading readiness. *Annals of Dyslexia, 38*, 203–225.

Ball, E. W., & Blachman, B. A. (1991). Does phoneme segmentation training in kindergarten make a difference in early word recognition and developmental spelling? *Reading Research Quarterly, 26*, 49–66.

Ball, S., & Bogatz, G. A. (1970). *The first year of "Sesame Street": An evaluation*. Princeton, NJ: Educational Testing Service.

Barnhart, J. E. (1991). Criterion-related validity of interpretations of children's performance on emergent literacy tasks. *Journal of Reading Behavior, 23*, 425–444.

Baron, J. (1977). Mechanisms for pronouncing printed words: Use and acquisition. In D. LaBerge & S. J. Samuels (Eds.), *Basic processes in reading: Perception and comprehension* (pp. 175–216). Hillsdale, NJ: Erlbaum.

Baron, J. (1985). *Rationality and intelligence*. Cambridge, England: Cambridge University Press.

Barr, R. C. (1974–1975). The effect of instruction on pupil reading strategies. *Reading Research Quarterly*, 10, 555–582.

Barr, R. C. (1984). Beginning reading instruction: From debate to reformation. In P. D. Pearson (Ed.), *Handbook of reading research* (pp. 545–581). New York: Longman.

Beach, R., & Hynds, S. (1991). Research on response to literature. In R. Barr, M. L. Kamil, P. B. Mosenthal, & P. D. Pearson (Eds.), *Handbook of reading research*: (Vol. 2, pp. 453–489). New York: Longman.

Bean, T. W., & Steenwyk, F. L. (1984). The effect of three forms of summarization instruction on sixth graders' summary writing and comprehension. *Journal of Reading Behavior*, 16, 297–306.

Bell, R. Q. (1968). A reinterpretation of the direction of effects in studies of socialization. *Psychological Review*, 75, 81–95.

Bereiter, C., & Bird, M. (1985). Use of thinking aloud in identification and teaching of reading comprehension strategies. *Cognition and Instruction*, 2, 131–156.

Berkowitz, S. J. (1986). Effects of instruction in text organization on sixth-grade students' memory for expository reading. *Reading Research Quarterly*, 21, 161–178.

Bertelson, P., & De Gelder, B. (1989). Learning about reading from illiterates. In A. M. Galaburda (Ed.), *From reading to neurons* (pp. 1–23). Cambridge, MA: MIT Press.

Blachman, B. A. (1991). Phonological awareness: Implications for prereading and early reading instruction. In S. A. Brady & D. P. Shankweiler (Eds.), *Phonological processes in literacy: A tribute to Isabelle Y. Liberman* (pp. 29–36). Hillsdale, NJ: Erlbaum.

Bond, G. L., & Dykstra, R. (1967). The cooperative research program in first-grade reading instruction. *Reading Research Quarterly*, 2, 5–142.

Bradley, L. (1989). Predicting learning disabilities. In J. Dumont & H. Nakken (Eds.), *Learning disabilities: Vol. 2. Cognitive, social, and remedial aspects* (pp. 1–18). Amsterdam: Swets Publishing.

Bradley, L., & Bryant, P. E. (1983). Categorizing sounds and learning to read—a causal connection. *Nature (London)*, 301, 419–421.

Bradley, L., & Bryant, P. (1991). Phonological skills before and after learning to read. In S. A. Brady & D. P. Shankweiler (Eds.), *Phonological processes in literacy: A tribute to Isabelle Y. Liberman* (pp. 37–45). Hillsdale, NJ: Erlbaum & Associates.

Brown, A. L., Bransford, J. D., Ferrara, R. A., & Campione, J. C. (1983). Learning, remembering, and understanding. In J. H. Flavell & E. M. Markman (Eds.), *Handbook of child psychology: Vol. 3. Cognitive development* (pp. 77–166). New York: Wiley.

Brown, A. L., & Day, J. D. (1983). Macrorules for summarizing texts: The development of expertise. *Journal of Verbal Learning and Verbal Behavior*, 22, 1–14.

Brown, A. L., Day, J. D., & Jones, R. S. (1983). The development of plans for summarizing texts. *Child Development*, 54, 968–979.

Brown, R., & Coy-Ogan, L. (1993). The evolution of transactional strategies instruction in one teacher's classroom. *Elementary School Journal*, 94, 221–233.

Brown, R., Pressley, M., Van Meter, P., & Schuder, T. (1996). A quasi-experimental validation of transactional strategies instruction with low-achieving second grade readers. *Journal of Educational Psychology*, 88, 18–37.

Bruck, M. (1992). Persistence of dyslexics' phonological awareness deficits. *Developmental Psychology*, 28, 874–886.

Bruck, M., & Treiman, R. (1990). Phonological awareness and spelling in normal children and dyslexics: The case of initial consonant clusters. *Journal of Experimental Child Psychology*, 50, 156–178.

Bruck, M., & Treiman, R. (1992). Learning to pronounce words: The limits of analogies. *Reading Research Quarterly*, 27, 374–398.

Bus, A. G., & van IJzendoorn, M. H. (1988). Mother-child interactions, attachment, and emergent literacy: A cross-sectional study. *Child Development*, 59, 1262–1272.

Bus, A. G., van IJzendoorn, M. H., & Pellegrini, A. D. (1995). Joint book reading makes for success in learning to read: A meta-analysis on intergenerational transmission of literacy. *Review of Educational Research*, 65, 1–21.

Byrne, B., & Fielding-Barnsley, R. (1993). Evaluation of a program to teach phonemic awareness to young children: A 1-year followup. *Journal of Educational Psychology*, 85, 104–111.

Carpenter, P. A., Miyake, A., & Just, M. A. (1994). Working memory constraints in comprehension: Evidence from individual differences, aphasia, and aging. In M. A. Gernsbacher (Ed.), *Handbook of psycholinguistics* (pp. 1075–1122). San Diego, CA: Academic Press.

Carver, R. P. (1990). *Reading rate: A review of research and theory*. San Diego, CA: Academic Press.

Castle, J. M., Riach, J., & Nicholson, T. (1994). Getting off to a better start in reading and spelling: The effects of phonemic awareness instruction within a whole language program. *Journal of Educational Psychology*, 86, 350–359.

Catts, H. (1989). Defining dyslexia as a developmental language disorder. *Annals of Dyslexia*, 39, 50–64.

Chall, J. S. (1967). *Learning to read: The great debate*. New York: McGraw-Hill.

Chi, M. T. H., Glaser, R., & Farr, M. J. (Eds.). (1988). *The nature of expertise*. Hillsdale, NJ: Erlbaum.

Chomsky, N. (1965). *Aspects of the theory of syntax*. Cambridge, MA: MIT Press.

Cipielewski, J., & Stanovich, K. E. (1992). Predicting growth in reading ability from children's exposure to print. *Journal of Experimental Child Psychology*, 54, 74–89.

Clarke, L. K. (1988). Invented versus traditional spelling in first graders' writings: Effects on learning to spell and read. *Research in the Teaching of English*, 22, 281–309.

Clymer, T. (1963). The utility of phonic generalizations in the primary grades. *Reading Teacher*, 16, 252–258.

Cochran-Smith, M. (1984). *The making of a reader*. Norwood, NJ: Ablex.

Collins, C. (1991). Reading instruction that increases thinking abilities. *Journal of Reading*, 34, 510–516.

Conners, C. K. (1971). Cortical visual evoked response in children with learning disorders. *Psychophysiology*, 7, 418–428.

Cornell, E. H., Sénéchal, M., & Broda, L. S. (1988). Recall of picture books by 3-year-old children: Testing and repetition effects in joint reading activities. *Journal of Educational Psychology*, 80, 537–542.

Crain-Thoreson, C., & Dale, P. S. (1992). Do early talkers become early readers? Linguistic precocity, preschool language, and emergent literacy. *Developmental Psychology*, 28, 421–429.

Cunningham, A. E. (1990). Explicit versus implicit instruction in phonemic awareness. *Journal of Experimental Child Psychology*, 50, 429–444.

Cunningham, A. E., & Stanovich, K. E. (1990). Assessing print exposure and orthographic processing skill in children: A quick measure of reading experience. *Journal of Educational Psychology*, 82, 733–740.

Cunningham, A. E., & Stanovich, K. E. (1991). Tracking the unique effects of print exposure in children: Associations with vocabulary, general knowledge, and spelling. *Journal of Educational Psychology*, 83, 264–274.

Dahl, K. L., & Freppon, P. A. (1995). A comparison of innercity children's interpretations of reading and writing instruction in the early grades in skills-based and whole language classrooms. *Reading Research Quarterly*, 30, 50–74.

Delpit, L. D. (1986). The silenced dialogue: Power and pedagogy in educating other people's children. *Harvard Educational Review*, 58, 280–298.

Dempster, F. N. (1985). Short-term memory development in childhood and adolescence. In C. J. Brainerd & M. Pressley (Eds.), *Basic processes in memory development: Progress in cognitive development research* (pp. 209–248). New York: Springer-Verlag.

Duffy, F. H., & McAnulty, G. (1990). Neuropsychological heterogeneity and the definition of dyslexia: Preliminary evidence for plasticity. *Neuropsychologica*, 28, 96–103.

Duffy, G. G. (1991). What counts in teacher education? Dilemmas in educating empowered teachers. In J. Zutell & S. McCormick (Eds.), *Learner factors/teacher factors: Issues in literacy research and instruction: Fortieth yearbook of the National Reading Conference* (pp. 1–18). Chicago: National Reading Conference.

Duffy, G. G., & Roehler, L. R. (1989). Why strategy instruction is so difficult and what we need to do about it. In C. B. McCormick, G. Miller, & M. Pressley (Eds.), *Cognitive strategy research: From basic research to educational applications* (pp. 133–154). New York: Springer-Verlag.

Duffy, G. G., Roehler, L., & Herrmann, G. (1988). Modeling mental processes helps poor readers become strategic readers. *Reading Teacher, 41*, 762–767.

Duffy, G. G., Roehler, L. R., Sivan, E., Rackliffe, G., Book, C., Meloth, M., Vavrus, L. G., Wesselman, R., Putnam, J., & Bassiri, D. (1987). Effects of explaining the reasoning associated with using reading strategies. *Reading Research Quarterly, 22*, 347–368.

Durkin, D. (1978–1979). What classroom observations reveal about reading comprehension instruction. *Reading Research Quarterly, 15*, 481–533.

Ehri, L. C. (1980). The development of orthographic images. In U. Frith (Ed.), *Cognitive processes in spelling* (pp. 311–338). London: Academic Press.

Ehri, L. C. (1984). How orthography alters spoken language competencies in children learning to read and spell. In J. Downing & R. Valtin (Eds.), *Language awareness and learning to read* (pp. 119–147). New York: Springer-Verlag.

Ehri, L. C. (1987). Learning to read and spell words. *Journal of Reading Behavior, 19*, 5–31.

Ehri, L. C. (1991). Development of the ability to read words. In R. Barr, M. L. Kamil, P. B. Mosenthal, & P. D. Pearson (Eds.), *Handbook of reading research* (Vol. 2, pp. 383–417). New York: Longman.

Ehri, L. C. (1992). Reconceptualizing the development of sight word reading and its relationship to recoding. In P. B. Gough, L. C. Ehri, & R. Treiman (Eds.), *Reading acquisition* (pp. 107–143). Hillsdale, NJ: Erlbaum.

Ehri, L. C., & Robbins, C. (1992). Beginners need some decoding skill to read words by analogy. *Reading Research Quarterly, 27*, 12–27.

Ehri, L. C., & Wilce, L. S. (1987). Does learning to spell help beginning readers to learn whole words? *Reading Research Quarterly, 22*, 47–65.

Ehrlich, M.-F., Kurtz-Costes, B., & Loridant, C. (1993). Cognitive and motivational determinants of reading comprehension in good and poor readers. *Journal of Reading Behavior, 25*, 365–381.

El-Dinary, P. B., Pressley, M., & Schuder, T. (1992). Becoming a strategies teacher: An observational and interview study of three teachers learning transactional strategies instruction. In C. Kinzer & D. Leu (Eds.), *Literacy research, theory, and practice: Views from many perspectives. Forty-first Yearbook of the National Reading Conference* (pp. 453–462). Chicago: National Reading Conference.

Elley, W. B. (1989). Vocabulary acquisition from listening to stories. *Reading Research Quarterly, 24*, 174–187.

Ericsson, K. A., & Smith, J. (Eds.). (1991). *Toward a general theory of expertise*. Cambridge, England: Cambridge University Press.

Feitelson, D. (1988). *Facts and fads in beginning reading*. Norwood, NJ: Ablex.

Feitelson, D., Kita, B., & Goldstein, Z. (1986). Effects of listening to series stories on first graders' comprehension and use of language. *Research in the Teaching of English, 20*, 339–356.

Fisher, C. W., & Hiebert, E. H. (1990). Characteristics of tasks in two approaches to literacy instruction. *Elementary School Journal, 91*, 3–18.

Fitzgerald, J. (1995). English-as-a-second-language learners' cognitive reading processes: A review of research in the United States. *Review of Educational Research, 65*, 145–190.

Flavell, J. R., Miller, P., & Miller, S. (1993). *Cognitive development* (3rd ed.). Englewood Cliffs, NJ: Prentice-Hall.

Fletcher, J. M., Shaywitz, S. E., Shankweiler, D. P., Katz, L., Liberman, I. Y., Stuebing, K. K., Francis, D. J., Fowler, A. E., & Shaywitz, B. A. (1994). Cognitive profiles of reading disability: Comparison of discrepancy and low achievement definitions. *Journal of Educational Psychology, 86,* 6–23.

Flood, J. (1977). Parental styles in reading episodes with young children. *Reading Teacher, 30,* 864–867.

Flowers, D. L., Wood, F. B., & Naylor, C. E. (1991). Regional cerebral bloodflow correlates of language processes in reading disability. *Archives of Neurology (Chicago), 48,* 637–643.

Foorman, B. R. (1994). The relevance of a connectionist model of reading for "The great debate." *Educational Psychology Review, 6,* 25–47.

Galaburda, A. M., Sherman, G. F., Rosen, G. D., Aboitz, F., & Geschwind, N. (1985). Developmental dyslexia: Four consecutive patients with cortical anomalies. *Archives of Neurology (Chicago), 35,* 812–817.

Galin, D. (1989). EEG studies in dyslexia. In D. J. Bakker & H. van der Vlugt (Eds.), *Learning disabilities: Vol. 1. Neuropsychological correlates and treatment.* Amsterdam: Swets Publishing.

Gambrell, L. B., & Bales, R. J. (1986). Mental imagery and the comprehension-monitoring performance of fourth- and fifth-grade poor readers. *Reading Research Quarterly, 21,* 454–464.

Gambrell, L. B., & Jawitz, P. B. (1993). Mental imagery, text illustrations, and children's story comprehension and recall. *Reading Research Quarterly, 28,* 264–273.

Gaskins, I. W., Anderson, R. C., Pressley, M., Cunicelli, E. A., & Satlow, E. (1993). Six teachers' dialogue during cognitive process instruction. *Elementary School Journal, 93,* 277–304.

Goodman, Y. M. (Ed.). (1990). *How children construct literacy: Piagetian perspectives.* Newark, DE: International Reading Association.

Goswami, U. (1986). Children's use of analogy in learning to read: A developmental study. *Journal of Experimental Child Psychology, 42,* 73–83.

Goswami, U., & Bryant, P. (1992). Rhyme, analogy, and children's reading. In P. B. Gough, L. C. Ehri, & R. Treiman (Eds.), *Reading acquisition* (pp. 49–63). Hillsdale, NJ: Erlbaum.

Graham, S., & Harris, K. R. (1994). The effects of whole language on children's writing: A review of literature. *Educational Psychologist, 29,* 187–192.

Griffith, P. L. (1991). Phonemic awareness helps first graders invent spellings and third graders remember correct spellings. *Journal of Reading Behavior, 23,* 215–233.

Gross-Glenn, K., Duara, R., Yoshii, F., Barker, W. W., Chen, J. Y., Apicella, A., Boothe, T., & Lubs, H. A. (1988). PET-scan reading studies of familial dyslexics [Abstract]. *Journal of Clinical and Experimental Neuropsychology, 10,* 34–35.

Guthrie, J. T., Schafer, W., Wang, Y. Y., & Afflerbach, P. (1995). Relationships of instruction to amount of reading: An exploration of social, cognitive, and instructional connections. *Reading Research Quarterly, 30,* 8–25.

Haller, E. P., Child, D. A., & Walberg, H. J. (1988). Can comprehension be taught? A quantitative synthesis of "metacognitive" studies. *Educational Researcher, 17*(9), 5–8.

Harris, A. J., & Sipay, E. R. (1990). *How to increase reading ability: A guide to developmental and remedial methods.* New York: Longman.

Harter, M. R. (1991). Event-related potential indices: Learning disabilities and visual processing. In J. E. Obrzut & G. W. Hynd (Eds.), *Neuropsychological foundations of learning disabilities: A handbook of issues, methods, and practice* (pp. 437–473). San Diego, CA: Academic Press.

Heath, S. B. (1982). What no bedtime story means: Narrative skills at home and school. *Language in Society, 11,* 49–76.

Hier, D. B., LeMay, M., Rosenberger, P. B., & Perlo, V. P. (1978). Developmental dyslexia: Evidence for a subgroup with a reversal of cerebral asymmetry. *Archives of Neurology (Chicago), 35,* 90–92.

Hoffmann, R. R. (1992). *The psychology of expertise: Cognitive research and empirical AI.* New York: Springer-Verlag.

Horn, C. C., & Manis, F. R. (1987). Development of automatic and speeded reading of printed words. *Journal of Experimental Child Psychology, 44,* 92–108.

Hulme, C., & MacKenzie, S. (1992). *Working memory and severe learning difficulties.* Hillsdale, NJ: Erlbaum.

Hutchins, E. (1991). The social organization of distributed cognition. In L. Resnick, J. M. Levine, & S. D. Teasley (Eds.), *Perspectives on socially shared cognition* (pp. 283–307). Washington, DC: American Psychological Association.

Huttenlocher, J., Haight, W., Bryk, A., Seltzer, M., & Lyons, T. (1991). Early vocabulary growth: Relation to language input and gender. *Developmental Psychology*, 27, 236–248.

Hynd, G. W., & Semrud-Clikeman, M. (1989). Dyslexia and brain morphology. *Psychological Bulletin*, 106, 447–482.

Idol, L. (1987). Group story mapping: A comprehension strategy for both skilled and unskilled readers. *Journal of Learning Disabilities*, 20, 196–205.

Idol, L., & Croll, V. J. (1987). Story-mapping training as a means of improving reading comprehension. *Learning Disability Quarterly*, 10, 214–229.

Iversen, S., & Tunmer, W. E. (1993). Phonological processing skills and the reading recovery program. *Journal of Educational Psychology*, 85, 112–126.

Jernigan, T. L., Hesselink, J. R., Sowell, E., & Tallal, P. A. (1991). Cerebral structure on magnetic resonance imaging in language- and learning-impaired children. *Archives of Neurology (Chicago)*, 48, 539–545.

Johnson, D., & Myklebust, H. R. (1967). *Learning disabilities: Educational principles and practice*. New York: Grune & Stratton.

Juel, C. (1988). Learning to read and write: A longitudinal study of 54 children from first through fourth grades. *Journal of Educational Psychology*, 80, 417–447.

Juel, C., Griffith, P. L., & Gough, P. B. (1986). Acquisition of literacy: A longitudinal study of children in first and second grade. *Journal of Educational Psychology*, 78, 243–255.

Kail, R. (1991). Processing time declines exponentially during childhood and adolescence. *Developmental Psychology*, 27, 259–266.

Kail, R. (1992). Processing speed, speech rate, and memory. *Developmental Psychology*, 28, 899–904.

Katz, R. B., Shankweiler, D., & Liberman, I. Y. (1981). Memory for item order and phonetic recoding in the beginning reader. *Journal of Experimental Child Psychology*, 32, 474–484.

King, D. F., & Goodman, K. S. (1990). Whole language: Cherishing learners and their language. *Language, Speech, and Hearing Services in Schools*, 21, 221–227.

Kucan, L. (1993, December). *Uncovering cognitive processes in reading*. Presented at the annual meeting of the National Reading Conference, Charleston, WV.

LaBerge, D., & Samuels, S. J. (1974). Toward a theory of automatic information processing in reading. *Cognitive Psychology*, 6, 293–323.

Larsen, J. P., Hoien, T., Lundberg, I., & Ødegaard, S. (1990). MRI evaluation of the size and symmetry of the planum temporale in adolescents with developmental dyslexia. *Brain and Language*, 39, 289–301.

Lehr, S. (1988). The child's developing sense of theme as a response to literature. *Reading Research Quarterly*, 23, 337–357.

Levin, J. R., & Pressley, M. (1981). Improving childrens' prose comprehension: Selected strategies that seem to succeed. In C. M. Santa & B. L. Hayes (Eds.), *Children's prose comprehension: Research and practice* (pp. 44–71). Newark, DE: International Reading Association.

Liberman, I. Y., & Liberman, A. M. (1990). Whole language versus code emphasis: Underlying assumptions and their implications for reading instruction. *Annals of Dyslexia*, 40, 51–76.

Liberman, I. Y., Mann, V. A., Shankweiler, D., & Werfelman, M. (1982). Children's memory for recurring linguistic and nonlinguistic material in relation to reading ability. *Cortex*, 18, 367–375.

Lovett, M. W., Borden, S. L., DeLuca, T., Lacerenza, L., Benson, N. J., & Blackstone, D. (1994). Treating the core deficits of developmental dyslexia: Evidence of transfer of learning after phonologically- and strategy-based reading training programs. *Developmental Psychology*, 30, 805–822.

Lovett, M. W., Ransby, M. J., Hardwick, N., Johns, M. S., & Donaldson, S. A. (1989). Can dyslexia be treated? Treatment-specific and generalized treatment effects in dyslexic children's response to remediation. *Brain and Language*, 37, 90–121.

Lundberg, I. (1991). Phonemic awareness can be developed without reading instruction. In S. A. Brady & D. P. Shankweiler (Eds.), *Phonological processes in literacy: A tribute to Isabelle Y. Liberman* (pp. 47–53). Hillsdale, NJ: Erlbaum.

Lundberg, I., Frost, J., & Peterson, O. (1988). Effects of an extensive program for stimulating phonological awareness in preschool children. *Reading Research Quarterly*, 23, 263–284.

Lyon, G. R., Newby, R. E., Recht, D., & Caldwell, J. (1991). Neuropsychology and learning disabilities. In B. Y. L. Wong (Ed.), *Learning about learning disabilities* (pp. 376–406). San Diego, CA: Academic Press.

Mann, V. A. (1984). Longitudinal prediction and prevention of early reading difficulty. *Annals of Dyslexia*, 34, 117–136.

Markman, E. M. (1977). Realizing that you don't understand: A preliminary investigation. *Child Development*, 46, 986–992.

McBride-Chang, C. (1995). What is phonological awareness? *Journal of Educational Psychology*, 87, 179–192.

McBride-Chang, C., Manis, F. R., Seidenberg, M. S., Custodio, R. G., & Doi, L. G. (1993). Print exposure as a predictor of word reading and reading comprehension in disabled and nondisabled readers. *Journal of Educational Psychology*, 85, 230–238.

McCaslin, M. M. (1989). Whole language: Theory, instruction, and future implementation. *Elementary School Journal*, 90, 223–229.

McConkie, G. W., Zola, D., Blanchard, H. E., & Wolverton, G. S. (1982). Perceiving words during reading: Lack of facilitation from prior peripheral exposure. *Perception & Psychophysics*, 32, 271–281.

McIntyre, E., & Pressley, M. (Eds.). (1996). *Balancing elementary literacy instruction: Teaching skills in whole language settings*. Newton, MA: Christopher-Gordon.

McKenna, M. C., Stratton, B. D., Grindler, M. C., & Jenkins, S. J. (1995). Differential effects of whole language and traditional instruction on reading attitudes. *Journal of Reading Behavior*, 27, 19–44.

Meyers, J., Lytle, S., Palladino, D., Devenpeck, G., & Green, M. (1990). Think-aloud protocol analysis: An investigation of reading comprehension strategies in fourth- and fifth-grade students. *Journal of Psychoeducational Assessment*, 8, 112–127.

Morrow, L. M. (1989). *Literacy development in the early years: Helping children read and write*. Boston: Allyn & Bacon.

Morrow, L. M. (1990). Preparing the classroom environment to promote literacy during play. *Early Childhood Research Quarterly*, 5, 537–554.

Morrow, L. M. (1992). The impact of a literature-based program on literacy achievement, use of literature, and attitudes of children from minority backgrounds. *Reading Research Quarterly*, 27, 251–275.

Morrow, L. M., O'Connor, E. M., & Smith, J. K. (1990). Effects of a story reading program on the literacy development of at-risk kindergarten children. *Journal of Reading Behavior*, 22, 255–275.

Morrow, L. M., & Weinstein, C. S. (1986). Encouraging voluntary reading: The impact of a literacy program on children's use of library corners. *Reading Research Quarterly*, 21, 330–346.

Moshman, D. (1982). Exogenous, endogenous, and dialectical constructivism. *Developmental Review*, 2, 371–384.

Neuman, S. B., & Roskos, K. (1992). Literacy objects as cultural tools: Effects on children's literacy behaviors in play. *Reading Research Quarterly*, 27, 203–225.

Nickerson, R. S., Perkins, D. N., & Smith, E. E. (1985). *The teaching of thinking*. Hillsdale, NJ: Erlbaum.

Ninio, A. (1980). Picture-book reading in mother-infant dyads belonging to two subgroups in Israel. *Child Development*, 51, 587–590.

Oakhill, J. (1993). Children's difficulties in reading comprehension. *Educational Psychology Review, 5*, 223–237.

Oakhill, J. V., & Patel, S. (1991). Can imagery training help children who have comprehension problems. *Journal of Research in Reading, 14*, 106–115.

O'Connor, R. E., Jenkins, J. R., & Slocum, T. A. (1995). Transfer among phonological tasks in kindergarten: Essential instructional content. *Journal of Educational Psychology, 87*, 202–217.

Olson, R. K., Kliegl, R., Davidson, B. J., & Foltz, G. (1985). Individual and developmental differences in reading disability. In G. E. MacKinnon & T. G. Waller (Eds.), *Reading research: Advances in theory and practice* (Vol. 4, pp. 1–64). Orlando, FL: Academic Press.

O'Sullivan, J. T., & Pressley, M. (1984). Completeness of instruction and strategy transfer. *Journal of Experimental Child Psychology, 38*, 275–288.

Palincsar, A. S., & Brown, A. L. (1984). Reciprocal teaching of comprehension-fostering and monitoring activities. *Cognition and Instruction, 1*, 117–175.

Pearson, P. D., & Dole, J. A. (1987). Explicit comprehension instruction: A review of research and a new conceptualization of instruction. *Elementary School Journal, 88*, 151–165.

Pearson, P. D., & Fielding, L. (1991). Comprehension instruction. In R. Barr, M. L. Kamil, P. B. Mosenthal, & P. D. Pearson (Eds.), *Handbook of reading research*: (Vol. 2, pp. 815–860). New York: Longman.

Pellegrini, A. D., Perlmutter, J. C., Galda, L., & Brody, G. H. (1990). Joint reading between black head start children and their mothers. *Child Development, 61*, 443–453.

Pennington, B. F., Groisser, D., & Welsh, M. C. (1993). Contrasting cognitive deficits in attention deficit hyperactivity disorder versus reading disability. *Developmental Psychology, 29*, 511–523.

Pennington, B. F., Van Orden, G. C., Smith, S. D., Green, P. A., & Haith, M. M. (1990). Phological processing skills and deficits in adult dyslexics. *Child Development, 61*, 1753–1778.

Perfetti, C. A., & Lesgold, A. M. (1977). Discourse comprehension and sources of individual differences. In M. A. Just & P. A. Carpenter (Eds.), *Cognitive processes in comprehension*. Hillsdale, NJ: Erlbaum.

Peterson, M. E., & Haines, L. P. (1992). Orthographic analogy training with kindergarten children: Effects of analogy use, phonemic segmentation, and letter-sound knowledge. *Journal of Reading Behavior, 24*, 109–127.

Pflaum, S. W., Walberg, H. J., Karegianes, M. L., & Rasher, S. P. (1980). Reading instruction: A quantitative analysis. *Educational Researcher, 9* (7), 12–18.

Phillips, L. M. (1988). Young readers' inference strategies in reading comprehension. *Cognition and Instruction, 5*, 193–222.

Pratt, A. C., & Brady, S. (1988). Relation of phonological awareness to reading disability in children and adults. *Journal of Educational Psychology, 80*, 319–323.

Pressley, G. M. (1976). Mental imagery helps eight-year-olds remember what they read. *Journal of Educational Psychology, 68*, 355–359.

Pressley, M. (1994). Commentary on the ERIC whole language debate. In C. B. Smith (Moderator), *Whole language: The debate* (pp. 187–217). Bloomington, IN: ERIC/REC.

Pressley, M., & Afflerbach, P. (1995). *Verbal protocols of reading: The nature of constructively responsive reading*. Hillsdale, NJ: Erlbaum.

Pressley, M., El-Dinary, P. B., Gaskins, I., Schuder, T., Bergman, J., Almasi, L., & Brown, R. (1992). Beyond direct explanation: Transactional instruction of reading comprehension strategies. *Elementary School Journal, 92*, 511–554.

Pressley, M., El-Dinary, P. B., Stein, S., Marks, M. B., & Brown, R. (1992). Good strategy instruction is motivating and interesting. In A. Renninger, S. Hidi, & A. Krapp (Eds.), *The role of interest in learning and development* (pp. 333–358). Hillsdale, NJ: Erlbaum.

Pressley, M., Gaskins, I. W., Cunicelli, E. A., Burdick, N. J., Schaub-Matt, M., Lee, D. S., & Powell, N. (1991). Strategy instruction at Benchmark School: A faculty interview study. *Learning Disability Quarterly, 14*, 19–48.

Pressley, M., Gaskins, I. W., Wile, D., Cunicelli, B., & Sheridan, J. (1991). Teaching literacy strategies across the curriculum: A case study at Benchmark School. In J. Zutell & S. McCormick (Eds.), *Learner factors/teacher factors: Issues in literacy research and instruction: Fortieth yearbook of the National Reading Conference* (pp. 219–228). Chicago: National Reading Conference.

Pressley, M., Johnson, C. J., Symons, S., McGoldrick, J. A., & Kurita, J. A. (1989). Strategies that improve memory and comprehension of what is read. *Elementary School Journal, 90*, 3–32.

Pressley, M., & Rankin, J. (1994). More about whole language methods of reading instruction for students at-risk for early reading failure. *Learning Disabilities Research & Practice, 9*, 157–168.

Pressley, M., Rankin, J., & Yokoi, L. (1996). A survey of the instructional practices of primary-level teachers nominated as effective in promoting literacy. *Elementary School Journal, 96*, 363–384.

Pressley, M., Schuder, T., SAIL Faculty and Administration, Bergman, J. L., & El-Dinary, P. B. (1992). A researcher-educator collaborative interview study of transactional comprehension strategies instruction. *Journal of Educational Psychology, 84*, 231–246.

Pressley, M., Yokoi, L., Rankin, J. L., Wharton-McDonald, R., & Mistretta, J. (in press). A survey of the instructional practices of grade-5 teachers nominated as effective in promoting literacy. *Scientific Studies of Reading*.

Rankin, J. L. (1993). Information processing differences of college-age readers differing in reading comprehension and speed. *Journal of Reading Behavior, 25*, 261–278.

Rankin, J. L., & Pressley, M. (in preparation). *A survey of the instructional practices of primary-level, special education teachers nominated as effective in promoting literacy*. Lincoln: University of Nebraska-Lincoln, Department of Special Education and Communicative Disorders.

Rayner, K., Inhoff, A. W., Morrison, R. E., Slowiaczek, M. L., & Bertera, J. H. (1981). *Journal of Experimental Psychology: Human Perception and Performance, 7*, 167–179.

Rice, M. L., Huston, A. C., Truglio, R., & Wright, J. (1990). Words from "Sesame Street": Learning vocabulary from viewing. *Developmental Psychology, 26*, 421–428.

Richgels, D. J. (1995). Invented spelling ability and printed word learning in kindergarten. *Reading Research Quarterly, 30*, 96–109.

Robbins, C., & Ehri, L. C. (1994). Reading storybooks to kindergartners helps them learn new vocabulary words. *Journal of Educational Psychology, 86*, 54–64.

Roehler, L. R., & Duffy, G. G. (1984). Direct explanation of comprehension processes. In G. G. Duffy, L. R. Roehler, & J. Mason (Eds.), *Comprehension instruction: Perspectives and suggestions* (pp. 265–280). New York: Longman.

Rosenblatt, L. M. (1978). *The reader, the text, the poem: The transactional theory of the literary work*. Carbondale: Southern Illinois University Press.

Rosenshine, B., & Meister, C. (1994). Reciprocal teaching: A review of nineteen experimental studies. *Review of Educational Research, 64*, 479–530.

Rosenshine, B., & Trapman, S. (1992, April). *Teaching students to generate questions: A review of research*. Paper presented at the annual meeting of the American Educational Research Association, San Francisco.

Roser, N., & Martinez, M. (1985). Roles adults play in prschool responses to literature. *Language Arts, 62*, 485–490.

Sawyer, D. J., & Butler, K. (1991). Early language intervention: A deterrent to reading disability. *Annals of Dyslexia, 41*, 55–79.

Scarborough, H. S. (1989). Prediction of reading disability from familial and individual differences. *Journal of Educational Psychology, 81*, 101–108.

Scarborough, H. S. (1990). Very early language deficits in dyslexic children. *Child Development, 61*, 1728–1743.

Scarborough, H. S., & Dobrich, W. (1994). On the efficiency of reading to preschoolers. *Developmental Review, 14*, 245–302.

Sénéchal, M., Thomas, E., & Monker, J.-A. (1995). Individual differences in 4-year-old children's acquisition of vocabulary during storybook reading. *Journal of Educational Psychology, 87*, 218–229.

Shaywitz, S. E., & Shaywitz, B. A. (1992). Learning disabilities and attention deficits in the school setting. In L. J. Meltzer (Ed.), *Strategy assessment and instruction for students with learning disabilities: From theory to practice* (pp. 221–241). Austin, TX: PRO-ED.

Short, E. J., & Ryan, E. B. (1984). Metacognitive differences between skilled and less skilled readers: Remediating deficits through story grammar and attribution training. *Journal of Educational Psychology*, 76, 225–235.

Shu H., Anderson, R. C., & Zhang, H. (1995). Incidental learning of word meanings while reading: A Chinese and American cross-cultural study. *Reading Research Quarterly*, 30, 76–95.

Siegel, L. S., & Ryan, E. B. (1988). Development of grammatical-sensitivity, phonological, and short-term memory skills in normally achieving and learning disabled children. *Developmental Psychology*, 24, 28–37.

Slavin, R. E., Karweit, N. L., & Wasik, B. A. (1994). *Preventing early school failure: Research, policy, and practice*. Boston: Allyn & Bacon.

Stahl, S. A., McKenna, M. C., & Pagnucco, J. R. (1994). The effects of whole language instruction: An update and reappraisal. *Educational Psychologist*, 29, 175–186.

Stahl, S. A., & Miller, P. D. (1989). Whole language and language experience approaches for beginning reading: A quantitative research synthesis. *Review of Educational Research*, 59, 87–116.

Stanovich, K. E. (1986). Matthew effects in reading: Some consequences of individual differences in the acquisition of literacy. *Reading Research Quarterly*, 21, 360–407.

Stanovich, K. E. (1988). Explaining the differences between the dyslexic and the garden-variety poor reader: The phonological-core variable-difference model. *Journal of Learning Disabilities*, 21, 590–604.

Stanovich, K. E., & Cunningham, A. E. (1993). Print exposure as a predictor of word reading and reading comprehension in disabled and nondisabled readers. *Journal of Educational Psychology*, 85, 211–229.

Stanovich, K. E., & West, R. F. (1989). Exposure to print and orthographic processing. *Reading Research Quarterly*, 24, 402–433.

Stuart, M., & Masterson, J. (1992). Patterns of reading and spelling in 10-year-old children related to prereading phonological abilities. *Journal of Experimental Child Psychology*, 54, 168–187.

Sulzby, E., & Teale, W. (1991). Emergent literacy. In R. Barr, M. L. Kamil, P. B. Mosenthal, & P. D. Pearson (Eds.), *Handbook of reading research* (Vol. 2, pp. 727–758). New York: Longman.

Swanson, H. L. (1992). Generality and modifiability of working memory among skilled and less skilled readers. *Journal of Educational Psychology*, 84, 473–488.

Swanson, H. L., & Cooney, J. B. (1991). Learning disabilities and memory. In B. Y. L. Wong (Ed.), *Learning about learning disabilities* (pp. 104–127). San Diego, CA: Academic Press.

Tangel, D. M., & Blachman, B. A. (1992). Effect of phoneme awareness instruction on kindergarten children's invented spellings. *Journal of Reading Behavior*, 24, 233–261.

Taylor, B. M. (1982). Text structure and children's comprehension and memory for expository material. *Journal of Educational Psychology*, 74, 323–340.

Taylor, B. M., & Beach, R. W. (1984). The effects of text structure instruction on middle-grade students' comprehension and production of expository text. *Reading Research Quarterly*, 19, 134–146.

Taylor, B. M., Frye, B. J., & Maruyama, G. M. (1990). Time spent reading and reading growth. *American Educational Research Journal*, 27, 351–362.

Taylor, D., & Strickland, D. (1986). *Family storybook reading*. Exeter, NH: Heinemann.

Torgesen, J. K., & Houck, D. O. (1980). Processing deficiencies of learning disabled children who perform poorly on the digit span test. *Journal of Educational Psychology*, 72, 141–160.

Treiman, R. A., & Baron, J. (1981). Segmental analysis ability: Development and relation to reading ability. In G. E. MacKinnon & R. G. Walker (Eds.), *Reading research: Advances in theory and practice* (Vol. 3). San Diego, CA: Academic Press.

Tunmer, W. E., Herriman, M. L., & Nesdale, A. R. (1988). Metalinguistic abilities and beginning reading. *Reading Research Quarterly*, 23, 134–158.

Uhry, J. K., & Shepherd, M. J. (1993). Segmentation/spelling instruction as part of a first-grade reading program: Effects on several measures of reading. *Reading Research Quarterly*, 28, 218–233.

Vauras, M., Kinnunen, R., & Kuusela, L. (1994). Development of text processing skills in high-, average-, and low-achieving primary school children. *Journal of Reading Behavior*, 26, 361–389.

Vellutino, F. R. (1979). *Dyslexia: Theory and research*. Cambridge, MA: MIT Press.

Venezky, R. L., & Johnson, D. (1973). The development of two letter-sound patterns in grade 1–3. *Journal of Educational Psychology*, 64, 109–115.

Wagner, R. K., Torgesen, J. K., Laughon, P., Simmons, K., & Rashotte, C. A. (1993). Development of young readers' phonological processing abilities. *Journal of Educational Psychology*, 85, 83–103.

Walczyk, J. J. (1994). The development of verbal efficiency, metacognitive strategies, and their interplay. *Educational Psychology Review*, 6, 173–189.

Weaver, C. (1994). *Understanding whole language: From principles to practice*. Portsmouth, NH: Heinemann.

Wharton-McDonald, R., Pressley, M., & Mistretta, J. (1996). *Outstanding literacy instruction in first grade: Teacher practices and student achievement*. Albany: University of Albany, State University of New York, Department of Educational Psychology and Statistics.

Whitehurst, G. J., Epstein, A. L., Angell, A. C., Payne, D. A., Crone, D. A., & Fischel, J. E. (1994). Outcomes of an emergent literacy intervention in head start. *Journal of Educational Psychology*, 86, 542–555.

Whitehurst, G. J., Falco, F. L., Lonigan, C. J., Fischel, J. E., DeBaryshe, B. D., Valdez-Menchaca, M. C., & Caulfield, M. (1988). Accelerating language development through picturebook reading. *Developmental Psychology*, 24, 552–559.

Williams, J. P. (1980). Teaching decoding with an emphasis on phoneme analysis and phoneme blending. *Journal of Educational Psychology*, 72, 1–15.

Williams, P. L., Reese, C. M., Campbell, J. R., Mazzeo, J., & Phillips, G. W. (1995). 1994 NAEP *Reading: A first look*. Washington, DC: U.S. Department of Education, Office of Educational Research and Improvement.

Wood, S. S., Bruner, J. S., & Ross, G. (1976). The role of tutoring in problem solving. *Journal of Child Psychology and Psychiatry*, 17, 89–100.

Yuill, N. M., & Oakhill, J. V. (1991). *Children's problems in text comprehension: An experimental investigation*. Cambridge, England: Cambridge University Press.

Yuill, N. M., Oakhill, J. V., & Parkin, A. J. (1989). Working memory, comprehension ability and the resolution of text anomaly. *British Journal of Psychology*, 80, 351–361.

CHAPTER

7

A Cognitive Perspective on the Assessment, Diagnosis, and Remediation of Reading Skills

JAMES M. ROYER

University of Massachusetts, Amherst

The assessment of any academic skill should begin with a decision regarding the purpose of assessment. Standardized reading tests adequately fulfill some purposes for measuring reading skill but not others. For instance, standardized tests provide school administrators and educational policy makers with valuable information about how a particular group of students is performing relative to other groups, but the tests contain little information that is relevant to the classroom teacher.

One reason that standardized tests provide little information of use to the classroom teacher is that the tests are based on the concept of a "general" curriculum and test content is directed to that hypothetical curriculum. Designing the test with a general curriculum in mind means that, in theory, no single school has an advantage on the test relative to other schools. It also means, however, that the test does not map precisely onto the instructional goals of any given school. This leaves classroom teachers questioning whether some of the variation in test performance is associated with differences between their instructional emphases and test content.

Another reason why standardized tests are of little use to classroom teachers is that they contain very little information that has diagnostic and prescriptive value. In the early grades, standardized tests contain reading subtests that measure word decoding skill, vocabulary knowledge, spelling ability, sentence comprehension and several kinds of syntactic and punctu-

Handbook of Academic Learning

ation knowledge (often referred to in tests as *language skills*). In the later grades, these measures are supplemented or replaced by global measures of reading comprehension and indexes of content knowledge (often attained using subject matter reading comprehension tests) in subjects such as science and social studies. These measures may tell teachers which students are good readers and which are poor readers (information they probably already know), but they tell them nothing about the nature of a reading problem a student is experiencing and what might be done to fix the problem.

The remainder of this chapter will be devoted to the description of reading assessment procedures that educators can use to identify the nature of reading problems, and to how the assessment procedures lead directly to educational interventions designed to repair the problems. The chapter begins with a broad overview of the diagnostic and prescriptive procedures that the author and his colleagues have developed, followed by a description of the theoretical underpinnings of the diagnostic and prescriptive procedures. This overview and description of theory is followed by a discussion of five properties an effective diagnostic and intervention system must have. The discussion of the properties a diagnostic system must have is followed by a description of the diagnostic and intervention procedures themselves, a discussion of how those procedures work in practice, and a presentation of evidence for the effectiveness of the procedures in the form of student case studies. The chapter concludes with an argument that reading assessment procedures that are useful to the classroom teacher must combine instructional and diagnostic purposes in a manner such that there is constant interplay between the two activities.

AN OVERVIEW OF THE LATAS MODEL OF ASSESSMENT AND EDUCATIONAL INTERVENTION

The techniques and procedures described in this chapter have evolved during nearly 20 years of research, much of which has been conducted at the Laboratory for the Assessment and Training of Academic Skills (LATAS) at the University of Massachusetts. The research program began with the desire to develop a procedure for measuring listening and reading comprehension that classroom teachers could use to develop comprehension tests based on materials used in their classrooms. The procedure that evolved from this goal was called the *Sentence Verification Technique* (SVT), and a considerable amount of research in the late 1970s and 1980s was devoted to establishing the reliability, validity, and practical utility of the technique as a measure of listening and reading comprehension. This research is summarized in Royer (1990, 1995) and Royer, Carlo, and Cisero (1992).

The SVT research convinced the author and his colleagues that they had developed a technique that could be used to assess listening and reading comprehension, but it also highlighted diagnostic and prescriptive issues that remained to be solved. That is, one could identify students who had difficulty understanding a particular text, but SVT assessments could not pinpoint the reasons for comprehension failure and provided no information about what could be done to fix the problem. The desire to know more about why comprehension failure occurs and what might be done to prevent it from happening led to the development of a computer-based assessment system called CAAS (computer-based academic assessment system). The CAAS allows one to measure the speed and accuracy of performance on a range of academic tasks. The focus of this chapter will be on reading assessment, but CAAS has also been used to measure math performance and specialized reading performance in subjects such as chemistry, social studies, and biology.

Several years of research using CAAS established that the system provides reliable assessments and considerable evidence has accumulated supporting its validity (Carlo & Royer, 1995; Carlo & Skilton Sylvester, 1994a, 1994b; Cisero, Royer, Marchant, & Jackson, 1995a, 1995b; Cisero, Royer, Marchant, & Wint, 1994; Greene & Royer, 1994; Royer & Sinatra, 1994; Sinatra & Royer, 1993; Wint, Cisero, & Royer, 1995). After establishing this base of psychometric research, the author and his colleagues began a program of research that used the diagnostic information provided by CAAS to develop instructional interventions designed to repair deficient reading and math skills. The academic intervention efforts initially involved students referred to LATAS by a clinical psychologist who had a practice that specialized in working with youth who had attention deficit disorder (ADD). In addition to having behavioral problems associated with ADD, the referred students also had academic problems that were either produced by their behavioral problems or arose because of a separate learning disability. Over time, word of mouth referrals brought in students with other types of learning problems, and the LATAS client list has come to include students with specific learning disabilities in reading, math, and writing.

The LATAS model of working with students experiencing learning problems begins with a comprehensive assessment of reading and math skills. The assessment process pinpoints poorly developed academic skills that are blocking progress, and an intervention program is implemented that is designed to strengthen the undeveloped skill. The bulk of the intervention efforts involve nightly practice sessions during which parents and students keep detailed records of progress. Once a week the student returns to LATAS where progress is checked with a CAAS assessment, and this assessment, in combination with an examination of home study records, results in either continuing the current intervention efforts or switching to higher-level skills that need to be developed.

The final step in the LATAS model occurs when students have repaired all of the lower-level skills that had blocked academic progress, whereupon attention turns to activities that will enhance performance in particular subject matter courses and the acquisition of strategies that can be used to assist academic learning in general. This phase of the intervention effort involves isolating and acquiring technical vocabulary and concepts in subject matter areas, and teaching students to use the subject matter index of their textbooks as a means of identifying and studying important content. This phase of the intervention effort also involves teaching students to develop semantic maps of courses they are taking (e.g., see Lambiotte, Dansereau, Cross, & Reynolds, 1989).

THE THEORETICAL UNDERPINNINGS OF THE LATAS DIAGNOSES AND INTERVENTIONS

The LATAS approach to reading diagnosis and remediation has been guided by the assumption that reading comprehension is essentially decoding plus speech comprehension, and by an amalgam of theory constructed from Anderson's (1983, 1993) Adaptive Control of Thought (ACT) theory, Perfetti's (1992) theory of the acquisition of reading skills, and perspectives on the automaticity and modularity of reading skills (e.g., Stanovich, 1990). The amalgamated theory, which is discussed in greater detail in Royer and Sinatra (1994), suggests that reading acquisition begins with the acquisition of the enabling skills of letter identification and phonological awareness.[1] These two enabling skills lead to the development of the "alphabetic principle," which is the realization on the part of the developing reader that there is a correspondence between letters and the sounds of spoken language.

With increased experience in processing graphemic information, the developing reader begins to transform conscious, strategic, activities into modularized processes that are "data driven." Data-driven processes are those that are automatically activated by the stimulus event. This modularization process is hierarchical and developmental. It is hierarchical in the sense that the reader begins from the simplest skill and moves progressively to more complex skills, and it is developmental in the sense that all readers acquire processes in the same order and the acquisition of those processes is mediated by practice in using the skills.

The first reading process to be transformed from a conscious strategic activity to a modularized activity is letter identification. Readers develop the

[1]It should be noted that Perfetti (1992) has argued that what he calls *reflective phonological awareness* is not a prerequisite for the acquisition of reading skills. He does argue, however, that "computational phonological awareness" is a necessary prerequisite. This distinction is theoretically important and has implications for instructing students who lack phonological awareness skills. However, it has no impact on the diagnostic and remediation activities at LATAS.

capability of automatically recognizing letters in a variety of stimulus guises. This is followed by the development of processing modules that recognize words. The modules that recognize words actually carry out two functions. The first is the identification of the word itself, and the second is the activation of the meanings of the word. It is important to note that the general act of reading words does not become modularized. Rather, the act of reading *particular* words becomes modularized. Beginning readers initially develop modularized processing capabilities for commonly experienced words and then add to their repertoire as experience increases. However, readers will always encounter unfamiliar words that require conscious attention, and anyone engaged in the study of new subject matter is constantly in the process of acquiring new modularized words.

When words have been successfully decoded, their meanings are deposited into working memory, where the interpretation of meaningful units occurs, presumably utilizing the same processes that govern speech comprehension. The fact that interpretation occurs in working memory has several important consequences. Working memory is limited in both capacity and duration. The exact limits of working memory capacity are a matter of some debate, but the range mentioned by most theorists is from four to nine units of information, with units being either individual elements such as the meaning of a word or a coherent "chunk" of information that could contain multiple elements (e.g., "founding fathers," which would decompose into Washington, Adams, Jefferson, etc.). The capacity of working memory places limits on our ability to derive an interpretation of messages containing many elements, and since individuals vary in working memory capacity, it is also a source of individual differences in comprehension ability.

The second attribute of working memory, its limited duration, is more important for the purposes of this chapter. Information deposited in working memory that is not consciously maintained via a strategy such as rehearsal typically decays within 10 to 15 seconds. The implication of this attribute of working memory can be illustrated by discussing what happens when a reader tries to understand the following sentence: *Soccer is a game that requires great agility and endurance.*

For the moment, assume that the reader is skilled and that the eye rests on each word in the sentence, except the article *a*, during the reading act. From eye movement research (e.g., Rayner & Pollatsek, 1989), we know that a typical fixation during reading lasts approximately 250 milliseconds, and that the transition movement (called a *saccade*) between fixations takes 100 milliseconds. Given these numbers, a little arithmetic suggests that it would take a skilled reader approximately 3 seconds to deposit the meaning of the words from the sentence into working memory so that an interpretation could take place.

Now consider what might happen with a reader who is slow to recognize words. If a reader were to take 2 seconds to recognize a word, the process of depositing the meaning of words from the sentence into working memory would exceed 15 seconds, and it is entirely possible that the meaning of early words would decay from working memory before the meaning of all of the words could be obtained. If this happens, it is impossible for the reader to comprehend the sentence. To foreshadow what will come, disabled readers often have word recognition times that exceed two seconds.

The LATAS diagnostic and remediation process is based on the theoretical assumptions just briefly outlined. We assume that many (not all) reading problems are due to slow or inaccurate processing at some level in the cognitive system, and the diagnostic process is designed to identify those processes. The remediation effort that follows is designed to make those processes fast and accurate.

Research on the practicality and effectiveness of the LATAS approach has been guided by an attempt to satisfy five criteria for an effective reading diagnostic and instruction system. A discussion of the criteria and the extent to which LATAS activities satisfy the criteria is provided in the next section.

FIVE CHARACTERISTICS OF TEACHER-USEFUL READING DIAGNOSIS AND REMEDIATION

In a recent article describing CAAS as a reading diagnostics procedure, Royer and Sinatra (1994) suggested four characteristics that successful reading diagnostic procedures should have: (1) the procedures must be reliable and valid, (2) the procedures must yield patterns of performance that are consistent with cognitive developmental theories of reading, (3) the procedures must provide specific information about the nature of the reading difficulty a student is experiencing, and (4) the procedures must provide diagnoses that lead to prescriptive procedures that alleviate to a demonstrable degree the reading problems the student is experiencing. Another characteristic will be added to the list in this chapter: (5) teacher-useful diagnostic and instructional procedures must be capable of using materials drawn from the local curriculum and teachers should to be able to use the procedures to develop their own assessment and instructional procedures with minimal training. The remainder of this section will discuss the extent to which LATAS procedures satisfy the first two criteria and the major sections to follow will discuss evidence indicating that LATAS procedures can satisfy the remaining three criteria.

Reliability and Validity of LATAS Procedures

The major tools used in the LATAS diagnostic and instructional activities are SVT listening and reading comprehension tests and CAAS reading tasks.

Royer (1995) has summarized the evidence regarding the reliability of SVT tests. He reports that the reliability of SVT tests range from .5 to .9 depending on the length of the test. Short tests based on three passages that can be administered in 15–20 minutes have reliabilities in the lower range and longer tests based on six passages that require approximately an hour to administer have reliabilities in the upper range.

CAAS assessments involve obtaining response time and accuracy measures on from 20 to 60 separate stimulus events for each CAAS task (specific tasks will be described in a later section). Gale Sinatra's (1989) Ph.D. dissertation, which was completed at LATAS, examined the reliabilities of five reading tasks used in CAAS and found they had reliabilities that exceeded .9 in every task.

Establishing the validity of any assessment procedure is an ongoing task (Messick, 1980), and validity research is continuing on all of the LATAS assessment instruments. A great deal of evidence has accumulated on the validity of SVT tests, however, and some evidence is available on the validity of CAAS assessments. Royer (1995) reviews evidence that SVT tests have the following properties relevant to their validity: (1) performance on SVT tests varies with reading skill, (2) performance on SVT tests varies with text difficulty, (3) SVT tests measure the comprehension of complete passages, (4) SVT test performance improves as a function of relevant instruction, (5) SVT performance covaries with working memory capacity, (6) SVT listening and reading comprehension covary in a theoretically sensible manner, and (7) SVT performance displays good convergent and divergent relational properties in that SVT scores are related to other measures they should be related to and are not related to measures they are not supposed to be related to.

Royer and Sinatra (1994; Sinatra & Royer, 1993) described evidence relevant to the question of whether CAAS assessments provide valid indexes of reading competence. This evidence indicated that (1) CAAS performance varied as a function of grade level with students in higher grades performing better than students in lower grades, (2) students within the same grade who were reading in high-level basal readers performed better on CAAS tasks than students reading in lower-level basal readers, and (3) CAAS performance varied as a function of teacher ratings of student reading skill.

Additional evidence regarding the validity of CAAS has shown that patterns of CAAS performance for students with previously diagnosed learning disabilities differ from CAAS patterns obtained from students who have no learning disabilities. Cisero et al. (1994), for example, found markedly different CAAS profiles for three groups of college students: (1) students with diagnosed specific reading disabilities, (2) students with learning disabilities in areas other than reading, and (3) students who did not have a learning disability. A follow-up study then showed that, within a group of students diagnosed as having a specific reading disability, there were interesting variations in patterns of CAAS performance that were consistent with other indexes of the difficulties being experienced by the student (Cisero et al., 1995, 1996). The same study also identified an instance of what appeared to be a misdiagnosis. This involved a student who had been diagnosed as having a learning disability, but CAAS evidence and other evidence suggested that she had no learning disability.

Finally, Carlo and Skilton Sylvester (1994a) have reported a study that provides evidence that the CAAS system is valid for the purpose of assessing developing English language skills in a population of non-English-speaking adults enrolled in an English-as-a-second-language course. Their research showed that English CAAS performance could be used to predict English reading comprehension performance.

Consistency between Reading Development Theory and LATAS Assessments

The second attribute that Royer and Sinatra (1994) suggested a reading diagnostic system should have is that the information derived from the system be consistent with theories of reading development. Several types of evidence suggest that LATAS assessments have this attribute.

Reading Development Theory and SVT Performance

Reading researchers have long assumed that there is an intimate relationship between listening and reading comprehension (e.g., Danks, 1980; Horowitz & Samuels, 1987; Sticht, Beck, Hauke, Kleinman, & James, 1974), and this presumed relationship has served as a testing ground for evaluating the match between reading developmental theory and SVT assessment. The proposed relationship between listening and reading comprehension has varied from strong forms, which essentially say that reading is decoding plus listening comprehension (e.g., Carroll, 1977), to weak forms, which suggest that the variety of cues available to assist the comprehension process is far greater in listening than in reading but the underlying psychological processes are nonetheless heavily interrelated (Kleinman & Schallert, 1978). Both the strong and the weak forms assume that listening comprehension performance imposes a developmental cap on reading comprehension ability. That is, during the period when reading skills are being developed, listening comprehension should exceed reading comprehension given comparable presentations of text in each modality. Royer, Kulhavy, Lee, and Peterson (1986), Royer and Sinatra (1994), and Royer, Sinatra, and Schumer (1990) provided support for this hypothesis using SVT tests to measure listening and reading comprehension.

Reading Development Theory and CAAS Performance

Sinatra and Royer (1993) have provided evidence indicating that CAAS assessments are consistent with expectations derived from cognitive developmental theories of reading acquisition. They conducted a longitudinal study of the reading performance of students enrolled in grades 2, 3, and 4 that utilized a precursor to the CAAS assessment system. The study tested hypotheses derived from Perfetti's (1992) theory that describes the acquisition of reading skills. Perfetti's theory makes predictions about the developmental role that word identification ability plays in reading comprehension. Specifically, the theory suggests that variation in the speed and accuracy of word identification performance would play relatively little role in reading comprehension with very young children (e.g., grade 2 students). The reason for this is that word identification skills are so poorly developed that nearly all children use slow and inefficient procedures to identify words and variation in reading comprehension is associated primarily with variation in the extent of prior knowledge and the utilization of conscious reasoning and inferential strategies, rather than with variation in speed and accuracy of word identification. However, as students mature, some begin to develop modularized word identification abilities whereas others lag behind. This idea leads to the prediction that variation in word identification performance should be a potent predictor of reading comprehension performance for students in the middle elementary grades (e.g., grades 3 and 4). Finally, as students continue in their reading development, the modularity of word identification skills should be attained by most students and variation in word identification performance should again make relatively little contribution to reading comprehension performance.

Sinatra and Royer (1993) provided evidence supporting two of the suppositions derived from Perfetti's (1992) theory. Specifically, the data they collected using CAAS indicated that variation in word identification ability was not a predictor of reading comprehension in grade 2 but was a potent predictor in grades 3 and 4. Walczyk (1990), using data collection procedures similar to those used in CAAS, has also provided evidence that reading comprehension in grade 4 is related to variation in word identification performance. Finally, Walczyk (1995), again using procedures similar to those in CAAS, has shown that reading comprehension is not normally influenced by variation in word identification performance in mature readers (it does come into play, however, under conditions where readers are pressed to read rapidly). This finding is again consistent with cognitive developmental theories of reading acquisition.

Having described evidence consistent with the interpretation that the SVT and CAAS procedures used in the LATAS model are reliable, valid, and yield measures that are consistent with theories of reading development, I will now turn to a discussion of the degree to which the LATAS diagnostic procedures provide specific information about the nature of the difficulty the reader is experiencing.

Profiles of Reading Skills Provided by LATAS Assessments

The third criterion that Royer and Sinatra (1994) identified for a successful reading diagnostic system was that it provide specific information about the nature of the reading difficulties a student is experiencing. This section of the chapter provides information relevant to this criterion in the form of common profiles we see on the LATAS assessments. We have developed these profiles over a period of years through extensive research with both disabled and nondisabled readers (e.g., Cisero et al., 1995a; Wint *et al.*, 1995).

The LATAS Assessment Process

The reader should be aware that most of the students who have been referred to LATAS have been subjected to multiple assessments by their school system, private psychologists, and on occasion, medical centers specializing in the assessment of learning disabilities. We make copies of those assessments and compare LATAS assessments with those previous ones. Very often, a good deal of correspondence is found between the overall picture derived from the LATAS assessments and those derived from other procedures. However, we believe that the "fine-grained" LATAS assessments have advantages over other procedures when it comes to devising and monitoring instructional interventions. By *fine grained*, we mean that LATAS assessments are highly sensitive detectors of skill deficiencies and they can actually detect competence gains associated with a single day's practice. We do not use traditional assessment procedures, but we are certain that procedures that collect only accuracy information are not as sensitive to academic accomplishment and gain as those such as CAAS that also collect response time information.

Our general assessment strategy is to assess the entire range of activities involved in performance of an academic task. In the case of reading, we begin with the measurement of very simple performances, such as the recognition of letters and words, and proceed to complex performances, involving the comprehension of paragraph length material. We use SVT tests to assess reading and listening comprehension of text passages and CAAS assessments to assess lower-level reading skills.

Several different levels of the CAAS reading system have been developed: an elementary version, suitable for administration to students in grades 2–5; a middle school version, appropriate for students in grades 6–8; and an adult version, which can be administered to students in grade 9 and beyond.

In addition, the elementary version of the reading tasks is available in Spanish. CAAS tasks can be set up so that students respond using either button presses or vocal responses into a microphone. Most of the research we conduct at LATAS uses vocalization responses. The reading skills measured by the CAAS system are the following:

- *Simple response time*. This task involves presenting +++ or *** on the computer screen. The student responds into the microphone with a star or a plus. This task has proven to be very useful in differentiating students who have specific academic difficulties from those who have general cognitive deficits.
- *Letter naming*. A lower case or upper case letter appears on the computer screen and the student says the name of the letter into the microphone.
- *Word naming*. Words of varying difficulty appear on the screen and the student speaks the word into the microphone. The CAAS elementary word task contains 240 words, 40 of which are randomly sampled (10 from four categories varying in difficulty) to conduct a CAAS assessment.
- *Pseudoword naming*. Pronounceable nonwords (produced by altering words in the word task) appear on the screen and the student pronounces the nonword into the microphone. This task is identical to the word task except for the stimuli.
- *Concept activation*. The student is told that pairs of words will appear on the screen that either belong or do not belong to a named category. When the words appear, the student says "yes" (they belong to the same category) or "no." Again, assessments are conducted by sampling from a large pool of items.
- *Semantic processing of sentences*. A sentence appears on the screen that has a blank in it and a word appears above the blank and another below the blank. The words vary in semantic appropriateness and the student says the name of the word into the microphone. Assessments are conducted by sampling from a large pool of items.

Prototypical Profiles of Disabled and Nondisabled Readers

The reading profiles presented in this section have been developed through an extensive program of research that has involved collecting SVT reading and (sometimes) listening profiles from several thousand students (grade 3 to adult) over the years and from collections of CAAS profiles from several hundred grade 1 to adult students. Most of these profiles have been collected from nondisabled readers, although some of our field research and all of the research conducted with LATAS clients has involved readers with disabilities. Prior to presenting profiles of readers with varying types of reading difficulties, it is important to recognize that not all of the students who have

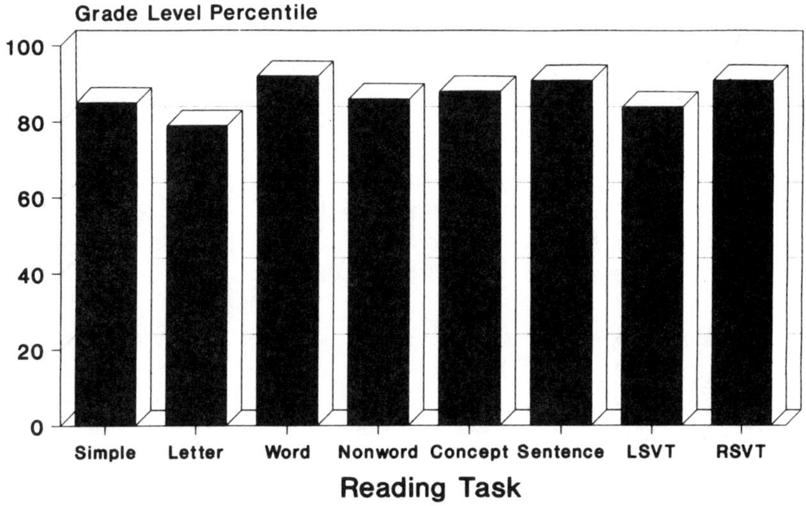

FIGURE 1
Good reader performance profile on LATAS tasks.

a particular type of disability will display the profile we describe as being characteristic of that disability. The longer we work with students with disabilities, the more impressed we are with the differences among students who have been placed in common diagnostic categories. The labeling of profiles that will be presented here is for exposition in this chapter. In practice, at LATAS, we tend not to use diagnostic labels because the labels have little utility in developing instructional interventions. That is, our instructional interventions are driven by the nature of the academic deficiency the student displays, rather than by a diagnostic label.

Figures 1–6 display grade level percentiles on SVT and CAAS tasks for categories of students we have observed in our research activities. The CAAS data in the figures are an index created by combining accuracy and response times.[2]

Figure 1 displays a profile that is commonly seen in students who are good readers. Performance is generally high on all of the assessment tasks and reading SVT performance is slightly higher than listening SVT performance. The reason that reading performance exceeds listening performance has to do with the nature of the test administration process. Listening SVT tests are administered using an audiotape recorder, and the student has one opportunity to comprehend the aurally presented passages and test ques-

[2]The technique that we use to combine speed and accuracy indexes is interesting in and of itself. Anyone interested in more information about the technique should contact the author.

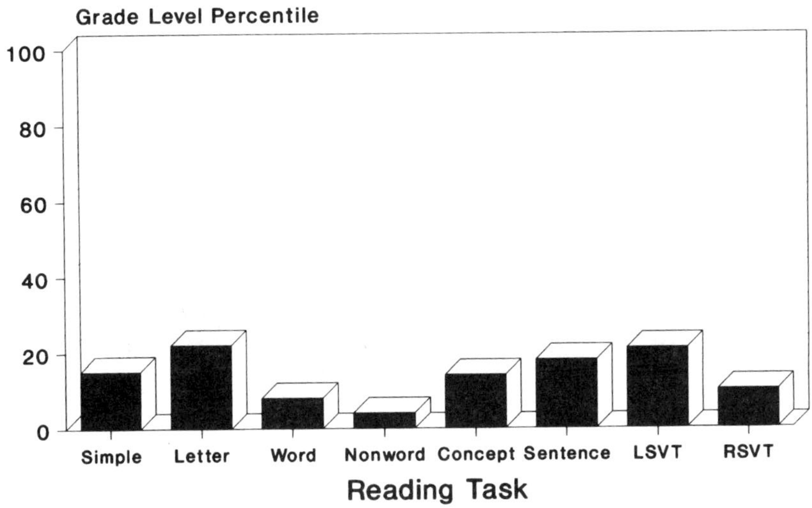

FIGURE 2
Global cognitive deficit performance profile on LATAS tasks.

tions. In contrast, students completing the reading SVT test can freely inspect the passage until they are ready to answer the test questions. This gives the student who is a good reader an advantage on the reading section

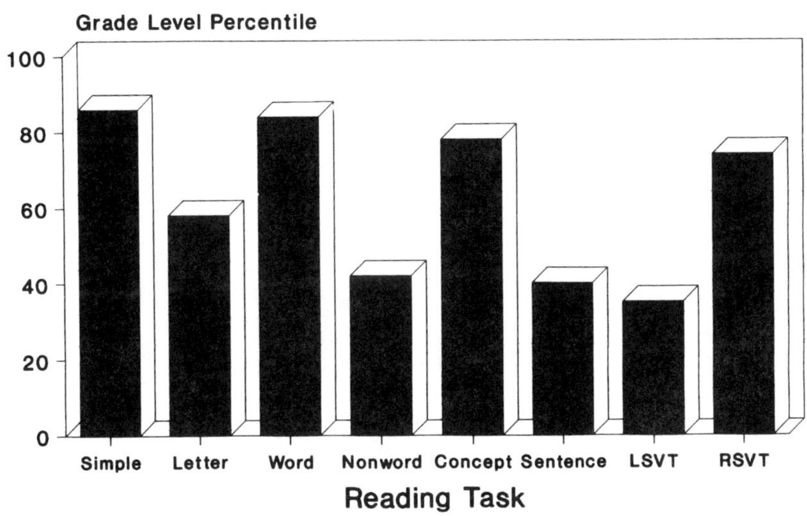

FIGURE 3
ADD profile performance profile on LATAS tasks.

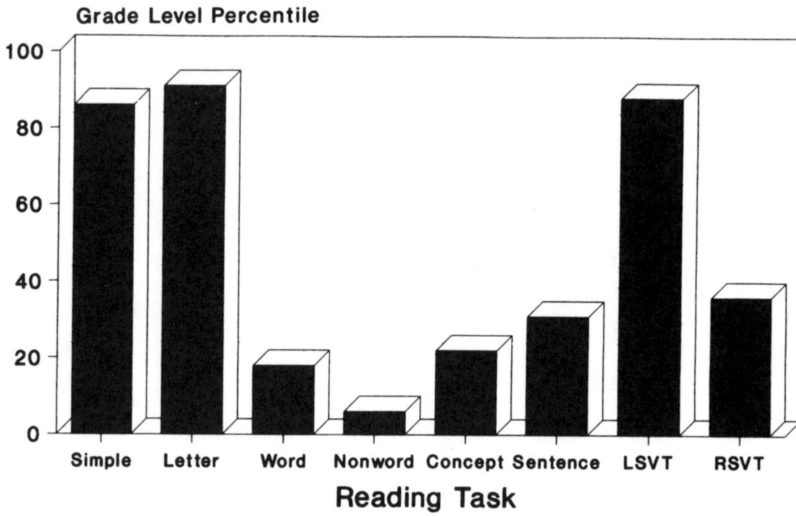

FIGURE 4
Specific reading disability performance profile on LATAS tasks.

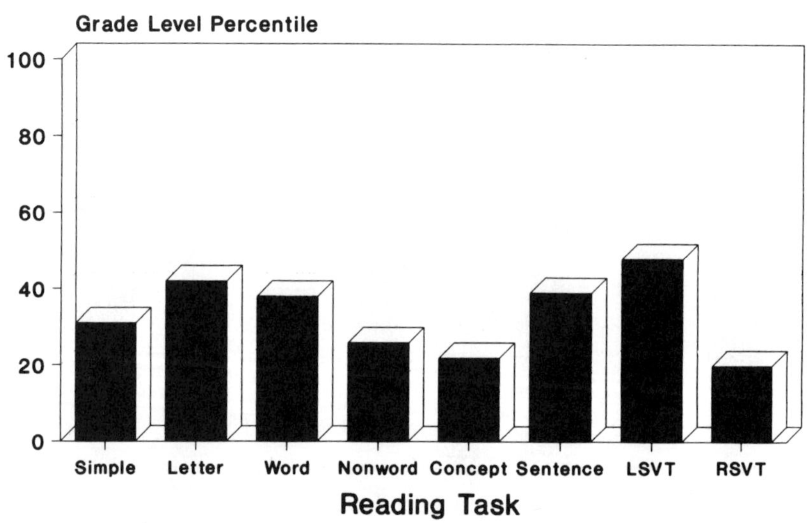

FIGURE 5
Garden variety poor reader performance profile on LATAS tasks.

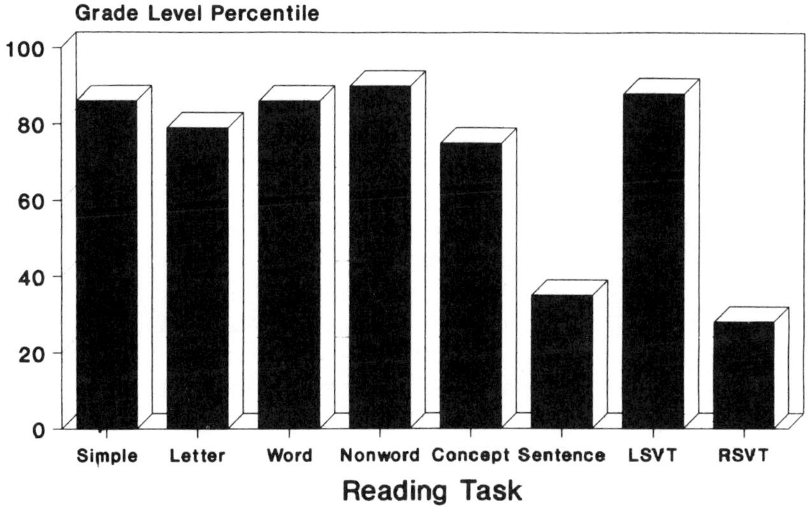

FIGURE 6
Meaning deficit performance profile on LATAS tasks.

of the test. Note, however, that the poor reader who cannot comprehend the written material might very well perform better on the listening test than on the reading test, as will be seen in a later profile.

Figure 2 is a profile that we call the *global cognitive deficit profile*, characterized by poor performance on all of the LATAS tasks. The global cognitive deficit profile demonstrates the utility of the LATAS assessments for sorting out diagnostic alternatives. Imagine, for instance, that the only thing a diagnostician knew about the student in Figure 2 was that he performed poorly on a reading comprehension test. The diagnostician might propose several competing explanations for the poor reading performance aside from the possibility that the student lacked reading skill. Vision problems is one possibility, but notice that the LATAS assessment makes the vision reason less probable because the explanation is not consistent with equally poor performance on both the listening and reading SVT test. Another possible reason for poor reading performance is that the student lacks the prior knowledge necessary to interpret the reading passages. This explanation is also consistent with the examinee's poor performance on the listening SVT test. However, the lack of background knowledge explanation would not explain why the student would perform at low levels on the simple response time and letter perception tasks on the CAAS battery. Yet another reason for poor reading performance might be a lack of fluency in the language of assessment; however, again this explanation would not necessarily be consistent with poor performance on a perceptual task such as the simple response time task. A final explanation that is consistent with the entire pattern of data is that the examinee has a global cognitive deficit that depresses performance in both language-based and perceptual tasks.

Figure 3 presents a profile that we sometimes see with children who have attention deficit disorder, sometimes accompanied by hyperactivity (ADHD). We administer both the listening and reading SVT tests individually in a quiet room. ADD children seem able to maintain concentration on a reading SVT test for the half-hour or so that it takes to administer the test. However, it appears that their attention wanders in the listening condition. Though we have no direct evidence this is true, we believe that the opportunity to look around the room during administration of the listening test allows the ADD student to "tune in and tune out" while listening to the passages and the test questions. In contrast, while reading the student's eyes tend to remain focused on the printed page, making the examinee less subject to distraction, with the result that reading performance exceeds listening performance. The distractibility of ADD students carries over to CAAS tasks, where a variety of patterns are seen. Sometimes, a relatively constant pattern of performance can be seen on lower-level tasks but with depressed performance on higher-level tasks, which probably results from the lack of academic progress caused by the inability to concentrate on instructional activities while in school. Other ADD students are characterized by substantial variability both within and between testing sessions. Sometimes, they perform exceptionally well on one task only to completely bomb on the next one. Sometimes they drop or gain as much as 40 percentile points from one test administration to another.

The profile in Figure 4 is one that we commonly see with students who have been diagnosed (by diagnosticians outside of LATAS) as having a specific reading disability. The characteristic pattern for this type of student is that listening performance is considerably better than reading performance, and performance on the CAAS reading tasks is depressed relative to performance on the simple and letter tasks. We also find that relative performance on the nonword task is typically poorer than word performance for the specific reading disability student. This result is consistent with the view that many students with a specific reading disability suffer from the inability to utilize phonemic knowledge in the word identification process (e.g., Stanovich & Siegel, 1994). Finally, we often see another pattern in our specific reading disability students that may be a unique characteristic of the students we work with. As the profile in Figure 4 shows, our specific reading disability students typically have relative performance on the concept and sentence tasks that is better than their performance on the word and nonword tasks. This may be an artifact, in that the students we work with who have a specific reading disability are uncommonly bright, and they may be using superior vocabulary and strategic knowledge to overcome to some degree their poor word processing capabilities.

Figure 5 displays a typical profile of a "garden variety poor reader." The reader's performance hovers around the average to below average range on all of the tasks. Notice that the garden variety poor reader's profile is differentiated from the specific reading disability profile in Figure 4 by the fact that the specific reading disability student displays superior performance on the listening SVT test and on the simple and letter CAAS tasks.

Finally, Figure 6 displays a profile that we call the *meaning deficit* profile. The student's performance on the reading SVT test is depressed, as is performance on the sentence processing task on the CAAS, but the remainder of the student's performance is average to above average. We have found that this type of student is a matter of great puzzlement to teachers who depend to a large extent on oral reading capability as a means of judging a student's reading competence. The meaning deficit student is often a superior oral reader, but has difficulty extracting the meaning of what he or she is reading.

The reader might note that the different profiles depicted in Figures 1–6 suggest different intervention strategies for each of the readers. The good readers are doing fine and should be left alone. Students with global comprehension deficits and the garden variety poor readers are reading about as well as could be expected given the comprehension cap imposed by their listening comprehension performance and their limited low-level processing skills. Before reading performance could be expected to improve for these readers, instructional interventions would have to eliminate the global barriers and improve lower-level processing capabilities. The ADD student with the profile depicted in Figure 3 could be provided a quieter, less distracting place to work or could use medication to reduce levels of distractibility (as an aside, we have often assessed ADD students under medicated and nonmedicated conditions and difference in performance in the two states is striking). The specific reading disability student depicted in Figure 4 could profit from direct reading instruction designed to eliminate skill deficits that are blocking reading comprehension performance. Finally, the meaning deficiency student depicted in Figure 6 might profit from instruction that teaches students strategies for extracting the meaning from text (see, for example, Palincsar & Brown, 1984). For example, the interventions might consist of activities like predicting what will come next at various points in a reading exercise and summarizing the gist of material that has just been read.

THE RESULTS OF INSTRUCTIONAL INTERVENTIONS BASED ON LATAS ASSESSMENTS

The fourth criterion that Royer and Sinatra (1994) identified for an effective reading diagnostic system was that diagnoses must lead to prescriptions for educational interventions that alleviate the reading difficulties of the student. Evidence regarding the extent to which the LATAS model satisfies this criteria will be presented in the form of three case studies of students who have received services from LATAS.

Case Study 1. JS

JS came to LATAS in December 1994, at the middle of his grade 6 school year. He has been diagnosed as having ADD and has been receiving medication during the school day since the fifth grade. JS and his family have been working with a clinical psychologist on behavioral problems at home for several years, and he was referred to LATAS by the clinician. In addition to his behavioral disorder, JS has a long history of academic difficulties, and he underwent his first core evaluation when he was in grade 3. The evaluation resulted in him receiving special education services, and until the middle of the sixth grade, he went to a resource room for reading instruction. His resource room placement ended when he walked out of the bathroom one morning with a noose around his neck and informed his mother that he would hang himself if he had to keep going to the resource room with the "dumb kids." JS's grades were in the C to low C range in reading, language arts, and spelling and in the B to B+ range in math, social studies, and science.

JS did not take the SVT listening and reading comprehension tests during his initial visits to LATAS because at that time we did not have norms for the test. However, he did take the CAAS battery and his results on that battery are presented in Figure 7. For the moment, the reader should only attend to the "initial" assessment bars in Figure 7.

JS's CAAS profile generally matched the profile that we have seen for students with a specific reading disability. His simple and letter performance was in the average to low average range, his word performance was poor, his nonword performance was very poor, and his performance on the concept and sentence processing tasks was in the average range. In addition, JS's performance on the math component of the CAAS assessment was above average. Our assessment results with JS were similar to those obtained on other assessments he had undergone. As an example, here is a quote from a psychoeducational evaluation that was completed during grade 5.

> His fluid reasoning and processing speed performances were low average. This indicates that he may need some additional time to think through the information before responding. Research has indicated that students who have reading disabilities tend to score lower on tasks which involve processing speed and results suggest that even though academic performance develops, some students may continue to have difficulty with the basic rapid processing of symbols into young adulthood.

This evaluation led to the following prescriptions (also from the psychoeducational evaluation) for helping JS with his academic difficulties:

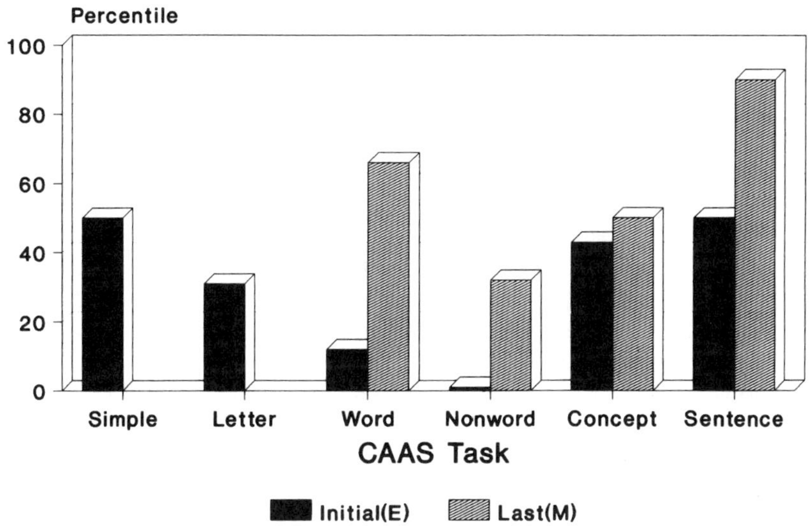

FIGURE 7

JS's initial and last percentile performance on CAAS reading tasks.

Classroom modifications to accommodate for processing speed should include:

1. allowing additional time to complete tasks
2. emphasizing accuracy, not speed
3. reducing the volume of work so that it can be completed in a reasonable amount of time

These academic prescriptions for JS illustrate the largest difference between what LATAS attempts to do and what, in our experience, is current educational practice. Current educational practice says that, if you find a learning problem, you change the system to accommodate to the problem. Almost always the accommodation is to slow down the pace of instruction. The LATAS model takes the opposite approach. We do not want to change the system (which is not to say that it does not need changing), we want to change the student. In JS's case, we wanted to speed up the slow processing that seemed to be the basis of his academic difficulties.

Before describing the interventions we used with JS, I would like to comment on his nonword performance and on whether it makes instructional sense to address his weaknesses in this skill. We have decided not to conduct direct instruction on recognition of nonwords because it does not seem sensible to teach students to recognize nonwords when we could be teaching them to recognize words. We have also chosen to not conduct direct instruction in phonics skills that might result in improved performance in both word and nonword recognition. Our reasoning is that students who have a reading disability caused by a phonological core deficit are unlikely to be able to derive considerable benefit from phonics instruction (see Stanovich & Siegel, 1994, for a description of phonological core deficits). We have no direct evidence from our lab that this is true, but we do know that many of the students we see at LATAS have had extensive instruction in phonics skills at school with little obvious benefit.

Aside from performance on the nonword task, it is apparent that JS's weakest reading skill is word identification. Accordingly, our initial intervention efforts were focused on building his word recognition skill to the point where he had a large corpus of words that could be automatically recognized without conscious thought. Our intervention consisted of sending JS and his parents home with four pages of 40 words at grade 4–6 level drawn from the Dale and O'Rourke (1976) word lists. Five nights a week JS sat down with a parent and named the words on each of the four pages as fast as possible while trying to maintain accuracy. The parent recorded the time per page, corrected his pronunciation of any words that he missed (after the timed trial), and then JS computed the mean time per page and recorded the time on his home graph, which is shown in Figure 8. When JS's home performance on the 160 initial words indicated that he had reached a plateau in skill development, he was given another set of 40 words, and this continued until he had achieved sight word mastery of four sets of 160 words (640 total words).

JS's home graph, shown in Figure 8, illustrates several interesting aspects of the home training. Note that his word naming performance begins at 70 seconds per page (1.75 seconds per word) and he reaches a plateau on the first word set at around day 19 of training at about 25 seconds per page (.62 seconds per word). His performance on set 2 begins on day 25 and starts at about the same place as with set 1 (about 70 seconds per page), but it takes him only 13 days of training to reach a plateau. On word set 3, he begins at a much lower level than on the previous sets (about 38 seconds per page), and he takes only five days to plateau at around .7 seconds per word. I will return to a discussion of this pattern, where practice causes the student to start faster and reach a plateau sooner when new material is encountered, after a description of the next phase of our interventions with JS.

After JS had attained very rapid sight recognition of the 720 grade 4–6 words, we began an intervention designed to achieve automatic activation of the meaning of the words. In the word meaning exercise, JS went through the same word lists he had mastered in the word naming exercise, but now when he looked at each word he said anything that came to mind that indicated that he knew the meaning of the word. He might say a synonym or antonym or provide some relevant context (e.g., saying "lightbulb" if the word was electric). Again, he went through the lists as fast as possible and a parent timed each of the four pages and JS computed his mean performance and plotted it on his home graph. Figure 9 shows JS's performance on three

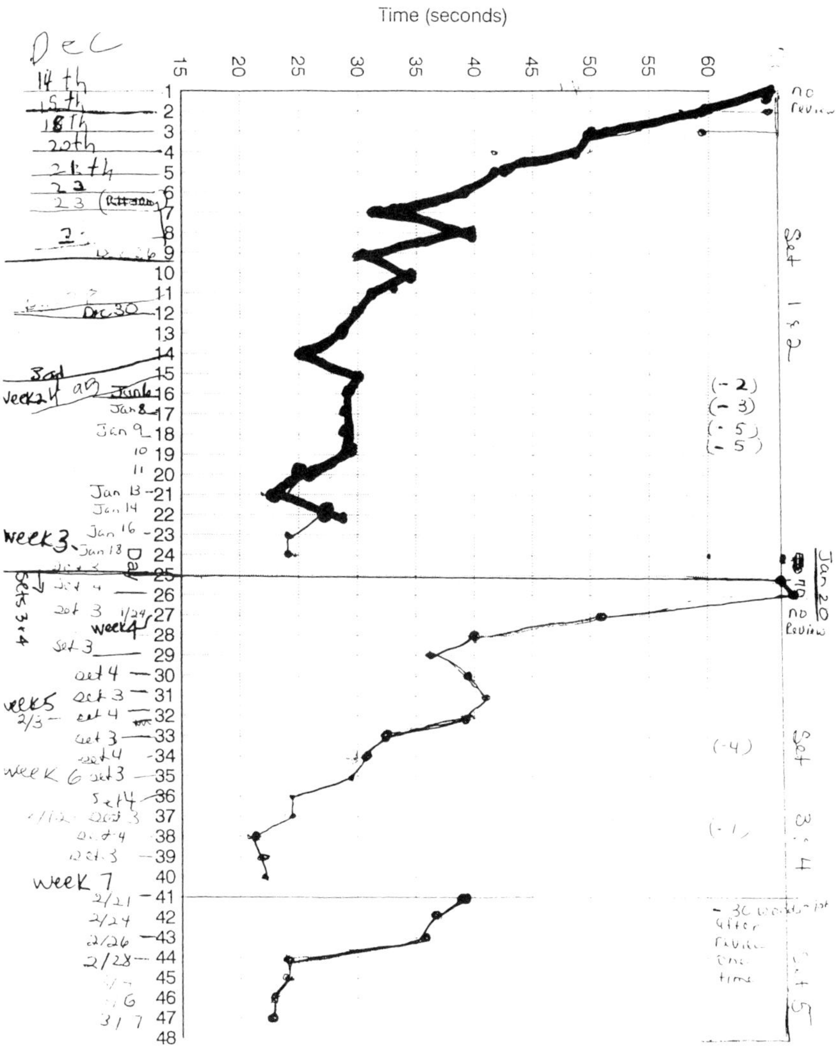

FIGURE 8
JS's home graph for word naming response times.

of the word sets. Note that he starts out at around 155 seconds per page (4 seconds per word) and he reaches a plateau at day 9 at about 70 seconds (1.75 seconds per word). On the second set he started at about 90 seconds per page and reached a plateau after six days at about 60 seconds per page; and on set three he started at about 110 seconds, but got down to about 65 seconds per page in two days.

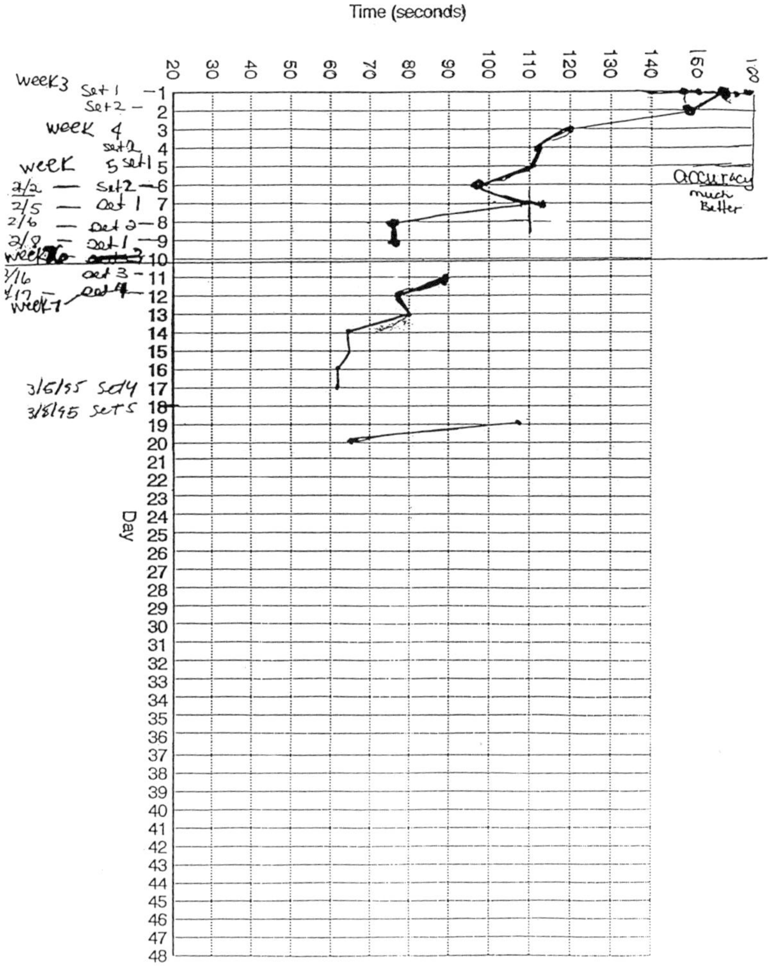

FIGURE 9

JS's home graph for word meaning response times.

The home graphs that all LATAS students produce (of which Figures 8 and 9 are illustrations) have had an unanticipated impact. A problem I anticipated as we developed our intervention activities was difficulty in keeping students on task. I devised several direct reward-for-performance strategies that I expected to put into play as soon as enthusiasm for the practice sessions waned. However, much to our surprise, the dropping line on the graph has captivated every student we have worked with. For students who have had a long history of academic failure, the concrete demonstration of growing academic skill in the form of a dropping line on a graph turned out to be enormously self-reinforcing. We have instituted a "LATAS" game that allows students to gain rewards for gains on their weekly CAAS assessments, but we have never had to institute procedures for rewarding students for home performance.

The pattern where JS, as a function of practice, got progressively faster the first time he worked on new material and progressively faster at attaining plateau levels of performance is typical of almost all of the students we have worked with. It seems obvious that the concentrated practice with an emphasis on speed produces a capability that transfers to new material. A similar finding has been reported by Johnson and Layng (1992), using techniques very similar to those used at LATAS. The metaphor may not be apt, but it is as if the student is building a mental "word munching" muscle that enables faster acquisition of new words.

During the time JS was involved in home practice, he returned on a weekly basis to LATAS, where he retook the CAAS reading battery. These assessments, which were conducted for the most part using materials different from those being studied at home, provided an independent measure of his progress and information that contributed to the decision to switch JS to more difficult words or from naming to meaning exercises. JS's progress on the CAAS assessments in the time frame from December 1994 to August 1995 is illustrated in the Last bars in Figure 7. Figure 7 shows JS's grade 6 percentiles on the CAAS elementary tasks when he first arrived at LATAS (Initial, E), and his performance on the most recent middle school level CAAS (Last, M). The change from the CAAS elementary level tasks (suitable for students in grades 2–5, although also normed on middle school students) to the middle school tasks (suitable for students in grades 6–8) occurred because JS's level of performance on the elementary tasks was beginning to approach the ceiling. As can be seen in Figure 7, JS's CAAS performance indicates that he has progressed from having poor skills (relative to his grade peers) on easy material to having average to good skills on age-appropriate reading material. The exception to this generalization is his performance on the nonword task, which remains poor relative to performance on the other reading tasks. The failure to affect nonword performance to the same degree as other skills could have to do with the nature of JS's reading disability. That is, if he has a phonological core deficit, it might be difficult for him to make much progress on developing a skill that requires him to use phonemic analysis capabilities.

Earlier it was mentioned that JS started at a faster pace on new words with increasing practice and he reached a performance plateau faster as a function of practice, both were evidence of practice-related transfer. Figure 7 also provides evidence of practice-related transfer. The intervention activities during the time frame depicted by Figures 7, 8, and 9 consisted of exercises designed to build fluency in word recognition and the activation of word meanings. Note, however, that JS's sentence processing performance has increased markedly, and he now discerns the meaning of middle school level

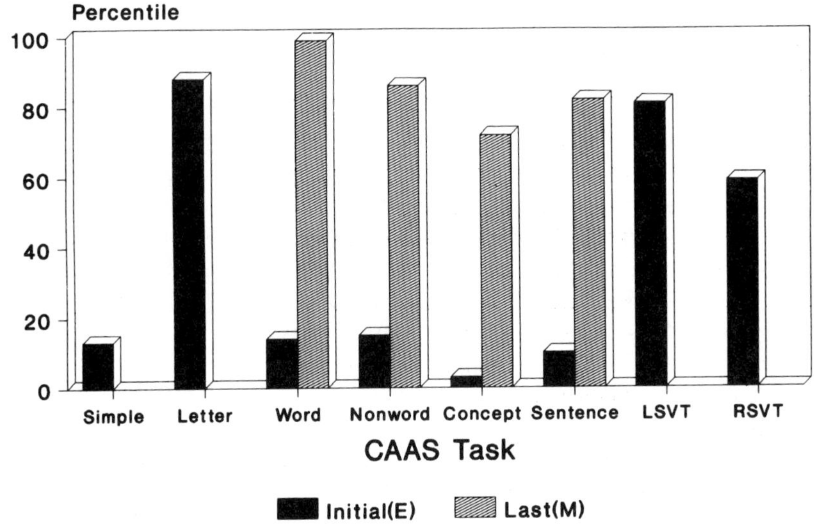

FIGURE 10

GC's initial and last percentile performance on LATAS reading tasks.

sentences faster and more accurately than the majority of his peers. We interpret this to mean that the skills that JS has been building at the level of identifying words and activating their meaning have enabled him to be a more efficient processor of sentence-length written material.

Case Study 2. GC

GC came to LATAS in August 1994, shortly before he started the eighth grade. Like JS, he had been diagnosed as having ADD and was medicated during school hours. His academic performance in the elementary grades was in the average range but at about grade 5 his performance began to deteriorate markedly. His grade point average for his grade 7 school year was in the D minus range, and he received four Fs in core academic subjects during the four marking periods of the school year. His performance on the reading sections of standardized tests was consistently low, although somewhat variable. For instance, at the beginning of grade 7 he scored at the 34th percentile, and at the beginning of grade 8, at the 4th percentile. His math, social studies, and science performance on the standardized tests was in the average range.

GC's pattern of performance on the SVT and CAAS tests is depicted by the "initial" bars in Figure 10. He scored at the 81st percentile on a SVT listening comprehension test and at 59th percentile on the reading comprehension test. As was the case with JS, we initially assessed GC on the elementary level of the CAAS tasks, and his performance on the tasks is depicted by the "initial" bars in Figure 10. GC's pattern of performance is somewhat unusual in that we generally see substantial correspondence between performance on the simple task and performance on the letter task, but GC's performance on these two tasks is very different. One clear pattern that is obvious though in Figure 10 is that GC's performance is considerably depressed on all of the CAAS reading tasks.

GC arrived at LATAS with an "attitude," and he was convinced that he was going to have to do things that were appropriate for children much younger than he (a belief derived from his experiences in special education classes). Accordingly, we wanted to give him a challenging activity. We settled on doing word naming training using commercially available English vocabulary words (*Vis Ed* cards). The words come in boxes of 1000 words and are challenging even for college level readers (e.g., *permeate, etymology, prevaricator, gyration, nefarious*). Our intervention consisted of having GC select 80 words from the box, divide them into piles of 20, and pronounce each of the 20 words with the help of his parent. He then repiled the 20 words and named them as fast as possible with his parent recording the time. This procedure was repeated with the remaining three piles of 20 words, and GC then computed the mean time per pile and recorded the time on his home graph. GC and his parent would repeat this exercise five nights a week, taking a new stack of 80 cards each night. Using this procedure, it took GC 12 practice nights to make it through the box, whereupon he started again. During this phase of training no effort was made to teach GC the meaning of the words.

GC's home word naming graph is presented in Figure 11. As can be seen in the graph, GC made no progress during the first nine days of training. However, at day 10 his performance began to improve and that improvement continued until he leveled off at about day 26. During this period of precipitous drop in naming times, GC became very involved in his performance, and he asked around day 20 what the world record was for word naming, because he thought he could beat it. As you can see from his graph, he got to the point where he could do any 20 words in box of 1000 words in about 14 seconds, a time that very well may be around the world record.

After it was obvious that GC had reached a plateau on the word naming exercise, we began word meaning training. This activity was identical to the word naming training except that rather than naming the word, GC said anything that came to mind that indicated that he knew the meaning of the word. GC's home graph for the word meaning exercise is presented in Figure 12. Again the graph shows steady gains in his ability to provide an indication of the meaning of the boxed words.

As was the case with JS, we also monitored GC's progress with repeated CAAS assessments. His performance on the last CAAS assessment he took (in June 1995) is depicted in Figure 10 by the "last" (M) bars. During training we also moved GC from the elementary version of the CAAS tasks to the

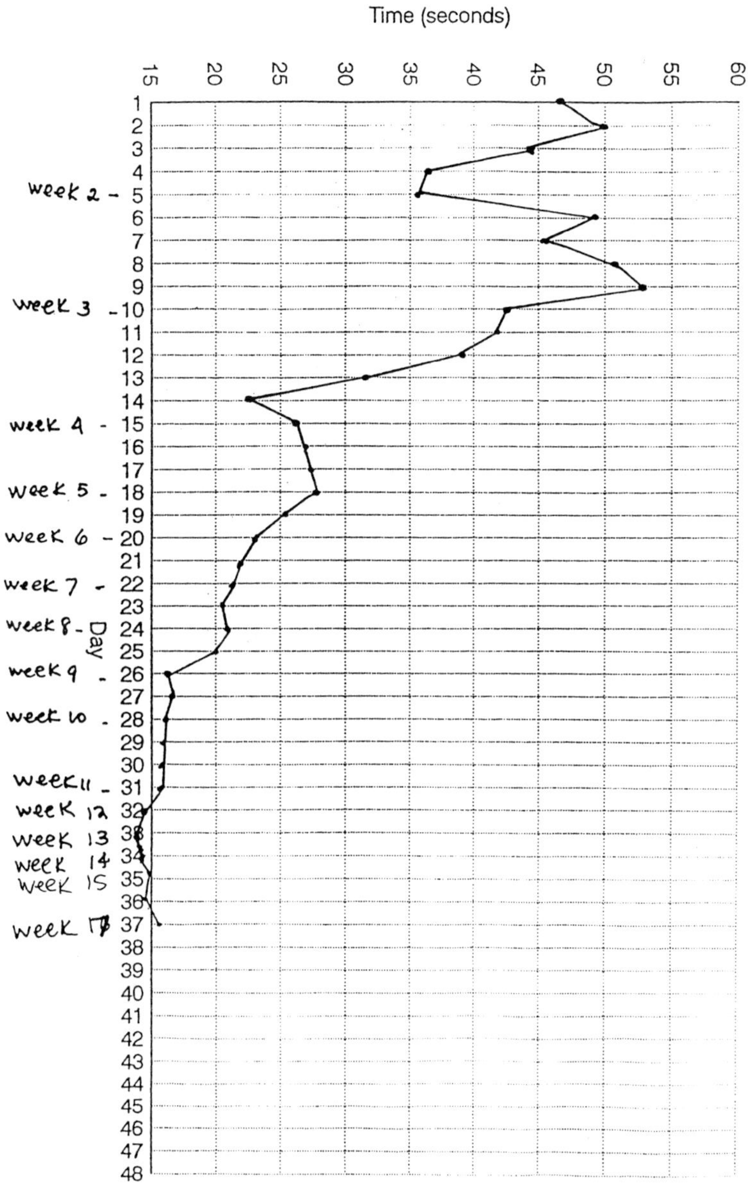

FIGURE 11

GC's home graph for word naming response times.

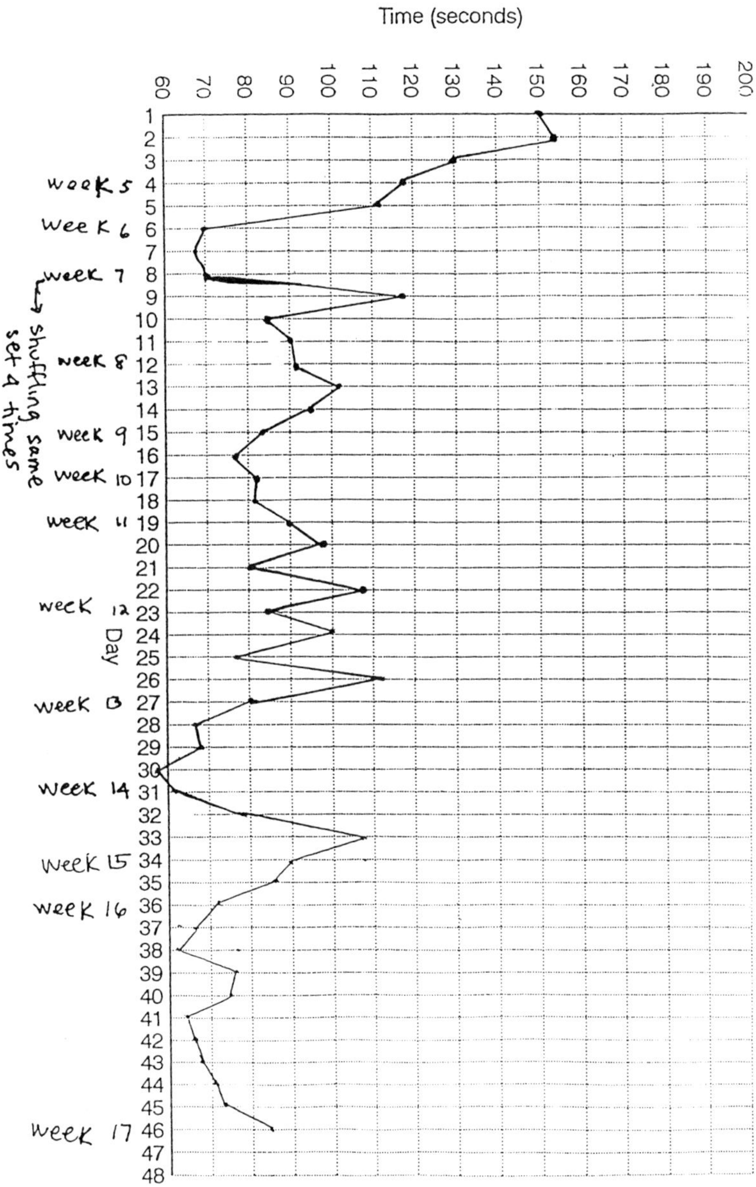

FIGURE 12
GC's home graph for word meaning response times.

middle school version, because he was approaching the ceiling on the elementary tasks. GC's performance on the CAAS tasks again provides evidence of a transfer of skills. We never worked directly on sentence processing. Nonetheless, GC's performance on the sentence comprehension task moved from the 14th percentile on the elementary version of the task to the 81st percentile on the middle school version of the task. GC's academic performance also showed modest improvement during the year he was at LATAS, in that his grade point average for his grade 8 year was in the C− range and he received not a single F during the school year. GC no longer receives services from LATAS, but the clinical psychologist who is working with GC and his parents called recently and reported that he had a B minus average on his most recent grade 9 report card and that he was running for class president. Both of these accomplishments would have been outside of the LATAS staff's range of imagination when we first met GC.

Case Study 3. JB

JB is a third grade student who came to LATAS on the recommendation of the mother of another student we were working with. JB initially received a core evaluation from her school near the beginning of the third grade, followed by an evaluation by a clinical psychologist specializing in learning disabilities. Both evaluations indicated that JB had developmental dyslexia. The tests administered during these evaluations indicated that JB's reading level was at least one year behind her peers.

The results of JB's initial LATAS assessments (May 1995) are presented by the "initial" bars in Figure 13. As can be seen in the figure, JB's performance on the simple and letter CAAS tasks was above average, but her performance on the remaining tasks was well below average. JB's pattern of performance on the SVT tests is noteworthy as it is contrary to the pattern we ordinarily see with students who have a specific reading disability. Specifically, JB's listening performance was well below her reading performance whereas that pattern is normally reversed for students with a specific reading disability. We are not sure why this happened but it is noteworthy that JB has had a long history of ear infections and had tubes in her ears during the first evaluation. It is possible that she simply did not hear the SVT passages very well.

We began JB's intervention with practice on four pages of "word family" lists. The lists were constructed by arranging words with common endings into four columns on a page with each page containing approximately 30 words. For instance, one column might contain words with *ale* endings (*ale, bale, sale, dale,* etc.), another *at* endings, and so on. Every night JB would sit down with a parent and go through a page of words as fast as possible while maintaining accuracy. The average time per page would be calculated and

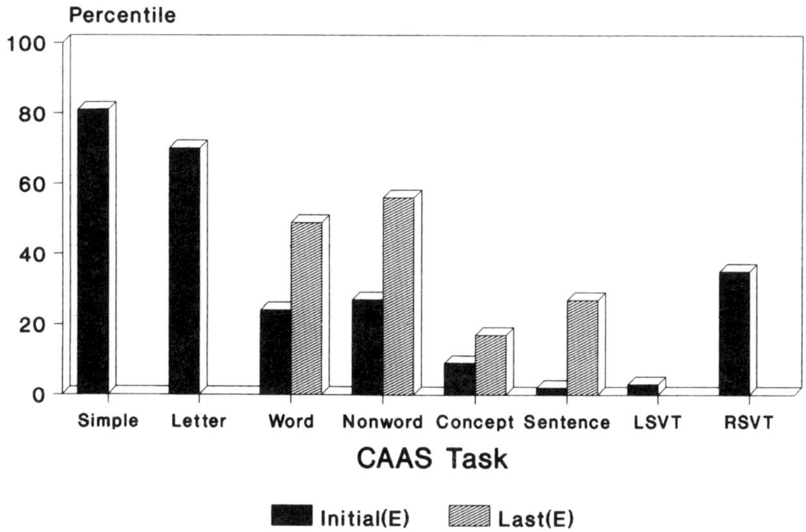

FIGURE 13
JB's initial and last percentile performance on LATAS reading tasks.

recorded on her home graph. When she achieved mastery of one set (four pages) of word families, we gave her another. When she had attained mastery of three sets of word family lists (approximately 360 words), we gave her practice lists that consisted of the same words she had been studying but arranged in random order. She is currently (October 1995) on her third set of randomly arranged word families. During this training period JB would return to LATAS once a week where she retook the CAAS assessments.

JB's home graph on the randomly presented word family lists is depicted in Figure 14. JB's record of home practice presents a particularly striking example of the transfer that I described earlier. JB's first practice session on set 1 words took her 113 seconds (2.8 seconds per word) and she reached a plateau at approximately 45 seconds on day 10. Her first session with set 2 took her 102 seconds on average (2.5 seconds per word) and she reached a plateau 11 days later at 32 seconds per page. She began set three at 62 seconds per page (1.5 seconds per word) and she reached a plateau in six days at about 40 seconds per page (1 second per word).

JB's progress on the elementary level CAAS tasks is depicted by the "final" bars in Figure 13. As can be seen in the figure, she has attained normal third grade performance on the word and nonword naming tasks and improved her competence to a considerable degree on the category and sentence processing tasks.

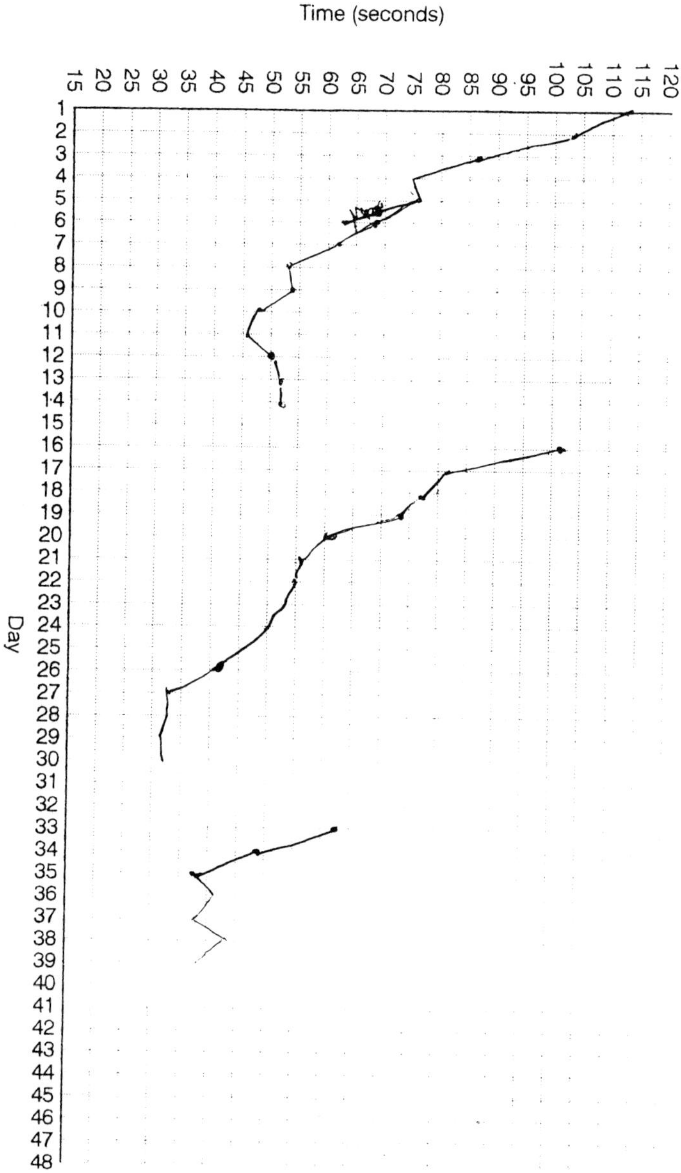

FIGURE 14
JB's home graph for word naming response times.

OTHER INTERVENTION STRATEGIES USED AT LATAS

Once we repair lower-level problems that are blocking student progress, we work on developing specific and general skills that are designed to help a student's school performance. Several of these techniques can be illustrated in our work with KK, a student enrolled in the 11th grade.

Our approach to improving KK's course performance involves a variant of procedures that have been described already and some techniques that have not been described thus far. The familiar procedure involves isolating the technical vocabulary encountered in a course of study and using our word naming and word meaning tasks to attain fluency of that vocabulary. For instance, we copied all of the terms listed in the glossary of KK's chemistry textbook and are having KK alternate between nights of working on general vocabulary terms (from the *Vis Ed* vocabulary box) and nights of working on chemistry terms. Similar to the situation with general vocabulary, when KK reaches the point where she can name the technical terms in under 1 second per item, we will switch to training on the meaning of the terms. We are also monitoring KK's progress using the CAAS system. We have created a word naming CAAS task that contains the words KK is studying in her chemistry home practice activities, and her performance on the task provides an index of the degree to which she is attaining word recognition mastery.

The previously unmentioned procedures that we are using to work on KK's course performance include a technique to help her identify important material to be studied from her textbooks and a procedure designed to provide her with a visual map of the course content she is studying. The technique for identifying important content involves developing a study and self-test list using the subject matter index of a textbook. Say, for instance, that KK is expected to study and take a test on Chapter 2 of her book, which is covered by pages 20–45. We have her go into the subject matter index of the book and write down every entry (and page number) that appears between pages 20 and 45. She will then be instructed to study the chapter, and use the index listings as self-study questions. If she can successfully answer the question suggested by the entry, she goes on to the next entry. If she cannot answer the question, she goes to the page number beside the entry and restudies the material. She will continue this process until she can answer questions about the entry generated both by herself and by a parent. The logic of the subject index study procedure is that many students with learning problems have difficulty differentiating important material from unimportant material. Authors presumably place content they believe to be important in the subject index, hence study of that material is one way to concentrate study on important information.

The final technique we plan to use with KK to help her in her course work is a variant of semantic mapping procedures that have shown by a number of researchers to enhance learning (see Lambiotte et al., 1989, for a review of this literature). Our usage of the procedure will be to develop reasonably high-level visual depictions of the content of each of the textbooks that KK will be using during her 11th grade school year. Ideally, these depictions will provide a "big picture" perspective that will assist her in the learning process.

USER-FRIENDLY PROPERTIES OF THE LATAS PROCEDURES

The final properties that a teacher-useful assessment and intervention procedures should have are twofold. The procedures should be able to be based on local curriculum materials, and teachers should be capable of developing the assessment and intervention procedures without extensive training. Both the SVT assessments and the CAAS assessments have these properties.

Teacher-Friendly Properties of SVT Tests

SVT research (summarized in Royer, 1995) demonstrates that SVT listening and reading comprehension tests can be based on virtually any text sample. Examples of materials that have been used in studies include material from college level textbooks (e.g., Royer, Marchant, Sinatra, & Lovejoy, 1990), from elementary level textbooks (e.g., Royer, Hastings, & Hook, 1979), from medical information materials (Ramos & Bayona, 1991), from abstracts of psychology journal articles (Royer, Lynch, Hambleton, & Bulgareli, 1984), from manuals used in military training (Royer, Tirre, Sinatra, & Greene, 1989), from scripts to be read on educational radio in a developing country (Anzalone & Mathima, 1989), and from videotapes of classroom interactions (Clark, 1994). The wide variety of materials that have been used as the basis for SVT tests indicates that it should be possible to base tests on local curriculum materials.

It is also possible to easily train people to develop SVT tests. At this time, I know of projects that have involved training SVT test development procedures to teachers in bilingual education programs, mainstream classroom teachers, educators in Grenada, Agency for International Development personnel in Guatemala and Belize, and graduate and undergraduate students enrolled in a university. Royer (1995) describes a training process that has proven to be effective in a variety of settings.

The Open-Ended Architecture of CAAS

All of the test content and test control properties of CAAS are in the form of easily edited ASCII files. This means that anyone with even a modicum of computer skill can change the parameters of the testing procedure and insert his or her own content into any of the CAAS tasks. Moreover, the assessments themselves are easy to administer, in that the CAAS system is menu driven and requires very little computer competence on the part of the test administrator. This means that teachers could construct CAAS tasks based on materials that were drawn from their instructional curriculums and then administer the tests themselves.

FINAL COMMENTS

This chapter has described assessment procedures and instructional activities that can be used by teachers who work with students who are having reading problems. The assessment procedures and the instructional activities used by LATAS are highly interrelated. The assessment procedures are designed to provide a fine-grained picture of a student's reading competency and identify specific skills that should be targeted by the intervention activities. Assessment continues as the instructional interventions are implemented and it provides indexes that are used to change the nature of the interventions the students are receiving. This means that interventions are highly individualized. Each student has an intervention plan based on his or her own competency profile, and changes are made in instructional interventions as a function of individual progress. We believe that this constant interplay between assessment and intervention is essential to help students who are truly learning disabled.

In this chapter I have presented data from only 3 of the students with whom we have worked, but data from 10 others show comparable levels of progress. The results we have obtained from most of them suggests that the LATAS procedures have significantly improved their academic functioning. Our results are largely restricted, though, to demonstrations that LATAS techniques change performance on home graphs and LATAS assessments. At this point we have accumulated very little evidence regarding the impact where it really counts, in the classroom and on standardized tests. Collection of data on the impact in these arenas is an important goal of future research.

Another research agenda we are trying to implement is to determine if some of the techniques that we have developed at LATAS will work in a school setting. LATAS staff are currently working with special education teachers in an elementary school and a high school in an effort to determine whether the techniques that we use at LATAS can be implemented in their schools.

Before completing the chapter I want to note that not all of the students we have worked with have been success stories. Five students began the LATAS program and dropped out before they had made the progress we felt they might have made. Four of these students were adolescents who had

ADD. Adolescents with ADD are difficult to work with and the clinical research literature documents the failure of most efforts to positively influence either their behavioral disorders or accompanying academic problems (Barkley, Fischer, Edelbrock, & Smallish, 1990; Hinshaw, 1992). Our experiences with these students has led to a policy where we will not work with high school age students with ADD who are having behavioral difficulties either at home or at school. The students we worked with who dropped out were not willing to invest the work necessary to make academic gains using the techniques we had devised. Since we believe that the unwillingness to practice academic tasks is associated with the general defiance exhibited by many older students with ADD, we choose to invest our efforts with younger children where there might be more positive payoff.

The fifth failure experience we had was a girl in grade 5 who had a specific math disability. Our math intervention efforts, which are similar to those we use in reading, involved nightly practice of math facts accompanied with weekly evaluations on the CAAS system. The girl we were working with had a general performance anxiety that had negatively affected her performance in a variety of areas including sports, playing a musical instrument, and school functioning, particularly in math. During CAAS assessments and home practice sessions she would exhibit signs of considerable stress and her mother reported that on one occasion she had even fainted. Several weeks into our training activities, her mother elected to stop the program, believing that the stress being induced could not be compensated for by the gains that she was making.

Acknowledgments

I thank Barbara Greene, Maria Carlo, Cheryl Cisero, Gale Sinatra, Loel Tronsky, and the rest of the LATAS staff for the contributions they have made to the research described in this chapter and for their comments on a draft of this chapter. Correspondence with the author should be sent to James M. Royer, Department of Psychology, University of Massachusetts, Amherst, MA 01003.

References

Anderson, J. R. (1983). *The architecture of cognition*. Cambridge, MA: Harvard University Press.

Anderson, J. R. (1993). *Rules of the mind*. Hillsdale, NJ: Erlbaum.

Anzalone, S. A., & Mathima, S. S. B. (1989). *Final external evaluation: Radio technology training* II (Project RETT II). Arlington, VA: Institute for International Research.

Barkley, R. A., Fischer, M., Edelbrock, C. S., & Smallish, L. (1990). The adolescent outcome of hyperactive children diagnosed by research criteria: I. An 8 year perspective follow-up study. *Journal of the American Academy of Child and Adolescent Psychiatry*, 29, 546–557.

Carlo, M. S., & Royer, J. M. (1995). *The cross-language transfer of component reading skills*. Article submitted for publication.

Carlo, M. S., & Skilton Sylvester, E. E. (1994a). *Cognitive components in L2 reading: A study of Adults Learning to Read English-as-a-Second-Language*. Philadelphia: University of Pennsylvania, National Center on Adult Literacy.

Carlo, M. S., & Skilton Sylvester, E. E. (1994b). *Validation of an English language assessment used with English as a Second Language adult literacy learners*. Philadelphia: University of Pennsylvania, National Center on Adult Literacy.

Carroll, J. B. (1977). Developing parameters of reading comprehension. In J. T. Guthrie (Ed.), *Cognition, curriculum, and comprehension* (pp. 1–15). Newark, DE: International Reading Association.

Cisero, C. A., Royer, J. M., Marchant, H. G., & Jackson, S. (1995). *Can the Computer-based Academic Assessment System (CAAS) be used to identify reading disability?: A look at the CAAS profiles of reading disabled college students*. Poster presented at the annual meeting of the American Educational Research Association, San Francisco.

Cisero, C. A., Royer, J. M., Marchant, H. G., & Jackson, S. J. (1996). *Using the Computer-based Academic Assessment System (CAAS) to identify reading disability in college students: A replication*. Paper presented at the 1996 annual meeting of the American Educational Research Association.

Cisero, C. A., Royer, J. M., Marchant, H. G., & Wint, F. (1994). *Diagnostic identification of dyslexic and learning-disabled college students using the Computer-based Academic Assessment System (CAAS)*. Poster presented at the annual meeting of the American Educational Research Association, New Orleans, LA.

Clark, C. L. (1994). *An experimental study of the ability of novice and experienced teachers to comprehend classroom interaction*. Unpublished master's thesis, Arizona State University, Tempe.

Dale, E., & O'Rourke, J. (1976). *The living word vocabulary*. Elgin, IL: Field Enterprises Educational.

Danks, J. H. (1980). Comprehension in listening and reading: Same or different? In J. H. Danks & K. Pezdek, *Reading and understanding*. Newark, DE: International Reading Association.

Greene, B. A., & Royer, J. M. (1994). A developmental review of response time data that support a cognitive component model of reading. *Educational Psychology Review, 6*, 141–172.

Hinshaw, S. P. (1992). Academic underachievement, attention deficits, and aggressions: Comorbidity and implications for intervention, *Journal of Consulting and Clinical Psychology, 60*, 893–903.

Horowitz, R., & Samuels, S. J. (Eds.). (1987). *Comprehension oral and written language*. San Diego, CA: Academic Press.

Johnson, K. R., & Layng, T. V. J. (1992). Breaking the structuralist barrier: Literacy and numeracy with fluency. *American Psychologist, 47*, 1475–1490.

Kleinman, G., & Schallert, D. L. (1978). Some things the reader needs to know that the listener doesn't. In P. D. Pearson & J. Hansen (Eds.), *Reading: Disciplined inquiry in process and practice. Twenty-Seventh Yearbook of the National Reading Conference* (pp. 138–142). Clemson, SC: National Reading Conference.

Lambiotte, J. G., Dansereau, D. F., Cross, D. R., & Reynolds, S. B. (1989). Multirelational semantic maps. *Educational Psychology Review, 1*, 331–368.

Messick, S. (1980). Test validity and the ethics of assessment. *American Psychologist, 35*, 1012–1227.

Palinscar, A. S., & Brown, A. L. (1984). Reciprocal teaching of comprehension-fostering and monitoring activities. *Cognition and Instruction, 1*, 117–175.

Perfetti, C. A. (1992). The representation problem in reading. In P. B. Gough, L. Ehri, & R. Treiman (Eds.). *Reading acquisition* (pp. 145–174). Hillsdale, NJ: Erlbaum.

Ramos, D., & Bayona, J. (1991). *Testing patient comprehension and the comprehensibility of educational materials using the Sentence Verification Technique* (Tech. Rep.). Rochester, NY: University of Rochester Medical School.

Rayner, K., & Pollatsek, A. (1989). *The psychology of reading*. Englewood Cliffs, NJ: Prentice-Hall.

Royer, J. M. (1990). The Sentence Verification Technique: A new direction in the assessment of reading comprehension. In S. M. Legg & J. Algina (Eds.), *Cognitive assessment of language and math outcomes* (pp. 144–191). Norwood, NJ: Ablex.

Royer, J. M. (1995). *The Sentence Verification Technique: A practical procedure for measuring listening and reading comprehension*. Article submitted for publication.

Royer, J. M., Carlo, C. S., & Cisero, C. A. (1992). School-based uses for the Sentence Verification Technique of measuring listening and reading comprehension. *Psychological Test Bulletin, 5*, 5–19.

Royer, J. M., Hastings, C. N., & Hook, C. (1979). A sentence verification technique for measuring reading comprehension. *Journal of Reading Behavior, 11*, 355–363.

Royer, J. M., Kulhavy, R. W., Lee, J. B., & Peterson, S. E. (1986). The Sentence Verification Technique as a measure of listening and reading comprehension. *Educational and Psychological Research, 6*, 299–314.

Royer, J. M., Lynch, D. J., Hambleton, R. K., & Bulgareli, C. (1984). Using the Sentence Verification Technique to assess the comprehension of technical text as a function of level of expertise. *American Educational Research Journal, 21*, 839–869.

Royer, J. M., Marchant, H. G., Sinatra, G. M., & Lovejoy, D. A. (1990). The prediction of college course performance from reading comprehension performance: Evidence for general and specific factors. *American Educational Research Journal, 27*, 158–179.

Royer, J. M., & Sinatra, G. M. (1994). A cognitive theoretical approach to reading diagnostics. *Educational Psychology Review, 6*, 81–113.

Royer, J. M., Sinatra, G. M., & Schumer, H. (1990). Patterns of individual differences in the development of listening and reading comprehension. *Contemporary Educational Psychology, 15*, 183–196.

Royer, J. M., Tirre, W. C., Sinatra, G. M., & Greene, B. A. (1989). The assessment of on-line comprehension of computer presented text. *Journal of Educational Research, 82*, 348–355.

Sinatra, G. M. (1989). *Implementation and initial validation of a computer-based system for the assessment of reading competencies*. Unpublished doctoral dissertation, University of Massachusetts, Amherst.

Sinatra, G. M., & Royer, J. M. (1993). The development of cognitive component processing skills that support skilled reading. *Journal of Educational Psychology, 85*, 509–519.

Stanovich, K. E. (1990). Concepts in developmental theories of reading skill: Cognitive resources, automaticity, and modularity. *Developmental Review, 10*, 72–100.

Stanovich, K. E., & Siegel, L. S. (1994). Phenotypic performance of children with reading disabilities: A regression-based test of the phonological-core variable-difference model. *Journal of Educational Psychology, 86*, 24–53.

Sticht, T. G., Beck, L. J., Hauke, R. N., Kleinman, G. M., & James, J. H. (1974). *Auding and reading: a developmental model*. Alexandria, VA: Human Resources Research Organization.

Walczyk, J. J. (1990). Relation among error detection, sentence verification, and low-level reading skills in fourth graders. *Journal of Educational Psychology, 82*, 491–497.

Walczyk, J. J. (1995). Testing a compensatory-encoding model. *Reading Research Quarterly, 30*, 396–408.

Wint, F. T., Cisero, C. A., & Royer, J. M. (1995). *Poor readers have different problems as revealed by the Computer-Based Academic Assessment System*. Paper presented at the annual meeting of the American Educational Research Association, San Francisco.

CHAPTER

8

Psychological Foundations of Elementary Writing Instruction

STEPHEN L. BENTON
Kansas State University

Teachers historically have placed less emphasis on writing skills than on reading skills. It was not until the first Conference on College Composition and Communication, in 1949, that English teachers began to emphasize K–12 writing instruction. Even into the 1980s, the essence of elementary literacy instruction was on reading and spelling (Squire, 1991).

Today, elementary teachers are doing a better job of teaching students how to write (Palincsar & Klenk, 1992). However, in some areas of writing instruction, they can do better. In many instances, students passively receive knowledge that is decontextualized from the setting in which it will be used. This is in contrast to the view that writing is a tool for communicating in real-life contexts. Students must understand that writing is a problem-solving process in which much learning can occur (Palincsar & Klenk, 1992). Rather than simply responding to a teacher's writing assignment, students need to initiate writing to express themselves, to accomplish tasks, or to learn something. In this chapter, I review theories of learning and development that have implications for helping teachers and students achieve these goals.

As shown in Table 1, several psychological theories influence contemporary elementary writing instruction: endogenous development, exogenous learning, functionalism, and dialectical constructivism. Endogenous developmentalists argue that learning to write is a natural process that develops within learners as they are exposed to literate environments. Exogenous learning methods emphasize direct instruction in basic skills such as handwriting, phonemic awareness, and spelling. Functionalism suggests that

Handbook of Academic Learning

TABLE 1
Major Theories and Models of Writing

Theoretical View	Definition	Concepts	Implications
Endogenous development	Writing skills develop before children can write competently; writers create knowledge about writing	Emergent literacy, whole language; cultural compatibility	Have print-rich classrooms; display students' writing; allow for exploration; integrate elements of literacy
Exogenous learning	Knowledge is acquired from the environment	Handwriting instruction, phonemic awareness training, spelling instruction	Vary writing materials and instruments; train students in phonological skills; accomodate to spelling disabilities
Functionalism	Writing is a process that involves critical thinking and communicating in the real world	Long-term memory, task environment, writing processes; expressive, transactional, and poetic writing	Draw upon students' knowledge and interests; allow students write to express, to do, and to learn
Dialectical constructivism	Writing is recontextualization and social construction of knowledge	Knowledge retrieval, expression verification; zone of proximal development	Young writers can revise and adapt prose to audience expectations with teacher or peer assistance

writing is a complex problem-solving process that involves false starts, regressions, and ongoing revision. Young writers learn best when they write for real audiences, and when they write to experience, to do, and to learn. Dialectical constructivists believe young writers are capable of adapting their writing to different audiences and revising their own and other's writing. Writers socially negotiate meaning through interactions with others. In the pages that follow, I elaborate on each of these theoretical positions and discuss their implications for elementary writing instruction.

ENDOGENOUS DEVELOPMENT

The essence of endogenous development is that individuals create knowledge about writing within their own memory structures rather than acquire information from the environment (Moshman, 1990). Endogenous developmentalists vary along a continuum of nativism and constructivism in their views about the origin of knowledge. The nativist position stresses genetic influences (e.g., Chomsky, 1980; Keil, 1981). Constructivists emphasize that writers actively construct knowledge from their experiences (Piaget, 1983, 1985). In both cases, what the student does internally may be more important than what the teacher does.

Some aspects of endogenous development are found in the concept of emergent literacy. Literacy refers to reading, writing, speaking, and listening skills, each of which is important for success in school and life. The concept of *emergent literacy* means children begin to develop these skills before they can actually read, write, speak, or spell competently. Learners therefore are neither *ready to read and write* nor *unable to read and write*. They vary along a continuum of emerging literacy skills.

Although reading is the most important element of literacy, learners should be competent in all forms of language acquisition and expression. Elements of literacy share common communication processes. For example, moderate correlations exist between reading achievement and writing quality (Benton, Corkill, Sharp, Downey, & Khramtsova, 1995) and between reading achievement and syntactic complexity in writing (Benton et al., 1995). Furthermore, poor readers tend to become poor writers (Juel, 1988). Students who read children's literature write more maturely than those who read only basals (Eckhoff, 1984), and the relationship between reading and writing becomes stronger as students mature (Loban, 1976). Reading and writing, therefore, no longer are taught separately but together (Pearson, 1985).

The notion of endogenous development also seems to underlie the *whole language* movement. Whole language programs view learning to read and write as natural processes. Children learn to read and write indirectly through exposure to literate environments (Stahl, McKenna, & Pagnucco, 1994). Whole language is student centered in that it focuses on the language of students rather than on the language of textbooks. The teacher's role is to provide opportunities for students to express themselves in writing (Simmons, 1991).

Whole language programs have potential for improving students' writing (Graham & Harris, 1994). Students in whole language classrooms spend more time writing than students in conventional classrooms. Teachers in whole language classrooms emphasize choices in writing topics, student ownership, authentic writing tasks, and student self-evaluation. Students write meaningful assignments in environments that are supportive and nonthreatening. Within such environments, writing and spelling skills have the potential to develop endogenously.

Development of Writing Skills

The development of writing skills begins with discovery and invention (Salinger, 1992). Young writers experiment at an early age by representing their ideas in drawing and printing. Children begin to scribble between 12 to 18 months of age, to draw between ages 2 to 3, to use letters from ages 3 to 4, to invent spellings in kindergarten, and to write conventionally by the end of first grade (Allen & Carr, 1989; Strickland & Freeley, 1991). Teachers should encourage students' writing explorations and inventions by providing opportunities to write across the curriculum (Allen & Carr, 1989). Young students should draw and write about real events in their lives and then read their written works to classmates (Graves, 1983).

From kindergarten through second grade, students experiment with writing by drawing and scribbling; by writing messages, grocery lists, or short stories; by taking notes; and by adding punctuation marks to letters and words (Graves, 1983). Oftentimes, children talk to themselves as they draw or write (Dyson, 1983), or they talk to each other to generate and develop ideas (Allen & Carr, 1989). Teachers should listen to students and use that information to make decisions about writing instruction.

At the end of grade 2, many students become more concerned about whether their writing is meaningful to an audience. They want their writing to look like their basals (Graves, 1983). By ages 8 to 9, children can coordinate three writing systems: semantic (i.e., meaning), syntactic (i.e., structure), and graphophonemic (i.e., sound-to-letter rules). Writers at this age are capable of two kinds of writing: *personal* (e.g., journals, diaries) and *practical* (e.g., reports, letters). Teachers can develop personal writing by exposing students to good literature and having students write frequently in journals. Teachers can foster practical writing by assigning compositions and conducting writing conferences (Strickland & Freely, 1991). Writing conferences, in which students meet individually with the teacher, are described in a later section of this chapter.

As students progress through grades 4–12, their writing gradually becomes lengthier (Hunt, 1965; Loban, 1976). They use more noun clauses, subordinate clauses, and adjectives (Hunt, 1965). The development of lengthier writing is important, because, among older writers, measures of text length correlate with ratings of text quality (Benton, Kiewra, Whitfill, & Dennison, 1993).

Connections between Home and School

The quality of children's home life and their parents' involvement influence the development of writing skills. Students of low socioeconomic status are at a marked disadvantage in terms of expressive language abilities (Tierney & Pearson, 1983). Parents can play a key role by reading or telling stories to their children. Preschool children whose parents read to them extensively use features of formal written language, rather than informal oral language, when writing a story in response to a picture (Purcell-Gates, 1992).

Teachers should become familiar with students' home lives, particularly when students' cultures differ from the majority population. Minority students have lower achievement scores and higher dropout rates, on average, possibly because of the "cultural clash" between the home and school environments (Garcia, 1992). Teachers can foster "cultural compatibility" by integrating students' home language and culture into the writing curriculum. For example, Moll and Diaz (1987) taught teachers about Hispanic and Filipino students' cultural and linguistic home environments. The teachers then incorporated that information into the writing curriculum. Students wrote on topics familiar to them and were permitted to write first drafts in their native language. Consequently, they became more enthused about writing, and they wrote more frequently.

Development of Spelling Skills

During the last two decades, several researchers have studied the development of spelling ability. (For a review of this literature, see Brown, 1990). What was initially perceived as a two-stage model of spelling development—inability to spell versus spelling competence—has progressed into five stages: precommunicative, semiphonetic, phonetic, transitional, and competent spelling (Gentry, 1981). The essence of the stage model is that students' spelling errors indicate distinct stages of development. Therefore, whole language advocates believe that teachers should not demand correct spelling because it will simply emerge naturally (Gentry, 1981).

At the *precommunicative stage*, preschool children recognize and write letters of the alphabet but possess no sound-to-letter rules (i.e., knowledge that each letter has a designated sound) or knowledge of left-to-right progression. Learners may mix numbers with letters and upper case with lower case letters. For example, in trying to spell *monster*, the child might write *btBpa*.

In *semiphonetic spelling*, children in grades 1 and 2 learn that certain letters represent specific sounds (i.e., sound-to-letter rules) and that letters are written from left to right. Spelling usually does not extend beyond three to four letters, as in *left* for *elephant*. At the level of *phonetic spelling*, third and fourth grade students are more adept at connecting letters with sounds and at using suffixes and prefixes. They also understand the role of silent vowels and know how to use tenses. An example of phonetic spelling might be *mostr* for *monster*.

Transitional spellers, usually students in grades 4 through 6, have knowledge about basic spelling rules, consonant doubling, and stressed versus unstressed syllables. Transitional spellers might spell *monster* as *monstur*. *Competent spellers*, however, recognize that the second spelling—*monstur* looks incorrect. They have constructed an extensive memory of correctly spelled words they can visualize easily.

Summary

Emergent literacy reminds teachers that writing skills are as important as reading skills and that instruction should integrate all forms of literacy.

Whole language programs give students the opportunity to write in environments that support and reward writing. Writing and spelling skills flourish in print-rich classrooms that make students' home and school lives compatible. These endogenously developmental perspectives have done much to improve writing in elementary classrooms. However, an endogenous developmental approach may not enable all learners to acquire writing skills. Less-skilled writers might not learn to write effectively without some teacher intervention (Harris & Graham, 1992; Mather, 1992). In addition, students might not learn handwriting and spelling skills without direct instruction. In response to such concerns, elementary teachers can turn to exogenous learning methods.

EXOGENOUS LEARNING

Exogenous learning stems from the empiricist assumption that knowledge is acquired from the environment and therefore can be learned (Moshman, 1982). One may take either the perspective of social learning (Bandura, 1977) or information-processing theory (e.g., Bransford, 1979). In either case, the teacher provides direct instruction in basic language and writing skills.

In practice, exogenous learning is seen in the skills-based approach to elementary writing instruction (Needels & Knapp, 1994). The essence of the skills-based approach concerns teaching specific skills, such as spelling, handwriting, sentence structure, paragraph construction, word usage, and grammar. In the paragraphs that follow, I consider how the skills-based approach can be applied effectively in teaching handwriting, phonemic awareness, and spelling.

Handwriting

Although keyboarding is becoming more prevalent in elementary classrooms, word processing has not replaced handwriting as the primary means of written communication (Graham & Weintraub, 1996). In fact, computerized notebooks now enable learners to enter information with a pen instead of a keyboard. Handwriting, therefore, must remain an important component of elementary writing instruction.

Good handwriting mechanics are related to academic success. For example, writers who must allocate considerable time and attention to handwriting may forget ideas or may write less coherently. Slow handwriting may affect how long students take to complete assignments, how well they take notes, how frequently they write, or how they feel about their writing ability (Graham, 1992). The quality of students' handwriting can also affect the grades students receive on writing assignments, because teachers' judgment about writing quality is related to measures of writing legibility. Furthermore, elementary-age children with good handwriting also tend to do well in other basic skills (e.g., reading, spelling, mathematics).

Typically, students make dramatic improvements in handwriting quality (on indexes of formation, alignment, size, etc.) from grades 2 to 3 until they reach a plateau in grade 4 (Hamstra-Bletz & Blote, 1990; Mojet, 1991; Ziviani & Elkins, 1984). By grades 5 and 6, formal handwriting instruction is relatively uncommon; consequently, legibility decreases (e.g., more ambiguous letters, diminishing spaces between letters and words). Some students therefore may benefit from occasional reviews of formal handwriting instruction (Graham & Weintraub, 1996). However, formal handwriting instruction may have little impact once students have established personal styles (Simner, 1981).

Contrary to what teachers might expect, young students' ability to print legibly is not highly correlated with students' cursive writing. Small to moderate correlations (.04 to .40) have been found between printed manuscript and cursive writing samples on measures of letter formation, size, slant, spacing, and alignment (Armitage & Ratzlaff, 1985). So, drilling students on legible printing will not necessarily produce good cursive writers.

An alternative method, *slanted manuscript*, is offered in some classrooms to facilitate the transition from printed manuscript to cursive writing. Thurber (1983) modified the traditional printed manuscript alphabet so that letters are slanted and so that they more closely resemble cursive style. As yet, however, no evidence supports the assertion that slanted manuscript is more rhythmical, faster, or more conducive to learning cursive writing (Graham, 1992).

Elementary classroom teachers sometimes use special writing instruments to facilitate good handwriting. The *primary* or "beginner's" *pencil* is larger in diameter than a regular pencil, and the lead in the primary pencil is relatively bigger. Supposedly, the primary pencil enables correct finger position, reduces finger movements and cramping, and is easier to control (Graham, 1992). However, findings regarding the relative superiority of the primary pencil are equivocal. Therefore, students should be allowed to use a variety of writing instruments when practicing handwriting (Graham, 1992; Graham & Weintraub, 1996).

Some teachers also supply elementary students with wide-lined paper. Advocates argue that wide-lined paper may decrease the strain on children's eyesight and allow greater freedom of movement while writing. As with writing instruments, researchers recommend that teachers allow for variety (Coles & Goodman, 1980; Graham & Weintraub, 1996). Supplying only one kind of paper may restrict children who must adapt to various kinds of writing materials throughout their life.

Phonemic Awareness

Phonemes are the meaningful sounds of a language. *Phonemic awareness* refers to knowing about sound patterns in letters and words and about how to

TABLE 2
Methods of Spelling Instruction

1. Use the test–study procedure.
   Test students over new words at the beginning of the week. Give immediate feedback so that students can then concentrate on words they mispell. Retest at the end of the week.
   Distribute the introduction of new words across several days rather than present them en masse on Monday.
2. Make spelling a regular part of each day's activities.
   Spend from 10 to 15 minutes per day.
   Spend no more than 75 minutes per week.
3. Individualize instruction.
   Form spelling groups by establishing a frustration level ranging from 50% to 70% correct. Spend more time and use different instructional techniques with students below the frustration level.
4. Use sensory learning.
   Students who are good spellers can visualize words in memory.
   Have students who are poor spellers trace over correctly spelled words, trace words in the air, and visualize tracing words in their mind.
   Test students on whether words look correct.
5. Use group learning activities.
   Teach students in small groups of four rather than one-to-one.
   Have students study spelling words in pairs. One student orally expresses each word and the other spells it. After a brief time period, have students switch roles.

From Brown (1990).

blend and delete phonemic segments. Phonemic awareness is essential for making the transition from semiphonetic to phonetic spelling.

Students demonstrate phonemic awareness in several ways. When presented a stimulus (i.e., word or nonsense word) aurally, they must be able to repeat it correctly. They must also be able to identify a particular phoneme in a stimulus (e.g., /*t* / in *velt*) and delete a sound (e.g., saying *cat* without the /*k* / sound). Finally, students must be able to express orally the correct response to a given visual stimulus (McBride-Chang, 1995).

Because not all students develop phonemic awareness endogenously, some believe teachers should use exogenous learning methods to bring about such awareness (Castle, Riach, & Nicholson, 1994; O'Connor, Jenkins, & Slocum, 1995). Castle et al. (1994) studied the effects of phonemic awareness training on five-year-olds enrolled in a whole language program. Students randomly assigned to a training group participated in phonemic games twice a week over 10 weeks. Examples of games included matching picture cards that had the same initial, medial, or final phoneme; and matching picture to letter cards that had the same phoneme as the initial sound in the picture. Students randomly assigned to the control group participated in whole language activities, such as story writing and invented spelling. At the post-test, the training group outperformed the control group on measures of phonemic awareness and spelling.

Phonemic awareness training may be particularly beneficial to students with low phonological skills. O'Connor et al. (1995) randomly assigned kindergartners with low phonological skills to either of two training groups or to a control group. Students in the first training group participated in tasks requiring auditory blending and segmenting. For example, students practiced blending sounds, as in SSS*aaack*; they pointed to pictures that matched names of objects; and they identified the phonemes corresponding to particular sounds within a word. Students in the second training group participated in similar activities plus letter–sound and word–sound matching. Students in the control group participated in letter–sound matching only. Students in both training groups improved their phonological skills and achieved phonemic awareness to a level comparable with that of higher-skilled children.

Spelling

Teachers also use exogenous methods when teaching spelling. Some innovative methods of teaching spelling include (1) introducing only a few new words at a time, (2) giving students immediate feedback and requiring them to correct spelling errors, (3) using visual imagery (e.g., requiring students to trace new spellings in the air or in their mind), or (4) using group tutoring (Brown, 1990). Table 2 lists other methods of spelling instruction.

Students with spelling disabilities may find exogenous learning methods particularly beneficial. Two categories of spelling disabilities are phonological dysgraphia and lexical dysgraphia. Students with *phonological dysgraphia* can retrieve stored representations of correctly spelled words in memory (i.e., the lexicon) but cannot sound out words. They can spell familiar words but have difficulty with new or unfamiliar words. Students with *lexical dysgraphia* are unable to retrieve the lexicon, but they can sound out words using phonological rules. These students have trouble spelling words that are phonologically irregular, such as *choir* (Brown, 1990).

Teachers should make accommodations for students with spelling disabilities. For example, such students should be permitted a dictionary during tests and writing assignments. In addition, although teachers should give feedback about spelling errors, they should not consider misspellings in determining a student's grade.

Summary

The skills-based approach makes sense when teaching handwriting, phonemic awareness, and spelling. Skills-based instruction may be particularly beneficial to students of low income, students whose native linguistic patterns are different from standard English, and students with spelling disabilities (Needels & Knapp, 1994). However, when used exclusively, such exogenous methods may not be as effective as they are when combined with a whole language approach.

When teachers use exogenous learning methods, they tend to emphasize *correct* writing. They focus on the products of students' writing rather than on the processes of how to write well. In the next section, I consider the processes involved in writing for meaningful communication.

FUNCTIONALISM

Functionalism is a school of thought that considers how organisms adapt to their environment. Functionalism finds its roots in Darwinian evolutionary theory and the writings of American psychologists William James, John Dewey, and James Angell. Contemporary functionalists consider the procedural knowledge and cognitive processes related to success in academic tasks. Functional views of writing emphasize the problem-solving processes underlying effective writing.

Janet Emig's *The Composing Process of Twelfth Graders* (1971) was the starting point for the emphasis researchers and teachers place on writing processes. Emig observed students as they wrote and then conducted interviews with them. She found that the linear model of writing processes (i.e., prewriting, writing, revising) was outdated. She observed false starts, regressions, and errors as writers moved in and out of planning, drafting, and revising. Graves (1973) conducted the same kind of research with elementary students and found similar results.

In response to the emphasis on writing processes, Flower and Hayes (1981) proposed a model of writing based on verbal protocol analyses of writers as they composed. The Flower and Hayes (1981) model has three main components: the task environment, long-term memory, and writing processes. Elements in the *task environment* include the writing topic, the intended audience, motivating factors, and elements of text already produced (e.g., notes, outlines, drafts). Within *long-term memory*, writers store knowledge of the topic, audience, and types of writing forms (expository, narrative, etc.). The writer's knowledge interacts with the task environment to influence the iterative *writing processes* of planning, translating, and reviewing.

Planning involves three subprocesses: generating, organizing, and goal setting. Writers generate ideas by retrieving relevant information about the writing topic from long-term memory and the task environment. Writers organize ideas by constructing a meaningful structure that matches readers' expectations. In goal setting, writers plan how to convey their ideas in a meaningful way to the intended audience. In *translating*, writers transform ideas into written text. Translating requires knowledge of vocabulary and the rules of standard written language. *Reviewing* is a continual process that involves the writer's evaluation and revision of text according to internal standards and perceived audience expectations.

The Flower and Hayes model has led researchers to investigate variables that influence writing, most notably the writer's knowledge and interests, elements in the task environment, and the writer's working-memory processes. In the sections that follow, I discuss these variables and suggest implications for elementary writing instruction.

The Writer's Knowledge

Students need two basic types of knowledge to be effective writers: discourse knowledge and topic knowledge (Benton & Kiewra, 1987). *Discourse knowledge* concerns what students know about how to write. It "consists of schemata for various discourse forms, procedures and strategies involved in instantiation of those schemata, and local sentence-generation procedures (including grammatical knowledge)" (McCutchen, 1986, p. 432). *Topic knowledge* refers to students' specific knowledge related to the writing topic (e.g., baseball, soccer, volleyball). Topic knowledge is important because

> Intuition and experience suggest that when students write to a topic about which they have a great deal of well-integrated knowledge, their writing is more likely to be well organized and fluent; conversely, when students know little about a topic, their writing is more likely to fail. (Langer, 1984, p. 28)

Discourse Knowledge

Discourse knowledge is related to students' proficiency in expository (Benton & Kiewra, 1986; Benton, Kiewra, & Bean, 1988) and narrative (Benton et al., 1995; McCutchen, 1986) writing. Typically, researchers measure discourse knowledge using standardized tests of verbal ability, such as the California Achievement Test (CAT; McGraw-Hill, 1985) Reading score, the American College Testing (ACT; American College Testing Program, 1989) English Usage Test, or the Test of Standard Written English (TSWE; College Board, 1983).

Among elementary students, discourse knowledge explains observed developmental differences between grade levels in students' local coherence in writing (McCutchen, 1986). Among middle-school students, discourse knowledge (CAT Reading score) is related to *syntactic maturity*, the number of grammatically correct words found in a students' writing sample, and to *thematic maturity*, the ability to write a logical narrative organized around a theme (Benton et al., 1995). Among college students, Benton et al. found a low, but significant, correlation between discourse knowledge (ACT English Usage Test) and syntactic maturity ($r = .20$).

The relationship between discourse knowledge and writing has to do mostly with the translating process. Translating requires transforming ideas (semantics) into written symbols that satisfy the constraints of the standard rules of the language (e.g., syntax). Ample discourse knowledge enables writers to translate rapidly and accurately. Evidence for this comes from research requiring skilled and less-skilled writers to unscramble scrambled letters, words, sentences, and paragraphs (Benton, Kraft, Glover, & Plake, 1984). Among both high school and undergraduate students, skilled writers perform these tasks faster and more accurately than less-skilled writers. In addition, college students' performance on these tasks is positively related to their discourse knowledge.

Young students construct discourse knowledge by reading, listening to others read, and practicing writing. In addition, students benefit from *sentence combining*. Sentence combining requires that students combine sets of sentences into increasingly complex sentence structures (Hillocks & Smith, 1991). Sentence combining enhances students' syntactic maturity and the overall quality of their writing (O'Hare, 1973). In a review of sentence-combining studies conducted from 1973 to 1982, Hillocks and Mavrogenes (1986) found that 60% yielded significant positive effects, 30% yielded non-significant positive effects, and 10% yielded negative or no effects. The average effect size of sentence combining on writing quality is .35 standard deviations (Hillocks, 1986). Disadvantaged students seem to benefit most from sentence combining (Ross, 1971).

Sentence combining benefits students for several reasons (Crowhurst, 1983). First, students practice writing sentences. Second, students construct new sentences. Third, students may become more proficient at translating, freeing them to devote more attention to planning processes. Although researchers disagree about whether sentence combining has long-lasting effects on the quality of students' writing, young writers most likely benefit more from this method than from traditional grammar instruction (Hillocks & Smith, 1991).

Topic Knowledge

Topic knowledge is related to qualitative measures of both narrative (Benton et al., 1995; DeGroff, 1987; McCutchen, 1986) and expository (McCutchen, 1986) writing among elementary, middle school, and undergraduate students. The more students know about a topic, the less effortful it is for them to retrieve and generate ideas in written composition (Kellogg, 1987). For the student with vast topic knowledge, ideas come so rapidly that writing becomes automatic to the point where the pen cannot keep up with the generating process. Consequently, the planning process is highly automated when students know a great deal about a topic.

Elementary (DeGroff, 1987), middle school, and undergraduate (Benton et al., 1995) students with high topic knowledge generate a greater proportion of topic-relevant ideas in narrative passages than do students with low topic knowledge. Conversely, writers with low topic knowledge generate a greater proportion of topic-irrelevant ideas. In addition, the narrative writing of middle school and undergraduate students with high knowledge is more thematically mature than that of students with low knowledge (Benton et al., 1995). Students with high topic knowledge apparently exert less effort to retrieving ideas, which frees them to devote more attention to organizing their thoughts around a theme. In contrast, writers with relatively less topic knowledge probably devote more effort searching long-term memory for topic-related ideas, and less attention is available for organizing them. Teachers, therefore, should assess students' knowledge about a topic before giving writing assignments. Teachers should also allow students some choice in the selection of writing topics.

The Writer's Interests

Psychologists have long asserted that interest directs attention and enhances learning (Dewey, 1913; James, 1890; Thorndike, 1935). They have recently begun to consider the role that interest plays in writing (Benton et al., 1995; Hidi, 1990; Hidi & Anderson, 1992; Hidi & McLaren, 1990). Theoretically, individuals may vary with respect to *individual* interest, which emerges from one's history of interaction with an object or a stimulus, and *situational* interest, which pertains to the specific characteristics of an event or object that capture one's interest (Hidi, 1990). Whereas individual interest is a relatively enduring preference for certain topics, activities, or events; situational interest is more of a temporary emotional state in response to stimulation (Hidi, 1990; Renninger, 1990; Schiefele, 1990). For example, across time people develop long-lasting individual interests about such things as baseball, periods in history, or hobbies. In contrast, situational interest may arise more suddenly from something that occurs in the environment, such as a dynamic presentation or a discrepant classroom event.

Researchers have found that interindividual differences in interest are related to narrative writing. Middle school students with high individual interest in a topic can write well-organized narratives that match those of undergraduate students (Benton et al., 1995). Controlling for grade level and topic knowledge, Benton et al. found that students with high individual interest in a topic write narratives that are more logical and better organized than those of less interested students.

Intraindividual differences in interest are also related to narrative writing. At the elementary level, fourth and sixth graders are more motivated to write about topics they find interesting than about topics they find less interesting (Hidi & McLaren, 1990). In addition, older students write better about topics they find interesting than about topics they find less interesting (Albin, Benton, & Khramtsova, in press). Undergraduate students in the Albin et al. (in press) study completed brief interest inventories about the topics of baseball (a relatively high-interest topic) and soccer (a relatively low-interest topic). They then wrote narratives about one-half inning of baseball and about one-half of a soccer game, counterbalanced. Students wrote a greater proportion of topic-relevant ideas and evidenced greater thematic maturity on the baseball story. In contrast, they generated a greater proportion of topic-irrelevant ideas in the soccer story. These findings indicate that teachers should expect variability in the quality of students' writing, depending upon the writing topic. Again, students should have some choice in writing topics.

Elements in the Task Environment

Partially produced text influences writing processes (Benton et al., 1993). Partial text may include notes, outlines, or sentences already written that provide a plan for writing. Reviewing such external records reduces memory load and frees attentional capacities so that the writer can generate ideas (Kellogg, 1988). In addition, having topic-relevant information available in the task environment improves the quality of students' writing (Benton et al., 1993; Kellogg, 1988; Langer, 1984).

For example, Benton et al. (1993) randomly assigned undergraduates to one of three kinds of note-taking conditions: conventional, outline, or matrix. Conventional notes are the notes that students ordinarily take without training or aid. They typically are brief, verbatim accounts of the lecture. Outline notes are recorded on a framework that lists the lecture's major topics and subtopics in a linear fashion and that provides spaces between ideas for note taking. Matrix notes are recorded in a framework that is two dimensional. The framework lists the topics across the top of the page and the subtopics vertically along the left margin. Students record notes within the intersecting cells of the matrix.

In Experiments 1 and 2, Benton et al. (1993) examined the effects of immediate versus delayed writing following a videotaped lecture. Across both experiments, students who took and referred to their own notes outperformed those who took notes but wrote without their notes. Referring to notes enhanced indicants of the generating (i.e., number of words and ideas) and organizing (i.e., cohesion and coherence) processes in expository writing. After a one-week delay (in Experiment 2), the effect of external storage (i.e., recorded notes) on generating was significantly greater than it was without a delay. The elapsed time between listening to the lecture and writing the essay rendered the notes more valuable.

In a subsequent experiment, students listened to a lecture without taking notes. One week later, students returned and were given either no notes or complete conventional, outline, or matrix notes. (Complete notes contained all of the recorded lecture information.) Students who referred to any type of complete notes generated more words in their writing than students who wrote without notes. Students who referred to complete matrix or outline notes generated more ideas than students who wrote without notes. In addition, students who referred to complete outline or matrix notes wrote more coherent essays than students who wrote without notes.

These findings indicate that writers benefit from recorded notes in the task environment. Information presented in an organized framework may be particularly beneficial. Even elementary students can create text based on information presented in a matrix framework (Bereiter & Scardamalia, 1987). Although taking notes from a lecture is relatively less common in elementary than in secondary education, upper elementary teachers should teach students how to take notes. Secondary and postsecondary education students often take notes to acquire information (Palmatier & Bennett, 1974). Note taking, therefore, is an important writing skill that should be taught at the elementary level.

Researchers have had some success in teaching young students how to take notes (Laidlaw, Skok, & McLaughlin, 1993; Peck & Hannifin, 1983). Peck and Hannifin (1983) trained sixth graders to take notes by cuing them to pay attention, to select main ideas, and to maintain pace with the rate of instruction. However, the effect of note-taking training depended upon students' intelligence and verbal ability. Similarly, Laidlaw et al. (1993) found that, in a sample of fifth and sixth graders, skilled readers were better note takers than less-skilled readers. Less-skilled readers simply copied material from a text rather than summarized and organized the information.

Teachers should also continue to emphasize the value of referring to externally stored information during writing. This recommendation may seem trite until one realizes that most novice writers write off the top of their heads (Graesser, Hopkinson, Lewis, & Bruflodt, 1984). Despite the emphasis teachers place on note taking and outlining, most novice writers do very little planning before writing, and few make use of their notes or outlines (Hillocks, 1986).

Working-Memory Processes

The number of processes involved in writing can overload the limited capacity of young writers' working memories (Schallert, 1991). To test the relationship between working-memory information processing capabilities and the quality of students' writing, Benton, Kraft et al. (1984) compared better and poor college and high school student writers (defined by judges' holistic impressions of a sample of students' writing) on a letter-reordering task. The letter-reordering task required that students respond to a series of consonants displayed one at a time on a computer screen. After the last of five letters in a sequence was displayed, students had to reorder the letters held in working memory into alphabetical order. Across several trials, better writers performed faster and more accurately than did poorer writers.

Benton, Kraft et al. (1984) found no significant differences between better and poorer writers on grade point averages or standardized achievement test scores. This suggests that the best explanation for better writers' superior performance on the letter-reordering task is working-memory information processing differences.

Other authors have also found that individual differences in working memory processes are related to elementary students' writing (McCutchen, Covill, Hoyne, & Mildes, 1994; Whitaker, Berninger, Johnston, & Swanson, 1994). Whitaker et al. (1994) found that, among fourth, fifth, and sixth grade writers, performance on a verbal working-memory task correlated with writing tasks involving translating and reviewing. Similarly, McCutchen et al. (1994) found that skilled elementary and middle school writers showed more fluent sentence-generation processes than did less-skilled writers. In addition, skilled writers were faster at making lexical decisions about whether words—presented on a microcomputer—were "real" or "phony." These findings suggest that working-memory and retrieval processes are more fluent for skilled than for less-skilled young writers.

Such differences indicate that teachers should be patient during young students' early attempts at writing. Young students perform basic tasks (e.g., spelling, punctuation) methodically and with error. Teachers may wish to break down writing processes into small components (e.g., brainstorming, outlining, writing a rough draft). They should also begin with simple writing assignments, and they should allow plenty of time for practicing writing. Writing skills become more automated with practice.

The Functions of Writing

The functional approach to writing instruction also emphasizes the role of context. In some sense, all academic learning, not just writing, has become decontextualized (Cohen & Riel, 1989). Students usually learn academic skills in environments outside the context in which they will be required to apply them. In fact, students' lack of audience awareness in writing may be an artifact of the way they are taught to write (i.e., primarily for the teacher). By emphasizing the functions of writing, teachers recontextualize writing by requiring students to write meaningfully for real audiences. Writing is viewed as a tool for learning rather than as a means for displaying knowledge acquired (Applebee, 1991).

In their analysis of over 2000 samples of students' writing, Britton and colleagues (Britton, Burgess, Martin, McLeod, & Rosen, 1975) learned that writing functions for students in expressive, transactional, and poetic ways. *Expressive* writing is closely tied to the writer's experiences and interpretations. Writers write to experience, such as when they compose letters, keep diaries or journals, or write creatively. *Transactional* writing accomplishes some goal. Writers write to do something, such as to interact with a computer, write memos, or complete forms. *Poetic* writing allows for contemplation. Writers write to learn, such as when they write a report or answer study questions (Moore, Moore, Cunningham, & Cunningham, 1986).

Researchers have investigated the poetic or writing-to-learn function as a tool for constructing knowledge from texts or lectures. Restricted writing (e.g., answering adjunct or study questions) following reading is helpful for short-term retention of facts (Newell & Winograd, 1989). However, restricted writing does not affect long-term retention because students typically limit their focus to narrow aspects of what they have read (i.e., intentional learning).

Another type of restricted writing is note taking. Taking notes during a lecture may enhance encoding of information because the process of recording notes leads to a more generative processing of the lecture than simply listening or reading (Peper & Mayer, 1986). However, in a review of the literature on note taking, Kiewra (1985) found that the effects of taking notes are equivocal. In some cases, taking notes has increased memory for a lecture beyond that of simply listening; in other cases, it has not.

Benton et al. (1993) also found that taking notes, without the opportunity for review, does not influence generating or organizing processes in college students' essay writing beyond that of simply listening. This is because note taking requires only transcribing information, which involves simply recording thoughts that someone else has organized previously (Durst & Newell, 1989).

To foster a more lasting effect on learning, teachers should assign analytic writing. *Analytic writing* requires students to formulate an extended response that integrates information from a text (Durst & Newell, 1989). When students are required to think about what they have read and write about it in a manner that goes beyond mere summarizing, they construct a deeper understanding (Newell, 1984). However, teachers should not assume that writing analytically is better than reviewing notes in preparation for a test. Students who write essays following a lecture, instead of reviewing their notes, do no better on tests than students who only review their notes (Kiewra, Benton, Kim, Risch, & Christensen, 1995).

Summary

The emphasis on writing processes made the stage model (i.e., prewriting, writing, revising) obsolete and established that writing is a problem-solving process. Teachers now consider the writer's knowledge and interests when assigning writing. They understand the complexities of working-memory processes that occur during writing. The functionalist approach to writing instruction emphasizes purpose and context. Students write to express, to do, and to learn. Students can increase their learning of material when they write analytically.

In spite of its influence on research and instruction, the functional view of writing is incomplete because it portrays writing as a single, solitary process (Schallert, 1991). Psychologists now emphasize the constructive and social nature of writing (Faigley, 1986; Nystrand, 1986). The psychological foundations for these views can be found in dialectical constructivism.

DIALECTICAL CONSTRUCTIVISM

The essence of dialectical constructivism is that learners construct knowledge through their interaction with the environment (Byrnes, 1992; Moshman, 1982; Vygotsky, 1962). Neither the individual nor the environment is the sole source of knowledge. The cognitive and social realms are interconnected. Young writers socially negotiate their knowledge about how to write (Derry, 1992). Students learn how to write, not by having rules presented to them and then practicing those rules, but by interacting with others to complete meaningful tasks in realistic situations (Langer, 1991). Teachers can practice dialectical constructivism in the classroom by viewing writing as recontextualization and as social constructivism.

Writing as Recontextualization

Young writers actively construct knowledge. Rather than passively acquire information, they select, interpret, and organize information, assimilating it into existing knowledge structures. Writers construct meaning through a process called *recontextualization*, which involves reconstructing an event in a meaningful way for the reader. For example,

> A toddler on her first December 24 visit to Trafalgar Square may acquire the label "tree" to refer to the centre of attention of the Christmas celebrants. She may call the caroling "sing", and the products at the Kiosks "nuts." This young language learner is acquiring verbal tools to negotiate new social–cognitive transactions by decontextualizing her experiences. When she is in elementary school and is asked by her teacher to write about a favorite family vacation ritual, she might depict the same scene, keeping in mind what her reader needs to know to understand that the tree is not simply a naturally growing conifer, and that the singing and the nuts are both seasonal specialities. She might, then, characterize the tree as a Christmas tree, and even detail its appearance; she might name a particular carol or hymn that was sung; and she might evoke the taste of warm, roasted chestnuts. (Cameron, Hunt, & Linton, 1996).

The young writer in this example uses linguistic and social knowledge to construct a shared meaning between herself and the reader. She "recontextualizes" her experience in Trafalgar Square for the readers' comprehension and enjoyment.

Teachers can observe young writers recontextualize in several ways. First, writers recontextualize when they adapt their writing to specific audiences, referred to as *knowledge accessing* (Cameron et al., 1996). If students can vary the meaning or style of their writing depending upon the audience—for example, the teacher versus a friend—they are recontextualizing an experience to make sense to the reader. Second, writers recontextualize when they modify text semantically and syntactically through *expression verification* (Cameron et al., 1996). Students demonstrate expression verification when they revise their text in response to feedback from the teacher or from other students. Further evidence for recontextualization is found when students make outlines before writing and when they write coherently. To write coherently, students must check their writing against the informational needs of the audience.

Traditionally, researchers have assumed that young writers do little knowledge accessing (Bereiter & Scardamalia, 1987). Some have argued that young writers write egocentrically for themselves rather than for the reader (Flower, 1985). Novice writers supposedly engage in knowledge telling, which is characterized by (1) spending little time in planning, (2) writing without adapting to the informational needs of the reader, (3) writing incoherently, (4) being unable to form arguments in writing, (5) engaging in very little revision, and (6) evidencing little problem solving in writing (Cameron et al., 1996).

However, young writers apparently can engage in knowledge accessing (Edmunds, Cameron, & Eglington, 1988; Kroll, 1984). For example, Kroll (1984) asked nine-year-olds to write letters to a city peer and to a farm-dwelling adult. The children successfully adapted the content of their letters to the different audiences. Similarly, Edmunds, Cameron, and Eglington (1988) asked second, fourth, and sixth grade students to write letters to audiences that varied in age and location. The children were asked to pretend their dog just had puppies. They were told to write individuals, requesting them to give a puppy a home. Edmunds et al. scored each letter on 12 categories of audience-directed statements, such as context-creating statements (e.g., introduction, statement of the problem), descriptive statements (e.g., physical descriptions), and appeal statements (e.g., flattery, sympathy, enticements). Children at all grade levels adapted their writing to the nature of the audience. Whereas second graders relied more on pleading and sympathy, fourth graders used descriptive statements primarily, and sixth graders used both descriptive and appeal statements. Although the strategies constructed by second graders were relatively less sophisticated than those of older writers, young writers were clearly aware of the need to construct convincing arguments for their readers.

Young writers also engage in expression verification or revision (Edmunds, Cameron, Linton, & Hunt, 1988). Participants in the Edmunds, Cameron, Linton, and Hunt (1988) study were students in grades 2 through 5 who were trained to diagnose flaws in someone else's writing. Following the training, children revised two texts: one containing semantic flaws, the other containing syntactic and spelling flaws. The percentages of flaws revised correctly ranged from 35% in grade 2 to 55% in grade 3 to 75% in grades 4 and 5.

In a subsequent study, Edmunds, Cameron, Linton, and Hunt (1988) asked writers to revise their own texts. The percentages of flaws revised correctly were similar to those in the previous study. Such findings demonstrate that elementary students can revise someone else's and their own writing, which is evidence for expression verification.

Empirical evidence for knowledge retrieval and expression verification confirms that elementary students recontextualize or reconstruct knowledge in writing. Teachers can facilitate recontextualization in students' writing through social constructivism.

Writing as Social Constructivism

When writing is considered a social activity, the teacher's role is to initially provide guidance and direction when students need assistance. The point at which students need assistance is the zone of proximal development (Vygotsky, 1962). The *zone of proximal development* is the difference between what students can handle on their own and what they can accomplish with assistance from a knowledgeable person. Teachers provide such assistance through scaffolding. In *scaffolding*, the teacher provides as much help as needed for the learner to accomplish the task. Teachers provide scaffolding in several ways including prewriting discussions, writing conferences, procedural facilitation, peer response or peer editing teams, group summary writing, and computer technology.

Prewriting Discussions

One example of scaffolding is prewriting discussions between the teacher and the student. Moll and Diaz (1987) taught teachers to conduct prewriting discussions with Hispanic and Filipino students. After attending a seminar, teachers and students engaged in prewriting discussions about writing and methods for generating and organizing ideas. Prior to these teacher–student dialogues, the students wrote infrequently, and when they did write they wrote only for their teacher. After implementing prewriting discussions, the teachers reported that students increased their enthusiasm about writing, wrote more frequently, and showed greater understanding about assigned writing topics.

Writing Conferences

Writing conferences offer another opportunity for teacher–student interaction. In writing conferences, students meet individually with their teacher to deal with either the content or the mechanics of something the student has written. The teacher can question the student about intended meaning or about the student's thoughts during writing. The student may also write for the teacher or the teacher may model writing for the student.

Procedural Facilitation

Procedural facilitation refers to external supports that ease the burden of writing and enable writers to perform independently (Bereiter & Scardamalia, 1987). One type of external support is teacher *cues* related to the writing assignment. Scardamalia, Bereiter, and Goelman (1982), for example, cued fourth and sixth graders to continue writing by saying (after the child appeared finished writing), "You're doing fine," or "Can you write some more?" After cuing, students in both grade levels increased the quantity of ideas generated, and fourth graders improved the quality of their texts.

Teachers can also facilitate students' writing with *questions* (Benton & Blohm, 1986, 1988; Benton, Glover, & Plake, 1984; Blohm & Benton, 1991). Benton, Glover, and Plake (1984) randomly assigned undergraduate students to either a control (no question) group, a lower-order question group (i.e., a group that received knowledge-level questions related to the writing topic), or a higher-order question group (i.e., a group that was taught to ask themselves questions requiring analysis, synthesis, and evaluation). During the first four weeks of training, students in the higher-order question group were taught to ask themselves such questions as the following before and during writing: "What is the gist of the desired response?" "Are there different approaches to the topic I haven't considered?" and "Have I thought of why, how, when, and what?" In the fifth session, the questions were withdrawn, and students were instructed to generate their own questions. Across five different expository writing assignments, students in the higher-order question group wrote essays that contained more ideas than those from the control group.

In addition, Benton and Blohm (1988) found that relatively concrete prewriting questions (e.g., "What might restaurants do to reduce wastefulness of potatoes?") lead college writers to generate more details and examples in their expository writing than abstract questions (e.g., "What impact has wastefulness in America had on hunger?"). Blohm and Benton (1991) also discovered that college students who are cued to create their own prewriting questions write essays that contain more examples and explanations than the essays of students who respond to experimenter-generated questions.

Postwriting questions can also facilitate the revising process. Students who receive questions after writing an expository essay, and who are then allowed 15 minutes to revise, add more details to their essays than students who revise without postwriting questions (Benton & Blohm, 1986). In a study conducted with fifth and sixth graders, Graham, MacArthur, and Schwartz (1995) randomly assigned students to one of three revising conditions: general revising, with the goal of making the paper better; general revising, with the goal of adding three things to make the paper better; and general revising, with the goal of writing down five things to make the paper better. Students in the second and third groups made more meaning-based changes and wrote qualitatively better papers than students in the first group.

Another way to provide procedural facilitation for beginning writers is to use think sheets. *Think sheets* prompt writers to respond to questions such as "Who am I writing for?" "Why am I writing this?" and "What do I know?" Think sheets facilitate students' self-questioning and self-instructing by providing a window into the thinking of skilled writers, prompting student awareness and use of problem-solving strategies, and modeling the inner self-talk of self-regulated writers (Englert, 1992).

Peer Response and Peer Editing Teams

Peer response teams are composed of from two to five students. One student writes, and the other members of the team respond to what was written. For example, Vukelich (1986) taught second graders how to ask peers questions about their writing. Peer questioning followed by rewriting texts led to improvements in students' writing. To be successful, (1) initial responses should focus on what the writer did well, (2) negative responses should be stated as questions, (3) responses may be either oral or written, and (4) the writer should not be allowed to respond immediately to the students' comments (Moore et al., 1986).

Peer editing teams consist of small groups of students who help a writer with the mechanics of writing. Responses are directed toward spelling, punctuation, word usage, word choices, and so forth. In one study, a reciprocal peer editing strategy helped learning disabled fourth through sixth graders make more revisions and write higher-quality papers relative to students in a control group (MacArthur, Schwartz, & Graham, 1991). Students in the reciprocal peer editing group worked in pairs to help each other improve their writing.

In spite of their benefits, peer response and peer editing teams should not replace the teacher as evaluator (Newkirk, 1984). Writing conferences should be used intermittently with peer response and peer editing teams so that students learn about the informational needs of several audiences (Moore et al., 1986).

Group Summary Writing

Group summary writing requires that students first listen as the teacher reads a passage orally. The students then reconstruct the important points they heard, and the teacher lists these on the board so that all students can see them. Students then use the notes to reconstruct the passage at the students' reading level.

Computer Technology

Computer technology offers a number of advantages for scaffolding instruction:

1. Young children learn editing and revising skills faster if they write on word processors than if they write by hand (Daiute, 1985).
2. Students can write for longer time periods because word processing eases the physical strain of handwriting.
3. Students may improve their attitude about writing because they complete a clean, finished product rather than a messy first draft.
4. Students may be less fearful of writing because they can correct errors easily.
5. Students write lengthier prose because they can devote more attention to planning than to concerns about mechanics.
6. Computers provide greater opportunity for peer collaboration (Roswell & Natchez, 1989).

For ideas about how to use word processors to increase peer collaboration, see Roswell and Natchez (1989, pp. 246–247).

Word processing programs can also provide scaffolding for teaching spelling, vocabulary, synonyms and antonyms, grammar, punctuation, capitalization, and word usage. Over 40 programs can provide feedback to students about their spelling, style, diction, and other writing mechanics (Bruce, 1991). However, Brown (1990) reviewed literature on the utility of computers for teaching spelling and found that computers are no more effective than traditional spelling instruction and that they require greater teacher time and effort.

Some computer programs also provide scaffolding for students to explore language structures. For example, Rubin created *Storymaker* (as cited in Mikkelsen, 1984) which helps students create and manipulate text by representing a story structure as a tree consisting of nodes and branches. The nodes contain sentences or paragraphs from which students choose branches to follow in creating a story.

Other computer programs enable communication among peer writers. Electronic mail provides a link among students who collaborate on writing projects. *Mailbag* (Rubin & Bruce, 1986) is an example of an electronic mail system that allows writers to share ideas with each other and the teacher. (See Bruce, 1991, for a review of specific computer programs designed for writing instruction.)

These examples demonstrate that teachers can provide scaffolding in several ways. To be successful at scaffolding, teachers should follow certain guidelines (Applebee, 1991):

1. *Encourage student ownership*. When students express their own views and defend them in writing, they develop critical thinking skills. As Blohm and

Benton (1991) observed, students benefit from constructing their own prewriting questions. Teachers should also allow students to choose their own writing topics (Benton et al., 1995; Graves, 1983).

2. *Provide appropriate instruction*. Begin at the child's developmental level. Identify students' zones of proximal development: what they can do by themselves versus what they can do with assistance. Offer guidance until the student can write independently.

3. *Provide support*. Teachers provide support by creating meaningful prewriting activities, conducting prewriting discussions, cuing students to write more, providing questions, and using computer technology.

4. *Collaborate with students*. Teachers and students should work together on writing projects. Advances in computer technology enable teachers and students to construct text together by projecting a computer screen with an LCD panel or similar instrument. When collaborating with students, teachers should not evaluate students' writing until late in the writing process.

5. *Foster student internalization*. Students should have opportunities to initiate writing rather than to just respond to the teacher's writing assignments. Students must learn that writing is a tool for communicating and for thinking critically.

Summary

Dialectical constructivists emphasize interaction between teachers and students and between peers. Scaffolding helps learners clarify misunderstandings about writing assignments. Students learn to write for a purpose: to communicate. But, by itself, this approach to writing instruction would be ineffective. Students can also benefit from endogenous developmental, exogenous learning, and functional approaches to writing instruction. Teachers therefore will best serve elementary students by adopting an eclectic approach that combines the four theoretical foundations described in this chapter. I describe such an approach in the section that follows.

AN ECLECTIC APPROACH TO ELEMENTARY WRITING INSTRUCTION

Table 1 reveals the major concepts and implications that follow from the theoretical positions reviewed in this chapter. With these in mind, I make the following recommendations for elementary writing instruction:

1. Teach composition skills early and often.
2. Integrate instruction in reading, writing, handwriting, spelling, listening, and speaking so that learners see connections among all forms of literacy.

3. Fill the classroom with printed materials and provide plenty of opportunities for writing. Provide a variety of handwriting instruments and materials. Construct a writing center to emphasize the importance of developing writing skills.
4. Display students' writing to instill motivation and give writing the status it deserves. Allow students to read aloud their written works to classmates.
5. Permit playful, explorative writing (e.g., drawing, invented spelling).
6. Encourage parent involvement in classroom writing activities and homework assignments. Strive for compatibility between the home and school environments.
7. Teach basic skills such as handwriting, phonemic awareness, and spelling.
8. Use sentence combining to develop students' discourse knowledge.
9. Allow students choice in writing topics.
10. Be tolerant of students' early attempts at writing, and allow plenty of time for practicing and revising.
11. Teach students how to take notes and how to write from external sources.
12. Require young students to write for different audiences and purposes.
13. Use peer response and peer editing teams.
14. Conduct prewriting discussions and writing conferences.
15. Provide scaffolding that enables student ownership and internalization.

In conclusion, elementary teachers face diverse classrooms of developing writers. Writing skills can emerge in the midst of such diversity if teachers provide opportunities for social interactions among students who write about real problems and for diverse audiences. Teachers must lead students to advanced levels of writing ability so that students learn to write in order to experience, to do, and to learn.

References

Albin, M., Benton, S. L., & Khramtsova, I. (in press). *Individual differences in interest and narrative writing. Contemporary Educational Psychology.*

Allen, J., & Carr, E. (1989). Collaborative learning among kindergarten writers: James learns how to learn at school. In J. Allen & J. Mason (Eds.), *Risk makers, risk takers, risk breakers: Reducing the risks for young literacy learners* (pp. 30–74). Portsmouth, NH: Heinemann.

American College Testing Program. (1989). *The enhanced ACT assessment.* Iowa City, IA: Author.

Applebee, A. N. (1991). Environments for language teaching and learning: Contemporary issues and future directions. In J. Flood, J. M. Jensen, D. Lapp, & J. R. Squire (Eds.), *Handbook of research on teaching the English language arts* (pp. 549–556). New York: Macmillan.

Armitage, D., & Ratzlaff, H. (1985). The non-correlation of printing and writing skill. *Journal of Educational Research, 78,* 174–177.

Bandura, A. (1977). *Social learning theory.* Englewood Cliffs, NJ: Prentice-Hall.

Benton, S. L., & Blohm, P. J. (1986). Effect of question type and position on measures of conceptual elaboration in writing. *Research in the Teaching of English*, 20, 98–108.

Benton, S. L., & Blohm, P. J. (1988). Elaboration of ideas in prose production. *Journal of Experimental Education*, 56, 60–66.

Benton, S. L., Corkill, A. J., Sharp, J. M., Downey, R. G., & Khramtsova, I. (1995). Knowledge, interest, and narrative writing. *Journal of Educational Psychology*, 87, 66–79.

Benton, S. L., Glover, J. A., & Plake, B. S. (1984). Employing adjunct aids to facilitate elaboration in writing. *Research in the Teaching of English*, 18, 189–200.

Benton, S. L., & Kiewra, K. A. (1986). Measuring the organizational aspects of writing ability. *Journal of Educational Measurement*, 23, 377–386.

Benton, S. L., & Kiewra, K. A. (1987). Cognitive factors in academic abilities. In R. R. Ronning, J. C. Conoley, J. A. Glover, & J. C. Witt (Eds.), *The influence of cognitive psychology on testing: Vol. 3. Buros-Nebraska Symposium on Measurement and Testing* (pp. 145–190). Hillsdale, NJ: Erlbaum.

Benton, S. L., Kiewra, K. A., & Bean, R. O. (1988). Attributes of organizational ability related to writing ability. *Contemporary Educational Psychology*, 13, 87–89.

Benton, S. L., Kiewra, K. A., Whitfill, J., & Dennison, R. (1993). Encoding and external-storage effects on writing processes. *Journal of Educational Psychology*, 85, 267–280.

Benton, S. L., Kraft, R. G., Glover, J. A., & Plake, B. S. (1984). Cognitive capacity differences among writers. *Journal of Educational Psychology*, 76, 820–834.

Bereiter, C., & Scardamalia, M. (1987). *The psychology of written composition*. Hillsdale, NJ: Erlbaum.

Blohm, P. J., & Benton, S. L. (1991). Effect of prewriting interventions on production of elaboration in informative writing. *Journal of Research and Development in Education*, 24, 28–32.

Bransford, J. D. (1979). *Human cognition: Learning, understanding, and remembering*. Belmont, CA: Wadsworth.

Britton, J., Burgess, T., Martin, N., McLeod, A., & Rosen, H. (1975). *The development of writing abilities* (pp. 11–18). London: Macmillan Education.

Brown, A. S. (1990). A review of recent research on spelling. *Educational Psychology Review*, 2, 365–397.

Bruce, B. (1991). Roles for computers in teaching the English language arts. In J. Flood, J. M. Jenson, D. Lapp, & J. R. Squire (Eds.), *Handbook of research on teaching the English language arts* (pp. 536–541). New York: Macmillan.

Byrnes, J. P. (1992). Categorizing and combining theories of cognitive development and learning. *Educational Psychology Review*, 4, 309–343.

Cameron, C. A., Hunt, A. K., & Linton, M. J. (1996). Written expression as recontextualization: Children write in social time. *Educational Psychology Review*, 8, 125–150.

Castle, J. M., Riach, J., & Nicholson, T. (1994). Getting off to a better start in reading and spelling: The effects of phonemic awareness instruction within a whole language program. *Journal of Educational Psychology*, 86, 350–359.

Chomsky, N. (1980). On cognitive structures and memory development. In R. S. Siegler (Ed.), *Children's thinking: What develops?* (pp. 73–96). Hillsdale, NJ: Erlbaum.

Cohen, M., & Riel, M. (1989). The effect of distant audiences on students' writing. *American Educational Research Journal*, 26, 143–159.

Coles, R., & Goodman, Y. (1980). Do we really need those oversized pencils to write with? *Theory Into Practice*, 19, 194–196.

College Board. (1983). *Test of Standard Written English*. Princeton, NJ: Author.

Crowhurst, M. (1983). Sentence combining: Maintaining realistic expectations. *College Composition and Communication*, 34, 62–72.

Daiute, C. (1985). *Writing and computers*. Reading, MA: Addison-Wesley.

DeGroff, L. C. (1987). The influence of prior knowledge on writing, conferencing and revising. *Elementary School Journal*, 88, 105–118.

Derry, S. J. (1992). Beyond symbolic processing: Expanding horizons for educational psychology. *Journal of Educational Psychology*, 84, 413–418.

Dewey, J. (1913). *Interest and effort in education*. Boston: Riverside Press.

Durst, R. K., & Newell, G. E. (1989). The uses of function: James Britton's category system and research on writing. *Review of Educational Research*, 59, 375–394.

Dyson, A. (1983). The role of oral language in early writing processes. *Research in the Teaching of English*, 17, 1–30.

Eckhoff, B. (1984). How reading affects children's writing. In J. M. Jensen (Ed.), *Composing and comprehending* (pp. 105–114). Urbana, IL: ERIC/RCS.

Edmunds, G. A., Cameron, C. A., & Eglington, K. (1988). Audience adaptation in persuasive letters. Paper presented at the annual meeting of the American Educational Research Association, New Orleans, LA.

Edmunds, G. A., Cameron, C. A., Linton, M. J., & Hunt, A. K. (1988). Children's text revision [Abstract]. *Canadian Psychology*, 29, 224.

Emig, J. (1971). *The composing process of twelfth graders*. Urbana, IL: National Council of Teachers of English.

Englert, C. S. (1992). Writing instruction from a sociocultural perspective: The holistic, dialogic, and social enterprise of writing. *Journal of Learning Disabilities*, 3, 153–172.

Faigley, L. (1986). Competing theories of process. *College English*, 48, 527–542.

Flower, L. S. (1985). *Problem-solving strategies for writing* (2nd ed.). San Diego, CA: Harcourt Brace Jovanovich.

Flower, L. S., & Hayes, J. R. (1981). A cognitive process theory of writing. *College Composition and Communication*, 32, 365–387.

Garcia, E. E. (1992). "Hispanic" children: Theoretical, empirical, and related policy issues. *Educational Psychology Review*, 4, 69–94.

Gentry, J. R. (1981). Learning to spell developmentally. *Reading Teacher*, 34, 378–381.

Graesser, A., Hopkinson, P. L., Lewis, E., & Bruflodt, H. (1984). The impact of different information sources on idea generation. *Written Communication*, 3, 341–363.

Graham, S. (1992). Issues in handwriting instruction. *Focus on Exceptional Children*, 25, 1–14.

Graham, S., & Harris, K. (1994). The effects of whole language on children's writing: A review of literature. *Educational Psychologist*, 29, 187–192.

Graham, S., MacArthur, C., & Schwartz, S. (1995). Effects of goal setting and procedural facilitation on the revising behavior and writing performance of students with writing and learning problems. *Journal of Educational Psychology*, 87, 230–240.

Graham, S., & Weintraub, N. (1996). A review of handwriting research: Progress and prospect from 1980 to 1994. *Educational Psychology Review*, 8, 7–88.

Graves, D. H. (1973). Children's writing: Research directions and hypotheses based upon an examination of the writing processes of seven-year-old children. *Dissertation Abstracts International*, 34, 6255A.

Graves, D. H. (1983). *Writing: Teachers and children at work*. Portsmouth, NH: Heinemann.

Hamstra-Bletz, L., & Blote, A. (1990). Development of handwriting in primary school: A longitudinal study. *Perceptual and Motor Skills*, 70, 759–770.

Harris, K., & Graham, S. (1992). Self-regulated strategy development: A part of the writing process. In M. Pressley, K. Harris, & J. Guthrie (Eds.), *Promoting academic competence and literacy in school* (pp. 277–309). San Diego, CA: Academic.

Henderson, E. H., & Templeton, S. (1986). A developmental perspective of formal spelling instruction through alphabet, pattern, and meaning. *Elementary School Journal*, 86, 305–316.

Hidi, S. (1990). Interest and its contribution as a mental resource for learning. *Review of Educational Research*, 60, 549–571.

Hidi, S., & Anderson, V. (1992). Situational interest and its impact on reading and expository writing. In K. A. Renninger, S. Hidi, & A. Krapp (Eds.), *The role of interest in learning and development* (pp. 215–238). Hillsdale, NJ: Erlbaum.

Hidi, S., & McLaren, J. (1990). The effect of topic and theme interestingness on the production of school expositions. In H. Mandl, E. DeCorte, N. Bennett, & H. F. Friedrich (Eds.), *Learning and instruction: European research in an international context* (Vol. 2, pp. 295–308). Oxford, England: Pergamon.

Hillocks, G. (1986). *Research on writing composition*. Urbana, IL: ERIC Clearinghouse.

Hillocks, G., & Mavrogenes, N. (1986). Sentence combining. In *Research on written composition: New directions for teaching* (pp. 134–141). Urbana, IL: ERIC/NCRE.

Hillocks, G., & Smith, M. (1991). Grammar and usage. In J. Flood, J. M. Jenson, D. Lapp, & J. R. Squire (Eds.), *Handbook of research on teaching the English language arts* (pp. 591–603). New York: Macmillan.

Hunt, K. W. (1965). Grammatical structures written at three grade levels (NCTE Rep. No. 3). Urbana, IL: National Council of Teachers of English.

James, W. (1890). *The principles of psychology*. London: Macmillan.

Juel, C. (1988). Learning to read and write: A longitudinal study of 54 children from first through fourth grades. *Journal of Educational Psychology*, 80, 437–447.

Keil, F. C. (1981). Constraints on knowledge and cognitive development. *Psychological Review*, 88, 197–227.

Kellogg, R. T. (1987). Effects of topic knowledge on the allocation of processing time and cognitive effort to writing processes. *Memory & Cognition*, 15, 255–266.

Kellogg, R. T. (1988). Attentional overload and writing performance: Effects of rough drafts and outline strategies. *Journal of Experimental Psychology*, 14, 355–365.

Kiewra, K. A. (1985). Investigating note-taking and review: A depth of processing alternative. *Educational Psychologist*, 20, 23–32.

Kiewra, K. A., Benton, S. L., Kim, S., Risch, N., & Christensen, M. (1995). Effects of note-taking format and study technique on recall and relational performance. *Contemporary Educational Psychology*, 20, 172–187.

Kroll, B. M. (1984). Audience adaptation in children's persuasive letters. *Written Communication*, 1, 407–427.

Laidlaw, E., Skok, R. L., & McLaughlin, T. F. (1993). The effects of notetaking and self-questioning on quiz performance. *Science Education*, 77, 75–82.

Langer, J. A. (1984). The effects of available information on responses to school writing tasks. *Research in the Teaching of English*, 18, 27–44.

Langer, J. A. (1991). Literacy and schooling: A socio-cognitive perspective. In E. H. Hiebert (Ed.), *Literacy for a diverse society* (pp. 9–27). New York: Teachers College Press.

Loban, W. (1976). *Language development: Kindergarten through grade twelve*. Urbana, IL: National Council of Teachers of English.

MacArthur, C. A., Schwartz, S. S., & Graham, S. (1991). Effects of a reciprocal peer revision strategy in special education classrooms. *Learning Disabilities Research and Practice*, 6, 201–210.

Mather, N. (1992). Whole language reading instruction for students with learning disabilities: Caught in the cross fire. *Learning Disabilities Research and Practice*, 7, 87–95.

McBride-Chang, C. (1995). What is phonological awareness? *Journal of Educational Psychology*, 87, 179–192.

McCutchen, D. (1986). Domain knowledge and linguistic knowledge in the development of writing ability. *Journal of Memory and Language*, 25, 434–444.

McCutchen, D., Covill, A., Hoyne, S. H., & Mildes, K. (1994). Individual differences in writing: Implications of translating fluency. *Journal of Educational Psychology*, 86, 256–266.

McGraw-Hill (1985). *California Achievement Test—Reading*. New York: Author.

Mikkelsen, N. (1984). Talking and telling: The child as storymaker. *Language Arts*, 61, 229–239.

Mojet, J. (1991). Characteristics of the developing handwriting skill in elementary education. In J. Wann, A. Wing, & N. Sovik (Eds.), *Development of graphic skills: Research, perspectives and educational implications* (pp. 53–75). London: Academic Press.

Moll, L., & Diaz, R. (1987). Teaching writing as communication: The use of ethnographic findings in classroom practice. In D. Bloome (Ed.), *Literacy and schooling* (pp. 193–221). Norwood, NJ: Ablex.

Moore, D. W., Moore, S. A., Cunningham, P. M., & Cunningham, J. W. (1986). *Developing readers and writers in the content areas*. New York: Longman.

Moshman, D. (1982). Exogenous, endogenous, and dialectical constructivism. *Developmental Review, 2*, 371–384.

Moshman, D. (1990). Rationality as a goal of education. *Educational Psychology Review, 2*, 335–364.

Needels, M. C., & Knapp, M. S. (1994). Teaching writing to children who are underserved. *Journal of Educational Psychology, 86*, 339–349.

Newell, G. N. (1984). Learning from writing in two content areas: A case study/protocol analysis of writing to learn. *Research in the Teaching of English, 18*, 265–287.

Newell, G. N., & Winograd, P. (1989). The effects of writing on learning from expository text. *Written Communication, 6*, 196–217.

Newkirk, T. (1984). How students read student papers: An exploratory study. *Written Communication, 1*, 283–306.

Nystrand, M. (1986). *The structure of written communication: Studies in reciprocity between writers and readers*. Orlando, FL: Academic Press.

O'Connor, R. E., Jenkins, J. R., & Slocum, T. A. (1995). Transfer among phonological tasks in kindergarten: Essential instructional content. *Journal of Educational Psychology, 87*, 202–217.

O'Hare, F. (1973). *Sentence combining: Improving student writing without formal grammar instruction*. Urbana, IL: National Council of Teachers of English.

Palincsar, A. S., & Klenk, L. (1992). Examining and influencing contexts for intentional literacy learning. In C. Collins & J. N. Mangieri (Eds.), *Teaching thinking: An agenda for the 21st Century* (pp. 297–316). Hillsdale, NJ: Erlbaum.

Palmatier, R. A., & Bennett, J. M. (1974). Note-taking habits of college students. *Journal of Reading, 18*, 215–218.

Pearson, P. D. (1985). *The comprehension revolution: A twenty-year history of process and practice related to reading comprehension* (Reading Education Rep. No. 57). Urbana: University of Illinois, Center for the Study of Reading.

Peck, K. L., & Hannafin, M. J. (1983). The effects of notetaking pretraining and the recording of notes on the retention of aural instruction. *Journal of Educational Research, 77*, 100–107.

Peper, R. J., & Mayer, R. E. (1986). Generative effects of note-taking during science lectures. *Journal of Educational Psychology, 78*, 34–38.

Piaget, J. (1983). Piaget's theory. In P. H. Mussen (Series Ed.) & W. Kessen (Vol. Ed.), *Handbook of child psychology: Vol. 1: History, theory, and methods* (4th ed., pp. 103–128). New York: Wiley.

Piaget, J. (1985). *The equilibration of cognitive structures: The central problem of intellectual development*. Chicago: University of Chicago Press.

Purcell-Gates, V. (1992). Roots of response. *Journal of Narrative and Life History, 2*, 151–161.

Renninger, K. A. (1990). Children's play interests, representation, and activity. In R. Fivush & J. Hudson (Eds.), *Knowing and remembering in young children* (pp. 127–165). Cambridge, MA: Cambridge University Press.

Ross, J. (1971). A transformational approach to teaching composition. *College Composition and Communication, 22*, 179–184.

Roswell, F. G., & Natchez, H. (1989). *Reading disability: A human approach to evaluation and treatment of reading and writing difficulties*. New York: Basic Books.

Rubin, A. D., & Bruce, B. C. (1986). Learning with QUILL: Lessons for students, teachers, and software designers. In T. E. Raphael (Ed.), *Contexts of school-based literacy* (pp. 217–230). New York: Random House.

Salinger, T. (1992). Critical thinking and young literacy learners. In C. Collins & J. N. Mangieri (Eds.), *Teaching thinking: An agenda for the 21st century* (pp. 319–332). Hillsdale, NJ: Erlbaum.

Scardamalia, M., Bereiter, C., & Goelman, H. (1982). The role of productive factors in writing ability. In M. Nystrand (Ed.), *What citizens know: The language, process, and structure of written discourse* (pp. 173–210). New York: Academic Press.

Schallert, D. L. (1991). The contribution of psychology to teaching the language arts. In J. Flood,

J. M. Jenson, D. Lapp, & J. R. Squire (Eds.), *Handbook of research on teaching the English language arts* (pp. 30–39). New York: Macmillan.

Schiefele, U. (1990). The influence of topic interest, prior knowledge and cognitive capabilities on text comprehension. In J. M. Pieters, K. Breurer, & P. R. J. Simons (Eds.), *Learning environments* (pp. 323–338). Berlin: Springer.

Simmons, J. S. (1991). The junior high school years. In J. Flood, J. M. Jenson, D. Lapp, & J. R. Squire (Eds.), *Handbook of research on teaching the English language arts* (pp. 320–330). New York: Macmillan.

Simner, M. L. (1981). The grammar of action and children's printing. *Developmental Psychology, 17,* 866–871.

Squire, J. R. (1991). The history of the profession. In J. Flood, J. M. Jenson, D. Lapp, & J. R. Squire (Eds.), *Handbook of research on teaching the English language arts* (pp. 3–17). New York: Macmillan.

Stahl, S. A., McKenna, M. C., & Pagnucco, J. R. (1994). The effects of whole-language instruction: An update and a reappraisal. *Educational Psychologist, 29,* 175–186.

Strickland, D. S., & Freeley, J. T. (1991). Development in the elementary school years. In J. Flood, J. M. Jenson, D. Lapp, & J. R. Squire (Eds.), *Handbook of research on teaching the English language arts* (pp. 286–302). New York: Macmillan.

Thorndike, E. L. (1935). *Adult interests.* New York: Macmillan.

Thurber, D. (1983). *D'Nealian manuscript—An aid to reading development* (CS 007 057). Arlington, VA: ERIC Document Reproduction Service.

Tierney, R. J., & Pearson, P. D. (1983). Toward a composing model of reading. *Language Arts, 60,* 568–580.

Vukelich, C. (1986). The relationship between peer questions and seven-year-olds' text revisions. *National Reading Conference Yearbook, 35,* 300–305.

Vygotsky, L. S. (1962). *Thought and language.* Cambridge, MA: MIT Press.

Whitaker, D., Berninger, V., Johnston, J., & Swanson, H. L. (1994). Intraindividual differences in levels of language in intermediate grade writers: Implications for the translating process. *Learning and Individual Differences, 6,* 107–130.

Ziviani, J., & Elkins, J. (1984). An evaluation of handwriting performance. *Educational Review, 36,* 249–261.

CHAPTER

9

Teaching Composition: Current Theories and Practices

REBECCA E. BURNETT AND LEE-ANN MARIE KASTMAN

Iowa State University

While there is a more than two-century history of teaching writing to secondary-level students in the United States, there is little agreement about the most effective way to teach composition. For much of this history, teachers have been influenced by a perspective that provided formal models, encouraged students to learn rules of grammar and style, and presumed the value of abstract and often moralistic topics. However, this structured, rule-based approach, while one of the common approaches in the 19th century and much of the 20th century, is not the only way to teach writing. A handful of 19th-century texts, used initially (and primarily, though not exclusively) in secondary schools, offered an alternative. These early 19th-century texts encouraged young writers to focus on the processes of writing, draw on their own observations, reflect on their own experiences, plan, freewrite, use heuristics to discover information, and use their own voice (Schultz, 1995).

In this chapter, we take the position that this alternative approach—this focus on the processes and strategies of writing—not only has a solid historical foundation but also forms the basis for some of the most effective practices for teaching writing in secondary schools. These practices provide fertile ground for research about teaching writing; of course, the results of this research circle back to inform evolving practices. What practices seem most effective? While we agree that students need to learn conventional forms and develop analytical strategies, we also see writing as a way for students to explore beliefs (their own and others'), their communities, and their worlds. Writing helps students stretch their thinking, develop

Handbook of Academic Learning

communication strategies useful to future academic and workplace experiences, and share in new experiences—as Lillian Bridwell-Bowles says, "to dream, to think in new cycles, and to have visions for the future that are hopeful" (1995, p. 47).

We believe that one way students learn to be functional and effective writers is to use writing regularly—as a way to express themselves, solve their problems, argue their points. Learning to write is not a matter of students' mastering modes of discourse (such as narrative, exposition, or argument); instead, as Richard Larson explains, learning to write involves achieving "a specific purpose with a reader or group of readers" (1992, p. 35).

We also believe that students need to be able to talk about the processes and products of writing that are part of their personal, community, and workplace lives. These processes and products, of course, are always integrated, always inseparable. Sometimes pedagogy simply decides to focus on one or the other. All writing is created using some process, whether or not students can articulate it. No process exists except as an abstraction unless a product is created. In asserting our position, we argue that writing is a dynamic, communicative, constructive, contextual, and collaborative activity.

Writing is *dynamic*. Ideas and events influence and are influenced by writing. Simply put, the very act of writing often changes writers' ideas—stimulating new points of view, calling up new images, enabling previously unexamined connections. Sometimes writing persuades and challenges writers as they work. And the resulting documents are often provocative forces that soothe or cajole readers, provide new information, slant perspectives, and stimulate insights. Writing never is neutral, never objective for writers or readers.

Writing is *communicative*. Writing communicates *about* something; there must be subject matter. Some agree with Maxine Hairston that "Writing courses . . . should not be *for* anything or *about* anything other than writing itself, and how one uses it to learn and think and communicate" (1992, p. 179). Others argue that writing courses are ideal places to explore issues and ideas related to a range of topics—from literature and great ideas to conflicts emerging from sexism, racism, and multiculturalism. A risk of making a writing course the site for exploring content other than the students' own writing processes is that the content (ranging from great ideas to multiculturalism) will be seen by some students as more important than what they need to learn about the complexities of writing (David, Gordon, & Pollard, 1995). As students learn to manage the complexities of writing about a broad range of topics for various purposes and audiences, they need help in monitoring and examining their own writing processes.

The meaning conveyed in writing is always *constructed* and interpreted, by both writers and readers. Meaning is not inherent in the marks on the page (or electronic blips on a screen). Instead, meaning is constructed and interpreted from the prior histories, current situations, and future expectations of both writers and readers as they interact with the text. This interaction may be between a writer and herself when, for example, a writer keeps a personal journal in which to reflect on ideas and events. The interaction may also be between a writer and an individual or small group, perhaps in a letter, perhaps in a proposal to a community group. Or the interaction may be between a writer and a broader, less familiar audience, perhaps in a newspaper editorial, perhaps in a poem in the *New Yorker.* Regardless of the audience, intimate or wide ranging, meaning is shaped within the writer and reader and by the interpretive interaction between them.

Writing is *contextual*. To some, the term *context* simply means the linguistic context of a word. For example, the word *bat* on a page by itself is ambiguous. It can be an animate or inanimate noun, a verb, or an adjective. Even putting the word in a sentence helps only a little. "Casey's at bat"—is that Casey in the poem, Casey Stengel, or eight-year-old Casey Greenough who lives next door? "Pick up the bat"—is the bat the aluminum athletic equipment left on the lawn or the little brown bat that squeezed its way through a crack in the attic window frame? Now, however, when teachers and researchers refer to context, they generally refer both to "contexts for the production of writing . . . [and] eventual contexts of use for written texts" (Chin, 1994, p. 446). Some contexts for the *production* of writing include the task, the occasion, and the situation in which writers work. Some contexts of *use* for written texts include the purposes, audiences, and uses to which the text is put, whether intended by the writer or not.

Writing is *collaborative*. Writers depend on interaction with others—whether in thought, text, observation, or personal contact—to consider and reconsider, shape and reshape their ideas. Because writers live and learn (and write) in a social environment, their ideas are stimulated and refined by their interactions. If a writer ever huddled in a Parisian garret, shivering from cold while scratching words onto sheets of paper, he was only alone physically. The voices of his conversations and experiences and readings would influence the interpretation of ideas and words.

As we write this chapter, our own perspective is shaped by our combined experience: two decades of teaching writing in public secondary schools and another two decades of teaching and tutoring writing in colleges and universities. By both temperament and training, we are teachers of writing. But we are also researchers about writing, theorists interested in explaining the nature of writing, and, certainly not least, we ourselves are writers. From our experiences as teachers, researchers, theorists, and practitioners, we offer a perspective that is strongly influenced by our belief that students should be actively engaged in developing strengths as individuals and as members of a community. They learn both abstractions and applications and then reflect on them as they build a repertoire of experiences as writers.

In this chapter, we encourage an approach to teaching writing that is dynamic, communicative, constructive, contextual, and collaborative. In doing this, we first describe conventional approaches to teaching writing and discuss additional theoretical perspectives that we believe influence the way writing is taught. Then we identify sites and situations for teaching writing: in composition classes, in literature classes, in applied communication, in writing across the curriculum, in community settings. After examining problems that must be addressed in virtually every school (remedial–basic writers and assessment and evaluation), we identify important sources of support for teachers of writing (writing centers and technology). Throughout the chapter, we include boxed examples from exemplary educators who describe their classroom practices. We conclude by suggesting that focusing on processes and strategies helps students be better prepared to engage in dialogue, leading to writing that is influenced by and influences others.

CONVENTIONAL APPROACHES TO TEACHING WRITING

Composition teachers have generally approached their teaching in one of three ways, often referred to as a current–traditional approach, a neoromantic (expressivist) approach, or a neoclassicist (rhetorical) approach. Each approach has a long history, each has committed supporters, and each has distinct benefits and limitations as far as students are concerned. Each approach has a different primary focus: on the text, the writer, or the audience. In practice, of course, the distinctions among these approaches are not nearly as neat and clear-cut as simple definitions make them seem; experienced teachers often describe their teaching as an amalgam of various approaches.

Current–Traditional Approach

Teachers using a current–traditional approach encourage students to focus on the text. This attention to the printed word, whether crafted with a pen or a computer, evolves from the 19th-century view that we can teach "mental habits" and the "craft" but not the "mysteries" of writing (Schultz, 1995; Young, 1982). Because teachers emphasizing a current–traditional approach encourage students to give their primary attention to the structure, organization, and correctness of their text, they often emphasize rules and use handbooks to define and illustrate those rules of grammar, mechanics, and style. Attention given to textual conventions sometimes overshadows attention to individual voice, writing processes, social context, or meaning making. A current–traditional approach assumes there is a "correct" way to write, a way that can be taught (Dasenbrock, 1993), a way that depends on learning to use grammatical and mechanical conventions of language.

This current–traditional approach often uses what George Hillocks calls a *presentational mode* of instruction (1984, 1986), which is characterized by

> (1) relatively clear and specific objectives, e.g., to use particular rhetorical techniques; (2) lecture and teacher-led discussion dealing with concepts to be learned and applied; (3) the study of models and other materials which explain and illustrate the concept; (4) specific assignments or exercises which generally involve imitating a pattern or following rules that have been previously discussed; and (5) feedback following the writing, coming primarily from teachers. (1986, pp. 116–117)

In a meta-analysis of research studies about effective ways to teach composition, Hillocks concluded that the presentational mode is "the most common and widespread [with the teacher dominating the activity and] with students acting as passive recipients of rules, advice, and examples of good writing" (1986, p. 246). Unfortunately, it was "the least effective mode examined—only about half as effective as the average experimental treatment" (1986, p. 247).

A primary risk of a current–traditional approach is that writing is not usually seen as related to critical thinking and problem solving. Instead, the assumption is that writing is simply the act of articulating ideas that already exist, of putting the right words in the right order using the right conventions. Success is often measured by correctness rather than insight. Since the text is the focus, students often produce writer-based prose rather than reader-based prose.

A second risk is that the current–traditional approach potentially ignores both the individual cognitive and collective social factors that influence writers (Berlin, 1988; Flower & Hayes, 1977). The current–traditional approach has been criticized for ignoring the nature of the community in which writers and writing are situated (Hillocks, 1984, 1986). However, theorists such as Thomas Kent (1992) suggest that, in fact, we cannot teach writing as a codifiable process; however, we can teach a great deal *about* writing—for example, grammar, mechanics, analytical methods, coherence, cognitive strategies, logic, text conventions, genres, and so on. Simply put, there is a difference between learning to write and learning about aspects of writing.

Neoromantic (Expressivist) Approach

Teachers using a neoromantic or expressivist approach most often encourage students to focus on themselves as individual writers rather than on the text or the social context in which they create their text. Richard Young asserts that in this approach "the intellect is no better guide to understanding reality than nonlogical processes are, and that the act of composing is a kind of mysterious growth fed by what Henry James called 'the deep well of unconscious celebration'" (1982, p. 132).

Expressivist approaches to writing concentrate on the individual. In discussing expressivism, James Berlin explains that "Discovering the true self in writing will simultaneously enable the individual to discover the truth of the situation which evoked the writing, a situation that, needless to say, must always be compatible with the development of the self . . ." (1988, p. 485). Teachers who use an expressivist approach typically design situations that encourage both intellectual probing and, as Young notes, "occasions that stimulate the creative process" (1982, p. 133). Teachers using this approach usually believe that while they can teach the conventions of writing, they cannot teach the art (magic, mystery, and glamor) of writing. Instead, they can provide opportunities and encouragement for the art.

A neoromantic or expressivist approach often uses what George Hillocks calls a *natural process mode* of instruction (1984, 1986), which is characterized by

> (1) generalized objectives, e.g., to increase fluency and skill in writing; (2) free writing about whatever interests the students, either in a journal or as a way of "exploring a subject"; (3) writing for audiences of peers; (4) generally positive feedback from peers; (5) opportunities to revise and rework writing; and (6) high levels of interaction among students. (1986, p. 119)

In his meta-analysis of research studies about effective ways to teach composition, Hillocks concluded that the natural process mode of instruction is "about 25 percent less effective than the average experimental treatment, but about 50 percent more effective that the presentational mode" (1986, p. 247).

A neoromantic or expressivist approach often refers "to the teacher as a 'facilitator' whose role is to free the student's imagination and promote growth by sustaining a positive classroom atmosphere" (Hillocks, 1984, p. 143). As the box by John Forssman (Ames High School in Ames, Iowa) shows, some extraordinarily successful teachers are devoted to an expressivist approach. John Forssman's fervor and commitment are repaid by students who not only learn to write but also, years later, recall his class as one of their most positive educational experiences.

In addition to the notable successes of a neoromantic or expressivist approach (Rico, 1988), it has some risks. One risk is that success is often judged by effort rather than results. Students who try hard, who are diligent, who stay focused on the task are often rewarded for their energy rather than their achievement.

Another risk is that students may produce writer-based prose rather than reader-based prose. While teachers want to encourage students to develop the competence and confidence to express themselves, a narrow, often egocentric writing may emerge. These students need to realize that a collective voice may often be more powerful, more likely to be heard. James Berlin focuses on this objection when he explains that

> expressionistic rhetoric is inherently and debilitatingly divisive of political protest, suggesting that effective resistance can only be offered by individuals, each acting

The Spiritual Connection: An Expressivist Approach to Teaching Writing

The poet Coleman Barks talks about the golden light he sees in the Tennessee Valley for about 10 minutes each day. For him, these minutes are "moments of ecstasy." He refers to them as "marvelous moments of eternity."

That same golden light coats many pieces of our lives, and serious writers have always known this. As a high school composition teacher, part of my job is to help my students discover the golden light in pieces of their own lives. Often it is a matter of refining their perceptions, so they can see the natural light in themselves and in their surroundings; or, as one of my students wrote, "We need to listen to ourselves and to our surroundings because truth lies in everything."

For my composition students to see the golden light in their lives in what Willa Cather said "is there about us always," their perceptions must truly be "made finer." Marcel Proust wrote, "The real voyage of discovery consists not in seeking new landscapes but in having new eyes." Or, as one of my more perceptive students wrote, "Mining the gold in a book means getting the most out of a book so that it can help the best come out of you."

To help my students genuinely discover this invisible connection between the spiritual and material worlds, I have them focus on definite pieces of their own lives—their golden ideas, their golden questions, their golden moments, their golden images, their golden power spots, their golden people. I encourage them to focus on these six golden pieces of their lives and to personally discover how they are coated with the natural light of heaven. Gold is my metaphor for refining the perception of my students and for illuminating specific pieces of their lives in terms of their full spirituality.

John Forssman
Ames High School
Ames, Iowa

> alone. Given the isolation and incoherence of such protest, gestures genuinely threatening to the establishment are difficult to accomplish. (1988, p. 487)

Therefore, students need to be taught to articulate their position in relation to others and to provide citations for ideas derived from others.

A third risk is that the focus is most often on the writer's creativity. The risk of encouraging individual creativity is forgetting that knowledge is not created by a lone individual; rather, an individual interacts with and interprets situational and social circumstances, with memories of prior conversations and experiences, with reactions stimulated by reading and rereading the current text. Simply put, an individual's creativity is made possible by interaction with and interpretation of the broad social context.

Neoclassical (Rhetorical) Approach

Teachers using a neoclassical or rhetorical approach encourage students to focus on the audience more than on the text or on themselves as writers. The importance of audience (and other rhetorical factors such as context, purpose, and organization) was articulated initially by rhetoricians such as Aristotle, who in *Metaphysics* argued that artists and authors are "wiser not in virtue of being able to act, but of having the theory for themselves and knowing the causes" (cited in Young, 1982, p. 134). Understanding the underlying elements that influence writing rather than simply having a knack for writing encourages students to consider factors such as audience, context, purpose, and organization that influence their generation of a text.

A neoclassical or rhetorical approach often uses what George Hillocks calls an *environmental mode* of instruction (1984, 1986), which is characterized by

> (1) clear and specific objectives, e.g., to increase the use of specific detail and figurative language; (2) materials and problems selected to engage students with each other in specifiable processes important to some particular aspect of writing; and (3) activities, such as small-group problem-centered discussions, conducive to high levels of peer interaction concerning specific tasks. (1986, p. 122)

In his meta-analysis of research studies about effective ways to teach composition, Hillocks concluded that the environmental mode of instruction is the "most effective" because it "brings teacher, student, and materials more nearly into balance and, in effect, takes advantage of all resources of the classroom." According to Hillocks, "[T]he environmental mode is over four times more effective than the traditional presentational mode and three times more effective than the natural process mode" (1986, p. 247).

In classrooms that emphasize a neoclassical or rhetorical approach, students often learn *heuristics* (as opposed to rules). (*Heuristic* is defined by Linda Woodson as "a method of solving problems; a series of steps or questions which are likely to lead to a solution of a problem" [1979, p. 28]. She also quotes Richard Young who defines *heuristic* as "specific plans for analyzing and searching which focus attention, guide reason, stimulate memory, and encourage intuition"; cited in Woodson, 1979, p. 29.) Learning heuristics implies a generic conception of processes and supports the notion that imaginative acts can be stimulated and nourished. Heuristics, which are available for virtually all phases of composing, imply that these phases can be carried out deliberately and rationally (Young, 1982). Whether these heuristics are successful depends, in part, on students' ability to understand their own processes of writing and to use the feedback they receive about their work (Sitko, 1993).

Conversation of Discovery: Collaborative Planning as a Heuristic

Collaborative planning gives my students—from my sophomores suspicious of any activity involving a pencil or a keyboard to my AP [advanced placement] seniors writing about *King Lear*—a chance to think more about rhetorical elements and to improve their image of themselves as writers. During collaborative planning, students pose questions to each other, questions about the rhetorical aspects of writing that they don't have the experience or confidence to ask themselves. I give students a "starter list" of questions that encourages then to investigate each other's purposes, key points, audiences, organization and textual support, as well as the overall designs of their papers.

My students usually adapt my questions as they provoke each other to provide explanations and rationales for their responses. So Melanie asked Kirsten, who was writing a paper about the famous person she'd chosen for an evening of conversation, not only "Who's the focus of your paper?" but also "*Why* would you choose Saddam Hussein?"

Collaborative planning also encourages my students' self-discovery. When Sharon and I read the transcript of her taped planning session with Scott, she was able to see that she'd had a good key idea in her draft; Scott simply helped her focus and refine her idea: "I wasn't sure when I came to class ... what to write about, but [after the collaborative planning session with Scott], when I got my notes at home, everything fell together."

Collaborative planning gives my students a clear starting place for their own planning and revising, gives them a window on their writing process, and gives me a way to help them see their own strengths.

Leslie Byrd Evans
Steel Valley High School
Munhall, Pennsylvania

As the box by Leslie Byrd Evans (Steel Valley High School, Munhall, Pennsylvania) shows, a heuristic such as collaborative planning can have a powerful influence on students' writing. Collaborative planning is an interactive heuristic that encourages writers to work in pairs or small groups to ask each other questions about rhetorical elements that experienced writers often ask themselves (Flower, Wallace, Norris, & Burnett, 1994).

During the past 20 years, this rhetorical approach has been adopted by many teachers focusing on writing processes. This focus on processes resulted from research that attempted to model the cognitive processes writers use (Flower & Hayes, 1981a, 1981b; Hayes, Flower, Schriver, Stratman, & Carey, 1987; Scardamalia & Bereiter, 1987). Recently, writing research has examined the complex contexts in which writing occurs: classrooms, workplaces, communities. This recognition that the social component is critical marks an important development in writing research, with attention to both the social and cognitive aspects of writing.

As with the current–traditional and the expressivist approaches, the rhetorical approach has limitations. For example, writing process research, unfortunately, has often been translated for the classroom into an oversimplified three-step process—prewriting, writing, and revision—that ignores the recursive nature of writing processes and students' ability to determine what works most effectively for them. Thus, attention to processes that writers use is sometimes inappropriately codified into a rigid, inviolate process that student writers are forced to follow. Another limitation occurs because writing processes too frequently are portrayed as linear rather than recursive, as absolute rather than flexible (organic) so that heuristics become rules rather than approaches to solving a problem.

CURRENT THEORETICAL PERSPECTIVES ABOUT TEACHING WRITING

While most secondary school teachers use a current–traditional, expressivist, or rhetorical approach to teach writing, they now have the opportunity to consider two relatively new theoretical perspectives, social construction and externalism, that provide insights about the teaching of writing. Even more than expressivist or rhetorical approaches, social constructionist and externalist perspectives focus on the act of writing for a particular purpose and a particular audience.

The social constructionist and externalist perspectives, although at odds with each other, both disagree with a current–traditional approach to teaching writing. A current–traditional approach is often referred to as *foundationalist*, a reliance on rules of grammar, structures, and conventions, all of which combine to form a foundational "truth" that can be taught about writing. In contrast, social constructionists such as Kenneth Bruffee (1993) claim that knowledge is socially constructed and that teachers ought to encourage environments that foster discussion and dialogue. Those not yet satisfied with constructionist views that all knowledge is socially constructed have explored yet another approach, externalism, which focuses on communicative interactions and interpretations among individuals, including individuals in the classroom. Social construction and externalism both lend support, in very different ways, to alternative approaches (as suggested by Schultz in the opening of this chapter) to teaching composition—approaches that view writing as dynamic, communicative, constructive, contextual, and collaborative.

Social Construction

Social construction centers around the notion of community—the idea that knowledge is located not in individuals but in communities. (For a detailed description of the social perspective, see Thralls & Blyler, 1993.) This concept is important in writing classrooms because of social constructionists' underlying assumption that learning and writing depend on group interaction; thus, activities and assignments are frequently in some way collaborative. Collaborative writing groups have a number of potential advantages for students, including increased solidarity among group members, more sophisticated written products, and increased awareness of writing processes. (For a detailed description of peer response groups, see DiPardo & Freedman, 1988.)

Without preparation, however, student writing groups often encounter problems because of unproductive conflict, either interpersonal conflict (caused by personality differences) or procedural conflict (caused by disagreements about schedules, meeting places, and agendas). Learning about how their own behavior influences a group can help students reduce negative behaviors that cause unproductive conflicts and increase positive behaviors that invite interaction. Positive behaviors can help group members as they make decisions that lead to consensus (Kastman, 1994).

The way student writers talk with each other—whether part of collaborative planning, collaborative writing assignments, or peer review workshops—influences the quality of their collaborative decision making and, eventually, the quality of the writing. Collaborators whose conversation leads too quickly to consensus tend not to engage in productive conflict, what is often called *substantive conflict* (Burnett, 1993a, 1993b). Substantive conflict occurs when writers raise alternatives or voice explicit disagreements about any of the rhetorical decisions they have to make, including the content. Students who engage in substantive conflict often make more informed, thoughtful, and appropriate decisions about their writing.

Students can examine their own conversations, both written (printouts from computer interactions) and oral (transcripts from small group discussions), to track the ways in which their decision making has led to their written products (Bell-Maetereau, 1994; Latimer & Spoto, 1994; Reagan, 1994; Sperling, 1994; Villanueva, 1994). These analyses help students better understand their writing processes, including the way they deal with complex issues and resolve unproductive conflict (Rodby, 1994; Villanueva, 1994; Zeni, 1994).

A social-constructionist perspective encourages students to question authority and the factors that enable them to see others (as well as themselves) as authoritative. In writing classes, students may be encouraged to question authoritative figures from their reading or community. Students may also be encouraged to question broader social authority—for example, advertising—to discover societal myths and the structures that create them. As students explore and write about authority, they may consider factors such as gender, fitness, race, ethnicity, education, economics, and social status. These factors can be useful for analyzing literature and authors as well as contemporary issues and events. For example, these factors are as critical in understanding what motivated Nathaniel Hawthorne, Charlotte Brontë, Jorge Luis Borges, or Alice Walker as they are in understanding why certain television programs are popular. Equally important, these factors can help students understand themselves as writers. How, for example, does their own gender or race or social status influence their writing.

In writing classes, students can explore authority simply by examining how their class is hierarchically structured. Susan Miller describes such an examination: "We [the teacher and students] will reason together about the dynamics of making assignments, the anxieties of being evaluated and of evaluating, the status of 'expertise'" (1994, pp. 291–292). Miller explores how students may become authorities in a class through evaluating themselves and others, participating in class design, and creating writing assignments.

Some social constructionists want students to use writing as a vehicle to explore and respond to social issues in our culture. Thus, they extend social constructionist boundaries to include what is called a *social–epistemic perspective*; that is, concern with issues of power (ideology) in the construction of knowledge. A social-epistemic perspective focuses on issues of oppression and empowerment; writing teachers using this radical pedagogy often encourage students to explore and respond to oppressive social acts.

Thomas Fox (1994) comments about the way the extension of these boundaries affects collaborative pedagogy: "One of the staples of radical pedagogy has been the transformation of private individual experience into knowledge of collective oppression. In this fact, for me, lies the promise of collaborative learning for radical pedagogy" (p. 113). An example of this radical pedagogy is provided by Dale Sullivan (1990). Sullivan embraces a social-epistemic approach, which he asserts is supported by an apprenticeship model of teaching (p. 382). In this apprenticeship model, Sullivan suggests that teachers create assignments that will immerse students into a "discourse community of industry and the larger discourse community of public citizenship" (p. 382). To do this, Sullivan provides students with a particular case study, asks students to take sides on the case (to provoke resistance and critical thought), and enacts a process of deliberation about the case. The approach requires students to carefully study the issue and as a group form a collective objection to the issue at hand; their position forms the basis for their collaborative paper. Sullivan argues that the apprenticeship model provides experience for students by immersing them in an industrial or technological issue. (For a detailed discussion of cognitive apprenticeships, see Collins, Brown, & Newman, 1989.)

Like other approaches, social construction has limitations when used as the basis for teaching writing. A major limitation is that teachers may not be sufficiently trained to help their students avoid or manage problems that can subvert collaborative interaction, the central teaching strategy of social constructionism. For example, individual dissenting voices may be subordinated or marginalized if a group concedes to a majority position without sufficient discussion (known as *groupthink*). Or students may find themselves embroiled in seemingly unresolvable conflicts and, thus, may never reach consensus if they are not taught ways to negotiate disagreements.

In summary, then, a social-constructionist approach to composition encourages students to be aware that they are part of a community, writing about ideas that are reflective of and shaped by that community. Assignments that reinforce a social-constructionist approach typically encourage students to engage in dialogue, decision making, consensus, and exploration of authority as critical parts of their composing.

Externalist Perspective

Unlike social constructionists, externalists argue that our understanding of the world is based on our communicative *interactions* with others and our *interpretations* of those interactions. These interactions and interpretations are determined by individuals rather than by groups or communities.

Social construction has been criticized by some as an "iron cage" because of the limitations that consensus places on a group (Spellmeyer, 1994, p. 83). This view, held by theorists such as Thomas Kent (1991), Reed Way Dasenbrock (1993), and Gregory Clark (1994), suggests that collaborative assignments may discourage individual interpretation in the process of the group forming a consensus. In any interaction, including those in classrooms, reaching a consensus may not adequately allow for individual interpretation or dissension. In response to this shortcoming, externalists advocate what they call a dialogic and intersubjective (communicating with other individual language users) approach to teaching composition; that is, assignments should encourage students to explore their ideas as they are situated in relation to others' ideas, including the teacher's. This exploration occurs through interaction that may or may not result in consensus or agreement about ideas.

An externalist perspective requires, according to Spellmeyer (1994), the need "to reconceive social life in ways that make room for change and difference as well as likemindedness, that allow us to acknowledge intersubjectivity but also the reality of dissent" (p. 86). The "reality of dissent" plays itself out in intersubjective exchanges that *allow* for dissent (Davidson, 1993, p. 2). An externalist approach to writing encourages students to consider a variety of viewpoints about writing. They are encouraged to articulate the ways in which their ideas are situated with or in contrast to other viewpoints.

A central concept for externalism is *interpretation* of meaning (that is, language as interpretation; Kuhn, 1991). Any two individuals may share beliefs, but to share beliefs or ideas, we must stand in some interpretive relation to others, even if the other is us. For externalists, writing is one *kind* of communicative interaction, one in which student and teacher interact with one another and actively interpret one another's utterances. An externalist approach to writing instruction is centered on agency and a student writer's ability to communicate effectively.

Language as interpretation focuses on the communicative acts surrounding language. For some externalists, such as Donald Davidson, language has meaning only when it has been spoken and communicated with others (1993, p.1). According to Thomas Kent, "externalists hold that propositional attitudes—our beliefs, intentions, desires, and so forth—derive from our public interactions with other language users and with the world." Kent explains that when a teacher supports an externalist approach, students explore their own ideas in relation to "other language users and the world" (1991, p. 430).

There is a downside to an externalist approach. One problem is that such pedagogy is extremely time consuming because of demands for frequent student–teacher conferences (the interaction and interpretation) about papers. While students can benefit from such extensive feedback, most daily school schedules do not provide time for regular and often lengthy conferences. A second potential problem is that externalist pedagogy does not claim that writing can be taught at all. Even though externalists argue that teachers should acknowledge the importance of rhetorical knowledge, they believe that the best teachers can do is give students conventions of discourse (rules of grammar and mechanics, strategies for cohesion and coherence, and so on).

SITUATIONS FOR TEACHING WRITING

Regardless of the approach and theoretical perspective, writing is taught in a variety of secondary school classes. Writing, of course, is taught in classes designated specifically for composition, but it is also taught in other situations: in literature classes, in applied contexts, in writing-across-the-curriculum programs, and in the community. Schools that recognize the importance of writing incorporate a number of these situations to meet the needs and interests of a diverse group of students. Each situation provides teachers with opportunities to teach writing as a dynamic, communicative, constructive, contextual, and collaborative activity.

Writing in Composition Classes

Many secondary schools offer separate courses in basic and advanced composition. Sometimes these are quarter- or semester-long workshops required of all students during their first year; other times these are semester-long electives available to junior and senior students. These courses may cast a broad net that touches on a range of writing: *personal writing* (ranging from journals to personal narratives to short stories); *academic writing* (ranging from essays to term papers to lab reports); and *applied communication* (ranging from business letters to informative brochures to proposals). Sometimes these courses concentrate in-depth in one area (just personal writing or academic writing or applied communication); others times these courses offer less depth but a broader range of assignments. Regardless of the depth or breadth, in most situations, these composition courses encourage students to consider the audience, context, purpose, organization, and style of their writing.

One of the most important things students can learn is the *context of their writing*; that is, the situation in which their writing originates and is used. Tied to context is *purpose*, which is always implicitly or explicitly persuasive, even if there are other primary purposes such as conveying information. Students also need to identify and analyze their intended *audience* and then adapt their writing to that audience. Students need help as they learn to adjust factors such as content complexity, paragraph and sentence structure, vocabulary, examples, and explanations to meet the needs and expectations of their audience. And students need to learn their options for the *organization* of their writing, choices influenced by the way they interpret the expectations of the audience, context, and purpose. Recent research indicates that providing students with more information about the topic, purpose, and audience seems to positively affect the quality of the papers they write, with 11th graders able to make better use of rhetorical information than 9th graders (Oliver, 1995).

Finally, students need to learn techniques to improve their writing *style*. On a global level, style may be broadly interpreted as selecting the appropriate genre (learning to differentiate, for example, the style for a personal essay from the style for a newspaper article). On a local level, learning about style helps students with prose and paragraph structure (Mendelson, 1988; Selzer, 1989), cohesion and coherence (Beene, 1988; Campbell, 1989), "given–new" constructs (Kent, 1984) in which students connect previously mentioned subjects to newly introduced subjects, and readability (Huckin, 1983; Markel, 1993; Redish, Battison, & Gold, 1985) so that they can better connect ideas between sentences, create topic sentences, eliminate wordy phrases, and strengthen overall organization and expression.

The box by Barbara Toohey (Westford Academy, Westford, Massachusetts) shows how a class in American studies helps students capitalizes on the important connections between reading and writing. Students become more skillful readers by focusing on these factors: the context (situation, problem, or occasion) for the document they are reading, the audience who needed the information, the purposes of the document (both writer purpose and audience purpose), and options for appropriate genres and ways to organize

Reading to Help Writing in American Studies

This year as part of an American Studies team I have been able to tap into the breadth of the American experience in order to teach literature and composition. Since making connections is an essential part of understanding, the interdisciplinary approach is a natural fit for teaching writing and thinking skills. By providing the historical, social, cultural, and philosophical contexts in which literary works are produced, students see creative expression as part of a total picture, rather than as something that occurs in isolation.

Reading Thoreau's "Civil Disobedience" while examining the Mexican war and the activities of abolitionist John Brown makes Thoreau's ideas much more assessable. Students can appreciate the climate in which Thoreau's essay was written. The intensity and conviction of his voice can be appreciated as one that speaks to many generations.

Students find that they understand why a particular genre can be appropriate for an age. If the Puritans saw God in every aspect of their lives, it made sense to use diaries and journals to record that involvement. If the harshness of the Civil War made romantic idealism impossible, the "brass and bombast" rejected by Henry Fleming in *The Red Badge of Courage* seems inevitable.

I have found that giving students options as they approach a writing assignment is another way to have them consider audience, purpose, and context. Assuming the identity of a Civil War soldier writing a letter home requires different skills than that of a politician drafting a speech, a journalist describing a battle or a black slave recording his thoughts. Exposing students to Ken Burns's series on the Civil War, the photographs of Matthew Brady, the movie *Glory,* and *The Autobiography of Frederick Douglass* offers them multiple perspectives from which to draw. Students see that each genre is suited to accomplishing a purpose and that style is closely linked to intent and audience.

Barbara Toohey
Westford Academy
Westford, Massachusetts

the text to accomplish the purpose for the intended audience (Flower et al., 1994). The interdisciplinary team of teachers (English and social studies) then asks students to consider these same factors when doing their own writing.

Teaching Writing in Literature Classes

Traditional approaches to teaching literature focus on the literature itself, on discussions and analyses of close readings (formalist interpretations) of particular genres, periods, cultures, or authors. Writing in such literature classes typically leads to assignments that ask students to write in a genre somewhat (or perhaps entirely) unfamiliar to them, since most of them have read little (or no) literary criticism as they respond to texts that may have been only superficially contextualized for them.

Teachers who shift from a focus on genre, period, culture, or author to a focus on the responses of students themselves move these students out of the role of passive recipients. These teachers generally believe that a large part of the value of literature comes from the connections students make between their reading and their lives rather than from "some illusory unspecifiable absolute or 'correct' reading" (Rosenblatt, 1978, p. 140). These teachers recognize that secondary students seldom read on their own because they plan to become literary critics; instead, students who read literature independently read for pleasure and, perhaps, reflection. These teachers believe that both pleasure and reflection give students something legitimate to say about literature, and they encourage both free and structured responses that are supported by the text and students' experiences with situations similar to those in the text.

Among the techniques that encourage students' free responses to literature are brief writing periods "intended to force the students into solitary, unassisted thought about the work read and to obtain that thought from them so that it can be discussed by the group" (Probst, 1988, p. 42). These responses typically fall into broad categories that teachers can use to evaluate individual ranges of response (Probst, 1988, pp. 56–61): personal feelings and memories provoked by the literature; topical responses about issues in the literature; interpretations about the accuracy, relevance, or value of the literature; comments about formal elements in the literature such as rhythm schemes or images; broader literary concerns related to the literature such as genre, period, culture, biographical influences, and media (for example, how do movies of Jane Austen's work differ from her novels?). Students can write again following small-group and whole-class discussions, revisiting and refining their original, tentative responses, reflecting on them to see whether their original ideas have changed and whether they now recognize other perspectives.

Alternatively, teachers may encourage more focused, structured written responses that

> ask the students to respond to a certain aspect of the work: the motivation of a character, the influence of the setting on the mood, the nature of the conflict between two characters, the values implicit in the choices characters make, or the values and beliefs of the writer as shown in the work. (Probst, 1988, p. 46)

Probst points out that while such assignments are more complicated and demanding, they are also more constrained and thus may sacrifice students' most vivid connections with the text. If too much emphasis is placed on responding to teacher-generated questions, students may come to see literature simply as a basis for classroom exercises rather than as a source for pleasure and reflection.

Reader response approaches to literature can also generate longer response papers, both free and structured, that ask students to identify and elaborate "their own reactions to a work and [trace] them as far back into their own history and as deeply into the text as they can" (Probst, 1988, p. 46). These papers typically are part of an extended conversation about the literature, rather than simply texts for teachers to correct and return. Thus, these longer papers, whether responding to questions posed by the teacher or by the students themselves, can serve as the basis for student–teacher conferences as well as for small-group and whole-class discussions. (For extended discussion about ways to incorporate writing into literature classes, see Bleich, 1975; Probst, 1988.)

One example of an approach in which students respond to literature is described in the box by Elizabeth Foster (Chelmsford High School, Chelmsford, Massachusetts). She encourages students to interact with and sometimes even interrogate texts as they work out their own interpretations of events, actions, and ideas. Such an approach presumes that students, as readers of the text, have legitimate responses. Their understanding does not come from being told what to interpret but rather from their involvement with the text and in their writing about it. This writing forces them to be participants rather than observers (Burnett, 1992; Burnett & Foster, 1985, 1988).

Writing Related to Applied Contexts

While the overwhelming majority of writing in secondary school English classes is related to literature or academic composition, this is not the only writing that is done. For many years, secondary schools offered a course in business writing, usually taught by business education teachers and often focused on correctness (as an extension of courses in dictation and transcription) and models (formulas for standard memos, letters, and short reports). While this current–traditional, prescriptive approach is still used in a few schools, the shift is strongly toward using a rhetorical approach in what is now broadly called *applied communication*.

The emphasis of well-designed applied communication courses is on oral, visual, and written communication related to workplace situations, for students on academic tracks as well as for students in vocational programs. Recently, nonacademic writing has ranged from technical communication to tech prep programs (workplace communication courses designed to meet the needs of the middle 50% of the student population).

All versions of applied communication—courses in journalism, business communication, tech prep, and technical communication—appear most ef-

Metaphoric Masks: A Persona Approach to Increase Student Involvement with Literature

My literature students—from ninth graders reading *Romeo and Juliet* and *Of Mice and Men* to seniors reading *Hamlet* and *Tess of the D'Ubervilles*—actively and enthusiastically explore connections between reading and writing because of the persona approach that I encourage. A persona approach requires the student reader/writer to adopt a persona, to assume a role much as an actor does in a play—essentially a metaphoric mask.

Once students take on the voice, the persona, of a character from the literature they are studying, they probe the text for clues to help them better understand the character. For example, one student searched the text of *Macbeth* to compose a letter from Malcom to the Scottish nobles in which he identifies his kingly qualities and attempts to persuade them to assist him in overthrowing Macbeth. Another student produced a clever speech as the Wife of Bath, interpolating Chaucer's words with her own as she gave advice to young women about dealing with the men in their lives.

Responding to persona assignments gives students the opportunity to interpret literature in a way that makes it relevant to their own lives as well as to stretch the boundaries of the genre they already know and venture to experiment with new genre. In every grade and level that I teach, persona assignments kindle an enthusiasm for literature that spills over into lively class discussions as well as concern and commitment in their writing.

Elizabeth Foster
Chelmsford High School
Chelmsford, Massachusetts

fective when the approach is rhetorical; that is, when students learn to manage the elements of audience, context, purpose, organization, and style. A major element of this approach is seeing writing as problem solving, so students are encouraged to see writing as part of a larger process: articulating a problem, establishing a position about the problem, locating and organizing information, creating an effective argument, selecting appropriate support (Flower & Hayes, 1981a, 1981b). Understanding these rhetorical elements and processes that use them helps students create documents that are purposeful and functional.

A rhetorical approach uses tools, heuristics like collaborative planning (mentioned earlier), to address individual situations (Mitchell & Smith, 1989). Not only are the factors of audience, context, purpose, organization, and style important, but students also need to consider other rhetorical factors. For example, learning to address the four purposes for reading documents—reading to assess, reading to learn, reading to do, and reading to learn to do (Redish, 1987)—helps students become more skillful writers in practical situations. Student writers also need to consider that context is expanded to include the organizational or institutional context in which and for which they are writing, as well as the expectations and conventions of those organizations (Driskell, 1989; Southard, 1989). Finally, the design of information is central in teaching nonacademic writing, since visual organization and presentation dramatically influence readers (Barton & Barton, 1987, 1993; cf. Tufte, 1983, 1990). Teachers can give students tools for analyzing design elements (Kostelnick, 1989, 1990) and strategies for creating documents in which information is accessible and appealing to readers (Hartley, 1985; White, 1988).

The box written by Janet Hyden (Great Oaks Institute of Technology and Career Development, Cincinnati, Ohio) provides a clear description of one way to approach applied communication in a vocational–technical high school. The situation here is complicated by students with minimal skills and negative attitudes. The philosophy Janet Hyden uses and the kinds of assignments she designs encourage her students to begin to develop skill and confidence in communication.

While Janet Hyden describes a course in a vocational–technical high school, technical communication is also taught in academic high schools to a range of students, from advanced placement to non-college track. Sometimes technical communication is embedded with literature as part of year-long courses; other times it is taught as a separate term-long elective. Sometimes technical communication is taught in conjunction with a science teacher, so students, for example, take an advanced biology course in anatomy and physiology and also an English course in technical communication. Sometimes the goals are more modest, as when an English teacher and algebra teacher collaborate to help students use writing to work through math problems (Venne, 1989).

The alternative to a rhetorical approach is a formulaic, genre-driven approach, which provides students with formats suitable for various conventional situations or occasions. Such an approach is convenient for simple communication tasks. The problem is that students do not necessarily have the tools to know when the formula is appropriate and when it is not. A rhetorical approach gives students these necessary tools (Allen, 1990; Blyler, 1993; Rymer, 1993).

Writing across the Curriculum

Because writing is "the responsibility of every discipline and of no discipline" (Russell, 1992, p. 25), composition has value for teachers in other disciplines, a value articulated in writing-across-the-curriculum (WAC) programs. Discipline-specific courses often include written, oral, or visual communication assignments, yet teachers of these courses may not have specific knowl-

Changing Attitudes and Improving Communication: Technical Communication for Vocational Students

One challenge in teaching a technical communication course to high school senior vocational students is persuading them that their ability to express themselves clearly and directly will have a direct bearing on success as they work as auto mechanics, medical assistants, and electricians. These practical, hands-on students too often view reading, writing, and speaking as just more useless school stuff.

One strategy that works is providing authentic audiences and purposes for writing whenever possible. When classroom writing has a practical purpose—to get something done—these students work with a great deal of attention and diligence. At first, our team of technical communication teachers generated all the ideas for authentic assignments. Now, not only do many students originate their own projects, but their lab teachers and other staff members often request the documents our students create.

For years students bombarded our assistant superintendent with memos persuading him to approve funds for new computers for technical communication classes. They have sent illustrated reports to our campus director persuading him to revise an outdated student dress code. One student wrote a memorandum to appeal (successfully) a Saturday school punishment.

Student collaboration has produced the most effective documents. Our Child Learning program operates a nursery school. When their lab instructor requested redesigned forms (for medical emergency, tuition payment, permission slip, and lesson plan), student teams produced them. Four dental assisting students designed a guide to vocational programs that we now present to all visiting prospective students. Culinary Arts students designed a customer-comment card. Personal Computer Technology students designed a questionnaire to help English teachers assess computer skills and attitudes of incoming students.

Students come to realize that information has value only when it can be successfully communicated to someone who needs it—and that communicating effectively can be as challenging and rewarding as building a product.

Janet Hyden
Great Oaks Institute of Technology and Career Development
Cincinnati, Ohio

edge about designing, assigning, or evaluating communication assignments. Writing-across-the-curriculum programs offer support for teachers who seek to improve and who want or need supplemental guidance for communication instruction. The WAC movement began in the mid-1970s (Russell, 1992).

Since the movement began, discussion has included theory, implementation, history, pedagogy, and administration of WAC programs.

WAC programs run counter to this century-long tradition in English departments of teaching composition as a separate subject (Berlin, 1988; Russell, 1991). Because they promote the integration of composition in discipline-specific courses, WAC programs are difficult to implement and even more difficult to maintain. Most scholars of WAC advocate an integrated, slow approach (Herrington & Moran, 1992; Young, 1991), as WAC programs take time to develop. "WAC programs require patience. Ten—or thirty—years may not be enough to change century-old . . . priorities and classroom practices" (Russell, 1992, p. 191).

In addition to gradual development, WAC programs require support from all parties involved, from those who need the services as well as those who provide the services. This support requires that faculty assumptions about knowledge, language, and learning be discussed and shared. Because disciplines may have different assumptions about these concepts, establishing a dialogue about writing among departments and disciplines is difficult. Nevertheless, this dialogue is important—even critical—for building a base for WAC programs. It is important that differences come to the surface so that the teachers involved in WAC programs understand how to best address the differences and build a common understanding of theories about learning, assumptions about knowledge, and assumptions about language (Bazerman, 1992; Britton, 1992; Langer, 1992).

The box by Pamela Childers (The McCallie School, Chattanooga, Tennessee) shows that successful WAC units, courses, and programs—both planned and serendipitous—generate remarkable enthusiasm among faculty and students and provide opportunities for integrated, long-term learning. However, like any interdisciplinary team effort, planning and presenting WAC programs take time and energy beyond that required for individual teaching.

Writing Related to Community

A particularly engaging and difficult approach to writing helps students learn more about the way we perceive and understand our worlds. Thus, students are encouraged to extend their study of writing beyond the classroom to include the home, community, and workplace. The argument for this approach is that students write best when they are given real-life consequences and involved in true collaboration, not when they are placed in classroom settings with contrived assignments and the teacher as audience.

One approach is to bring community situations into the classroom. For example, students can become activists in local or regional controversies, writing letters to newspapers, community leaders, and local, regional, and national politicians. In one instance, the political action of high school soph-

Bugs and Drugs: WAC from Tropical Rain Forests

When I began directing my second WAC-based writing center in a secondary school, I tried to visit as many classes as possible in all disciplines. I wanted to open dialogues with people who were already interested in using writing in their disciplines. In a discussion with one of the science teachers, Peter LaRochelle, I mentioned that I had taught biology when I did my student teaching. He suggested that we could team teach an experimental honors biology class the next year by teaching the class part of the time in the WAC writing center.

The following year we began our project with a year-long focus on rain forests. Peter had spent time in the rain forests of Ecuador, so his experiences and photographs would be an essential part of the project's success. As our text, we used *Tropical Nature,* a collection of essays by Adrian Forsyth and Ken Miyata (1984). I offered suggestions for writing activities and parallel readings while Peter focused on the biology of the rain forest. When we got to the chapter on plants and insects emitting toxic defenses against herbivores ("Bugs and Drugs"), I suggested that we all read Hawthorne's "Rappacini's Daughter" to see how accurate the author was in describing the poisonous plants. The writing that resulted from this exercise was a learning experience for all of us. It also began a continued and now well-established involvement between the science department and the WAC writing center.

Just this year, three teachers of integrated science grabbed me on the first day of school so that I could help them set up an appropriate WAC activity for the beginning of the course. Science teachers also won the WAC faculty grants last year. The conversations continue, and the science teachers spread the word of the value of WAC.

Pamela Childers
The McCallie School
Chattanooga, Tennessee

omores in Illinois influenced a local community to hold public hearings and move ahead the construction of a new sewer and water treatment plant (Scharle, 1993). On a smaller scale, teachers can develop units from the multipage letters that charities send to appeal for money. Based on students' assessment of the letters' persuasive appeals and legitimacy of needs, students create presentations to convince their audience (classmates, parents, community representatives, and so on) that a particular charity deserves financial support (VanderStaay, 1990).

Another approach moves the students into the community. One of the best-known examples of student writing emerging from the community (with documents that have a real audience, a clear context, a legitimate purpose,

Community Literacy:
Addressing Pregnancy, Street Violence, and Police Brutality

However deeply disguised beneath bulky trench coats or masked by ski caps pulled down almost over their eyes, many at-risk urban teenagers hunger to learn, to write, and to have *a say.* On city streets where lines of conflict are demarcated by gang graffiti, these teens hunger for an alternative kind of literacy—something different than school-based or street-graffiti literacies. Many at-risk urban teenagers, sick of the stress that violence creates, have stories to tell. They want to change their communities and get on with their dreams of becoming rap artists or pediatricians or army officers. They are looking for places to connect and be heard by people in power.

Marginalized by poverty and stigmatized by threatened adults, urban teenagers are seldom invited inside large institutions in their neighborhoods: hospitals, city halls, post offices, churches, urban universities, and community colleges. Often targeted as *problems,* urban teenagers are seldom regarded as working partners in building and sustaining community life nor are they invited to participate in policy conversations that influence their lives.

The Community Literacy Center—a community/university collaboration between an historic settlement house in Pittsburgh and Carnegie Mellon University—gathers groups of urban at-risk teens and college-age mentors to address pressing justice issues that affect teenagers within city neighborhoods. In 10-week projects, urban teenagers—supported by mentors—analyze issues such as teen pregnancy, gang violence, police brutality, and the spread of urban curfews and then present their perspectives in writing to the mayor in televised news conferences before the media. When they are not invited to the table where policy decisions that shape their lives are made, they send documents that speak from a youth perspective.

Community literacy enables teenagers to be heard. It is a powerful forum guided by an explicit set of literate practices that enable urban teens to write and connect with officials in power and to influence the issues and policies that affect their lives.

Wayne Peck
Community Literacy Center
Pittsburgh, Pennsylvania

an established genre) is *Foxfire* magazine, which was started in 1966 as a way to motivate students and give them the opportunity to learn academic skills while reporting their community's cultural heritage (Olmstead, 1988).

As the box by Wayne Peck (Community Literacy Center, Pittsburgh, Pennsylvania) shows, involving at-risk students in research and writing projects can turn lives around. The Community Literacy Center's after-school program for high school students extends their opportunities by providing them with a way to develop communication skills as they study, write, publish, and distribute newsletters and position papers for members of the community. Since 1990, groups of inner-city teens, with facilitators and mentors from the community and from Carnegie Mellon University, have taken on a number of complex issues that are close to their lives: teen pregnancy, drugs, the elderly, housing, teen recreation opportunities, gangs, and violence. Programs such as the ones developed by the Community Literacy Center change the way writing is taught by moving students into the community, blurring the boundaries among disciplines, questioning boundaries among genres, and extending the boundaries of media (Peck, Flower, & Higgins, 1995).

MANAGING COMPLEXITIES AND COMPLICATIONS IN TEACHING WRITING

In the process of creating effective alternatives for teaching writing, teachers need to address a number of complexities and complications. Two of the most widespread concerns that complicate the teaching of writing include providing help for basic writers and handling the challenge of assessment and evaluation.

Remedial or Basic Writers

The term *basic writer* describes writers who have inordinate difficulty with writing. These writers might have problems with conventions of standard English grammar, may be fearful or apprehensive about writing (Rose, 1985), or may have reading disabilities or other learning disabilities. Despite its original conception, the term *basic writers* need not be synonymous with *remedial writers*. As Lunsford and Sullivan (1990) carefully point out, basic writers include any beginning writers, who may or may not be remedial.

Basic writers have a diversity of problems: "Basic writers have consistent trouble starting a piece of writing, expressing ideas clearly, and revising what they have written" (Sheridan-Rabideau & Brossell, 1995, p. 22). Another problem basic writers may experience is a "gap" between spoken and written English. Mina Shaughnessy described this gap:

> An English-speaking student is already a maker of statements that not only sound like English but sound like him. . . . Such a student does not need to learn how to make statements but how to write them at least as well as he speaks them. (Shaughnessy, 1994, p. 108)

Teachers can help basic writers in a number of ways including support groups (actually a form of peer review) and protocol analyses.

Some teachers have tried forming support groups for writers to help alleviate problems that basic writers face (Fitzgerald, Mulvihill, & Dobson, 1991). Supporters are trained to offer constructive feedback to help writers identify and respond to problems readers have with their texts (Burnett, 1994). Effective support groups create an open, accepting environment in which writers can safely contribute and receive feedback. Often whole-class groups are too large to achieve the same open effect; instead, smaller support groups are valued for the comforting environment they provide: "The practical yet safe environment that offers underprepared students the writing experiences they need is the one to be honored" (Sheridan-Rabideau & Brossell, 1995, p. 26). Even though support groups can help basic writers, such groups also provide important support for all student writers.

Protocol and other oral analyses can also be used to help reduce problems of basic writers. Flower and Hayes's protocol analysis has provided a solid model of this oral technique. In protocol analysis, students speak aloud and taperecord all their thoughts and ideas as they plan and draft their papers (Flower & Hayes, 1977). With training, students can then review their tapes and pinpoint areas of difficulty in their writing process. Over a sequence of assignments, students can usually identify patterns of problems that interfere with readers' interpretations of their writing. Protocol analyses also help students see problems that occur when their oral communication is transformed into written communication; this insight may especially help writers who experience writer's block.

Sometimes basic writers have a combination of complications that make teaching writing extraordinarily difficult. The box by Sherry Hulsey and Candice McDonald (Oñate High School, Las Cruces, New Mexico) shows one way that these experienced teachers help their basic writers get started and feel some sense of accomplishment. These basic writers not only have limited skills but also negative attitudes that contribute to sporadic attendance and behavioral problems.

Assessment and Evaluation

One of the most difficult and stressful parts of teaching writing is assessment and evaluation. Central to issues surrounding assessment and evaluation is the question of whether a teacher's responsibility is to correct the papers or help the students. A focus on the papers tends to result in assessment and evaluation that concentrate on correctness. A focus on the students tends to concentrate on communication. We define *assessment* as the feedback students receive—whether from themselves, peers, teachers, or outside readers—that provides information and advice about a range of topics from audience reactions to adherence to grammatical and mechanical conventions. Ideally, this formative feedback is used to help students revise their work rather than simply to justify their grades. We define *evaluation* as the

Prime the Pump: Reaching out to Basic Writers

One of the most difficult parts of writing is getting started, so we begin each class with a nonthreatening activity to increase the confidence of the basic writers in our classes—students in grades 9–12, most of whom have had almost no success with writing. The students come to expect ten minutes of free writing in their spiral notebooks at the beginning of each class.

We put one prompt—usually a first-person completion—on the board before students come into class. The 30 students in each class start writing as soon as the bell rings.

- One of my earliest memories is . . .
- I believe that the best excuse for being late is . . .
- At Thanksgiving my family always . . .
- I agree/disagree that the U.S. troops should be sent to . . .

Topics such as these form the basis for our daily prompts:

- Describe the best place to be alone
- Explain the best kind of pet to own
- List ten things that make you angry, happy, sad, relieved
- Describe a favorite meal, car, relative, teacher
- Describe the best brand of a product
- Describe an embarrassing experience
- Tell about the hardest thing you've ever learned to do
- Explain how you or someone you know got a broken arm, leg, or other injury

Students write for the full ten minutes (with music *we* select playing in the background), producing at least one page a day; some write much more. There are always memorable pieces:

Katie's account of being abused by her boyfriend
Roberto's description of his ideal car
Naomi's reactions to the death of her brother
Tina's description of her little boy being sick
Shawn's explanation how he'd run the school

By the end of the first month, each student has at least 20 pages of writing; by the end of the semester, each has at least 75 pages. At the end of the year, students include more than 150 pages of free writing as part of the individual books of their own work that they laminate and bind.

Sherry Hulsey and Candice McDonald
Oñate High School
Las Cruces, New Mexico

class or institutional policy of assigning summative grades or some other formal response to student work. Regardless of the approach to assessment and evaluation, the task of reading and responding constructively and productively to student writing is burdensome when class sizes and student loads are excessive. The Secondary Section of the National Council of Teachers of English recommends that programs, districts, and states implement staffing plans so that by the year 2000 English–language arts teachers have "class sizes of not more than 20 students and a work load of not more than 80 students" (Secondary Section of NCTE, 1990).

Despite current burdensome student loads, many teachers spend hundreds of hours a year outside their classrooms and preparation periods correcting and responding to papers, expending a great deal of time in marking local-level violations of conventions, but often spending less time addressing global rhetorical concerns such as audience and purpose. For example, a study that looked at teacher comments on 3000 student papers reported that only 11% of all the comments,

> even with liberal interpretation, [could] be considered to be about purpose. . . . Even rarer were comments about the writer's approach toward audience, with only 6% of papers mentioning anything about audience considerations such as tone or voice. . . . Since most textbooks, and many teachers, put considerable stress on the two large issues of purpose and audience . . . ,

the lack of attention in teacher comments to these rhetorical issues is surprising (Connors & Lunsford, 1993, p. 212).

Because little research supports the practice of marking every instance of local-level violations of conventions, composition specialists encourage writing teachers to try other approaches—for example, helping their students learn to analyze their errors rather than counting them (Shaughnessy, 1977). There are numerous alternative methods to assess and evaluate student writing. Whether a particular method is appropriate depends largely on the needs of the students and the nature of the writing task. Teachers often consider these alternatives:

- *Alternative focus for assessment*: holistic assessment
- *Alternative medium for delivering assessment*: taped comments
- *Alternative breadth of assessment*: portfolio

The rater—whether individual student, small groups of students working collaboratively, or the teacher—can use refocus assessment by using one of several types of *holistic assessment* to sort or rank writing according to a set of features or criteria (Cooper, 1977):

- *Essay scale* ranks a set of papers according to agreed-on criteria; one piece is placed at the top, another at the bottom, the rest are ranked in between.

- *Analytic scale* uses 10 or 12 agreed-on text features to assess each paper on a general scale such as high–medium–low or 1–10.
- *Dichotomous scale* uses a series of yes–no statements about key text features to assess each paper.
- *Feature analysis* focuses on one particular aspect of each paper—for example, structure or adaptation to audience.
- *Primary trait scoring* focuses on several selected aspects of a paper relevant to the type of discourse—for example, 5Ws + H in news articles (Lloyd-Jones, 1977).

Drawbacks to holistic scoring include lack of time and skill to train the raters (whether students or teachers) and the mistaken public perception that "correcting everything" is the way to help students become better writers. Benefits include articulating selected criteria for assessment, focusing on manageable areas for revision, and involving students in assessment.

Taped comments, an alternative medium for delivering assessment, enable teachers or other reviewers to use a tape cassette to record comments. Rather than marking the paper, teachers or other reviewers read and comment, providing students with detailed observations. These readers, of course, can comment on violations of text conventions, but the emphasis is certainly on their responses as readers. The comments can be structured according to the criteria used for assessment (for example, comments about whether the paper is adapted for the audience, fulfills its purpose, is effectively developed and organized, and so on).

Seldom is any time saved; taping comments is usually every bit as time consuming as writing comments. The benefits come from the amount of feedback students receive and from the personal nature of the response. In the time teachers allot to commenting on a paper, say 20 minutes (this including the time it takes to read and assess a paper), they usually can *say* much more than they can *write*. And, of course, students benefit from hearing the inflection and intonation of the reaction.

Portfolios, an alternative for increasing the breadth of assessment, reduce the emphasis on immediate summative evaluation and increase the emphasis on students' formative development over a period of weeks, months, or years. Assessment and evaluation, then, are based not on a single paper but on a series of papers, often revised, that demonstrate students' increasing understanding and skill (Luce-Kapler, 1996; Raines, 1996). Portfolios give students the opportunity to be the primary evaluators of their own work and develop a meta-cognitive sense of their progress as they identify patterns in their own writing.

Unlike collection folders in which students simply place completed work, portfolios involve students' reflections and analyses of selected papers through a series of drafts and over a period of time. Students' reflections and analyses come in a variety of ways, including completing self-assessment forms or grids, writing captions to accompany their papers, or writing periodic one-page reflections and analyses. Students do not necessarily become better writers, but they become more reflective and articulate about the full range of their literacies (Sunstein, 1992).

Despite their benefits, portfolio systems may be problematic. Having a portfolio system may conflict with institutional and public ways of looking at excellence. Specifically, portfolios highlight *difference*; in contrast, conventional forms of evaluation such as tests measure *sameness* (Sunstein, 1992). Simply put, portfolios do not promote what many see as a central feature of grading: competition with others. Furthermore, portfolios do not work if teachers and administrators ignore the overarching principle that portfolios are designed to reflect students' voices; therefore, portfolios should be created and maintained by students, not assembled by teachers. Also, many teachers and administrators do not realize how time consuming portfolios can be, taking time and resources for ongoing training, implementation, and maintenance.

The responsibility for assessment, whether using a portfolio system or some other approach, should be shared between the teachers and the students. One of the characteristics of experienced, successful writers is their ability to accurately assess their own work. How does a paper address the intended audience? How is it appropriate for the context? How does it fulfill the purpose? How does it effectively develop and organize the information? Recent views about assessment and evaluation encourage the involvement of students in the process. As the box by Linda Boxleitner (The International School, Bellevue, Washington) shows, assessment and evaluation are generally productive when students participate in shaping the criteria for assessing their work and know these criteria will be used for ongoing assessment of drafts (formative assessment) as well as for final paper grades (summative evaluation). In the process of this interaction, students learn concepts and vocabulary for discussing their writing and, thus, can develop skills for monitoring their own progress (Duke & Sanchez, 1994).

For comments about their papers, whether made by teachers or peers, whether written or taped, to make sense, students need to understand the comments and be able to link these comments to their own text. There is support for the view that students have a variety of reasons for withdrawing from the revision process after they have received feedback. Figure 1 shows a sequence of possible decisions student writers might make when considering what to do with feedback comments.

Simply saying that students are not responsive to the feedback they receive is inadequate. Immediately after receiving feedback, students may withdraw from the process if the feedback does not make sense to them. If it makes sense to them, students assess the feedback. But if they disagree that the problem is legitimate, again, they may withdraw. If they agree that there is a problem, they then need to decide whether the problem is the fault of

Student Editors, Student Benchmarks: Involving Students in Assessment

During my first years of teaching, I evaluated student writing based on three criteria: content, organization, and the "great etceteras" of grammar, mechanics, spelling, capitalization. Twenty-three years later, my evaluation focuses on criteria students have identified as valuable for the type of writing.

My task as a teacher of writing is to help my students discover their abilities to be their own best editors. The most difficult part of this task is enabling students to take ownership of their writing. To facilitate their "buying in," I ask students in my classes to look at three to five papers generated by other students for the same assignment. My initial goal is for them to rank order the papers. Young writers easily perceive the difference between excellent, mediocre, and ineffective communication. After they rank order sample papers, they brainstorm what worked in the most effective paper and what was missing or poorly executed in the poorest paper. The class reaches a consensus on benchmarks for excellence for each individual assignment.

Where overall purpose is blatantly clear, students are outspoken about what works. I'm flexible about their phrasing. For instance, one group evaluating essays may agree that "be" verbs dominate a weak paper and want them replaced by stronger verbs. Another group may classify that same weakness as repetition. What they call it doesn't matter; that they have included the criteria is central.

Once students have decided upon criteria for excellence, they begin their own rough drafts, which usually seem easier when built on the easy-to-understand criteria the students themselves have identified. Next, using a holistic scale based on their own criteria, students assess their own and another person's essays. At the beginning of the year, I sometimes also holistically assess their rough drafts. Most students create higher quality revisions than the ones they do when I alone specify the criteria for excellence.

Linda Boxleitner
The International School
Bellevue, Washington

the writer (in which case, they will keep going) or with the reader (in which case, they will stop). If they assume responsibility for the problem, they then need to locate the problematic place in the text. If they cannot, they stop. If they do locate the problem in the text, they need to decide whether to fix it. If they think too much effort is needed for the change that may result, they will stop. If they do decide to fix the problem, they need to have the

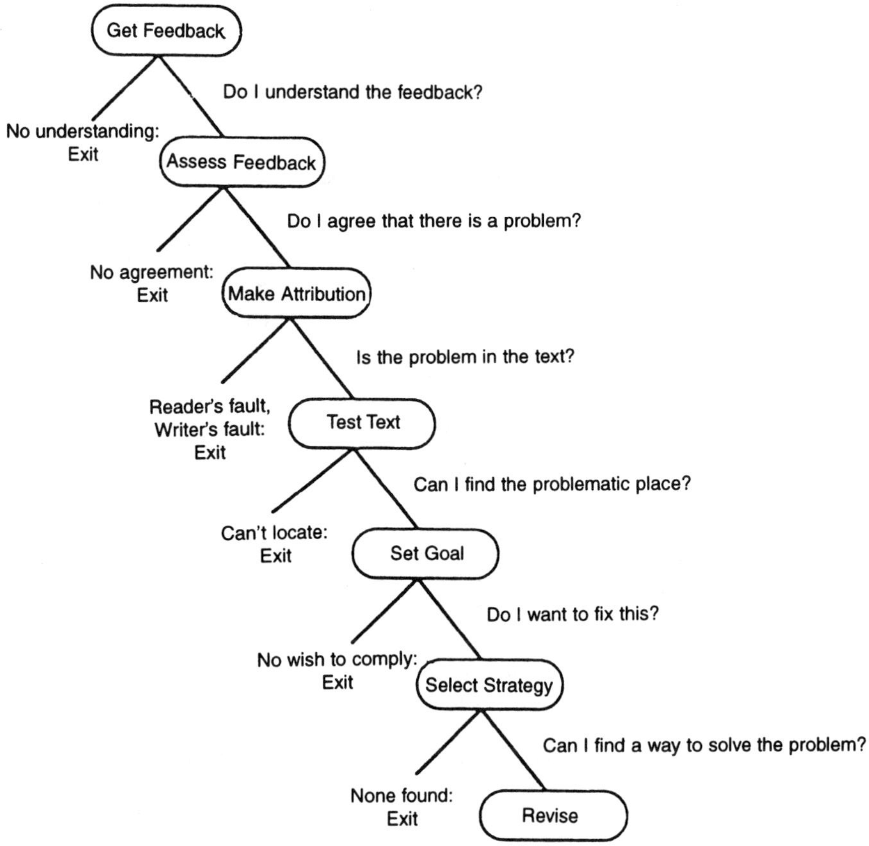

FIGURE 1
Decision tree of revising after feedback (from Sitko, 1993, p. 183).

necessary skills or strategies. Without the necessary skills, students are stuck, even if they understand and agree with the feedback.

SUPPORT FOR TEACHING WRITING

Teaching writing as a dynamic, communicative, constructive, contextual, and collaborative activity should depend on more than teachers' remarkable intellects, imaginations, and energies. Among the sources of support for teachers are two of special importance: writing centers and technology.

Writing Centers

Many schools have found that establishing a writing center reduces the pressure on classroom teachers to respond to every problem of every student, especially in large heterogeneous classes. Writing centers, usually staffed by professionals, typically provide individual tutoring and small-group conferencing for students who lack the ability, attitude, or preparation to develop as successful writers unless they have additional guidance. Students who seek help in writing centers frequently have problems in managing local-level conventions of mechanics and grammar; more important to their development as writers, though, is their lack of understanding of the processes and global concepts they need. More recently, schools are supporting writing centers that provide support for all students, not just basic writers, who want a second pair of eyes, another perspective.

In recent years, writing centers have struggled to proclaim that their primary responsibility is to help students develop their writing processes and global concepts, *not* to pose as a "fix-it shop" (North, 1984). The movement toward long-term writing improvement is heavily supported as a concept, yet sometimes difficult for administration to support financially because immediate results are not obvious and direct causal links (between the writing center and improved writing) are difficult to establish. Such frustrations have been noted in a number of publications (e.g., Olson, 1984). As a result of strongly felt beliefs that writing centers are beneficial, research about writing centers—for example, about group tutoring, peer tutoring, and administrative issues—is growing and providing demonstrable support for their benefits (Wolff, 1991). Specifically, writing centers have been shown to help students develop critical thinking skills (Harris, 1995), collaborate (Brooks, 1991; Lunsford, 1991), and revise their papers (Fulwiler, 1992). Tutors are encouraged, in the spirit of collaboration, to engage in dialogue with students—to encourage students to talk about their writing rather than focus on errors of mechanics and grammar (Brooks, 1991; Harris, 1995; Sperling, 1991).

Even when a school has no writing center, some of the practices used in writing centers can be incorporated into individual classes. One of the most fruitful approaches is a variety of peer groups, used for collaborative planning (discussed earlier) as well for peer editing.

Technology

Computers in writing classrooms and labs should be used as more than fancy typewriters. In fact, if computers are used simply as a way for students to create a neat printout of a paper they have already written and revised by hand, then the electronic capabilities are being wasted. Students benefit more through making continued use of computers, not as tools for typing, but as tools for research, document design, discussion, and correspondence.

A number of successful computer technologies support tasks and interactions critical to a writing class (Burnett, White, & Duin, in press). Regardless of the technology, however, the central focus should remain on communication, not on the technology (Selfe, 1988):

- *Planning, drafting, editing, and producing documents.* Most word processing software such as Microsoft Word allows writers to plan, outline, cut and paste, copy chunks of text, reorder lists, check spelling, check grammar, and so on. Drafting and revising with word processing software encourages students to try major revisions that might be too tedious or time consuming without the technology. Students can also use groupware such as Lotus Notes, Microsoft Access, and PrepEditor to work with collaborators on the same draft at the same time or at different times. These collaborators might be in the same class or in another class (which may be in a different school or even in a different state or country).
- *Designing visuals, documents, and presentations.* Software such as Cricket Graph enables students to design and produce visuals such as tables, graphs, diagrams, and drawings to embed in their documents. Most sophisticated word processing software enables writers to design accessible, appealing, professional-looking documents. Software for desktop publishing such as PageMaker offers writers even more options as they design and produce documents. Presentation software such as PowerPoint and Persuasion gives writers the capability to produce transparencies or slides, handouts, and speaker's notes from an outline.
- *Exchanging messages.* Students can participate in real-time or delayed-time exchange of messages about their projects. Tools for *real-time* discussion include IRCs (Internet relay chats), MOOs (multiuser object-oriented environments), World Wide Web chat systems, and desktop videoconferencing systems. Tools for *delayed-time* exchange of messages include electronic mail, computer conferencing, and listservs, all of which give students the opportunity to read comments from others, reflect on them, and then compose their own responses when they wish. With real-time and delayed-time exchange of messages, students may carry on personal correspondence or participate in (or listen in on) small-group or extended-group discussions.
- *Retrieving and publishing information through the* Internet. Students can now extend their information-gathering resources (for term papers, personal opinion essays, background sections in lab reports, and so on). Tools such as Gopher give users access to every member library in the world that has computerized the list of its holdings. The World Wide Web (WWW) enables students to track down information on almost any topic, with access to information from government agencies, universities, companies, and a wide range of researchers. Students can also post their own work. WWW has hundreds of home pages produced by students in elementary schools, middle and junior high schools, and high schools.

Using computer tools shapes student learning in ways different from the traditional classroom. By necessity, students become immersed in networks

Negotiating Poetry On-line: Computers and Poetry

I use networked computers to help students learn how to write essays about poems. I regularly use Emily Dickinson's "As Imperceptibly as Grief" and Jack Hirschman's "This Neruda Earth." When students arrive in the lab, they type their responses about the poems into the appropriate Daedalus Interchange conference (Dickinson or Hirschman). Then they begin reading each other's responses and choose to join a conference about one poem or the other. When one conference includes half the students, the late deciders automatically must join the other conference.

In one class, the Dickinson conference students, for example, were soon exchanging information: a female student had learned about the "Amazing Grace" hymn rhyme scheme of Dickinson's poems in high school, and a male student, who had taken a women's literature class, contributed the concept that women poets frequently use "mutable images," like flowers, in their poems; others commented on looking up some hard words, like *perfidy* and *harrowing;* many commented on Dickinson's use of capitalization and personification, but soon it was time to be off to the main conference to type their polished in-class essays.

The experience of negotiating meaning with other readers, seeing what others made of the same lines, and noticing where others sought insights and generalizations (about poetic forms, about women writers, about how the change of seasons feels) helped each reader to see how these pieces contributed to a feeling of competence about creating a reading of a poem. The conference becomes a community of readers who write much longer, more thoughtful individual essays than the initial reader responses they'd typed in an hour before.

Rosanne G. Potter
Iowa State University
Ames, Iowa

of dialogues and information, and they are required to communicate within these networks through computer interaction. This allows students to contribute their individual thoughts and ideas to a larger group discussion and network. The box by Rosanne Potter shows how her students use networked computers to share responses to poems and then to draw from those collective responses as they create their own essays about a poem.

Another use of computer technology is with computer-mediated tutoring programs. For example, students at the University of Minnesota and students in a local Minneapolis high school work together, with the university students acting as tutors for the high school students who are revising drafts of papers. The students are linked so that they have simultaneous video, audio, and text. The computer monitors (one in front of the high school student and another in front of the university mentor) show the high school student's text and a cameo picture of the other person; the voices come over a telephone receiver. Recent research (Duin, in press) shows important growth in the high school students' writing and equal advances in the university students' skills as tutors.

Composition is being taught in computer classrooms more and more frequently in certain schools. Computer use is one of the most dramatic ways in which socioeconomic differences show themselves in public schools. Some schools misuse and underutilize computers, relegating their students to using drill-and-practice software. Other schools more appropriately encourage students to use computers as tools to develop cognitive and literacy skills. Teachers can become advocates for appropriate uses of technology by becoming critics as well as users; by learning about important technology issues such as access, design, ideologies that directly affect their students; by actively contributing suggestions to software designers and manufacturers about ways to improve products; by using software as a text for class study—a source to examine for cultural, linguistic, and ideological perspectives (Selfe & Selfe, 1994).

CONCLUSION

In this chapter, we encourage teachers to approach writing as dynamic, communicative, constructive, contextual, and collaborative. The reality of teaching is not choosing a single approach but constantly negotiating among competing demands and goals. Knowing about the range of well-researched options enables teachers to draw productively from them as the field of composition constantly changes. Both rigorous research and exemplary practices support an approach that focuses on processes and strategies that help students develop the ability to write for specific purposes and for specific readers. To fulfill their purposes and address readers, students engage in dialogue that contributes to their sense of place in the world, an understanding of how they are influenced by that world, and an awareness of their ability to influence that world. Their sense of place and understanding supports and infuses their writing; their awareness of process enables them to manage their writing; their strategies give them the skills to plan and carry out their writing.

Acknowledgments

We thank the following colleagues for their helpful comments and insightful observations in reviewing this chapter: Andrea Breemer Frantz, Thomas Kent, Elizabeth Carros Keroack, Bruce Penniman, and David Russell.

References

Allen, J. (1990). The case against defining technical writing. *Journal of Business and Technical Communication*, 4(2), 68–77.

Barton, B. F., & Barton, M. S. (1987). Simplicity in visual representation: A semiotic approach. *Journal of Business and Technical Communication*, 1(1), 9–26.

Barton, B. F., & Barton, M. S. (1993). Modes of power in technical and professional visuals. *Journal of Business and Technical Communication*, 7(1), 138–162.

Bazerman, C. (1992). From cultural criticism to disciplinary participation: Living with powerful words. In A. Herrington & C. Moran (Eds.), *Writing, teaching, and learning in the disciplines* (pp. 61–68). New York: Modern Language Association.

Beene, L. (1988). How can functional documents be made more cohesive and coherent? In L. Beene & P. White (Eds.), *Solving problems in technical writing* (pp. 108–129). Oxford, England: Oxford University Press.

Bell-Maetereau, R. (1994). Breaking boundaries, solving problems, giving gifts: Student empowerment in small group work. In S. B. Reagan, T. Fox, & D. Bleich (Eds.), *Writing with new directions in collaborative teaching, learning, and research* (pp. 247–264). Albany: State University of New York Press.

Berlin, J. (1988). Rhetoric and ideology in the writing class. *College English*, 50(5), 477–494.

Bleich, D. (1975). *Readings and feelings: An introduction to subjective criticism*. Urbana, IL: National Council of Teachers of English.

Blyler, N. (1993). Theory and curriculum: Reexamining the curricular separation of business and technical communication. *Journal of Business and Technical Communication*, 7(2), 218–245.

Bridwell-Bowles, L. (1995). Freedom, form, and function: Varieties of academic discourse. *College Composition and Communication*, 46(1), 46–61.

Britton, J. (1992). Theories of the disciplines and a learning theory. In A. Herrington & C. Moran (Eds.), *Writing, teaching, and learning in the disciplines* (pp. 47–60). New York: Modern Language Association.

Brooks, J. (1991). Minimalist tutoring: Making the student do all the work. *Writing Lab Newsletter*, 15(6), 1–4.

Bruffee, K. (1993). *Collaborative learning: Higher education, interdependence, and the authority of knowledge*. Baltimore: Johns Hopkins University Press.

Burnett, R. E. (1992). Persona as pedagogy: Engaging students in Shakespeare. In R. P. Merrix & N. Ranson (Eds.), *Professing Shakespeare now: Through theory into practice* (pp. 243–255). Lewiston, NY: Edwin Mellen Press.

Burnett, R. E. (1993a). Conflict in collaborative decision-making. In N. R. Blyler & C. Thralls (Eds.), *Professional communication: The social perspective* (pp. 144–162). Newbury Park, CA: Sage.

Burnett, R. E. (1993b). Decision-making during the collaborative planning of coauthors. In A. M. Penrose & B. M. Sitko (Eds.), *Hearing ourselves think: Cognitive research in the college writing classroom* (pp. 125–146). Oxford, England: Oxford University Press.

Burnett, R. E. (1994). Interactions of engaged supporters. In L. Flower, D. Wallace, L. Norris, & R. E. Burnett (Eds.), *Making thinking visible: Writing, collaborative planning, and classroom inquiry* (pp. 67–82). Urbana, IL: National Council of Teachers of English.

Burnett, R. E., & Foster, E. (1985). *Shakespeare persona*. Littleton, MA: Sundance.

Burnett, R. E., & Foster, E. (1988). *American persona*. Littleton, MA: Sundance.

Burnett, R. E., White, C. I., & Duin, A. H. (1997). Locating collaboration: Reflections, features, and influences. In K. Staples & C. Ornatowski (Eds.), *Theory, program, and program design in technical communication*. Norwood, NJ: Ablex.

Campbell, K. S. (1989). Structural cohesion in technical texts. *Journal of Technical Writing and Communication*, 21(3), 221–237.

Chin, E. (1994). Redefining "context" in research on writing. *Written Communication*, 11(4), 445–482.

Clark, G. (1994). Rescuing the discourse of community. *College Composition and Communication*, 45(1), 61–74.

Collins, A., Brown, J. S., & Newman, S. E. (1989). Cognitive apprenticeship: Teaching the crafts of reading, writing, and mathematics. In L. Resnick (Ed.), *Knowing, learning, and instruction: Essays in honor of Robert Glaser* (pp. 453–494). Hillsdale, NJ: Erlbaum.

Connors, R. J., & Lunsford, A. A. (1993). Teachers' rhetorical comments on student papers. *College Composition and Communication*, 44(2), 200–223.

Cooper, C. R. (1977). Holistic evaluation of writing. In C. R. Cooper & L. Odell (Eds.), *Evaluating writing* (pp. 3–31). Urbana, IL: National Council of Teachers of English.

Dasenbrock, R. (1993). The myths of the subjective. *Journal of Advanced Composition*, 13(1), 1–32.

David, D., Gordon, B., & Pollard, R. (1995). Seeking common ground: Guiding assumptions for writing courses. *College Composition and Communication*, 46(4), 522–532.

Davidson, D. (1993). Language philosophy, writing, and reading. *Journal of Advanced Composition*, 13(1), 1–32.

DiPardo, A., & Freedman, S. W. (1988). Peer response groups in the writing classroom: Theoretical foundations and new directions. *Review of Educational Research*, 58(2), 119–49.

Driskell, L. (1989). Understanding the writing context in organizations. In M. Kogen (Ed.), *Writing in the business professions* (pp. 125–145). Urbana, IL: National Council of Teachers of English.

Duin, A. H. (in press). Case studies of computer-mediated mentoring: File exchange and desktop videoconferencing. In R. E. Burnett & A. H. Duin (Eds.), *Collaboration in technical communication: Research perspectives*. Hillsdale, NJ: Erlbaum.

Duke, C. R., & Sanchez, R. (1994). Giving students control over writing assessment. *English Journal*, 83(4), 47–53.

Fitzgerald, S., Mulvihill, P., & Dobson, R. (1991). Meeting the needs of graduate students: Writing support groups in the center. In R. Wallace & J. Simpson (Eds.), *The writing center: New directions* (pp. 133–144). New York: Garland.

Flower, L. S., & Hayes, J. R. (1977). Problem-solving strategies and the writing process. *College English*, 39(4), 449–461.

Flower, L., & Hayes, J. R. (1981a). A cognitive process theory of writing. *College Composition and Communication*, 32(4), 365–387.

Flower, L., & Hayes, J. R. (1981b). Images, plans, and prose. *Written Communication*, 1(1), 120–160.

Flower, L., Wallace, D. L., Norris, L., & Burnett, R. E. (Eds.). (1994). *Making thinking visible: Writing, collaborative planning, and classroom inquiry*. Urbana, IL: National Council of Teachers of English.

Fox, T. (1994). Race and gender in collaborative learning. In S. B. Reagan, T. Fox, & D. Bleich (Eds.), *Writing with new directions in collaborative teaching, learning, and research* (pp. 111–122). Albany: State University of New York Press.

Fulwiler, T. (1992). Writing and learning American literature. In A. Herrington & C. Moran (Eds.), *Writing, teaching, and learning in the disciplines* (pp. 156–173). New York: Modern Language Association.

Hairston, M. (1992). Diversity, ideology, and teaching writing. *College Composition and Communication*, 42(2), 179–93.

Harris, M. (1995). Talking in the middle: Why writers need writing tutors. *College English*, 57(1), 27–41.

Hartley, J. (1985). *Designing instructional text* (2nd ed.). New York: Nichols.

Hayes, J. R., Flower, L., Schriver, K., Stratman, J. F., & Carey, L. (1987). Cognitive processes in revision. In S. Rosenberg (Ed.), *Advances in applied psycholinguistics* Vol. 2, (pp. 176–240). Cambridge, England: Cambridge University Press.

Herrington, A., & Moran, C. (Eds.). (1992). *Writing, teaching, and learning in the disciplines*. New York: Modern Language Association.

Hillocks, G. (1984). What works in teaching composition: A meta-analysis of experimental treatment studies. *American Journal of Education*, 93(1), 133–170.

Hillocks, G. (1986). *Research on written composition*. Urbana, IL: National Council of Teachers of English.

Huckin, T. (1983). A cognitive approach to readability. In P. V. Anderson, R. J. Brockmann, & C. R. Miller (Eds.), *New essays in technical and scientific communication: Research, theory, practice* (pp. 90–110). Farmingdale, NY: Baywood.

Kastman, L.-A. M. (1994). *Gender and communication: The value of relational behaviors for collaborative leadership in small group interaction*. Unpublished master's thesis, Iowa State University, Ames.

Kent, T. (1984). Paragraph production and the given-new contract. *Journal of Business Communication*, 21(4), 45–66.

Kent, T. (1991). On the very idea of a discourse community. *College Composition and Communication*, 42, 425–445.

Kent, T. (1992). Externalism and the production of discourse. *Journal of Advanced Composition*, 12(1), 57–74.

Kostelnick, C. (1989). Visual rhetoric: A reader-oriented approach to graphics and designs. *Technical Writing Teacher*, 16(1), 77–88.

Kostelnick, C. (1990). The rhetoric of text design in professional communication. *Technical Writing Teacher*, 17(3), 189–202.

Kuhn, T. (1991). The interpretive turn. In D. R. Hiley, J. F. Bohman, & R. Shusterman (Eds.), *The interpretive turn* (pp. ix–24). Ithaca, NY: Cornell University Press.

Langer, J. (1992). Speaking of knowing: Conceptions of understanding in academic disciplines. In A. Herrington & C. Moran (Eds.), *Writing, teaching, and learning in the disciplines* (pp. 69–85). New York: Modern Language Association.

Larson, R. L. (1992). Classes of discourse, acts of discourse, writers, and readers. *English Journal*, 81(8), 32–36.

Latimer, M., & Spoto, P. (1994). Collaboration and world view. In S. B. Reagan, T. Fox, & D. Bleich (Eds.), *Writing with new directions in collaborative teaching, learning, and research* (pp. 265–282). Albany: State University of New York Press.

Lloyd-Jones, R. (1977). Primary trait scoring. In C. R. Cooper & L. Odell (Eds.), *Evaluating writing* (pp. 32–66). Urbana, IL: National Council of Teachers of English.

Luce-Kapler, R. (1996). Narrating the portfolio landscape. *English Journal*, 85(1), 45–49.

Lunsford, A. (1991). Collaboration, control, and the idea of a writing center. *Writing Center Journal*, 12(1), 3–10.

Lunsford, A., & Sullivan, P. A. (1990). Who are basic writers? In M. G. Moran & M. J. Jacobi (Eds.), *Research in basic writing: A bibliographic sourcebook* (pp. 17–30). New York: Greenwood.

Markel, M. (1993). Techniques of developing forecasting statements. *Journal of Business and Technical Communication*, 7(3), 360–366.

Mendelson, M. (1988). Teaching arrangement inductively. *Journal of Business Communication*, 25(2), 67–83.

Miller, S. (1994). New discourse city: An alternative model for collaboration. In S. B. Reagan, T. Fox, & D. Bleich (Eds.), *Writing with new directions in collaborative teaching, learning, and research* (pp. 283–300). Albany: State University of New York Press.

Mitchell, J. H., & Smith, M. K. (1989). The prescriptive versus the heuristic approach in teaching technical communication. In B. E. Fearing & W. K. Sparrow (Eds.), *Technical writing: Theory and practice* (pp. 117–127). New York: Modern Language Association.

North, S. (1984). The idea of a writing center. *College English*, 46(5), 433–446.

Oliver, E. I. (1995). The writing quality of seventh, ninth, and eleventh graders, and college freshmen: Does rhetorical specification in writing prompts make a difference? *Research in the Teaching of English*, 29(4), 422–450.

Olmstead, K. J. (1988). Expanding cultural awareness: Wigginton on cultural journalism. *English Journal*, 77(3), 32–35.

Olson, G. (Ed.). (1984). *Writing centers: Theory and administration*. Urbana, IL: National Council of Teachers of English.

Peck, W., Flower, L., & Higgins, L. (1995). Community literacy. *College Composition and Communication*, 46(2), 199–222.

Probst, R. E. (1988). *Response and analysis: Teaching literature in junior and senior high school*. Portsmouth, NH: Boynton/Cook/Heinemann.

Raines, P. A. (1996). Writing portfolios: Turning the house into a home. *English Journal*, 85(1), 41–45.

Reagan, S. B. (1994). Collaborative learning in the graduate classroom. In S. B. Reagan, T. Fox, & D. Bleich (Eds.), *Writing with new directions in collaborative teaching, learning, and research* (pp. 197–212). Albany: State University of New York Press.

Redish, J. (1987). Reading to learn to do. *Technical Writing Teacher*, 15(3), 223–233.

Redish, J. C., Battison, R. M., & Gold, E. S. (1985). Making information accessible to readers. In L. Odell & D. Goswami (Eds.), *Writing in non-academic settings* (pp. 129–153). New York: Guilford.

Rico, G. L. (1988). Against formulaic writing. *English Journal*, 77(6), 57–58.

Rodby, J. (1994). Community and communitas: Collaboration in an adult ESL class. In S. B. Reagan, T. Fox, & D. Bleich (Eds.), *Writing with new directions in collaborative teaching, learning, and research* (pp. 141–156). Albany: State University of New York Press.

Rose, M. (Ed.). (1985). *When a writer can't write*. New York: Guilford.

Rosenblatt, L. M. (1978). *The reader, the text, and the poem: The transactional theory of the literary work*. Carbondale: Southern Illinois University Press.

Russell, D. (1991). *Writing in the academic disciplines, 1870–1990: A curricular history*. Carbondale: Southern Illinois University Press.

Russell, D. (1992). American origins of the writing-across-the-curriculum movement. In A. Herrington & C. Moran (Eds.), *Writing, teaching, and learning in the disciplines* (pp. 22–44). New York: Modern Language Association.

Rymer, J. (1993). Collaboration and conversation in learning communities: The discipline and the classroom. In N. Blyler & C. Thralls (Eds.), *Professional communication: The social perspective* (pp. 179–195). Newbury Park, CA: Sage.

Scardamalia, M., & Bereiter, C. (1987). Knowledge telling and knowledge transforming in written composition. In S. Rosenberg (Ed.), *Advances in applied psycholinguistics* (Vol. 2, pp. 142–175). Cambridge, England: Cambridge University Press.

Scharle, C. M. (1993). The lesson that flew: A political-action primer for students. *English Journal*, 82(7), 39–43.

Schultz, L. M. (1995). Elaborating our history: A look at mid-19th century first books of composition. *College Composition and Communication*, 45(1), 10–30.

Secondary Section of the National Council of Teachers of English. (1990). *Lost in the crowd: A statement on class size and teacher work load*. Urbana, IL: National Council of Teachers of English.

Selfe, C. L. (1988). The humanization of computers: Forget technology, remember literacy. *English Journal*, 77(6), 69–71.

Selfe, C. L., & Selfe, R. J., Jr. (1994). The politics of interface: Power and its exercise in electronic contact zones. *College Composition and Communication*, 45(4), 480–504.

Selzer, J. (1989). Arranging business prose. In M. Kogen (Ed.), *Writing in the business professions* (pp. 37–64). Urbana, IL: National Council of Teachers of English.

Shaughnessy, M. (1977). *Errors & expectations: A guide for the teachers of basic writing*. New York: Oxford University Press.

Shaughnessy, M. (1994). Some new approaches toward teaching. *Journal of Basic Writing*, 13(1), 103–116.

Sheridan-Rabideau, M. P., & Brossell, G. (1995). Finding basic writing's place. *Journal of Basic Writing*, 14(1), 21–26.

Sitko, B. M. (1993). Exploring feedback: Writers meet readers. In A. M. Penrose & B. M. Sitko (Eds.), *Hearing ourselves think: Cognitive research in the college writing classroom* (pp. 170–187). New York: Oxford University Press.

Southard, S. (1989). Protocol and human relations in the corporate world: What interns should know. In W. O. Coggin (Ed.), *Establishing and supervising internships* (pp. 65–77). Association of Teachers of Technical Writing.

Spellmeyer, K. (1994). On conventions and collaboration: The open road and the iron cage. In J. Clifford & J. Schilb (Eds.), *Writing theory and critical theory* (pp. 73–95). New York: Modern Language Association.

Sperling, M. (1991). Dialogues of deliberation: Conversation in the teacher-student writing conference. *Written Communication* 8(2), 131–162.

Sperling, M. (1994). Speaking of writing: When teacher and student collaborate. In S. B. Reagan, T. Fox, & D. Bleich (Eds.), *Writing with new directions in collaborative teaching, learning, and research* (pp. 227–246). Albany: State University of New York Press.

Sullivan, D. L. (1990). Political-ethical implications of defining technical communication as a practice. *Journal of Advanced Composition*, 10(2), pp. 375–86.

Sunstein, B. (1992). *Portfolio portraits*. Portsmouth, NH: Heinemann.

Thralls, C., & Blyler, N. R. (1993). The social perspective and professional communication: Diversity and directions in research. In N. R. Blyler & C. Thralls (Eds.), *Professional communication: The social perspective* (pp. 3–34). Newbury Park, CA: Sage.

Tufte, E. R. (1983). *The visual display of quantitative information*. Cheshire, CT: Graphics Press.

Tufte, E. R. (1990). *Envisioning information*. Cheshire, CT: Graphics Press.

VanderStaay, S. (1990). Charitable topics: Research, writing, and speaking. *English Journal*, 79(3), 52–54.

Venne, G. (1989). High-school students write about math. *English Journal*, 78(1), 64–66.

Villanueva, V. (1994). On writing groups, class, and culture: Studying oral and literate language features in writing. In S. B. Reagan, T. Fox, & D. Bleich (Eds.) *Writing with new directions in collaborative teaching, learning, and research* (pp. 123–140). Albany: State University of New York Press.

White, J. V. (1988). *Graphic design for the electronic age*. New York: Watson-Guptill.

Wolff, W. C. (1991). Writing services: A new role for the writing center and faculty. In R. Wallace & J. Simpson (Eds.), *The writing center: New directions* (pp. 110–132). New York: Garland.

Woodson, L. (1979). *A handbook of modern rhetorical terms*. Urbana, IL: National Council of Teachers of English.

Young, R. (1982). Concepts of art and the teaching of writing. In J. J. Murphy (Ed.), *The rhetorical tradition and modern writing* (pp. 130–141). New York: Modern Language Association.

Young, R. (1991). Designing for change in a writing-across-the-curriculum program. In V. A. Chappell, M. L. Buley-Meissner, & C. Anderson (Eds.), *Balancing acts* (pp. 141–160). Carbondale: Southern Illinois University Press.

Zeni, J. (1994). Oral collaboration, computers, and revision. In S. B. Reagan, T. Fox, & D. Bleich (Eds.), *Writing with new directions in collaborative teaching, learning, and research* (pp. 213–226). Albany: State University of New York Press.

CHAPTER

10

Developing Student Understanding in Elementary School Mathematics: A Cognitive Perspective

MEGAN LOEF FRANKE
University of California, Los Angeles

DOUGLAS A. GROUWS
University of Iowa

Cognitive science, what we know about how individuals learn and develop, has already changed the face of mathematics education, especially in elementary schools. We have moved away from focusing only on drill and recitation to thinking more about problem solving and hands-on activities. However, as we continue to learn more about how individuals learn, we must also continue to reflect on our teaching of mathematics and adapt accordingly.

The breadth and depth of work in cognitive psychology that addresses how children learn has been synthesized in a number of places (Calfee, 1981; Gardner, 1985; Posner, 1989; Resnick & Ford, 1981; Schoenfeld, 1987). Our goal here is not to provide another literature review but rather to think through how considering the individual as a learner and part of a social context can help us understand current implications from cognitive science for engaging children in mathematics and the ramifications of instantiating these ideas in the classroom context. Theories of cognitive science do not

Handbook of Academic Learning

lead to a single view of classrooms, instead they offer principles from which decisions can be made about teaching mathematics.

Theorists and researchers like Jean Piaget and Lev Vygotsky have helped us come to understand that children come to school with rich stores of knowledge developed from interacting with and within their environments (Piaget, 1954, 1973; Vygotsky, 1978). Children can learn without explicitly being told, although others play a significant role in an individual's learning. The ideas of Piaget and Vygotsky have influenced theory and practice in a variety of ways. Often you hear teachers say that children construct knowledge rather than receive knowledge. Teachers report that children must be actively engaged in learning. Teachers and researchers alike are curious about what children are thinking. Our current understanding of how children learn and develop, often building on the work of Piaget, Vygotsky, and others (Chi, Glaser, & Rees, 1982; Miller, Galanter, & Pribram, 1960; Newell & Simon, 1972; Rumelhart & Norman, 1978), allows for more specific links to teaching than the earlier theories of cognitive science.

Developments in cognitive science convey a way of understanding different aspects of the mind and modeling individual thinking and learning (Chi, Glaser, & Rees, 1982; Newell & Simon, 1972; Schneider & Shiffrin, 1977; and others, see Calfee, 1981, or Resnick & Ford, 1981). This understanding of mental capacity and functioning has allowed researchers to go beyond thinking about the more general, yet powerful, notion that children learn from interacting with their environment to begin to document more specifically the development of children's thinking within various content domains.

Currently, cognitive science researchers are debating the extent to which knowledge is socially constructed. The tension between thinking about the individual learner and the individual as a part of a social group provides a forum for understanding what cognitive psychology offers teachers of elementary school mathematics. Building on the work of Piaget, one can think about the learner gaining knowledge by interacting with his or her world, the focus here is on active individual construction and reflection (see the work of von Glasersfeld, 1984, in press Steffe, Cobb & Von Glaserfeld, 1988). As Cobb (1994) describes, constructivists who focus on the individual learner are concerned with (1) the quality of individual interpretive activity, (2) the development of ways of knowing at the specific level, and (3) the participants' interactive composition of classroom social norms and mathematical processes. This is not to say that focusing on individual construction ignores the relevance of the environment or social interactions. Social interaction does come into play, as the individuals interact with their environment and their reflection on these interactions lead to modifications and accommodations in their learning structures.

Sociocultural theorists advocate that learning occurs within social interaction and thus the social setting, participants, and interactions play a significant role in any individual's learning. Researchers differ in the degree to which they consider learning as occurring within an individual. A sociocultural perspective recognizes that knowledge and understanding are constructed when individuals engage socially in talk and activity about shared problems or tasks, that making meaning involves communication where individuals are introduced to a culture by more skilled others, and that individuals appropriate cultural tools through their involvement in the activities of the culture (see the work of Brown, Collins, & Duguid, 1989; Carraher, Carraher, & Schliemann, 1985; Greeno, 1991; Lave, 1988; Lave & Wenger, 1991; Saxe, 1991; Vygotsky, 1978). Some researchers view the individual as possessing no knowledge that can be seen as separately residing within the person, others suggest that, although knowledge is socially constructed, an individual does possess some individual knowledge. Learning mathematics from either perspective can be viewed as a process of enculturation into the practices of intellectual communities. Classroom practices are viewed as an instantiation of the culturally organized practices of schooling.[1]

One way to understand the issues underlying the constructivist and sociocultural perspectives is to examine the role of the teacher within each perspective. The teacher, from the constructivist perspective, focuses on the sensory motor and conceptual activity of the individual, while attempting to understand the social and cultural basis of the learner's personal experiences. The micro-culture, from the constructivist perspective, does not exist apart from the teacher's and students' attempts to coordinate their individual activities. From the sociocultural perspective, learning is seen as a process of mutual appropriation, in which the teacher and students use each other's contributions. The teacher's responsibility when negotiating mathematical meaning is to appropriate the students' actions into the wider system of mathematical practices. So, within the constructivist perspective, learning occurs through adaptation and therefore reflection, while within the sociocultural perspective, the focus is on appropriating and therefore communication. Although each perspective has a different focus, different assumptions, and varied implications, each perspective can play a role in teaching and learning mathematics.

Cobb (1994) argues that rather than viewing these two perspectives as being at odds with one another, we can think of them as each constituting the background for the other. According to Cobb, "coordination of the perspectives leads to the view that learning is a process of both self-organization and a process of enculturation that occurs while participating in cultural practices, frequently while interacting with others" (p. 18). Hence, as teachers, the perspective taken, constructivist or sociocultural, will be driven by the particular issue or dilemma teachers currently are attempting to understand or help their students to understand.

[1]This is a simplified account of the constructivist and sociocultural views of learning. There are points of view in both camps that do not necessarily fall at either extreme.

Developing understanding is a cornerstone of both cognitive science and mathematics education. Creating meaning for issues related to the development of mathematical understanding enables us to reflect on what cognitive science has to say about teaching and learning mathematics. We begin by laying out a cognitive science view of understanding, and we build on this by specifically discussing issues related to the development of understanding in particular mathematical domains. We then discuss the specific implications of both our view of understanding and the development of children's mathematical thinking for the teaching and learning of mathematics.

UNDERSTANDING

One significant impact of theories of cognitive science on mathematics education has been an expanded view of what it means for someone to understand. Research in cognitive science has provided insight into what occurs in the minds of individuals and thus enables us to begin to conceptualize and document what it means to understand (Gardner, 1985). The work in cognitive science about how individuals think is not inconsistent with work in mathematics education. Much of what has been learned in mathematics education is conceptually consistent with what we have learned from cognitive science (Brownell, 1935; Polya, 1957). What the work in cognitive science now adds is a more precise view of modeling human thought. The evolution of these models has already had an impact on the thinking of many mathematics educators. The combined work in cognitive science, in conceptualizing the nature of learning and modeling individual thought, and in mathematics education, in characterizing the learning of mathematics, creates the opportunity for rethinking what constitutes mathematical understanding for a child.

To determine whether a child understood within a behavioral paradigm, the speed and accuracy of the child's solution would have been examined. However, research now shows that a child can solve a problem accurately by using a memorized procedure and not understand. Research shows that two children can solve the same problem in the same amount of time, get the same answer, and have very different understanding of the problem. A child who quickly answers "7" to the problem "3 + 4" does not necessarily understand addition. The child may know only the fact and little else about the process of adding. Through work in cognitive science we can now begin to articulate not only what it would mean to specifically understand a problem like three plus four but also what generally characterizes understanding.

Conceptualizing understanding from a cognitive science point of view requires a sense of how cognitive scientists model the thinking process. Cognitive scientists believe that within the mind of the individual exists a body of knowledge best described as a series of relationships (Gardner, 1985).

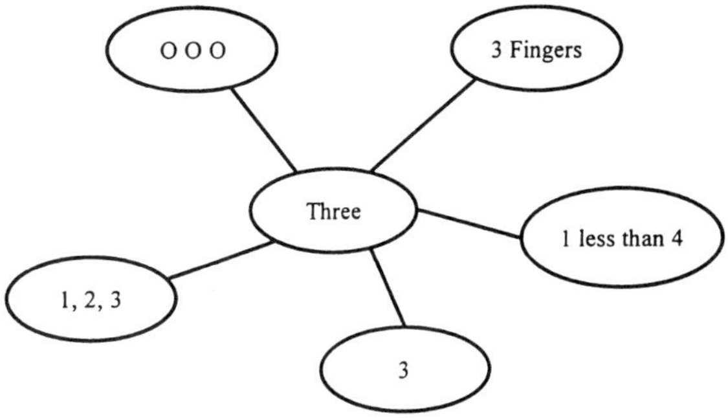

FIGURE 1
Possible representation of an individual's concept of 3.

When you think of cat, you automatically think about other things. These other things, other pieces of knowledge, are those pieces of knowledge related to your notion of cat. Cognitive scientists describe and characterize the relationships in an individual's mind through models of internal representation. There is no one model of individual thinking, the various theorists have developed different models of the individual's internal relationships (Gardner, 1985). Yet across the various cognitive models of thinking, consistencies do exist. The most obvious and universal consistency is that relationships among ideas can be viewed as a series of connections. So, if when thinking about cat you thought about Siamese, animal, or clean, within your internal representation we would find that each of these bits of information would be connected to the concept of cat and potentially connected to each other as well. In mathematics, an individual's concept of 3 might be linked to a representation of three fingers, a set of three counters, the numeral 3, or the counting sequence 1, 2, 3 (see Figure 1). Each individual creates her own connections.[2] The connections an individual constructs vary based on an individual's access to information, the relationships being connected, and the number of times the relationships are activated or used over time.

Connections

The connections between ideas enable an individual to search her mental structure, moving from connection to connection, in an attempt to gain access to and combine information, so that it can be purposely put to use. An individual who is unable to gain access to a piece of information cannot use it. A successful search of one's mental connections depends on (1) the types

[2] In all cases the pronouns refer to males and females. We have chosen to use female pronouns for ease of reading.

of information that have been connected, (2) how they have been connected (what information is connected to what other information), and (3) the strength of the connections (how clearly the ideas are linked or thought of together).

Searching

Searching one's mental structure for information can be thought of in much the same way one might think about negotiating the way from one location to another. Certain variables will be critical in successfully negotiating one's way, (1) how many of the streets in the possible paths you know in relation to other streets, (2) whether the streets to be traveled are connected systematically in one's mind, and (3) how often one has traveled the path, or pieces of the path, that one intends to take.

Think about traveling to a friends home where you have never been. If you were given one set of directions (a linear set of connections) to follow that listed the street names and turns, and you followed it exactly, you would most likely arrive without difficulty. However, your route may not have been the most efficient. The person giving directions may have worried you would get lost and therefore gave you the simplest possible, but not the most direct, path to follow. You may also find that you made a wrong turn, came to a detour, or ran into traffic. If you know only one way to get to your friend's house and do not know the surrounding streets, changing your route to accommodate the impasse becomes difficult. However, if you knew some of the main streets surrounding the route you are taking and were to come to some sort of impasse, you would be able to use the streets that you did know to help you find your way. With some knowledge of the surrounding streets as you continue to visit your friend's house, you will be able to develop the most efficient route as well as develop mechanisms for when detours occur. As you create these routes you may also develop routes that are contextually sensitive. For instance, you may have a route that you travel only when it is 5:00 on a weekday and another route you travel on Saturday mornings. You may have another route you take when it is raining. If your friend's house is close to a restaurant that you frequent or a store you shop at regularly, you can use that information to think about various ways to reach your destination. You then know that, if you turn the wrong way you will have a sense of *how* to efficiently get yourself back on track. If your friend's house happens to be down the block from a place you go to consistently, you can probably travel there without even thinking about where you are going. The only danger is that you may end up at the consistently traveled place and then realize you were going to your friend's house. Here, the connections in your path are so strong that changing or adjusting your route takes thought. Searching your memory is much the same. Solving a mathematics problem encompasses many of the same principles, if you think about solving problems as searching your mental space.

If I have only one solution path for a given problem and the problem posed does not stimulate me to think about one of the ideas in my path, I will not know how to get started. If I get started on my solution path and I get stuck because something in the problem does not quite fit with how I have thought about it in the past, it becomes difficult to know how to adjust. If I can think of another problem that is similar to this one and then use another path to help me, I am more likely to have success. If the problem posed is like ones I have already solved many times, I can use the same solution path that I have always used. To increase the possibility of being able to solve a variety of problems, using a variety of paths, the individual will need multiple connections in her mathematical knowledge and the connections must be organized in ways that reduce the number of routes searched in figuring out how to solve the problem.

Understanding Mathematics

Understanding mathematics is based on the number, types, and organization of connections that exist for an individual. Understanding occurs as representations get connected into increasingly structured and cohesive networks. The connections that create networks form several kinds of relationships including similarities, differences, and inclusion and subsumption (Hiebert & Carpenter, 1992). An individual who *understands* is seen as having multiple connections to a variety of different pieces of information, an intricate web if you will. Often these connections are strong from continued use. Yet, having more than isolated bits of knowledge is not enough to constitute understanding, connections must be developed in a way that creates ways of efficiently searching ones mental space. Connections can be conceptualized as organized in some form of a hierarchy.

Hiebert and Carpenter suggest that both types of representation, webs and hierarchies, can coexist. An individual can create a cognitive structure that begins building in a hierarchical manner and then expands in a weblike fashion or vice versa. Let us return to the example of 3 + 4. A child could possess a rich web of connections that includes information like images of three cats and three cookies or the idea that 3 is a numeral, can be represented by three fingers, can be represented by three objects, can be considered a counting sequence 1, 2, 3, and so on (see Figure 2). If asked to solve the problem 3 + 4, the individual might think about the numeral 3, which in turn is connected to the picture of her three fingers and then count 1, 2, 3, and thus create her own solution path.

Representations

Within mathematics and mathematics education, we spend a great deal of time focusing on and discussing representations, both internal and external. As we discussed understanding, we focused on the internal representations

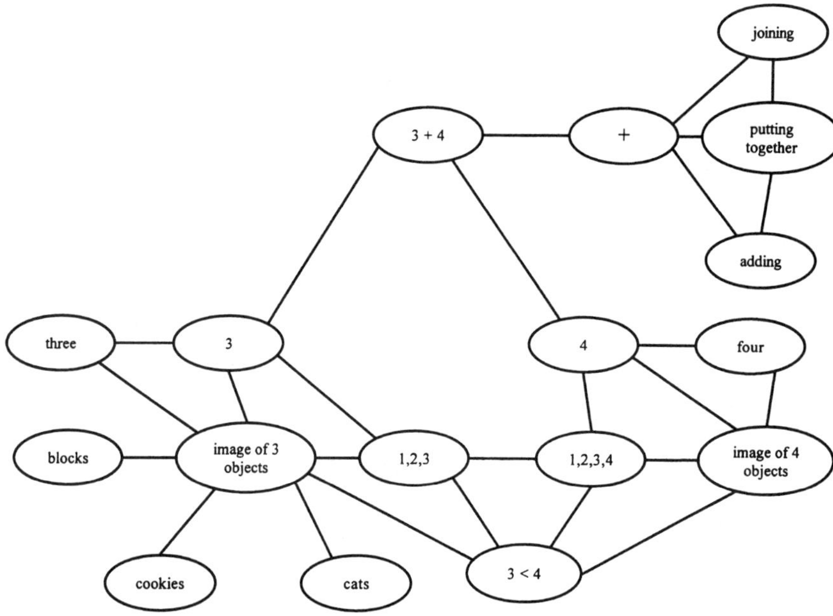

FIGURE 2
Possible representation of an individual's cognitive structure for 3 + 4.

created by the individual. However, external representations also play a significant role in the development of understanding. The nature of an external mathematical representation influences the nature of the internal mathematical representations (Greeno, 1988; Kaput, 1992). External representations can include materials that children use to solve problems; symbols, pictures, essentially any physical form (written or concrete) that a child uses to represent the problem; and its solution. In the context of understanding as we have now defined it, the external representations that children engage become critical to the internal representations they form. The external representations interact with the internal representations that a child already possesses. The external representations also interact with the other external representations that a child engages, just as internal representations interact with each other.

External representations can enable an individual to construct connections between internal representations. When a child works with a particular external representation it may bring to mind another idea that she has that has not yet connected to the mathematical idea being considered. For example, a child may have an internal representation of addition that includes bringing together sets of objects. Yet, as the child interacts with counters in solving an addition problem, she may notice at some point that she can use the counters to keep track of the second set and not form the first set at all. These interactions with the counters affect the child's internal representation. Now the child has connected the idea of keeping track of the second set to addition and bringing together both sets.

Watching a child's engagement with external representations also provides a window into her internal representations. For instance, if a child were to make three tally marks and then four more tally marks to solve 3 + 4, we would have a sense that the child's internal representation of addition included representing the quantities in groups using tally marks as well as counting.

Individuals' internal representations also drive their interpretation of any external representation with which they come into contact. A child may not bring the knowledge a teacher expects to the work with the external representation. If a child cannot easily relate her interactions with particular materials to existing internal representations (networks), she may not interpret the materials in the way that the teacher expects and then she may generate only haphazard connections within her networks.

Summary

Developing understanding is a dynamic process. A process that takes a very long time and one that may never be complete. On the one hand, conceptualizing understanding as we have creates a situation where understanding does not develop in a linear, time-sequenced manner; rather students seem to build mathematical understanding sporadically, and seemingly nonsystematically (Hiebert, Wearne, & Taber, 1991; Steffe & Cobb, 1988). On the other hand, this view of mathematics would rarely if ever characterize a student as possessing no understanding. Almost always an individual has some pieces of knowledge that are relevant to her understanding of the mathematics. As teachers, we need to find out what the students do know and understand so that it can be built on. Few individuals, we could say, understand nothing about 3 + 4, even young children can quantify the set of three showing that they understand that three counters can represent the quantity 3. So, rather than focusing on whether the student understands or does not, the focus becomes what degree of understanding an individual articulates or demonstrates. The other implication of this conceptualization of understanding is that we may not always know what a child understands. Just because a child fails to articulate does not mean that she does not understand, and because a child chooses not to articulate in one setting does not mean that she would not in a different setting with different students. It therefore becomes the teachers' responsibility to begin to understand how to learn about their students' existing mathematical understanding.

In the past it was often thought that what was critical in mathematical learning was the information acquired. Once the information was acquired, understanding could be developed by making connections between the existing knowledge (Nolan, 1973). However, now it seems that the incoming information must be connected to some other piece of knowledge for connections to continue to be built. This suggests that teachers need to know about their students' existing mathematical ideas so that new knowledge is not isolated from existing knowledge. If we are going to help students build understanding, we need to provide opportunity for the students to make multiple connections among their mathematical ideas, to think about these ideas on multiple occasions, so they can both strengthen the relationships and build hierarchies with their connections.

CHILDREN'S THINKING

Building in specific ways on the work in cognitive science, researchers in mathematics education have developed frameworks delineating children's thinking in various mathematical domains. Researchers have examined children's thinking in counting (Gelman & Gallistel, 1978; Steffe, von Glasersfeld, Richards, & Cobb, 1983) addition and subtraction (Briars and Larkin, 1984; Carpenter, 1985; Carpenter & Moser, 1982; Resnick, 1982; Riley, Greeno, & Heller, 1983), multiplication and division (Ball, 1990; Carpenter, Ansell, Franke, Weisbeck, and Fennema, 1993; Greer, 1992; Kouba, 1989; Tirosh & Graeber, 1990), place value (Carpenter, Ansell, Levi, Franke, & Fennema, 1995; Fuson, 1990; Fuson et al, 1994; Hiebert & Wearne, 1992; Kamii & Joseph, 1988), and fractions (Baker, 1994; Bennett, 1995; Mack, 1990; Post, Harel, Behr, & Lesh, 1991; Streefland, 1993) as well as others (some of the content domains are addressed in the upper grades chapter; see Williams, this volume). The findings within and across mathematical domains are strikingly robust. Children from different parts of the country with various backgrounds are solving problems in quite similar, principled ways. The nature and strength of these findings reinforces how valuable this information can be for a teacher. A teacher in Los Angeles and a teacher in rural Wisconsin can both expect to see similar strategies, related in principled ways, that match the frameworks developed by researchers studying children's thinking.

The research describing children's mathematical thinking is reported both in detail and in summary in a number of different places (Carpenter, 1985; Fuson, 1992). Our intent here is to provide a sense of what the research has to offer and how it might affect the teaching of mathematics in kindergarten through sixth grades. We will use the work in addition and subtraction as a way to illustrate the depth, breadth, and value of this work.

Researchers studying children's thinking in addition and subtraction outline both a set of problems that characterize the domain itself and a range of strategies children typically use to solve the various problems. Often the problems that a first grade teacher uses in addressing addition and subtraction in her classroom are of three or maybe four types. Children are asked to solve problems like those seen in Table 1. However, researchers, in listening to children, have found that children can solve addition and subtraction problems of a much wider range and difficulty.

Four basic classes of addition and subtraction problems can be identified, based on how children think about solving problems. Within each problem class, the problems involve the same type of action or relation. The problems can be characterized as involving a (1) joining action, (2) separating action, (3) part–part–whole relation, or (4) comparison situation. Within each class, different types of problems can be identified based on which quantity is the unknown (see Table 2). The distinctions within and across problem classes are clearest when examining how children solve the different problems.

Students use a range of strategies to solve the different addition and subtraction problems. In the following excerpt Carpenter and his colleagues (Carpenter, Fennema, & Franke, in press) demonstrate how a student solved three different problems that most adults would solve by subtracting.

> Teacher: "TJ had 13 chocolate chip cookies. At lunch he ate 5 of those cookies. How many cookies did TJ have left?"
>
> Rachel: Puts out 13 counters, removes 5 of them, and counts the counters that remain. "There are 8."
>
> Teacher: "Good. Now here's the next one. Janelle has 7 trolls in her collection. How many more trolls does she have to buy to have 11 trolls?"
>
> Rachel: First puts out a set of 7 counters and adds counters until there is a total of 11. She then counts the counters she added to the initial set to find the answer. "Four."
>
> Teacher: "That's good. Here's one more. Willy has 12 crayons. Lucy has 7 crayons. How many more crayons does Willy have than Lucy?"
>
> Rachel: Makes two sets of counters, one containing 12 counters and the other containing 7. She lines up the two sets in rows so that the set of 7 matches the set of 12, and counts the unmatched counters in the row of 12. "Five more."

Rachel's solutions to these problems illustrate that children do not think of all addition problems or subtraction problems as alike. Rachel did not take away to solve each of these "subtraction" problems. She chose a different strategy to solve each problem. However, there was consistency in her responses. In each case, Rachel directly modeled the action or relationship described in the problem. Rachel did what the problem asked, in the order the problem stated. Specifically, the first problem involved separating 5 from 13, the second involved adding more to the 7 until there were 11, and the third involved comparing two quantities. In each case Rachel's strategy mirrors these relationships. Rachel's strategies reflect the action in the problem and the location of the unknown.

As children engage in solving problems their strategies develop. Direct modeling strategies, like Rachel's, are replaced initially by counting strategies, which are essentially abstractions of the direct modeling strategies. A counting strategy for Rachel's second problem would be thinking 7 and then

TABLE 1
Typical Addition and Subtraction Word Problems

Addition:
Anthony had 5 stickers. His teacher gave him 3 more stickers. How many stickers does Anthony have altogether?
Subtraction:
Andrea has 8 goldfish. She gave 3 of her goldfish to Claire. How many goldfish does Andrea have left?
Part–part–whole:
There are 7 girls and 5 boys waiting in line. How many children are waiting in line?

counting 8, 9, 10, 11 and keeping track of the counts (four) as she goes along. Although counting strategies continue to reflect the actions in the problems, they are more efficient and require a more sophisticated conception of number than direct modeling with manipulatives. As Rachel developed in her understanding you would be likely to see her solve the problem by using what she knew about 10, 7 + 3 is 10, and one more is 11, 3 + 1 is 4. The continued development of more abstract symbolic procedures can be characterized as progressive abstractions of children's attempts to model action and relations depicted in problems. Eventually Rachel would see this problem as a subtraction problem and know 11 − 7 at the recall level.

The research on children's thinking in addition and subtraction demonstrates that children intuitively solve word problems by modeling the action and relations described in them (Carpenter et al., in press). The research shows that when children are given the opportunity to solve problems with a choice of materials available, children as young as kindergarten can solve many addition and subtraction problems as well as multiplication and division problems by modeling. Children then continue to develop in the use of counting strategies, derived facts, and recall of number facts.

Based on this evidence, researchers have developed frameworks of problems that distinguish between them and identify the relative difficulty of such problems. (A more complete description of distinctions among problems and the strategies children use to solve them can be found in Carpenter, 1985; Carpenter, Carey, & Kouba, 1990; Carpenter, Fennema, & Franke, in press).

Within each of the content domains where children's thinking is being investigated we have learned both about how children develop in their thinking and about the content domain itself. We also continue to learn more about the possibilities for using this information in instruction (see Fennema, Carpenter, Franke, & Carey, 1992; Fennema, Carpenter, Franke, Levi, Jacobs, & Empson, in press).

Specifically, we have learned that the domain of addition and subtraction can be conceptualized as including different types of problems, varying in

TABLE 2
Addition and Subtraction Problems Drawn from Research on Children's Thinking

Joining Action:

Result unknown

Anthony had 5 stickers. His teacher gave him 3 more stickers. How many stickers does Anthony have altogether?

Change unknown

Anthony had 5 stickers. How many more stickers does he have to collect to have 11 stickers altogether?

Start unknown

Anthony had some stickers. He bought 5 more stickers. Now Anthony has 11 stickers. How many stickers did Anthony have to start with?

Separating Action:

Result unknown

Andrea has 8 goldfish. She gave 3 of her goldfish to Claire. How many goldfish does Andrea have left?

Change unknown

Andrea won 11 goldfish at the school fair. She gave some of her goldfish to her brother. Now she has 8 goldfish left. How many goldfish did Andrea give to her brother?

Start unknown

Andrea had some goldfish in her fish bowl. She took 8 fish out of her fishbowl and she still had 3 goldfish left in the bowl. How many goldfish did Andrea have in her fishbowl to begin with?

Part–Part–Whole (no action):

Whole unknown

There are 7 girls and 5 boys waiting in line. How many children are waiting in line?

Part unknown

There were 11 children playing soccer. Five of the children were boys. How many girls were playing soccer?

Comparison:

Difference unknown

Keisha has 13 toy cars. Tomas has 5 toy cars. How many more toy cars does Keisha have than Tomas?

Compare quantity unknown

Tomas has 5 toy cars. Keisha has 8 more than Tomas. How many toy cars does Keisha have?

Referent unknown

Keisha has 13 toy cars. She has 5 more toy cars than Tomas. How many toy cars does Tomas have?

actions and unknowns. We have learned that the degree to which a problem can be modeled determines its difficulty. We know that certain types of problems elicit certain strategies. We can identify the range of strategies children use to solve the problems and how the children's strategies are related.

Strategies develop subsequent to children modeling and before children memorize the number facts. We know that children most likely will be able to tell you that 3 + 3 is 6 before they will be able to tell you that 3 + 4 is 7. We know what problems to pose to help determine what children understand about the domain.

More generally, we know that, rather than assuming that children cannot solve any problems when they come to school, we now know that children come to school with knowledge that helps them think about how to solve addition and subtraction problems. We know there is a sequence to the developmental progression of children's strategies that can help teachers decide what problems to pose and why. We have learned that, even though individual children may vary in their responses, some strategies can serve as benchmarks to help teachers understand what to expect in the development of the children's strategies and mathematical understanding. We have learned that, in many cases, children use strategies before they have been formally taught to use them. And when talking about the need to connect children's existing knowledge to new knowledge, we now have a sense of what the existing knowledge may be.

IMPLICATIONS

Listening

Everything we are learning from theory, research, and practice suggests that listening to students do mathematics is critical. Developing understanding, as put forth in this chapter, requires that teachers find out what their students know. Listening to students enables teachers to find out specific information about the solution methods students employ, to create communication in the classroom, to provide opportunities for students to learn from each other, and to provide opportunities for children to rehearse their solution methods to gain greater understanding. The research on understanding and children's thinking helps us both to understand why each aspect of listening to students is critical and to create specific ideas of what these broader ideas may mean in the classroom context.

Listening for Specificity

Many teachers are beginning to see the need for carefully listening to students describe their solutions to problems. However, theory suggests that it may not be sufficient to recognize that children are using a number of different strategies (Franke, Fennema, Carpenter, Ansell, & Behrend, 1996). For classroom practice to build mathematical understanding, it may be necessary for the teacher to identify the specific strategy a child uses and elaborate on how that strategy fits with others children use to solve that type of problem. For instance, if a teacher were to pose a problem like 70 − 26, she may notice that the children solved the problem in a number of different ways. The teacher may recognize that some of the children's strategies used counters and that some of the strategies involved paper and pencil. This knowledge would allow the teacher to predict in a general way what the child would do with a similar problem. This knowledge, however, would not necessarily help the teacher know what problem to pose next in creating additional learning opportunities nor enable the teacher to predict what strategy might develop next in the student's repertoire. However, knowing that one child modeled the problem, by putting out 70 unit counters, taking away 26 of those counters and then counting the remaining counters, while another child put out 7 ten blocks, took away 26 counters by counting, 1, 2, 3, 4, . . . , 26 on the ten bars, eliminating two blocks and six squares from the third block, and counting the remaining units to find the answer, the teacher would be able to make a more specific determination about what to do next. Both children used counters, but they used them differently. The different ways they used the counters reflects the children's understanding of the concept of 10. Neither child was able to operate using tens to solve the problem. The first child does not use tens at all and the second child uses tens to set up the problem but not to find the solution. In this case a teacher might decide to pose a problem that would stretch the child's thinking and create an opportunity for the child to build knowledge about tens, like 55 − 35 or 38 + 20. Having specific knowledge of children's thinking can allow for specific decisions to be made about how to build on children's mathematical thinking within individual interactions and within the context of the classroom (Carpenter, Fennema, & Franke, in press).

Knowing the specific strategy can also help a teacher know when to ask a question of an individual child and what question to ask. In the case of the second child, a teacher could ask "show me how you used these" (pointing to the tens). Focusing the child's attention on the tens, the teacher could say, "What if the problem were 70 take away 20, what would you do?" and then return to engaging with the problem 70 − 26. Knowing the specific strategies a child uses can enable a teacher to better provide opportunities for children to connect their existing knowledge to new knowledge and thus develop understanding.

Creating opportunities for connections to be made among existing knowledge or between existing knowledge and new knowledge is facilitated by a teacher listening to what a child says and reflecting on how that fits with what else the teacher knows about the child and children's thinking. If a teacher hears from a child that she solved a problem, six groups of 21, by putting out six groups of 21 unit counters and counting them all, the teacher knows the child modeled the problem. The teacher can then think about what other types of problems this child solves using a modeling strategy.

The teacher can consider that the child has not used knowledge of ten as a unit to solve the problem (a possible solution would have been to put out six groups of two ten counters and one unit counter). The teacher can then reflect about what she knows about the development of children's thinking. She may want the child to begin moving toward using tens to represent the numbers in the problem, putting out the counters in groups of ten and counting by ones to figure out how many counters there are. Based on this information, the teacher can think about what problems she might pose to help the children begin to build on what they know about modeling to incorporate knowledge of operating on tens. The teacher could pose a problem similar to six groups of 21, but use numbers conducive to initially using ten counters, like three groups of 10. The children would have the opportunity with a few tens to put out groups of ten and still count by ones if need be. The teacher's ability in this example to think through the children's thinking and think about how to build on that knowledge, demonstrates how critical it can be to listen to the specifics of children's thinking and go beyond listening for surface features.

This is not to say that teachers always need to or do make these specific kinds of decisions, often teachers do not; but having the needed information allows them to do so if they find it necessary. Teachers regularly report that they find it extremely useful to be able to identify a child's strategy. One of the most striking consistencies across teachers who successfully create classroom environments where children's mathematical understanding develops is not what their classrooms look like but rather the teachers' specific talk about their children's solution strategies and how these strategies fit with the development of understanding within the domain (Carpenter, Fennema, & Franke, in press; Franke et al., 1996).

Communicating

Building communication in the classroom requires that teachers listen to students and students listen to each other. The Curriculum and Evaluation Standards (National Council of Teachers of Mathematics [NCTM], 1989) and the Professional Standards for Teaching Mathematics (NCTM, 1991), as well as other research reports and policy documents, argue for creating mathematical communication in the classroom. However, often little is said about how to create this communication, creating a perception that developing communication in the classroom is easy. If we realize that in any kind of communication those participating must be able to understand at some level what is being said (for conversation to be sustained), then communicating mathematically begins to sound quite complicated. Teachers and students must understand and talk about their own thinking and listen, understand and talk about the thinking of others.

To communicate mathematically, teachers must be able to identify what each child is saying, so that she and her students can ask questions that stimulate discussion and add to the conversation by building on what was previously said. Consider a child sharing a rather complicated strategy to a problem. One option for the teacher would be to thank the child for sharing and move on by asking another child to share her solution. Another option would be to ask the child specific questions about the strategy, to try to help the child articulate her thinking, and to enable the other children to figure out aspects of what the child has done. The first option is certainly a viable alternative, but in most cases it will not lead to the most productive learning for either the child sharing or for the rest of the class. This option also does not foster communication. The teacher must be able to identify the strategy the child is using to make a decision about how to respond and whether to pursue building communication. The teacher must also be prepared for another child in the class to pursue the same strategy. Without knowing enough about the child's strategy and thinking about this strategy, the teacher will have a difficult time deciding how to pursue what was said and how to continue to create communication.

Communication in the classroom also requires a restructuring of the mathematics conversation from teacher to student to student to student with the teacher participating in the dialogue. This requires that the teacher find ways that the students can come to listen and understand one another. If the teacher does not listen, the children are not likely to listen. A student who does not feel that someone is listening may not be as likely to explicitly articulate her thinking. I remember particularly well a classroom visit where a child began sharing her strategy with me. The child began explaining and after about 30 seconds of her explanation I could identify, based on what she was saying and the way she had configured her materials, the strategy the child was using. I told the child that I could see what she was doing and thanked her for sharing with me. As I began to move on and hear another child's strategy, she looked up at me and told me that she needed to show me the whole thing, she was not finished. I proceeded to watch and listen as the child completed her explanation. I then watched the children share their strategies with the class. I noticed that the children were not allowed to cut short their explanations. The teacher or another student would typically ask for more information. The children in this class were learning that they needed to articulate their entire strategy to make sure all of the people in the class had an opportunity to understand. I had not allowed the child the opportunity to articulate her thinking and had cut off communication; the child knew better. I also had not allowed the child to continue learning both about her strategy and about how to communicate.

Listening to students as a way to foster communication cannot be limited to listening to children talk about their strategies. Oftentimes when solving problems, children use some form of external representation. This representation may range from a set of counters to a set of numbers written down to help the child think about the problem. Whatever the representation, it is a part of the child's thinking about the problem. The representation serves as a picture of how the child is viewing the mathematical relationships in the problem. Not only is the child's representation critical to how the child understood the problem, it can also serve as a vehicle for helping other children understand what the child was thinking. In Sue Gehn's third grade mathematics classroom, the children all get out of their desks to go over and see and listen to a child share her thinking about a problem. The children ask each other questions about how the materials or written numbers were used. They discuss the differences in solutions when different representations were used. Children's representations can stimulate other children to make connections and access information they may not have otherwise considered. If the representations the child uses are a window into how the child was thinking about the problem, the students as well as the teacher need access to this information to come to some understanding of the child's thinking. Further, sharing representations can foster discussion of the mathematical relationships in the problem.

Children communicating about mathematics in the classroom are not just learning mathematics. They are learning about effective communication and specifically about articulating their thoughts in ways their audience will understand. In this situation children learn mathematics as they learn to communicate. Learning mathematics and learning to communicate each incorporate critical goals for children. When learned together, children can make connections between communication issues and mathematics. Students need to learn how to say what they are thinking, adjust their explanations to fit the context of the situation and the audience, learn to listen to one another, and value each other's knowledge. Teachers provide the opportunities that foster children's mathematical communication. Listening to students can enable a teacher to begin to create these opportunities.

Learning from Others

The need for communication in the classroom not only gives children the opportunity to articulate their own thinking and acknowledges them for having their own unique thoughts, it also allows children to learn from each other. Research suggests that children, and adults, develop understanding as they interact within their social environment (Carraher et al., 1985; Lave, 1988; Saxe, 1991). This means that, together, the students and the teacher are constructing understanding. The development of understanding for one child affects and is dependent on the understanding of others, others they come in contact with. So, not only are students learning from listening to each other, they are constructing understanding that depends on others. One child may bring one piece of information that elicits a particular piece from another child and then this feeds back to the first child. The child may not come to understand the mathematics in the same way if she were in a different environment with different children. Even within the context of a single classroom, during different activities and under differing conditions, children may chose to solve problems in different ways.

Rehearsing Strategies

Listening to children implies that teachers will encourage children to talk about their thinking. As we have described, the advantages to this may go beyond the teacher learning about the children's thinking; namely, the development of children's communication skills and the encouragement of the coconstruction of mathematical meaning. There may be yet an additional individual benefit to children describing their thought processes (Hiebert et al., in press). Children may continue to gain in understanding through the process of telling. In its most simple form, we see this increase in understanding as children explain their solution processes, notice places in their solution that do not make sense, and make appropriate adjustments. The child may have miscounted, misinterpreted the problem, miscalculated, or something else, but in the process of sharing her explanations she makes adjustments that build on her initial thinking. In a more complex form, the children may also, through their explanations, come to see how they could have created an alternative or more sophisticated solution. Consider again the child who was able to solve the problem 70 − 26 by initially putting out the tens but then counted by ones to complete the solution. We might observe that, as this child was explaining her solution, that she recognized that she could have taken away the entire ten bar instead of taking away the units one at a time. Describing the strategy in words and actions for others provides an opportunity for the child to think through the problem again, to create connections, and to see patterns in what she has done.

Background Knowledge

The research and theories of learning suggest that teachers need knowledge that will enable them to anticipate and understand children's strategies. Listening to children's strategies and providing opportunities for children to build on them—thinking about what questions to ask or what problems to pose next—is quite different from checking to see if a child got the right answer. Sometimes the children rattle off their strategies at a speed that is difficult to follow. It is almost like listening to someone who speaks a language that you do not, it sounds like it is all going by so fast, but when you learn to speak the language it does not seem so. Knowing what to expect from the children will allow the teacher to hear what the child is saying. Knowing what to expect also enables the teacher to know what a child, who was unable to complete her thoughts, was attempting to do. The teacher then has an idea of what questions to ask the child. The teacher who has little idea of what the child's solution is about or where it is going has few options for helping the student. The teacher can ask the child to repeat her thinking or move on to another child, but these options are of limited value. This is not to say that a teacher will always know what strategy a child used or was trying to use, but increased knowledge will ensure that the teacher will often know the strategy, and when she does not, she will at least know some of the possibilities.

Learning about children's strategies also helps teachers understand the mathematics content. Many teachers report knowing more and thinking differently about mathematics after beginning to listen to their students' thinking and after acquiring knowledge about the development of children's mathematical thinking. One teacher told us,

> You know, I've learned a lot just from listening to some of these kids. I'm thinking, wow, I never figured it out that way. But you know, I even find myself using some of their ways. I mean, it's a riot. And that's what's kind of neat about this.

Teachers who are able to solve a problem like "Who planted more of his or her garden, Marty who planted $2/3$, Jackie who planted $5/6$, or Dawne who planted $10/16$?" by manipulating garden plots and trying to make them the same size, while still representing the correct proportion planted (lining up two two-thirds representations next to each other to make four-sixths so that it could be compared to the five-sixths), begin to see where the need for a common denominator comes from. These are mathematical ideas that many of us have not thought too much about. We know the procedure to use to find a common denominator, but that represents the extent of our knowledge. Reproducing children's strategies forces us to think about how the strategy works, if it is generalizable, and how it fits with other strategies that children may use. Thinking about these issues provides an opportunity for teachers to build mathematical understanding.

Problem Selection

The problems that children confront during mathematics class play a significant role in the development of their understanding (Hiebert et al., in press). The problems determine what and how children are going to be thinking about the mathematics. The problems can facilitate connections being made between one idea and another. There are a number of ways to think about using problems as a way to develop understanding. One way to think about problem posing is to create and pose problems that are sufficiently open-ended to elicit a variety of different strategies. The rationale underlying this is that children could come to the problem with varied types of understanding and yet still solve the problem in ways that makes sense to them. The children here are building on their own types of understanding, rather than having someone else decide what the next step will be. Another way to conceptualize this process is to think about developing problems that systematically build on one another and provide specific opportunities for the children to build understanding with a particular concept. For instance, a teacher who wanted to provide opportunities for children to develop counting strategies by building on what the students already know might pose a series of problems as follows:

1. Chris has 6 cookies. His dad gave him 5 more cookies, how many cookies does Chris have now?
2. Jennifer had 8 books on her bed. Her little brother brought over 3 more books. How many books does Jennifer have on her bed?
3. Eloise picked 11 flowers from the garden. She gave 2 of them to her grandmother. How many flowers did Eloise have left?
4. Carolynn has 3 goldfish. Her mom gave her 9 more goldfish for her birthday. How many goldfish does Carolynn have now?

The first problem allows the teacher to identify the strategies children are using. The next two problems encourage counting strategies by the problem structure and the number relationships. The final problem allows the teacher to begin to determine if a child can count on from the larger number and not just from the first number she comes to in the problem. A teacher may choose to pose more that one of each of these problems and to present the problems over a series of days, or the teacher may do it in one day. The teacher's decision should be based on the strategies she sees her students using and what she knows about her students' problem-solving tendencies. Notice also that these problems can be solved by children even if they do not use counting strategies. The problems are ones that all children in the class should be able to solve in ways consistent with their understanding.

Another teaching option includes the teacher posing a problem where the sequence of solutions a child might use is fairly well articulated and then the teacher adds some solution constraints to encourage use of a particular strategy. The teacher might say, "I want you to solve this problem without using paper and pencil," or after the children have finished, ask them if they can think of another way to solve this problem.

Knowing a range of problems for a given content domain and the strategies children typically use to solve them can provide support for teachers as they create opportunities for their students to build mathematical understanding.

Teaching Tools

Teachers use a wide variety of teaching tools as they conduct lessons that focus on increasing student learning. No doubt the use of particular teaching tools is propagated in part through teachers sharing ideas about what works well in their classrooms and what does not; that is, the sharing of the "wisdom of practice" among colleagues accounts for the popularity of many tools. Unfortunately such sharing of ideas generally is not accompanied by a rationale that explains why things work. This sometimes leads to using teaching tools at inappropriate times and in poorly chosen ways. Cognitive psychology provides a rationale for why many of these tools work well and also potential explanations as to why they work better in some classrooms than others (see, for example, Hiebert & Carpenter, 1992). Manipulative materials and various forms of technology are two examples of tools frequently used in teaching mathematics and where cognitive psychology provides insight into how and why they are effective in particular contexts.

Manipulative Materials

Historically, a universal guideline for conducting a good mathematics lesson at the elementary school level has been to use manipulative materials. The assumption underlying this instructional principle is that the presence of concrete material ensures that learning takes place, indeed in many quarters the assumption is that the mere presence of concrete material ensures that meaningful learning takes place. Reviews of research (e.g., Suydam & Higgins, 1977) and, more recently, meta-analyses of studies of the use of manipulative materials in mathematics teaching (e.g., Sowell, 1989) have tended to support this view when they conclude that using manipulatives produces greater student achievement gains than not using them. Therefore, it is not surprising that manipulative materials have become commonly used instructional tools in many mathematics classrooms. Unfortunately, the unfettered use of manipulatives may not accomplish the instructional goals their use was intended to achieve.

A careful examination of the research literature on the use of manipulative materials shows that results across research studies are more uneven than a broad overview of these studies initially suggests. In fact, in some studies achievement differences between students using concrete materials and those not using them are negligible and in some cases even negative (see, for example, Fennema, 1972), even among studies that are carefully controlled and monitored and that use the same manipulatives (Thompson, 1992). Among studies that used base-ten blocks, for instance, some studies reported little impact on student learning from the use of concrete materials (Labinowicz, 1985; Resnick & Omanson, 1987), although other studies demonstrated significant positive results, including increased skill levels and deeper levels of understanding for those children using manipulatives (Fuson & Briars, 1990; Hiebert & Wearne, 1992). Given the undeniable potential of manipulative materials to influence meaningful student learning and the promising impact they might have on student disposition (Sowell, 1989), it is important to search for factors that influence their effectiveness and strive to understand the nature of this influence on the learning process.

The key to understanding the differential impact of manipulative materials may lie in some of the principles of cognitive science that we have discussed previously. For example, we emphasized the importance of connections, representations, and the learning context in the cognitive science perspective on student learning and understanding of mathematics. Each of these factors may play a significant role in the successful use of manipulative materials in the classroom.

In the realm of connections salient to the effective use of manipulatives, the connection between the material being used in the classroom and previous student experience with the material outside the classroom setting merits discussion. Student outside experience may range from no experience (for example, with Unifix Cubes) to extensive familiarity (for example, with money). When experience with a particular manipulative is lacking, a new network of relationships must be constructed from scratch and connected to appropriate networks already in place. This is a time-consuming process in an environment where adequate instructional time is often in short supply. When extensive familiarity and experience is present from the onset, students can immediately begin the learning process by building on their previous experience. When working with money, for example, student knowledge of the equivalent value of 10 pennies and 1 dime can be helpful in developing the place value concepts in our base-ten number system. Starting with familiar material has clear advantages and teachers should strongly consider this factor in selecting materials for classroom use. Of course, if a manipulative is suitable for use in connection with developing many forthcoming mathematical ideas in the curriculum, then it may be worthwhile to take the instructional time necessary to develop an unfamiliar manipulative into a familiar one.

Some caution in implementing the preceding advice about using materials familiar to students is in order. Inherent problems may accompany existing student experience. Consider again the use of money in mathematics teaching. As Hiebert and Carpenter (1992) point out, in our culture it is unusual to let money stand for other objects. Thus, high-level awareness of the relative value of a dime and a penny may be quite helpful initially. But, it may not be easy to use money in later instruction, when an important use of manipulatives is to represent what is happening in a problem context, such as in a situation where one is trying to find the number of desks in all the first grade classrooms when one knows the number in each room. Specifically, using money to represent the number of desks in a classroom may be quite unnatural and confusing for children because of the mismatch between the current task and their previous uses of money, whereas using tongue depressors to represent desks (bundled in groups of ten when appropriate) may be much less artificial for students and thus allow them to concentrate more deeply on the problem at hand. The lesson here is that short-term and long-term effects must be considered concomitantly in choosing manipulatives for instructional use.

Another connection that may differentially affect the impact of the use of manipulatives is the relationship between existing student quantitative structures and the manipulatives used in instruction. On one hand, the material being used may fit well with the cognitive structures in place and learning may not only proceed smoothly but be enhanced. On the other hand, conflict or a mismatch between cognitive structures and the material being used can slow or even disrupt the pace of learning. To illustrate this situation, consider two popular manipulatives used to develop place value concepts and computational skills: base-ten blocks and colored chips. The distinguishing feature between these materials that is relevant to this discussion is that base-ten blocks are used in a way that the relative size of the pieces is directly proportional to the values assigned to them. This is not the case with colored chips. When using base-ten blocks, small cubes (units) are used to represent ones, rows of ten units joined together (rods) are used to represent tens, and ten rods are joined together (flats) represent hundreds, and so on. Thus, as one increases by a multiple of ten going from ones to tens to hundreds, the size of the materials used to represent them increases 10-fold at each stage, too. As natural as this seems, this is not true for many manipulatives, including colored chips. When using chips, the white chips are assigned a value of 1, the blue chips a value of 10, and the red chips a value of 100. Since the chips are all the same size, color alone determines their value. This means that students must focus on color and ignore any previous notions about size–value relationships that might interfere with correct interpretation. The use of so-called nonproportional teaching aids, such as colored chips and the abacus, is not necessarily inappropriate, but decisions concerning how and when to use them must be carefully determined and take into account existing student conceptions and where the lesson in question fits into the sequence of lessons forming the instructional unit. Failure to do so may affect student learning and the results of a research study.

In the preceding discussion, the use of manipulatives in problem solving such as finding the total number of desks in a number of classrooms was mentioned. This might be considered an example of how representation, our second factor in understanding the use and power of manipulatives, comes into our discussion. In this case, a manipulative (tongue depressor) is used to stand for another object (student desk) in solving a real-life problem. The role of representation, however, quickly becomes more complex when one moves from solving a problem to the relationship between representations and manipulatives in the context of student conceptual learning. The increase in complexity is due, in part, to the need to consider internal representations, how things are represented in a student's cognitive structure; external representations, how things are represented in the physical world; and finally the relationship between internal and external representations. We cite one example to demonstrate the complexity and the importance of representation.

A brief visit to a mathematics classroom quickly reminds us that abstract symbols are a part of mathematics and mathematics instruction. At the very earliest grade levels students use written number symbols to represent "how many." These numerals are an example of an external representation, an external representation considerably more abstract than using a collection of base-ten blocks to represent the same quantity. If we consider just base-ten blocks and written numerals, we can begin to understand the complexity of learning tasks that involve manipulatives and symbol representations. The student here must develop connections between the base-ten blocks and the written symbols. These relationships include those between internal representations of numerals and materials, between the external representations of the numerals and materials, and between the internal representations and the external representations. Failure to attend to any one of the three can cause learning problems in the long run, as students create isolated information. An example may clarify the point.

Many students learn to externally manipulate written numerals in an addition exercise like 24 + 37 using base-ten blocks to determine and record the correct sum of 61. The extent to which this external activity is linked in a meaningful way to existing internal representations involving the blocks, numbers, and quantitative notions is often questioned by mathematics educators trying to find causes for learning difficulties that appear later, when the student is trying to learn a related process (36 − 19) or to solve a real-life word problem. Without the internal connections between representations and the connections between the internal and the external representations, long-term learning is impaired. Encouraging a child to use an external representation unrelated to her internal representation may lead only to confusion or rote memorization. This suggests that expecting all children to use the same external representation in a learning situation may be problematic. Ignoring any of these relationships between representations, by failing to carefully develop them in instruction, can result in learning that appears successful on the surface but is destined for problems in the future. Of course, some of these difficulties may arise quickly and, as such, account for some of the uneven results from studies of the effects of manipulative materials.

The third and final factor in our consideration of manipulative materials is the learning context. Previously, we emphasized the many advantages that can accrue when social interaction between teacher and student and among students is prominent in a mathematics learning situation. This interaction is affected by and related to the instructional use of manipulative materials. The social interaction is affected by the presence and use of materials because they provide a common referent for discussion. Materials, for example, can be an especially helpful means of explaining one's solution to a problem. Given the current emphasis on examining multiple problem solutions, an important reason for using materials to help explain one's thinking is not only to convey one's thinking clearly in a way likely to be successful but to make it easier to compare the solution to a different one that has also been explained using the same materials. Social interaction also is related to the meaningful use of manipulatives, because it can call attention to the salient features of the material and promote disregarding those features irrelevant to the materials use in representing the mathematical situation. For example, when an abacus is being used, the importance of the position of the rod that represents hundreds can come out in discussion, as can the fact that the color of the disk used to record a value on an abacus is immaterial. Similarly with colored chips, the importance of color is brought to the foreground through interaction and the relative position of the chips is relegated to the background because it does not affect the value represented. Social interaction can also help establish the relationships among internal and external representations, and thus the effects of social interaction on the effective use of manipulatives can be both direct and indirect. Children, for example, will choose different external representations based on who they are interacting with and on their interpretation of what the other children know (Ansell, 1995; Carpenter, Fennema, & Franke, in press).

In summary, we have shown that the selection and use of manipulative materials can be guided by central ideas from cognitive science. In particular, connections, representation, and social interaction are some of the ideas that seem to hold special importance. Although our understanding of the relationships between these ideas and the use of manipulative materials in mathematics instruction is still emerging, careful reflection on the relationships, as instructional decisions are being made, will result in improved teaching practice and increased student learning.

Technological Tools

Both the variety and the frequency of use of technological tools in mathematics teaching is increasing. Many teachers use videotapes, calculators, computer software, CD-ROMs, and videodiscs as part of their mathematics lessons. More recently, the use of technology in teaching has expanded to include having students exchange electronic mail messages to discuss problem solutions, use the Internet to gather realistic data for problem posing and problem solving, and use quick-take cameras to capture geometric ideas in real-world settings. It is beyond the scope of this chapter to discuss each of these tools and its use individually. For example, the value of using calculators to enhance student learning has been discussed regularly (e.g., Grouws, 1995) and, therefore, will not be discussed here. Nevertheless, it is helpful to examine connections between technological tools and cognitive science in general to illustrate relationships between them and to provide a basis for further thought about instructional decisions and curriculum development.

The use of computer software can help students develop skills in a mathematical context. The importance of skills such as the ability to sense a pattern, to organize one's thinking, to communicate one's thinking, and to represent ideas and data are advocated in mathematics curriculum recommendations such as the NCTM Standards (NCTM, 1989) and in educational psychology textbooks (Woolfolk, 1995). The development of each of these skills can be aided by technology, and the resulting learning can be partially explained by cognitive psychology.

Patterns are at the heart of mathematics (Dossey, 1992; Steen, 1988), and therefore the ability to recognize them is essential and should be a central objective in every mathematics classroom. Cognitive science suggests that working with patterns in a variety of perceptually and conceptually different settings develops the ability to identify new patterns. This use of variation promotes the development of a broad network of connections among the patterns explored by the learner. When a new pattern is examined, the features embedded in it are linked in some way to the student's existing cognitive network and thus a new pattern is identified. The pattern is also tied into the existing cognitive framework. Software can be a useful instructional tool in helping children develop the foundation network needed for the additional learning of patterns to take place. For example, some commercial software packages (e.g., King's Rule®, O'Brian, 1995) provide contexts for students to identify numerical patterns at a variety of levels of complexity. These programs center on providing a number of examples of a pattern in the form of a list, letting students make a conjecture as to the pattern, and then having students test their conjecture by suggesting additional examples that fit the pattern. The computer provides feedback and also assessment tasks. In other software programs (e.g., *Tesselmania*, 1994), students can construct geometric shapes that tile the plane and then, on command, the computer displays the resulting tessellation. This type of program provides experience with a wide array of geometric patterns. Finally, general tool programs, such as a spreadsheet (e.g., *Microsoft Works*, 1992), can be used to develop pattern recognition. Spreadsheets, by design, lend themselves to constructing new rows or columns of data based on functions that operate on existing rows or columns of numeric or alphabetic data. Thus, this software can be used by teachers to generate a wide variety of data patterns and activities where students develop skills in detecting patterns. We can see that, within just a small number of software programs, students can gain valuable experience with a wide variety of patterns, including patterns in perceptually different settings such as spreadsheets and lists, and in a variety of conceptually different settings, such as geometric and numerical contexts.

Representation of data and ideas is central to the discipline of mathematics (Janvier, 1987) and the use of mathematics in the real world. Therefore, in different forms and at different levels of complexity, the development of representation skills should be a part of the mathematics curriculum at every grade level. At the elementary school level, students should summarize basic fact knowledge in the form of charts, record data they collect in tables, display information using bar and line graphs, and write their predictions and conclusions from activities using prose and number sentences. Computer software exists that facilitates students making graphs (e.g., *Graphers*; Edwards, 1994), recording data they collect from simulations (e.g., *Puzzle Tanks*; O'Brian, 1988), displaying information they collect in table and graph form (e.g., *Microsoft Works*, 1992), communicating their ideas through words and simple equations by use of any standard word processing package, and developing many other representational skills.

How information is represented mentally and the ease with which an individual can move from one representational form to another (e.g., from a table to a graph) is a cornerstone to understanding how meaningful learning takes place and how what is learned can be transferred to new situations. As such, representation is a key component of cognitive science and the related research on teaching and learning. Most cognitive scientists emphasize the importance of not only representations but the ability to move easily back and forth between representations. In mathematics at the elementary school level, for example, this involves the ability to move between a number sentence (simple equation), a table of related values, and a graph of the relationship. The teaching implication here is that all three modes of representation are important, as is the relationship among them. Software designed to develop these modes of representation and foster the ability to move between them is being developed (see, for example, Kaput, 1992) and these kinds of software packages should be very valuable tools in teaching these important ideas.

In summary, many skills that are deemed important in mathematics, including pattern recognition and representation, are also important components of cognitive psychology. There are opportunities to develop these skills within the mathematics curriculum at the elementary school level. The development of these skills and many others can be facilitated by the use of technological tools. Thus, the relationship between cognitive science, curriculum, and instruction is a closely knit one that bears attention as we seek to improve student learning in mathematics.

Curriculum Use and Selection

Curriculum has always been a significant issue in teaching and learning mathematics. Significant because most teachers use a formal mathematics curriculum, usually a textbook. Yet, until recently, textbooks have changed little to become consistent with a cognitive science view of the development of understanding. In the not too distant past, elementary school mathematics textbooks contained mostly exercises aimed at drill and practice, with many exercises on a page and few problems developed in a context children might understand. Currently, publishers of mathematics textbooks and other curricula materials, as well as research projects, are developing materials consistent with a cognitive science view of learning and teaching. Our intent here is not to review these curricula but rather to focus on how cognitive science can direct the use and selection of curriculum materials.

Curriculum Use

In thinking about developing understanding in relation to the use of curricular materials, what is critical is that the curriculum the teacher chooses becomes a tool. The teacher uses the curriculum as a tool to provide opportunity for her students to build mathematical understanding. The focus is on how teachers use the curriculum. We know perfect curricula do not exist. The curriculum must be interpreted and implemented by the teacher. Thus, how the materials get used, no matter how structured the curricula, depends on the knowledge and perspectives through which a given teacher filters the information. Two teachers with different knowledge and beliefs can take the same curriculum materials and use them in very different ways. So, using a curriculum to develop understanding from a cognitive science point of view requires that the teacher think about her students, what they know and understand (culturally, socially, and academically), and then decide what experiences her students need. The curriculum plays two roles in this scenario. First the curriculum materials can serve as a tool for helping the teacher think about where the students could be going with their thinking, not just in terms of scope and sequence but in terms of the development of children's mathematical thinking. The second way the curricula can act as a tool is by providing activities and problems that the teacher might use with her students once she has decided what concepts she wants her students to engage. For instance, rather than following the sequence of the textbook, the teacher finds that many of her students are developing an understanding of operating on groups of items, so she skips to the section in her book that deal with multiplication and division. She then looks at what the curriculum materials have to offer and decides if they are appropriate for her children, both in terms of the content being addressed and the contexts available, and then she decides what she will use and not use. Here the teacher is allowing children's thinking to drive her decisions about the curriculum instead of allowing the curriculum materials to drive those decisions. This becomes critical if our intent is to create opportunity for students to make connections; fewer opportunities will exist if the teacher does not take into account the children's mathematical thinking.

Textbooks, both past and present, contain many activities or tasks that focus on developing speed and accuracy. These goals are not necessarily consistent with building understanding, so the opportunity provided will not necessarily allow for listening to students, discussing multiple solutions, or integrating technology. This does not mean that the materials cannot be used; however, the teacher would need to find ways for the children to connect their practice of the mathematical idea to conceptions of what underlies what they are practicing, so they create a more intricate web of connections. A child who is completing a page of addition problems with numbers below 20 should be able to connect this to real-life experiences where she might use adding numbers this size, that the adding symbol means putting together, joining, or combining, and so on. Speed and accuracy that will stay with children and be used over and over throughout their lives needs to be connected to other aspects of the children's mathematical knowledge.

Curriculum Selection

When choosing materials for students, teachers search for those that will enable them to teach mathematics in the ways that match their preferred methods. Adopting a view of mathematics learning that includes developing understanding based on a cognitive paradigm requires rethinking about the materials to be used in the classroom. Choosing a curriculum based on the theories and research put forth in this chapter requires revisiting our earlier discussions on the implications from cognitive science for teaching: listening to children, fostering classroom communication, understanding children's backgrounds, deciding which problems to pose, and using teaching tools.

The teacher must first decide whether the curriculum she has chosen adequately allows her to accomplish goals related to building children's mathematical understanding. For instance, does the curriculum provide opportunities for the teacher to have the children discuss their thinking with their classmates? Does the curriculum include problems that lend themselves to multiple solutions or problems that build on one another in a manner consistent with the development of children's thinking? Do the suggested activities allow the teacher to easily determine the children's prior knowledge? Are teaching tools appropriately integrated into the curriculum?

Many available curricula do not meet the criteria just described; however, this may be asking the impossible. It may be that the teacher will always have to select from a set of imperfect curricula and then create and use it in ways that connect with her students. Because the focus of many of the activities in past curricula were teacher centered or directed and emphasized speed and accuracy, a teacher would have to make major adjustments in the curriculum to build understanding and incorporate things like communication and showing solutions previously mentioned. For instance, a teacher might take a page of exercises related to the multiplication facts (given that she felt the children had a basic understanding of multiplication) and have the children circle the exercises for which they know the fact at a recall level, without solving them. The teacher might then have them solve exercises that involve factors that are "one more" or "one less" than one of the exercises circled. So a child who knows 7×7 would then solve 7×8, using what she knows about 7×7. Or the teacher may use the same page to build a deeper understanding of multiplication by having the children write word problems for three of the number sentences on the page. In both modifications the children are connecting what they already know with something new.

Some curriculum may provide more guidance and support for the teacher than others. Some curriculum may help teachers by providing information related to building and understanding children's thinking, and some may help teachers decide what activities and problems to use. But for the foreseeable future, teachers will need to take the lead in creating an environment conducive to building understanding. Here, the curriculum becomes another tool for the teacher, a tool that must often be modified and adjusted to accomplish desired goals.

CONCLUSIONS

Within this chapter we provided a way of thinking about the teaching and learning of mathematics from a cognitive science perspective. One of the most critical aspects of this perspective is that theories of cognitive science raise issues for thinking about learning and teaching, yet provide no single view. The characterization of understanding put forth is based on a mental model view of cognitive science; however, this must be interpreted within the sociocultural perspective. This combination of perspectives creates the opportunity to focus on the individual, with the goal being to learn how that individual thinks about mathematics, yet to always keep in mind that the individual cannot be understood outside her social context. The students with whom an individual interacts, the knowledge the individual and the other students bring in relation to one another, the cultures of the students and their previous experiences affect the individual learner and our interpretation of that learning. Although this may sound challenging for the teacher in a classroom of 30 or more students, research in both cognitive science and mathematics education provides information that can facilitate the teachers' learning about their students and then provide support as teachers make decisions about what they have learned. Together, perspectives of cognitive science and mathematics education have created a view of understanding with direct implications for learning and teaching. Tools are available for gaining access to student thinking, in terms of both what it means to elicit thinking and communicate about it and for understanding how a child's thinking fits into a broader developmental progression of children's domain-specific mathematical thinking. The challenge remains for teachers to continue to develop specifics of practice based on such perspectives.

References

Ansell, E. (1995). *Understanding children's strategy use as classroom activity*. Unpublished doctoral dissertation, University of Wisconsin-Madison.

Baker, S. (1994). *The development of children's fraction thinking in a first grade classroom*. Unpublished doctoral dissertation, University of Wisconsin-Madison.

Ball, D. L. (1990). Prospective elementary and secondary teachers' understanding of division. *Journal for Research in Mathematics Education*, 21, 132–144.

Bennett, T. R. (1995). *Developing an understanding of fractions: An investigative study of student's thinking and cognitive development*. Unpublished doctoral dissertation, University of California, Los Angeles.

Briars, D. J., & Larkin, J. (1984). Ann integrated model of skill in solving elementary word problems. *Cognition and Instruction*, 1, 245–296.

Brown, J. S., Collins, A., & Duguid, P. (1989). Situated cognition and the culture of learning. *Educational Researcher*, 18(1), 32–42.

Brownell, W. A. (1935). Psychological considerations in the learning and teaching of arithmetic. In W. D. Reeve (Ed.), *The teaching of arithmetic. Tenth Yearbook of the National Council of Teachers of Mathematics* (pp. 1–31). New York: Columbia University, Teachers College.

Calfee, R. (1981). Cognitive psychology and educational practice. *Review of Research in Education*, 9, 3–73.

Carpenter, T. P. (1985). Learning to add and subtract: An exercise in problem solving. In E. A. Silver (Ed.), *Teaching and learning mathematics problem solving: Multiple research perspectives* (pp. 17–40). Hillsdale, NJ: Erlbaum.

Carpenter, T. P., Ansell, E., Levi, L., Franke, M. L., & Fennema, E. (1995, April). *The development of multidigit addition and subtraction in two first grade classes*. Paper presented at the annual meeting of the American Educational Research Association, San Francisco.

Carpenter, T. P., Ansell, E., Franke, M. L., Weisbeck, L., & Fennema, E. (1993). A study of kindergarten children's problem-solving processes. *Journal for Research in Mathematics Education*, 24, 428–441.

Carpenter, T. P., Carey, D. A., & Kouba, V. (1990). A problem solving approach to the operations. In J. Payne (Ed.), *Mathematics for the young child* (pp. 111–132). Reston, VA: National Council of Teachers of Mathematics.

Carpenter, T. P., Fennema, E., & Franke, M. L. (in press). Cognitively guided instruction: A knowledge base for reform in primary mathematics instruction. *Elementary School Journal*.

Carpenter, T. P., & Moser, J. M. (1982). The development of addition and subtraction skills. In T. P. Carpenter, J. M. Moser & T. A. Romberg (Eds.), *Addition and subtraction: A cognitive perspective* (pp. 9–24). Hillsdale, NJ: Erlbaum.

Carraher, T. N., Carraher, D. W., & Schliemann, A. D. (1985). Mathematics in the streets and in schools. *British Journal of Developmental Psychology*, 3, 21–29.

Chi, M. T. H., Glaser, R., & Rees, E. (1982). Expertise in problem solving. In R. J. Sternberg (Ed.), *Advances in the psychology of human Intelligence* (pp. 7–75). Hillsdale, NJ: Erlbaum.

Cobb, P. (1994). Where is the mind? Constructivist and sociocultural perspectives on mathematical development. *Educational Researcher*, 23(7), 13–20.

Dossey, J. (1992). The nature of mathematics: Its role and influence. In D. A. Grouws (Ed.), *Handbook of research on mathematics teaching and learning* (pp. 39–48). New York: Macmillan.

Fennema, E. (1972). Models and mathematics. *Arithmetic Teacher*, 18, 635–640.

Fennema, E., Carpenter, T. P., Franke, M. L., & Carey, D. A. (1992). Learning to use children's mathematical thinking: A case study. In R. Davis & C. Mather (Eds.), *Schools, mathematics, and the world of reality* (pp. 93–117). Needham Heights, MA: Allyn & Bacon.

Fennema, E., Carpenter, T. P., Franke, M. L., Levi, L. Jacobs, V. R., & Empson, S. B. (in press). Mathematics instruction and teachers; beliefs: A longitudinal study of using children's thinking. *Journal for Research in Mathematics Education*.

Franke, M. L., Fennema, E., Carpenter, T. P., Ansell, E., & Behrend, J. (1996). *Understanding teachers' self-sustaining change in the context of elementary school mathematics*. Manuscript submitted for publication.

Fuson, K. C. (1990). Conceptual structures for militant numbers: Implications for learning and teaching multidigit addition, subtraction, and place value. *Cognition and Instruction*, 7, 343–403.

Fuson, K. C. (1992). Research on whole number addition and subtraction. In D. Grouws (Ed.), *Handbook of research on mathematics teaching and learning* (pp. 243–275). New York: Macmillan.

Fuson, K. C., & Briars, D. J. (1990). Using a base-ten blocks learning/teaching approach for first- and second-grade place-value and multidigit addition and subtraction. *Journal for Research in Mathematics Education, 21*, 80–206.

Fuson, K. C., Wearne, D., Hiebert, J., Human, P., Murray, H., Olivier, A., Carpenter, T. P., & Fennema, E. (1994, April). *Children's conceptual structures for multiunit numbers at work in addition and subtraction*. Paper presented at the annual meeting of the American Educational Association, New Orleans, LA.

Gardner, H. (1985). *The mind's new science*. New York: Basic Books.

Gelman, R., & Gallistel, C. R. (1978). *The child's understanding of number.* Cambridge, MA: Harvard University Press.

Greeno, J. G. (1988). *Situations, mental models, and generative knowledge* (Rep. No. IRL 88-0005). Palo Alto, CA: Institute for Research on Learning.

Greeno, J. G. (1991). Number sense as situated knowing in a conceptual domain. *Journal for Research in Mathematics Education, 22*, 170–218.

Greer, B. (1992). Multiplication and division as models of situations. In D. Grouws (Ed.), *Handbook of research on mathematics teaching and learning* (pp. 276–296). New York: Macmillan.

Grouws, D. A. (1995). Mathematics. In G. Cawelti (Ed.), *Handbook of research on improving student achievement* (pp. 97–110). Arlington, VA: Educational Research Service.

Hiebert, J., & Carpenter, T. P. (1992). Learning mathematics with understanding. In D. Grouws (Ed.), *Handbook of research on mathematics teaching and learning* (pp. 65–97). New York: Macmillan.

Hiebert, J., Carpenter, T. P., Fennema, E., Fuson, K., Wearne, D., Murray, H., Olivier, A., & Human, P. (in press). *Designing classrooms for learning mathematics with understanding.* Portsmouth, NH: Heinemann.

Hiebert, J., & Wearne, D. (1992). Links between teaching and learning place value with understanding in first grade. *Journal for Research in Mathematics Education, 22*, 98–122.

Hiebert, J., Wearne, D., & Taber, S. (1991). Fourth graders gradual construction of decimal fractions during instruction using different physical representations. *Elementary School Journal, 91*, 321–341.

Janvier, C. (1987). Representation and understanding: The notion of function as an example. In C. Janvier (Ed.), *Problems of representation in the teaching and learning of mathematics* (pp. 67–72). Hillsdale, NJ: Erlbaum.

Kamii, C., & Joseph, L. (1988). Teaching place value and double column addition. *Arithmetic Teacher, 35*(6), 48–52.

Kaput, J. (1992). Technology in mathematics education. In D. A. Grouws (Ed.), *Handbook of research on mathematics teaching and learning* (pp. 515–556). New York: Macmillan.

Kouba, V. (1989). Children's solution for equivalent set multiplication and division problems. *Journal for Research in Mathematics Education, 20*, 147–158.

Labinowicz, E. 1985. *Learning from students: New beginnings for teaching numerical thinking.* Menlo Park, CA: Addison-Wesley.

Lave, J. (1988). *Cognition in practice: Mind, mathematics and culture in everyday life.* Cambridge, England: Cambridge University Press.

Lave, J., & Wenger, E. (1991). *Situated learning: Legitimate peripheral participation.* Cambridge, England: Cambridge University Press.

Mack, N. K. (1990). Learning fractions with understanding: Building on informal knowledge. *Journal for Research in Mathematics Education, 21*, 16–32.

Microsoft Works. (1992). [Computer software]. Everet, WA: Microsoft Corporation.

Miller, G. A., Galanter, E., & Pribram, K. (1960). *Plans and the structure of behavior.* New York: Holt, Rinehart & Winston.

National Council of Teachers of Mathematics (NCTM). (1989). *Curriculum and evaluation standards for school mathematics.* Reston, VA: Author.

National Council of Teachers of Mathematics (NCTM). (1991). *Professional standards for teaching mathematics.* Reston, VA: Author.

Newell, A., & Simon, H. (1972). *Human problem solving*. Englewood Cliff, NJ: Prentice-Hall.

Nolan, J. D. (1973). Conceptual and rote learning in children. *Teachers College Record*, 75, 251–258.

O'Brian, T. C. (1988). *Puzzle Tanks* [Software]. Pleasantville, NY: Sunburst Communications.

O'Brian, T. C. (1995). *King's Rule: Mathematics and discovery* [Software]. Pleasantville, NY: Sunburst Communications.

Piaget, J. (1954). *The construction of reality in the child*. New York: Basic Books.

Piaget, J. (1973). *To understand is to invent*. New York: Grossman.

Polya, G. (1957). *How to solve it* (2nd ed.). New York: Grossman.

Posner, M. I. (Ed.). (1989). *Foundations of cognitive science*. Cambridge, MA: MIT Press.

Post, T. P. R., Harel, G., Behr, M. J., & Lesh, R. (1991). Intermediate teachers' knowledge of rational number concepts. In E. Fennema, T. P. Carpenter, & S. J. Lamon (Eds.), *Integrating research on teaching and learning mathematics* (pp. 177–198). Albany: State University of New York Press.

Resnick, L. B. (1982). Syntax and semantics in learning to subtract. In T. P. Carpenter, J. Moser, & T. A. Romberg (Eds.), *Learning to add and subtract: A cognitive perspective* (pp. 136–155). Hillsdale, NJ: Erlbaum.

Resnick, L. B., & Ford, W. W. (1981). *The psychology of mathematics for instruction*. Hillsdale, NJ: Erlbaum.

Resnick, L. B., & Omanson, S. F. (1987). Learning to understand arithmetic. In R. Glaser (Ed.), *Advances in instructional psychology* (Vol. 3, pp. 41–95). Hillsdale, NJ: Erlbaum.

Riley, M. S., Greeno, J. G., & Heller, J. I. (1983). Development of children's problem solving ability in arithmetic. In H. P. Ginsburg (Ed.), *The development of mathematical thinking* (pp. 153–196). New York: Academic Press.

Rumelhart, D. E. & Norman, D. A. (1978). Accretion, tuning and restructuring: Three modes of learning. In J. W. Cotton & R. Klatzky (Eds.) *Semantic factors in cognition*. Hillsdale, NJ: Erlbaum.

Saxe, G. B. (1991). *Culture and cognitive development: Studies in mathematical understanding*. Hillsdale, NJ: Erlbaum.

Schneider, W., & Shiffrin, R. M. (1977). Controlled and automatic information processing: I. Detection, search, and attention. *Psychological Review*, 84, 1–66.

Schoenfeld, A. H. (1987). Cognitive science and mathematics education: Overview. In A. H. Schoenfeld (Ed.), *Cognitive science and mathematics education* (pp. 1–31). Hillsdale, NJ: Erlbaum.

Sowell, E. J. (1989). Effects of manipulative materials in mathematics instruction. *Journal for Research in Mathematics Education*, 20, 498–505.

Steen, L. A. (1988). The science of patterns. *Science*, 240, 611–616.

Steffe, L. P., & Cobb, P. (1988). *Construction of arithmetical meanings and strategies*. New York: Springer-Verlag.

Steffe, L. P., Cobb, P., & von Glasersfeld, E. (1988). *Construction of arithmetical meanings and strategies*. New York: Springer-Verlag.

Steffe, L. P., von Glasersfeld, E., Richards, J., & Cobb, P. (1983). *Children's counting types: Philosophy, theory, and application*. New York: Praeger.

Streefland, L. (1993). Fractions: A realistic approach. In T. P. Carpenter, E. Fennema, & T. Romberg (Eds.), *Rational numbers: An integration of research* (pp. 289–326). Hillsdale, NJ: Erlbaum.

Suydam, M. N., & Higgins, J. L. (1977). *Activity-based learning in elementary school mathematics: Recommendations from research*. Columbus, OH: ERIC Center for Science, Mathematics, and Environmental Education.

Tesselmania. (1994). [Software]. Minneapolis: Minnesota Educational Computing Corporation.

Thompson, P. W. (1992). Notations, conventions, and constraints: Contributions of effective uses of concrete materials in elementary mathematics. *Journal for Research in Mathematics Education*, 20, 123–147.

Tirosh, D., & Graeber, A. O. (1990). Evoking cognitive conflict to explore preservice teacher's thinking about division. *Journal for Research in Mathematics Education*, 21, 98–108.

von Glasersfeld, E. (1984). An introduction to radical constructivism. In P. Watzlawick (Ed.), *The invented reality* (pp. 17–40). New York: Norton.

von Glasersfeld, E. (in press). Sensory experience, abstraction, and teaching. In L. P. Steffe (Ed.), *Constructivism in education*. Hillsdale, NJ: Erlbaum.

Vygotsky, L. S. (1978). *Mind and society: The development of higher psychological processes*. Cambridge, MA: Harvard University Press.

Woolfolk, A. E. (1995). *Educational psychology*. Needham Heights, MA: Allyn & Bacon.

CHAPTER

11

Mathematics (Grades 7–12)

STEVEN R. WILLIAMS
Brigham Young University

INTRODUCTION

I have approached the writing of this chapter mindful of a metaphor borrowed from Bernard Forscher (1963) by way of Begle and Gibb (1980). In this metaphor, scholars are thought of as builders, and the edifices they build are explanations or understandings. Research consists mostly of constructing these edifices, paying attention both to the buildings themselves and to the stuff of which buildings are made, the individual bricks, or "facts." Researchers give systematic care to both the gathering of individual facts and the building of understanding. Unfortunately, as Begle and Gibb warn us, scholarly work can sometimes focus too narrowly on the individual bricks, without paying enough attention to the buildings.

In this case, the building I wish to construct is an understanding of how outstanding secondary mathematics classrooms work and how to encourage their development. I am interested primarily in assisting efforts to improve student learning in secondary mathematics classrooms and not so much in transmitting the results of individual studies of learning algebra or geometry as offering a lens by which to view both the purposes and processes of these classrooms. In doing so, I hope to avoid the mistake of concentrating on individual bricks at the expense of the buildings themselves. Excellent reviews of the literature are readily available (Grouws, 1992; Putnam, Lampert, & Peterson, 1990; Wagner & Kieran, 1989, are some starting points), so this chapter will not exhaustively review the research literature. Instead, I hope to bring to light a few of the major issues that drive the current reform movement, and suggest directions for implementing reforms in classrooms.

Handbook of Academic Learning

Three complementary movements in mathematics education have informed the writing of this chapter: (1) emerging views of what mathematics is, (2) the movement toward constructivism as a framework for explaining teaching and learning in mathematics, and (3) the reform movement in mathematics education as represented by the three documents, the *Curriculum and Evaluation Standards for School Mathematics* (National Council of Teachers of Mathematics [NCTM], 1989), the *Professional Standards for Teaching Mathematics* (NCTM, 1991), and the *Assessment Standards for School Mathematics* (NCTM, 1995), known in what follows as the *Curriculum Standards*, the *Teaching Standards*, and the *Assessment Standards*, respectively. Drawing on these movements, I begin with a critical look at both traditional and newly emerging views of mathematics, and what they imply for teaching and learning in the secondary mathematics classroom. Next, I review constructivist thought as interpreted in the scholarly literature of mathematics education, providing brief descriptions of several complementary branches of the constructivist family tree. I then elaborate on how views of mathematics and constructivist theory relate to the reform movement and how all three combine to suggest specific instructional practices. I next provide a few examples of blueprints for success—studies of student learning and classroom life that illustrate constructivist principles in the spirit of the reform movement. Finally, I provide some cautionary tales of reform and summary comments.

A NEW LOOK AT MATHEMATICS

Beginning a discussion of teaching and learning mathematics from within mathematical philosophy might seem to be a largely academic exercise, especially to those interested primarily in improving instruction. Increasingly, however, it is recognized that the nature of mathematics itself is a fundamental issue affecting teaching and learning. Any serious discussion of students' construction of mathematical knowledge must address what it means to know mathematics, and all scholarly work that attempts to address students learning mathematics must make assumptions about this issue, whether or not they are made explicit. As Reuben Hersh reminds us, "Ideas have consequences. One's conception of what mathematics *is* affects one's conception of how it should be presented. One's manner of presenting it is an indication of what one believes to be most essential in it" (1986, p. 13). In this passage, Hersh was pointing out the plausibility of a connection between a formalist philosophy of mathematics and the formal expository style prevalent in mathematics journals. However, the point is equally well taken as it applies to pedagogical exposition. One's beliefs about what mathematics is, about what is essential to mathematics, must certainly be reflected in pegadogical choices about what to teach and how to teach it (for a discussion of research on how teachers' knowledge and beliefs affect instruction, see Fennema & Franke, 1992; Thompson, 1992).

It is important to understand that this careful examination of beliefs about mathematics is more than an academic exercise. As an example, consider the discussions that take place in a school where any new approach to teaching mathematics is being attempted side by side with more traditional approaches.[1] Sides are taken quickly, and discussions about what can and cannot be done by students from the other course make their way into the workroom and sometimes into the classroom. Students and parents quickly become aware that something different is being taught. The debate that takes place is not really about whether students can perform a trigonometric substitution or a partial fraction decomposition, or perform three-digit by three-digit multiplications on paper. The argument is about what is basic to mathematical learning; whether, for example, conceptual understanding, in the face of altered procedural competence, should really "count" as legitimate mathematical knowledge. Beliefs about what counts as legitimate mathematical knowledge are based directly on views of what mathematics is all about.

Still, working mathematicians tend to ignore such philosophical issues, choosing instead to simply do mathematics. Cannot practicing teachers do the same? After all, we have fairly well-defined curricular responsibilities: algebra, geometry, trigonometry, calculus. Surely these can be taught, and taught well, without concern for philosophical foundations. Unfortunately, ignoring foundational beliefs does not mean adopting a neutral stance. Rather, it means that those beliefs go unexamined, and pedagogical possibilities become limited to what has always been done. If those who choose to ignore history are doomed to repeat it, those who choose not to examine their views of mathematics are doomed to replicate those views in their classrooms.

The Contrast between Knowing and Doing Mathematics

Work in mathematics education brings this issue into sharp focus. Welch (1978) describes typical instruction in mathematics classrooms two decades ago:

> In all math classes I visited, the sequence of activities was the same. First, answers were given for the previous day's assignment. The more difficult problems were worked by a teacher or a student at the chalkboard. A brief explanation, sometimes none at all, was given of the new material, and problems were assigned for the next day. The remainder of class was devoted to working on the homework while the teacher moved about the room answering questions. The most noticeable thing about math classes was the repetition of this routine. (p. 6).

[1] This can apply to almost any reform, from *new math*, through the use of calculators in elementary classrooms, right up to ongoing arguments in university mathematics departments about the value of "reform calculus."

Romberg and Carpenter (1986) point out that such routine is symptomatic of a belief that mathematics is a "static, bounded discipline" (p. 851), divorced from inquiry and largely divorced from reality. They go on to suggest that mathematics has been fragmented into concepts, facts, skills, and procedures, which are then arranged into courses, topics, and lessons, and that knowledge of these isolated facts and concepts has become a replacement for knowledge of how to *do* mathematics. Hence, knowledge of facts and procedures are valued, even though by themselves they may not provide students with the ability to deal mathematically with problems that they confront. This has been the case, with few exceptions, for the better part of a century (see Stanic, 1986, for a review of how our current mathematics curriculum has developed).

The *Curriculum Standards* (NCTM, 1989) argues that this view does justice neither to mathematics, nor to the idea of understanding mathematics:

> First, "knowing" mathematics is "doing" mathematics. A person gathers, discovers, or creates knowledge in the course of some activity having a purpose. This active process is different from mastering concepts and procedures. We do not assert that informational knowledge has no value, only that its value lies in the extent to which it is useful in the course of some purposeful activity. (p. 7)

Thus, the measure of students' mathematical understanding is their ability to engage in mathematical behavior, to have what the *Curriculum Standards* call *mathematical power*, "the ability to explore, conjecture, and reason logically, as well as the ability to use a variety of mathematical methods effectively to solve nonroutine problems" (NCTM, 1989, p. 5).

A starting point, then, is to focus on the doing of mathematics, as opposed to the learning of mathematics as a collection of distinct facts and procedures, to be applied at some future date. This leads directly to the question of what "doing" mathematics entails. It is here that modern philosophy of mathematics can be of use. The directions we explore in the philosophy of mathematics will lead us naturally to constructivism as a philosophy of learning.

Mathematics as Practice

Traditional philosophies of mathematics have in common a search for a *foundation* on which mathematics can be built. Doing mathematics has been seen, on the one hand, as discovering the truths of an immutable, rational, and consistent mathematical reality "out there" somewhere. This *Platonist* view explains why mathematics is useful (because it uncovers truth about the world) but traditionally has problems explaining how we gain access to these truths. On the other hand, mathematics has also been seen as essentially a mental game, using logic to arrive at mathematical results from agreed-on axioms with no necessary connection to the real world. This view avoids the problems of how humans gain access to mathematical truth (they create it), but has more problem explaining why mathematics is so useful in solving real-world problems. Of these two views, the second, *formalist* position has had the greater impact on school mathematics as we know it. It is exactly this formalist view of mathematics that Hersh (1986) discusses as undergirding secondary mathematics instruction. He makes a strong case that changes in classroom teaching depend on directly confronting the formalist viewpoint:

> The criticism of formalism in the high schools has been primarily on pedagogic grounds: "This is the wrong thing to teach, or the wrong way to teach." But all such arguments are inconclusive if they leave unquestioned the dogma that real mathematics is precisely formal derivations from formally stated axioms. . . . The real issue is not, What is the best way to teach? But, What is mathematics really all about? To discredit formalism in pedagogy, one must challenge its philosophical base. . . . Controversies about high school teaching cannot be resolved without confronting problems about the nature of mathematics. (p. 13)

Formalism is often supported by an implicit theory of mathematics learning, what Skovesmose (1993) has called a *monological* view. This view suggests that gaining knowledge is essentially an individual activity, involving one's senses; interaction with others is not a necessary feature of learning. Although Skovesmose does not see these two views as strictly compatible, both views have been used to justify much of traditional mathematics instruction: teachers impart formal rules and procedures to students, who are largely responsible for making sense of them (or just memorizing them) and being able to demonstrate individually that they can apply those procedures properly. Mathematics becomes memorizing rules and procedures and knowing when to apply them.

Various authors in philosophy, education, and sociology have recently outlined new approaches to the philosophy of mathematics (cf. Restivo, Van Bendegem, & Fischer, 1993; Tymoczko, 1986). These new approaches contrast with the more traditional views just outlined and have in common a concern for the social aspects of mathematics. These new philosophers of mathematics argue against a view of mathematics as a static, bounded discipline or as a body of canonized truths to be mastered. Rather, they emphasize the way in which mathematical knowledge is arrived at in practice: conjecture, discussion, justification, refutation, and modification, all in a social arena. In doing so, they argue for a *fallibilist* view of mathematics, giving up the search for a metaphysical foundation and suggesting that mathematical truth, like scientific truth, is subject to revision. Moreover, they insist that the production of knowledge is inherently social. As Restivo (1993) suggests, individual mathematicians do not create mathematics. Rather, *math worlds*—"networks of human being communicating in arenas of conflict and cooperation, domination and subordination" (p. 249)—actually create mathematics. Nicholas Goodman describes it this way:

> Mathematical truth, unlike a mathematical construction, is not something I can hope to find by introspection. It does not exist in my mind. A mathematical theory, like any other scientific theory, is a social product. It is created and developed by the dialectical interplay of many minds, not just one mind. . . . Each generation of mathematicians rethinks the mathematics of the previous generation, discarding what was faddish or superficial or false and recasting what is still fertile into new and sharper focus. (1986, p. 87)

Thus, mathematics is a human creation, developed to serve human ends, and modified as needed to meet those ends. This explains mathematics' usefulness in describing our world, and why mathematical truth needs to be judged not only formally, that is, from the point of view of logical consistency, but from empirical grounds as well.

Freudenthal (1987) supports this view when he calls for a *realistic* view of mathematics. He argues that

> mathematics, from both the historical and individual perspectives, starts in reality. Mathematical structures are not presented to the learner so that they might be filled with realities (or rather, pseudo-realities). They arise, instead, from reality itself, which is not a fixed datum, but expands continuously in man's individual and collective learning process. (p. 280)

This view of mathematics has served as a foundation for curriculum development in the Netherlands as well as the United States (Romberg *et al.*, 1993).

Summary

This brief introduction to modern philosophy of mathematics is not sufficient to describe a complete, consistent philosophy of mathematics. These emerging philosophies are in their infancy, and a good deal of work remains ahead. Nor has my treatment been exhaustive. Other reasonable and useful frameworks exist for discussing the nature of mathematical knowledge. My major intention is to bring to light the implied criticism of traditional views, particularly as they relate to learning and teaching school mathematics. Traditional mathematics instruction is based on views of mathematics that are increasingly untenable. This includes viewing mathematics (1) as something done long ago or far away, transmitted through teacher and text to students; (2) as involving formal rules requiring memorization and a good deal of individual mental work; and (3) as absolute and infallible, not open to debate, discussion, or modification. On the other hand, basing instruction on fallibilist views of mathematics underscores the importance of the social construction of mathematical knowledge and suggests that mathematics is best learned within a community of discourse and best viewed as a quasi-empirical science, subject to hypotheses, conjecture, refutation, and revision.

In any attempt to deal with mathematics learning, beliefs about what we are teaching are critical. Choosing not to teach traditional mathematics may have as profound an affect as choosing not to teach mathematics traditionally. As I will argue, beliefs about mathematics weave together with beliefs about learning to inform practice. To change practice requires a change in the mathematics we teach.

CONSTRUCTIVISM AND REFORM IN MATHEMATICS EDUCATION

A Brief Overview of Constructivist Thought in Mathematics Education

Constructivism in various forms has become what might be called the "state religion" of mathematics education. It would be very difficult to find a mathematics educator who did not claim to be a constructivist. This is not to say that all those who claim to be constructivists would agree on what constructivism is or even on how mathematics should be taught. A wide range of beliefs fall under the general label of *constructivism*, and it seems important to examine briefly these beliefs and what they mean for instruction.

Steffe and Kieren (1994) trace the roots of constructivism in mathematics education most directly to the work of Jean Piaget and the interpretation given his work by Ernst von Glasersfeld. Constructivism emerged in the context of efforts to account both for behaviorism's apparent failure and the epistemological problems of how knowledge of the outside world (e.g., mathematical structures) could be gained internally. Von Glasersfeld's is a two-pronged attack. He asserts that "a) knowledge is not passively received but actively built up by the cognizing subject; [and] b) the function of cognition is adaptive and serves the organization of the experiential world, not the discovery of ontological reality" (von Glasersfeld, 1989, p. 162). Those who accept both of these propositions are called *radical* constructivists, while those who accept only the first are called (by their radical siblings) *trivial* constructivists. Specifically, radical constructivists reject the flow of anything like "information" between a teacher and a student, insisting that "knowledge cannot be *transferred* to the student by linguistic communication," but instead "language can be used as a tool in a process of guiding the student's construction" (von Glasersfeld, 1989, p. 163). By way of analogy to evolutionary processes, radical constructivists suggest that cognitive structures are molded by testing their viability against the world. Therefore, they speak of a cognitive construction *fitting* with the world if it works well enough for the cognizing subject to achieve its goals. By contrast, they categorically deny any match between a cognitive construction and what it is supposed to represent. This contrast between a construction *fitting* the world, in the sense of providing a viable organization and predictive ability, and a construction *matching* some ontological reality, is central to radical constructivism. To quote von Glasersfeld (1983), "From an explorer who is condemned to seek 'structural properties' of an inaccessible reality, the experiencing organism now turns into a builder of cognitive structures intended to solve such problems as the organism perceives or conceives" (p. 50).

In many ways, trivial constructivism is less problematic and less controversial than radical constructivism. Probably the majority of those who say they are constructivists, or that their teaching is constructivist, have in mind the first of von Glasersfeld's two propositions but not necessarily the second. For many whose primary concern is day-to-day classroom life, the finer philosophical nuances of radical constructivism may not seem to matter.[2] Indeed, a wide range of beliefs that can be called *constructivist* take no hard stand on von Glasersfeld's second proposition. Lyddon and McLaughlin (1992) discuss four essentially different kinds of constructivist thought, two of which are radical constructivism and theories like Piaget's that depend on dialectic interplay between person and environment. In addition, they discuss two other constructivist schools of thought that have wide acceptance in the mathematics education community.

The first includes various cybernetic theories of cognition. Such theories typically assume the existence of some sort of mental representation of knowledge and equate understanding with the quality or integrity of these representations. In mathematics education, attempts to describe understanding have attended in large part to the organization of knowledge representations, and are hence constructivist in this sense. Heibert and Carpenter (1992) describe this viewpoint well:

> A mathematical idea or procedure or fact is understood if it is part of an internal network. More specifically, the mathematics is understood if its mental representation is part of a network of representations. The degree of understanding is determined by the number and the strength of the connections. (p. 67)

Understanding, then, is characterized by robust representations that are rich in connections. A good deal of work in mathematics education is done with this general view of understanding in mind.

Lyddon and McLaughlin's fourth general school of constructivism has also had broad acceptance in mathematics education, where it is usually called *social constructivism* (Ernst, 1991). The fundamental proposition underlying social constructivism is that knowledge is a product of social processes and not solely an individual construction. Lyddon and McLaughlin, for example, describe Gergen's (1985) social constructionist views as seeking "to place knowledge not exclusively in the minds of single individuals . . . or in the

[2] In fact, I agree with Slife and Williams (1995) that such philosophical issues do matter, indeed, that they have a real effect on practice. However, as Slife and Williams also suggest, this view is not universally accepted.

environment . . . but rather in the processes of social exchange and linguistic construction that set conceptual parameters on personal categories of understanding" (p. 95). From this view, social processes cannot be divorced from knowledge production.

It should be clear that social constructivism is in harmony with the fallibilist views of mathematics discussed earlier. Ernst (1991) makes these connections explicit, taking social constructivism as a philosophy of knowledge production in mathematics and suggesting that accounts of learning, teaching, and mathematical practice could be developed in parallel ways. As I will argue, social constructivism, both as a philosophy of learning and as a philosophy of knowledge production in mathematics, is compatible with much of the current reform movement in mathematics education.

Before leaving this brief overview of constructivism in mathematics education, it must be mentioned that I make no claims of exhaustive description. The works of Vygotsky (1962), the work in activity theory (Leont'ev, 1978), and the symbolic interactionist tradition (Mead, 1934; Mehan, 1979), to name just a few, all have strong similarities to various versions of constructivism. For the purposes of this chapter, however, it is enough to highlight the major trends.

Constructivism, Mathematics, and the Reform Movement

The reform movement in mathematics education, as represented by the *Standards* documents, resonates both with constructivist ideas and with emerging views of mathematics. As discussed previously, the *Curriculum Standards* (NCTM, 1989) focus on *doing* mathematics as the fundamental aspect of knowing mathematics. They also discuss at length the historical changes in mathematics that have taken place with the advent of computing technology. They call for more attention to mathematics as a way of quantifying problems in many disciplines, and suggest that "students need to experience genuine problems regularly" (p. 10). This supports both Freudenthal's focus on realistic mathematics and a view of mathematics as a tool to better understand and manage our world. Finally, the *Curriculum Standards* suggest that "individuals approach a new task with prior knowledge, assimilate new information, and construct their own meanings" (p. 10) and supports understanding as connected knowledge in the sense of Heibert and Carpenter (1992). Clearly, there is a strong constructivist undercurrent in reform.

Social constructivist ideas can also be seen in the reform documents. The Standards for Teaching, in *Professional Standards for Teaching Mathematics* (NCTM, 1991), for example, emphasize task selection and structuring mathematical discourse about those tasks as a major part of describing instructional practice. The document explores at length the teachers' role in discourse, the students' role in discourse, and ways of enhancing discourse. This focus on knowledge production though discourse (which includes questioning, conjecturing, and providing and evaluating evidence) is closely aligned with both the theories of mathematics we discussed earlier and social constructivist views of how mathematical understanding is produced.

Although constructivist theories and new views of mathematics are not the sole driving forces behind the reform movement, it seems clear that major threads from the recommendations of the reform documents, the basic tenets of constructivism, and the emerging views of mathematics all intertwine to produce a set of common recommendations for mathematics instruction. In the next few sections, I briefly discuss some of these recommendations.

Recommendations for Reform

Intellectual Authority

One issue that pervades reform efforts in mathematics education is the idea of intellectual authority; that is, who validates mathematical knowledge produced in the classroom. At one time, of course, this was exclusively the teachers' job and in some sense it still is. The teacher has the responsibility to guide knowledge production in useful ways. The *Teaching Standards* (NCTM, 1991) state it well:

> For the discourse to promote student learning, teachers must orchestrate it carefully. Because many more ideas will come up than are fruitful to pursue at the moment, teachers must filter and direct the students' explorations by picking up on some points and by leaving others behind. Doing this prevents student activity and talk from becoming too diffused and unfocused. . . . Beyond asking clarifying or provocative questions, teachers should also, at times, provide information and lead students. (p. 36)

To a much greater degree, however, the responsibility for validation of correct mathematics is being turned over to students or at least shared between teacher and students. Validation of mathematical reasoning is given by the community of scholars in which the construction is taking place, so that when a student provides an answer to a mathematical problem, the answer is not just checked by the teacher but subjected to questioning by the class. Reasoned explanation, justification, and argument are increasingly expected of students when they do mathematics. Not surprisingly, this parallels the process of knowledge production in mathematics as a discipline. Proofs are produced and subjected to the scrutiny of others in the field and decisions are made regarding their usefulness, appropriateness, generalizability, and so forth.

Rich Mathematical Tasks

Another aspect of reform teaching that seems closely linked to constructivist ideas is the importance of task selection. The *Teaching Standards* make it clear that the environment in which students work, the kinds of tasks they work on, should be chosen to facilitate students' construction of useful knowledge. Tasks must be chosen that are rich mathematically, and time must be given to explore the mathematics in those tasks. Discourse among students and teachers, as appropriate, can facilitate the exploration. In general, it is also assumed that sufficiently rich tasks facilitate connections between mathematical topics, and so lead to the building of more connected knowledge, in the sense that Heibert and Carpenter (1992) discuss.

A Focus on Student Understanding

A fundamental aspect of constructivist theory that applies to instruction is the importance of forming models of students' understanding. Confrey (1990) states:

> When one applies constructivism to the issue of teaching one must reject the assumption that one can simply pass on information to a set of learners and expect that understanding will result. Communication is a far more complex process than this. When teaching concepts, as a form of communication, the teacher must form an adequate model of the students' ways of viewing an idea and s/he then must assist the student in restructuring those views to be more adequate from the students' and from the teachers' perspective. (p. 109)

This is the core idea behind the constructivist teaching experiment, in which a teacher bases instructional decisions on his or her understanding of students' constructions. Knowledge of students' thinking becomes a critical factor in constructivist teaching of any kind.

The focus on student understand implies a need for teachers to gain reliable information on students' understandings as a basis for instructional decisions. Thus, constructivist teachers rely on a wide range of information, verbal and nonverbal, to assess students conceptions. To the extent that teachers can be provided with information on students' thinking, they can successfully use it to plan instruction (see Franke & Grouws, this volume; Carpenter, Fennema, Peterson, & Carey, 1988).

Balancing Conceptual and Procedural Knowledge

A final important aspect of the reform movement that seems tied to constructivist ideas is a concern for conceptual understanding as opposed to procedural knowledge. The epistemological question "What counts as mathematical knowledge?" has for some time been answered by mathematical formalists, who had a very strong affect on curriculum and practice. For example, Kleiner and Movshovitz-Hadar (1990) discuss how what we know as modern symbolic algebra grew out of a formalist philosophy of mathematics. Today, it is much more accepted that formalisms are of less importance than the ability to apply mathematics to real-world situations. Although the tensions between formalism and practicality have been present to some extent for decades (Kleibard, 1992; Kleiner & Movshovitz-Hadar, 1990; Stanic, 1986), it is now widely accepted that it is important for all students to make mathematical connections, not only between different areas of mathematics but between mathematics and areas of application. With this comes an emphasis on conceptual knowledge as opposed to procedural knowledge (Heibert & Lefevre, 1986).

Summary

The constructivist zeitgeist in mathematics education merges nicely with emerging philosophies of mathematics to support reform in mathematics classrooms. In general, the reform movement calls for classrooms in which students construct mathematical knowledge through engaging in rich mathematical tasks and discourse about those tasks. The teachers' role in these classrooms shifts from an authoritative dispenser of information to facilitator of discourse and construction, concerned with individual students' understanding. Finally, the focus shifts to students' conceptual understanding and away from disconnected procedural knowledge. In what follows, I examine a few examples of such classrooms and instructional practice commensurate with the reform movement.

A FEW EXEMPLARY STUDIES

A great deal of work at the elementary level has been done in support of these reform goals (see the chapter by Franke & Grouws, this volume). Much of the foundational work that helps us understand social construction of knowledge in mathematics seems to be taking place prior to the middle school years (Cobb, Wood, & Yackel, 1991; Lampert, 1990). Indeed, indications are that, although secondary school teachers claim to be well aware of the Standards documents, their use of pedagogical practices is much less aligned with the Standards than those of elementary school teachers (Weiss, Matti, & Smith 1994). Stories of reform in secondary classrooms have only begun to reach the literature. However, I can point to some studies that discuss the kinds of classes and instructional practices discussed here.

Healy's Build-a-Book Geometry

Healy (1993) reports on a high school geometry course he developed in 1987. The class used no textbook, but instead built their own geometry book by starting with three "given facts" (the only geometric knowledge ever provided by the teacher) and compiling "discovered truths," definitions, and so forth on which the class agreed. On the first day of class, students were randomly assigned to small groups. The groups were given sheets that contained only a statement at the top, one of three given facts: parallel lines never meet, a triangle contains 180 degrees, a linear pair contains 180 degrees. They were instructed to write on the sheets the comments of group members about the given statements. Following each class period, the teacher would read the comments of the groups, and choose some to be the statements for discussion on the next day. Over time, the statements emerging from the groups would be brought before the class, who would vote on whether they should be included in the geometry book.

When students had questions about the meaning of terms, groups would be given the task of coming up with a class definition for the terms. These were debated (sometimes hotly) among the whole class and, when consensus was achieved, became part of the class book. Students were allowed to use any sources they wished, provided they were able to explain and support what they found. They also used the Geometric Supposer (Schwartz & Yerushalmy, 1985–1988) software to test conjectures. Students were evaluated using questions from the geometry book they built, and the tests were corrected using definitions and discovered truths from the book.

Healy reports considerable success, including increased passing rates for geometry and increased student interest. He also notes that grades and SAT preparation were not sacrificed. However, the real story to be told is from the students themselves, and he offers several excerpts from students writing about the class. The students' reactions range from shock, disbelief, and anger at the first of the year to gradual acceptance and on to enjoyment at the end. As one student put it, "You actually have to use a part of your brain you don't use very often in school. The thinking part. The class questions and situations force you to think. . . . I love it. I love being forced to think." (p. 103).

The description of build-a-book geometry illustrates several of the aspects of constructivist theory discussed earlier. Most obviously, perhaps, it illustrates that individual students' mathematical knowledge can be constructed in a social arena, where ideas are subjected to public scrutiny. In this class, mathematical knowledge was (tautologically) social knowledge. Determining the usefulness of ideas, the validity of arguments, and the value of concepts, each involved social processes. This gave the students a different view of mathematics: "I think our book will be better (than other books) because ours was made by normal humans" (p. 104). Mathematics becomes something normal humans can do, rather than something only geniuses do (see Schoenfeld, 1989). It is not surprising that, in this context, several worthwhile goals beyond mathematical knowledge were achieved. Students learned a good deal about their own capabilities and to express themselves, as one student said, "keeping our personal feelings to ourselves."

A second aspect of social constructivist thought illustrated by Healy's course is the importance of teachers surrendering intellectual authority. Healy noted that it takes "from 1 to 3 months for the mystique surrounding the teacher to be minimized by the discoveries students make" (p. 87), during which time the teacher is unable to ask questions or participate in class activities. In this case, Healy is radically departing from his traditional role and giving responsibility for the class to the students. He concludes: "1. Students need to have ways of assuming authority and responsibility for their own learning. 2. If one permits students to exercise authority and responsibility, many of them learn to do so" (p. 104).

A Study of Four Extraordinary Mathematics Teachers

Phillip, Flores, Sowder, and Schappelle (1994) examined the background, mathematical knowledge, beliefs about mathematics and about teaching mathematics, and classroom practices of four extraordinary middle school teachers. The intent of the study was to find commonalities among excellent teachers to inform the professional development of other teachers. The authors' findings support the contention that the goals of the reform movement can be met in ordinary classrooms.

In general, the four teachers' content knowledge was linked to their pedagogical practice. That is, they tended to have deeper, more connected understanding of mathematical topics they had taught. The authors suggest that these teachers learned mathematics "with their students in mind" (p. 162) when they participated in graduate courses or inservice activities. The four teachers also had distinctive beliefs about mathematics, and about what it means to teach and to learn mathematics. All four seemed to reject mathematics as a collection of procedures, algorithms, or facts, in favor of a view of mathematics as a language or as a way of thinking. A vision of mathematics as sense making figured heavily in these teacher's conceptions; as one teacher put it, "My primary focus is understanding. I want those kids to know not just how to do it, but why it works" (p. 166).

In addition, the teachers were sensitive to individual differences in students' understanding. The authors concluded that "all four teachers appeared to approach this difficult task by presenting lessons that contained challenges for all levels of students" (p. 167). As one teacher put it,

> I try to be very, very conscious of the reality that all of these people in the room have an incredible variety of prior knowledge and experience, and they're all coming into this learning that I think I want to have happen at exactly the same time with this diversity. And, so what I try to really concentrate on is: Am I presenting this information in ways that allow multiple entry levels and allow accessibility by kids of all abilities? . . . And am I aware? How do I know? What do I do, and how do I know if kids are not getting it? (p. 168)

Finally, these four teachers had a common core of beliefs about the role of teachers and students in the mathematics classroom, particularly in relation to the idea of intellectual authority. The authors point out that all of the teachers saw themselves as facilitators, rather than as dispensers of information. They greatly downplayed the use of a textbook, using it mainly as an aid in thinking about the mathematical tasks they wanted to present. In addition, the teachers encouraged students to produce their own reasons for the correctness of mathematical propositions or answers in the class, rather than providing explanations of why the students were or were not correct.

A typical day in the classrooms of these teachers differed greatly from the description offered by Welch (1978) previously. Teachers tended to begin class with a problem or situation related to the previous lesson and used this to assess whether students were ready for more activities or needed more time on previously discussed topics. In general, lessons focused on activities, often group activities, that involved using appropriate manipulatives. Each lesson included time for students to write in journals. The authors noted an atmosphere of expectation that students "demonstrate, explain, and justify answers" (p. 175). Perhaps most descriptive is the following observation: "We did *not* observe any detailed teacher explanations, any work on exercise sets (individually or otherwise), any commitment to carefully follow the textbook, or any standard sequencing of classroom activities" (p. 175).

The practices and beliefs of the teachers in this study reflect many of the constructivist notions described earlier: concern for individual students' understanding and prior knowledge, a sharing of intellectual authority, a commitment to knowledge production as a social as well as an individual activity, a focus on mathematics as something to *do* rather than something to *know*. These teachers demonstrate that implementing desired reforms are possible. However, as the authors of the study point out, such reform is not possible without support. These teachers sought out support groups that allowed them time and opportunity to reflect on their practice; they, too, constructed knowledge of mathematics and mathematical pedagogy in the social context of a community of learners. Continued support of this kind seems critical for continued movement toward the goals of reform.

A Case Study from the QUASAR Project

A third example of a successful classroom comes from a report of the QUASAR project by Williams and Baxter (1996). This project, funded by the Ford Foundation and centered at the Learning Research and Development Center at the University of Pittsburgh, has as its goal the demonstration that it is "both feasible and responsible to implement instructional programs that foster the acquisition of mathematical thinking and reasoning skills by students attending middle schools in economically disadvantaged communities" (Silver & Lane, 1993, p. 12). The project selected schools in various cities and established a partnership between school personnel and resource partners from local colleges and universities. These partners worked together to develop and implement programs of instruction that addressed the particular needs of their students.

As part of their efforts, QUASAR project staff documented how classroom instruction occurred at each school (cf. Stein, Grover, & Silver, 1991). Project staff visited each school numerous times informally and made more formal documentation visits three times a year. Each documentation visit included videotaping and observation of three successive days in classrooms, as well as interviews with teachers, students, school personnel, and resource partners. These data provided the basis for Williams and Baxter's analysis.

As part of their analysis they describe a typical day in the classroom of one exceptional teacher they call Ms. H. It has much in common with the typical days in classrooms of the teachers in the Phillip et al. study:

> In a typical lesson Ms. H presented a problem from the curriculum on the overhead projector. Her problem presentation was usually lean, with little elaboration. Students then worked on the problem in small groups, using manipulatives and calculators as needed. They were encouraged to talk the problem over, share ideas and possible solution strategies, and explain their thinking to one another. Finally, the whole class discussed the problem, with several students going to the overhead projector and using it to explain their thinking with drawings or manipulatives. This sequence of problem presentation, small-group work and whole-class discussion was often repeated a number of times during a lesson. (p. 29)
>
> There was more student talk in this classroom than one would expect in a traditional mathematics classroom where the teacher is the center of conversation. In addition, we saw important developments in *what* students said. Ms. H's students contributed substantively to class discussions. Their responses to teacher questions were thoughtful and at times original, reflecting their efforts to understand mathematical ideas. In addition, students talked to each other in meaningful ways: They built on each other's ideas and questioned each other's thinking rather than merely supplying right answers. (p. 32)

As in the previous study, it is clear that intellectual authority became shared among members of the class. Students were expected to justify their work and to ask questions of other students. They were expected to explore and discuss numerous paths though the problem. They were expected and encouraged to make connections. A very strong sense was gleaned from both interviews with Ms. H and from observations of classroom practice of the importance of constructing understanding.

Williams and Baxter (1996) coined the term *discourse-oriented teaching* to describe the teaching they saw in Ms. H's classroom, although they contend that hers is a reasonable interpretation of the reform movement and of constructivist principles. Williams and Baxter noted that Ms. H spent a good deal of time discussing and modeling expected social behaviors, setting up the norms for mathematical discussions in class. They referred to this as building a *social scaffolding*, which helps students to direct their mathematical discourse in productive ways. With the social scaffolding in place, the hope was that student discussions about rich mathematical tasks would build an *analytic scaffolding* to support the construction of useful mathematical knowledge. Ms. H tended to spend a lot of time on social scaffolding, helping students learn to act as their own support when discussing mathematical ideas.

Summary

It seems safe to draw a few general conclusions from the examples just discussed. These generalization are my own, but I believe they are in keeping with the best knowledge we have of building successful constructivist classrooms at the secondary level.

1. Students' constructions are important, meaningful, and need to be taken seriously. Successful teachers are those who gather information on how their students think and use it as a basis for selection of mathematical tasks. In all three cases, teachers gathered information on a daily basis and used it to decide when to go on and how to select tasks.
2. Mathematical understanding can be constructed within a social context where teachers and students share responsibility for validating mathematical ideas and concepts. This provides students with a more reasonable view of the social nature of mathematical knowledge, and supports the belief that knowing mathematics involves their *doing* mathematics, including subjecting their mathematical ideas to public scrutiny.
3. Mathematically rich tasks that are designed to require time, effort, and exploration provide an excellent context for mathematical discussion, and hence knowledge production. This is contrasted with the traditional use of procedural exercises from textbooks or worksheets.
4. Teachers need the opportunity to reflect on their own understanding of mathematics, teaching, and learning. In all three cases discussed, the teachers reflected frequently on their own knowledge of mathematics, how to deal with specific mathematical concepts, their goals for instruction, and their practice. In the absence of such reflection, attempts to alter a classroom culture are extremely difficult. Moreover, making the changes discussed in the examples—leaving behind textbooks, withdrawing from traditional leadership roles in the classroom, focusing on individual understanding of students in a large class—can be an overwhelming burden. Without support, many of us will become discouraged and fall back on our traditional ways of doing things.

I feel about this list much as I feel about the list of activities my doctor provides to improve my general health (exercise, eat well, get rest, reduce stress). They are sensible, even commonsensible. They are backed by good scholarship. We have, in some sense, known for a long time that they were important. And they all seem curiously difficult to implement. I hope that a focus on the philosophies that guide these recommendations renders them more tractable, and worth the considerable effort it will take to implement them in practice.

SOME CAUTIONARY TALES

In this final section I consider some cautionary tales that come from attempts to change mathematics instruction and other aspects of classroom culture in ways consistent with the general constructivist philosophy of the reform movement. My purpose here is to alert those who attempt such changes to a few blockades that might be encountered so that they can be better prepared or, at least, know they are not alone.

Dilemmas of Discourse-Oriented Teaching

In the example from the QUASAR project, Williams and Baxter (1996) argued that real changes had taken place in Ms. H's classroom. However, they also note "trade-offs" involved in Ms. H's decisions to engage in discourse-oriented teaching. Classroom conversations showed genuine frustration by the students and the teacher. Williams and Baxter pointed out that Ms. H was a strong believer in her interpretation of constructivist theory: she believed she needed to take a hands-off, noninterventive role in her students' learning of mathematics. Through selections of good tasks from a reform-oriented curriculum, orchestrating the discourse, and setting expectations for what was expected in small-group and whole-class discourse among students, Ms. H believed that she was assisting students in building a scaffold for the creation of mathematical knowledge. Part of this scaffold was social and part was analytic, and the responsibility for building it was shared among the teacher, the student, and the curriculum and tasks. However, having set up this scaffold did not mean that the instruction always flowed smoothly to desired ends. Williams and Baxter focus on two kinds of situations in which problems arose.

Among the problems that Williams and Baxter (1996) point out are the ritualizing of discourse and the radical contextualizing of discourse. Some students' explanations suggested that they viewed the discourse as a ritual; that is, as an end in itself rather than a means to an end. In one example, Ms. H asked students to explain how they had arrived at an answer. Eventually, after extended questioning, one student told Ms. H that they "worked in groups." The student knew that working together was required, and they had indeed worked in groups, but had not arrived at a group understanding. The work as a group and the discourse among group members was a ritual they performed with no real purpose. In other cases, students would seem to ask questions of one another when they already knew the answer, apparently to fulfill the expectation that they ask questions. The questions were not genuine but were part of a ritual of the classroom.

Students would also radically contextualize discourse. Students are very good at finding out what the teacher expects, and when those expectations shift from procedural mathematical knowledge to conceptual knowledge within a social realm, students may still use the discourse only to please the teacher and not to build legitimate knowledge. Williams and Baxter (1996) give an example of a group of students who, over the course of a class period, were able to go through the motions of group discourse about problems while still operating on a largely procedural level. They aimed only at accomplishing the task as they saw it and not on letting their discussion promote understanding. Setting up excellent tasks and norms for engagement did not necessarily communicate to students what was expected and what they should be gaining, nor did it guarantee their cooperation (see Edwards & Mercer, 1987, for a discussion of these issues in "discovery" classrooms).

Classroom Interactions

A second kind of cautionary tale comes from a two-year project on classroom communication in middle school classrooms funded by the National Science Foundation. Two different reports from that project point to the importance of attending to beliefs of the students in the reform process. The first report, by Walen (1993), deals specifically with the role of teachers' questions and answers. Walen spent most of a year in two algebra classes of a teacher who was attempting to initiate reforms. The teacher hoped to encourage class discussions, sense making, and the construction of understanding by her students. Walen studied this process though extensive classroom observations, journal exchanges and interviews with six students who acted as key informants, and whole-class questionnaires based on interviews and observations.

Walen points out that traditional classroom interaction follows what Mehan (1979) calls the initiation–response–evaluation (IRE) pattern of classroom instruction. Here, teachers initiate a verbal interaction, typically by asking a question. A student or students will give a response, and the teacher will evaluate that response (e.g., say it is correct) before initiating another interaction. In the past, teachers' questions have been largely rhetorical; they knew the answers and were using the questions to test students' knowledge of facts or sometimes as attention-getting or disciplinary devices. As teachers adopt the philosophy of reform and attempt to create communities of learners in which they play a legitimate role, they will tend to ask questions that are actually questions to them; that is, broader questions for which discussion and exploration are necessary.

During these early phases of reform, students are still used to more traditional kinds of questions. Walen reports that in the classrooms she studied, both kinds of questions were used, and students had a difficult time deciding when questions were legitimate and when they were largely part of an IRE pattern. Students in her study overwhelmingly believed that teachers ask questions to which they already know the answer, to find out if students know the answer or if students are listening or to determine whether it is time to move on to a new topic.

Walen reports on one memorable incident, where the class was exploring the generalization of a rule for multiplying two-digit numbers by 11 (add the two digits together and place the result between the two digits to get the three-digit answer). This was a genuine problem for the teacher, who had not before considered how to generalize the rule. The class struggled for some time with conjectures and attempted justifications that students' methods would work every time. The teacher encouraged students to persevere, explored connections between algorithms, and facilitated the search for patterns. At one point, the following dialogue occurred (from Walen, 1993, p. 192):

Pat: I don't think there is a pattern.
Teacher: I bet there is.
Fred: She knows how (confidently, to the other students).
Teacher: No, I don't. I've never done this before. I'm learning just like you are.
Fred: Liar (challenging tone followed by nervous laughter).
Teacher: I have *never* done this before.

The teacher's last line was spoken with obvious irritation, which almost immediately dissolved as she reinterpreted Fred's statement. At this point, however, the classroom discussion took on a different character. Increasingly, the class and teacher fell back on the IRE pattern that they were used to. By way of explanation, Walen suggests that Fred, and other students in the class, had trouble negotiating rules for discussions when the familiar IRE pattern was displaced. In this example, Fred fell back on the informal patterns he would use with other students as a model for discourse. Moreover, he failed to understand that the teacher was playing a different role; she really did not have the answer, but this was outside his realm of experience. When these expectations led to conflict, both teacher and student returned to more comfortable and established patterns of discourse.

For Walen, the message is that students and teachers together need to work toward a joint understanding of new discourse patterns. "Both the teacher and students had difficulty in knowing how to modify the existing classroom structure, how to maintain existing changes during problematic episodes, and how to evaluate their progress." (p. 219). More explicit attention needs to be paid to the changes we are asking students to make, and how students' beliefs and social needs combine to make those changes difficult. Walen concludes, "Ultimately, without addressing student concerns for changing the classroom environment, reform movements in mathematics education have little chance of continued success." (p. 226)

Conflicting Worldviews

A study by Ivey (1994) explored students' *worldviews* as one way of getting at the idea of students' concerns. She uses the work of Pepper (1942, 1982) to discuss how students' basic worldviews affect their participation in mathematics class. Pepper argues that humans rely on root metaphors, such as machines or living organisms, to understand their experience and that such metaphors affect the way they view the world in general. Hence, worldviews are strong internal belief systems that can affect many areas of students' lives.

Ivey (1994) tells the stories of students in a prealgebra class of one teacher who was attempting to implement reforms in his teaching. Ivey combined extensive classroom observations with interviews of 10 key student informants to describe how traditional and emerging classroom cultures clashed. In addition, she evaluated the worldviews of two of her informants in detail, demonstrating how worldviews interact with the classroom culture to either inhibit or enhance movement toward reform.

One student, Urissa, is described as having a consistently *mechanistic* worldview. This worldview has as its root metaphor the machine. Those with this worldview tend to see the world in terms of cause and effect. Descriptions of truth tend to be quantitative, focusing on measurables (how much, how often, when, where), and explanations have the flavor of descriptions of how the machine—the causes, effects, actions, and reactions—works.

A second student, Lisa, was described as having a *contextual* worldview. The root metaphor for this worldview is an act in context. Descriptions of truth involve interpretations of actions and experiences as they unfold in context and explanation often consists of anecdotes, stories told of experiences that bring out pertinent connections. Lisa's responses to interview questions were frequently grounded in the context of her everyday experience, the narrative of her life.

Ivey (1994) also uses the work of Misshauk (1979) to identify two cultures in the classroom she studied and describes how these students reacted to the different cultures. One was a traditional, mechanistic culture described by Ivey as one in which "the teacher is the sole authority, the teacher allocates time and space, and the teacher questions students in order to evaluate them" (p. 105). The second was an organic culture that reflected the teacher's desire for change. In this new culture, students' roles were less distinctive; they were given more freedom and authority in deciding how to work and when they were on the right track. The teacher's management style was more permissive, allowing movement around the class, more noise and confusion. He delegated more authority. Finally, the teacher and students relied more on oral, rather than written, communication.

Ivey argues that these two students acted in ways consistent with their worldviews and that their actions were dramatically different. On one occasion, when the class was discussing divisibility rules, Urissa volunteered the rule for divisibility by four. The teacher, Mr. Scott, validated the rule by restating it and showing a few examples. At this point, Lisa conjectured a different rule for divisibility by four, involving multiplying the first and last digits together. In this case, Mr. Scott responded differently. Even when Lisa found that the rule did not work for some two-digit numbers, Mr. Scott searched for counter examples among three- and four-digit numbers. In the midst of this searching, the class considered the number 320, and the product of 3 and 0, which is 0. Mr. Scott asked if 0 was a multiple of 4, and Lisa argued that it was, because "0 times any number is 0." Eventually, a counterexample was found, and the class moved on. Ivey (1994) concludes:

> The important point, for this analysis, was the difference between the effect of Urissa's actions on the class and the effect of Lisa's actions. Even in what was primarily a mechanistic lesson—rules were stated with no justification, and examples were given of their uses—Lisa was able to act in a contextual way. Her search of connections between the examples listed on the board led to a much richer class discussion. (p. 123)

Ivey also discusses the roles Urissa and Lisa played in small group work, in which the culture of the classroom was more organic. Urissa was successful in turning small group work into the kind of work she was used to. When compelled to work in groups, she would work individually and only compare answers with other group members. She refrained from participating in group discussions, except on rare occasions when she would explain her solution by describing the algorithm she had used to obtain it. Lisa, on the other hand, was eager to engage in group discussion. Even when doing individual seatwork, Lisa would engage in informal group discussions whenever Mr. Scott would allow it. She sometimes worked as a liaison between groups, in an effort to connect more students' ideas with hers. Justification was a normal part of her working in groups, to the extent that she provided it as part of her normal discourse in groups.

The point, for Ivey, is that "both Lisa and Urissa were able to substantively change the course of particular classroom activities to make them more consistent with their particular world views" (p. 137). When confronted with a new culture at odds with her worldview, Urissa modified the new culture to make it conform more with her expectations. On the other hand, Lisa was able to adopt the new culture at a high level of expertise, because it was consistent with her worldview. Ivey concludes,

> Students' world views are powerful influences on their responses to new cultural expectations. As current reform efforts are tantamount to cultural change, students'

> world views have important consequences for reform efforts. Failure to address new expectations for students in explicit ways will lead to classroom difficulties. . . . What must be done . . . is to recognize the power of a student's world view to shape her or his actions in the classroom and even to partially shape instruction itself, and to consider ways of dealing with differing world views in the classroom. (p. 142).

Summary

The cautionary tales of this section point to one aspect of the complexity of change. Other problems might include lack of administrative support, incompatible teachers' beliefs, or parental expectations. My intention is to point to the students as important but frequently overlooked players in the reform process and to the ways in which their views of reform can have a profound effect on individual teachers' success.

CONCLUSION

In this chapter I attempted to provide a rationale for recommendations on improving secondary mathematics instruction. While I attempted to ground my recommendations in solid research, I also attempted to show the philosophical background that informs both the recommendations and the research. In part, this is due to my conviction that individual teachers, given time and support, will find good ways to teach, provided they have clear visions of *what teaching and learning mathematics means*. I have tried to provide a window to the best current thinking on these issues.

One critical point remains to be made. In *Wrestling with Change*, Lew Romagnano (1994) reports on a collaborative project with a first year teacher in which they worked together in two ninth grade general math classes to implement the kinds of reforms we have discussed in this chapter. Some but not all of Romagnano's recommendations parallel those brought to light in this chapter: the need for teachers to develop their own understanding of mathematical ideas, the need for rich mathematical tasks, the need to negotiate new classroom traditions with students, and the need to work through traditional practices such as grading and tracking in light of these new classroom traditions. However, the message that emerges most strongly for me from Romagnano's work is the idea that teaching involves managing dilemmas and that changing teaching will bring to light a new set of dilemmas to manage (see also Lampert, 1985). Such dilemmas as when and how much to tell students (as opposed to letting them discover), how best to assess and assign grades to students, and how to make reforms in the context of pressures from school policy must be managed, and many may not be solvable. Romagnano argues that teachers need to reconsider their roles as teachers to include managing these dilemmas. "They can then apply the same knowledge, judgement, and creativity they bring to other aspects of their work to the task of coping with the dilemmas of change" (p. 174).

Returning to the metaphor with which I began, I feel that the individual bricks needed to build a reformed classroom are becoming increasingly easy to come by. As teachers, we gather facts about students and classroom life all the time. What I have attempted to provide is a scaffold on which to stand as we attempt to build from that information a better classroom. With that scaffold in place, good teachers can successfully build the kinds of classrooms that are equal to the vision of reform.

References

Begle, E. G., & Gibb, E. G. (1980). Why do research? In R. J. Shumway (Ed.), *Research in mathematics education* (pp. 3–19). Reston, VA: National Council of Teachers of Mathematics.

Carpenter, T. P., Fennema, E., Peterson, P. L., & Carey, D. A. (1988). Teachers' pedagogical content knowledge of students' problem solving in elementary arithmetic. *Journal for Research in Mathematics Education*, 19(5), 385–401.

Cobb, P., Wood, T., & Yackel, E. (1991). A constructivist approach to second grade mathematics. In E. von Glasersfeld (Ed.), *Radical constructivism in mathematics education* (pp. 157–176). Boston: Kluwer Academic Publishers.

Confrey, J. (1990). What constructivism implies for teaching. In R. B. Davis, C. A. Maher, & N. Noddings (Eds.), *Constructivist views on the teaching and learning of mathematics* (Journal for Research in Mathematics Education Monograph Series, No. 4, pp. 107–122). Reston, VA: National Council of Teachers of Mathematics.

Edwards, D., & Mercer, N. (1987). *Common knowledge: The development of understanding in the classroom*. London: Routledge.

Ernst, P. (1991). *The philosophy of mathematics education*. New York: Falmer Press.

Fennema, E., & Franke, M. L. (1992). Teachers' knowledge and its impact. In D. A. Grouws (Ed.), *Handbook of research on mathematics teaching and learning* (pp. 147–164). New York: Macmillan.

Forscher, B. K. (1963). Letter to the editor. *Science*, 142, 329.

Freudenthal, H. (1987). Mathematics starting and staying in reality. In I. Wirszup & R. Streit (Eds.), *Developments in school mathematics around the world: Proceedings of the UCSMP International Conference on Mathematics Education, 28–30 March, 1985* (pp. 279–295). Reston, VA: National Council of Teachers of Mathematics.

Gergen, K. J. (1985). The social constructionist movement in modern psychology. *American Psychologist*, 40, 266–275.

Goodman, N. (1986). Mathematics as an objective science. In T. Tymoczko (Ed.), *New directions in the philosophy of mathematics* (pp. 79–94). Boston: Birkhäuser.

Grouws, D. A. (Ed.). (1992). *Handbook of research on mathemtics teaching and learning*. New York: Macmillan.

Healy, C. C. (1993). Discovery courses are great in theory, but. . . . In J. L. Schwartz, M. Yerushalmy, & B. Wilson (Eds.). *The geometric supposer: What is it a case of?* (pp. 85–104). Hillsdale, NJ: Erlbaum.

Heibert, J., & Carpenter, T. P. (1992). Learning and teaching with understanding. In D. A. Grouws (Ed.), *Handbook of research on mathematics teaching and learning* (pp. 65–97). New York: Macmillan.

Heibert, J., & Lefevre, P. (1986). Conceptual and procedural knowledge in mathematics: An introductory analysis. In J. Heibert (Ed.), *Conceptual and procedural knowledge: The case of mathematics* (pp. 1–27). Hillsdale, NJ: Erlbaum.

Hersh, R. (1986). Some proposals for reviving the philosophy of mathematics. In T. Tymoczko (Ed.), *New directions in the philosophy of mathematics* (pp. 9–28). Boston: Birkhäuser.

Ivey, K. M. C. (1994). *World views in the mathematics classroom: Students translating beliefs into actions*. Unpublished doctoral dissertation, Washington State University, Pullman.
Kleibard, H. M. (1992). *Forging the American curriculum: Essays in curriculum theory and history*. New York: Routledge.
Kleiner, I., & Movshovitz-Hadar, N. (1990). Aspects of the pluralistic nature of mathematics. *Interchange*, 21(1), 28–35.
Lampert, M. (1985). How do teachers manage to teach? Perspectives on problems in practice. *Harvard Educational Review*, 55(2), 178–194.
Lampert, M. (1990). When the problem is not the question and the solution is not the answer: Mathematical knowing and teaching. *American Educational Research Journal*, 27, 29–63.
Leont'ev, A. N. (1978). *Activity, consciousness and personality*. Englewood Cliffs, NJ: Prentice-Hall.
Lyddon, W. J., & McLaughlin, J. T. (1992). Constructivist psychology: A heuristic framework. *Journal of Mind and Behavior*, 13(1), 89–108.
Mead, G. H. (1934). *Mind, self, and society*. Chicago: University of Chicago Press.
Mehan, H. (1979). *Learning lessons: Social organization in the classroom*. Cambridge, MA: Harvard University Press.
Misshauk, M. J. (1979). *Management: Theory and practice*. Boston: Little, Brown.
National Council of Teachers of Mathematics (NCTM). (1989). *Curriculum and evaluation standards for school mathematics*. Reston, VA: Author.
National Council of Teachers of Mathematics (NCTM). (1991). *Professional standards for teaching mathematics*. Reston, VA: Author.
National Council of Teachers of Mathematics (NCTM). (1995). *Assessment standards for school mathematics*. Reston, VA: Author.
Pepper, S. C. (1942). *World hypotheses: A study in evidence*. Berkeley: University of California Press.
Pepper, S. C. (1982). Metaphor in philosophy. *Journal of Mind and Behavior*, 3, 197–205.
Phillip, R. A., Flores, A., Sowder, J. T., & Schappelle, B. P. (1994). Conceptions and practices of extraordinary mathematics teachers. *Journal of Mathematical Behavior* 13(2), 155–180.
Putnam, R. T., Lampert, M., & Peterson, P. L. (1990). Alternative perspectives on knowing mathematics in elementary schools. In C. B. Cazden (Ed.), *Review of research in education* (Vol. 16, pp. 57–150). Washington, DC: American Educational Research Association.
Restivo, S. (1993). The social life of mathematics. In S. Restivo, J. P. Van Bendegem, & R. Fischer (Eds.), *Math worlds: Philosophical and social studies of mathematics and mathematics education* (pp. 247–278). Albany: State University of New York Press.
Restivo, S., Van Bendegem, J. P., & Fischer, R. (Eds.). (1993). *Math worlds: Philosophical and social studies of mathematics and mathematics education*. Albany: State University of New York Press.
Romagnano, L. (1994). *Wrestling with change: The dilemmas of teaching real mathematics*. Portsmouth, NH: Heinemann.
Romberg, T. A., Allison, J. L., Clarke, B. A., Clarke, D. M., Middleton, J. A., Pedro, J. D., Smith, M. E., & Spence, M. (1993). *A blueprint for maths in context: A connected curriculum for grades 5–8* (Revised). Madison, WI: Wisconsin Center for Education Research.
Romberg, T. A., & Carpenter, T. P. (1986). Research on teaching and learning mathematics: Two disciplines of scientific inquiry. In M. C. Wittrock (Ed.), *Handbook of research on teaching* (3rd ed., pp. 850–873). New York: Macmillan.
Schoenfeld, A. (1989). Explorations of students' mathematical beliefs and behavior. *Journal for Research in Mathematics Education* 20, 338–355.
Schwartz, J., & Yerushalmy, M. (1985–1988). *The geometric supposer*. Pleasantville, NY: Sunburst.
Silver, E. A., & Lane, S. (1993). Balancing considerations of equity, content quality, and technical excellence in designing, validating and implementing performance assessments in the context of mathematics instructional reform: The experience of the QUASAR project. Pittsburgh, PA: Learning Research and Development Center, University of Pittsburgh. (ERIC Document Reproduction Service No. ED 361 370)

Skovesmose, O. (1993). The dialogical nature of reflective knowledge. In S. Restivo, J. P. Van Bendegem, & R. Fischer (Eds.), *Math worlds: Philosophical and social studies of mathematics and mathematics education* (pp. 162–181). Albany: State University of New York Press.

Slife, B. D., & Williams, R. N. (1995). *What's behind the research? Discovering hidden assumptions in the behavioral sciences.* Thousand Oaks, CA: Sage Publications.

Stanic, G. M. A. (1986). The growing crisis in mathematics education in the early twentieth century. *Journal for Research in Mathematics Education, 17,* 190–205.

Steffe, L. P., & Kieren, T. (1994). Radical constructivism and mathematics education. *Journal for Research in Mathematics Education, 25*(6), 711–733.

Stein, M. K., Grover, B. W., & Silver, E. A. (1991). Changing instructional practice: A conceptual framework for capturing the details. In R. Underhill (Ed.), *Proceedings of the thirteenth annual meeting of the North American Chapter of the International Group for the Psychology of Mathematics Education* (pp. 36–42). Blacksburg: Virginia Tech Department of Curriculum and Instruction.

Thompson, A. (1992). Teachers' beliefs and conceptions: A synthesis of research. In D. A. Grouws (Ed.), *Handbook of research on mathematics teaching and learning* (pp. 127–146). New York: Macmillan.

Tymoczko, T. (1986). *New directions in the philosophy of mathematics.* Boston: Birkhäuser.

von Glasersfeld, E. (1983). Learning as a constructive activity. In J. C. Bergeron & N. Herscovics (Eds.), *Proceedings of the fifth annual meeting of the North American Chapter of the International Group for the Psychology of Mathematics Education* (pp. 41–68). PME-NA: Montreal.

von Glasersfeld, E. (1989). Constructivism in education. In T. Husen & T. N. Postlethwaite (Eds.), *The International Encyclopedia of Education, Supplementary Volume* (pp. 162–163). Oxford, England: Pergamon.

Vygotsky, L. S. (1962). *Thought and language.* Cambridge, MA: MIT Press.

Wagner, S., & Kieran, C. (Eds.). (1989). *Research issues in the learning and teaching of algebra.* Reston, VA: National Council of Teachers of Mathematics; Hillsdale, NJ: Erlbaum.

Walen, S. B. (1993). *An analysis of students' knowledge of the mathematics classroom.* Unpublished doctoral dissertation, Washington State University, Pullman.

Weiss, I. R., Matti, M. C., & Smith, P. S. (1994). *Report of the 1993 national survey of science and mathematics education.* Chapel Hill, NC: Horizon Research.

Welch, W. (1978). Science education in Urbanville: A case study. In R. Stake & J. Easley (Eds.), *Case studies in science education* (pp. 5-1–5-33). Urbana: University of Illinois.

Williams, S. R., & Baxter, J. A. (1996). Dilemmas of discourse-oriented teaching in one middle school mathematics class. *The Elementary School Journal, 97*(1), 21–28.

CHAPTER

12

The Teaching and Learning of Elementary Science

KENNETH TOBIN
Florida State University

The traditions of teaching elementary science are set within a context of how most elementary schools are structured. For the most part, students are arranged in class groupings and one teacher is assigned to teach the class in all subject matter areas. In addition, elementary science has not been regarded as a staple compared to mathematics, reading, and writing. Because of the strong emphasis on teaching students to read, write, and master basic skills in arithmetic, the priority for teaching science is usually at best at the second tier of significance. Furthermore, in relation to other subject matter areas, the predominantly female elementary teaching profession does not feel confident to teach science and within that context it is not surprising to find that science is taught infrequently in many elementary classrooms (Briscoe & Lorsbach, 1991).

Even when science is taught regularly, two major problems call for attention. First, teachers with a limited background in science feel dependent on textbooks and can implement a program that uses commercial texts to emphasize science as the learning of facts and vocabulary. Second, a movement in the 1960s resulted in science being accepted as hands on. At this time massive funding from the National Science Foundation and other government agencies fueled a plethora of projects in which curricular resources (e.g., teacher guides, student workbooks, kits of materials and equipment) were prepared to address the problems of teaching and learning of elementary science. At its best, the hands-on movement emphasized student enjoyment of science in a problem-solving environment, and at its worst, worksheets were used to guide materials-centered activities that were prescriptive and formulaic. The hands-on movement in elementary science placed into the foreground the significance of concrete activities with manipulatives and placed into the background the conceptual aspects of science. When manipulatives were used extensively the links between the hands-on activities and the development of meaningful conceptual understandings were elusive in many classrooms (Kuhn, 1993).

The most recent decade also has produced a flurry of activity in terms of curriculum resources for elementary teachers. These resources have endeavored to incorporate the potential of technology into the suggested approaches to learning science and also have addressed the problems alluded to in the introduction to this chapter. At issue now, as it always has been, is how to bring these new resources into classrooms in such a way as to enhance the scientific literacy of elementary students. Traditions die hard, and social forces are in place that favor maintenance of the status quo. Past efforts at reforming science education have seen sporadic uptake of promising approaches, and of course, some exemplary teachers always have been doing exceptional things in science education. However, the problems have been persistent and international studies of science achievement suggest that students in the United States are falling behind their peers in other countries. Such comparisons, as somber as they might be, mask an even more significant issue, that approaches to the teaching of science in elementary grade levels are problematic throughout the world.

LEARNING SCIENCE THROUGH COPARTICIPATION

Science is regarded as a form of discourse that has evolved as a relatively recent activity of humankind. The goal of science is to make sense of a universe of phenomena in terms of knowledge that is viable. To be accepted as scientific, knowledge must meet several tests. First, it must be coherent with other viable knowledge claims. Second, it must be accepted by members of the scientific academy through a process of peer review. Third, it must withstand conceptual and empirical challenges in repeated attempts to refute its viability. Skeptical acceptance of scientific knowledge claims is a part of what is considered acting scientifically. Thus, even at the earliest of stages, an idea is carefully scrutinized in relation to what else is known and efforts are made to refute the claims associated with the knowledge. In the event that the knowledge withstands those tests, the activity of gaining acceptance becomes increasingly social as attempts are made to convince others of the acceptability of what is claimed. When viewed in this way it is apparent that science can be viewed as a form of argument during which ideas are formulated and then argued out in a social forum in which efforts are made to persuade peers to a particular point of view. The process necessarily involves the production of evidence and discussions about the extent to which the evidence fits the knowledge claim. As is the case with other forms of discourse, conventions and skills are also a part of science. In the past, efforts to characterize these methods have led to oversimplification, with the identification of the science processes, which then were enshrined into approaches to curriculum in a manner implying that such processes had a generic character that transcended the subject matter. In this chapter, the conventions, manipulative skills, and process skills are regarded as linked to subject matter, and approaches to teaching and learning science are regarded as most fruitful when the processes and subject matter are interwoven.

If science is viewed as a form of discourse, then learning science can be considered learning a new way to make sense of experience. *Discourse*, as it is used here, refers to a "social activity of making meanings with language and other symbolic systems in some particular kind of situation or setting" (Lemke, 1995, p. 8). Lemke also noted that:

> Instead of talking about meaning making as something that is done by minds, I prefer to talk about it as a *social practice* in a community. It is a kind of *doing* that is done in ways that are characteristic of a community, and its occurrence is part of what binds the community together and helps to constitute it as a community. In this sense we can speak of a community, not as a collection of interacting individuals, but as a system of doings, rather than a system of doers. (p. 9)

In an elementary science community one might expect to see students engage in ways such that the discourse of a class would become more science like over time. If the essence of science is to examine the coherence of evidence and knowledge claims then one might expect a form of discourse in elementary science classrooms that involved students routinely in arguments over the efficacy of the warrants for knowledge claims. As has been advocated by Kuhn (1993), science could be regarded as a form of argument in which emerging conceptual understandings are related to evidence and the fit with canonical science.

If students are to learn science as a form of discourse it seems imperative that they be able to adapt their language resources as they practice science in a setting in which others who know science assist them to learn by engaging activities in which they coparticipate (Roth, 1995). As used here, *coparticipation* implies the presence of a shared language that can be used by all participants to communicate with one another such that meaningful learning occurs. The shared language must be negotiated and would enable all participants in a community to engage the activities of the community. In such a setting, knowledge claims that made no sense would be clarified and discussion would occur until a learner was satisfied that he or she now understood. In a setting in which coparticipation was occurring, students would have the autonomy to ask when they did not understand and the focus always would be on what students know and how they can re-present what they know.

Students would not feel that they could not understand and that their only recourse was to accept what was being said as an article of truth based on a faith that others understand the warrants for the viability of the claim. Thus, coparticipation would involve discussions in which participants tested one another's understanding and were sensitive to their roles as both teachers and learners.

One way to think of the roles of the students and teacher in an environment of coparticipation is that students come to know by engaging at the elbows of those who do know. Students receive opportunity to practice and observe others practice, and at any time a person might be a teacher and a learner with respect to others in the community. Coparticipation implies a concern for facilitating one another's learning, and peer teaching is a critical element of such an environment. During interactions, respect would be shown for the knowledge of others and efforts would be made to find out why particular claims were regarded as viable. There would be concern for knowing in a way that is scientific and the knowledge that is learned within the community would be consistent with canonical science. Within this evolving knowledge community, concern would be shown for what is known by learners at any given time and how they can re-present what they know. A teacher can structure activities in which students engage such that they can use their existing knowledge to make sense of what is happening and build new understanding on a foundation of extant knowledge. The focus of the teacher on the re-presentations of the learner is what is most critical about a coparticipatory environment. The mediating role of the teacher is focused not only on what students know and how they can re-present what they know but also on the identification of activities that can continue the evolutionary path of the classroom community toward the attainment of agreed-on goals. Thus, the concern is beyond re-presentation and also involves mediating the constructions of a discourse that becomes increasingly scientific in its character.

CONTEXTUAL ISSUES

In the late 1970s, Anyon (1981) explored how social class of elementary students related to the way knowledge was re-presented in the school curriculum. She viewed social class as composed of such factors as occupational status, income level, and relationships to the system of ownership of physical and cultural capital, the structure of authority at work and in society, and to the content and process of the work in which an individual engages. The schools participating in the study were differentiated by income level and the kind of work that characterized most parents. Five schools were involved: two working class schools (lower than 40th percentile in family income;

parents in unskilled or semiskilled occupations), one middle class school (40th–80th percentile in family income; parents employed as teachers, accountants, middle managers), one affluent professional school (above 90th percentile in family income; parents highly paid doctors, television or advertising executives, and other affluent professionals), and one executive elite school (above the 99th percentile in family income; parents vice-presidents or more advanced corporate executives).

Even though all schools were subject to the same state requirements, striking differences were observed in the manner in which science curricula were enacted. For example, in working class schools, the expectations of teachers for the performance of students were lower than in the other schools. Although some instances were reported in which teachers endeavored to go beyond simple facts and skills, there was evidence of a teacher belief that students did not benefit greatly from the activities and would use such knowledge infrequently. In working-class schools, emphasis was on physical control and few efforts were observed to enthuse and motivate students. Anyon described passive (refusal to engage or less than enthusiastic engagement in learning activities) and active resistance of students to the teacher enacting the curriculum. She concluded that what counts as knowledge in working class schools is fragmented facts, isolated from the context and connection to each other or to wider bodies of meaning. The curriculum was perceived to consist of procedures to allow students to carry out tasks that were largely mechanical.

Anyon described the middle class school as reflecting a theme of possibility. Education was seen as a valuable commodity to get a job or to go to college. Knowledge was regarded as more conceptual in middle class than working class schools and was perceived as being separate from the efforts of students to learn. Students were anxious about tests and grades.

In the affluent professional school, there was a perception that students learn from experience and attempts to discover. Learning to think was valued, and it was felt that students should not just regurgitate facts but should immerse themselves in ideas. The use of curricular resources from the *Elementary Science Study* (Education Development Center, 1971) provided students with experience in problem-oriented activities. Anyon described the school as being focused on extreme individualism; there were attempts to individualize instruction and an emphasis on individual expression and development. Knowledge was regarded not only as conceptual but as open to discovery, construction, and meaning making. It was not always given. There seemed to be an awareness that knowledge was constructed by individuals but served social goals as well.

The teachers at the executive elite school attempted to teach more subject matter and more difficult concepts than in any other school. Excellence was the theme of this school. Knowledge was not regarded as a product of an individual's attempts to make sense but was considered to be academic, intellectual, and rigorous, a product of disciplined inquiry and rational thought. Throughout the school curricular resources from the *Elementary Science Study* or *Science a Process Approach* (American Association for the Advancement of Science, 1975) were used to promote reasoning and intellectual development. Children were more intense in competition than in other schools, were under pressure to excel, and were exhorted to produce top-quality performance and get into the best colleges.

Although the Anyon study was undertaken more than 15 years ago the implications are so profound that all teachers should look closely at their expectations and examine whether or not the curriculum is shaped by social forces that tend to differentiate opportunities to learn in ways that reflect social class. Certainly students from homes that differ in social class will bring different discursive resources with them to school and will have sets of expectations of schooling that reflect their personal histories. However, as teachers examine what students know, how they can re-present what they know, and how to structure learning environments to mediate the learning of their students, it is imperative that the goals for all students be ambitious and egalitarian.

White (1996) described the school and home as different discourse communities and an associated lack of fit that made it difficult for some students to experience science in a meaningful way. Her study used interview and classroom observation to foreground the voices of the children as they made sense of their science classroom and schooling. The major implications of the study for the teaching and learning of science in grades K–6 relate to the use of language and the manner in which the home is regarded as a resource to support learning. The study suggested that the African-American students who participated had difficulties in making connections between their everyday language and the language used in science. White questioned the value of using a language in the classroom that is often inaccessible to most students. She advocated the use of a negotiated language that enabled students to learn science using written and oral language, incorporate "personal and colloquial" terms, and show scientific knowledge as connected to knowers. To benefit students who do not use standard English in the home, White emphasized the importance of teachers making explicit thematic relationships that previously might have been regarded as implicit in the language. Teachers might teach students how the language of science differs from everyday language. White noted that, for students to become adept in its use, they should be given chances to use the language of science in a context in which a teacher is available to assist them to build bridges between the language of the home and the evolving language of the classroom. According to White, through explicit actions of the teacher, the language and relationships encountered in the science curriculum may become "less mystical" and within the grasp of a majority of students. White exhorted teachers to acknowledge that

> We can no longer stand on the traditional practices, values, and referents of our subject and insist that only the children modify their understanding and language until it fits and mimics our own and our subjects. If we truly desire more children to succeed in schooling and in science, then our beliefs, practices and language must also change to more closely "fit" with the referents with which our students view their world and ours. (p. 62)

White advocated that teachers find ways "in which the school community may better organize its customs, practices, and language to reduce the gap between the discourses of the home and school." She commented that, although each child spent more than a half of every day at home, teachers rarely made efforts to learn about the home environment and how it could promote learning science. At best, there was a one-way transmission of information of how the home can be adapted to improve the success of a currently unsuccessful child. The home environment was not seen as a source of capital to enhance learning but something that needed to be changed. Accordingly, for most students a gulf between the discourse of the home and the school was a detriment to their learning. White cautioned that

> Teachers and administrators need to invite parents into classrooms and administrative meetings, to listen to their views about how schooling might better meet their child's needs. . . . More than only listening, the school community should then act on parents' advice, and seek to modify those practices and customs of the school which are especially difficult for parents to support. In the classroom too, some practices and customs may need to be altered. In return, a more comprehensive investment of time with parents, explicitly demonstrating and practicing some of the thinking skills valued by the school, might enable parents to construct a more complete image of what is involved in school learning. Perhaps with greater varieties of behaviors accepted as a result of these negotiations, more of the children at home and in class will be free to engage in thinking and learning. (p. 60)

Muire (1996) undertook a study of the needs of elementary teachers with respect to the teaching of science in Florida. The study is highly significant because it examines teacher needs in relation to what is happening and how important teachers perceive what is happening. In addition, these analyses are related to the policy environment in a state that is increasingly diverse. Accordingly, the study provides insights into some of the reasons elementary curricula have not changed in the ways envisioned in the myriad reports that have urged reform for more than a decade (e.g., Hurd, 1993; Rutherford & Ahlgren, 1990).

On the basis of responses from more than 500 teachers, Muire identified nine critical areas of need: resources for teaching, curriculum, technology, assistance, time, professional development, assessment, class size, and power/control. The most frequently cited resource needs, each listed by almost 50% of the teachers, were manipulatives and materials. All resource needs were closely related to support for students to learn science and included textbooks, workbooks, and kits. Muire reported that the highest priority of need, identified by more than a third of the respondents, related to hands-on materials, manipulatives, and basic supplies needed to actively involve students. Muire concluded that "Florida's elementary teachers seem to be motivated, with respect to providing materials-rich learning environments for their students" (p. 30). However, as Muire indicated, the survey of what was happening in the classrooms taught by the same teachers who expressed the need for manipulatives, was that most teachers used lecture, weekly or daily, to disseminate science information to their students. Lecture was regarded by a significant number of teachers as an important strategy to use in elementary science. These data suggest that teachers may need assistance to enact the curriculum in ways that do not emphasize lectures and textbooks to the same degree. Muire provides evidence for this assertion, in that the second highest category of need was ideas for improving teaching and learning. The specific needs suggested by teachers related to science curricula, integrated curricula, hands-on curricula, cooperative learning ideas, problem-solving activities, standards-based assessment, and alternative assessment. The results suggest that teachers are familiar with strategies they might employ to improve learning of science and recognize that they need assistance to implement them in a satisfactory way.

Muire indicated that the amount of time spent on hands-on experiences in Florida's elementary classrooms decreased from 1991 to 1993. This trend in the data may have been associated with the relatively high incidence of lectures and use of textbooks and also a shortage of suitable materials to employ in hands-on activities. The failure of school systems to provide staff development that focuses on the needs of teachers also might have contributed to a fall off in the use of hands-on activities. Further evidence of the need for additional staff development is that, although teachers perceived the importance of studying fewer topics in more depth, approximately 60% reported they did not know how to accomplish this and were in need of assistance.

The third highest need expressed by elementary teachers related to technology. Teachers requested more computers, more software, and more calculators. It is possible that a lack of knowledge of what was available and how it might be used restricted teachers from suggesting what they need. For example, with the explosion of the World Wide Web and its subsequent application as a teaching resource, it is now likely that teachers would have more sophisticated needs related to accessing the World Wide Web and use of the Internet. Despite a marked increase in the number of computers available in elementary schools, the data reported by Muire suggest that in 1993 the extent they were used to enhance the learning of science was less than might be expected. Teachers perceived the importance of using computers to enhance instruction but did not use them, presumably because they have not yet adapted their curricula to the extent that computers can play an integral role. Muire also reported that the use of interactive media and telecommunication were limited in elementary science curricula. Most teachers in the study did not perceive the use of telecommunication to be of importance, and this has implications for staff development.

Although one might take issue with particular needs expressed by teachers, it seems paramount to ascertain what those needs are and attend to them in a direct manner. Even if the intention is to convince teachers that their needs are not as important as issues they have failed to mention, it is an imperative for improving the quality of teaching and learning science to build support systems associated with the identified needs of elementary teachers. As a starting point, it might be wise to plan an educational program that focuses on research and theory associated with each of the needs identified by teachers. The goals of such a program might be to identify teacher needs and provide experiences that will lead to the needs being satisfied or reset as priorities.

Muire analyzed the policy climate in Florida that led to critically low schools being identified and targeted for special treatment. What is interesting about Muire's analysis is that, whereas national- and state-level reports recommended reforms to promote transformational learning of science and considerable local freedom to pursue science topics that were of relevance to students, the policy decision to identify critically low schools appears to be driving curricula toward basic skills, possibly to the detriment of efforts to change science curricula toward the visions encapsulated in many reform documents (e.g., National Research Council, 1996). What is clear from Muire's analysis is the vast number of social forces that constrain what teachers feel they must do in the enactment of science curricula. These forces are interactive and a decision to increase the stakes of state-level tests can have a major impact not only on the subjects being tested but on the curriculum as a whole as schools place greater emphasis on meeting the minimum standards required of mandated tests.

FOCUSING ON THE LEARNER

Driver, Squires, Rushworth, and Wood-Robinson (1994) compiled an impressive review of the manner in which children constructed understandings of a large variety of science-related concepts. In their discussion of children coming to know science, they emphasized the significance of the social dimension of learning in the following way: "Science ideas, which are constructed and transmitted through the culture and social institutions of science, will not be discovered by individual learners through their own empirical inquiry: learning science involves being initiated into the culture of science" (p. 6).

Driver and her colleagues indicated that a teacher was essential if students are to build understanding congruent with accepted science. They advocated a form of teaching that focused on childrens' thinking and suggested the following list of activities as suited to promoting understandings of science: written statements, posters, card sort, thought experiment, design and make, explain, checklist–questionnaire, predict and explain, and practical experiments. The list contains some hands-on activities but breaks away from the notion that hands-on science is sufficient and embraces the idea that learners need access not only to physical experiences but also to the concepts and models of conventional science. Driver et al. noted that "Experience by itself is not enough. It is the sense that students make of it that matters" (p. 7). Consistent with Kuhn's notion that effective learning of science would involve a form of argument in which knowledge claims were related to evidence was the claim made by Driver and her colleagues that "the relationship between evidence and theory is not only an important facet of the nature of science, it is also a critical issue in children's learning of science" (p. 6).

Watters and English (1995) investigated scientific reasoning in a sample of 182 students from 14 elementary schools in Australia. Their interest was primarily to apply a model for information and cognitive processing to learning science (Luria, 1973). Watters and English focused on a relational understanding of science concepts, which involves the facility to manipulate mentally and perform operations with mental models. The authors noted that catering for individual differences needs to involve the provision of multimodal experiences, including the use of diagrams and collaborative grouping to allow individuals to construct their own unique representations of knowledge. Watters and English concluded that enhanced learning should occur when teachers begin to focus on problem solving in learning environments that encourage individual explorations and construction of models.

Because assessment is a social act usually enacted in a classroom, it is important to examine the roles of teachers and students in assessment situations. Teachers often use metaphors to make sense of a role such as assessment. For example, teachers frequently see their role as an assessor in terms of being a fair judge (Tobin & Tippins, in press). They perceive their role in terms of ascertaining what students know and weighing the students' knowledge claims against the principal dimensions of canonical knowledge; that is, the knowledge that has been accepted as viable by an eminent group of scientists. As a fair judge, it is important for the teacher to ask about the most important parts of the disciplinary knowledge and be impartial in their judgment. In terms of this metaphor, the judge decides on the focus for the assessment tasks and whether or not performance is adequate. The students' roles are to know what is most important and thereby prepare to demonstrate what they know about these parts of a course and their knowledge when called on to do so. If students do not learn what is to be assessed, they rarely have the opportunity to show a fair judge that they learned other things and could have performed adequately on other tasks. The goals of a learner can shape not only what is learned but the manner in which it is learned and how at a later time that knowledge can be enacted in a performance task. The relative importance of learner goals to what is being learned and how knowledge can later be enacted has implications for the design and use of assessment tasks.

If a teacher adopts a role that is constrained by a fair judge metaphor, the possible actions of students in assessment tasks will be constrained by the teacher's role. Thus, in such a scenario, students will be judged by their teacher in terms of their performance on tasks selected by the teacher and administered at a time judged by the teacher to be suitable. In terms of the relative power of the teacher and students, it seems clear that the teacher has considerable power compared to students.

Murphy (1995) noted that students should be provided with tasks that allow them to express their interests and understanding in a manner that suits them. However, in such tasks students will see different problems and offer different solutions, thereby making it difficult to compare responses. Such assessments provide teachers with what they need in terms of evidence of students' understanding. Teachers can act on the insights provided to enable individuals to develop further their scientific understanding in ways that are integrated with their existing knowledge of the world and themselves.

Constructivism recognizes the central role of the learner in all parts of the process of constructing, reconstructing, and enacting knowledge. The best an outsider, such as a teacher, can do is to mediate in the process of constructing, reconstructing, and enacting knowledge. Accordingly, it makes sense to find ways of assessment that acknowledge the central role of the learner. From a constructivist point of view, assessment can be regarded as an opportunity for students to show what they have learned. If assessment is conceptualized in this way, it is apparent that students potentially have more power to select the foci for assessment tasks, when their knowledge will be assessed, and what would constitute a satisfactory level of performance. Such an approach overcomes a number of the problems associated with assessment under the fair judge metaphor and kindred conceptualizations.

To understand assessment from a constructivist point of view, it is useful to think about the concept of action. When an individual enacts knowledge, or performs, several aspects need to be considered. First, there is a behavioral part, something that is observed, such as a written description or the manipulation of materials to effect a desired outcome. Second is a belief that a particular behavior is appropriate in the circumstances. Third is the context in which the belief is grounded and the behavior is enacted. Fourth is the goal set of the individual, an important set of beliefs that constrains all components of the action. Other components of action also might be focused on. For example, a significant component of the context is the consequences for behaving in a particular manner. Irrespective of what a student knows, that student might deem it wise to behave in a particular way in the context of a teacher assessing his or her knowledge. In this example, a student might have as a goal to be assessed as satisfactory on an assessment task. The context for the action of the student might be a performance task to be judged by a teacher who has taught the class how to determine the relative density of liquids, for example, in a given way. Despite knowing how to solve the problem in a different way, in the circumstances, the student might decide that the consequences of behaving differently than what he or she believes to be the teacher's expectations would constitute too great a risk of not attaining the goal. Accordingly, the student behaves in a way consistent with the methods taught by the teacher to employ in problems of the type to be solved in this instance.

In a context of coparticipation, it is important that students use a variety of modes to show what and how they know. When this is done, conversations can focus on the re-presentations and new learning can connect from what is already known. A very common way of re-presenting what is known involves the inscriptions of students. Hayes, Symington, and Martin (1994) studied the manner in which drawing was used in science classes by students in grades 1 and 2, where the extent to which they can write is limited. They noted that the students enjoyed drawing and found it an effective way of communicating their ideas about science. The drawings appeared to assist the teacher to understand the students' thinking. In addition, the drawings were foci for conversations, and students learned to use them as a basis for framing questions of one another and the teacher.

Hayes et al. were cautious in the extent to which they would generalize their findings, pointing out that the strategies associated with the use of drawings was important. An important contextual factor is that the drawings were not an end in themselves, a product to be completed for a grade, but a part of a discourse community endeavoring to become more sciencelike. The drawings served a purpose of facilitating communication. They were a device to demonstrate the knowledge of students, and discussions therefore could occur in relation to what was known, making it possible for students to connect what and how they know to new learning. Patterns of interaction that might suggest coparticipation did not occur immediately but appeared to evolve over time. This tendency may have greater salience to teachers than the authors of the study have indicated. The use of drawings as representations of what and how students know is not going to occur automatically. If diagrams are to have the type of application desired by Hayes et al., then teachers and learners will have to draw in ways that will explicate what and how they know. And if the drawings are to be useful in learning science, then students and the teacher need to develop interaction patterns that focus conversations on the meanings given the drawings.

The videotape prepared by the Science Media Group at the Harvard Smithsonian Center for Astrophysics (1995) also featured the representations of very young elementary students. Here the students' diagrams were critical links between hands-on activities and learning. An essential part of the diagram, encouraged by the teacher, was the invented spelling of students. Prior to beginning to write about what they had learned, the teacher encouraged all students to use their invented spelling. The teacher then moved around the class to discuss the diagrams and read the texts with her students. Thus, at this level, the invented spelling of students became a part of the shared discourse of the class. The expectation that this discourse would evolve as a consequence of the learning was overt in the activities of the class. Over time, evidence was presented to depict everyday language being replaced by the language of science and invented spelling being replaced by standard English.

One way of designing an approach to assessment that is consistent with constructivism is to use portfolios as repositories for students' knowledge. The portfolio, conceptualized as a container, can be used as a place for students to place artifacts that represent what they have learned. An artifact would be evidence of learning and can be the focus for discussions between students or with a teacher and a student. A system of assessment and learning built around portfolios affords the advantage of providing students with power to decide which artifacts to place in the container, how to describe what each artifact represents, and to engage in an interactive manner about the artifact and what it represents. Via artifacts, students and teachers can engage in rich conversations about what is known and how learning has changed over time. An artifact that is no longer relevant to the understanding of an individual can be removed or retained as an example of how learning has occurred over time. Students have considerable power in such a system, but so too do teachers, as they focus their attention on ascertaining what students know and how they are making sense of the artifacts that they have chosen to include in their portfolios.

Performance tasks in science usually involve the use of materials to engage a task, identify a problem, and seek solutions. Materials are frequently manipulated, measurements are taken, and calculations are made as data are manipulated in a process of problem solving. Students are given a common task, but they are allowed to seek solutions in their own way and they can interact with assessors about the meanings given the tasks, what they mean by their solutions, and how they justify the selection of one solution over another. The potential for interaction diminishes the problems of misunderstanding the intended meanings of the assessor and the assessed but do little to address the power imbalances inherent in many assessment systems.

Within most educational cultures, assessment provides a driving force for the implemented curriculum. To the extent that assessment tasks provide students with a reason to learn facts and algorithms by rote and to suppress their own voices with respect to the powerful voices of canonical knowledge, there is a dire need for the reform of science assessment. At the present time, the approaches to assessment fit well with transmission models of teaching and learning. One set of traditional practices supports the other and provides a conservative force in opposition to well-intentioned reform efforts. Teaching, learning, and assessment practices form a coherent set that leads most learners to a situation where they are disempowered by science. Memorization and rote application of algorithms characterize the experiences of many students, who will readily acknowledge that they do not understand science. If the approach to assessment were to be reformed so that the assessment system would focus on the extent to which students make sense of scientific ideas and can enact their knowledge in problem settings, then it is possible that students would adapt their approaches to learning so that they could be successful in performing on assessment tasks in an acceptable way. What I am suggesting is that there is some potential in using the assessment system as an engine for the reform of elementary science teaching and learning. However, there is a cautionary note, reform occurs in a culture that has its traditions and associated expectations. If the approaches to assessment are to be reformed in such a way that learners have more power than is traditionally the case, not only teachers and students will need to be educated as to the efficacy of the changes. New ways of thinking will have to be pervasive throughout the culture, if changes to the methods of assessment are to be initiated and sustained.

ORGANIZING STUDENTS FOR LEARNING

This section examines the manner in which the environment can be organized to facilitate student learning. A variety of activities are discussed in terms of the idea that the teacher is best able to mediate the learning of students by attending to the manner in which they engage tasks. The activities discussed are small group, whole class, textbook, and laboratory.

Small-Group Activities

If the route to the facilitation of learning is via coparticipation, then it makes sense to organize students for learning so that they can interact with others and use the shared language they are constructing. A variety of grouping patterns can promote learning and will be considered here. However, small groups have been advocated as one way to organize students for higher levels of learning. In a review of the relationship between cooperative learning and the teaching and learning of science, Tobin, Tippins, and Gallard (1994) noted that "although studies of cooperative learning in the context of science education abound, . . . the focus of these studies has not been so specifically on the learning process." This is no longer the case. Good,

McClaslin, and Reys (1992) identified many difficulties with small-group learning that can arise when proper conditions for learning cooperatively are not created and sustained.

Group learning comprises a number of quite different activities, all of which assume that learning requires discussion among group members before completing a task. Linn and Burbules (1993) distinguished cooperative learning where a task is divided into parts and group members each complete a part, collaborative learning where two or more students work together to arrive at an agreed-on solution to a problem, and tutored learning where one student teaches another. They indicated that any small group activity might involve a combination of one or more of these types.

Noddings (1989) examined some of the theoretical and empirical factors associated with small group learning and concluded that the issues that needed to be considered prior to implementing group activities included the purposes of the groups, group membership, roles of teacher and students, the nature of the activities in which students will engage, and the manner in which group outcomes will be evaluated. Is group learning equally effective for all educational goals? Linn and Burbules identified cognitive, social, and workplace skills as three goal areas often associated with small-group learning. According to Linn and Burbules, group learning is usually effective for brainstorming and generating ideas and usually ineffective for planning activities. However, they cautioned that successful groups are trained to generate ideas and accept and elaborate on the ideas of others without criticizing them. Learning in a social setting, including a small group, can occur by students appropriating the ideas of others by building on someone else's idea to create an idea they could not have created alone. Linn and Burbules (1993) noted that

> Collaboration succeeds when students are effective at communicating their ideas and able to help other group members see why their idea contributes to the group goal. It also depends on group adherence to a form of discourse that values argument, reliance on evidence, and explanation. (p. 112)

A premise underlying this chapter is that the discourse of an elementary class will evolve over time from the discourse of the home toward a discourse of science. Linn and Burbules identified two aspects of life in everyday situations that are unhelpful in terms of making progress toward a scientific form of discourse, a tendency to remain silent about conflicting evidence or to assert with authority. If students are to make progress in terms of not remaining silent and not asserting on the basis of faith, then they will need practice in relating evidence to knowledge claims. Such practice will no doubt take place in a variety of activity settings, including small group activities. Can students accept multiple alternative solutions and then choose the best from among them? There appears to be no sound reason to expect students to do this automatically, and it is acknowledged that students would have to learn the value of doing this and then learn how to do it. A confounding factor in making progress in this regard would appear to be the perceived status of certain peers and peer pressure to maintain the status quo. For example, an idea generated by a person with the highest status is often accepted without being subjected to tests of its viability. Linn and Burbules commented that often the status accorded an individual has little to do with scientific aptitude. Thus, ideas that are not viable may be accepted on the authority of a student who has status for reasons unrelated to his or her knowledge of science. In addition to increasing the probability that students will accept "incorrect" knowledge as correct without first considering other alternatives is a danger that group members will reinforce status differences and stereotyped behavior. Linn and Burbules warn that male students may discredit females and minorities and reinforce views of science as a male domain. Group activities may be less equitable than autonomous learning activities for females

Science educators must be concerned about whether students in groups learn and also whether the knowledge the group constructs is viable. Groups might construct a consensus that is at odds with canonical science. To address this potential problem teachers would need to review the consensuses reached in small groups and facilitate the development of a whole-class-level consensus that can be compared with the views accepted by scientists as correct. Indeed access to the knowledge accepted by scientists through texts and other sources of information about science appeals as a necessary part of any elementary science program. Even in a class where small-group work occurs frequently, it is anticipated that levels of consensus will be negotiated and final agreed-on knowledge claims would be tested with canonical science.

Battistich, Solomon, and Delucchi (1993) described how the effects of cooperative learning on students' academic achievement and social development are a function of the quality of group interaction. They asserted that group efforts often may involve negative interactions that reduce interpersonal attraction and may actually impede the learning and achievement of some students. Battistich et al. indicated that pressures toward conformity and concurrence seeking in groups may lead to unproductive collaboration and unreflective decision making that solidify misconceptions or lead to compromises that combine the worst, rather than the best, of members' ideas. They identified a need to incorporate procedures for improving group interaction and management skills and for creating and maintaining group norms for interpersonal cooperation and concern. They suggested that, throughout lessons, teachers might emphasize the interpersonal values that were relevant to group activity (e.g., fairness, concern for others, responsibility).

Linn and Burbules (1993) commented that students who ask questions that are answered benefit from group learning. They then raised a question about students who are ignored. This question relates directly to research undertaken in mathematics by King (1993), who observed forms of student passivity during small-group cooperative learning, especially among low-achieving students. Low expectations for the performance of low achievers was fueled by self-perceptions and the reinforcing perceptions of their high-achieving peers. In small-group activities, the engagement of low achievers was mediated by the dominant leadership style of some high achievers, interpersonal relations among group members, their relative inability to make a positive impact on the progress of the group, and the reinforcing effects of their negative self-perceptions with regard to personal progress in mathematics. King noted that because low achievers enjoy learning and working in small groups, educators need to overcome the problems associated with small-group learning. Among the suggestions King made for elementary teachers, to allow for the development of cooperative skills, were these: students should rotate roles within groups, tasks should be selected to enable progression from simple to complex and from short duration to relatively long duration, students should be permitted to practice assigned roles, and successful experiences for small groups should be promoted. Teachers were encouraged to closely monitor the progress of low achievers and alter prevailing status differentials with a goal of establishing more equal rates of participation among low and high achievers.

Corno (1992) observed that one reason why students enjoy group activities is that they often mix learning and relationship building activities. She advocated that teachers provide support and create activities for students to challenge themselves and others while they pursue goals and grow comfortable with criticism. Corno suggested that teachers might mediate less in the learning of students in small-group activities because "the value of peers over teachers in delivering external prompts appears to rest on students' common worldviews at various ages, which lead to developmentally appropriate queries and comments" (p. 79). The suggestion highlights the place of student verbal interaction in the negotiation of a shared discourse. Accordingly, teachers need to strike a balance between effective mediation and over*engineering*, by gradually relinquishing control of certain processes and objectives. The assumption is that the students will assume responsibility for the control relinquished by the teacher and employ their greater autonomy to pursue activities to enhance their learning and engagement in relevant and meaningful tasks. If the increased autonomy leads to coparticipation for students then small groups indeed can promote meaningful learning.

Whole-Class Activities

During this constructivist era there seems to be a widespread perception that it is not desirable to employ whole-class activities in science. Rather than adhering to such a generalized assertion it might be more fruitful to focus on the roles of teachers and learners and inquire as to the types of whole class activities that might be conducive to learning. The focus of a whole-class activity must be on enhancing the learning of all students and the roles of students should necessitate active engagement and coparticipation in the shared language of the classroom. Analogously, the roles of the teacher ought to be active and focused on mediating the learning of all students.

Experienced elementary teachers will often have students sit together on a mat or in a semicircle. The purpose of doing this is to bring the students together in such a way that they can focus on the teacher whose role is to conduct a whole-class activity. Of course, the focus need not be a teacher, it could just as easily be a peer as was demonstrated in mathematics education in the problem-centered learning approaches advocated by Wheatley (1991) and Cobb (1991). In the problem-centered approaches in mathematics, students led whole class discussions in a process of developing negotiated consensuses about what they had learned from earlier small-group work. These whole-class sessions were interactive and continued for up to 45 minutes. In these examples, the active engagement of students was supported by earlier small-group activities in which they engaged with a peer in problem solving. They could use the language and volunteer to lead the whole class discussion when they wanted to make a contribution.

Demonstrations are potentially useful foci in science because they can provide events around which concepts can be built. For example, in a lesson shown in a videotape from the Harvard Case Studies Project (Science Media Group, 1995), a teacher employs a demonstration that shows the prongs of a tuning fork being plunged into a glass of water. The teacher moves around a semicircle in which her students are seated and allows individuals to describe what they observed. Quickly the class constructs a shared experience around which vibrations and the pitch of musical notes are associated. Throughout the lesson on sound the students participated in a variety of activities that included whole-class, small-group, and individualized settings. At all times the teacher demonstrated her knowledge of students of this age and mediated their engagement in such a way that they remained focused and were permitted to employ the shared language of the class to make visible what they knew at a particular point in time. Whole-class activities certainly were not taboo, but were used to provide variation and to create experiences that were shared, in a negotiated sense, with the entire class. In such activities the teacher's goals were not to disseminate or transmit knowledge but to facilitate the negotiation of a shared experience at the whole class level.

In my review of the use of an extended wait time in teaching and learning (Tobin, 1987), it was clear that teachers should provide time for students to process speech in whole-class settings. The review suggests that bursts of speech should be punctuated with intervals of 3–5 seconds of silence, not for others to begin to speak, but for all to think about what has been said and make sense of it. During these periods of silence students can begin to connect what they are learning to what they already know and think about what else they know that might be relevant to what they are learning. Thus, they will reconstruct extant knowledge, make connections, identify contradictions and consistencies, and formulate questions that need to be resolved. The arguments that Kuhn (1993) has suggested might characterize science are carried out in the minds of individuals in the silent periods between bursts of speech. During those intervals of silence the teacher can reflect on what he or she has already said and consider what is to be said next. In addition, the teacher can monitor the body language of students and formulate strategies for changing the ways in which individuals engage. The inclusion of 3–5 second intervals of silence also increases the potential of noninteractive whole class activities to become interactive. Students have the time to construct questions and explanations and indicate a willingness to contribute to ongoing conversations.

Wait time is not seen as a mechanical device to be used in a technical way but as a way to provide time for reflection in action, to allow the social context to mediate the personal constructions of individuals. As students acquire the language of the speaker they need time to assign meaning, reconstruct relevant extant knowledge, and examine the fit of what they are hearing with what they know. The learner has much to do and a continual barrage of talk from the teacher or another student will interfere with building meaningful conceptual relationships. If teachers use wait times of 3–5 seconds and students do not engage in the processes mentioned previously, then the odds are that they will not learn in the way that I envision here. It is important, therefore, for students to have a clear idea of their roles as learners, so that they recognize the purpose of opportunities such as short but regular intervals of silence to making sense, elaborate, and clarify. In addition, if opportunities to reflect are not provided and students understand the purpose of regular periods of silence for their own learning, they can request additional opportunity to think things through. To use an extended wait time appropriately is not to pause after every sentence, but to pause when it is appropriate and for a time that is appropriate in the context. Research has shown that, on average, the required pause time is 3–5 seconds, but what an average hides is that there will be times when pauses of 10–15 seconds are desirable and other times when less than a quarter of a second is optimal to link sentences to one another.

Rowe (1983), in a series of studies undertaken at the college level and following after her wait time studies, explored the value of longer periods of time away from the input of a teacher in whole-class settings. Although her initial studies were conducted in college classes, we conducted a set of studies in middle and high school classes (e.g., Tobin & Espinet, 1989) in which we adapted Rowe's 10–2 method to ensure that in every 10 minutes of instruction there was at least 2 minutes for students to look back over what had happened in the previous 8 minutes. What we did in those studies was to create groups of two in which students discussed questions related to what was covered by the teacher in the previous 8 minutes. These review questions allowed students to use their own words to make sense of what had happened previously and also to reconstruct relevant prior knowledge and examine the fit of what they were learning to what they knew already. Breaks of this type are consistent with building a shared language and creating an environment in which coparticipation occurs. Once again, it would not be essential for this to occur for 2 minutes of every lesson in a mechanical way. The 10–2 method serves as a reminder to break up whole class activities with small group and individualized activities such that students can make sense of what is happening. I see the 10–2 method as being applicable to elementary classrooms so long as it is not seen as a panacea to be used irrespective of context.

Textbook Activities

There has been a tendency for present day science educators to look at textbooks as a part of traditional practice that has to be downplayed. In part this is due to acceptance of the hands-on metonymy for science education. If an activity is not hands-on, then it is regarded as inappropriate. However, from the science as discourse perspective is quite apparent that approaches to science that include the use of a textbook can be very productive, as long as students can use the language of the textbook and construct ideas that lead to a meaningful learning of science. Calhoun and Rubba (1993) noted that textbooks are used more than 90% of the time by more than 90% of all science teachers. However, what type of science is portrayed in textbook-oriented curricula? Calhoun and Rubba reported that the textbooks they analyzed differed greatly in terms of the complexity of the treatment of scientific ideas. They noted that, within a textbook, the level of the treatment appeared to be similar but between textbooks there were marked differences. Their analyses looked at the number of propositions, cross linkages, and illustrative examples. They concluded that those textbooks in which concepts were interrelated were written at a more difficult conceptual level and were likely to be perceived as more difficult by students. What is of most importance with a textbook is that students, with the assistance of a teacher and peers, can create environments of coparticipation that include textual materials. If this occurs, then the text can be a way to link the science of the classroom to the worlds of scientists and applications of science outside universities and school buildings. As long as students can read them meaningfully, textbooks are one way of connecting science to technology and society.

Laboratory Activities

There has been some confusion about the role of the laboratory in science teaching and learning. I was quite surprised to find, in a study of high school teaching and learning, that teachers and students alike valued laboratory activities, enjoyed participating in them, and rated them as valuable learning experiences. In contrast to the positive statements from teachers and students, the labs we observed in that study were bedlam (Tobin & Gallagher, 1987). Students were unruly and uncontrollable and the teachers battled to maintain a safe environment let alone one that was conducive to learning. I conclude from this observation that the value that teachers and students have for laboratory activities relates to underlying beliefs about learning science rather than a critical analysis of the learning environments in laboratory activities in which they have participated. Similarly, it is commonplace for science educators to regard laboratory activities as the essence of science education. For example, Marek and Cavallo (1995) asserted "Scientific investigations in elementary school are essential" (p. 2). However, what are the purposes of laboratories? To some, they are opportunities for students to engage in problem-centered learning tasks (Wheatley, 1991). To others, laboratory activities provide the concrete experiences many have inferred optimize Piaget's notions of maximizing the learning of young children. They provide the hands-on learning that is thought to promote learning. Others maintain that the laboratory is the essence of science and to do science is to engage in laboratory activities.

There is a variety of reasons for doing laboratory activities, and these ought to be acknowledged. By making it possible to engage in laboratory activities, students can see what science is like by manipulating equipment and participating in activities not unlike those in which scientists have engaged. Getting involved in standard experiments, such as those associated with pendulums, melting, optics, sound, and studies of plants and animals provide students with insights into the nature of science. What is important here, as in all activities, is that students understand what they are doing and why they are doing it. Laboratory activities can assist in removing the mystique of science, making it comprehensible to all students. The use of laboratory activities to verify information derived from text sources also is an underrepresented activity in elementary schools. Putting knowledge to the test or ascertaining the warrants for given knowledge claims are at the essence of becoming literate in science. It is not essential for every activity to involve students in problem-solving tasks. In making that claim I do not want to play down the importance of problem solving as a way of learning or representing science. What I claim is that laboratory activities also can play important additional roles in science education. Other important reasons for getting involved in laboratory activities include learning the manipulative skills associated with measurement and building equipment for given purposes.

Recently I watched, for the first time, a television program called *Bill Nye, the Science Guy*. The grade 6 students with whom I shared this experience were completely entranced by the program. They watched an episode each Friday and their teacher built his science program around the episodes. This program was on our solar system and its magnitude. I was astonished at the high quality of the learning environment. The discussion after the videotape was superb as students recapped with their teacher the most salient points. The class wanted to replicate what they had seen on the videotape by drawing the orbits of the planets around the sun as ellipses, using a pencil, string, and thumb tacks. Actually, the teacher planned to do this and managed a lively postviewing discussion with the students such that the idea emerged as a consensus that was enthusiastically endorsed by his highly motivated students. Like Bill Nye and their teacher, these students loved science. Inwardly I groaned, thinking that the activity was way too advanced. The numbers were huge and I could not envision coparticipation occurring.

The laboratory activity that ensued occupied several weeks of science but involved all students in a sixth grade pod. At the end of the activity what had been accomplished was astonishing. The activity was conceptually difficult for the teacher, the students, and for me. I participated by reaching the World Wide Web to obtain the technical data about the eccentricity of the orbits and faxing the data to the class. The students used their calculators to generate the data they needed to plot the orbits and they were successful in re-creating the orbital patterns featured on the videotape. Throughout the activity the students, the teacher, and I were constantly challenged. The knowledge needed to complete the project that was negotiated with the 180 students was distributed throughout a community that included me and a prospective teacher. Throughout the task, we were all problem solving, focused on a shared goal of plotting the orbits to replicate what we had seen on television. What was important about the activity was that students were not excluded because of a distance between them and the data used to build the orbits. Coparticipation was a goal for everybody. We were sensitive to the problems of students not knowing what was happening and wanted to ensure that students all had chances to participate actively and meaningfully.

At the heart of what I consider to be a meaningful learning activity was a shared experience on a videotape of a television series on children's science. The shared event was brought into focus with a whole-class discussion in which students heightened their motivation to engage in subsequent hands-on activities, but with a purpose of re-creating the orbitals of the planets around the sun. Important ingredients to the success of the lesson was the high level of enthusiasm of all participants in this community and a willingness to commit the time to complete the project. In addition, the knowledge needed to complete the project was dispersed throughout the community and there was a visible willingness to seek out expertise and learn from those who had the knowledge. The boundaries of the learning community were permeable as necessary resources from outside the classroom were used to facilitate the accomplishment of the goal of plotting the orbits and the associated learning. All students were included in the activity and out-of-school time was willingly volunteered by many students to search for potentially relevant data and to learn skills that could be taught to others in the class.

A study by Marek and Cavallo (1995) examined the relationship between the learning opportunities that occurred when instruction was centered on the use of student generated data compared to teacher generated data. Essentially, they reported that the quality of engagement was superior when students used student-generated data. What can be gleaned from this study is the importance of students knowing about the data they are manipulating such that they can engage with understanding in conversations about it. In other words, the significance of the study undertaken by Marek and Cavallo is the focus it brings to the importance of coparticipation. If students are to learn and benefit from laboratory activities they need to have a full understanding of and participate in conversations about what they are doing. Marek and Cavallo stated that:

> The coordination of experiences was accomplished when students used the written language and symbols (the charts) and engaged in dialogue with one another about their developing thoughts and ideas. The use of oral and written language together with the development of the concept through the utilization of student-gathered data allows students to develop a "logical system." (p. 13)

In a study of the science learning of five- and six-year-olds, Butts, Hofman, and Anderson (1993) noted that there was no evidence that manipulation of objects helped children build a concept of floating and sinking. There was clear evidence that instructional experiences helped children develop a clearer concept of sinking and floating. They speculated that the success of children may have resulted from both manipulation and instructional experiences plus sufficient time to make sense of what they were learning. The authors concluded that it is essential for teachers of young children to provide them with direct experiences coupled with instructional conversations that include discrepant events. In a follow-up study, Butts, Hofman, and Anderson (1994) presented evidence that instructional conversations helped students develop a clearer concept of pitch. They concluded from this study that hands-on activities, a relevant videotape, and instructional conversations were significant contributors to children modifying their personal conceptual frameworks. The authors noted that:

> In the contemporary reform efforts, it may be that many teachers interpret the usefulness of "hands-on" experiences for children as meaning that if students are active in their science experiences, then they will be learning. In this study, we found this is

> not necessarily true. "Hands-on" experiences need to be coupled with instructional conversations. (p. 12)

EQUITY ISSUES

Hardly any issue is more important in science education than the participation and learning of minorities (Hodson, 1993). In the United States of America, for example, three significant minority groups, African-Americans, Hispanics from numerous Latin American countries, and Native Americans are underrepresented and underachieving in science education (Atwater, 1994). In addition, despite more than two decades of widespread research on gender equity and participation in science, the evidence suggests that females are still underrepresented in science and tend to achieve at lower levels than males (Kahle & Meece, 1994).

The challenges of educating minorities are widespread throughout the United States and the world, but at no level is the issue of greater importance than in elementary schools. Here students are just starting out on their journeys as learners of science and it is imperative that they experience success and enjoy science in the elementary years. To do this, it is critical that students perceive themselves as able to make sense of what is to be learned. Too often it seems as if, in these formative years, students begin to drop out of science because of inappropriate experiences in the classroom. However, the evidence suggests that students can get excited about science if efforts are made to involve them in appropriate activities. One of the elementary teachers interviewed by Muire (1996) noted that

> Those students who did not grasp concepts from books were able to express themselves through the use of recycled materials and increased whole class sharing and learning. Students with poor language skills were able to express themselves better while working on various hands-on projects. Activities become more student oriented. Behavior problems decreased and students with attention problems have been able to attend to these activities for longer periods of time. I have learned that authentic assessment is achieved much easier. Student participation has skyrocketed. (p. 43)

This section examines issues associated with ethnic, linguistic, and gender equity as they apply to the teaching and learning of elementary science.

Ethnic and Linguistic Minorities

A framework proposed by Ogbu (1992) allows us to examine teaching and learning of science in terms of sociocultural factors relating to the presence of minorities in a dominant culture. Voluntary minorities are those who have migrated to a country, more or less voluntarily, and desire more economic well being and, in many cases, greater political freedom. They usually experience initial difficulties due to language and culture as well as a lack of understanding of how the educational system works. However, unlike other minority groups, voluntary minorities gradually adapt to the mainstream culture and usually succeed academically. This group includes migrants from Asia to Western countries such as the United States of America, Canada, the United Kingdom, and Australia. Tobin and McRobbie (1996) described how Chinese Australians, whom they regarded as voluntary minorities, worked hard in the classroom to overcome the almost insurmountable barriers of limited English proficiency and a tendency for all classroom transactions to be undertaken in English. A second of Ogbu's categories, involuntary minorities, includes people who are in the mainstream culture against their will, due to historical factors such as slavery, conquest, colonization, and forced labor. Involuntary minorities often experience difficulties with school learning due, in part, to cultural inversion, a tendency to regard certain forms of behavior, events, symbols, and meanings as inappropriate because of their association with the mainstream culture. Fordham and Ogbu (1986) noted that peer pressure not to act white was a factor that limited the opportunities of some African-American students. Accordingly, teachers might recognize a tendency for some minorities in a classroom to reject the norms of the mainstream white culture and perhaps even endeavor to disrupt that environment. Rather than focus on compliance and the use of power it might be beneficial to explore alternative ways of implementing the curriculum such that all students can engage in ways that are meaningful and motivating to them.

Cultural inversion does not appear to be a problem for most voluntary minorities. According to Ogbu (1992, p. 9),

> voluntary minorities did not come to the United States expecting the schools to teach them in their own culture and language, although they are grateful if the schools do. Usually, they go to the school expecting and willing to learn the culture and language of the schools, and they also expect at least some initial difficulty in doing so.

Consequently, it is anticipated that students who are voluntary minorities will be, for the most part, committed to learning and generally prepared to make extra efforts to become acculturated. According to Ogbu (1992), among the voluntary minorities, there appears to be a collective orientation, or cultural capital (Bourdieu, 1977a, 1977b), toward making good grades in school and social pressure, including peer pressure, that encourages success. In addition, community pressure promotes quests for high grades and avoidance of ridicule, criticism, and isolation. Accordingly, voluntary minority students might be expected to support their learning by fully utilizing information and resources available in their schools as well as their cultural capital, which includes their native language. However, unless teachers make provision for them to employ their native language tools in bilingual activities they may find their learning environments less than optimal.

Members of a group that is regarded as consisting of voluntary minorities can assume the characteristics of involuntary minorities. In terms of the culture of science, it appears as if some groups of students participate minimally, against their will, for the minimum amount of time, and suffer from cultural inversion. They see the culture of science as inappropriate for them and reject it because they do not fit. Although students might construct themselves as interested in science and committed to learning with understanding (i.e., as voluntary minorities), they might feel as if they are swimming against a strong current as they endeavor to convince others of their goals. They will feel most comfort when their practices fit the expectations of others in the classroom. When a minority student walks into a classroom he or she is constructed by others in ways that partially reflect personal characteristics and partially those associated with belonging to an ethnic or cultural group. Those in the class, including the teacher, construct themselves and one another. Thus, each person, whether one likes it or not, is constructed in ways that take account of gender, ethnicity, and social class. Within a given society, each person will feel a pressure to adopt a set of roles that is consistent with the constructions of others, and when others interact with her or him, the expectations associated with those interactions might be mediated by a realization that the person with whom they are interacting is part of a minority group. Over a period of time, these pressures can lead some minority students to feel unwelcome in the culture and their practices can become more like those of involuntary minorities.

Ogbu argued that minority groups have castelike features; cultural baggage assigned by others with whom they interact. What seems most salient about this phenomenon is that often it is an invisible part of belonging to a culture. Neither the minority member who has to deal with this cultural baggage nor those who construct them as they do might be specifically aware of what is happening. The construction of self and nonself are a part of the daily routines of individuals in any social setting, a part of normal life within a cultural setting. The normal routines of constructing self and others are part of the problem of dealing with significant differences associated with the performance of minorities in science classes. Some teachers do not notice differences in the performance of minorities, and even when they are pointed out to them, they might recognize such differences as the way things are meant to be.

In the past several decades, refugees from political upheaval and repression, who are not included in Ogbu's categories, have contributed to significant increases in the populations of many Western countries and have challenged extant approaches to education. In addition to the language and other cultural obstacles they encounter when they arrive at school, frequently these students suffer from the trauma of fleeing their home countries, where they may not have been well educated. For example, although they might speak Spanish, students might be unable to write in Spanish or read and write in English. These students face cognitive and affective challenges in learning science and can benefit from a curriculum that focuses on the special problems they encounter and ways in which activities can be arranged to allow them to utilize their cultural capital in the production of learning.

Lee, Fradd, and Sutman (1995) noted that students from nonmainstream backgrounds had more difficulty with science knowledge and vocabulary compared to monolingual English students. Some did not have requisite science knowledge or experiences and others had the science concepts but lacked the specific vocabulary to communicate meaning. Many words were needed by limited English proficient (LEP) students to communicate ideas that could be communicated by English proficient students as short, concise statements. Problems such as these appear to be widespread and are not confined to the United States of America nor are they applicable only to students whose achievement is low. For example, Asian immigrants and refugees, most of whom have limited English proficiency, constitute a minority group in many Western countries where English is a native language and, in comparison to their English-speaking indigenous counterparts, they often are successful in science (Biggs, 1994). The magnitude of the challenges of teaching LEP students is heightened by a dearth of research and policy frames, which often require the language of teaching and learning to be English. There is evidence that a form of linguistic imperialism (Phillipson, 1992) underlies decisions to use English to enact the curriculum in linguistically diverse classrooms. Sweeney and Gallard (1996) reported that science teachers believed that

> LEP and cultural minority students must learn the English language in order to achieve any level of success within this country's education system, and within its wider mainstream society. Academic and/or social "success" within wider American society (or the "power world") is seen as being a possibility for minority cultures. This possibility relies on the extent to which minority culture "fits in" with or adapts to the mainstream or "majority" culture. In relation to LEP and cultural/language minority students, such adaptation requires a high level of proficiency in the English language. (p. 2)

Heath and Mangiola (1991) discussed peer tutoring as a way of fulfilling the promise of linguistic and cultural diversity in elementary classrooms. Like White (1996) they emphasized the critical role schools had in creating options for all students to use their language tools to learn. They noted that

> All students do not bring the same kinds of knowledge, language habits and strategies for learning to school, and that school is an institution that must take responsibility for presenting all students with a range of options for organizing knowledge and using language. (p. 14)

In contexts that build on their strengths and consider their learning needs, students develop meaning and improve their performance in science. The native language of an individual can be regarded as a form of cultural capital that can be used in the process of learning. Heath and Mangiola (1991) made it clear that they regarded students in linguistically and culturally diverse settings as having considerable promise that was not necessarily exploited through traditional approaches to teaching and learning. They advocated moves away from traditional approaches to teaching multilingual groups of students. They commented that

> acquiring the ability to talk about reading and writing is not dependent on the particular language used or on the particular learning context . . . the ability to talk and think "literately" is a fundamental skill that is transferable to all areas of academic performance. (p. 22)

Sweeney and Gallard (1996), who examined teachers' beliefs about teaching science to LEP students, reported that

> the cultural background of LEP/cultural minority students is seen by teachers as being "inferior" or less "advanced" than the mainstream US culture. Acquisition of facility in the English language is one main way in which they may gain access to a "better" culture which will ultimately be of academic and social benefit to them. (p. 2)

If such a belief is used as a referent for teaching elementary science, then one might expect all students to have to engage in English and adopt the cultural mores of the majority. In contrast, a principle of coparticipation would suggest that students employ all of their language resources including their native languages and English. Although this will provide a challenge for teachers who speak only English, strategies might be employed for all learners to employ all of their language tools even though interactions with the teacher would involve the use of English. Just as an early childhood teacher might collaborate with a child to make sense of invented spelling so too might teachers engage LEP students to make sense of inscriptions written in languages other than English. And just as the early childhood teacher encouraged the use of invented spelling so too might elementary teachers encourage the use of students' native languages.

Atwater (1994) noted that

> the best ways to teach children depend on the individual student's cognitive style. The more traditional ways of teaching science may not be as effective with underrepresented groups in science as are some of the active, relational, and holistic approaches. (p. 563)

A question that must be addressed by teachers in elementary grades is how to accomplish coparticipation for all learners in a class. From this perspective, a program that will benefit minorities is most likely to benefit all learners. If coparticipation is attained in the classroom, then all learners will be able to use a language that enables them to communicate effectively. They will be able to understand what is being said by others and will employ language tools to extend their understanding in the contexts of what they already know. Their cultural knowledge thereby becomes a form of capital rather than an obstacle that has to be overcome before learning can occur. In the special case of students for whom English is not a native language, and who have limited proficiency in English, it is apparent that strategies need to be employed to enable these students to use their native language and their developing English to communicate and make sense. Atwater (1994) also noted that when science is taught in the primary language of students and when they have access to bilingual visuals, science success is more apt to be within their reach.

Teemant and colleagues have examined issues related to the problems faced by LEP students endeavoring to learn science (Teemant, Bernhardt, Rodriguez-Muñoz, & Aiello, 1995). The authors drew the attention of teachers to three significant gaps that ought to be considered when teaching LEP students: between what they can understand in English and what they can speak in English, between what they can write in English and what they can write in their own native languages, and how they conceptualize in English and how they conceptualize in their own native language. The authors claim that students cannot wait until they speak English fluently to be deemed "ready" for science learning. The implication here is that it should be recognized that building proficiency in a second language, such as English, will take many years. Teachers should realize that helping bilingual students does not mean compromising science content. Because of the language limitations of LEP students, it may be necessary to make special provision for learning science, such as placing them with others who speak their native language. If that is not possible, it still might be beneficial to make it possible for students to use their native language in making summaries of what happened, in raising questions, and in providing answers to those questions. For LEP students, learning science could be a bilingual experience during which they are encouraged to use all of their language tools to make sense of science. Teemant et al. mention that teachers can help make science more accessible to LEP students through their adjustments to the lesson in progress. They specifically mention adjustments in how reading and writing activities are used to reinforce learning and basing the assessment of performance in science on multiple assessments. Atwater (1994) maintained that it is impossible to develop nonbiased assessment instruments and that the best science teachers can do is to use a variety of assessment techniques to determine their students' understandings of science. Teemant et al. caution that students' conversational fluency does not guarantee fluency in the type of language needed to make sense of science. The chief implication of this is to allow students to decide on the extent to which they employ their native language in the initial efforts to describe what is happening, to interpret data, and to interconnect understandings of science within a semantic network.

Gender Equity

Research on gender equity and science highlights a pervasive and continuing problem. Weinburgh (1995) conducted a meta-analysis of gender related differences and attitudes toward science. She reported that, based on 18 studies and more than 6000 subjects, boys had more positive attitudes than girls and that the correlation between attitudes and science achievement was about 0.5 for boys and girls. Boys had a more positive attitude toward all science subjects. Keeves and Kotte (1995) noted that the gender issue in science is very much an international one that is quite marked at the time of secondary schooling. The notion that follows from this is that the elementary grade levels and perhaps earlier are critical in terms of shaping the attitudes of children toward science. Harding (1995) explained that, by the time children are expected to participate in formal school science, they are considerably experienced in gender-appropriate activities. Kahle (1995) asserted that, if the gender issue in science is to be successfully addressed, the elementary school is the critical place for changes in formal and informal science curricula, classroom instruction and interactions, and in school structure and socialization.

Greenfield (1995) noted that girls remain behind boys in science achievement and interest at the upper grade levels, in part because they experience different situations in and out of school. She advocated the use of investigation-based, cooperative learning strategies and a closer connection of physical science with aspects of daily life. In an analysis of participation in science fairs over a period of 20 years Greenfield noted that girls are less likely than boys to do projects in the physical, earth, and mathematical sciences and their projects are less likely to involve scientific inquiry.

Research on gender-related differences in science performance and achievement in the elementary grade levels is mixed and often reflects the design of the study as much as substantive issues. For example, Shaw and Doan (1990) found that, for a sample of children from grades 2 and 5 from a city in southern Alabama, there were no statistically significant differences in achievement and attitudes toward science of boys and girls. However, for a sample of 11-year-olds in the United Kingdom differences in favor of boys occurred in physics-related activities, with those involving electricity consistently showing the largest differences for boys and girls (Harding, 1995). Harding described similar results in Norway, where girls achieved at a lower level only in fields such as electricity where they had less experience than boys. Interestingly, Parker and Rennie (1985) demonstrated that females achieved parity with males in their understandings of electricity when their teachers had completed a special in-service on gender equity. The suggestion is that changes in the dynamics of the classroom can lead to equality in terms of achievement even in fields where the initial experiences of females may place them at a relative disadvantage with respect to males in terms of what knowledge they have to build on at the start of a topic such as electricity.

There appears to be a consensus that a gender-inclusive curriculum should introduce a range of role models, create a friendly and nonthreatening atmosphere in which girls are considered special, contain alternative images of science, model the importance of cooperation and shared learning experiences during problem-solving exercises, provide extra time for girls to experience practical skill development, and portray the relevance of science to young women's lives (Parker, Rennie, & Fraser, 1995). According to Jorde and Lea (1995) gender-inclusive science should have a strong writing component and all children must be motivated and engaged from the beginning of each activity and structure and guidance as well as activities are essential if all students are to learn with understanding. Jorde and Lea also argued that an appropriate gender-inclusive program that is more suitable for girls will be more suitable for all children. They recommended that such programs contain different presentation forms, less content and more of an emphasis on understanding, teachers who perceive themselves as colearners, and total school involvement to increase enthusiasm and participation.

Kahle (1995) argued that much can be done to advance equitable science education by changing the image of science. Because girls and boys enter elementary school with equal interest in science but unequal science-building experiences, activity-based curricula provide girls with experiences that they are less likely than boys to bring to school. Kahle advocates changes in practices to assure equity in relation to the use of science instruments and materials, reading science-related books, and the quality and quantity of interactions with the teacher. Kahle explained that changes need to extend beyond the classroom to ensure equity in the corridors as well as the classrooms. She advocated that, in both the playground and in the classrooms, areas should be specified for quiet and adventurous activities, and boys and girls should be encouraged to participate in both types. Jorde and Lea (1995) commented that, unless teachers try activity-based curriculum materials in their own classrooms, gender-inclusive science will not become a reality no matter how exciting activity-based science is for children. However, what seems to lie in the background in this analysis and what might be of greatest significance in bridging the gap is to ensure that girls and boys coparticipate in the shared language that characterizes the science class. Manipulation of materials might be desirable for learning science meaningfully, but I do not regard it as either necessary or sufficient. However, if materials are available to be used in an activity, it is not reasonable for any participants, such as the most able boys, to monopolize its use to the exclusion of others who seek to use the materials. Coparticipation necessitates equal opportunity to access and appropriate learning resources.

CONCLUSIONS

Conceptualizing elementary science curricula in terms of learning communities brings to the foreground issues associated with interactions between participants in an ongoing process of creating a scientific discourse that is characteristic of that community. Coparticipation among the teacher and students requires all participants to communicate with one another using a shared language that evolves over time. Use of the language is a critical part of the learning process, as important as having hands-on experiences, as students engage the tasks that constitute the curriculum. Oral and written communication cannot be regarded as optional extras, components of an activity that are cut short or omitted when time is short. Hands-on activities occur for a purpose, to provide bases for interpretations in which emergent knowledge claims are related to evidence and plans are made to test them experimentally and ascertain whether or not the emergent knowledge fits with canonical science.

At issue in enacting the curriculum are the goals and expectations constructed for learners. The study by Anyon suggests that goals are shaped by the social class of the students in ways that reproduce society. Coparticipation to support the learning of science implies mutual adaptation of the home and school environments. The extant knowledge of students is not a liability and it is essential for teachers to identify the salient features of the students' discursive tools and enact the curriculum to build from this foundation. Since different students will start with different knowledge resources, the interaction of teachers and learners needs to be tailored to the resources available within the learning community.

The enacted science curriculum must take account of the students, the teachers, and the culture in which a particular school and its curricula are embedded. The notion that curricula can be transferred from one school to another is an oversimplification. There has been a tendency to make sweeping generalizations about what ought to happen in elementary science classes. For example, problem-centered learning approaches that involve small groups of students might be highly suitable for some learning communities and not as suitable for others. Whereas some classes might operate in a problem-centered mode every day for an entire year, others might utilize a wider range of resources and activities. Irrespective of the activity setting it is important for the teacher to focus on the manner in which each student engages. Meaningful learning can occur if coparticipation using a shared language is possible and the students engage in such a way as to employ all of their language resources.

The equity issues addressed in this chapter are not recent phenomena. One way to think about inequitable practices in elementary science is that they are supported by the society in which schools operate. Inequities continue because they are a "normal" way for schools to function and frequently are invisible to participants within the community. If equity is to be attained, there need to be new ways to look at the participation of students in learning tasks. One focus for teachers is to examine the manner in which students make sense of the shared language of the classroom and use it in the process of learning science. If students are unable or unwilling to engage in an appropriate manner, then learning is unlikely to occur as intended and the challenge for both the teacher and students is to redefine tasks such that full participation is possible. I am not advocating an individualized program of study for each student but a realization that, because of the differing resources available to learners, learning trajectories will necessarily be different from one learner to the next. Organizing students to learn not only from interactions with the teacher but also with peers is a challenge and a possible means of realizing the potential locked within the diversity that characterizes elementary science classes.

References

American Association for the Advancement of Science. (1975). *Science—A process approach*. Lexington, MA: Ginn.

Anyon, J. (1981). Social class and school knowledge. *Curriculum Inquiry*, 10, 55–76.

Atwater, M. (1994). Research on cultural diversity in the classroom. In D. L. Gabel (Ed.), *Handbook of research on science teaching and learning* (pp. 558–576). New York: Macmillan.

Battistich, V., Solomon, D., & Delucchi, K. (1993). Interaction processes and student outcomes in cooperative learning groups. *Elementary School Journal*, 94(1), 19–32.

Biggs, J. (1994). What are effective schools? Lessons from East and West. *Australian Educational Researcher*, 21(1), 19–39.

Bourdieu, P. (1977a). Cultural reproduction and social reproduction. In J. Karabel & E. H. Halsey (Eds.), *Power and ideology in education*. Oxford, England: Oxford University Press.

Bourdieu, P. (1977b). *Outline of a theory into practice*. New York: Cambridge University Press.

Briscoe, C., & Lorsbach, A. W. (1991). *Analysis of surveys of Florida principals regarding the preparation of elementary teachers in the areas of mathematics, science, computer technology and geography* (A report to the Education Standards Commission). Tallahassee: Florida Department of Education.

Butts, D. P., Hofman, H. M., & Anderson, M. (1993). Is hands-on experience enough? A study of young children's views of sinking and floating objects. *Journal of Elementary Science Education*, 5(1), 50–64.

Butts, D. P., Hofman, H. M., & Anderson, M. (1994). Is direct experience enough? A study of young children's views of sound. *Journal of Elementary Science Education*, 6(1), 1–16.

Calhoun, R. S., & Rubba, P. A. (1993). An examination of the conceptual structure and reading level of six sixth-grade science textbooks. *Journal of Elementary Science Education*, 5(2), 21–36.

Cobb, P. (1991). Reconstructing elementary school mathematics. *Focus on Learning Problems in Mathematics*, 12(2), 3–32.

Corno, L. (1992). Encouraging students to take responsibility for learning and performance. *Elementary School Journal*, 93(1), 69–83.

Driver, R., Squires, A., Rushworth, P., & Wood-Robinson, V. (1994). *Making sense of secondary science: Research into children's ideas*. London: Routledge.

Education Development Center. (1971). *A working guide to the Elementary Science Study*. Newton, MA: Author.

Fordham, S., & Ogbu, J. (1986). Black students' school success: Coping with the 'burden of acting White.' *Urban Review*, 18(3), 176–206.

Good, T., McClaslin, M., & Reys, B. (1992). Investigating work groups to promote problem solving in mathematics. In J. Brophy (Ed.), *Advances in research on teaching: Vol 3. Planning and managing learning tasks and activities* (pp. 115–160) Greenwich, CT: JAI Press.

Greenfield, T. A. (1995). An exploration of gender participation patterns in science competitions. *Journal of Research in Science Teaching*, 32(7), 735–748.

Harding, J. (1995). Science in a masculine strait-jacket. In L. H. Parker, L. J. Rennie, & B. J. Fraser (Eds.), *Gender, science and mathematics: Shortening the shadow* (pp. 9–21). Dordrecht, The Netherlands: Kluwer Academic Publishers.

Hayes, D., Symington, D., & Martin, M. (1994). Drawing during science activity in the primary school. *International Journal of Science Education*, 16(3), 265–277.

Heath, S. B., & Mangiola, L. (1991). *Children of promise: Literate activity in linguistically and culturally diverse classrooms*. Washington, DC: National Education Association.

Hodson, D. (1993). In search of a rationale for multicultural science education. *Science Education*, 77(6), 685–711.

Hurd, P. D. (1993). Comment on science education research: A crisis of confidence. *Journal of Research in Science Teaching*, 30(8), 1009–1011.

Jorde, D., & Lea, A. (1995). Sharing science: Primary science for both teachers and pupils. In L. H. Parker, L. J. Rennie, & B. J. Fraser (Eds.), *Gender, science and mathematics: Shortening the shadow* (pp. 163–174). Dordrecht, The Netherlands: Kluwer Academic Publishers.

Kahle, J. B. (1995). Equitable science education: A discrepancy model. In L. H. Parker, L. J. Rennie, & B. J. Fraser (Eds.), *Gender, science and mathematics: Shortening the shadow* (pp. 137–147). Dordrecht, The Netherlands: Kluwer Academic Publishers.

Kahle, J. B., & Meece, J. (1994). Research on gender issues in the classroom. In D. L. Gabel (Ed.), *Handbook of research on science teaching and learning* (pp. 542–557). New York: Macmillan.

Keeves, J. P., & Kotte, D. (1995). Patterns of science achievement: International comparisons. In L. H. Parker, L. J. Rennie, & B. J. Fraser (Eds.), *Gender, science and mathematics: Shortening the shadow* (pp. 85–101). Dordrecht, The Netherlands: Kluwer Academic Publishers.

King, L. H. (1993). High and low achievers' perceptions and cooperative learning in two small groups. *Elementary School Journal*, 93(4), 399–416.

Kuhn, D. (1993). Science as argument: Implications for teaching and learning scientific thinking. *Science Education*, 77(3), 319–337.

Lee, O., Fradd, S. H., & Sutman, F. X. (1995). Science knowledge and cognitive strategy use among culturally and linguistically diverse students. *Journal of Research in Science Teaching*, 32(8), 797–816.

Lemke, J. L. (1995). *Textual politics: Discourse and social dynamics*. London: Taylor & Francis.

Linn, M. C., & Burbules, N. C. (1993). Construction of knowledge and group learning. In K. Tobin (Ed.), *The practice of constructivism in science education* (pp. 91–119). Hillsdale, NJ: Erlbaum.

Luria, A. R. (1973). *The working brain: An introduction to neuropsychology*. Harmondsworth: Penguin.

Marek, E. A., & Cavallo, A. M. L. (1995). Passkeys to learning science in the elementary schools: The data and language of science. *Journal of Elementary Science Education*, 7(1), 1–15.

Muire, W. C. (1996). *An evaluation of elementary teachers' needs for mathematics and science teaching in Florida*. Tallahassee: Florida State University.

Murphy, P. F. (1995). Assessment practices and gender in science. In L. H. Parker, L. J. Rennie, & B. J. Fraser (Eds.), *Gender, science and mathematics: Shortening the shadow* (pp. 113–125). Dordrecht, The Netherlands: Kluwer Academic Publishers.

National Research Council. (1996). *National science education standards*. Washington, DC: National Academy Press.

Noddings, N. (1989). Theoretical and practical concerns about small groups in mathematics. *Elementary School Journal*, 89(5), 607–623.

Ogbu, J. U. (1992). Understanding cultural diversity and learning. *Educational Researcher*, 21(8), 5–14, 24.

Parker, L. H., & Rennie, L. J. (1985). *Teacher in-service as an avenue to equality in science and technology education* (pp. 226–234). Contributions to the Third GASAT Conference, Chelsea College, University of London.

Parker, L. H., Rennie, L. J., & Fraser, B. J. (Eds.). *Gender, science and mathematics: Shortening the shadow*. Dordrecht, The Netherlands: Kluwer Academic Publishers.

Phillipson, R. (1992). *Linguistic imperialism*. Oxford, England: Oxford University Press.

Roth, W.-M. (1995). *Authentic school science: Knowing and learning in open-inquiry science laboratories*. Dordrecht, The Netherlands: Kluwer Acadamic Publishers.

Rowe, M. B. (1983). Getting chemistry off the killer course list. *Journal of Chemical Education*, 60(11), 954–956.

Rutherford, F. J., & Ahlgren, A. (1990). *Science for all Americans*. New York: Oxford University Press.

Science Media Group. (1995). *The case of Ingrid* (Case Studies: Modules 1, 2, rough cut No. 2). Cambridge, MA: Harvard Smithsonian Center for Astrophysics.

Shaw, E. L., & Doan, R. L. (1990). An investigation of the differences in attitude and achievement between male and female second and fifth grade science students. *Journal of Elementary Science Education*, 2(1), 10–15.

Sweeney, A., & Gallard, A. J. (1996). *Minority students in the science classroom: Issues of language, class, race and culture*. Tallahassee: Florida State University.

Teemant, A., Bernhardt, E. B., Rodriguez-Muñoz, M., & Aiello, M. (1995). *Bringing science and second language learning together: What every teacher needs to know*. Columbus, OH: National Center for Science Teaching and Learning.

Tobin, K. G. (1987). The role of wait time in higher cognitive level learning. *Review of Educational Research*, 57(1), 69–95.

Tobin, K. G., & Espinet, M. (1989). Impediments to change: An application of peer coaching in high school science. *Journal of Research in Science Teaching*, 26, 105–120.

Tobin, K. G., & Gallagher, J. J. (1987). What happens in high school science classrooms? *Journal of Curriculum Studies*, 19, 549–560.

Tobin, K. G., & McRobbie, C. (1996). The significance of limited English proficiency and cultural capital to the performance in science of Chinese-Australians. *Journal of Research in Science Teaching*, 33(3), 265–282.

Tobin, K. G., & Tippins, D. (in press). Metaphors as seeds for learning and the improvement of science teaching. *Science Education*.

Tobin, K. G., Tippins, D. J., & Gallard, A. (1994). Teachers as learners in the reform of science education. In D. Gabel (Ed.), *Handbook for research on science teaching* (pp. 45–93). New York: Macmillan.

Watters, J. J., & English, L. D. (1995). Children's application of simultaneous and successive processing in inductive and deductive reasoning problems: Implications for developing scientific reasoning skills. *Journal of Research in Science Teaching*, 32(7), 699–714.

Weinburgh, M. (1995). Gender differences in student attitudes toward science: A meta-analysis of the literature from 1970 to 1991. *Journal of Research in Science Teaching*, 32(4), 387–398.

Wheatley, G. H. (1991). Constructivist perspectives on science and mathematics learning. *Science Education*, 75, 9–21.

White, R. (1996). *Barriers to learning science: Bridging gaps between the languages of the home and school science classrooms*. Tallahassee: Florida State University.

CHAPTER

13

Meaningful Learning in Science: The Human Constructivist Perspective

JOEL J. MINTZES
University of North Carolina at Wilmington

JAMES H. WANDERSEE
Louisiana State University

JOSEPH D. NOVAK
Cornell University

CLASSROOM LEARNING IN SCIENCE

Although natural science, in one form or another, has been a significant part of the secondary school curriculum for well over a century (Montgomery, 1994), serious thinking about theory, research, and practice did not fully emerge in the United States until the late 1950s and early 1960s. The launch of the Soviet spacecraft Sputnik in October 1957 shocked a complacent nation and ushered in a "golden age" of curriculum development in science and mathematics. The Russian technological achievement was viewed as a threat to national security and an embarassment to a country that prided itself on its scientific and technical prowess. Blame was laid on an insufficiently rigorous science curriculum, and soon money flowed from Washington. In 1953, the earliest year of NSF activity, $21,000 was allocated for science education; by 1959, that figure had grown to over $22 million (Duschl, 1990). Products of these curriculum development activities included such well-known materials as PSSC Physics, CHEM Study, and BSCS Biology.

Handbook of Academic Learning

Early efforts during this frenzied period were driven largely by the practical demands of creating new materials. Basic theorizing about the structure of knowledge and the nature of learning certainly existed in the work of B. Bloom (1956), Bruner (1960), Easley (1959), Schwab (1960), Tyler (1949), and others, but curriculum efforts and research as it then existed, were tied only loosely to theory. Hotbeds of intellectual activity such as Harvard, Stanford, Berkeley, and the Universities of Illinois and Minnesota were investing much of their time in developing and testing teaching materials. The accepted view of classroom learning was dominated by a theory of operant conditioning (Skinner, 1954) with its heavy emphasis on molding behavior through reinforcement and its proscription against investigating the workings of the human mind. In educational practice, "behavioral objectives" were de rigueur, and "programmed instruction" was viewed as the most promising innovation of the day.

Gradually, during the period 1962–1965, science educators turned their attention toward contemporary work in applied learning theory, epistemology, and the philosophy of science. Among the most influential works of the time were the writings of Ausubel (1963), Gagné (1965), and Piaget (1964) in learning; Kuhn (1962) and Popper (1959), in philosophy; and Vygotsky (1962) and Chomsky (1965) in language and semantics. Without question, the work of Jean Piaget was to have the greatest impact on science curriculum development, especially at the elementary school level, where well-funded projects such as the Science Curriculum Improvement Study (SCIS), the AAAS–Science a Process Approach, and the Elementary Science Study (ESS) were heavily influenced by his stage theory of cognitive development.

At the secondary school level, however, disciplinary specialists from biology, chemistry, and physics dominated curriculum development efforts, and their commitment to rigorous, "accelerated" science programs often resulted in clashes with those espousing developmental views. For example, in a seminal report based on conferences at Cornell and Berkeley that served to introduce Piaget to the science education community, the conference conveners tell us that, "The revival of interest in the work of Jean Piaget on cognitive development in children has served as a leveling agent to the aspirations of curriculum reformers bent on ignoring children's cognitive development in the name of acceleration" (Ripple & Rockcastle, 1964). This nascent tension between "stage theory" developmentalists and reformers influenced by contemporary work on the structure of knowledge (Ausubel, 1963) would reach its apogee in the period 1965–1980 (Herron, 1978; Novak, 1977a, 1977b).

Although the work of David P. Ausubel was known to the science education community, it attracted relatively little attention at first. To many, the central insight advanced by Ausubel (1968) seemed murky and even uninspired; that is, "The most important single factor influencing learning is what the learner already knows. Ascertain this and teach him [sic] accordingly."

How could this formulation guide research and curriculum development? Contributing to the difficulty was Ausubel's tortured and inscrutable writing style that many found impossible to understand. To Novak (1965) and his graduate students, however, Ausubel's work provided a framework for understanding a vast spectrum of seemingly unrelated educational events (Novak, 1977c); and eventually in elaborated form (Ausubel, Novak, & Hanesian, 1978; Novak & Gowin, 1984), the work launched an immensely rich and fruitful research tradition, capturing the attention of a whole new generation of workers in science education and related disciplines (Wittrock, 1994).

Inspired largely by Ausubel's work and beginning in the early 1970s, a steady stream of mostly young investigators began to focus their efforts on "what the learner already knows." The foundation set by Ausubel was further reinforced by an emerging epistemology that had its roots in Kelly's (1955) personal construct theory. The notion that knowledge is a personal, idiosyncratic, and socially negotiated construction and that individuals often construct knowledge that is at variance to the scientifically accepted view led to a *constructivist* perspective on learning that has received wide support in the science education community (Driver & Easley, 1978). This view has been strengthened by an immense avalanche of research on students *alternative conceptions* in science and by recent work in the emerging field of cognitive science.

In this chapter we review some of this research, focusing particularly on studies that support a new synthesis of learning theory, epistemology and philosophy of science. The new synthesis, which has been dubbed *human constructivism* (Novak, 1987, 1993a, 1993b), provides a useful framework for understanding why instruction often fails and why we need to focus on conceptual change by helping students *learn how to learn* in science.

RESEARCH IN SCIENCE LEARNING: THE CONTEXT OF METACOGNITION

Since the early seventies substantial progress has been made in the exploration of human learning. Science educators have contributed significantly to this work, particularly in efforts that address how students understand and misunderstand central concepts in the biological and physical sciences. A second line of related research has developed alongside and largely in isolation of the efforts in science education by workers in the emerging discipline of cognitive science (Carey, 1986). Among other questions, this work has examined how learners structure and use knowledge in science-related domains. The products of these two research programs provide strong support for a Human Constructivist (Novak, 1987, 1993a, 1993b) view of learning and for a variety of metacognitive classroom strategies. In this section we provide an overview of these research traditions and their findings.

Understanding Concepts in the Natural Sciences ("Ascertain This")

Perhaps the most important contribution made by researchers in science education over the past 25 years has been the massive effort to explore the empirical evidence for Ausubel's "prior knowledge" hypothesis. How do students understand concepts in the natural sciences? With the cumulative weight of several thousand studies to support us, we now feel enough evidence has been garnered to advance a modest set of assertions or knowledge claims (Novak & Gowin, 1984) about the ideas students bring with them to their science classes and the effects these notions have on subsequent learning (Wandersee, Mintzes, & Novak, 1994).

The first of these claims, and the one that has received the most empirical support, is that *learners are not "blank slates" or "empty vessels," rather they bring with them to their formal study of science concepts, a finite but diverse set of ideas about natural objects and events; often these notions are inconsistent with explanations offered by scientists and science teachers*. These notions have been variously labeled (Abimbola, 1988); however, at this point the term *alternative conceptions* (P. Hewson, 1981) is apparently preferred by more researchers than any other.

At latest count (Pfundt & Duit, 1994), just under 3500 studies have addressed issues related to students' alternative conceptions in science. Of this number, approximately 50% have focused simply on identifying, describing, and documenting the frequencies of these ideas; with studies on physics concepts predominating, followed by those in biology, chemistry, and earth science, in descending order of frequency.

In physics, the earliest and most influential studies investigated students' conceptions of basic Newtonian mechanics (Champagne, Klopfer, & Anderson, 1980; Clement, 1982; diSessa, 1982; McCloskey, 1983; Minstrell, 1982; Viennot, 1979). Many students, regardless of age or prior experience, appear to subscribe to a kind of Aristotelian notion of moving bodies. In contrast to the Newtonian view, these students hold that moving objects are kept in motion by a constant force, and in the absence of a force, the objects are either at rest or slowing down. These views have been elicited from many students who have been asked to predict the course of a moving body acted on by an outside force. The result, as diSessa describes it, is "a collision" between an Aristotelian worldview and a Newtonian reality.

The fundamental structure of matter is another domain that has been investigated thoroughly by several researchers (Novick & Nussbaum, 1978, 1981; Nussbaum, 1985). Recently, we had occasion to work with the Science Education Department at the Harvard–Smithsonian Center for Astrophysics on the PBS television miniseries A *Private Universe* (Corporation for Public Broadcasting, 1995). In the course of that production we interviewed Jody, a 12th grade student enrolled in an advanced placement (AP) chemistry course at an affluent suburban Boston high school, and Jamie, a middle school student enrolled in a prestigious preparatory school in Cambridge, Massachusetts. The interviews were based directly on Nussbaum's studies and focused on the particulate model of matter. The videotaped discussions revealed that even students who have been exposed to the advantages of a costly, high-quality education often subscribe to alternative conceptions. In this case, both Jody and Jamie held to a common continuous, "raisin cake" model of matter in which atoms are imbedded in a kind of fluid matrix or an infinite regression of progressively smaller particles. The notion that matter consists of particles surrounded by empty space seems to be universally problematic.

Students' ideas about energy and its conservation have been well documented (Bliss & Ogborn, 1985; Duit, 1981; Solomon, 1982, 1983, 1984). Among the most difficult problems in this domain is the inability of many students to think about an idealized world where friction plays no role. In our interviews on *A Private Universe*, we queried elementary, middle, and high school students about their views of energy conservation. Although many of the students had been introduced to common classroom demonstrations such as one focusing on the period of a pendulum, they were unable to apply their learning in new situations; for example, predicting the height reached by a metal ball on its return trip along a parabolic surface. These findings seem to confirm Solomon's conclusions that good physics students must learn to live in two worlds; the world of science and the "life world," where the laws of physics are mediated by friction. Apparently, only a small proportion of students learn to navigate both worlds successfully.

The nature of electric circuits and optical phenomena are two additional domains that have proven difficult for large numbers of students. Our interviews on electric circuits were based on a substantial accumulation of recent research (Fredette & Clement, 1981; Joshua, 1984; Osborne, 1981; Shipstone, 1984). In the episode on circuits, Mr. C, a 25-year veteran of the high school science classroom, teaches his 11th and 12th grade physics students about series and parallel circuits. Jennifer, whom Mr. C calls "a typical student," was interviewed before and after the lessons. When asked to explain the flow of current through a simple circuit consisting of a light bulb, a set of wires and a battery, Jennifer suggested that positively charged particles emanating from the top of the battery collide in the filament with negatively charged particles originating at the bottom of the battery. This "clashing currents" model is very common and, in Jennifer's case and many others, the ideas are not substantially altered by instruction. In fact, the postinstruction interview revealed that Jennifer had actually acquired a whole new set of alternative notions.

Our interviews on light and vision were equally revealing. As suggested in previous research (Eaton, Anderson, & Smith, 1983; Shapiro, 1994; Stead & Osborne, 1980), even well-educated college students subscribe to a set of common misconceptions about optical phenomena. In interviews for A

Private Universe, virtually all of the recent Harvard graduates with whom we spoke were unable to explain the workings of a mirror. One bright fifth grader attending a working class elementary school in Cambridge, Massachusetts, offered an idea about light and vision that has been documented at virtually every grade level. Conor had the notion that light rays emanating from the eyes illuminate objects enabling us to see them.

Findings such as these provide strong evidence for two additional knowledge claims: *the alternative conceptions that students bring to formal science instruction cut across age, ability, gender, and cultural boundaries; and furthermore these ideas are often tenacious and resistant to extinction by conventional teaching strategies*.

Since our last analysis of students' alternative conceptions in the life sciences (Mintzes, Trowbridge, Arnaudin, & Wandersee, 1991; Wandersee, Mintzes, & Arnaudin, 1989), a proliferation of several hundred additional studies has provided a strong foundation for understanding how students view biological concepts in domains as diverse as cellular respiration (Songer & Mintzes, 1994), sexually transmitted diseases (Benton, Mintzes, Kendrick, & Solomon, 1994), and evolutionary theory (Trowbridge & Wandersee, 1994).

Arguably, the most significant and best documented work has focused on such difficult issues as plant nutrition (Barker & Carr, 1989; Eisen & Stavy, 1988; K. Roth, Smith, & Anderson, 1983; Wandersee, 1983, 1986) and natural selection (Bishop & Anderson, 1990; Brumby, 1984; Good et al., 1992; Hallden, 1988; Jungwirth, 1975).

Based on Wandersee's (1983, 1986) cross-age study of students' understanding of plant nutrition, we videotaped the explanations of photosynthesis offered by some 20 middle school students before and after instruction on the topic. The instruction included lecture–discussions, textbook readings, and a conventional laboratory session that focused on starch as a principal storage product of photosynthesis. Our interviews with Jon were replayed for his teacher, Mr. H, an articulate veteran of the middle school science classroom.

Of several questions we posed, the most revealing query targeted the source of plant biomass: "Where does most of the 'stuff' in this log come from?" Jon suggested that most of the weight of a plant comes from the soil, with additional contributions from water and sunlight. Even after instruction Jon failed to identify carbon dioxide as a principal source of biomass, although when asked he was able to reproduce a complete and correctly balanced equation for photosynthesis. Jon's explanation is characteristic of a large proportion of students, including all of the Harvard graduates we interviewed (Figure 1).

Subsequent to the interviews, Mr. H reviewed the videotapes and registered disappointment and considerable surprise at Jon's explanations, suggesting perhaps that the experiments his students performed that term were atypical and less effective than the lessons he usually plans. Probing further

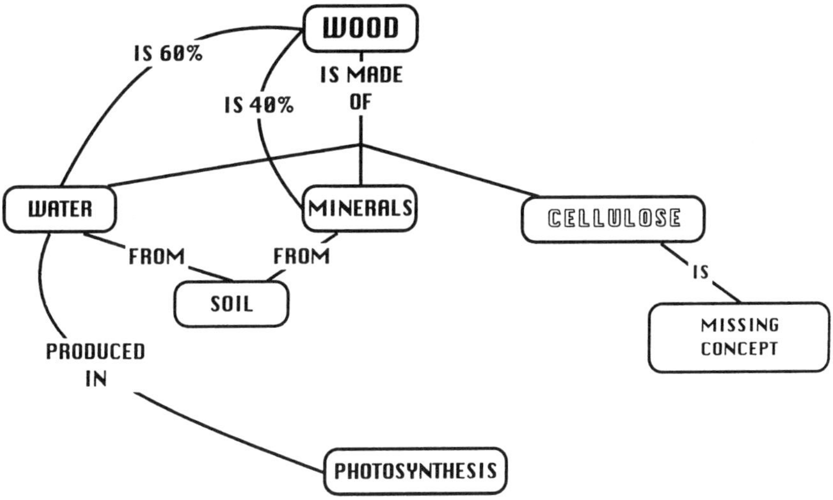

FIGURE 1
Jon's ideas about photosynthesis.

into Jon's explanation, however, revealed something quite different. When asked directly about carbon dioxide as a possible source of plant biomass, Jon dismissed the idea explaining, "that's impossible" because air has no weight. Jon's reasoning is good but a basic misconception about gases and the structure of matter has led him astray. Unfortunately, Mr. H failed to recognize that the source of Jon's misunderstanding was rooted in a domain that seemed to him distantly related to photosynthesis.

Episodes such as this in biology and in virtually all other areas of science instruction illustrate another of our knowledge claims: *a learner's prior knowledge interacts with knowledge presented in formal instruction, resulting in a diverse set of unintended learning outcomes*. Mr. H's lessons were well prepared, but Jon "missed the point." It appears that regardless of the teacher's intentions, students construct their own meanings and often those meanings are at variance with the scientifically accepted view. Evidence of this has been found in all science subjects and at every instructional level (Eaton, Anderson, & Smith, 1984; Gilbert, Osborne, & Fensham, 1982; Happs, 1985; Smith & Anderson, 1984).

The study of students' understanding of natural selection provides a good example of yet another of our knowledge claims: *students' explanations of natural phenomena often resemble theories offered by previous generations of scientists and natural philosophers*. In the exegesis of his stage theory of learning, Piaget (1970) went considerably further than this, suggesting, "The fundamental hypothesis of genetic epistemology is that there is a parallelism between progress made in the rational and logical organization of knowledge and the corresponding psychological processes." Most science education researchers today would eschew this strong interpretation; however, many now feel that the similarities between students' ideas and the discarded ideas of scientists offer a valuable heuristic opportunity to help students wrestle with their own conceptual shortcomings (Wandersee, 1986).

Understanding evolutionary theory is central to understanding biology. Unfortunately, a significant body of recent research suggests that the principal mechanism of evolutionary change, that is, natural selection, is poorly understood by large numbers of students (Good et al., 1992). Additionally, in many cases, it appears that resistance to conceptual change in this domain can be traced to strong and often unexamined emotional commitments rooted in theological explanations of natural phenomena (Lawson & Worsnop, 1992). However, even students who reject theological explanations are constrained by the limitations of understanding chance or random events, probability, variation, adaptation, geologic time, genes in populations, and other concepts (Mintzes, 1992). As a result, even those who have taken several college-level biology courses revert to a kind of Lamarckian explanation when asked to describe the nature of evolutionary events (Brumby, 1984).

Lamarckian theory (1809) employs three overriding principles to account for change in biological systems: (1) the principle of needs (changes in the environment cause changes in the needs of living organisms), (2) the principle of use and disuse (frequent use of a body part strengthens and enlarges it, while disuse weakens and reduces it), and (3) the principle of inheritance of acquired characteristics (traits that are acquired as a result of interaction with the environment are passed to the next generation). Each of these ideas has been well documented in explanations offered by science students. For example, a substantial number of respondents assert that Africans have developed dark skin because they need to be protected from the sun's rays; that animals dwelling in the dark develop small eyes because they fail to use them frequently, and that mice having their tails clipped for several generations will give birth to offspring with shorter tails (Bishop & Anderson, 1990; Engel-Clough & Wood-Robinson, 1985).

A substantial number of studies have focused on students' understanding of chemical concepts. Perhaps the most important investigations have addressed multiple ways students view the structure and transformation of matter (Andersson, 1986, 1990; Stavy, 1988, 1989). The overwhelming weight of evidence suggests that the majority of learners have difficulty conceptualizing the microscopic and submicroscopic properties of atoms and molecules in solid, liquid, and gaseous states and the transformation of matter in chemical reactions. In one study of 12–16-year-olds (Andersson, 1990), students suggested that atoms of different substances differ in overall shape: some are square, some rectangular, and others triangular. Another common finding is the observation that learners assign the chemical properties of elements and compounds to the atoms and molecules of which they are composed, resulting in "drippy" water molecules, yellow phosphorous atoms, and copper atoms that can be hammered into an infinite number of shapes. Findings such as these suggest that many of the ideas students embrace are an attempt to construct meaning from direct personal experience. Water is wet, so water molecules must be made of small droplets.

The origin of students' scientific explanations has been a subject of considerable speculation; however, the best available evidence supports the view that *alternative conceptions are a product of a diverse set of personal experiences, including direct observation of natural objects and events, peer culture, everyday language, and the mass media as well as teacher's explanations and instructional materials*. It appears that virtually every source of scientifically acceptable knowledge may also serve as a vehicle for promoting misconceptions (Ameh & Gunstone, 1985; Barras, 1984; Cho, Kahle, & Nordland, 1985; M. Hewson, 1985; Kenealy, 1987; Lawson, 1988; Mintzes, 1989). Perhaps most disconcerting is the finding that common instructional practices, including those of good teachers and textbooks, are a major source of misunderstanding. It seems that errors and misleading information inevitably find their way into scientific explanations despite the best efforts of instructional developers, publishers, and editors. This problem is compounded when students "misinterpret" otherwise sound explanations.

In our interviews with students attending an inner-city middle school in Boston, we asked subjects to draw what they might see in a microscopic view of a glass of water. Many of them drew water molecules surrounded by a blue field. When queried about the blue field, many of the youngsters said it was water. At first we dismissed this explanation as yet another instance of a continuous model of matter with no known source. Later, however, we had an opportunity to examine a copy of the students' textbook, a widely adopted edition of an integrated science book distributed by a major national publisher. There in the chapter on "states of matter" was an artistically appealing but grossly misleading four-color line drawing depicting water molecules floating in a blue liquid.

Unfortunately, considerable evidence now suggests that *teachers often subscribe to the same alternative conceptions as their students* (Ameh, 1987; J. Bloom, 1989; Enochs & Gabel, 1984; Feher & Rice, 1987; Ogunniyi & Pella, 1980). Very often the scientific education teachers themselves receive is inadequate. Ms. S, our Boston middle school teacher, admitted that she held many of the same misconceptions as her students. Like many middle school science teachers, she received a bachelors degree in elementary education and felt most comfortable teaching social studies in the upper elementary grades. However, when the school system introduced the 6–8 middle school arrangement, a shortage of science teachers necessitated her present assignment, which she accepted with some trepidation. Recent studies suggest that Ms. S is not atypical of many of those teaching middle school science (Darling-Hammond & Hudson, 1990).

This pattern is even gloomier at the elementary school level. In one study (Lawrenz, 1986), 300 teachers were told that iron rusts when it combines with oxygen. They were then asked whether rust weighs more, the same as, or less than the iron from which it comes. Only 36% of the teachers reasoned that the rust weighs more than the iron.

Conceptual Change in the Natural Sciences ("and Teach Him Accordingly")

The product of some 25 years of work and 3500 studies reveals that learners often fail to understand central concepts in the sciences and that failure to understand is a result of difficulties encountered in attempting to construct meaning. Furthermore, it appears that these difficulties are widespread and not necessarily limited to students of low ability, even those enrolled in our finest institutions experience similar problems.

At this point it appears that the central issue facing science educators is how to effect lasting change in the way students understand concepts (Wandersee et al., 1994). Within the framework of Ausubel's (1963) original formulation, the research community has spent many years ascertaining "what the learner already knows"; the time has come to focus attention on how to "teach him accordingly." To do so is not a simple matter. It requires an in-depth analysis of how scientific knowledge is structured and restructured as students engage in meaningful learning of formal disciplines and what teachers might do to facilitate these processes. Although research in this area is still in its infancy, we now think that sufficient evidence exists to support several additional claims.

The most comprehensive claim is that *successful science learners develop elaborate, strongly hierarchical, well-differentiated, and highly integrated frameworks of related concepts as they construct meanings* (Ausubel et al., 1978). Additionally, there is now good evidence that scientific thinking, reasoning, processing, or as some prefer to call it, *problem solving* is a product of a complex set of neural events that requires priming and successive activation of closely related concepts within these hierarchical frameworks (Collins & Loftus, 1975). While the neurological basis for scientific thinking remains conjectural (Anderson, 1992; Lawson, 1994), it is clear that *the ability to reason well in the natural sciences is constrained largely by the structure of domain-specific knowledge in the discipline*, which accounts for many of the differences seen in the performance of novices and experts in science-related fields (Carey, 1986; Chi, Glaser, & Farr, 1988; Hirschfeld & Gelman, 1994). Evidence for these claims comes from a variety of sources, including studies on learning in physics (Chi, Feltovich, & Glaser, 1981; Larkin, McDermott, Simon, & Simon, 1980), biology (Atran, 1990;

Gobbo & Chi, 1986; Keil 1989; Markham, Mintzes, & Jones, 1994), medicine (Lesgold et al., 1988; Patel, Groen, & Frederikson, 1986), and computer programming (Adelson & Soloway, 1988; Soloway, Ehrlich, Bonar, & Greenspan, 1982).

The relationship between cognitive structure and conceptual change is a matter of considerable speculation (West & Pines, 1985). It is apparent that *conceptual change requires a restructuring of the knowledge framework, and this in turn results from the making and breaking of connections between concepts and sometimes the replacement or substitution of one concept with another.* The epistemological conditions underlying these cognitive events have been discussed at length by others (Laudan, 1984; Posner, Strike, Hewson, & Gertzog, 1982).

In the view of many cognitive scientists, significant change in the way learners understand natural phenomena results from both the gradual and orderly elaboration and refinement of an existing framework as well as radical alterations that necessitate the introduction of entirely new superordinate concepts. *Weak restructuring* (Carey, 1987), *tuning*, and *accretion* (Rumelhart & Norman, 1978) are labels that have been applied to the former and *strong* or *radical restructuring* to the latter. Carey has shown that both types of restructuring occur in the acquisition of biological concepts during childhood. Nussbaum (1989) has pointed out that the distinction between gradual and rapid change bears close resemblance to the "normal" and "revolutionary" events that characterize historical periods of scientific activity described by Kuhn (1962). Others have suggested that the weak and strong restructuring of conceptual change are analogous to the gradual processes of natural selection and the rapid events of punctuated equilibrium, the mechanisms that are thought to underlie evolutionary change.

Whether these analogies are useful or not, it appears from longitudinal studies that successful science learners engage in both forms of restructuring (Novak & Musonda, 1991). Recent studies in college biology suggest that strong restructuring is characteristic of early phases in the formal classroom learning of a new domain (Pearsall, Skipper, & Mintzes, in press). Over the course of the learning period, however, the incidence of strong restructuring declines substantially while the frequencies of gradual elaborative processes remain relatively stable. It appears that the early period in a learning episode challenges students with a series of major conceptual hurdles or "critical junctures" that must be successfully navigated if meaningful learning is to occur (Trowbridge & Wandersee, 1994). What are the instructional implications of these findings?

In this chapter and elsewhere (Novak & Gowin, 1984; Wandersee, Mintzes, & Novak, 1994), we advocate conceptual change approaches that focus on helping students learn how to learn. We generally embrace White and Gunstone's (1989) conclusion, "If metalearning can be taught, then the problem of how to bring about conceptual change may be solved." This view is supported by a large body of research suggesting that *successful learners in the natural sciences habitually employ strategies that enable them to plan, monitor, control, and regulate their own learning* (Chi et al., 1988; Larkin, 1983). Before turning to meta-learning strategies, however, we review several conceptual change approaches that have been tried by others and offer a new theoretical synthesis that supports our present views.

Although specific recommendations and emphases vary considerably, it appears to us that the most comprehensive proposals for addressing conceptual change in science have several common features (Scott, Asoko, & Driver, 1992). Typically these include an orientation or "messing about" followed by an elicitation or externalizing phase, a modification or restructuring phase, and a practice or application phase. In some proposals an additional phase focusing on meta-cognition is also included. Furthermore, while several of the proposed interventions are fairly generic in scope and might be employed in a wide range of circumstances (e.g., "cooperative learning," the "learning cycle"), others are targeted to address quite specific conceptual difficulties (e.g., analogies, confrontation, computer simulations). As suggested elsewhere (Wandersee et al., 1994), we think it quite likely that success in changing students' conceptions will require a significant number of strategies that can be used in various combinations as the needs of individual learners demand. At the heart of all conceptual change strategies is the knowledge restructuring component.

Among the earliest and best documented attempts at restructuring are Nussbaum's efforts to teach the particulate model of matter in the gaseous phase through conceptual conflict (Novick and Nussbaum, 1978, 1981; Nussbaum, 1989, 1993; Nussbaum & Novick, 1981). The 10-lesson sequence is intended for middle school students and begins with 4 lessons designed to teach the following propositions: (1) matter is composed of submicroscopic particles, and (2) the particles are surrounded by empty space. The orientation phase begins with several experiments designed to demonstrate that air occupies space, has weight, is a mixture of several gases, and can perform work. Lesson 3 is an elicitation or "exposing event" in which students imagine donning a pair of "magic glasses" and thinking about how air in a flask might look before and after partial evacuation of the flask. Drawings reveal that many students subscribe to a continuous, nonparticulate model of matter.

In the fourth lesson, the students are led to "invent" the particle idea through a "discrepant event," which is designed to create dissonance between the preconception and an observed phenomenon that cannot be explained by the preconception. In this lesson, students discover that gases contain "empty space" by attempting to explain the compression of air in a syringe. Nussbaum emphasizes the importance of getting students to clarify and defend their views and to seek supporting evidence as they explain their theories to others. Subsequent lessons in the sequence introduce the notion of particle movement through additional exposing and discrepant events involving the diffusion of gases.

Another well-documented effort in restructuring is found in the work of Clement and his coworkers at the University of Massachusetts (Camp & Clement, 1994; Clement, 1987; Clement, Brown, & Zeitsman, 1989). The focus of this work is on teaching the principles of mechanics through the use of analogies. The most recent publication offers a set of nine lessons intended for high school physics students that address forces exerted by static objects, relative motion, friction, gravity, inertia, and Newton's third law of dynamics.

As an example, in the first lesson students are introduced to static forces through a "target problem" that poses the question, "If a book is placed on a table, does the table exert an upward force on the book?" To encourage active participation and reflection, students are asked to commit themselves initially by voting. The vote is followed by a discussion of 15–20 minutes in which the teacher elicits responses and alternative explanations and attempts to clarify the reasons students offer for their positions.

Following the discussion, the teacher performs a demonstration that introduces an "anchoring example," which provides a concrete referent that is easily understood. In this instance, the anchor is a hand pushing down on a bedspring. "Does the bedspring exert a force on the hand?" On observing the demonstration students are asked how the situations of the hand and the book compare and to provide an explanation or rationale. The anchor is then followed by several "bridging examples" that are successively closer to the target; that is, a book on a soft foam pad, a book on a flexible board. These demonstrations are followed by another discussion in which students are encouraged to challenge each others' explanations. A second vote is then taken.

After the second vote the teacher introduces a "springy atomic model" and students are encouraged to think about the solid table as a collection of atoms bound together by springlike bonds. This phase culminates in an attention-getting demonstration, in which the teacher stands on a solid table deflecting a laser beam that bounces off the table onto a mirror. The demonstration is followed by a third vote, a summary, and a homework assignment.

Undoubtedly the best documented and most extensive work on knowledge restructuring has been done by Driver and her colleagues at the Children's Learning in Science (CLIS) project at the University of Leeds in the United Kingdom (Carmichael et al., 1990). In the 15 years of its existence, this group has developed and tested curricular materials in areas as diverse as the particulate nature of matter, energy, decomposition, Newtonian mechanics, and plant nutrition, to name a few. Recent work on strategies for teaching air pressure (Scott, 1993) and light (Asoko, 1993) provides some promising new techniques.

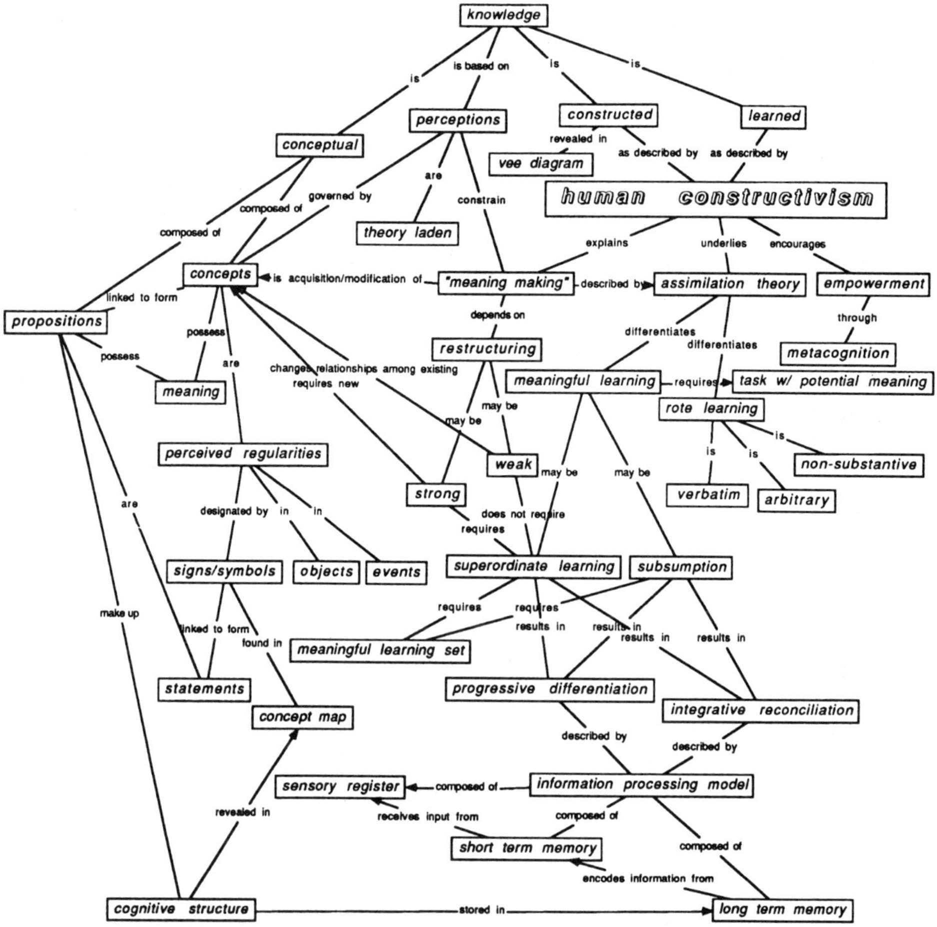

FIGURE 2
The human constructivist perspective.

HUMAN CONSTRUCTIVISM: THE NEW SYNTHESIS

Our present view of learning, which we have called *human constructivism*, is an effort to integrate the psychology of human learning and the epistemology of knowledge production (Novak, 1987, 1993a, 1993b). In it we emphasize the process of "meaning making," the acquisition and modification of concepts and concept relationships as the unique and central activity of human minds, an activity based on the use of language to represent regularities in the natural world. Our perspective on meaning making emerges directly from Ausubel's (1963, 1968) assimilation theory and has been heavily influenced by Kelly's (1955) efforts in personal construct theory, postpositivist thinking in the philosophy of science (Kuhn, 1962; Toulmin, 1972), contemporary work in epistemology (Gowin, 1982; Rorty, 1979; von Glasersfeld, 1989; Vygotsky, 1962), and advances in the cognitive sciences (Atkinson & Shiffrin, 1968; Carey, 1987; Collins & Loftus, 1975; Miller, 1956; Simon, 1974). Our thinking on meaning making has been publicized in a variety of venues (Novak, 1985, 1987, 1988, 1989a, 1989b, 1993a, 1993b, 1993c); however, we will attempt here to sketch out its essential elements (Figure 2).

Concepts

Since meaning making is a matter of modifying or changing concept relationships, we begin with the concept of concept. We define *concepts*, the basic units of meaning, as perceived regularities in objects or events that are designated by a sign or symbol. A familiar example will serve to illustrate. The concept chair is designated in the English language by a five letter word. This linguistic designation serves as a useful shorthand for a set of perceived regularities that enables us to think and speak efficiently. Normally, concrete concepts (or "natural categories") are constructed at an early age in response to interactions with objects, events, and people in our immediate environment. As a result, by the age of 18–24 months, most infants construct an understanding of chair that includes some of the following recurring regularities: a chair is an object composed of a seat, a back, and four legs that is used for sitting.

Over a period of months and years however, this early construction is modified as a result of our direct interaction with chairs and related objects and events. It is further modified through social interaction with other individuals whose personal constructions differ from our own in subtle or sometimes dramatic ways. These interactions cause us to elaborate or expand on and constrain or limit our original meanings: barber chairs have no legs; some "nonchairs" (bar stools) may have a seat, a back, and four legs; chairs may be used for taming lions; highchairs have a tray. As we elaborate on or constrain our early concepts by connecting them to newer concepts, we build complex, hierarchically organized webs of interrelated propositions in a process that Ausubel (1963) called *meaningful learning*.

Meaningful Learning

The distinction between rote and meaningful learning is certainly the most important of Ausubel's contributions: meaningful learning serves as the critical process in conceptual change. By *meaningful learning*, we refer to the nonarbitrary, nonverbatim, substantive incorporation of new knowledge into long-term memory. Meaningful learning requires a strong and deliberate commitment to forging links between new knowledge and relevant aspects of prior knowledge that constitute the learner's existing cognitive structure. Ausubel refers to this commitment as a *meaningful learning set*. When this commitment is lacking or when the learner's prior knowledge is inadequately structured, new knowledge is incorporated in an arbitrary, verbatim fashion, an event that Ausubel calls *rote learning*. Unfortunately, rote learning accounts for a substantial portion of school learning, including that occurring in most science classrooms.

In Ausubel's original formulation, meaningful learning is a product of essentially four processes: subsumption, superordinate learning, integrative reconciliation, and progressive differentiation. *Subsumption* occurs when new and less-inclusive concepts are linked to more general, higher-order concepts present in the learner's cognitive structure; for example, when students learn that certain unicellular organisms may be classified as "animals", the latter concept assumes substantively new meaning. Subsumption is undoubtedly the most common form of meaningful learning in science and accounts for much of the weak restructuring (i.e., tuning and accretion) that typifies conceptual change in schools. In *superordinate learning*, a new, more general and inclusive concept is linked to more specific concepts already a part of the learner's cognitive structure; for example, when students learn that visible light and radio waves represent different frequencies of electromagnetic energy. This kind of learning that accounts for much strong restructuring is the "stuff" of which creative activity is made; unfortunately, however, it is characteristic of only a small proportion of what goes on in public (and private) education.

As new concepts are added to cognitive structure either through subsumption or superordinate learning, the existing framework is *progressively differentiated*, resulting in a gradual clarification of concept meanings. Additionally, learners begin to delineate similarities and differences among existing concepts resulting in a more cohesive and integrated framework of knowledge. Among the most characteristic features of expertise in knowledge domains is the strongly differentiated and highly integrated nature of cognitive structure that enables the expert to recognize large patterns and regularities in that domain, to process information rapidly, and to represent problems at a deeper, more principled level than the novice. The best available evidence suggests that experts actually "see" the world differently than novices, and this perceptual superiority provides the expert with his or her competitive "edge."

Theory-ladenness

The notion that "what you see depends on what you know (and vice versa)" has become a commonplace in epistemology and the philosophy of science. Its roots are grounded in Kant's *Critique of Pure Reason* (1781) and the *Prolegom-*

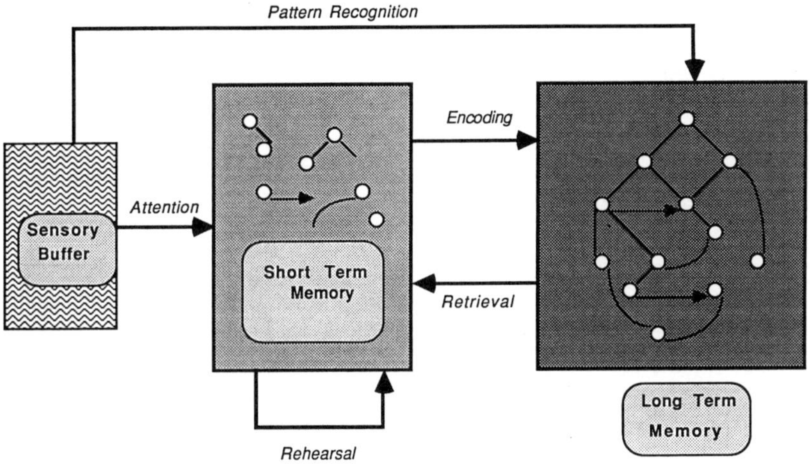

FIGURE 3
The information processing model.

ena to Any Future Metaphysics (1783), which attempted to reconcile the rationalist views of Descartes, Spinoza, and Leibniz with the empiricist tradition of Locke, Berkeley, and Hume. Among contemporary philosophers the idea that observation is theory laden has been associated most strongly with Kuhn's (1962) seminal work; more recently the notion has been borrowed by others (Osborne & Wittrock, 1983; Pope & Gilbert, 1983).

In our view, the concept of theory-ladenness constitutes a central link between a theory of learning based on Ausubelian principles and an epistemology of personal knowledge construction emerging from Kelly's (1955) work. The overwhelming weight of evidence supports the conclusion that learners selectively attend to and recognize patterns in environmental cues (i.e., objects and events), based on prior knowledge; that selective attention and pattern recognition govern perceptions; and that perceptions in turn constrain meaningful learning. This reciprocal relationship between prior knowledge, perception, and meaningful learning is at the heart of the constructivist argument and, within the context of information processing models (Atkinson & Shiffrin, 1968), has become something akin to the Central Dogma of the cognitive sciences (Figure 3).

Information Processing

Based on early work in the cognitive sciences, it is clear that sensory input, whether tactile, auditory, visual, olfactory, or gustatory, is registered in the cortex for a relatively short period of time; probably on the order of one second or less. However, sustained attention to sensory data rapidly moves information into consciousness or short-term memory (STM).

Short-term memory is the component of the information processing system where links are formed between sensory information and relevant aspects of prior knowledge. The capacity of STM is quite limited (7 ± 2 independent "chunks") and information that is not rehearsed or linked to existing concepts decays rapidly and is lost within a period of 15–30 seconds. The formation of links requires retrieving knowledge from long-term memory (LTM), consciously interpreting, evaluating, comparing, and contrasting new information with prior knowledge, and ultimately reconciling and assimilating new information by subsumption and superordinate learning.

The retrieval of relevant aspects of knowledge stored in LTM is consistent with a *spreading activation model* (Collins & Loftus, 1975) of information processing. This model suggests that bringing knowledge into consciousness involves the activation of relevant concepts in LTM and the subsequent spreading of this activation with decreasing strength through a network of related concepts. Concepts so activated are called into STM. Evidence (Rumelhart, 1989) further indicates that the time required to activate such a network precludes serial or sequential processing of information. Instead, it is probable that the activation of one concept initiates a cascade of activating impulses that spreads simultaneously in several directions. This notion of *parallel distributed processing* has received widespread support and is consistent with the known architecture of the cerebral cortex.

As far as we know, long-term memory is an information store of unlimited capacity and duration. However, the duration and ultimate value of knowledge stored in LTM depends critically on the structure of that knowledge. As Ausubel suggested over 35 years ago, learners who rely on the arbitrary, verbatim, nonsubstantive (i.e., rote) incorporation of information usually experience rapid decay and loss of knowledge, which accounts for much of the "forgetting" that typifies learning of school science.

The mode of knowledge representation in LTM has been a subject of continuing research and a substantial level of controversy and promises to remain in this state for some time to come (Gazzaniga, 1995). A number of workers have suggested that conceptual networks are only one of several ways knowledge may be represented in cognitive structure; other forms of representation may include the iconic or visual and the echoic or auditory modes, among others. For understanding classroom learning in science, the resolution of these issues has more than passing import, especially in an age when visual forms of communication are in the ascendance. In our view it is probable that knowledge in long-term memory is represented in a highly redundant network of tightly integrated, hierarchically organized conceptual nodes and that the semantic, iconic, and echoic forms of representation are inseparably linked. Furthermore, it is most probable that brain centers storing these cognitive representations are also tightly linked to cerebral and lower centers that control and regulate affective responses. Unfortunately, to our knowledge, research in this area is progressing at a relatively slow pace.

In addition to the problem of representation, some workers have made sharp distinctions among the types of knowledge stored in LTM. Tulving (1985), for example, has postulated two separate subsystems: one storing "semantic" memory and the other, "episodic" memory. In this view, the semantic system stores general knowledge of objects and events, while the episodic system contains temporally related personal experiences. Other researchers (McKoon, Ratcliff, & Dell, 1986) subdivide the semantic system into a component devoted to "declarative" knowledge (i.e., concepts, propositions) and one reserved for "procedural" knowledge (i.e., actions, skills, operations). At this point the evidence for these distinctions is not terribly strong and, in our view, of secondary significance for science teachers; accordingly, we prefer to make no such distinctions.

For most science teachers, the ultimate goal of the educational enterprise is to produce "scientifically literate citizens"; that is, citizens capable of "making meaning" or constructing knowledge about the natural world, especially knowledge that might be useful in novel, everyday situations. However, we have found that students typically need help in constructing knowledge and that teachers often have limited experience in providing this kind of help. With this in mind, we have devoted much of our research activity to the development and validation of strategies that empower students to learn meaningfully.

Empowerment

The elements of human constructivism we have briefly outlined are supported by recent work on two powerful heuristic devices, the concept map and the Vee diagram (Novak & Gowin, 1984). Employing these and several other devices (Fisher, 1990; Wandersee, 1987b) over a period of some 20 years has reinforced our view that any applied theory of learning, if it is to be of real value, must offer practical tools for the classroom practitioner.

Concept maps, concept circles, Vee diagrams, and the SemNet software are tools designed to help learners construct meanings through interactions with objects, events and other people. In the next section we focus on these tools and how they may be used to enhance meaning making in the natural sciences.

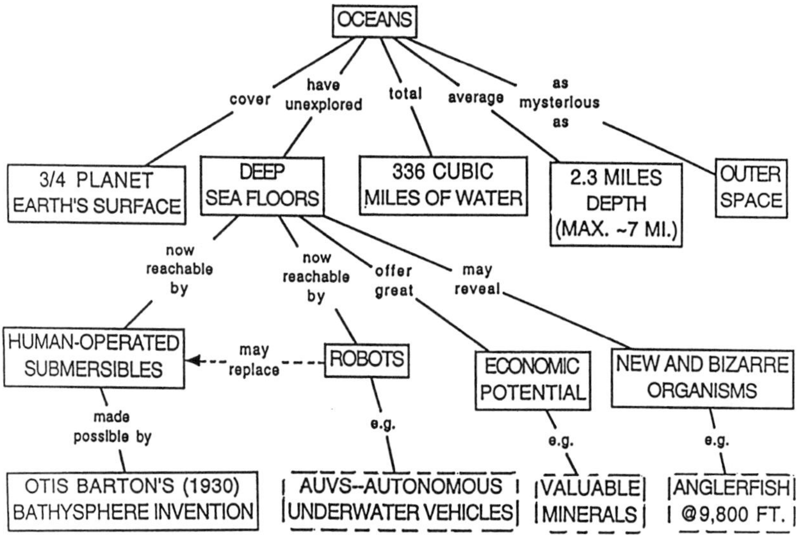

FIGURE 4
A concept map on exploring the ocean depths.

THE PRACTICE OF SCIENCE TEACHING: HOW META-COGNITIVE STRATEGIES CAN HELP

The Importance of Concept Mapping

Perhaps the most important meta-cognitive tool in science education today is the *concept map*. Invented by Novak and his research group at Cornell University in the early 1970s (Novak, 1972), it is now widely used not only in the United States but throughout the world. Hundreds of research studies have investigated the potential uses and learning outcomes of concept mapping in science teaching (cf. Al-Kunifed & Wandersee, 1990; Horton et al., 1993). Novak and Gowin (1984) made it the centerpiece of their handbook, *Learning How to Learn*, a publication devoted to the theory and application of meta-cognitive tools, now available in 10 languages worldwide. Subsequently, Novak and Wandersee (1990) edited the special issue, Perspectives on Concept Mapping, in the *Journal of Research in Science Teaching*. As recently pointed out (Wallace, Mintzes, & Markham, 1992), concept mapping was first developed as a science education research tool, but work with concept mapping involving thousands of students has lent empirical support to its effectiveness as a learning tool as well. We have found concept maps to be useful to science teachers in designing and improving curricula and in planning, carrying out, and evaluating instruction. Maps are useful especially in diagnosing conceptual problems in science learning. Students use them as aids to thinking, organizing, writing about, and studying science.

Characteristics of Concept Maps

Concept mapping is a meta-cognitive tool used for representing knowledge structures in content domains. Figure 4 depicts a concept map on exploring the ocean depths, as drawn from the domain of marine science. Each concept map has a treelike, two-dimensional form that represents a piece of knowledge as a semantic network. Several characteristic features are typically found in these representations: hierarchy, dendriticality (branchedness), nodes (concepts, constructs), and labeled links. As suggested in the previous section, a concept is a perceived regularity in objects or events that has been given a label (e.g., *cat* or *rain*). A construct is a higher-order (more abstract) concept, such as speed, which is composed of the concepts distance and time.

Like all concept maps, our oceans map is read from the top down, branch by branch, and contains the following concepts and constructs: oceans, earth's surface, deep-sea floor, volume of seawater, mean ocean depth, outer space, submersible, robot, economic potential, organism, bathysphere, autonomous underwater vehicle, valuable mineral, anglerfish.

The basic pattern of a concept map is dendritic (branched). The top or *superordinate* concept is the earth's oceans; the remaining concepts are *subordinate*; connected at various levels of hierarchy. *Examples* are enclosed by broken boxes and a *cross-link*, which bridges two different branches of the map, is indicated by a broken linking line. Most important, all of the linking lines appearing on this concept map have *linking words* associated with them. Two concepts joined by a linking word is termed a *proposition* and the resulting network of propositions in hierarchical array is used to represent a *knowledge structure*.

By examining such a knowledge structure constructed by a student, we can infer a great deal about his or her conceptual understanding. Salient features of such a map include the number and quality of scientifically acceptable propositions, the number and insightfulness of cross-link connections, the number and appropriateness of the map's levels of hierarchy, the extent of branching within the map, the precision of the linking words used in generating propositions, the number and quality of novel examples, and the aptness and choice of the superordinate concept.

Quantitative measures of map quality may be obtained by applying scoring rubrics (Novak & Gowin, 1984). Comparing the frequencies of salient features in a map over time gives us strong indication of conceptual change (Markham et al., 1994; Novak & Musonda, 1991).

We must point out that, unless the individual doing the scoring has a firm understanding of the knowledge domain, such scoring rubrics may yield misleading information. In addition, we caution that a concept map is simply a workable approximation of what the learner knows; maps are generally conservative estimates of the knowledge structure and typically capture 50% or less of a student's understanding. Novak and Musonda (1991) point out, "In practice, it is impossible to ascertain and illustrate the complete meaning held by an individual for any concept that has undergone significant differentiation." Furthermore it is important to recognize that a particular concept map may be regarded as simply a "snapshot in time" and offers but a fleeting picture of a dynamic and fluid process. Nonetheless, we argue that concept maps are significantly more robust than traditional assessment tools, assuming the mapmaker has practiced and received feedback prior to the assessment (Wandersee, 1987a).

Constructing a Concept Map

The process of map construction may be summarized as follows: (1) the mapmaker choses the knowledge domain, often by reviewing a section of textbook, a videotape, a journal article, a laboratory manual, or some lecture notes; (2) the most important concepts are arranged in hierarchical level, from general to specific, and important missing concepts are added; (3) the concepts are tentatively organized and reorganized into branching arrays, working from general to specific, branch by branch; (4) concepts are linked by lines and the lines are labeled to produce a set of interrelated propositions; (5) examples are added where appropriate at the terminus of any branch; (6) cross-links are added to represent integration among the branches, and (7) the mapmaker examines and reflects on his or her first draft, revising and redrawing it to improve its accuracy, precision, and graphic effectiveness. Although students typically construct concept maps with paper and pencil, special concept mapping software is readily available for those who prefer computer-based approaches (Stahl & Hunter, 1990).

Micromaps and Macromaps

A *micromap* (Trowbridge & Wandersee, 1994) is a concept map composed of approximately 12–15 *elements* (concepts, constructs, and examples), which is typically drawn from prior knowledge and supplementary sources. The limited map size encourages setting priorities and reduces the evaluation time to some 5 minutes per map, which effectively permits a one- or two-day turnaround time for a class and provides rapid feedback to students and helpful information for teachers. The effect of these micromaps is to limit the number of concepts a student must integrate and replace a large, single, and often cluttered, map with a series of smaller, overlapping maps.

In the study cited previously, college biology students were provided with five seed concepts or constructs, those the instructor was most interested in monitoring, and the learners supplied the remaining 7–10 map elements. Students chose or were supplied the appropriate superordinate concept. Results suggest that students increased their total study time by 37% as a result of the micromapping assignments. Furthermore, students reported spending an average of 48 minutes constructing each map, including at least two revisions each.

In contrast, a *macromap* (Trowbridge & Wandersee, 1995) is a concept map composed of elements drawn from a set of related micromaps and limited to the size of a micromap. It can be thought of as a map of maps, based on key concepts extracted from the upper levels of hierarchy in a set of related submaps. The macromap provides an overview of a broader piece of knowledge than that encompassed by a micromap; for example, an entire textbook chapter, a whole series of videotapes or a complete course unit. In our experience, students find the construction of a micromap less daunting than composing a larger map, and they have less trouble composing a macromap from component micromaps. Perhaps the most important feature of micromaps and macromaps is their limited size, which compels learners to focus on the "big ideas" rather than getting lost in the details of a knowledge domain.

Difficulties in Learning Concept Mapping

Many students develop their own idiosyncratic approaches to meaningful learning over the course of the elementary and secondary years; sometimes, they prefer their own methods to anything the teacher might introduce, such as concept mapping. Others have evolved strategies that afford a seemingly efficient route to rote learning and see no reason to adopt a new strategy that requires more reflection and conscious effort. We think it is especially important to remind science teachers of the importance of rewarding meaningful learning in their assessment of student progress. It is certainly little wonder that students opt for less effortful strategies, especially when meaning making is not recognized and encouraged. Our experience with concept maps has taught us that initial resistance to new learning strategies typically fades as students begin to recognize the value of meaningful learning and sense the empowerment it affords.

Another issue that science teachers should consider is that good concept mapping is an acquired skill, and students need time and considerable feedback to improve. When concept maps are first introduced, students typically display a wide range of difficulties; among the most common are (1) incorrect, imprecise, or missing linking words; (2) use of inappropriate examples or failure to include examples entirely; (3) absence or use of trivial cross-links; (4) failure to develop a strongly branching, hierarchical form resulting in a "stringy, linear" structure; (5) inclusion of more than a single concept in a box or node; (6) overuse of vague linking words (e.g., is related to, to be, to have); (7) clutter and graphic ineffectiveness; and (8) lack of concordance among superordinate concepts among students (Trowbridge & Wandersee, 1994).

Research on Concept Mapping

To date over 150 studies have been published on the effectiveness of the concept mapping technique. These studies run the gamut of grade level (K–16), subject matter (science, social studies, literature), and geographic locale (North America, Europe, Africa) as well as curricular and instructional variables (traditional and experimental). Unfortunately, experimental treatments differ substantially from one study to the next, making comparisons across studies virtually impossible. In our view, it is almost certainly premature to offer definitive conclusions about the effectiveness of concept mapping as a learning tool. Nonetheless we should indicate that the only meta-analysis performed to date, based on the results of 19 previous studies, concluded that concept mapping has moderate positive effects on student achievement and large positive effects on student attitudes (Horton et al., 1993).

Emerging from the 150 studies, one finds a large number of noteworthy and potentially important individual findings that provide strong support for the use of concept maps. Based on these findings, the following conclusions have been offered: *concept mapping helps students understand what meaningful learning is* (Arnaudin, Mintzes, Dunn, & Shafer, 1984); *it appears to enhance the integration and retention of knowledge* (Heinze-Fry & Novak, 1990); *it boosts recall in reading comprehension* (Armbruster & Anderson, 1980); *it produces better test scores, improved understanding of conceptual relations and patterns, and more cooperative class discussions* (Stice & Alvarez, 1986); *it reduces student anxiety levels and improves their perceptions of the subject matter* (Okebukola & Jegede, 1989); *it stimulates critical reading and changes students' metaphors of reading from absorbing information to making connections* (Davis, 1990); *it helps students become more strategic at developing and refining their knowledge* (Schwartz, 1988); and *it leads to student-centered, activity-oriented classes* (W. Roth, 1990).

Obviously, these conclusions remain tentative and should be seen as perhaps enticing invitations to further investigation. Nonetheless, the findings of these studies are encouraging, and if supported by further experimental evidence, they suggest that concept mapping offers a powerful aid to conceptual learning (Novak, 1990).

Other Metacognitive Tools in Science Teaching

While concept maps are useful in representing domains of scientific knowledge or parts of such domains, other metacognitive tools have different but complementary roles to play. In this overview, we will focus on four of them.

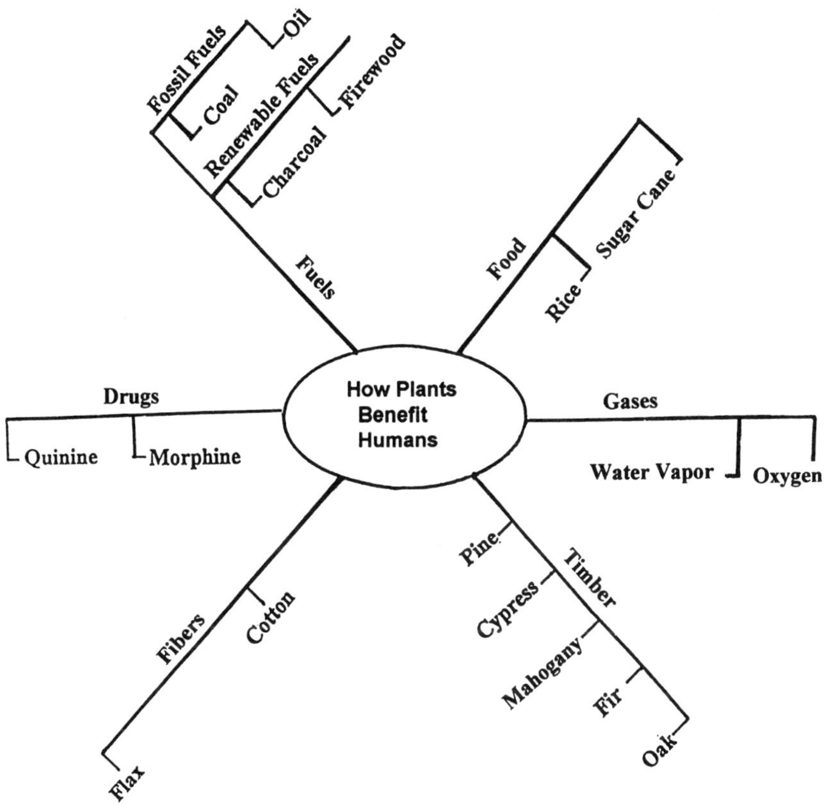

FIGURE 5
A concept web.

Ranging from "easy" to "more difficult," we consider these tools in order of the effort required by students to master them.

Concept Webs

The term *graphic organizer* is used in the reading research literature to mean any kind of two-dimensional visual reading comprehension framework (Readence, Bean, & Baldwin, 1985). *Concept webs* (also known as *spider maps*) are a type of graphic organizer developed by Hanf (1971) as a way of helping students take notes from a textbook. The *topical concept* is written in the center of the diagram and usually enclosed in a circle or ellipse. Lines radiating from the central ellipse are labeled with *subconcepts* (Bellanca, 1990), and sometimes these lines are branched (Figure 5) to subdivide the subconcept or provide *examples*. Although the linking lines have concept labels, they lack linking words, which, from a human constructivist perspective, is a common limiting feature of many graphic organizers. In our work with science students we have found that the meaning in a graphic organizer resides in the connections among concepts, and often students who claim to understand a topic cannot articulate these relationships when probed in depth about their representation.

We have found concept webbing to be a useful technique for brainstorming about a topic, to help individuals assemble and categorize a set of related concepts. In this capacity, concept webs may serve as "cognitive preludes" to more sophisticated forms of representation. While several authors (Jonassen, Beissner, & Yacci, 1993) have claimed that spider maps "depict the relationships between ideas in a content area," we have found that these relationships are not explicitly identified and the absence of hierarchical structure further limits the usefulness of the technique.

Concept Circle Diagrams

Wandersee (1987a, 1987b) invented the *concept circle diagram* while doing postdoctoral work at Cornell in biology education with Joseph Novak. The technique is now used at the elementary, middle school, high school, and college levels (Collette & Chiappetta, 1994; Hettich, 1992; Nichols, 1993; Nobles, 1993). It is designed to introduce students to concept-based learning by representing small clusters of concepts (no more than five) using rules for labeling, sizing, coloring, and positioning circles to depict inclusive or exclusive relationships between bounded, taxonomic-type concepts.

Students make their concept circle diagrams using commercially available drawing templates that are psychologically sized (Wandersee, 1987a). Thus, students may use the template to represent *relative quantities* (ratio: 1:2:3:4:5) or *ascribed importance* or *chronological sequence*.

On first glance, concept circle diagrams seems similar to the Venn diagrams used by logicians. Actually they are quite different. Venn diagrams typically are used to represent categorical propositions or syllogisms, with special shading and starring processes to depict intersection and no more than three circles per diagram.

The technique is based in part on the logic diagrams used by Leonhard Euler (1707–1783), which have been traced back to the famous circle of Apollonius (262–190 B.C.) (Cain, 1994). Euler's circles (*Lettres a une princesse d'Allemagne*, 1768) depicted five (now expanded to six) basic logical relationships (Figure 6). Wandersee has adapted these circles for use as a metacognitive tool grounded in a human constructivist perspective.

The tool is especially useful in depicting conceptual relationships of three types: whole–part, set–member, and has characteristics. Hoffman (1991) has shown that these three types account for approximately 50% of all conceptual relations regardless of domain; in the natural sciences they are espe-

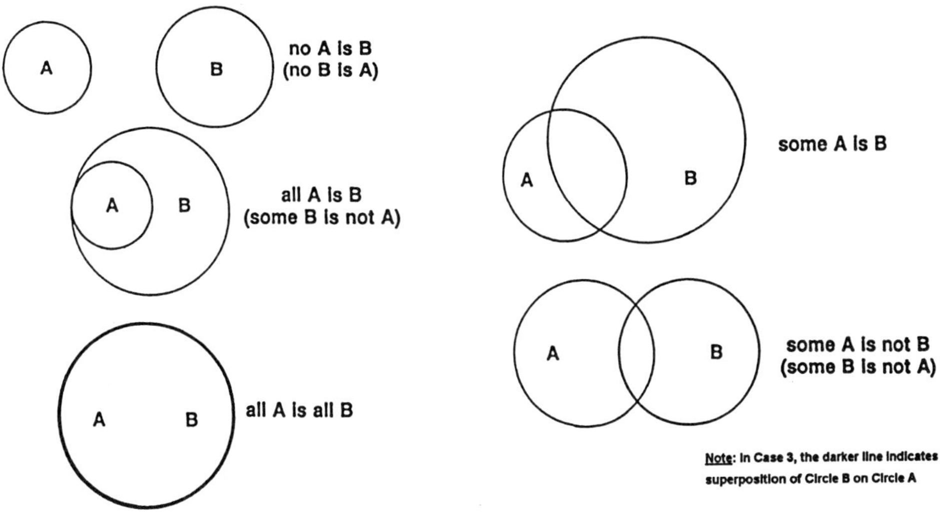

FIGURE 6
Euler's circles.

cially significant. Concept circles are ideal for depicting any or all three of these basic relationships when students are attempting to differentiate small clusters of concepts of the type typically taught in introductory science classes.

Because of its basic simplicity, concept circle diagramming provides a useful introduction to the nature of concepts, the relationshipships between them, and the differences in inclusiveness or exclusiveness among small sets of concepts. It can profitably precede work on concept mapping and serves as introduction to some of the ideas on which concept mapping builds. Younger children and lower-ability students especially like working with the templates and color coding their diagrams according to the 15 rules for diagram generation (cf. Collette & Chiappetta, 1994, p. 69). A concept circle diagram is a nice way to represent a period's work in the science classroom, working with a manageable set of concepts. *Telescoping* concept circles (Figure 7), the practice students most enjoy (Nobles, 1993), helps students connect one day's lesson to the next in a graphically enticing way.

Several scoring techniques have been developed that enable teachers to use concept circles as an evaluation approach. Nobles (1993) constructed scoring checklists that assign points for mastery of technique, graphic complexity, and conceptual sophistication. Nichols (1993) designed a scoring rubric for circle diagrams on the topic of insect metamorphosis that considers students' abilities to select and incorporate scientifically correct representations of insect stages and their ability to characterize these stages by

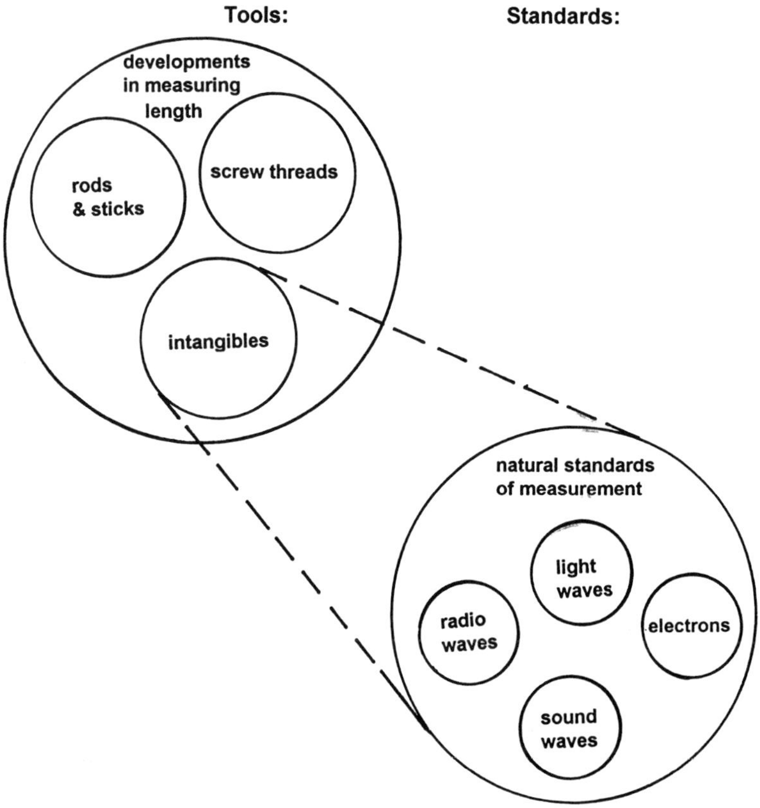

FIGURE 7

Telescoping in concept circles. Sample concept circle diagram: There have been three major developments in the measurement of length: use of independent rods and sticks; use of screw threads; and use of virtually unchanging intangibles such as sound waves, electrons, radio waves, and light waves—increasing precision and accuracy along the way.

structure and function. In short, concept circle diagrams have widespread applications for teaching and learning and also in assessing understanding of concepts and relationships.

Vee Diagrams

A *vee diagram* (Figure 8) is used to help students see and understand how science makes knowledge and value claims. It also helps them identify the components of knowledge making and presents these in a concise, coherent, and visual manner (Novak, 1989a). We think vee diagramming is profitably

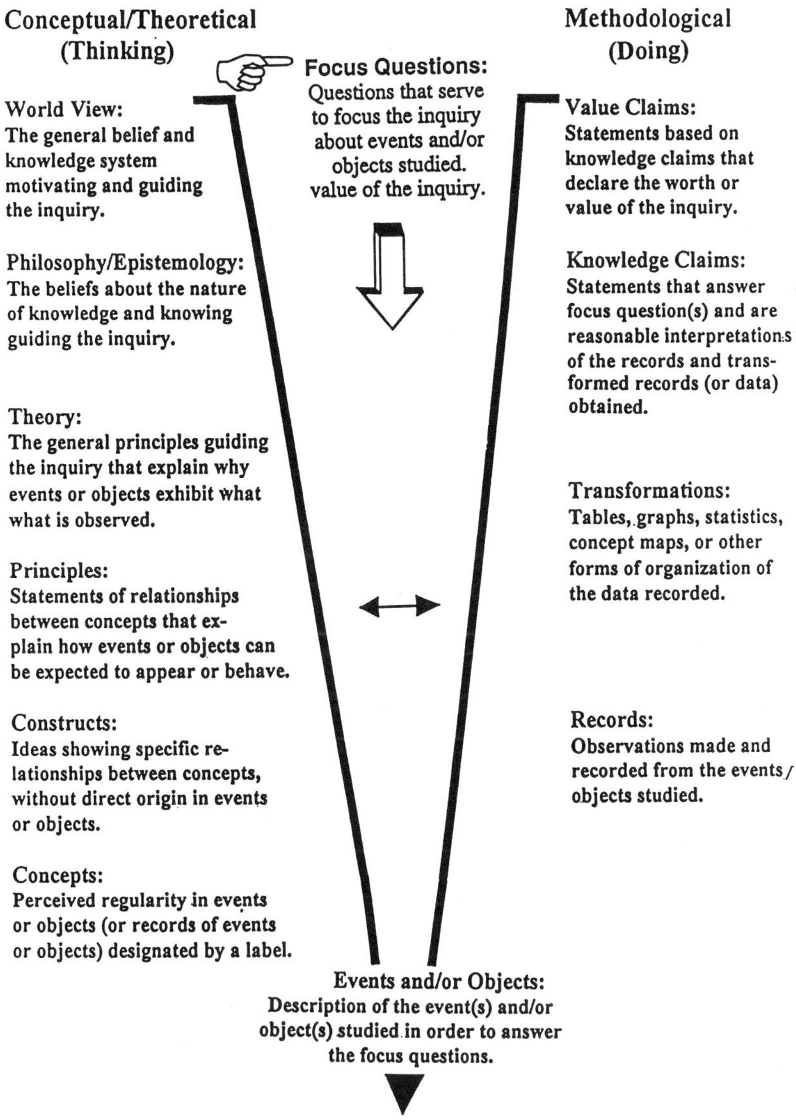

FIGURE 8
Gowin's vee diagram.

introduced after students are proficient at concept mapping, when they are familiar with some major components of the vee diagram; namely, concepts, objects, and events. While the concept map represents an existing

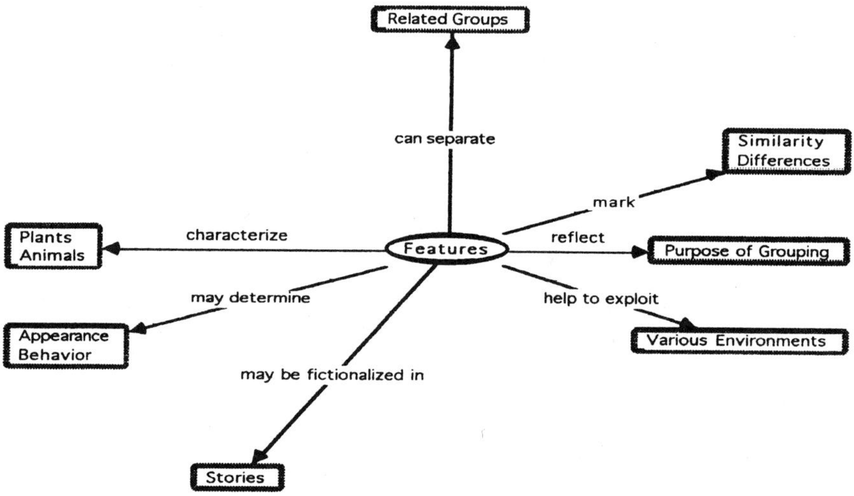

FIGURE 9
A semantic network.

knowledge framework, the vee diagram represents "how we come to know" what is represented on a concept map.

The vee diagram was invented by Cornell philosopher D. B. Gowin as an aid to understanding how knowledge is constructed in the sciences. This heuristic device is a result of Gowin's 20-year quest to help students understand how knowledge is produced and used (Novak & Gowin, 1984). In classroom practice, a blank form of the vee, with only the headings, would be given to the student who would then complete the diagram by synthesizing or analyzing an investigation and filling in the form with words, data, and graphics.

Science teachers find Gowin's vee particularly helpful in teaching students how knowledge is generated in the science laboratory or how to critically analyze a research report. A completed vee diagram may be interpreted by (1) reading the focus question(s); (2) looking at the objects or events to determine whether they will lead to valid and reliable answers; (3) reflecting on the concepts, constructs, principles, theories, philosophy, and worldview driving the investigation; (4) examining the records made of the objects and events to determine whether they are appropriate for answering the question(s); (5) analyzing the data transformations to decide whether they significantly distort the original data; and (6) reviewing the knowledge and value claims to ascertain whether they are consistent with the responses entered in all other categories of the diagram. Once students become comfortable with the vee diagramming technique, it can then be used to assess their understanding of particular knowledge constructions in the natural sciences.

We have found the vee diagram useful in helping students (and researchers) recognize the "conceptual goggles" through which they view the world (Novak, 1989a). Furthermore, the vee challenges both consumers and producers of knowledge to explicitly identify the route they have taken to particular knowledge and value claims. It also forces researchers to consider the possible value claims that might be made on completion of a study, thereby introducing an element of ethical introspection in the knowledge-making process. (Would Oppenheimer have agreed to head the Manhattan Project had he applied the vee first?)

Research on Gowin's vee is still in its infancy, however several studies offer very promising conclusions. For example: Vee-instructed students understand relationships between theory and method, ideas and observations, laboratory activities and class discussions (Gurley, 1982); Students using vee diagrams (and concept maps) in novel problem-solving activities outscore those who do not by a wide margin (Novak, Gowin, & Johansen, 1983); University biology students who employ vee diagrams (and concept maps) exhibit positive attitudes toward the subject they study and the laboratory activities in which they engage (Robertson, 1984).

Semantic Networks

Semantic networks (Figure 9) were first proposed by Quillian (1967) as a hierarchical model of human semantic memory, and his work led to many variations by other researchers. One basic assumption of Quillian's spreading activation model is that, at every level, general concepts offer access to more specific ones. Strictly speaking, concept maps are a form of semantic network; however, we think it is useful to differentiate between them and the semantic networks (SemNets) used by Fisher and her SemNet Research Group at San Diego State University. To Fisher (1992), a *semantic network* is "a network of concepts linked by named relations with associated text and images."

The research team headed by Fisher has developed a widely used semantic networking application for the Macintosh computer, which they call *SemNet*. This software is a powerful research tool that permits users to construct *n*-dimensional, computer-based networks containing thousands of concepts that can be analyzed for embeddedness, most frequently used relationships, and other characteristics.

In our view, concept maps and semantic networks are unique representational forms, each possessing inherent strengths and weaknesses. The concept map offers a graphically effective teaching and learning tool that is readily adapted to classroom use, but because concept maps are two dimensional, they sometimes become very complex and difficult to process visually. On the other hand, semantic networks are *n* dimensional, enabling them to capture large numbers of concepts and relationships and to analyze and display results in a graphically appealing form. However, constructing semantic networks requires schools to invest in costly computers, monitors, and printers. While semantic networks *can* be used for instructional purposes, knowledge is entered and displayed in a nonhierarchical form, which may be detrimental to efficient encoding and retrieval from long-term memory. As an analytical tool for research in large, information-rich domains, however, the SemNet software is a robust and flexible instrument. In general, we find ourselves in agreement with Fisher (1990), who suggested that "concept maps and semantic networking are complementary strategies that can be used effectively in tandem to help students learn, to help teachers teach, and to support cognitive research."

Concept webs, concept maps, vee diagrams, and semantic networks seem to fill different niches in meta-cognition. In our view, each has a decidedly significant role to play in learning how to learn. As Merlin Wittrock (1986) suggested, "we need research on the relation between the development of and the teaching of learning strategies and metacognitive processes"; "it seems quite possible that instruction in learning strategies and metacognitive processes, including awareness and control of one's own learning, can facilitate achievement."

A LOOK TOWARD THE FUTURE OF SCIENCE TEACHING

Harbingers of Change

As we approach the 21st century, it appears that Gowin's (1982) principal variables of educating (i.e., curriculum, teaching, learning, and governance) remain salient, but they are morphing rapidly and somewhat differentially in the nation's schools. Traditional patterns of schooling that once met the needs of an agrarian society are being rapidly reshaped and transformed by a host of social and economic factors, including tax issues, uneven population growth, the vanishing work ethic, welfare migration pressures, crime and personal security, information access, automation, single parenting, and many others. Currently, everything about schooling is open to question and the quest for perfect science teaching and learning continues. The nation's current "bugbear" appears to be "global economic competitiveness," replacing the communist threat of annihilation.

Trustworthiness Is a Key Issue

Shapin (1994) contends that the confident belief in knowledge is now a key issue in judging the worth of that knowledge. The index of truth telling is the trustworthiness of the knowledge makers. This pushes the *moral* to center stage. The key issue for us is this: is science a moral endeavor? Students are no longer content to learn what they are told by experts; science content must first be justified in terms of scientific literacy and scientific ethos and additionally in terms of its value in earning a livelihood.

The antiscience sentiment, driven by postmodern thought, has unduly emphasized the fallibility of science and given excessive weight to the social dimension of scientific knowledge making, while downplaying the role of nature as the arbiter of its truths. Therefore, it is no surprise that science teachers increasingly find students questioning *how we know what we know in science* and asking whether the lenses of science distort the natural objects and events we study. This means that science teachers need a firm grounding in relevant science content domains, as well as the history, philosophy, and sociology of science.

Science Content Is Necessary but Not Sufficient

To push the "lens analogy" a bit further, a new digital, electronic camera developed at the University of Illinois (Staff, 1995) contains a computer that selects the sharpest image of each object in its field of view and combines the images into a single photo, producing an elegantly focused picture regardless of variable distances between the objects and the lens system. Similarly, many now feel that excellence in science teaching and research therein benefits substantially from *multiple perspectives* (both qualitative and quantitative), each representing a distinct view of the learner's prior knowledge, the planned and enacted curricula, the learner's formative and summative performance, and the long-term effects of science learning.

From history, philosophy, and sociology of science; from the social studies, mathematics, and engineering; from the cognitive sciences, design, and technology; and from the spectrum and panoply of the sciences, new course content structures emerge and less powerful concepts, principles, and theories are jettisoned. *Depth* replaces *breadth* as the foremost instructional goal, and *coverage* is no longer deemed synonymous with *quality* in science teaching.

Scientists, teachers, administrators, and students collaborate in an evolving curriculum in which integration and elaboration of existing concepts become paramount, and the value accorded feeling and acting rises to equal status in triad with thinking. Thus, Gowin's (1982) goal of educating as the fluent integration of thinking, feeling, and acting is attained; students become autonomous learners, and rote procedural training takes its appropriate place in an educational system that focuses primarily on meaningful learning.

The Challenges of "Studenting"

Learning is the responsibility of the learner, and the conscious decision to learn meaningfully is one that only students can make. The teacher's parallel responsibility is to help students construct scientifically acceptable meanings for concepts encountered in the curriculum and evaluate their understanding of them—but, note, it is the student who must do the constructing. The student must come to realize that it is he or she who must attend classes regularly, engage willingly, and share meanings lucidly with peers and teachers. Given a safe and open classroom climate and a contemporary curriculum, the quality of one's education is chiefly self-controlled. One can expect schools to provide only *opportunities to learn*, seizing those opportunities is the student's job. Realistically, schools can be expected to provide no more than 50% of the motivational impetus to learn, the other half must be student generated.

In regard to the issue of "responsibility for learning," Barrett (1995) refers us to the 792-page study of Pascarella and Terenzini on the effects of college type on educational outcomes. Based on 2600 impact studies covering a period of almost 25 years, Pascarella and Terrenzini report, "The net impact of attending college (versus not attending college) tends to be substantially more pronounced than any differential impact attributable to attending different kinds of colleges (e.g., large/small, public/private, liberal arts/research, etc.)." The study also found no meaningful differences based on SAT scores, Ph.D.s on the faculty, student–faculty ratio, and so forth. With respect to success after college graduation, the original authors found "in excess of 98 percent of the differences in individual earnings is due to influences other than where one goes to college."

Accordingly, we think it reasonable to conclude that college learning experiences have been much more alike than previously thought, and differences in net learning impacts among students are more likely attributable to the degree to which students employ self-monitored, meaningful learning strategies than any college-specific curricular or instructional practices. Put somewhat differently, the principal difference between successful and unsuccessful students is the extent to which they "take charge" of their own learning.

In similar fashion, we are particularly inspired by meta-learning studies at the middle school level that show that "teachers and researchers have developed increasing respect for middle school students' capability to engage in extended and complex reasoning and their ability to foster it" (Schauble, Glaser, Duschl, Schulze, & John, 1995). These authors have been working on ways of using students' knowledge to guide instruction and on performance-based assessments that illuminate such knowledge. In our view, this work is powerfully illustrative of the improvement that can be achieved through attempts to empower science learners.

Trends That Impact the Future of Science Teaching

In conclusion we wish to cite the work of Marvin Cetron (1994), a futurist of international renown, who has identified a set educational trends that are likely to have substantial affect on America in the early 21st century. Among these trends are several that we believe will play an especially significant role in science education in the forseeable future.

The first of these trends is that the "half-life" of useable knowledge in business, industry, and the professions is rapidly declining. A generation ago, knowledge acquired in secondary school provided learners with the skills required to play a productive role in the work force over the course of a normal lifetime. Today skills often become obsolete even before the student collects his or her diploma. As a result, we can expect the demand for continuing, lifelong education and re-education (especially in scientific and technical fields) to grow rapidly in the years ahead.

Along with the growing demand for continuing education will be a rapid infusion of new technologies that promise to greatly improve access to and customization of instruction. Among these technologies will be advances in the application of computer and telecommunication delivery systems, including job-simulation stations, fiber optics, and interactive videodiscs, to name just a few. Experience with several generations of new technologies suggests that these innovations will have a disproportionate impact in science teaching and learning.

As demand for education grows and new technologies are implemented, schools will be called on to expand their customary operating schedules. Instead of the traditional 180-day school year, we can expect schools to remain open around the clock on a year-round basis serving a much more diverse student body, including adults in the labor force and senior citizens seeking ways to upgrade their skills and knowledge base.

As a result of new technologies and expanded service to the community, we can predict that the cost of public education will continue to rise. Rising costs will undoubtedly generate higher public expectations and a growing demand for accountability. Accordingly, we are likely to see substantial pressure to document school effectiveness through improved assessment approaches.

Unless new energy sources are rapidly developed, it is likely that commuting to and from schools will become more costly. Combined with the spread of computer and telecommunication technologies, this will support a growing tendency toward home and neighborhood schooling. As a result, individuals will learn more on their own and in small peer groups, adopting the scholar's mode of operation. Science teaching, which has traditionally relied on group work and laboratory-based activities, will come to rely more heavily on computer-based simulations and electronic sharing.

We close with Cetron's prediction that "improved pedagogy—the science of learning—will revolutionize education" (p. 32). In our view, this process has already begun and is seen in several of the meta-cognitive approaches described in this chapter. It is likely that most of the approaches we have described will be further developed and ultimately superceded by even more powerful tools. The one prediction we can make with utmost confidence is that the future will belong to those who learn how to learn.

References

Abimbola, I. (1988). The problem of terminology in the study of student conceptions in science. *Science Education*, 72, 175–184.

Adelson, B., & Soloway, E. (1988). A model of software design. In M. Chi, R. Glaser, & M. Farr (Eds.), *The nature of expertise* (pp. 185–208). Hillsdale, NJ: Erlbaum.

Al-Kunifed, A., & Wandersee, J. (1990). One hundred references related to concept mapping. *Journal of Research in Science Teaching*, 27, 1069–1075.

Ameh, C. (1987). An analysis of teachers' and their students' views of the concept "gravity." *Research in Science Education*, 17, 212–219.

Ameh, C., & Gunstone, R. (1985). Teachers' conceptions in science. *Research in Science Education*, 15, 151–157.

Anderson, O. (1992). Some interrelationships between constructivist models of learning and current neurobiological theory, with implications for science education. *Journal of Research in Science Teaching*, 29, 1037–1058.

Andersson B. (1986). Pupils' explanations of some aspects of chemical reactions. *Science Education*, 70, 549–563.

Andersson, B. (1990). Pupils' conceptions of matter and its transformations (age 12–16). *Studies in Science Education*, 18, 53–85.

Armbruster, B., & Anderson, T. (1980). *The effect of mapping on the free recall of expository text* (Tech. Rep. No. 160). Washington, DC: National Institute of Education. (ERIC Document Reproduction Service No. 182 735)

Arnaudin, M., Mintzes, J., Dunn, C., & Shafer, T. (1984). Concept mapping in college science teaching. *Journal of College Science Teaching*, 14, 117–121.

Asoko, H. (1993). First steps in the construction of a theoretical model of light: A case study from a primary school classroom. In J. Novak (Ed.), *Proceedings of the third international seminar on misconceptions and educational strategies in science and mathematics*. [Distributed electronically]. Ithaca, NY: Cornell University, Department of Education.

Atkinson, R., & Shiffrin, R. (1968). Human memory: A proposed system and its control processes. In K. Spence & J. Spence (Eds.), *The psychology and learning and motivation: Advances in research and theory* (Vol. 2, pp. 89–195). New York: Academic Press.

Atran, S. (1990). *Cognitive foundations of natural history*. Cambridge, England: Cambridge University Press.

Ausubel, D. P. (1963). *The psychology of meaningful verbal learning*. New York: Grune & Stratton.

Ausubel, D. (1968). *Educational psychology: A cognitive view*. New York: Holt, Rinehart & Winston.

Ausubel, D., Novak, J., & Hanesian, H. (1978). *Educational psychology: A cognitive view*. New York: Holt, Rinehart & Winston.

Barker, M., & Carr, M. (1989). Teaching and learning about photosynthesis: Part I. An assessment in terms of students' prior knowledge. *International Journal of Science Education*, 11, 49–56.

Barras, R. (1984). Some misconceptions and misunderstandings perpetuated by teachers and textbooks. *Journal of Biological Education*, 18, 201–206.

Barrett, W. (1995, August 4). Opinion: Better ways to measure quality. *Chronicle of Higher Education*, p. B3.

Bellanca, J. (1990). *The ccoperative think tank: Graphic organizers to teach thinking in the cooperative classroom*. Palatine, IL: Skylight Publishing.

Benton, J., Mintzes, J., Kendrick, A., & Solomon, R. (1994). Alternative conceptions in sexually-transmitted diseases: A cross-age study. *Journal of Sex Education and Therapy*, 19, 165–182.

Bishop, B., & Anderson, C. (1990). Students' conceptions of natural selection and its role in evolution. *Journal of Research in Science Teaching*, 27, 415–428.

Bliss, J., & Ogborn, J. (1985). Childrens' choices of uses of energy. *International Journal of Science Education*, 7, 195–203.

Bloom, B. (1956). *Taxonomy of educational objectives: Handbook I. Cognitive domain*. New York: McKay.

Bloom, J. (1989). Preservice elementary teachers' conceptions of science, theories, and evolution. *International Journal of Science Education*, 11, 401–415.

Brumby, M. (1984). Misconceptions about the concept of natural selection by medical biology students. *Science Education*, 68, 493–503.

Bruner, J. (1960). *The process of education*. Cambridge, MA: Harvard University Press.

Cain, R. (1994). The circle of Apollonius: A discovery activity. *School Science and Mathematics*, 94, 85–88.

Camp, C., & Clement, J. (1994). *Preconceptions in mechanics: Lessons dealing with students' conceptual difficulties*. Dubuque, IA: Kendall/Hunt.

Carey, S. (1986). Cognitive science and science education. *American Psychologist*, 41, 1123–1130.

Carey, S. (1987). *Conceptual change in childhood*. Cambridge, MA: MIT Press.

Carmichael, P., Driver, R., Holding, B., Phillips, I., Twigger, D., & Watts, M. (1990). *Research on students' conceptions in science: A bibliography*. Leeds, UK: University of Leeds.

Cetron, M. (1994). An American renaissance: 74 trends that will affect America's future—and yours. *The Futurist*, 28, 27–38.

Champagne, A., Klopfer, L., & Anderson, J. (1980). Factors influencing the learning of classical mechanics. *American Journal of Physics*, 48, 1074–1079.

Chi, M., Feltovich, P., & Glaser, R. (1981). Categorization and representation of physics problems by experts and novices. *Cognitive Science*, 5, 121–152.

Chi, M., Glaser, R., & Farr, M. (1988). *The nature of expertise*. Hillsdale, NJ: Erlbaum.

Cho, H., Kahle, J., & Nordland, F. (1985). An investigation of high school biology textbooks as sources of misconceptions and difficulties in genetics and some suggestions for teaching genetics. *Science Education*, 69, 707–719.

Chomsky, N. (1965). *Aspects of the theory of syntax*. Cambridge, MA: MIT Press.

Clement, J. (1982). Students' preconceptions in introductory mechanics. *American Journal of Physics*, 50, 66–71.

Clement, J. (1987). Overcoming students' misconceptions in physics: The role of anchoring intuitions and analogical validity. In J. D. Novak (Ed.), *Proceedings of the second international seminar on misconceptions and educational strategies in science and mathematics* (Vol. 3, pp. 84–97). Ithaca, NY: Cornell University, Department of Education.

Clement, J., Brown, D., & Zeitsman, A. (1989). Not all preconceptions are misconceptions: Finding "anchoring" conceptions for grounding instruction on students' intuitions. *International Journal of Science Education*, 11, 554–565.

Collette, A., & Chiappetta, E. (1994). Concept circles. *Science instruction in the middle and secondary schools* (3rd ed., pp. 68–70). New York: Macmillan.

Collins, A., & Loftus, E. (1975). A spreading activation theory of semantic processing. *Psychological Review*, 82, 407–428.

Corporation for Public Broadcasting. (1996). A *private universe* (A six-part television miniseries on students' alternative conceptions in science). M. H. Schneps (Director). New York: Author.

Darling-Hammond, L., & Hudson, L. (1990). Precollege science and mathematics teachers: Supply, demand and quality. *Review of Research in Education*, 16, 223–261.

Davis, N. (1990). Using concept mapping to assist prospective elementary teachers in making meaning. *Journal of Science Teacher Education*, 1, 66–69.

diSessa, A. (1982). Unlearning Aristotelian physics: A study of knowledge based learning. *Cognitive Science*, 6, 37–75.

Driver, R., & Easley, J. (1978). Pupils and paradigms: A review of the literature related to concept development in adolescent science students. *Studies in Science Education*, 5, 61–84.

Duit, R. (1981). Understanding energy as a conserved quantity-remarks on the article by R. U. Sexl. *European Journal of Science Education*, 3, 291–301.

Duschl, R. (1990). *Restructuring science education*. New York: Teachers College Press.
Easley, J. (1959). The physical science study committee and educational theory. *Harvard Educational Review*, 29, 4–11.
Eaton, A., Anderson, C., & Smith, E. (1983). When students don't know they don't know. *Science and Children*, 20, 7–9.
Eaton, A., Anderson, C., & Smith, E. (1984). Students' misconceptions interfere with science learning: Case studies of fifth grade students. *Elementary School Journal*, 84, 365–379.
Eisen, Y., and Stavy, R. (1988). Students' understanding of photosynthesis. *American Biology Teacher*, 50, 208–212.
Engel-Clough, E., & Wood-Robinson, C. (1985). Childrens' understanding of inheritance. *Journal of Biological Education*, 19, 304–310.
Enochs, L., & Gabel, D. (1984). Preservice elementary teachers' conceptions of volume. *School Science and Mathematics*, 84, 670–680.
Feher, E., & Rice, K. (1987). A comparison of teacher-student conceptions in optics. In J. D. Novak (Ed.), *Proceedings of the second international seminar on misconceptions and educational strategies in science and mathematics* (Vol. 2, pp. 108–117). Ithaca, NY: Cornell University, Department of Education.
Fisher, K. (1990). Semantic networking: The new kid on the block [Special issue]. *Journal of Research in Science Teaching*, 27, 1001–1018.
Fisher, K. (1992). SemNet: A tool for personal knowledge construction. In P. Kommers, D. Jonassen, & J. Mayes (Eds.), *Cognitive tools for learning* (pp. 63–75). New York: Springer-Verlag.
Fredette, N., & Clement, J. (1981). Student misconceptions of an electric circuit: What do they mean? *Journal of College Science Teaching*, 10, 280–285.
Gagné, R. (1965). *The conditions of learning*. New York: Holt, Rinehart & Winston.
Gazzaniga, M. (1995). *The cognitive neurosciences*. Cambridge, MA: MIT Press.
Gilbert, J., Osborne, R., & Fensham, P. (1982). Children's science and its consequences for teaching. *Science Education*, 66, 623–633.
Gobbo, C., & Chi, M. (1986). How knowledge is structured and used by expert and novice children. *Cognitive Development*, 1, 221–237.
Good, R., Trowbridge, J., Demastes, S., Wandersee, J., Hafner, M., & Cummins, C., (Eds.) (1992). *Proceedings of the evolution education research conference*. Baton Rouge: Louisiana State University.
Gowin, D. B. (1982). *Educating*. Ithaca, NY: Cornell University Press.
Gurley, L. (1982). *Use of Gowin's vee and concept mapping strategies to teach students responsibility for learning high school biological sciences*. Unpublished doctoral dissertation, Cornell University, Ithaca, NY.
Hallden, O. (1988). The evolution of the species: Pupil perspectives and school perspectives. *International Journal of Science Education*, 10, 541–552.
Hanf, M. (1971). Mapping: A technique for translating reading into thinking. *Journal of Reading*, 14, 225–230.
Happs, J. (1985). Cognitive learning theory and classroom complexity. *Research in Science and Technological Education*, 3, 157–174.
Heinze-Fry, J., & Novak, J. (1990). Concept mapping brings long-term movement towards meaningful learning. *Science Education*, 74, 461–472.
Herron, D. (1978). Role of learning and development: Critique of Novak's comparison of Ausubel and Piaget. *Science Education*, 62, 593–605.
Hettich, P. (1992). Concept circles. *Learning skills for college and career* (pp. 205–208). Pacific Grove, CA: Brooks/Cole.
Hewson, M. (1985). The role of intellectual environment in the origin of conceptions: An exploratory study. In L. H. T. West & A. L. Pines (Eds.), *Cognitive structure and conceptual change* (pp. 152–161). Orlando, FL: Academic Press.
Hewson, P. (1981). A conceptual change approach to learning science. *European Journal of Science Education*, 3, 383–396.
Hirschfeld, L., & Gelman, S. (1994). *Mapping the mind: Domain specificity in cognition and culture*. Cambridge, England: Cambridge University Press.

Hoffman, R. (1991). *Use of relational descriptors by experienced users of a computer-based semantic network.* Unpublished master's thesis, San Diego State University, San Diego, CA.

Horton, P., McConney, A., Gallo, M., Woods, A., Senn, G., & Hamelin, D. (1993). An investigation of the effectiveness of concept mapping as an instructional tool. *Science Education, 77,* 95–111.

Jonassen, D., Beissner, K., & Yacci, M. (1993). *Structural knowledge: Techniques for representing, conveying, and acquiring structuralknowledge.* Hillsdale, NJ: Erlbaum.

Joshua, S. (1984). Students' interpretation of simple electrical diagrams. *European Journal of Science Education, 6,* 271–275.

Jungwirth, E. (1975). Preconceived adaptation and inverted evolution (a case study of distorted concept formation in high school biology). *Australian Science Teachers Journal, 21,* 95–100.

Kant, I. (1781). *Critique of pure reason.* Translated with introduction by N. Smith (1958). New York: Modern Library.

Kant, I. (1783). *Prolegomena to any future metaphysics.* Translated with introduction by P. Lucas (1971). Manchester: Manchester University Press.

Keil, F. (1989). *Concepts, kinds, and cognitive development.* Cambridge, MA: MIT Press.

Kelly, G. (1955). *The psychology of personal constructs.* New York: Norton.

Kenealy, P. (1987). A syntactic source of a common "misconception" about acceleration. In J. D. Novak (Ed.), *Proceedings of the second international seminar on misconceptions and educational strategies in science and mathematics.* (Vol. 3, pp. 278–292). Ithaca, NY: Cornell University, Department of Education.

Kuhn, T. (1962). *The structure of scientific revolutions.* Chicago: University of Chicago Press.

Lamarck, J. B. (1809). *Philosophie zoologique, ou exposition des considérations relatives à l'histoire naturelle des animaux.* Paris. (Reprinted in English by University of Chicago Press, Chicago, IL. 1984).

Larkin, J. (1983). The role of problem representation in physics. In D. Gentner & A. Stevens (Eds.), *Mental models* (pp. 75–98). Hillsdale, NJ: Erlbaum.

Larkin, J., McDermott, L., Simon, D., & Simon, H. (1980). Models of competence in solving physics problems. *Cognitive Science, 4,* 317–348.

Laudan, L. (1984). *Science and values.* Berkeley: University of California Press.

Lawrenz, F. (1986). Misconceptions of physical science concepts among elementary school teachers. *School Science and Mathematics, 86,* 654–660.

Lawson, A. (1988). The acquisition of biological knowledge during childhood: Cognitive conflict or tabula rasa? *Journal of Research in Science Teaching, 25,* 185–199.

Lawson, A. (1994). Research on the acquisition of science knowledge: Epistemological foundations of cognition. In D. Gabel (Ed.), *Handbook of research on science teaching and learning* (pp. 131–176). New York: Macmillan.

Lawson, A., & Worsnop, W. (1992). Learning about evolution and rejecting a belief in special creation: Effects of reflective reasoning skill, prior knowledge, prior belief and religious commitment. *Journal of Research in Science Teaching, 29,* 143–166.

Lemonick, M. (1995, August 14). Mysteries of the deep—Scientists are set to conquer the last frontier: The ocean floor. *Time,* pp. 52–60.

Lesgold, A., Rubinson, H., Feltovich, P., Glaser, R., Klopfer, D., & Wang, Y. (1988). Expertise in a complex skill: Diagnosing x-ray pictures. In M. Chi, R. Glaser, & M. Marshall (Eds.), *The nature of expertise* (pp. 311–342). Hillsdale, NJ: Erlbaum.

Markham, K., Mintzes, J., & Jones, M. G. (1994). The concept map as a research and evaluation tool: Further evidence of validity. *Journal of Research in Science Teaching, 31,* 91–101.

McCloskey, M. (1983). Naive theories of motion. In D. Gentner & A. Stevens (Eds.), *Mental models* (pp. 299–325). Hillsdale, NJ: Erlbaum.

McKoon, G., Ratcliff, R., & Dell, G. (1986). A critical evaluation of the semantic-episodic distinction. *Journal of Experimental Psychology: Learning, Memory and Cognition, 12,* 295–306.

Miller, G. (1956). The magic number seven, plus or minus two: Some limits on our capacity for processing information. *Psychological Review, 63,* 81–97.

Minstrell, J. (1982). Explaining the "at rest" condition of an object. *Physics Teacher*, 20, 10–14.

Mintzes, J. (1989). The acquisition of biological knowledge during childhood: An alternative conception. *Journal of Research in Science Teaching*, 26, 823–824.

Mintzes, J. (1992). Proposal for a research agenda on conceptual change in evolutionary biology. In R. Good, et al. (Eds.), *Proceedings of the evolution education research conference* (pp. 153–156). Baton Rouge: Louisiana State University.

Mintzes, J., Trowbridge, J., Arnaudin, M., & Wandersee, J. (1991). Children's biology: Studies on conceptual development in the life sciences. In S. Glynn, R. Yeany, & B. Britton (Eds.), *The psychology of learning science* (pp. 179–202). Hillsdale, NJ: Erlbaum.

Montogomery, S. (1994). *Minds for the making*. New York: Guilford.

Nichols, M. (1993). *A cross-age study of students' knowledge of insect metamorphosis: Insights into their understanding of evolution*. Unpublished doctoral dissertation, Louisiana State University, Baton Rouge.

Nobles, C. (1993). *Concept circle diagrams: A metacognitive learning strategy to enhance meaningful learning in the elementary school classroom*. Unpublished doctoral dissertation, Louisiana State University, Baton Rouge.

Novak, J. (1965). A model for the interpretation and analysis of concept formation. *Journal of Research in Science Teaching*, 3, 72–83.

Novak, J. (1972). Audio-tutorial techniques for individualizing science instruction in the elementary school. In H. Triezenberg (Ed.), *Individualized science: Like it is* (pp. 12–23). Washington, DC: National Science Teachers Association.

Novak, J. (1977a). Epicycles and the homocentric earth: Or what is wrong with stages of cognitive development? *Science Education*, 61, 393–395.

Novak, J. (1977b). An alternative to Piagetian psychology for science and mathematics education. *Science Education*, 61, 453–477.

Novak, J. (1977c). *A theory of education*. Ithaca, NY: Cornell University Press.

Novak, J. (1985). Metalearning and metaknowledge strategies to help students learn how to learn. In L. West & A. L. Pines (Eds.), *Cognitive structure and conceptual change* (pp. 189–209). Orlando, FL: Academic Press.

Novak, J. (1987). Human constructivism: Toward a unity of psychological and epistemological meaning making. In J. D. Novak (Ed.), *Proceedings of the second international seminar on misconceptions and educational strategies in science and mathematics* (Vol. I, pp. 349–360). Ithaca, NY: Cornell University, Department of Education.

Novak, J. (1988). Learning science and the science of learning. *Studies in Science Education*, 15, 77–101.

Novak, J. (1989a). *Introduction to vee diagramming*. Unpublished manuscript, Cornell University, Ithaca, NY.

Novak, J. (1989b). The use of metacognitive tools to facilitate meaningful learning. In P. Adey (Ed.), *Adolescent development and school science* (pp. 227–239). London: Falmer Press.

Novak, J. (1990). Concept maps and vee diagrams: Two metacognitive tools to facilitate meaningful learning. *Instructional Science*, 19, 29–52.

Novak, J. (1993a). Human constructivism: A unification of psychological and epistemological phenomena in meaning making. *International Journal of Personal Construct Psychology*, 6, 167–193.

Novak, J. (1993b). Meaningful learning: The essential factor for conceptual change in limited or inappropriate propositional hierarchies (LIPHS) leading to empowerment of learners. In J. Novak (Ed.), *Proceedings of the third international seminar on misconceptions and educational strategies in science and mathematics* [Distributed electronically]. Ithaca, NY: Cornell University, Department of Education.

Novak, J. (1993c). A view on the current status of Ausubel's assimilation theory of learning. In J. Novak (Ed.), *Proceedings of the third international seminar on misconceptions and educational strategies in science and mathematics* [Distributed electronically]. Ithaca, NY: Cornell University, Department of Education.

Novak, J., & Gowin, D. B. (1984). *Learning how to learn*. New York: Cambridge University Press.

Novak, J., Gowin, D., & Johansen, G. (1983). The use of concept mapping and knowledge vee mapping with junior high school science students. *Science Education*, 67, 625–645.

Novak, J., & Musonda, D. (1991). A twelve-year longitudinal study of science concept learning. *American Educational Research Journal*, 28, 117–153.

Novak, J., & Wandersee, J. (Eds.). (1990). Perspectives on concept mapping [Special issue]. *Journal of Research in Science Teaching*, 27, 923–1079.

Novick, S., & Nussbaum, J. (1978). Junior high school pupil's understanding of the particulate nature of matter: An interview study. *Science Education*, 62, 273–281.

Novick, S., & Nussbaum, J. (1981). Pupils' understanding of the particulate nature of matter: A cross-age study. *Science Education*, 65, 187–196.

Nussbaum, J. (1985). The particulate nature of matter in the gaseous phase. In R. Driver, E. Guesne, & A. Tiberghien (Eds.), *Children's ideas in science* (pp. 124–144). London: Milton Keynes.

Nussbaum, J. (1989). Classroom conceptual change: Philosophical perspectives. *International Journal of Science Education*, 11, 530–540.

Nussbaum, J. (1993). Teaching about vacuum and particles, why, when and how: A research report. In J. Novak (Ed.), *Proceedings of the third international seminar on misconceptions and educational strategies in science and mathematics* [Distributed electronically]. Ithaca, NY: Cornell University, Department of Education.

Nussbaum, J., & Novick, S. (1981). Brainstorming in the classroom to invent a model: A case study. *School Science Review*, 62, 771–778.

Ogunniyi, M., & Pella, M. (1980). Conceptualizations of scientific concepts, laws and theories held by Kwara State, Nigeria secondary school science teachers. *Science Education*, 64, 591–599.

Okebukola, P., & Jegede, O. (1989). Students' anxiety towards and perception of difficulty of some biological concepts under the concept mapping heuristic. *Research in Science and Technological Education*, 7, 85–92.

Osborne, R. (1981). Children's ideas about electric current. *New Zealand Science Teacher*, 29, 12–19.

Osborne, R., & Wittrock, M. (1983). Learning science: A generative process. *Science Education*, 67, 489–508.

Patel, V., Groen, G., & Frederikson, C. (1986). Differences between students and physicians in memory for clinical cases. *Medical Education*, 20, 3–9.

Pearsall, N. R., Skipper, J., & Mintzes, J. (in press). Knowledge restructuring in the life sciences: A longitudinal study of conceptual change in biology. *Science Education*.

Pfundt, H., & Duit, R. (1994). *Students' alternative frameworks and science education*. Kiel, Germany: Institute for Science Education.

Piaget, J. (1964). Cognitive development in children: Development and learning. *Journal of Research in Science Teaching*, 2, 176–186.

Piaget, J. (1970). *Genetic epistemology*. New York: Columbia University Press.

Pope, M., & Gilbert, J. (1983). Personal experience and the construction of knowledge in science. *Science Education*, 67, 193–203.

Popper, K. (1959). *The logic of scientific discovery*. New York: Basic Books.

Posner, G., Strike, K., Hewson, P., & Gertzog, W. (1982). Accommodation of a scientific conception: Toward a theory of conceptual change. *Science Education*, 66, 211–227.

Quillian, M. ((1967). Word concepts: A theory and simulation of some basic semantic capabilities. *Behavioral Sciences*, 12, 410–430.

Readence, J., Bean, T., & Baldwin, R. (1985). *Content area reading: An integrated approach* (2nd ed.). Dubuque, IA: Kendall/Hunt.

Ripple, R. E., & Rockcastle, V. N. (1964). Piaget rediscovered: A report of the conference on cognitive studies and curriculum development [Special issue]. *Journal of Research in Science Teaching*, 2, 165–267.

Robertson, M. (1984). *Use of video-tape simulated recall interviews to study the thoughts and feelings in an introductory biology laboratory*. Unpublished masters thesis, Cornell University, Ithaca, NY.

Rorty, R. (1979). *Philosophy and the mirror of nature*. Princeton, NJ: Princeton University Press.

Roth, K., Smith, E., & Anderson, C. (1983). *Students' conceptions of photosynthesis and food for plants*. East Lansing: Michigan State University, Institute for Research on Teaching.

Roth, W. (1990, April). Map your way to a better lab. *Science Teacher*, pp. 31–34.

Rumelhart, D. (1989). The architecture of the mind: A connectionist approach. In M. Posner (Ed.), *Foundations of cognitive science* (pp. 133–160). Cambridge, MA: MIT Press.

Rumelhart, D., & Norman, D. (1978). Accretion, tuning and restructuring: Three modes of learning. In J. Cotton & R. Klateky (Eds.), *Semantic factors in cognition* (pp. 37–53). Hillsdale, NJ: Erlbaum.

Schauble, L., Glaser, R., Duschl, R., Schulze, S., & John, J. (1995). Students' understanding of the objectives and procedures of experimentation in the science classroom. *Journal of the Learning Sciences*, 4, 131–166.

Schwab, J. (1960). The teaching of science as inquiry. In J. Schwab & P. Brandwein (Eds.), *The teaching of science* (pp. 1–103). Cambridge, MA: Harvard University Press.

Schwartz, R. (1988). Learning to learn vocabulary in content area textbooks. *Journal of Reading*, 32, 108–118.

Scott, P. (1993). Overtures to obstacles: Teaching and learning about air pressure in a high school classroom. In J. Novak (Ed.), *Proceedings of the third international seminar on misconceptions and educational strategies in science and mathematics* [Distributed electronically]. Ithaca, NY: Cornell University, Department of Education.

Scott, P., Asoko, H., & Driver, D. (1992). Teaching for conceptual change: A review of strategies. In R. Duit, F. Goldberg, & H. Niedderer (Eds.), *Research in physics learning: Theoretical issues and empirical studies* (pp. 310–329). Kiel, Germany: Institute for Science Education.

Shapin, S. (1994). *A social history of truth: Civility and science in seventeenth-century England*. Chicago: University of Chicago Press.

Shapiro, B. (1994). *What children bring to light*. New York: Teachers College Press.

Shipstone, D. (1984). A study of children's understanding of electricity in simple DC circuits. *European Journal of Science Education*, 6, 185–198.

Simon, H. (1974). How big is a chunk? *Science*, 183, 482–488.

Skinner, B. F. (1954). *Verbal behavior*. New York: Appleton-Century-Crofts.

Smith, E., & Anderson, C. (1984). Plants as producers: A case study of elementary science teaching. *Journal of Research in Science Teaching*, 21, 685–698.

Solomon, J. (1982). How children learn about energy or does the first law come first? *School Science Review*, 63, 415–422.

Solomon, J. (1983). Learning about energy: How pupils think in two domains. *European Journal of Science Education*, 5, 49–59.

Solomon, J. (1984). Prompts, cues and discrimination: The utilization of two separate knowledge systems. *European Journal of Science Education*, 6, 63–82.

Soloway, E., Ehrlich, K., Bonar, J., & Greenspan, J. (1982). What do novices know about programming? In A. Badre & B. Shneiderman (Eds.), *Directions in human-computer interactions* (pp. 87–122). Norwood, NJ: Ablex.

Songer, C., & Mintzes, J. (1994). Understanding cellular respiration: An analysis of conceptual change in college biology. *Journal of Research in Science Teaching*, 31, 621–637.

Stahl, H., & Hunter, S. (1990). *CMap 2.0* [Computer program for concept mapping]. Ithaca, NY: HSSH (Exceller Software).

Staff. (1995, August). Camera combines near and far sight. *Popular Mechanics*, 172 24.

Stavy, R. (1988). Children's conception of gas. *International Journal of Science Education*, 10, 553–560.

Stavy, R. (1989). Students' conceptions of matter. In P. Adey (Ed.), *Adolescent development and school science* (pp. 273–282). London: Falmer Press.

Stead, B., & Osborne, R. (1980). Exploring students' conceptions of light. *Australian Science Teachers Journal*, 26, 84–90.

Stice, C., & Alvarez, M. (1986). *Hierarchical concept mapping: Young children learn how to learn* (*A viable heuristic for the primary grades*) (Center of Excellence, Basic Skills for the Disadvantaged Reading/Writing. Component Rep. No. 5). Nashville: Tennessee State University. (ERIC Document Reproduction Service No. ED 274 946)

Toulmin, S. (1972). *Human understanding: The collective use and evolution of concepts*. Princeton, NJ: Princeton University Press.

Trowbridge, J., & Wandersee, J. (1994). Identifying critical junctures in learning in a college course on evolution. *Journal of Research in Science Teaching*, 31, 459–473.

Trowbridge, J., & Wandersee, J. (1995) *How do graphics presented during college biology lessons affect students' learning?* Manuscript submitted for publication.

Tulving, E. (1985). How many memory systems are there? *American Psychologist*, 40, 385–398.

Tyler, R. W. (1949). *Basic principles of curriculum and instruction*. Chicago: University of Chicago Press.

Viennot, L. (1979). Spontaneous reasoning in elementary dynamics. *European Journal of Science Education*, 1, 205–221.

von Glasersfeld, E. (1989). Cognition, construction of knowledge, and teaching. *Synthese*, 80, 121–140.

Vygotsky, L. (1962). *Thought and language*. Cambridge, MA: MIT Press.

Wallace, J., Mintzes, J., & Markham, K. (1992). Concept mapping in college science teaching: What the research says. *Journal of College Science Teaching*, 22, 84–86.

Wandersee, J. (1983). Students' misconceptions about photosynthesis.: A cross-age study. In H. Helm & J. Novak (Eds.), *Proceedings of the international seminar on misconceptions in science and mathematics* (pp. 441–466). Ithaca, NY: Cornell University, Department of Education.

Wandersee, J. (1986). Can the history of science help science educators anticipate students' misconceptions? *Journal of Research in Science Teaching*, 23, 581–597.

Wandersee, J. (1987a). Drawing concept circles: A new way to teach and test students. *Science Activities*, 24, 9–20.

Wandersee, J. (1987b). Drawing concept circles: A way of revealing what the learner knows. In J. Novak (Ed.), *Proceedings of the second international seminar on misconceptions and educational strategies in science and mathematics* (Vol. I, pp. 506–520). Ithaca, NY: Cornell University, Department of Education.

Wandersee, J., Mintzes, J., & Arnaudin, M. (1989). Biology from the learners' viewpoint: A content analysis of the research literature. *School Science and Mathematics*, 89, 654–668.

Wandersee, J., Mintzes, J., & Novak, J. (1994). Research on alternative conceptions in science. In D. Gabel (Ed.), *Handbook of research on science teaching and learning* (pp. 177–210). New York: Macmillan.

West, L. H. T., & Pines, A. L. (1985). *Cognitive structure and conceptual change*. Orlando, FL: Academic Press.

White, R., & Gunstone, R. (1989). Metalearning and conceptual change. *International Journal of Science Education*, 11, 577–586.

Wittrock, M. (1986). Students' thought processes. In M. Wittrock (Ed.), *Handbook of research on teaching* (3rd ed., pp. 297–314). New York: Macmillan.

Wittrock, M. (1994). Generative science teaching. In P. Fensham, R. Gunstone, & R. White (Eds.), *The content of science* (pp. 29–38). London: Falmer Press.

PART III

Learning to Learn

CHAPTER

14

Inductive Reasoning and Problem Solving: The Early Grades

GARY D. PHYE
Iowa State University

Most of the academic standards that have been developed during the 1990s have made reference to learning outcomes such as creative thinking, critical thinking, reasoning, and problem solving. In this discussion, I will not be considering the topic of creative thinking. At first glance, these learning outcomes not only appear to be reasonable but also well-defined goals for classroom instruction. The latter, agreement as to what is meant by each of these terms, can present the greatest obstacle for most classroom teachers. This is not a surprising state of affairs, since researchers and theorists are also in disagreement (Galotti, 1989). This disagreement involves not only theoretical positions as to how each of these terms are defined but also issues of formal versus everyday reasoning.

Actually, from a teaching perspective, it may be best to think of the formal versus everyday reasoning issue as a problem for theorists to debate. As a classroom teacher, I tend to think of them as different ends on a scale or continuum. When introducing the topic of reasoning, I typically start with formal reasoning examples. I like to start with formal reasoning examples because they are well-defined problems and I can generate numerous other examples for practice. Once the basic procedures and rules are understood, I can then make connections with everyday reasoning problems. This is basically a teaching-for-transfer approach that reflects a constructivist perspective to academic learning and remembering.

Handbook of Academic Learning

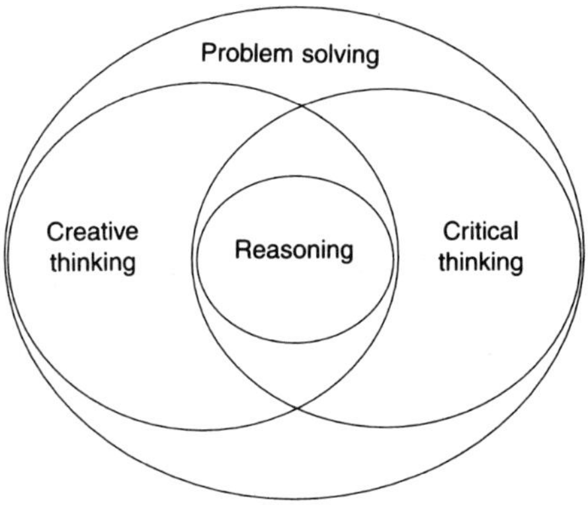

FIGURE 1
Higher-order thinking skills.

In this chapter, I am going to build on some of the basic themes introduced in Chapter 2. First, we will consider where reasoning "fits" within the context of higher-order thinking skills. This section will include references to reviews of curriculum programs that have been developed to promote thinking, reasoning, and problem-solving skills in the United States and Europe. The second section of this chapter contains a brief discussion of cognitive intervention and academic achievement, where teaching may involve individual students, small groups of students, or entire classrooms. The third section will introduce a cognitive training program for children from ages 6 to 10 that teaches inductive reasoning and problem-solving skills. This program has been used extensively in Germany and has been recently introduced in the United States (Klauer & Phye, 1994) and the Netherlands (Klauer, Resing, & Slenders, 1996).

HIGHER-ORDER THINKING SKILLS

Is reasoning distinct from problem solving discussed by Richard Mayer (Chapter 15) or critical thinking discussed by David Olsen (Chapter 16)? The answer is both yes and no (how is that for a philosophical answer?). The answer to our query is *yes* in the sense that formal reasoning involves a set of procedures and rules that characterize a particular way of thinking. The answer is *no* in the sense that reasoning is typically involved as an important part of both critical thinking and problem-solving activities. One way of conceptualizing the relationship among these three types of higher-order thinking skills is a visual map first suggested by Robert Ennis (Hanson, 1989). From this perspective (Figure 1), one can better appreciate the interrelated nature of these higher-order thinking skills. As a total package, these skills represent those cognitive intellectual abilities that make possible, learning to learn. These higher-order thinking skills provide the cognitive foundation for self-regulated learning or expertise in the classroom.

Classroom Instruction

Can higher thinking skills be taught? Yes! Can higher-order thinking skills be learned? Yes. Will students then demonstrate the ability to use higher-order thinking skills in the classroom? Maybe. A basic assumption frequently made in the classroom is that, if something is taught, it should automatically be reflected in future classroom activities. After all, is this not the way the curriculum is structured and is this not the way most textbooks are designed?

In the best of all possible classrooms, where all students are equally prepared, highly motivated, have made an effort to learn and remember, and are interested in the task at hand, this assumption may be accurate. However, after spending 25 years in the classroom, I am still in search of this classroom for even one week. The assumption that this condition will prevail across a semester or an academic year is wishful thinking, I suspect. Before we decide that the whole idea is not worth pursuing, let us first re-examine our assumptions.

Teaching Thinking Skills

Can higher-order thinking skills be taught? The obvious answer to this question is yes. There are a number of ways this can be accomplished. A knowledgeable teacher can embed these higher-order thinking skills in everyday instructional strategies or methods regardless of the nature of the curriculum found in a particular school. Some administrators not trusting their teachers may opt for a curriculum approach where a learning-to-learn course is taught at a particular grade level. With the emphasis on technology in the classroom, computer software will continue to be developed that is advertised as "teaching" thinking skills. A frequently asked question is, "Which approach is best?" I suspect that this is the wrong question. A better question might well be, "How do we better take advantage of resources by integrating all three approaches?" Each approach has its strengths and weaknesses. At the present time, I do not see one approach as so successful that we can ignore the others.

Even teachers who exhibit the prototypical teaching skills identified by Sternberg and Horvath (1995) as teaching expertise must have available appropriate resources. Sternberg and Horvath's (1995) expert teacher is viewed as well versed in content knowledge, highly skilled in terms of pedagogical knowledge, and approaching classroom teaching from a problem-solving perspective. This prototypical teacher is flexible in dealing with the constraints found in her or his classroom and insightful in the use of resources. In a "nutshell," the classroom teacher is the most important component in the teaching of higher-order thinking skills. However, even the expert teacher requires sufficient resources. In this regard, intervention programs, software packages, special classes added to the curriculum, and the like are viewed as resources that the teacher can draw on for teaching of thinking skills.

Learning Thinking Skills

Can higher-order thinking skills be learned? The answer is yes. This assumption is shared by the chapter authors in Part II where each author discusses teaching students *how* to learn within specific content areas (the 3Rs plus science). This assumption however, must not be translated into the corollary assumptions that all students learn at the same rate or to the same level of expertise. The caveat in this case being individual differences in prior knowledge and cognitive abilities. Further, there is more to the learning of higher-order thinking skills than just rules, strategies, procedures, meta-cognition, plans, or ideas. This "something else" is often referred to as attitude, mindfulness, volition, or motivation (see Chapters 3 and 4).

Of the aforementioned terms used to describe this "something else," attitude is probably understood best by most of us and has the advantage of wider applicability. Using a common dictionary definition (Soukhanov, 1984), *attitude* is defined as "a state of mind or feeling." I am of course referring to *student attitude*. Whether fostered at home or in the classroom (ideally both), an attitude of reasoning, critical thinking and problem solving is a critical foundation for classroom performance. Otherwise, even capable students will exhibit *anti-intellectual* classroom behavior because it might mark them as someone who does not fit in socially. On the other hand, in the college classroom I have seen *anti-intellectual* behavior taking the form of "Don't bother me with this higher-order thinking stuff. Tell me what I need to do to get out of this course and let me get my degree." Unfortunately, on occasion, I have heard this comment from prospective teachers.

It strikes me that, as teachers, we are all in the same situation—the classroom. Our classrooms reflect to a large extent our attitude toward the subject content we teach and *how* we expect students to use that knowledge (see Chapter 2) Consequently, classroom research is needed that looks at the causal relations among (1) teacher modeling of expertise as defined previously, (2) teacher expectations for students defined in terms of thinking and problem solving, and (3) demonstration by students of the higher-order thinking skills being taught. This research by its very nature would be developmental in design, requiring longitudinal studies to assess change within and between grades.

Thinking Demonstrated

Will students use higher order thinking skills. Maybe! As teachers we may have expectations as described above and still find it isn't enough. As teachers we must develop classroom assessment activities that will allow us to observe the application or *strategic transfer* (Chapter 2) of the higher-order thinking skills we have been teaching and consequently expect our students to demonstrate. This, of course, is one of the advantages of an assessment plan that includes performance assessment developed around authentic reasoning, critical thinking, and problem-solving tasks. Unfortunately, the following scenario is repeated time and time again in college classrooms. I think however, parallel situations occur at all classroom levels.

Most college professors would claim they are teaching a course that requires the use of highly developed abstract thinking and problem-solving skills for students to be successful. This comment, in fact, might be made by a psychology professor during the first class meeting. Students note this expectation on the part of the teacher and then structure their reading and study activities accordingly. Further, let us assume the students are self-directed learners with prior experience and practice in using higher-order thinking skills and are sophomores or juniors. However, these students have heard such expectations expressed in other classes. In some classes, higher-order thinking skills were assessed because professors developed classroom exams that required demonstrating such skills. In other classes, although the same expectations were voiced by professors, the assessment activities required only the recognition of facts, definitions from lectures, and material straight out of the text. Given this background of experience, what decisions are made concerning planning a study program for the first exam?

Actually many students use the first exam as feedback for future learning in the course. If the first assessment activity requires the use of higher-order thinking skills, the students will typically structure subsequent study for exams with this in mind. Consequently, the learning experience is geared toward the development of *both* declarative and procedural knowledge with an emphasis on being able to use such knowledge to solve academic problems. If the first exam requires *only* declarative knowledge about the lecture notes or the textbook, students will develop a study plan that involves learning only declarative knowledge. In this latter case, a professor may be teaching psychology from a critical thinking and problem-solving perspective and assuming that students are engaged in learning those critical thinking and problem-solving skills. In fact, those students who continue to attend class will see critical thinking and reasoning being demonstrated by the professor but will plan and organize their study strategies at the level of declarative knowledge. After all, that is what is going to be on the next exam. Consequently, these students will *know about* critical thinking and reasoning in psychology but will probably not *know how to use* these higher-order thinking skill with any proficiency.

This scenario was developed at the college level even though young children are the focus of this chapter. This was done intentionally for two reasons. First, the point to be make is that the problem exists at all levels of education in this country. Students are not dumb. If you want them to learn higher-order thinking skills, the demonstration of these skills must be required. This requirement must be part of the accountability system for both students and teachers whether we are talking first grade or doctoral programs. The second reason for using a college classroom scenario is to remind us that prospective teachers who cannot demonstrate critical thinking, reasoning, and problem-solving skills will have difficulty modeling these skills in their classroom when they enter the profession.

In summary, teachers must possess three aspects of *pedagogical* knowledge to help students acquire higher-order thinking skills. First and foremost is a combination of content knowledge and an understanding of how higher-order thinking skills are used in the content area, plus knowledge of the cognitive processing capabilities of the children being taught. The second is an ability to model the thinking skills within the content area being taught and the communication of learning expectations to students. The third aspect of pedagogical knowledge is the ability to develop an assessment system that provides evidence of the higher-order thinking skills being taught. Finally, while teachers are the most critical element for effectively teaching higher-order thinking skills, even expert teachers need resources. It is this topic to which we now turn.

Resources

The questions we have been addressing are not new. Further, the cognitive training program to be introduced later is not the only approach to teaching reasoning and problem solving skills. The teaching of higher-order thinking skills has a history in this nation's educational system as well as the educational systems in other countries. Three resources that I have found helpful for developing a better understanding of existing programs are *Thinking Skills Instruction: Concepts and Techniques* edited by Heiman and Slomianko (1987), *Teaching Thinking* edited by Coles and Robinson (1989), and *Really Raising Standards: Cognitive Intervention and Academic Achievement* by Adey and Shayer (1994).

The first volume (Heiman & Slomianko, 1987) is an anthology published by the National Education Association (NEA). The strength of this volume is the wide coverage of topics and approaches taken to the teaching of thinking skills. Many of the prominent theorist and directors of programs devoted to teaching thinking skills have contributed to this book. The second volume (Coles & Robinson, 1989) is a British publication and reflects what is happening in England at the current time. This volume is good reading because the individual chapter authors situate their discussion and examples within a classroom setting. Consequently, the particular approach to teaching thinking skills being discussed is embedded within a content area and grade level. This makes the examples provided quite meaningful and emphasizes the British perspective that the teaching of thinking skills should be situated within subject matter domains and grade level. The third volume (Adey & Shayer, 1994) is also a British publication. This monograph is written for the scholar or researcher and raises the question of whether or not it is feasible to design cognitive intervention programs to promote academic achievement. The strength of this work is its comprehensive review of different types of intervention programs, the emphasis on demonstrated success for various programs, and an in-depth discussion of strengths and weaknesses of various programs. Together, these three volumes provide an overview of perspectives taken in the United States and Great Britain concerning teaching higher-order thinking skills.

COGNITIVE INTERVENTION

Most of a teacher's day is spent providing students with domain-specific information. During the primary or elementary grades, the school day is typically structured around specific courses (e.g., language arts from 9:30 until 10:15; math from 10:15 until 11:00). Within each of these class periods, effective teachers teach not only declarative but procedural knowledge. As discussed in Chapter 2, teaching procedural knowledge would involve the teaching of strategies and procedures as well as facts, vocabulary, numbers, and so forth. This teaching of procedural knowledge involves not only helping students understand *what* is to be learned, but *how* to use the knowledge they have acquired. In many classrooms, strategy instruction and regular instruction go hand in hand (Brown, Bransford, Ferrara, & Campione, 1983).

However, as previously mentioned, teaching thinking skills does not automatically ensure that all students will learn these skills. When faced with this situation, one intervention technique involves changing the setting. Here, we use settings ranging from individualized instruction to working cooperatively in small groups. At this point, cognitive intervention can take different approaches. One approach is to alter the materials to be learned. This would involve teaching to a student's cognitive strengths and avoiding the student's weaknesses. An alternative is to first try to change the learner. This alternative involves teaching thinking strategies geared to specific assignments and teaching meta-cognitive strategies that can be used across specific assignments in a subject matter domain. Depending on the nature of the student's problem, one or more of these intervention approaches may be employed. Emphasis in teaching domain-specific strategies and meta-cognitive strategies can be noted in Chapters 6 through 13 of this book. The greater emphasis on domain-specific strategies is not meant to emphasize teaching of domain strategies to the exclusion of meta-cognitive strategies. Rather, the emphasis is on the fact that they are different kinds of strategies and have differing applications.

While the terms are frequently encountered in the educational psychology literature, considerable confusion remains concerning what is meant by *cognitive strategies* and *meta-cognitive strategies*. Looking to research in developmental psychology provides a basis for clarification. In this literature, *meta-cognition* has been used to refer to (1) knowledge about cognition and (2) the regulation of cognition. Research investigating children's knowledge about their own cognition reveals that it is a rather late developing ability. This meta-cognitive "awareness" relates to each person's personal naive theory about his or her own thinking, reasoning, and problem-solving skills.

The second cluster of research studies pertains to activities used to regulate and oversee learning. These strategies include the processes of *planning* learning activities (looking ahead), *monitoring* activities during learning, and *checking* learning outcomes. These meta-cognitive strategies are thought to be general in their utility and relatively age independent. In other words, these meta-cognitive strategies are used to oversee and regulate learning and can be taught in the primary or elementary grades. For readers who have taken a learning-to-learn course, you will immediately recognize these as study strategies we teach when helping students become self-regulated learners.

In summary, we have identified reasoning, critical thinking, and problem solving as higher-order thinking skills and provided a means for considering how they relate. This was followed with a discussion of teaching higher-order thinking skills and references to a number of programs that have been developed both in the United States and Great Britain. Based on evidence that higher-order thinking skills can be taught as well as learned, consideration was given to the means of delivering instruction. Here, intervention programs employing the teaching of cognitive and meta-cognitive strategies were viewed as a viable approach. What follows is an in-depth review of a cognitive intervention program that has been used successfully in Germany, the Netherlands, and the United States.

COGNITIVE TRAINING FOR CHILDREN: A DEVELOPMENTAL PROGRAM OF INDUCTIVE REASONING AND PROBLEM SOLVING

Inductive Reasoning

Formal reasoning is typically thought of as having two distinct forms. One is inductive reasoning; the other is deductive. Since inductive reasoning is the form of reasoning taught with the training program, attention will be devoted exclusive to this topic. Inductive reasoning, as presented here, draws heavily on the *dialectical method* introduced by the German philosopher G. W. F. Hegel and is considered to be independent of his general philosophical system (Harris, 1983). Hegel's dialectical method can be used to better organize and understand the world, both inside and outside the classroom. As we will see, this dialectical method can be viewed as both a teaching method and a meta-cognitive strategy employed by a self-regulated learner. Basically, the dialectical method involves both critical thinking and problem solving and consists of three phases: (1) thesis, (2) antithesis, and (3) synthesis. This method provides *one* approach for organizing and attacking academic problems in the classroom that require memory-based processing (see Chapter 2). Specifically, This method appears to facilitate problem identification, which was identified in Chapter 2 as the first stage in the problem-solving process. If this initial stage of problem solving is successful (problem identification) the problem solving sequence may be successfully completed.

Simply stated, inductive reasoning is a form of structured thinking (as contracted with "random" or "off the wall" thinking), which helps us organize what we are asked to learn in the classroom. Given a complex set of ideas, concepts, facts, objects, problems, and so on, we ask, "How are these things alike?" (*thesis*). Having arrived at some working plan as to how our "things" are alike, we now ask, "How are they different?" (*antithesis*). Having noted the differences as well as the similarities, the third phase involves combining an awareness of similarities and differences to produce a new and higher form of knowledge (*synthesis*). As a teaching method, one immediately recognizes similarity to inductive teaching strategies suggested for the development of concepts and concept learning. Reading between the lines, one can also note similarities with the upper end of Bloom's taxonomy of cognitive objectives. In terms of teaching meta-cognitive strategies in the classroom (Borkowski & Muthukrishna, 1992), similarities abound. In terms of learning, a student who has internalized this procedure would be developing expertise in learning to learn.

Cognitive Training Program

This highly practical training program helps children in the primary or elementary grades (ages 6 to 10) achieve greater competence in problem solving and inductive reasoning. A number of studies in both Germany (Klauer, 1995) and the United States (Phye, 1995; Phye & Sanders, 1993) have shown significant transfer of the inductive reasoning and problem-solving skill taught. In the United States, training has been conducted with individual students (Phye, 1995) and in small groups (Phye & Sanders, 1993). In these cases, children involved in the training exercises demonstrated strategic transfer within a problem-solving domain (see Chapter 2). Most of the work reported by Klauer (1995) was conducted with entire classrooms using group instructional techniques. Our work has included both regular classroom students and special needs students who have been identified as learning disabled or "inclusion" students.

The program is made up of 10 lessons, each consisting of 12 very carefully developed *problems*. The entire program is made up of 120 problems. These 120 problems fall into the following six categories: generalization, discrimination, cross classification, recognizing relationships, differentiating relationships, and system construction. Thus, 20 inductive reasoning problems are taught using each of these *six basic types of inductive reasoning*, for a total of 120 problems. In our work, we typically teach three lessons a week. Each lesson takes approximately 20–25 minutes. With three lessons per week being scheduled, it takes between three and four weeks to complete the program. The basic training approach is one of training for transfer. This involves helping the child learn how to strategically transfer these basic inductive reasoning procedures to other academic tasks. The materials, the content, and the teaching methods have been designed from a developmental perspective.

Initial lessons are designed for children as young as six years of age. Teaching young children to develop the meta-cognitive strategy of making analytical and systematic comparisons (dialectical method) lies at the heart of the training program.

Program Elements

An overview of the program format can be seen in Table 1. The format in Table 1 reflects the types of problems, the type of processing procedures, and the order in which these problems are taught. Note that only generalization problems and recognizing relationship problems are taught during the first two lessons. Also, note the systematic manner in which the problems are presented for study and practice. In lesson 1, the first six problems are generalization problems and the next six are recognizing relationships problems. Further, the first six problems consist of three picture problems with concrete objects (blocks) and the next three consist of picture problems involving common objects. The second set of six problems that are used for teaching children how to recognize relationships are made up of three picture problems with concrete objects and three picture problems involving common objects.

Lesson 2 also teaches generalization and recognizing relationships. Notice that lesson two starts with problems having the same processing requirements as the problems that were taught during the second half of lesson 1. Then, the last half of lesson 2 returns to the type of processing procedure that introduced lesson 1. This systematic ordering of problems is characteristic of all 10 lessons. Also, in lesson 2, in addition to continuing

TABLE 1
Format of Cognitive Training for Children Program

	Types of Problems						Order of Presentation					
Lesson	GE	DI	CC	RR	DR	SC	GE	DI	CC	RR	DR	SC
1	3C			3C			1,2,3			7,8,9		
	3P			3P			4,5,6			10,11,12		
2	2C			2C			19,20			13,14		
	2P			2P			21,22			15,16		
	2L			2L			23,24			17,18		
3	2L	3C		2L			25,26	27,28,29		35,36		
		3P						30,31,32				
		2L						33,34				
4	1L	2C		1L	2C		42	43,44		37	38,39	
		2P			2P			45,46			40,41	
		2L						47,48				
5	1L		2C	1L	3C		49		50,51	54	55,56,57	
			2P		3P				52,53		58,59,60	
6	1L	1L	3C		2L		63	64	65,66,67		61,62	
			3P						68,69,70			
			2L						71,72			
7			1L	1L	2L	4C			73	74	75,76	77,78
						3P						79,80
						1L						81,82
												83,84
8		2L	2L		2L	1C	93,94	95,96			91,92	85,86
						2P						87,88
						3L						89,90
9	1S	1S	2L	1S	1L	3L	97	98	99,100	102	103	105,106
			1S		1S	1S			101		104	107,108
10	2S	2S	2S	2S	2S	2S	109	111	113	115	117	119
							110	112	114	116	118	120

Basic types of processing: GE, generalization; RR, recognizing relationships; CC, cross classifications; DI, discrimination; DR, differentiating relationships; SC, system construction.
Types of problems: C, problems with concrete objects (blocks); P, paradigmatic pictoral problems; L, pictorial problems from daily life; S, problems with symbols.
Number of problems per basic processing type: Problems with concrete objects (here blocks) (C) 5; Paradigmatic pictorial problems (P) 3; Pictorial problems from everyday life (L) 7; Problems with symbols (S) 3; Sum of problems per basic processing type 20.

with picture problems made up of blocks or common objects, picture problems depicting situations from everyday life are introduced. As one moves on to the following lessons, an increasing number of picture problems depict everyday life situations. Also, picture problems made up of symbols are introduced in lessons 9 and 10. All 120 problems that make up the 10 lessons are picture problems. Standard questions are provided for introducing each problem. Not only is a solution strategy provided for each problem, the type of processing procedure being taught is always identified for the teacher. Examples will be provided later during the discussion of teaching basic processing procedures.

In lesson 3, discrimination is introduced as a processing procedure, and in lesson 4 differentiating relationships is introduced. Cross-classification problems are introduced for the first time in lesson 5. System construction problems are first introduced in lesson 7. As mentioned earlier, no lesson is made up entirely of one type of problem. In lesson 3, three types of processing are taught. In lessons 4 through 8, four types of processing procedures are taught during each lesson. In lessons 9 and 10, all six types of processing procedures are taught.

Basic Processing Procedures

We have found that the training program is only as effective as the teacher using the program. Our experience has been that teachers and trainers having a working knowledge of the six basic processing procedures can handle any questions that arise during the course of teaching. In addition to verbally describing the logic that defines each processing procedure, a problem example taken from the program is provided as a referent.

Generalization

Generalization (GE) is the process whereby we determine the common attribute that can be used to group a number of objects. All objects differ from one another but share at least one attribute in common. Identification of the common attribute provides the basis for forming a common group, class, category, or concept. An attribute is what defines an object. For example, a red basketball is round (shape), made of rubber (its substance), and red (color). In this case, shape, substance, and color are attributes of a single ball. For example, a black bowling ball, a red basketball, and a white baseball could be grouped together on the basis of a common attribute (round shape), if we ask the question, "How are they alike?" In response to the question, "How are they different?" we would note differences in substance, color, and size. These are all attributes that define objects we call *balls*. In the training program, picture problems that involve teaching the generalization process are similar to those shown in Figure 2.

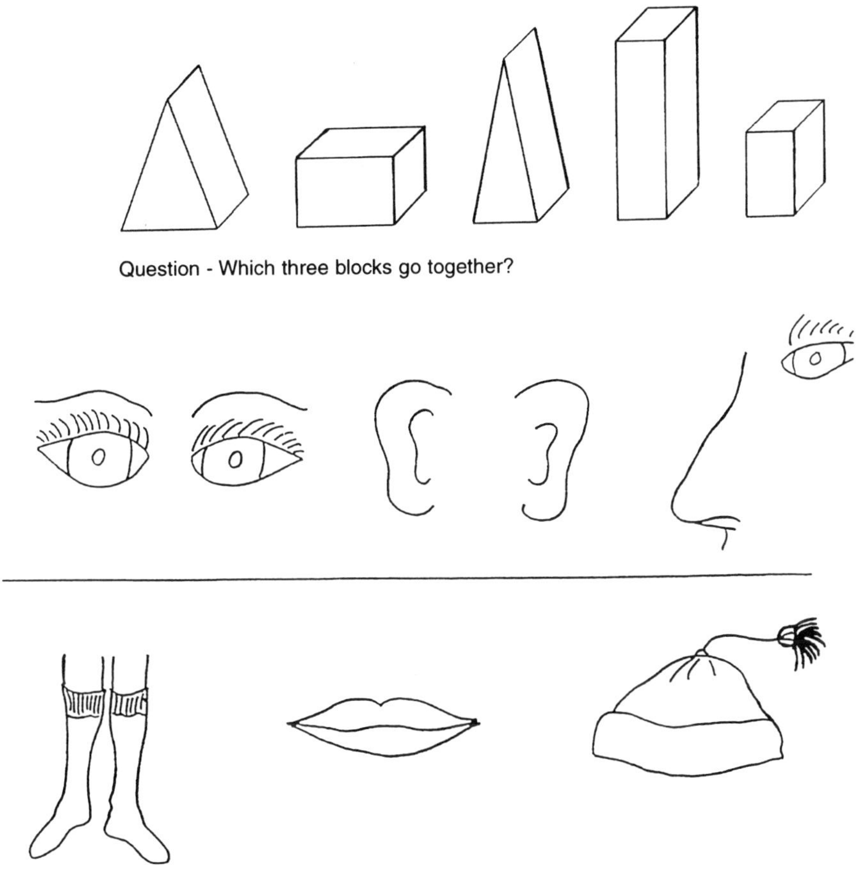

FIGURE 2
Teaching problems for the generalization procedure.

Discrimination

The second procedure that is taught in the program is discrimination (DI), the process of noting differences among objects with respect to attributes. In the training program, only one problem form is encountered, identification of the object that does not belong to the group. Whenever a picture problem of this type is encountered, the question is basically some form of, "Which one (or more) does not belong?" In the case of the problem shown in Figure 3, the number 2 does not fit because it is an even number. The other numbers are all odd numbers. It should be noted that with problems

9

3 2

5 7

FIGURE 3
Teaching problem for the discrimination procedure.

of this type, it is necessary to first look for a common attribute (generalization), then identify the single object that does not have the common attribute. The constraint "Which one does not belong?" was introduced by the question. Consequently, this reasoning procedure is one of first demonstrating how the objects are alike (they are single-digit real numbers) and how they are different (this one is an odd number).

Cross Classification

In the training program, cross-classification problems are also based on similarities and differences in attributes of objects. These problems are more complex, because they require the consideration of two attributes in combination rather than a single attribute. This procedure can be recognized as a Piagetian grouping activity, where two dimensions must be considered simultaneously. Two forms of cross-classification problems appear in the training program, these are shown in Figure 4. The question asked when teaching the problem shown in the top portion of Figure 4 is "In which box does the banana belong—or best fit?"

When teaching cross-classification problems, we also teach the child to recognize that this kind of problem requires a particular approach. First, we identify the two attributes that we are teaching. In this case the attributes are shape and class (fruit or not fruit). Starting with the apple in the upper left square we say "the apple is a fruit and it has a round shape." Then we ask, "how are the apple and pear alike and how are they different?" Answer, they are both fruit but the apple is round and the pear in long. The next comparison is the upper left square and the bottom left square. We ask "how are the apple and the ball alike" and "how are they different?" Answer, "they are both round but one is a fruit and the other is not." The next comparison is the upper right square (pear) and the lower right square (bat). How are they alike and how are they different? Answer, "they are both long, but one is

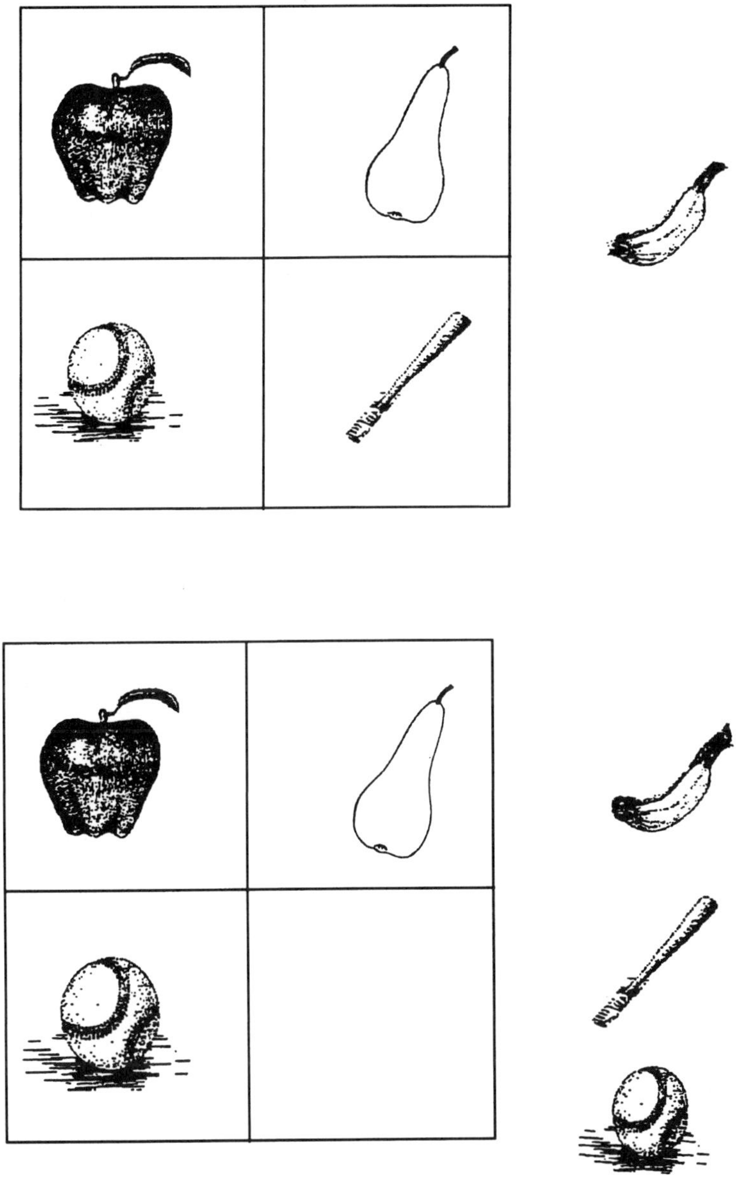

FIGURE 4
Teaching problems for the cross-classification procedure.

a fruit and the other is not." At this point, we return to the original question that framed the problem, "In which box would the banana belong?" Solution, "with the pear because it is a fruit but it is not round."

In terms of teaching, it is important for the teacher to first ask the question that accompanies every problem picture. Next, always start at the upper left quadrant and make the comparison with the upper right quadrant. Then the comparison sequence is from upper left to lower left followed by a comparison of the upper right with the lower right quadrant. When the problem takes the form shown in the bottom portion of Figure 4, the question is phrased, "which one of the objects over here (point to the right side of the plate) would best fit in the empty box?" In the training program, problems like those at the top of Figure 4 are encountered in earlier lessons than those shown at the bottom.

Recognizing Relationships

The same approach is used when teaching a procedure for recognizing relationships (RR) as was used when teaching the generalization procedure. The only difference is that instead of attributes defining the similarities and differences use for grouping and making comparisons, relationships define the problem. This is also the case when teaching the procedures of *differentiation of relationships* (DR) and *System Construction* (SC).

These three procedures involve teaching relationships that are more abstract and will probably require more assistance on the part of the trainer. For example, an attribute of an object can be determined by examining only that object in isolation (e.g., a red apple). Relationships requires at least two objects (or more) for a relationship to be determined. Further, attributes of an object do not change from one setting to the next (a red apple, is a red apple, is a red apple). However, I might have two red apples (one large and one medium size) and I ask a child, "Tell me, which one is larger?" Assuming the child responds appropriately, I might then take a small red apple out of a sack and ask the child to "Show me where this one would go." If the child places the small apple next to the medium apple, the child has demonstrates knowledge of a relationship. Teaching children to recognizing relationships is comparable to teaching generalization, differentiating relationships is comparable to teaching discrimination, and system construction is comparable to teaching cross classification. The primary difference is that attributes are used as the basis for teaching the first three procedures (GE, DI, and CC) and relationships the last three (RR, DR, and SC). Examples of picture problems that are used for teaching about relationships are shown in Figure 5.

A Constructivist Approach

In the training program a constructivist perspective can be identified in two ways. The influence of Piaget can be readily noted in terms of the nature of

A. Question - Continue the series above.

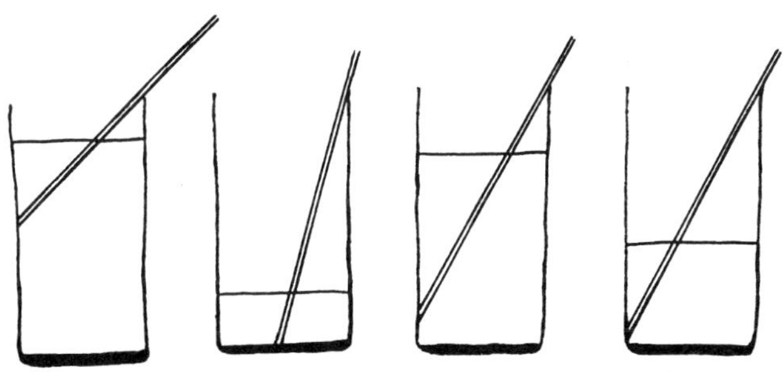

B. Question - How would you put the glasses in better order?

C. Question - Which one belongs in the empty box?

FIGURE 5

Teaching problems for the (a) recognizing relationships, (b) differentiating relationships, and (c) system construction procedures.

the tasks, and the influence of Vygotsky is apparent in the emphasis on guided discovery as a primary training method. "To Vygotsky, the training sessions are the most theoretically compelling periods of activity that take place during psychological research in that they represent the occasions during which learning occurs" (Smagorinsky, 1995, p. 199). In training sessions with an adult, the child learns how to use the mediational (reasoning) tools in what the teacher believes to be the most appropriate manner. The influence of this position, taken by Vygotsky, has influenced the way teaching and assessment is conducted when using the training program.

As mentioned in the examples of *how* an inductive reasoning procedure might be taught, each problem encountered involves some combination of teaching and assessment. If we can think of teaching as asking questions, checking responses, providing hints, prompts, even solutions, then teaching takes the form of guided discovery. As such, during the course of guiding the child through the problem-solving activity, numerous instances of checking occur to see what the child knows or can do. This checking is assessment. When effective teachers are training children in a complex activity, they do this all the time. Some assessment textbooks use the term *informal assessment* to describe such checking during teaching. Another term frequently applied to assessment that occurs during training is *dynamic assessment*. Dynamic assessment is viewed as a more formal, ongoing activity during training, because it provides a permanent record of progress. Both informal assessment and dynamic assessment reflect a view expressed by Vygotsky that data collection should occur during training not just on completion of training activities (Smagorinsky, 1995).

An example of dynamic assessment as employed with the cognitive training program (Phye, 1995) is provided in Figure 6. Figure 6 represents a layout of the 120 picture problems that make up the training program. The program contains 10 lessons, consisting of 12 problems to be taught during each lesson. As mentioned previously, we typically teach three lessons a week. While the forms in Figure 6 are used for formal assessment (permanent records), notice that only the problems (items) followed by an asterisk are formally assessed. The only difference between an assessment item and a nonassessment item is the following. In an assessment problem, the question initiating training is asked as usual, but teaching does not immediately commence. Rather, children are provided an opportunity to solve the problem on their own. Whether successful or unsuccessful, once it is apparent a child is finished, performance is recorded (yes/no). Then, the problem is taught as review for successful problem solvers or for learning by unsuccessful problem solvers. This procedure provides a child the opportunity to demonstrate the use of strategic transfer as a problem solving tool (see Chapter 2).

As can be seen in Figure 6, some of the assessment problems are designated on-task transfer problems and other are memory-based problems. This

Reporting Form

Name ______________________ Age ________

Lesson 1	Lesson 2	Lesson 3	Lesson 4	Lesson 5	Lesson 6	Lesson 7	Lesson 8	Lesson 9	Lesson 10
item 1	item 13	item 25* YN	item 37* YN	item 49* YN	item 61* YN	item 73	item 85* YN	item 97	item 109* YN
item 2	item 14	item 26* YN	item 38	item 50	item 62* YN	item 74	item 86* YN	item 98	item 110* YN
item 3	item 15	item 27	item 39	item 51	item 63	item 75* YN	item 87	item 99* YN	item 111* YN
item 4	item 16	item 28	item 40* YN	item 52* YN	item 64	item 76* YN	item 88	item 100* YN	item 112* YN
item 5	item 17* YN	item 29	item 41* YN	item 53* YN	item 65	item 77	item 89* YN	item 101	item 113* YN
item 6	item 18* YN	item 30	item 42* YN	item 54* YN	item 66	item 78	item 90* YN	item 102	item 114* YN
item 7	item 19	item 31	item 43* YN	item 55	item 67	item 79	item 91	item 103	item 115* YN
item 8	item 20	item 32	item 44* YN	item 56	item 68	item 80	item 92	item 104	item 116* YN
item 9	item 21	item 33* YN	item 45	item 57	item 69	item 81	item 93	item 105	item 117* YN
item 10	item 22	item 34* YN	item 46	item 58	item 70	item 82	item 94	item 106	item 118* YN
item 11	item 23* YN	item 35* YN	item 47	item 59* YN	item 71* YN	item 83* YN	item 95* YN	item 107* YN	item 119* YN
item 12	item 24* YN	item 36* YN	item 48	item 60* YN	item 72* YN	item 84* YN	item 96	item 108* YN	item 120* YN

Task transfer problems: 23, 24, 17, 18, 33, 34, 40, 41, 52, 53, 59, 60, 71, 72, 83, 84, 89, 90, 107, 108.
Memory-based transfer problems: 25, 26, 35, 36, 37, 42, 43, 44, 49, 54, 61, 62, 75, 76, 85, 86, 99, 100.
Lesson 10 is exclusively a memory-based transfer activity.
*Assessed items

Date of Lesson 1 ______________________

Date of Lesson 2 ______________________

Date of Lesson 3 ______________________

Date of Lesson 4 ______________________

Date of Lesson 5 ______________________

Date of Lesson 6 ______________________

Date of Lesson 7 ______________________

Date of Lesson 8 ______________________

Date of Lesson 9 ______________________

Date of Lesson 10 ______________________

FIGURE 6

Assessment format of cognitive training for children program.

designation is determined by the location of problems within a lesson. On-task problems occur in the middle or at the end of a lesson, following training with problems having the same procedure. Success in this case indicates strategic transfer during a learning episode (lesson) and is an indication of understanding "at the moment." Memory-based problems occur at the very beginning of a lesson and are the same procedure type (e.g., DI) as the problems being taught at the end of the previous lesson. In other words, to be successful children have to construct a solution using information stored in long-term memory. Strategic transfer is still being used as a tool for problem solving, but the child now demonstrates the ability to retrieve prior knowledge. Memory-based problems provide evidence of permanency or durability of learning during training.

Lesson 10 is the only lesson where all the problems are used for formal assessment. Interestingly, the 12 problems making up this lesson represent two examples of each of the six procedures being taught (GE, DI, CC, RR, DR, SC). Lesson 10 can be viewed as a comprehensive review that requires a demonstration of memory-based strategic transfer. Only in lesson 10 do we first go through all 12 problems and record performance before we go back and teach problems on which the child was unsuccessful.

CONCLUSION

Even if a you use a training program like the one described here, connections must continually be made with the regular curriculum being taught. In my own classroom, I find myself continually making reference back to previously taught examples, concepts, or procedures. With reference to the new material being learned and prior knowledge, I find myself using the dialectical method quite often. "How are they alike?" (compare). How are they different?" (contrast). "How can we synthesize (or integrate) what we *now* know to construct a new idea?"

Early in the chapter, I make the point that inductive reasoning and problem solving are attitudes as well as cognition skills. I believe that a dialectical teaching style promotes an attitude of inquiry, evaluation, and flexibility in thinking. When organizing what we know about a topic in terms of similarities and differences, we are looking backward in time to what we have previously learned. This is followed by looking forward in terms of developing a new idea or perspective based on the process of synthesis. I would suggest that such a teaching style provides the basis for the internalization of the method as a meta-cognitive strategy. As a consequence, some (not all) of our students may well develop into self-regulated academic learners.

References

Adey, P., & Shayer, M. (1994). *Really raising standards: Cognitive intervention and academic achievement.* London: Routledge.

Borkowski, J. G., & Muthukrishna, N. (1992). Moving meta-cognition into the classroom: "Working models" and effective strategy teaching. In M. Pressley, K. R. Harris, & J. T. Guthrie (Eds.), *Promoting academic literacy: Cognitive research and instructional innovation* (pp. 477–501). San Diego, CA: Academic Press.

Brown, A. L., Bransford, J. D., Ferrara, R. A., & Campione, J. C. (1983). Learning, remembering, and understanding. In P. H. Mussen (Ed.), *Handbook of child psychology* (Vol. 3, pp. 77–166), New York: Wiley.

Coles, M. J., & Robinson, W. D. (1989). *Teaching thinking: A survey of programmes in education*. Worcester, England: Bristol Press.

Galotti, K. M. (1989). Approaches to studying formal and everyday reasoning. *Psychological Bulletin*, 105, 331–351.

Hanson, J. (1989). The Oxfordshire skills programme. In M. J. Coles & W. D. Robinson (Eds.), *Teaching thinking: A survey of programmes in education* (pp. 81–89). Worcester, England: Bristol Press.

Harris, E. E. (1983). *An interpretation of the logic of Hegel*. Lanham, MD.: University Press of America.

Heiman, M., & Slomianko, J. (Eds.). (1987). *Thinking skills instruction: Concepts and techniques*. Washington, DC: NEA Professional Library.

Klauer, K. J. (1995, July). *Does a training program of inductive reasoning influence fluid intelligence and learning in children?* Paper presented at the Fifth Conference of the International Association of Cognitive Education, Lake Mohonk, NY.

Klauer, K. J., & Phye, G. D. (1994). *Cognitive training for children: A developmental program of inductive reasoning and problem solving*. Seattle, WA: Hogrefe & Huber.

Klauer, K. J., Resing, W. C. M., & Slenders, A. P. A. C. (1996). *Cognitive training voor kinderen: Ontwikkeling van het inductief redeneren bij kindereren*. Gottingen, Germany: Hogrefe Verlag fur Psychologie.

Phye, G. D. (1995, July). *Assessing inductive reasoning in the classroom*. Paper presented at the Fifth Conference of the International Association of Cognitive Education, Lake Mohonk, NY.

Phye, G. D., & Sanders, C. E. (1993, August). *Strategic transfer of inductive reasoning and problem solving strategies by young children*. Paper presented at the Fifth European Conference of the European Association for Research on Learning and Instruction, Aix en Provence, France.

Smagorinsky, P. (1995). The social construction of data: Methodological problems of investigating learning in the zone of proximal development. *Review of Educational Research*, 65, 191–212.

Soukhanov, A. H. (Ed.). (1984). *Webster's II: New riverside university dictionary*. Boston: Houghton Mifflin.

Sternberg, R. J., & Horvath, J. A. (1995, August-September). A prototype view of expert teaching. *Educational Researcher*, 24, 9–17.

CHAPTER

15

Incorporating Problem Solving into Secondary School Curricula

RICHARD E. MAYER
University of California, Santa Barbara

As educators, we expect secondary school students to be able to solve problems. In particular, we expect them to be able to engage in higher-order thinking in academic settings, ranging from writing a term paper about a historical issue to designing an experiment for a science fair. Yet, in spite of our expectations about students' problem solving, we sometimes fail to provide adequate opportunities for students to become problem solvers. All too often, problem solving becomes part of the hidden curriculum in high school and junior high school—a topic that we expect students to learn but often fail to teach (Mayer & Wittrock, 1996; Weinstein & Mayer, 1986). This chapter is based on the idea that it is time to take problem solving out of the hidden curriculum and place it as a highly visible part of every school subject.

How can we help students to develop into creative problem solvers? What do students need to know so that they will be able to create novel solutions to the problems they encounter? Why are some students able to take what they have learned and use it productively in a new situation? These are the kinds of questions that motivate this chapter on problem solving.

Increasingly, educational leaders have recognized the value of problem solving in education. Throughout the world, a call has gone out for a wider inclusion of problem solving in school curricula. Yet, while there may be a growing consensus for the inclusion of problem solving in schools, efforts at implementation have been hampered by a lack of understanding of the nature of human problem solving. To teach problem solving, teachers need to understand what problem solving is, how it should taught, where best to

Handbook of Academic Learning

TABLE I
Retention and Transfer Questions about a Passage on Lightning

Portion of Lesson on The Process of Lightning

Warm moist air near the earth's surface rises rapidly. As the air in this updraft cools, water vapor condenses into water droplets and forms a cloud. The cloud's top extends above the freezing level. At this altitude, the air temperature is well below freezing, so the upper portion of the cloud is composed on tiny ice crystals. Eventually, the water droplets and ice crystals become too large to be suspended by updrafts. As raindrops and ice crystals fall through the cloud, they drag some of the air in the cloud downward, producing down drafts. . . . Within the cloud, the moving air causes electrical charges to build. . . . The negatively charged particles fall to the bottom of the cloud, and most of the positively charged particles rise to the top. . . . A stepped leader moves downward in a series of steps. . . . As the stepped leader nears the ground, positively charged upward-moving leaders travel up from such objects as trees and buildings to meet the negative charges. . . . The two leaders generally meet about 165 feet from the ground. Negatively charged particles then rush from the cloud to the ground. . . . As the leader stroke nears the ground, it induces an opposite charge, so positively charged particles from the ground rush upward along the same path. . . . A return stroke produces the bright flash that people notice in a flash of lightning, but the current travels so quickly that its upward motion cannot be perceived . . .

Retention Test

Write a description of the process of lightning.

Transfer Test

What could you do to decrease the intensity of a lightning storm?
Suppose you see clouds in the sky, but no lightning. Why not?
What does air temperature have to do with lightning?
What causes lightning?

teach it, and when to begin instruction. After a brief introduction and historical overview, this chapter seeks to clarify these four issues concerning the teaching of problem-solving skill.

INTRODUCTION TO PROBLEM SOLVING

Before addressing these four target issues, it is useful to make some basic distinctions concerning retention versus transfer, rote versus meaningful learning, creative versus routine problem solving, and representation versus solution processes.

Retention and Transfer

Learning outcomes can be evaluated using two types of tests, retention and transfer. Retention tests measure the degree to which a student remembers the material that was presented. For example, a student may read a lesson about lightning, such as partially presented in the top of Table 1 (Mayer, Bové, Bryman, Mars, & Tapangco, 1996). A retention question would ask about material that is directly contained in the lesson, such as shown in the middle of Table 1. This is a retention question because the answer to it is contained in the lesson.

In contrast, transfer tests measure the degree to which a student can apply what was presented to a new situation. For example, a student who has read the lightning lesson could be asked to solve problems such as shown in the bottom of Table 1. Although the answers are not contained in the lesson, it is possible to use the presented information to make needed inferences. Thus, in correctly answering transfer questions, the student creates a solution to a problem based on the presented material.

Learning is often assessed through tests of retention. Yet, the ultimate goal of many instructional activities is the promotion of transfer. Increasingly, educators have come to recognize that evaluations of student learning should include both retention and transfer. This chapter focuses on transfer.

Rote and Meaningful Learning

Some students may perform well on retention but poorly on transfer. This pattern reflects rote learning—students have acquired the prescribed knowledge but are unable to use it.

In contrast, some students may perform well both on retention and transfer. This pattern reflects meaningful learning—students can take what they learned and apply it to a new situation that was not directly addressed during instruction.

When the goal of instruction is mastery of a specific behavior, then rote learning is sufficient. However, when the goal of instruction includes problem-solving transfer, then meaningful learning is called for. The instructional methods used to promote rote and meaningful learning differ, so it is important for teachers to choose methods that best suit their goals. Both rote and meaningful learning have a place in education, although the focus of this chapter is on meaningful learning.

Creative and Routine Problem Solving

It is useful to distinguish between creative and routine problem solving (Mayer, 1992b). In creative problem solving, the problem solver is confronted with a novel problem and must construct a solution plan that is new for him or her. Wertheimer (1959) refers to this as *productive thinking* because the problem solver must produce something new. For example, for most adults, writing a chapter on problem solving requires creative problem solving.

In general, most scholars use the term *problem solving* to refer to creative problem solving. Accordingly, problem solving is required when a person has a goal but does not know how to accomplish it. For example, in his classic monograph, *On Problem Solving*, Karl Duncker (1945) provided concise definitions of problem and problem solving:

> A problem arises when a living creature has a goal but does not know how this goal is to be reached. Whenever one cannot go from the given situation to the desired situation simply by action, then there has to be recourse to thinking. Such thinking has the task of devising some action which may mediate between the existing and the desired situations. (p. 1)

This definition is broad enough to cover the range of academic problem solving tasks that require creative solutions.

In contrast, routine problem solving occurs when a problem solver already knows a method for solving a given problem. Wertheimer (1959) refers to this as *reproductive thinking* because the problem solver simply reproduces a solution procedure that is already in his or her memory. For example, for most adults, solving a long division problem such as 568/14 requires routine problem solving.

According to classic definitions of *problem solving*, routine problem solving would not be considered to be problem solving at all. In this chapter, the focus is on creative problem solving.

Representation and Solution Phases in Problem Solving

The process of problem solving can be analyzed into two major phases, problem representation and problem solution (Mayer, 1992b). During the representation phase, the problem solver constructs a mental representation of the problem. For example, in solving an algebra word problem, representation includes translating each proposition of the problem into network of propositions and integrating this information into a coherent model of the situation being described in the problem. During the solution phase, the problem solver devises and carries out a plan for solving the problem. For example, in solving an algebra word problem, the solution would include planning which arithmetic operations to carry out and then executing the plan by actually making the computations.

Although training in problem solving often emphasizes the problem solution phase (particularly, executing a solution plan), many problem solvers have difficulty with the problem representation phase (particularly, integrating the presented information into a coherent mental representation of the situation). For this reason, this chapter focuses on the problem representation phase of problem solving.

HISTORICAL OVERVIEW: THREE THEORIES OF PROBLEM SOLVING

The increasing focus on problem solving as a legitimate goal of education is a natural consequence of changing theories of learning and teaching. Following previous historical analyses, I identify three metaphors in the psychology of thinking: thinking as response strengthening, thinking as information processing, and thinking as knowledge construction (Mayer, 1992b, in press).

Thinking as Response Strengthening

During the first half of the 20th century, the dominant metaphor of thinking was response strengthening. According to this view, problem solving involves strengthening and weakening responses or, more precisely, strengthening and weakening associations between problem situations and solution responses.

Based largely on research on animals in laboratory settings, the response strengthening view is epitomized in Thorndike's (1911/1965) classic research on how cats learned to escape from puzzle boxes. For example, Thorndike placed a hungry cat in a puzzle box with food outside but in sight. The cat could escape by pulling a loop of string that opened a trap door. On the first session, the cat engaged in many irrelevant behaviors, such as meowing and clawing at the wooden slates, before accidentally sweeping its paw into the loop of string. On each successive session, the cat engaged in fewer irrelevant responses and more rapidly pulled the loop of string that opened the door. According to Thorndike, each time the cat engaged in a behavior that led to displeasure, such as putting its paws through the slates and then not getting out of the box, it was less likely to engage in that response in the future. Similarly, each time the cat engaged in a behavior that led to pleasure, such as pulling the loop of string and getting out of the box, it was more likely to engage in that response in the future. Thorndike called this principle the *law of effect*, although today it is better known by its revised name of *reinforcement theory*.

If problem solving involves response strengthening, teaching involves dispensing rewards and punishments. The teacher becomes a dispenser of rewards and punishments. The student becomes a passive recipient of rewards and punishments such that when rewarded a response is automatically strengthened and when punished a response is automatically weakened. Thus, according to the response strengthening view, teaching problem solving involves creating situations in which the student must give an answer and then providing rewards for a correct answer or punishment for an incorrect answer. The most typical method for teaching of problem solving is drill and practice on a large set of exercises, such as the computational exercises often found in mathematics textbooks. For example, in a recent analysis of mathematics textbooks used in the United States, Mayer, Sims and Tajika (1995) found that almost half of the space is devoted to short, unsolved exercise problems.

A major shortcoming of the response strengthening view was its neglect of problem-solving transfer. The response strengthening view was ill-equipped to handle the question of how students solve a novel problem that they have never seen before. By the 1950s, a competing view was poised to replace response strengthening as psychology's dominant metaphor of thinking.

Thinking as Information Processing

Born in 1956 and developed in the 1960s and 1970s, the information processing metaphor views humans as processors of information. Like electronic computers, humans take in information as input in the form of symbols, apply mental processes that transform the information, and thereby create new output.

Based largely on research on humans in artificial laboratory settings, the information processing metaphor is epitomized by Newell and Simon's (1972) analysis of human problem solving on tasks such as solving the Tower of Hanoi problem. In this problem, a person is presented with three pegs. Several disks arranged from largest to smallest are on the first peg, and the problem solver's job is to move them to the same arrangement on the third peg. The problem solver may move one disk at a time and can never place a larger disk on top of a smaller disk. Newell and Simon asked people to think out loud as they solved the problem, and based on these protocols devised a computer program that simulated human problem solving. The program sought information, applied operators to the information, and then used the result as new information. The program is described more fully in Mayer (1992b).

If thinking involves processing information, then teaching problem solving involves helping students learn procedures for how to process information. For example, an important information processing strategy is to break a problem into smaller parts and then try to solve each part. The teacher becomes a dispenser of information about how to solve problems, and the students become recipients of information. It follows that the preferred method of teaching is to provide direct instruction in the processes for solving problems.

A major shortcoming of some versions of the information processing view was a rigid focus on information as a set of discrete symbols and processing as a set of discrete operators applied to symbols. Although applying procedures to a mental representation is an important part of problem solving, the information processing approach neglected another important aspect of problem solving; namely, how people come to construct a mental representation of the problem in the first place. The information processing approach did not adequately address the problem of how people understand and represent problems. By the 1980s, the need for a revision of the information processing metaphor was apparent.

Thinking as Knowledge Construction

During the 1980s and 1990s, thinking as knowledge construction gained ascendancy as psychology's third metaphor. Although the roots of a constructivist vision of cognition can be traced back to Piaget (1930) and Bartlett (1932), the knowledge construction view has come to dominate the field only within the past decade. The underlying premise of cognitive constructivism is that humans actively build their own knowledge. Rather than being a commodity that can be transferred from one person to another, new knowledge is constructed within the context of one's existing knowledge. Rather than being an algorithm applied to symbols, cognitive processing involves active construction including selecting, organizing, and integrating knowledge. According to this view, humans are sense makers who try to find meaning in what is presented to them.

The Gestalt psychologist Max Wertheimer (1959) provides an excellent example of the distinction between thinking by applying procedures and thinking by understanding. In teaching students how to compute the area of a parallelogram, a teacher may show students how to measure the height of a perpendicular line inside the parallelogram, how to measure the length of a base of the parallelogram, and how to multiply height times base to get the area. This method seems based on the information processing view, and according to Wertheimer does not lead to successful transfer on new area problems. An alternative method is to allow students to cut off a triangle from one side of a parallelogram and attach it to the other side, thus turning a parallelogram into a rectangle. Once students have achieved what Wertheimer calls *structural insight* into the relation between a parallelogram and a rectangle, they understand how to find the area of a parallelogram. This method is based on understanding and results in successful transfer to novel area problems.

In contrast to research on humans in artificial laboratory settings, the constructivist view follows from research on human problem solving in more realistic settings such as on academic tasks. According to the constructivist view, the learner is a knowledge constructor and the teacher is a cognitive guide who helps students work on authentic academic tasks. Teaching problem solving based on a constructivist metaphor involves discussion, modeling, and guided participation in representing and planning solutions for academic tasks.

FOUR RECOMMENDATIONS BASED ON A COMMONSENSE APPROACH TO PROBLEM SOLVING

Here are some basic principles about teaching problem solving:

1. The ability to solve problems is a general skill so that, when it is improved, problem solving performance will improve in domains ranging from writing essays to solving arithmetic word problems. For example, one can improve one's mind in general, through learning the mental discipline involved in certain subjects such as logic, geometry, or computer programming.
2. Like the training of any basic skill, the best way to learn how to solve problems is through regular mental exercises. In these exercises, one should give answers to problems and receive feedback on whether or not those answers were correct. In short, one can improve your problem-solving ability by practicing on giving the right answers to exercise problems.
3. Like any other important academic subject, problem-solving courses should be required for all students. The skills one learns in a problem-solving course will be useful in other courses taken.
4. Students cannot learn about higher-order thinking skills until they have mastered low-level basic skills. For example, students cannot learn how to design compositions until they know how to spell and punctuate, and they cannot learn how to solve arithmetic word problems until they have memorized their arithmetic facts.

These kinds of statements sound reasonable to many people and could be used as the basis for a program of instruction in problem solving. In short, they are examples of a commonsense approach to teaching problem solving. The problem with this approach, however, is that it can lead to unproductive conclusions. For example, each of these commonsense principles is contradicted by the growing research base in the field of problem solving. The statements help to highlight four fundamental issues concerning the teaching of problem solving: what to teach, how to teach, where to teach, and when to teach (Mayer, 1992a).

In summary, any program for teaching of problem solving is based on assumptions concerning the what, how, where, and when to teach. These issues should be addressed by anyone wishing to foster problem solving in students. In the following sections, I summarize each issue, provide examples, and describe representative research evidence.

What Is Problem-Solving Skill?

Issue

Should problem solving be taught as a single monolithic ability or as a collection of smaller component skills?

Example

The first commonsense recommendation concerns the "what" of problem solving. It seems to be based on the assumption that problem solving skill is a single monolithic ability. According to the single ability view, students need to exercise their mind in ways that will produce overall improvement in problem-solving ability. An implication of the "single ability" view is that the mind is some sort of mental muscle that can be exercised by studying certain school subjects. It follows that, when the mind is improved, performance on a wide variety of school tasks will improve.

At the turn of the century, this view—then known as the *doctrine of formal discipline*—was the dominant view among educational scholars. Subjects such as logic, geometry, and Latin were thought to produce proper habits of mind because they encouraged mental discipline and an orderly way of thinking. For example, the first Latin school in the United States was established in 1635 in Boston and Latin schools increased in number through the 19th century. Rippa (1980, p. 42) notes that "the main purpose was to teach boys to read, write, and speak Latin and to instruct them in the elements of Greek." For nine hours a day, for six days a week, for seven years, students memorized Latin and related subjects, all as a means of fostering "proper habits of mind" (Rippa, 1980, p. 42). In contrast, more recent advances in cognitive science suggest that mental ability can be viewed as a collection of component skills (Sternberg, 1990). A person's performance on any cognitive task depends on the degree to which he or she has mastered the component skills required for the task. Any academic task, ranging from essay writing to story problem solving, can be analyzed into component cognitive processes. For example, in a cognitive analysis of writing, Flower and Hayes (1980) identified three major cognitive processes in writing: planning, translating, and revising. According to the component process view of problem-solving instruction, success in becoming a writer involves developing each of these component skills, along with techniques for coordinating them.

Research

The doctrine of formal discipline and the Latin school movement it justified were rigorously tested in the early 1900s by a group of educational psychologists. For example, in a series of compelling studies, students who had mastered Latin fared no better in learning a new subject such as bookkeeping or shopwork than students who had not mastered Latin (Thorndike, 1924; Thorndike & Woodworth, 1901). More recently, similar claims about the mind-strengthening effects of learning computer programming languages such as Logo have been subjected to research tests. Paralleling the Latin results, students who had learned to program in Logo failed to show large improvements in problem solving skills not related to Logo (Mayer, 1988). In summary, the doctrine of formal disciple was rejected when the overwhelming preponderance of research showed that learning subjects like Latin (and, later, subjects like computer programming) did not transfer to learning of different subjects.

In contrast to the "single ability" view, current research in cognitive science suggests that problem-solving skill depends on a collection of smaller component skills and strategies for coordinating them.

How Should Problem-Solving Skill Be Taught?

Issue

Should problem-solving instruction emphasize the product of problem solving or the process of problem solving?

Example

The second commonsense recommendation addresses the issue of how to teach problem solving. In particular, the recommendation calls for an emphasis on producing the correct answer; that is, on the product of problem solving. It seems to be based on the response strengthening view of cognition, in which learning is based on rewarding correct answers and punishing incorrect answers.

For example, the product-based approach can be applied to the teaching students how to solve two-column problems such as $56 - 28 =$ ____. Students need to learn the procedure of borrowing from the upper digit in the tens column if the upper digit is less than the lower digit in the units column, subtracting the lower digit from the upper digit in the units column, writing the answer in the in the units column of the answer line, subtracting the lower digit from the upper digit in the tens column, and writing the answer in the tens column of the answer line. The student learns by applying this procedure to a large set of two-column subtraction problems and receiving feedback on each.

Although this drill-and-practice method is effective in improving the problem-solving performance of students, one might wonder what the students have learned. For example, Brownell & Moser (1949) have argued that emphasis on the product of problem solving results in rote learning that does not transfer easily to new problems. In contrast, Brownell and Moser proposed teaching students to understand the process of subtraction, by using concrete manipulatives. Each step in the subtraction process was modeled using bundles of sticks. For the problem $56 - 28 =$ ____, the student was given five bundles of 10 sticks and six single sticks. To take away 28, one of the bundles was opened, creating 16 single sticks, and eight of these were removed, yielding 8 single sticks. Of the remaining four bundles, two were removed, yielding two bundles, for a final answer of 28.

According to Brownell and Moser, students who learned by understanding the process of problem solving were better able to transfer what they had learned to solving three-column subtraction problems than were students who learned by rotely generating the product of problem solving. In short, Brownell and Moser sought to make arithmetic meaningful by changing the emphasis from product to process.

Research

In a classic study, Bloom and Broder (1950) demonstrated that a focus on the process of problem solving could lead to improvement in college students' problem-solving performance on academic tasks. The participants in the study were University of Chicago students who had difficulty in answering the questions on comprehensive examinations. The students were just as prepared and just as capable as the students who passed the exam, but they were unable to successfully solve the examination problems. For example, on the economics examination students were asked to determine whether policies such as reducing taxes, lowering the reserve that banks are required to hold against deposits, and encouraging the federal reserve banks to buy securities in the open market would control a possible extreme inflationary boom.

The training involved 10 to 12 sessions in which a remedial student (someone who could not pass the examination) and a model student (someone who could pass the examination) took turns in describing how they would solve a target problem. For example, first the model student would think aloud while solving a problem, describing each step in the thinking process. Then, the remedial student would do the same thing, and afterward compare the way that the students went about solving the problem. This procedure focuses on the process of problem solving by having students describe and compare their thinking processes. Students who participated in the training showed much greater improvement in their examination problem-solving performance than a group of matched control students who did not receive the training.

Bloom and Broder's study is important because it demonstrates the value of a focus on the process of problem solving. However, it is important to note that the students in the study already had an excellent background in their subject areas; that is, they had studied economics over the course of several years. According to Bloom and Broder, 10 hours of training in how to solve problems would not have been very useful for students who lacked this domain knowledge of economics.

Where Should Problem-Solving Skill Be Taught?

Issue

Should problem solving be taught in a general stand-alone course or be integrated within existing specific subjects?

Example

The third commonsense recommendation concerns the "where" of problem solving. It betrays an underlining assumption that problem solving is best learned as an isolated subject, separated from the context in which students are expected to work. For example, if we want students to improve in the skill of planning how to solve problems, we can teach them general procedures such as how to break a problem into parts. It does not matter what material we use for examples as long as the general principles of how to plan are well learned.

In contrast, current research in cognitive science suggests that problem solving is best learned within specific subjects such as mathematical problem solving, scientific problem solving, historical problem solving, creative writing, and so on. Rather than teaching problem solving as a decontextualized subject in its own right, this research suggests that problem solving should be embedded within a meaningful context for students. For example, teaching students how to plan an essay is quite different from teaching students how to plan a solution to a word problem.

Research

Recent ethnographic research has pointed to the domain specificity of problem solving; that is, problem solving skills learned within one context are rarely used in other contexts. Several researchers have shown that mathematical problem-solving strategies learned in a school setting are rarely used in out-of-school settings. For example, Lave (1988) asked people to determine the best buy for products such as a 10-ounce can of peanuts for 90 cents or a 4-ounce can of peanuts for 45 cents. The school-taught procedure is to compute the unit price for each can by dividing 10 into 90 (yielding 9 cents per ounce) and 4 into 45 (yielding 11.25 cents per ounce), and then selecting the can with the lowest unit price (i.e., the larger can). However, in a supermarket setting the unit-price procedure almost never is used; instead, many shoppers use a ratio procedure in which they reason that the larger can costs twice as much as the smaller can but contains more than twice as many ounces, so it is a better buy.

In a complementary study, Nunes, Schliemann, and Carraher (1993) found that street vendors could accurately carry out complex arithmetic computations in the context of their work but made many errors in solving identical problems posed in school. For example, to determine the cost of 10 coconuts at 35 cents each, a 12-year-old street vendor used a procedure of repeated addition, saying: "Three will be 105; with three more that will be 210. I need four more. That is . . . 315 . . . I think it is 350." However, given an arithmetic problem in a more formal school setting, the same child solved $35 \times 4 =$ ____ by writing 200 and saying "4 times 5 is 20, carry the 2; 2 plus

3 is 5, times 4 is 20." This research points to the failure of people to transfer a problem-solving procedure from one context to another, even though the same general procedure would work in both contexts.

A more classic demonstration of domain specificity of problem-solving skills comes from evaluations of a popular thinking skills program developed for elementary school children in the 1960s, the Productive Thinking Program (Covington, Crutchfield, & Davies, 1966; Covington, Crutchfield, Davies, & Olton, 1974). The Productive Thinking Program consisted of 15 cartoonlike booklets, each involving a mystery or detective story in which two children, Jim and Lila, sought to solve the case. The characters modeled basic thinking skills such as generating and testing hypotheses, and the booklet provided opportunities for the reader to do the same.

On the surface, the Productive Thinking Program appears to teach general problem solving skills, such as how to generate and test hypotheses. Indeed, when students were tested, the results showed that students who took the course outperformed control students on solving mystery and detective problems like those in booklet. However, when they were given dissimilar kinds of problem-solving tasks, the superiority of the trained group disappeared or was greatly reduced. As long as the context of the test problems was similar to the context of the training problems, students showed an improvement in problem-solving performance, but when the context of the test problems was dissimilar from the context of the training problems, the effect was much more difficult to find (Mayer, 1992b). These results point to the domain specificity of learning problem-solving skills. If problem-solving skills are often learned within the context they are taught, it follows that skills should be taught within specific subject matter domains rather than in general courses.

When Should Problem Solving Be Taught?

Issue

Should problem solving be taught mainly to older, experienced students who have mastered the basic skills in a subject area or should problem solving be taught to younger, inexperienced students who are novices in a subject area?

Example

The fourth commonsense recommendation is that students should learn about higher-order thinking skills only after they have mastered the prerequisite lower-level skills. This idea can be called *prior automatization* (Mayer, 1987a) because basic skills must become automatized before they are used in the context of higher-level tasks. An automatized skill requires no conscious attention or mental effort when it is applied, so students can use all their mental effort on the higher-order problem solving activity. For example, before a student can learn to solve arithmetic word problems (such as, "Tom has three marbles. Sue has two more marbles than Tom. How many marbles does Sue have?"), he or she must have memorized number facts (such as, $3 + 2 = 5$). Similarly, before a student can learn how to compose an essay (such as, on whether students should be allowed to select which subjects they study in elementary school), he or she must master correct spelling, punctuation, grammar, and handwriting.

A major criticism of the prior automatization view of when to teach problem-solving skills is that beginners in any subject domain must be condemned to years of drill and memorization of low-level skills before they can experience the joy of high-level thinking in the domain. An alternative is the *constraint removal* view—the idea that novices can learn to engage in high-level thinking in situations that do not require mastery of all the low-level skills. For example, in solving a word problem, the student who has not memorized addition facts may be required only to tell what to do (e.g., "add 3 and 2") or may use a calculator. Similarly, a student may be asked to write an essay without concern for spelling, punctuation, and grammar or simply give an oral presentation. These techniques remove the constraints of having to master low-level skills but allow the student to engage in some aspects of higher-level thinking in a subject domain. An important benefit of constraint-removal techniques is that novice students can engage in problem solving within the context of authentic academic tasks.

Of course, constraint removal is not an adequate long-term approach to teaching problem-solving skills because students must eventually automate their low-level skills. Research on expertise demonstrates that there is no substitute for the large and automatized knowledge base of experts (Chi, Glaser, & Farr, 1988). However, constrain removal allows students to develop expert-like thinking skills along with basic skills.

Research

Research on cognitive apprenticeship demonstrates how beginners in an academic field can learn to think like experts (Collins, Brown, & Newman, 1989; Tharp & Gallimore, 1988). In a cognitive apprenticeship, beginners are allowed to participate along with skilled practitioners on authentic tasks; that is, tasks that are important for the discipline such as learning how to determine the meaning of an historical document. The beginners may be allowed to carry out some of the parts of the task and receive some assistance from experts. Tharp and Gallimore (1988) refer to this technique as *assisted performance*, because students learn to perform authentic academic tasks but receive needed assistance from more skilled members of the community of learners.

Collins et al. (1989) have identified three features of cognitive apprenticeship: modeling, coaching, and scaffolding. In modeling, a teacher describes his or her cognitive processes while engaging in an academic task. For example, in trying to write a essay, the teacher may describe how he or she plans out the organization of the essay and decides which sources to read. In coaching, a teacher offers hints, comments, and critiques to a student who working on an academic task. For example, he or she may ask the student to describe the audience of the essay. In scaffolding, a teacher provides assistance to a student who is not able to carry out every part of a task. He or she may have to complete parts of the task that the student cannot do unaided.

One way of allowing novices to learn to think more like experts is through reciprocal teaching—an instructional technique in which students and teachers take turns in describing their strategies for a given task (Brown & Palinscar, 1989; Palinscar & Brown, 1984). For example, in one set of studies, a group of seventh grade students and a teacher worked on trying to make sense out of a difficult text passage. The students were learning how to use four widely acclaimed reading comprehension strategies: questioning, in which students generate appropriate questions for a passage; clarifying, in which students detect and correct potentially difficult portions of the passage; summarizing, in which students produce a concise summary for a passage; and predicting, in which students suggest what will come next in a passage.

At first, the teacher and students take turns in leading a discussion about the passage, including how to generate a question, summarize the text, clarify a portion of the text, and make a prediction. When disagreements arise, all participants reread the text and discuss options until consensus is reached. When a student leads the discussion, the teacher may periodically provide guidance on how to exercise the comprehension strategies and may offer critiques and support that allow the student to continue. As students become more proficient in using the comprehension strategies, the teacher will reduce the amount of assistance.

Brown and Palinscar (1989) compared junior high school students who learned reading comprehension techniques through reciprocal teaching with those who learned through more conventional techniques, such as direct instruction in each isolated skill. As predicted, the students who learned through reciprocal teaching showed a large improvement in their reading comprehension performance whereas the conventionally taught students did not. The gains were still strong, even when students were tested six months later.

These kinds of results support the idea that students can learn to engage in complex tasks involving problem solving, such as making sense out of a difficult reading passage, even before they have mastered each component skill. By working together on a challenging academic task, students become cognitive apprentices. By providing criticism and information as needed—that is, by providing expert scaffolding—teachers become cognitive guides.

The success of some cognitive apprenticeship techniques encourages the idea that instruction in higher-level thinking does not always need to be postponed until a student has fully mastered lower-level basic skills. Clearly, some level of competence in basic skills is required; for example, improving students' reading comprehension requires that they already know how to decode printed words. However, it is not necessary to wait until students have completely mastered component skills, such as how to summarize or how to clarify, before they learn how to engage in an authentic academic task such as interpreting a difficult text passage. In becoming a cognitive apprentice, students are able to learn both component skills and how to orchestrate them within the context of a complex task.

FOUR RECOMMENDATIONS BASED ON COGNITIVE CONSTRUCTIVIST RESEARCH

In contrast to the four commonsense recommendations, a review of the research on teaching problem-solving skills suggests alternative recommendations concerning what, how, where, and when to teach.

1. Concerning what to teach, a problem-solving curriculum should emphasize learning smaller component skills and techniques for coordinating them rather than improving the mind in general. Instead of trying to improve general intelligence, problem-solving instruction should focus on component skills—such as how to summarize a passage, how to represent a story problem in a diagram, how to plan an essay, or how to generate and test hypotheses in a mystery scenario—and how to coordinate them in the context of academic tasks.

2. Concerning how to teach, a problem-solving curriculum should emphasize the methods used for thinking about academic tasks (that is, the process of problem solving) rather than solely getting the correct final answer (that is, the product of problem solving). Instead of drill and practice on contrived and isolated parts of an academic task, students should engage in discussions of how to solve realistic academic problems.

3. Concerning where to teach, a problem-solving curriculum should be integrated into every subject area rather than presented as a stand-alone course. Teaching general strategies such as how to represent problems and plan solutions are ineffective because techniques for representing problems or planning solutions are different in each domain. It follows that basic thinking skills are best learned within the context of the kind of problems that students will be asked to solve.

4. Concerning when to teach, a problem-solving curriculum should allow students to work on interesting academic tasks before they have completely

mastered low-level skills rather than postpone higher-order thinking until all the low-level skills are mastered. By providing expert guidance, teachers can serve as cognitive guides to help students work together to gain competence on challenging academic tasks.

AN EXEMPLARY PROGRAM

As an example of a constructivist program for teaching problem solving skills at the secondary school level, my colleagues and I at the University of California, Santa Barbara, have developed a 20-day program to help prealgebra students improve their skills in representing algebra problems concerning functional relations (Brenner et al., 1995). The program was motivated by the observation that algebra courses can filter many students out of higher-level mathematics courses that are needed for admission to universities.

The major goal of the program was to help at-risk students become more effective mathematical problem solvers by helping them develop cognitive skills essential for success in algebraic reasoning; namely, constructing and using mathematical representations. In constructing a mathematical representation a student translates among verbal, symbolic, tabular, and graphic forms of functions, such as converting a verbal statement into a table or a table into a graph. In using mathematical representations, a student draws a conclusion based on one or more mathematical representations of functions, such filling in missing values in a table.

The unit was taught by the student's regular classroom teacher and was supported by an 80-page binder that contained information for each of the lessons. All of the lessons involved pizza, including choosing a pizza company for the school cafeteria, resolving a computer malfunction involving pizza invoices, using formulas to compare the advertising claims of rival pizza companies, using formulas to investigate the nutritional value of various kinds of pizza, and using graphs and tables in solving problems about profit and loss in various pizza companies. For example, in the computer malfunction lessons, students looked for patterns of errors in order forms and invoice sheets for a pizza maker, completed tables using a variable expression as a guide, generated graphs and tables based on the malfunction, and wrote about their interpretations of various graphs and tables. For each lesson, students together worked in small groups to help determine procedures for solving the problems, and received guidance and critiques from the teacher and other classmates along the way.

The program corresponds to each of the four constructivist recommendations for fostering problem solving in students. First, concerning what to teach, each lesson in the unit involved activities in which students learned to translate among verbal, tabular, graphical, and symbolic modes of representing a functional relation; and each lesson involved activities in which students learned to draw conclusions from one or more of these forms of mathematical representation of functions. Second, concerning how to teach, each lesson in the unit involved discussion and comparison of various methods for accomplishing mathematical tasks. Third, concerning where to teach, students learned mathematical problem solving skills within the context of realistic mathematical tasks such as determining which of three companies should get the pizza contract for the school cafeteria. Fourth, concerning when to teach, students who had not yet completely mastered lower-level skills, such as how to solve equations, learned to make sense out of pre-algebra problems as cognitive apprentices within small groups.

Does the pizza math unit work? To address this question, Brenner et al. compared the pretest to post-test changes in junior high school students who received the treatment in their classrooms with those who received conventional instruction on functions. As predicted, students who received the 20-day unit on mathematical representations showed a larger gain than conventionally taught students in their ability to represent algebra problems, such as being able to write an equation to correspond to a sentence expressing a functional relation. These results show that it is possible to help students acquire problem-solving skills that are essential for success in high school mathematics but that are not normally emphasized in the mathematics curriculum.

CONCLUSION

The search for teachable aspects of problem solving has had a long and somewhat disappointing history in the psychology of education (Mayer, 1987b). However, recent advances in educational psychology have helped to clarify some criteria for effective problem-solving programs. These include a focus on teaching of component skills rather than improving general intelligence, teaching the process of problem solving rather than only the product, teaching problem within the context of academic disciplines rather than as a separate course, and allowing beginning students to engage in problem solving on authentic academic tasks rather postponing instruction until all low-level skills are mastered. In short, the lesson to be learned from this review is that teaching problem solving in secondary school should be based on criteria concerning what, how, where, and when to teach.

These criteria should be viewed as a set of research hypotheses that need to be clarified and tested in appropriate empirical studies. Future research is needed to clarify the component processes in each academic discipline, such as Flower and Hayes's (1980) analysis of writing processes; effective ways to teach the process of problem solving, such as how Japanese schools encourage students to discuss mathematical problem solving strategies (Stevenson & Stigler, 1992); the nature of domain-specific learning, such as techniques for promoting effective transfer (Mayer & Wittrock, 1996); and the role of prerequisite skills in the learning of higher-order thinking skills, such as the effectiveness of cognitive apprenticeship (Collins et al., 1989). The constructivist vision of learning and cognition has stimulated exciting possibilities for promoting student problem solving. These possibilities form the basis for an important research agenda in the future.

References

Bartlett, F. C. (1932). *Remembering*. Cambridge, England: Cambridge University Press.

Bloom, B. S., & Broder, L. J. (1950). *Problem-solving processes of college students*. Chicago: University of Chicago Press.

Brenner, M. E., Brar, T., Duran, R., Mayer, R. E., Moseley, B., Reed, B. R., & Webb, D. (1995). The role of multiple representations in introducing students to algebra. In D. T. Owens, M. K. Reed, & G. M. Millsaps (Eds.), *Proceedings of the 17th annual meeting of the North American Chapter of the International Group for the Psychology of Mathematics Education* (Vol. 1, p. 229). Columbus, OH: Ohio State University.

Brown, A. L., & Palinscar, A. S. (1989). Guided, cooperative learning and individual knowledge acquisition. In L. B. Resnick (Ed.), *Knowing, learning, and instruction: Essays in honor of Robert Glaser* (pp. 393–451). Hillsdale, NJ: Erlbaum.

Brownell, W. A., & Moser, H. E. (1949). Meaningful versus mechanical learning: A study in grade III arithmetic. *Duke University Research Studies in Education* (No. 8). Durham, NC: Duke University Press.

Chi, M. T. H., Glaser, R., & Farr, M. J. (Eds.). (1988). *The nature of expertise*. Hillsdale, NJ: Erlbaum.

Collins, A., Brown, J. S., & Newman, S. E. (1989). Cognitive apprenticeship: Teaching the crafts of reading, writing, and mathematics. In L. B. Resnick (Ed.), *Knowing, learning, and instruction: Essays in honor of Robert Glaser* (pp. 453–494). Hillsdale, NJ: Erlbaum.

Covington, M. V., Crutchfield, R. S., & Davies, L. B. (1966). *The productive thinking program*. Berkeley, CA: Brazelton.

Covington, M. V., Crutchfield, R. S., Davies, L. B., & Olton, R. M. (1974). *The productive thinking program*. Columbus, OH: Merrill.

Duncker, K. (1945). On problem solving. *Psychological Monographs*, 58 (5, Whole No. 270).

Flower, L. S., & Hayes, J. R. (1980). Identifying the organization of writing processes. In L. W. Gregg & E. R. Steinberg (Eds.), *Cognitive processes in writing* (pp. 3–30). Hillsdale, NJ: Erlbaum.

Lave, J. (1988). *Cognition in practice*. Cambridge, England: Cambridge University Press.

Mayer, R. E. (1987a). *Educational psychology: A cognitive approach*. New York: Harper Collins.

Mayer, R. E. (1987b). The elusive search for teachable aspects of problem solving. In J. A. Glover & R. R. Ronning (Eds.), *Historical foundations of educational psychology* (pp. 327–347). New York: Plenum.

Mayer, R. E. (Ed.). (1988). *Teaching and learning computer programming*. Hillsdale, NJ: Erlbaum.

Mayer, R. E. (1992a). Teaching thinking skills in the sciences and mathematics. In D. F. Halpern (Ed.), *Enhancing thinking skills in the sciences and mathematics* (pp. 95–116). Hillsdale, NJ: Erlbaum.

Mayer, R. E. (1992b). *Thinking, problem solving, cognition* (2nd ed). New York: Freeman.

Mayer, R. E. (in press). Learners as information processors: Legacies and limitations of psychology's second metaphor. *Educational Psychologist*, 31.

Mayer, R. E., Bové, W., Bryman, A., Mars, R., & Tapangco, L. (1996). When less is more: Meaningful learning from visual and verbal summaries of textbook lessons. *Journal of Educational Psychology*, 88, 64–73.

Mayer, R. E., Sims, V., & Tajika, H. (1995). A comparison of how textbooks teach mathematical problem solving in Japan and the United States. *American Educational Research Journal*, 32, 443–460.

Mayer, R. E., & Wittrock, M. C. (1996). Problem solving transfer. In D. Berliner & R. Calfee (Eds.), *Handbook of research in educational psychology*. (pp. 47–62). Washington, DC: American Psychological Association.

Newell, A., & Simon, H. A. (1972). *Human problem solving*. Englewood Cliffs, NJ: Prentice-Hall.

Nunes, T., Schliemann, A. D., & Carraher, D. W. (1993). *Street mathematics and school mathematics*. Cambridge, England: Cambridge University Press.

Palinscar, A. S., & Brown, A. L. (1984). Reciprocal teaching of comprehension-fostering and monitoring strategies. *Cognition and Instruction*, 1, 117–175.

Piaget, J. (1930). *The child's conception of physical causality*. London: Kegan Paul.

Rippa, S. A. (1980). *Education in a free society: An American history*. New York: Longman.

Sternberg, R. J. (1990). *Metaphors of mind*. Cambridge, England: Cambridge University Press.

Stevenson, H. W., & Stigler, J. W. (1992). *The learning gap*. New York: Summit Books.

Tharp, R. G., & Gallimore, R. (1988). *Rousing minds to life*. Cambridge, England: Cambridge University Press.

Thorndike, E. L. (1965). *Animal intelligence*. New York: Hafner. (Original work published 1911)

Thorndike, E. L. (1924). Mental discipline in high school studies. *Journal of Educational Psychology*, 15, 1–22.

Thorndike, E. L., & Woodworth, R. S. (1901). The influence of improvement in one mental function upon the efficiency of other functions. *Psychological Review*, 8, 247–261.

Weinstein, C. E., & Mayer, R. E. (1986). The teaching of learning strategies. In *Handbook of research on teaching* (3rd ed., pp. 315–327). New York: Macmillan.

Wertheimer, M. (1959). *Productive thinking*. New York: Harper & Row.

CHAPTER

16

Critical Thinking: Learning to Talk about Talk and Text

DAVID R. OLSON
University of Toronto, Ontario, Canada

INTRODUCTION

Since the time of Plato, theories of thinking have veered between thinking of the mind as ideal, as composed of clear, logically related ideas and the mind as process, what actual people believe, decide, and say (Frye, 1976, p. 41). Educators, of course, aspire to improve on the latter by appeal to the former. That is, educators attempt to improve the quality of everyday thinking by appeal to the ideals of logic, mathematics, and science. The systematic study of the specialized arts and sciences is assumed to improve the more general quality of thinking. More recently, some researchers have attempted to approach the problem of thinking more directly rather than through the traditional subject matter disciplines. An example of this development is the recent concern with programs to foster critical thinking (Norris, 1992; Perkins, 1995). While a theory of how people think is the goal of a natural scientific research program, a theory of critical thinking is rather a propaedeutic, a corrective or prescriptive theory, a theory of how one ought to think if one is to be ideally rational. It is one that would allow us to "decide what to believe" or to exercise "the will to believe" (James, 1890/1950). Rather than simply allowing beliefs to form unreflectively, one is to choose one's beliefs and assess statements and beliefs rather than just forming or holding them.

The first task, that of describing how thinking ordinarily proceeds, has made important strides in the past decade. First, it has become clear that even good thinkers are not ideally rational. Even experts entertain beliefs on the basis of the skimpiest evidence and they are unlikely to abandon a

Handbook of Academic Learning

theory just because the evidence, to date, tends to run against it. They seek evidence that supports their theories while ignoring other equally well-collected counterevidence. Furthermore, the standards against which theories are judged tend to be those dictated by the scientific community rather than those dictated by nature (Latour & Woolgar, 1979). On the other hand, even if not ideally logical, thinking is informed by knowledge, including domain-specific theories (Carey & Spelke, 1994; Keil & Silberstein, 1996) and pragmatic reasoning schemes (Cheng & Holyoak, 1985), which give thinking impressive scope and depth.

The basis of much systematic thought is one's knowledge about a domain. Carey (1996) has proposed that even young children acquire three domain-specific forms of knowledge organized around three different implicit causal theories." Physical understanding is formulated in terms of mechanical causal relations between variables (force causes motion, pressure decreases volume, etc.); biological understanding, in terms of functional relations between variables (giraffes have long necks to allow them to reach the lofty leaves, you eat to live); and psychological understanding, in terms of intentional causes (he looked for his hat at X because he thought it was at X, she jumped high because she tried hard). The more elaborated the theory becomes the more powerful it is in anticipating and in explaining events.

Yet, there may be more to thinking than the domain-specific knowledge tied to particular disciplines. As mentioned, theories of critical thinking are attempts to come to grips with rules of thinking that apply across disciplines. To date, the results have been less than impressive, partly because they aspire to universality (as in the application of explicit rules of logic) and partly because of the infinite variety of devices that have been shown to be useful in one context or another, inventing a mnemonic to remember arbitrary associations, underlining texts while reading, creating indexical marginalia in books being read, creating visual schematics for organizing and remembering information, learning to distinguish between perception and inference or between facts and opinions and the like). What is lacking is a framework for approaching the problem of thinking critically in a way that is both general across domains and may be applied by learners.

In fact, the means are ready to hand. Epistemology is the theory of knowledge and its growth, the sustained examination of the question, "How does one know?" While the larger epistemological questions such as whether knowledge is invented or discovered will continue to be debated, the basic concepts needed for reflecting on what and how we know make up a significant part of ordinary language. Learning to make the distinctions and to appeal to them in "deciding what to believe" constitutes an important part of what we may think of as folk epistemology and provides an important resource for thinking critically.

One approach to the topic of folk epistemology is in terms of the theory of pragmatics of language use, the theory that attempts to set out the relations between expressions in a symbolic mode and the intentions of speakers or writers in using them (Austin, 1962; Grice, 1983; Searle, 1983). Pragmatic theory provides an analysis of discourse in terms of speech acts, which in turn may be analyzed in terms of content and attitude. *Content* refers to what is said; *attitude* refers to intention, specifically, what the speaker or writer wants the reader or listener to think or believe. All speech events involve both content and attitude. For example, in saying, "I'm sorry," I both express a content (my regret) and an attitude (an apology). However, in most contexts, content and attitude are so closely tied that we are unable to distinguish them. A sincere statement is likely to directly inspire belief rather than lead us to entertain the content while withholding believing it. Critical thinking, we suggest, is the deliberate application, in some contexts, of this type of analysis to utterances and, more important, to thoughts. Critical discourse, the appraisal of claims and assertions, is the public side of critical thought, the appraisal of the beliefs, hunches, and perceptions of one's own. Stated more technically, we may say that statements and thoughts have a content (what they are about) and an attitude (how they are held). Critical thinking is the act of distinguishing content from attitude and so assessing them separately. Thus one could entertain the same content either as a guess, a hunch, a hypothesis, a belief, or a conviction. Learning to do so is what is involved in learning to think critically. Critical thinking and reflective thinking are based on a similar set of considerations and are of a piece with "criticism" more generally: literary criticism, film criticism, architectural criticism and the like.

The tools for such analysis and reflection are part of ordinary language and involve such basic concepts as say, think, mean, and understand. Interestingly, children begin to exploit these basic concepts for representing the thoughts and utterances of others in the late preschool years. In a precedent-setting experiment, Wimmer and Perner (1983) showed that when they are about four years of age, children, for the first time, come to understand that another person may hold a belief that they themselves know to be false. If told a story about a person, Maxi, hiding a candy that is subsequently moved to a second location without Maxi's knowledge, children of three years will claim that Maxi will look for his candy in the new location. Four-year-olds, on the other hand, recognize that Maxi will look where he had left it. What the false belief task indicates is that children from about the age of 4 begin to distinguish the content of the belief from the attitude. They then assign different attitudes, Maxi believes it, I do not, from the content, that the candy is in the old location. At about the same time they begin to characterize such false beliefs using the verb *think*, "He thinks the candy is in the drawer." Thus, *think* from an early age is used to characterize a belief discrepant from the speaker's belief; it is used to express a distinctive attitude to another's belief and thus is the beginning of "critical" thinking. Specifically, for the first time they become able to entertain a belief without adopting it. Interestingly, if children can use verbs like *think, know, remember* to characterize the talk and thought of others, they can also use them to apply to their own former, now rejected, beliefs and utterances (Astington & Gopnik, 1988; see also Astington, 1994).

To think about what another thinks and why is one important aspect of critical thinking. Equally important is one's understanding of what one means. The concept of meaning is a complex philosophical one, and the verb *mean* is one of the most complex verbs in English (Ogden & Richards, 1923). *Mean* refers to intention whether in action or in speech. Children begin to characterize actions as intentional and distinguish them from accidental ones when they are three- or four-years-old (Lee, 1995.) Their understanding of intention in speech—that is, what someone means by what he or she says—is more complex. Understanding appears to develop in two stages. First, children begin to understand the distinction between what a speaker says and what the speaker thinks or wants, identifying what the speaker means with what the speaker thinks or wants. That allows them to distinguish true statements from false ones. Only later do they begin to understand the difference between what the speaker thinks and what he or she wants the listener to think. This allows them to understand such tropes as sarcasm and irony (Keenan, 1995; Winner, 1988; Winner & Leekam, 1991).

In an early study, Robinson, Goelman, and Olson (1983) found that, if preschool children knew the thought or wants of a speaker who then expressed that desire by means of an ambiguous statement such as, "Give me the blue flower," when in fact there are two blue flowers and the speaker wanted the larger of the two, they tended to report that the speaker had said, "Give me the large blue flower." This was taken as evidence that these children conflated what was said with what was meant. In another study (Torrance & Olson, 1987), children ranging in age from 5 to 10 years were told a story about a character, Lucy, who, wanting her new red shoes, asks only for her red shoes, two pairs of red shoes being available. On half the trials, Charlie Brown brings the wrong pair and the subjects are asked if Charlie "did what Lucy wanted him to do?" and again if Charlie "did what Lucy asked him to do?" or again if Charlie "did what Lucy said he should do?" The youngest children easily granted that he did not do what Lucy wanted but only when they were 8- to 10-years-old did they grant that Charlie had complied with what she had said or asked. When asked if Lucy had told him which shoes to bring, the five-year-olds replied, "Yes"; the older children replied, "No." Again such studies indicate that children begin to distinguish what is said, wanted, thought, and meant only in the early school years.

An added degree of subtlety appears when children are about eight years of age. A number of studies (Ackerman, 1981; Demorest, Silberstein, Gardner, & Winner, 1983; Winner, 1988) have shown that, although children recognize falsity and deception at an early age, they continue to have difficulty with sarcasm and irony. Therefore, although they may recognize an ironic remark—saying "Beautiful" when someone spills the milk—as false, they fail to recognize that the remark is intentionally false and they may fail to grasp that the speaker wants the listener to think that the act was far from beautiful. Keenan (1995) presented children with a series of stories with sarcastic utterances in them and specifically asked them what the speaker said, meant, and wanted the listener to think. All of the children studied could answer the first question quite easily. When asked what the speaker meant by a sarcastic utterance, even 6-year-olds could report what the speaker thought but it was not until they were about 10 years old that they could report what the speaker wanted the listener to think. Thus, thinking about what is meant appears to go through at least two stages. At first what is meant is taken to be what the speaker thinks; only later is it thought of in terms of audience-directed intention.

Children's ability to analyze critically the utterances of another person can also be examined through their mastery of modal verbs, verbs expressing possibility or necessity. Children show a precocious awareness of the differences between thinking and knowing, an understanding that is directly related to their understanding of the distinctions between the modal verbs *might be* and *must be* (Moore, Pure, & Furrow, 1990). Other studies have examined children's growing ability to criticize utterances involving such expressions. In one study (Babu, 1989; see Olson & Babu, 1992), children were told stories in which a character makes either a warranted or an unwarranted assertion, and the child subjects were asked first to describe the character's assertion and then to retell the story. The story has the following logical form. One character tells a second character that an object is in either A, B, or C. The second character then looks in A and, in one of the conditions, asserts, "It must be in C." That, of course, is an assertion based on an unwarranted inference. How do children represent that assertion? The subjects are asked a series of questions including, "Did he know that the object was not in B?" Even four- to six-year-olds respond, "No." Examples of eight-year-olds' responses include

1. "I think he guessed."
2. "I guess he forgot to open that box."
3. "He just guessed that it's not in there."
4. "He thought his mother probably forgot to put it in there."
5. "Yes . . . well, I think she thought if it's not in that cupboard, it must not be here [the other cupboard] and maybe mother forgot."
6. "He said probably in his head, it's not in here. He thought it's not there."
7. "No, maybe somehow he figured it out that it's not there."
8. "Well, he just assumed it's not there."

Notice that even four- to six-year-olds correctly acknowledge that the speaker could not *know* that the object was not in B because he had not looked in B.

By the time they are eight years old, they offer reasons why he may not have looked, including, "he guessed," "he thought," "he just guessed," "he said probably," "he figured," and most interesting, "he just assumed." This last child characterizes the action as based on an assumption. Furthermore most six- and eight-year-olds, when asked if the speaker knew it was in C after claiming, "It must be in C," asserted that he could not know it was in C because he had not checked B, whether or not it turned out actually to be in C. They recognized that the assertion was not warranted. This is paradigmatic thinking about thinking—the critical thinker, rather than merely remembering and reporting the assertion, characterizes that assertion in the light of how the speaker came to make the assertion and what the reporter knows about the true state of affairs. The child is characterizing an utterance from a theoretical point of view.

Second, child subjects were asked, "Why did he say that it must be in C?" Children's answers to this request for an explanation fall mainly into three categories: (1) empirical explanations, such as "because the chocolate is in the purse" or "because dad took the chocolate"; or (2) intentional explanations, which appeal either to (2a) action such as, "because he *wants* to play with his car" or (2b) to beliefs, "he thought it might be up there" or "because he knew/guessed/forgot his car is there"; or (3) deductive explanations, which appealed either to (3a) actions, such as "it's because he looked in this cupboard, it wasn't there, then he looked in the cupboard, it wasn't there, so he opened the purse"; or to (3b) deductive inferences, such as, "because if it wasn't in those cupboards it *must be* in the purse" or "after opening the cupboards she *thought it would be* in the paper bag, because that's the only place to look at" or "because his mother said 'If I forget to put it in the cupboard, it will still be in the purse,' Jim checked the cupboards, it wasn't there, so *it has to be* in the purse."

The percentages of each type of explanation given by children in the three age groups are shown in Figure 1. The youngest children tended to give empirical explanations, reporting some aspect of the empirical rather than the inferential or mental facts, such as, "Because the chocolate is there." Most common among the six-year-olds was an appeal to the logical implications of the actions: "Because he looked in the cupboards and it wasn't there." The eight-year-olds appeal to the same logic, the logic of necessity, but they mark the necessity not in terms of action but in terms of thought and beliefs, using modals such as *must be*, *has to be*, and *knew*.

The acquisition of this knowledge for characterizing the assertions of others shows up in the second method utilized in that study. Children were asked to retell the story that they had just been told. Interestingly, the youngest children provided a simple narration of action—he looked at A, it was not there, and so on. Bruner (1986) has described such narratives as involving a "landscape of action." By age 6, they begin to retell the story by appeal to the intentional states, the beliefs, knowledge, and desires of the charac-

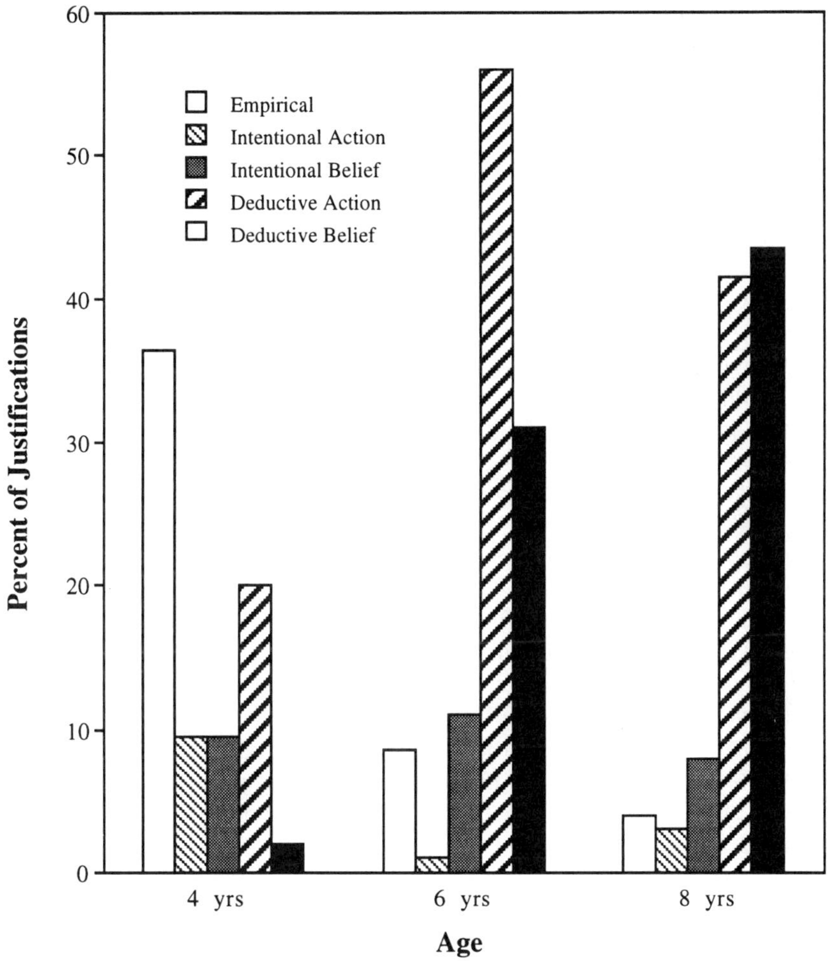

FIGURE 1
Percentage of empirical, intentional, and deductive justifications for speaker's expressions of inference offered by children at three age levels (adapted from Olson & Babu, 1992, p. 188).

ters in the story, what Bruner calls "the landscape of consciousness." Even if the original story made no reference to the intentional states of the characters, by eight years of age most children explain both action and utterances of characters by characterizing their mental states, that is, what the actors must have thought. Finally, there is a later development that appears among the eight-year-olds; namely, to characterize the inferences made in terms of logical necessity or lack of necessity using such expressions as "he knew it must be in C."

As children began to report the logical necessity of the inferences made by the characters in the stories, they also began to be more explicit in their setting out of the logical basis of the inferences. If we think of a syllogism as composed of a major premise, a minor premise, and a conclusion and think of the parts of the story in those terms, it is interesting to note that only the eight-year-old children thought it important to report the assertion that serves as the major premise of the inferential reasoning; namely, "He knew it was in either A or B or C." Younger children simply report the minor premise, "It wasn't in A," and the conclusion. As children get older, they increasingly recognize that the story could be characterized not merely as one of hunting for the hidden object but as testing the hypothetical possibilities and logical implications of the initial premise. They represent that logic in their description of the actions and utterances of protagonists.

Generally, such evidence suggests that, by the time they are eight or nine years old, children have mastered the basic concepts they need to represent utterances as inferences (figure out), assumptions (guess), warranted assertions (must be), true assertions (know), and false beliefs (think). This is the basic language needed for characterizing the beliefs and statements of themselves and others. While all children are clearly capable of such conceptual distinctions, it is not at all clear that all do. We suspect that there are important individual and cultural differences in both the ability to characterize statements in these ways and in the habit or disposition to do so when thinking (Jenkins & Astington, 1994). But these basic ways of talking about talk and thought is just the beginning of more elaborate ways of thinking about, that is, criticizing, utterances and beliefs.

LITERATE OR SCHOOLED MODES OF THOUGHT

Dewey (cf. Boydston, 1976) in his criticism of realism suggested that we substitute the notion of "taken as given" for the realist notion of the "given." What is given is merely a way of taking as someone has quipped. So, too, with beliefs. Beliefs can be held in a variety of ways beyond merely true and false, with conviction or tentatively, as posits or as inferences. Statements, too, can be offered or "taken" as more than merely acceptable or unacceptable, as literal or metaphorical, or as claims or conjectures, for example. Learning the ways of taking is a central feature of critical thinking. The way a belief or a statement is to be taken depends upon its warrant or justification and its relation to prior beliefs.

Scientific discourse provides a rich set of distinctions for the ways in which one can hold or express one's cognitive commitments. Latour and Woolgar (1979) analyzed the types of statements made by scientists as writers and critical readers. As writers, scientists prefer simple factual claims shorn of their rhetorical form. Yet, as readers, these same scientists work on other people's texts to recover their rhetorical form, asking themselves such questions as, "Who is saying this?" "Why is he or she saying this?" "What is he or she trying to get the reader to think?" and "Does he or she have any warrant for saying that?" In other words, they are skilled in deciding how to take the statements of others while at the same time writing their own texts in an impersonal form that makes those "ways of taking" largely invisible. Put another way, writers attempt to write texts as a series of logically related facts; critical readers, on the other hand, attempt to downgrade those putative statements of fact into mere expressions of opinion. Statements that resist such downgrading come to be taken as true and seen, often inappropriately, as autonomous and above criticism (Geisler, 1994).

Such discourse requires specialized language, and the mastery of that mode of discourse offers new ways of examining our beliefs and our claims. We can see this development by a brief look at the history of English vocabulary. English has two sets of vocabulary items. The common nouns and simple forms of oral speech are of Germanic origin; the more specialized terms are of Latin origin. Stevenson (1983, pp. 157–159) claims that more than 10,000 new words were introduced into English from scholarship Latin between 1500 and 1650 as English became the language of literature, science, philosophy, and government. Traugott (1987) adds, "This was a period of new developments in commerce with attendant needs for clarifying claims, asserting rights, reporting, assuring, and promising" (p. 40). In some cases, these terms were used first as mental verbs and only later as speech act verbs. In others, they were used first as directives and only later as assertives. Thus, *insist* was first used in sentences like: "I insist that you sit down," and only later was it used as an assertive speech act verb, as in "I insist that he sat down." The first gives an order, the second states a fact.

Further, the printing press, which had encouraged a flowering of literature, encouraged the development of rules and standards of expression, grammar, and spelling. Printing texts for a greatly enlarged reading public was a major factor in the standardization of language. That, together with an elaborate vocabulary adopted from Learned Latin, gave rise to what we may refer to as the *literate standard language*.

An important part of this "literate standard" is the set of speech act and mental state verbs that elaborate on that basic set—say, think, and mean—which as mentioned are part of ordinary, oral language. Speech act verbs are those that can take the place of the verb *say*, while mental state terms are those that can take the place of the verb *think*. An indication of the borrowing of terms for referring to what people say, write, and think, is given by Table 1.

The simple speech act and mental state verbs shown on the left of Table 1 are Indo–European and relatively ancient. The specialized verbs on the right are Latinate and added to English, either directly or via French, as

TABLE 1
Date of First Known Use in English of Some Speech Act and Mental State Verbs

Germanic		Latinate	
believe	OE	assert	1604
know	OE	assume	1436
mean	OE	claim	ME
say	OE	concede	1632
tell	OE	conclude	ME
think	OE	confirm	ME
understand	early ME	contradict	1570
		criticize	1649
		declare	ME
		define	ME
		deny	ME
		discover	ME
		doubt	ME
		explain	1513
		hypothesize	1596 (Greek)
		imply	ME
		infer	1526
		interpret	ME
		observe	late ME
		predict	1546
		prove	ME
		remember	ME
		suggest	1526

Note:
OE = Old English (before 1150)
ME = Middle English (1150–1350); late ME (1350–1450)
Source: The Oxford English Dictionary; adapted from Olson and Astington (1990). Reprinted from the *Journal of Pragmatics*, 14, D. R. Olson and J. W. Astington, Talking about text: How literacy contributes to thought, 705–721, 1990 by kind permission of Elsevier Science–NL, Sara Burgerhartstraat 25, 1055 KV Amsterdam, The Netherlands.

English came to be used for those functions that had, until then, been conducted largely or exclusively in Latin or in French.

Now why did there come to be such an elaboration and specialization of the verbs of saying and thinking? We suggested (Olson & Astington, 1990) that these are verbs used for criticizing and otherwise talking about text. The simpler set of verbs, *say*, *tell*, and the like, are used for talking about what a person says and what he or she means by it; the more elaborated set are used for talking not only about what a speaker says, but also about texts and their interpretations.

Why would textual commentators require a complex set of speech act verbs? Stated another way, why did the Scholastic philosophers invent them and why did the English writers and speakers borrow them? To see the precise functions of these verbs we must make a brief detour into the semantics of speech act and mental state verbs.

SPEECH ACT AND MENTAL STATE VERBS

Speech act and mental state verbs provide clear evidence for the extremely close relation between talk and thought. Austin (1962), Searle (1969), and Vendler (1972) have shown that mental state terms express the "sincerity" condition for speech acts. Thus, to *say* or *state* sincerely that it is raining, one must *believe* that it is raining; to *promise* sincerely to go swimming, one must *intend* to go swimming; to *request* sincerely a cookie, one must *desire* a cookie (Astington, 1992).

These terms provide the basic vocabulary for characterizing others' mental states (Astington & Olson, 1990). For example, I can say of myself, "I think it will rain" using a mental state verb *think*, but that is equivalent to saying "It might rain"; the mental state term is essentially interchangeable with the modal verb as an expression of uncertainty. However, if I want to mark another person's uncertainty, I cannot use the modal. To characterize his view I have to say, "John thinks that it will rain." Mental state verbs, it seems, are needed to characterize the states of others, even if they are not needed to characterize one's own. Indeed, as mentioned, when applied to the self, mental state terms are equivalent to expressions of possibility and certainty—"I think" versus "I know" expresses varying degrees of commitment to the truth of the proposition, not something about one's mental life.

Leech (1983) has analyzed the structure of assertive speech act verbs in terms of four basic factors: (1) prediction versus retrodiction, such as *predict* versus *report*; (2) public versus private assertion, such as *declare* versus *hint*; (3) confident versus tentative assertion, such as *affirm* versus *hypothesize*; and (4) informative versus argumentative assertion, such as *announce* versus *argue*. Furthermore, such verbs as *admit* and *agree* involve asserting something that is part of the adversary's position, while other assertive verbs such as *claim*, *assert*, *state*, and *argue* do not explicitly mark the adversary's position and, in this way, are like the verb *say*.

Thus, like the mental verbs *know* and *think*, which, as we saw earlier, can be used to indicate agreement or disagreement with the cognitive state of another person—if we agree, we say he knows; if we disagree, we say he thinks—the choice of the assertive verb does not depend purely on the attitude of the person whose speech is being characterized but also on the attitude of the reporter of the speech act. The reporter, in choosing a speech act verb, declares his or her own attitude to the speech act being reported whether agreement, disagreement, or abstention.

Because these verbs force the reporter to reveal his or her own stance in characterizing the mental states of others, they require an additional degree of subjectivity; that is, of consciousness of one's own beliefs and their relations to those of others. The acquisition of an elaborated set of terms for thought and talk allows distinctions to be made between related but distinguishable processes; for example, *infer* versus *remember, recall* versus *recognize*, and *describe* versus *explain*. And the process of ascribing these mental states and speech acts to others, as the choice among them depends upon one's own mental state, makes one more conscious of those states.

A major function of such meta-linguistic and meta-cognitive terms, then, is to characterize the utterances of others especially those utterances preserved in written text. Because such verbs were important in reporting and commenting on religious, bureaucratic, and philosophical texts, we suggest they were elaborated in Latin and subsequently borrowed into English. Their acquisition by children is an important part of the acquisition of *literate standard language*.

The role of this language is shown quite clearly in the work of Latour and Woolgar (1979) on the language of the scientific laboratory, which we mentioned briefly earlier. In an attempt to map the transition from the tentative formulation of ideas in the laboratory to the publication of scientific reports, the authors assigned the oral and written utterances into four classes, ranging from the most tentative conjectures ("could it be . . .") to the most declarative assertions ("The addition of X produces the effect of Y"). Interestingly, while the discourse in the laboratory belonged to the first class, the scientific reports were composed primarily of assertions of the last type. That is, published texts were presented as embodiments of truth. However, when these same writers read the publications produced by others from other laboratories, readers were quick to read the statements as if they were of the first kind, as claims, assumptions, and beliefs of the authors rather than embodied truths. Thus, equipped with an elaborate set of categories for ways of taking utterances and texts, scientists shifted easily from one mode to another in their thinking and writing.

In our laboratory, we examined school children's competence with these "ways of taking" written texts (Astington & Olson, 1990; see also Hall & Nagy, 1994; Siddqui, 1995). Senior elementary and high school students were asked to choose among the verbs *infer, hypothesize, concede, interpret, conclude, assume, doubt, remember, assert, imply, predict, confirm*, using items such as the following:

> Jane and Kate are arguing about which is the best place to eat. Jane thinks Harvey's is best but Kate thinks McDonald's is. Kate says that McDonald's is nearer, but Jane still thinks Harvey's is the best one to go to because the burgers taste better. *She says to Kate, "It's true McDonald's is nearer,* but I'd rather go to Harvey's."
>
> A. Jane contradicts Kate's point.
> B. Jane doubts Kate's point.
> C. Jane claims Kate's point.
> D. Jane concedes Kate's point.

> Bob is reading a scene from one of Shakespeare's plays for English homework. He comes to the lines: "that she may feel how sharper than a serpent's tooth it is to have a thankless child." He knows the words but he doesn't understand it, so he goes to ask his mother. *She says it means* "King Lear wants Cordelia to know how painful it is to have a child who is ungrateful."
>
> A. Bob's mother understands the lines.
> B. Bob's mother interprets the lines.
> C. Bob's mother criticizes the lines.
> D. Bob's mother defines the lines.

> Last week in science class, Mr. Jones showed Dave that an acid solution turns litmus paper pink. This week there is a test. The first question says, "What color will litmus paper be when you dip it in acid solution?" *Dave thinks that it will be pink.*
>
> A. Dave remembers that it will be pink.
> B. Dave hypothesizes that it will be pink.
> C. Dave infers that it will be pink.
> D. Dave observes that it will be pink.

All of these verbs are elaborated forms of the verbs *say* and *think*, which even the youngest children use appropriately. But, even high school students performed poorly on these items and many like them. For many of the items, students pleaded ignorance, for others such as the third item, for which the verb *remember* is correct, they were misled by the content. As the content of that item is science, many of the children were distracted by the alternative *hypothesize*. While the basic concepts of saying and thinking are in place, children have a considerable amount to learn about characterizing the utterances and beliefs of themselves more precisely. And learning to do so makes up an important part of learning to think (see Astington & Olson, 1990, for fuller details).

THE ROLE OF THE SCHOOL

On entering formal schooling at 5 or 6 years of age, children know a great deal, not only about the world but also about their own and others' beliefs and about the conditions and sources of knowledge. They have the basics of a folk epistemology. What they have yet to learn, and what falls to the schools to foster, is a set of concepts for thinking about the very activities children have been engaged in all along. The concepts children acquire for thinking about their own thinking are the very concepts that are important for teachers in dealing with children's thinking. Talk about thought provides a common core for both teachers and children to use in improving thinking. Consider, finally, two ways that this knowledge can be applied.

First, children have to learn how to take statements and hold beliefs. When children enter school they pay particular attention to the pragmatics of an expression, obeying or disobeying, agreeing or disagreeing with a speaker. They see through the utterance to the intention behind it, conflating what the sentence means with what the speaker means by it, as we pointed out earlier. They have yet to learn to entertain the content of the assertion somewhat independent of the attitude or belief of the speaker or writer who produced that assertion. Rather than simply agreeing or disagreeing with the speaker, the child has to go on to judge the truth or falsity of the assertion *whether or not it is believed by the speaker.* The student has to learn to assign his or her own attitude to that content. To illustrate, it is well known that children, from about the age of 2, are able to express their agreement or disagreement with a speaker. If an adult says "That's an apple" while pointing to an orange, the child is likely to reply, "No. Orange" (Pea, 1982). The child has rejected the assertion of the speaker. But not until after they are six- or seven-years-old can children judge the truth of sentences independent of their agreement or disagreement with the speaker (Astington, 1992). This understanding makes the acquisition of textual knowledge possible. It is a special orientation to knowledge that allows one to treat the semantics of an utterance independent of its pragmatics, truth being the primary semantic factor. Children must learn to go from the pragmatics of an expression to the semantics of that expression, from assertions to statements, if they are to understand the issues of truth and logic so important for reading and writing "decontextualized" or "autonomous" texts, texts of the sort they encounter in teachers' talk and in school texts.

The second point is the converse of the first. Students must learn to read textual statements as expressions of beliefs of the writer. Whereas in the first case children have to learn to set aside the pragmatics to focus on the semantics, in this second case they must again come to see through the semantics of expressions to the pragmatic functions of those expressions. Many writers have noted that, by the middle school years, children are quite competent in comprehending the texts they read and in recalling them, paraphrasing them, and extracting the gist. Indeed, schema theory provides a useful model for those aspects of comprehension (Anderson, Spiro, & Montague, 1977). What such models fail to account for is student's conspicuous failure in criticizing and otherwise evaluating the texts that they read (Geisler, 1994; Haas & Flower, 1988; Palinscar & Brown, 1984; Wineburg, 1991). This lack of criticism is perhaps a product of a respect for the official knowledge of the culture, conveyed, for example, in textbooks and a lack of respect for one's own ideas and beliefs.

The possibility of criticism of official, textbook knowledge and of building a bridge between personal and cultural knowledge depends on understanding that textbook knowledge is merely the expression of an author's intentions and beliefs. Criticizing statements requires that one not only evaluate the truth of the claims but also infer the intentions of an author that would have led to the formulation of such text. These were the questions that Latour and Woolgar (1979) found their critical readers asking: "Who is saying this? Why is he or she saying it? Is this a firm belief or a mere conjecture? Is there a warrant for that statement?" It is a matter of making an impersonal text personal.

The early school years are devoted, in part, to helping students treat statements as facts to be learned and organized into theoretical systems. Understanding textbooks, for example, requires children to find relations among the propositions expressed in the text. The author of those statements, to a large extent, is invisible. Indeed, some textbooks are written by a committee. The emphasized relations are those among propositions, not those between the propositions and the author's intentions and beliefs. Indeed, the authors become invisible. But this very stance makes some aspects of critical thinking difficult or impossible. Critical thinking about texts and beliefs requires that the thinker again come to see textual statements as expressions of some author's beliefs, beliefs that may be valid or invalid, relevant or irrelevant, decisive or indecisive. Critical reading and critical thinking are based on just this ability to recover the putative intentions of the writer and to examine their grounds.

Higher-order thinking, from the perspective we have developed, is nothing other than competence with the set of concepts for managing how beliefs are to be held and how statements are to be taken. It is a matter of the recognition of the attitude one takes to the content of one's own thoughts, and it is a matter of the correct assignment of illocutionary force to others' statements. The problem is particularly acute when dealing with authorless texts that provide no explicit indication of the intentions of the author. On the other hand, in learning to deal with such texts students have the opportunity to learn to exploit the resources of their folk epistemology for thinking about their own thinking and the thought of others.

The language for talking about thought and talk can be directly exploited in classrooms. First, teachers could be encouraged to pay close attention to how students intend their utterances to be taken and to help students become conscious of the force of their utterances. Questions such as "Is that an assumption or a hypothesis?" and "Is that a claim or is that evidence for some other claim?" not only will aid the teacher in understanding the thoughts of the student but will provide the conceptual categories in terms of which students may come to see their own utterances. Even young children can be asked questions such as "Do you really know that or are you just guessing?" and "Did you just think of that or did you remember it?" "Is that an assumption or an inference?" Such reflection can play a role in classroom discourse right from the start, not just in high school science, English, or history. Teachers need to talk more about what they themselves *think, know, expect, remember, wonder about, have decided on, guessed, assumed, inferred, concluded,* and so on and need to encourage students to do the same. By consciously introducing and using such language about thinking in the classroom, teachers will lead students to reflect on and articulate their own thinking and its expression. Teachers who make more use of meta-cognitive and metalinguistic language will have students who do the same, and these students will be better able to understand their own and others' beliefs and intentions; that is, how their own beliefs are held and how others' statements are to be taken.

Ways of talking about talk and thought are equally appropriate for talking about text. Texts are not to be learned; they are to be interpreted. Critical interpretation, in part, is a matter of deciding on how a text was intended by a writer and how it could be taken by a reader. Because written texts are fixed, they may become objects of reflection and analysis quite different from the more informal utterances encountered in a classroom. Hence, they provide an important context for sorting out ways of meaning and understanding.

Finally, it is worth repeating that the concepts we have discussed are not only useful for critically assessing the talk and texts of others. The very vocabulary useful to the teacher for helping the student understand how to take expressions and texts turns out to be appropriate for the learner for thinking about his or her own beliefs and statements; that is, for deciding what to believe. This, then, is a vocabulary for both teaching and for thinking (Olson & Bruner, 1996).

Acknowledgments

This chapter draws heavily from three earlier papers on this topic: Olson and Babu (1992), Olson and Astington (1990), and Olson and Astington (1993). I am grateful to the Spencer Foundation and to the Social Sciences and Humanities Research Council of Canada for their support.

References

Ackerman, B. (1981). Young children's understanding of a speaker's intentional use of a false utterance. *Developmental Psychology*, 17, 472–480.

Anderson, R. C., Spiro, R. J., & Montague, W. E. (Eds.). (1977). *Schooling and the acquisition of knowledge*. Hillsdale, NJ: Erlbaum.

Astington, J. W. (1992, April). *Children's understanding of truth*. Paper presented at the annual meeting of the American Educational Research Association, San Francisco.

Astington, J. W. (1994). *The child's discovery of the mind*. Cambridge, MA: Harvard University Press.

Astington, J. W., & Gopnik, A. (1988). Knowing you've changed your mind: Children's understanding of representational change. In J. W. Astington, P. L. Harris, & D. R. Olson (Eds.), *Developing theories of mind* (pp. 193–206). Cambridge, England: Cambridge University Press.

Astington, J. W., & Olson, D. R. (1990). Metacognitive and metalinguistic language: Learning to talk about thought. *Applied Psychology: An International Review*, 39, 77–87.

Austin, J. L. (1962). *How to do things with words*. Cambridge, MA: Harvard University Press.

Babu, N. (1989). *Children's understanding of the validity and truth of mental representations*. Unpublished doctoral dissertation, University of Toronto, Ontario Institute for Studies in Education, Toronto.

Boydston, J. A. (Ed.). (1976). *John Dewey: The middle works*, 1899–1924 (Vol. 2: 1902–1903). Carbondale: Southern Illinois University Press.

Bruner, J. S. (1986). *Actual minds, possible worlds*. Cambridge, MA: Harvard University Press.

Carey, S. (1996). Cognitive domains as modes of thought. In D. R. Olson & N. Torrance (Eds.), *Modes of thought: Explorations in culture and cognition* (pp. 187–215). New York: Cambridge University Press.

Carey, S., & Spelke, E. (1994). Domain-specific knowledge and conceptual change. In L. A. Hirschfeld & S. A. Gelman (Eds.), *Mapping the mind: Domain specificity in cognition and culture* (pp. 169–200). New York: Cambridge University Press.

Cheng, P. W., & Holyoak, K. J. (1985). Pragmatic reasoning schemas. *Cognitive Psychology*, 17, 391–416.

Demorest, A., Silberstein, L., Gardner, H., & Winner, E. (1983). Telling it as it isn't: Children's understanding of figurative language. *British Journal of Developmental Psychology*, 1, 121–134.

Frye, N. (1976). *Spiritus mundi: Essays on literature, myth, and society*. Bloomington: Indiana University Press.

Geisler, C. (1994). *Academic literacy and the nature of expertise: Reading, writing and knowing in academic philosophy*. Hillsdale, NJ: Erlbaum.

Grice, P. (1983). *Studies in the way of words*. Cambridge, MA: Harvard University Press.

Haas, C., & Flower, L. (1988). Rhetorical reading strategies and the construction of meaning. *College Composition and Communication*, 39, 30–47.

Hall, W. S., & Nagy, W. E. (1994). Theoretical issues in the investigation of the words of internal report. In I. Gopnik & M. Gopnik (Eds.), *From models to modules: Studies in cognitive science from the McGill workshops* (pp. 26–65). Norwood, NJ: Ablex.

James, W. (1950). *The principles of psychology*. New York: Dover. (Original work published 1890)

Jenkins, J. M., & Astington, J. W. (1994). *Cognitive factors and family structure associated with theory of mind development in young children*. Unpublished manuscript.

Keenan, T. R. (1995). *The role of echoic information in young children's comprehension of sarcasm*. Unpublished doctoral dissertation, University of Toronto, Ontario Institute for Studies in Education, Toronto.

Keil, F. C., & Silberstein, C. S. (1996). Schooling and the acquisition of theoretical knowledge. In D. R. Olson & N. Torrance (Eds.), *Handbook of education in human development* (pp. 621–645). Oxford, England: Blackwell.

Latour, B., & Woolgar, S. (1979). *Laboratory life: The social construction of scientific facts* (Vol. 80). London: Sage Library of Social Research, Sage Publications.

Lee, E. A. (1995). *Young children's representational understanding of intention*. Unpublished doctoral dissertation, University of Toronto, Ontario Institute for Studies in Education, Toronto.

Leech, G. N. (1983). *Principles of pragmatics*. London: Longman.

Moore, C., Pure, K., & Furrow, D. (1990). Children's understanding of the modal expression of speaker certainty and uncertainty and its relation to the development of a representational theory of mind. *Child Development*, 61, 722–730.

Norris, S. P. (Ed.). (1992). *The generalizability of critical thinking*. New York: Teachers College Press.

Ogden, C. K., & Richards, I. A. (1923). *The meaning of meaning*. New York: Harcourt, Brace & World.

Olson, D. R., & Astington, J. W. (1990). Talking about text: How literacy contributes to thought. *Journal of Pragmatics*, 14, 705–721.

Olson, D. R., & Astington, J. W. (1993). Thinking about thinking: Learning how to take statements and hold beliefs. *Educational Psychologist*, 28(1), 7–23.

Olson, D. R., & Babu, N. (1992). Critical thinking as critical discourse. In S. P. Norris, (Ed.), *The generalizability of critical thinking: Multiple perspectives on an educational ideal* (pp. 181–197). New York: Teachers College Press.

Olson, D. R., & Bruner, J. S. (1996). Folk psychology and folk pedagogy. In D. R. Olson & N. Torrance (Eds.), *Handbook of education in human development* (pp. 9–27). Oxford, England: Blackwell.

Palinscar, A. S., & Brown, A. L. (1984). Reciprocal teaching of comprehension-fostering and comprehension-monitoring activities. *Cognition and Instruction*, 1, 117–175.

Pea, R. D. (1982). Origins of verbal logic: Spontaneous denials by two- and three-year-olds. *Journal of Child Language*, 9, 597–626.

Perkins, D. (1995). *Outsmarting IQ: The emerging science of learnable intelligence*. New York: Free Press.

Robinson, E. J., Goelman, H., & Olson, D. R. (1983). Children's understanding of the relations between (what was said) and intentions (what was meant). *British Journal of Developmental Psychology*, 1, 75–86.

Searle, J. R. (1969). *Speech acts: An essay in the philosophy of mind*. Cambridge, England: Cambridge University Press.

Searle, J. R. (1983). *Intentionality: An essay in the philosophy of mind*. Cambridge, England: Cambridge University Press.

Siddiqui, S. K. (1995). *Cognitive consequences of exposure to print: A study of decontextualization and knowledge of mental state verbs*. Unpublished doctoral dissertation, University of Toronto, Ontario Institute for Studies in Education, Toronto.

Stevenson, V. (Ed.). (1983). *Words: The evolution of western languages*. Agincourt, Ontario: Methuen.

Torrance, N., & Olson, D. R. (1987). Development of the metalanguage and the acquisition of literacy: A progress report. *Interchange*, 18(1/2), 136–146.

Traugott, E. C. (1987). Literacy and language change: The special case of speech act verbs. *Interchange*, 18(1/2), 32–47.

Vendler, Z. (1972). *Res cogitans*. Ithaca, NY: Cornell University Press.

Wimmer, H., & Perner, J. (1983). Beliefs about beliefs: Representation and constraining function of wrong beliefs in your children's understanding of deception. *Cognition*, 13, 103–128.

Wineburg, S. (1991). On the reading of historical texts: Notes on the breach between school and academy. *American Educational Research Journal*, 28, 495–519.

Winner, E. (1988). *The point of words: Children's understanding of metaphor and irony*. Cambridge, MA: Harvard University Press.

Winner, E., & Leekam, S. (1991). Distinguishing irony from deception: Understanding the speaker's second-order intention. *British Journal of Developmental Psychology*, 9, 257–270.

PART IV

Assessment of Classroom Learning

CHAPTER

17

Classroom Assessment

WILLIAM D. SCHAFER
University of Maryland, College Park

INTRODUCTION

Assessment may be defined as gathering information that informs decision makers. It exists in many forms and occurs daily in classrooms. Stiggins (1991) has found that assessment-related activities, using this broad definition, can consume up to half of a teacher's professional time. Even using a more restricted definition, teachers can spend up to 10% of their time on formal testing, alone (Newman & Stallings, 1982). Assessment is clearly pervasive in classrooms.

Yet many teachers have received no formal assessment instruction. Schafer and Lissitz (1987) have found that only about half of teacher education programs nationally include an assessment course and that, in the remainder of the programs, major assessment topics are left untreated in required course work. Although standards exist for assessment understanding on the part of teachers (American Federation of Teachers, National Council on Measurement in Education, & National Education Association, 1990), Plake, Impara, and Fager (1993) have found that teachers average only 23.2 on a 35-item test tied directly to those standards. Indeed, Stiggins (1988) found that most teachers use their own experiences from when they were students plus suggestions from colleagues as the knowledge base for their assessment usage. He characterized instruction and technical help for practicing teachers in assessment as the area of most pressing need in education. Similarly, Wise, Lukin, and Roos (1991) found that, among practicing teachers, 55% use trial-and-error in their own courses to determine their uses of assessment and about half feel their assessment education has been inadequate.

Handbook of Academic Learning

The purpose of this chapter is to describe ways teachers can use assessment effectively to improve and document the achievement of their students. The difference between improving and documenting is important. Assessment used to improve instruction and learning is termed *formative*. These might be used for decision making by the teacher in identifying student strengths and weaknesses in prerequisite skills prior to an instructional unit or to monitor progress. They also may be used in decision making by the student. A student who understands the learning expectations of the teacher in concrete terms (i.e., exactly how he or she will be assessed) is equipped to evaluate his or her own progress toward those expectations and focus further study on needed material.

Assessment used to document achievement is called *summative*. Usually, these are the more formal activities that most people think of when they hear the word *assessment*, such as tests, quizzes, and rating scales. They may be used by the teacher to assign grades or in other ways to report student progress to others. Most standardized assessments are summative, although these are usually required by agencies outside the classroom (e.g., districts, states) and hence are outside the scope of this chapter.

The array of assessment approaches available to teachers is broad. Stiggins (1992) gave a typology that describes these by method (paper–pencil, performance or product assignment, or interpersonal communication) and by format (objective or subjective). They may be either teacher constructed or externally developed and further may be used for decision making by the teacher or the student.

Fortunately, relatively few criteria are needed to describe high-quality in assessment across this array of methods. This chapter describes those dimensions first and then discusses how various assessment methods may be used effectively by classroom teachers. It is assumed that the assessment is intended to inform a decision maker and therefore should provide information that is relevant for a decision-making purpose.

DIMENSIONS OF HIGH-QUALITY ASSESSMENT

In assessment, quality consists of validity, reliability, and practicability. Though these are traditional measurement concepts, their meanings apply across all assessment types.

Validity refers to the pertinence, to the decision maker, of the information generated by the assessment. Two fundamental questions need to be addressed. First, does the assessment process capture the breadth, or richness, of the domain of achievement about which the decision is to be made? For example, a history test used to provide information about achievement for a unit on the Civil War would not be very valid if it covered only dates, generals, and battles; would be even less valid if it covered only the Battle of Gettysburg; and would be invalid if it covered exclusively the Revolutionary War. Furthermore, a student studying for a Civil War test may only memorize facts if he or she does not know that the domain of achievement also requires higher-order thinking.

The second question is whether the assessment is affected by irrelevancies. Even in assessments that do capture the breadth of the domain, it is possible that the information they yield may be influenced by student characteristics that are not part of the domain, such as handwriting, verbal fluency, working speed, or achievement on previous units of instruction. This might occur if a teacher were to score a Civil War essay test, knowing whose papers he or she was reading and letting knowledge about how well each student did on the Revolutionary War unit affect the scoring. More troubling, but real, is the possibility that the outcomes of the assessment are affected by noneducational student characteristics such as gender, race, or religion.

The second quality dimension is reliability. A reliable assessment is dependable, generating information that accurately reflects stable characteristics of students. A teacher can make inferences about a student's achievement only by observing that student's behavior, or the results of such behavior, in either a contrived or a natural setting. If the student is behaving atypically, the inference will not be accurate; an assessment of the same domain at another time would likely yield different information even if the student's achievement did not change.

Regarding student production of behavior, three sources of unreliability are often differentiated: among different assessments of the same domain (e.g., between two tests), across different assessment times (occasions), and random lack of consistency (e.g., unpredictable student behavior). On paper–pencil tests, it has been shown that longer tests tend to balance out errors due to inconsistencies, and therefore multiple items are often used in an attempt to improve reliability (assuming that enough time is allowed for students to respond to all the items). In general, use of more assessment opportunities, whether in one sitting or over time, will tend to yield greater reliability.

Following student production, unpredictability of scoring, which is related to the objectivity of the assessment, is another aspect of reliability. Objective tests can be scored almost mechanically by comparison with an answer key. Subjective assessments, on the other hand, require inferences by the scorer (e.g., teacher) and are less consistent, both across scorers (interrater reliability) and within the same scorer (intrarater reliability). Since rating reliability is only one aspect of the general question of reliability, studying whether student responses can be scored consistently does not address all reliability concerns.

Unreliable assessments cannot be valid. Since unreliable assessments tap only capricious information, they cannot provide information that is of use to anyone, let alone a decision maker. However, a reliable test is not necessarily valid. For example, a teacher can reliably measure students' heights but those results would be invalid for assigning course grades.

Practicability, sometimes called *utility*, is the final dimension of assessment quality. The assessment should provide the right type of information, at the right time, be feasible, and result in desirable effects. This criterion may also be thought of as efficiency. The assessment should maximize needed information and positive outcomes and minimize unnecessary information and costs in terms of teacher time, student time, resources, and negative outcomes.

The aspect of practicability that has to do with the consequences of the assessment is important. When assessments are used formatively, it is expected that they help direct the activities of teachers in making instructional decisions and students in deciding what and how to study. When assessments are used summatively, decisions are made based on the resulting scores (e.g., grading, placement). All these decisions produce consequences. An assessment is more practical if its positive consequences are maximized and its negative consequences minimized. Most measurement professionals consider this to be a validity issue because it affects both what should be assessed and how it should be assessed, and they use the term *consequential validity* (e.g., Messick, 1995). It is included here under practicability because it involves value judgment about decision alternatives, part of a cost–benefit analysis, rather than hypotheses about whether the information an assessment yields is pertinent to the decision.

The next three sections describe different assessment methods: paper–pencil techniques, performance assessment, and interpersonal communication. Each has advantages and disadvantages. In general, a teacher who understands and can use these methods well will be able to employ assessment effectively for both formative (instructional) and summative (measurement) purposes. Techniques for interpreting assessments and a consideration of grading practices make up the remainder of this chapter.

PAPER–PENCIL ASSESSMENTS

Paper–pencil assessments come in many forms, all of which are common in classrooms and include true–false, multiple-choice, matching, short answer, or completion tests and essays. An essay is any item that requires a student to *construct* an extended response, such as a proof in mathematics or a strategy for a hypothesis test in science. The *selection* forms of paper–pencil assessments (true–false, multiple-choice, and matching), in which students are choosing from a limited list of options, can be answered quickly and scored mechanically, allowing broad coverage of the domain being assessed and efficient use of teacher time. To somewhat less extent, this is also true of short answer items, even though they do not involve selection, since students supply their own answers. But selection-type tests are difficult and time consuming to develop and assess only aspects of achievement that are consistent with their formats. The latter drawback need not be as limiting as many believe; selection items can be constructed to test a much broader range of student achievement, including higher-order thinking, than they are typically used for in schools. Selection formats are more conducive than others to reuse, which can decrease the time needed to construct such tests for new students.

Since an essay test has fewer items than an objective test, fewer essay items are needed. This means that an essay test is easier to construct. Essays also are able to assess aspects of production that cannot be reduced to choices, such as ability to organize thinking and communicate cogently. But they are more time consuming to score and, because of inherent subjectivity in scoring, more prone to rater unreliability and bias.

A general procedure for constructing paper–pencil tests is described next. Recommendations for developing and scoring selection and supply items are then discussed separately.

Describing the Domain: Tables of Specifications

The domain for an assessment of achievement includes the content it is intended to cover as well as the activities students are to accomplish using the content. It should not be surprising that these are the fundamental elements of a behavioral objective: the activity and the content. We infer achievement by observing what happens when students are asked to do something with something.

A table of specifications is an organizational device useful in test planning. It describes objectives in such a way that the types of items needed are identified, and it is useful in judging whether those items adequately cover the intended domain, thus yielding evidence helpful in making a subjective evaluation of the test's validity. Construction of a table of specifications takes place in several steps.

Step one entails listing the content areas that should be assessed. For example, if a test is to be constructed that covers criteria for evaluating assessments, the content areas could be validity, reliability, and practicability. A total of 100% is then divided among the content areas consistent with the importance of each; these will eventually represent the proportions of the test that cover each of the content areas. In our example, validity and reliability might each consume 45% of the test, and practicability 10%.

The second step is to use a taxonomy to list the activities of the cognitive domain. Here, the Quellmalz taxonomy (see Chapter 2) will be used. As with the contents, the thinking levels are each identified with percentages that sum to 100%. In this example, recall might be allocated 35%, analysis 5%, comparison 15%, inference 30%, and evaluation 15%.

TABLE 1
Table of Specifications for a Quiz on Evaluating Assessments

Activity	Content: Validity	Reliability	Practicability	Total
Recall	15	15	5	35
Analysis	5	0	0	5
Comparison	5	10	0	15
Inference	15	10	5	30
Evaluation	5	10	0	15
Total	45	45	10	100

The results of the first two steps are arrayed in a two-way table, activity and content (see Table 1). Each cell in the table is a combination of a level of thinking with a content area and thus represents a class of behavioral objectives that combines a category of activities (action verbs) and a category of content (material). For example, an item that combines recall with reliability might ask a student to name the sources of unreliability; an item that combines inference with validity might ask a student to construct an example of a test that is of questionable validity for a given purpose and suggest how its validity can be improved; and an item that combines analysis with practicability might ask a student to differentiate the features of a sample assessment that can make it impractical.

It should be pointed out that an item may on the surface look like a higher-order item but actually be a recall item. This will depend on the way the student is instructed. In the previous nonrecall examples, the particular activity may have been taught directly and, if so, the student is simply producing a memorized response. This is called the recall trap. To engage higher-order thinking, there must be some novelty.

The third and last step in constructing a table of specifications is to fill in cell percents so that they total the already fixed row and column percents. As can be seen in the example, the cell percents do not need to be proportional by rows or columns; some content areas may be more appropriate for certain activities than for others.

When the table is completed, the cell percents can be translated into the points available on the test. They then define the nature of the items that need to be written. For example, if this were to be a 20-item quiz, then one item is needed for each 5% in each cell. All that remains is to locate or write the items that correspond to the cells. When finished, the test is tied to the content domain through the table of specifications and the table thus becomes a device that facilitates judgment about the test's validity.

An important by-product of writing a table of specifications is that it forces attention to all the levels of activities. Based on an analysis of approximately

9000 test items written by classroom teachers, Fleming and Chambers (1983) found that the overwhelming majority were written to tap the recall level of thinking only. This suggests that very few of the behaviors that students are actually graded on assess higher-order thinking. Consequently, memorization becomes from the student's point of view, the fundamental learning outcome that educators desire. A table of specifications, however, forces the teacher to think about whether higher-order activities are desired and structure tests accordingly. These should include formative as well as summative assessments, so students know that higher-order outcomes are desired and understand how to accomplish them, using the particular content areas of the domain.

Using Selection Items

Selection items are those in which the correct (keyed) answers appear and the task of the student is to choose them. The most common examples are true–false, multiple-choice, and matching. In this section, some recommendations are given about writing these items effectively. It should be mentioned that selections items, especially multiple choice, are devalued by many education professionals. Unfortunately, this is more the result of how they are commonly used than it is due to inherent weaknesses. Selection items can engage higher-order thinking, although they are also very effective at assessing recall. While they should not be used exclusively, they are a valuable tool in the teacher's assessment arsenal.

Before we discuss multiple-choice items, you are invited to take the quiz in Figure 1. This example covers content based on the poem "Jabberwocky," by Lewis Carroll. You should answer all eight items, guessing if necessary; if you find you know little about this strange land, use whatever clues you can find in the quiz, itself. The answer key comes next, so complete the quiz, following its directions before you read on.

Each of these items can be answered using cues contained in the quiz. They provide examples of ways test-wise students can use incidental information to help them respond to selection items. The keyed response to item 1 is *a*, because there is repetition of a key word in the stem (the "question" part of the item) and one of the alternatives. To avoid this type of cue, try to make sure the alternatives are all parallel in that either they all do or they all do not contain key words in the stem. The second item is keyed *b* because it contains a qualifying phrase, which is typically found in keyed answers. The key for the third item is *c*. Each alternative in this item contains a word called a specific determiner because it either does or does not admit exceptions. Specific determiners such as *never* and *always* that do not admit exceptions are most common in incorrect alternatives (also called *decoys*, *distracters*, or *foils*). Words such as *sometimes*, *often*, and *usually* do admit exceptions and are more common in keyed alternatives. Both kinds of specific determiners

Directions: Circle the letter preceding one correct answer to each item. Each item is worth one point. Respond to all eight items. No correction for guessing will be applied. Time limit: 10 minutes. Good luck!

1. A sword is made vorpal through a process known as
   a. vorpalization
   b. whiffling
   c. calloohsion
   d. outgrabe

2. A jubjub bird is most likely to sing when
   a. toves gyre
   b. wood is tulgey, if it is brillig
   c. a bandersnatch is frumious
   d. a blade snicker-snacks

3. When days are brillig, then
   a. all toves slithe
   b. bandersnatches are always frumious
   c. foes are usually manxome
   d. no mome rath can ever galumph

4. A jabberwock burbles best in close proximity with an
   a. borogove
   b. bandersnatch
   c. slithing tove
   d. uffish

5. Among the reasons why the borogoves were mimsy were
   a. it was brillig and the toves gimbled
   b. the jabberwock was outgrabed
   c. the boy was beamish
   d. the callay was whiffling

6. What always appear when days are frabjous?
   a. borogoves and mome raths
   b. mome raths
   c. jubjub birds and mome raths
   d. mome raths and tumtums

7. Burbling near an uffish is most effective when done by a
   a. bandersnatch
   b. vorpal sword
   c. jabberwock
   d. beamish boy

8. a.
   b.
   c.
   d.

FIGURE 1

A "Jabberwocky" quiz.

should be avoided. The fourth item's keyed answer is *d*. This item contains a grammatical cue: the word *an* at the end indicates that the next word starts with a vowel sound and *uffish* is the only one that does. The fifth item's key is *a*, also for a grammatical reason. The stem indicates that more than one reason is asked for and choice *a* is the only option that has more than one. The sixth item's key is *b*. Note that, if choice *a*, *c*, or *d* were correct, since each includes mome raths, then *b* would also be correct. So only if *b* is correct can there be only one correct answer and the directions indicate that there is only one correct answer to each item. The seventh item is keyed *c*, based on item 4, where it was learned that a jabberwock burbles best next to an uffish. So the quiz has actually taught us something about "Jabberwocky" that we never learned from studying about it. The eighth item is keyed *d*. Notice that the answers thus far form a pattern. What is the next in the sequence: *a*, *b*, *c*, *d*, *a*, *b*, *c*, . . . ? Why *d*, of course.

Certain further recommendations should be followed to write effective multiple-choice items. The stem should present a clearly defined problem and is best if it can stand as a short answer item. The stem should not be explanatory, since stems that "teach" material not necessary for the item waste valuable time. The stem should be stated positively, since students expect to be choosing options that are "correct" or "best" and a change in ground rules should be avoided; if it is necessary, emphasize the change, such as by using capital letters and underlining to stress the negative word or words. The stem should also be simple; stems that contain many ideas can be interpreted differently by different students.

The options should be similar to each other in content and length, and all decoys should be plausible to the uninformed. It is too difficult a task to make rapid comparisons among complex alternatives, so the options should also be simple. Avoid "all of the above" as an option, which can be selected if two of the others are correct without evaluating the rest; and overinclusive options, since if two or more options cover all possibilities, the choice will likely be made ignoring the others. Finally, the position of the keyed option should be haphazard. This does not usually occur in teacher-made, multiple-choice tests. One reason may be that teachers typically do not wish to have examinees respond without reading all the options, perhaps because they want students to be aware of what their options are or perhaps because they have gone to a lot of trouble writing plausible, but wrong, answers and want the examinees to admire the results of all their hard work. Whatever the reason, the keyed alternative tends to be near the end of the option list, most commonly appearing next to last. An effective way to avoid this is to alphabetize the alternatives or place them in numerical order once they have been written for each item.

Describing flaws and suggesting ways to avoid them is intended to be used to eliminate them. Some teachers intentionally use flaws to key incorrect alternatives, feeling the decoys then become more attractive. But the trick is to get students responding to the content of the items, not to irrelevant cues, no matter which way they direct the students' responses. The test will then be more valid because its scores will not be affected by test-wiseness, which is not part of the domain being assessed (except on the "Jabberwocky" quiz).

Many of the flaws noted for multiple-choice items also apply to true–false items. For example, specific determiners should be avoided. The most important additional recommendation is to use only one idea for each item; if two or more ideas are to be tested, test them with two or more items. It is also desirable to phrase items positively (a negatively stated false item introduces unnecessary semantic complexity) and to have the numbers of true and false statements approximately equal.

Matching items consist of a list of items and a list of alternatives. They are very much like a homogeneous group of multiple-choice items, all with the same options. The most effective use of matching items occurs when the option list is short, about seven, and when the options may be reused, so that students are not using unselected options to respond to items they do not feel they know. The arrangement of the options should be in some logical order (e.g., alphabetic) and the basis on which items and options are matched should be clear to the students.

A useful variation on these formats is to use them after presenting students with new information that they are to interpret. The information may take the form of charts, paragraphs, tables, descriptions of experiments, and the like. This allows teachers to tap higher-order thinking and thus more complex learning outcomes but retain the advantages of objective test items.

Tests are usually best assembled by placing groups of the same item type together and items covering a subunit of content together. Items should not be split between pages. Since items sometimes have more than one answer that is correct and it is intended for the student to choose the better answer, it is recommended that the directions call for choosing the best, as opposed to the correct, answer, since those directions apply to both types. This also bolsters the teacher's defense when confronted with "creative" justifications for wrong answers in test review sessions. Finally, unless speed is being tested, enough time should be given so that all students can be expected to have an opportunity to answer all items.

A special concern on selection items is whether to encourage or discourage guessing. Although measurement professionals disagree on this issue, and disagree also about the adequacy of so-called corrections for guessing, the position taken here is that encouraging students to answer every item will lead to more valid assessment. The reason is that guessing is often done with partial information and students obtain proportionally about as many items right through guessing as they deserve. If guessing is discouraged, some will guess anyway and others will not guess at all, invalidly affecting their scores by introducing risk taking into the domain being measured. No correction for guessing formula can take these factors into account because all depend on an assumption that the probability of guessing a correct answer is based on a random process. Directions that say something like "answer every item; if you don't know the answer try to guess based on what you do know" can reduce the negative feeling many have about encouraging students to guess.

Using Supply Items

In contrast to selection items, supply items are those in which the student is either recalling or constructing the answer. Examples are short answer items, sometimes called *completion items*, and essays.

The major difference between short answer items and multiple-choice items is that essentially an infinite number of choices is available for short answer items. While this makes them resistant to guessing, it also makes scoring them less objective (e.g., does spelling count? or legibility?). Unexpected "right" answers are also possible. For example, the item, "*Common Sense* was written by ____" was intended by the teacher to be answered "Thomas Paine," but a student responded "1776." Should the student receive credit (it appeared in January 1776)? Some suggestions for writing short answer items are these: phrase each item so that only the desired response is correct (in the preceding example, a better item would have been "The author of *Common Sense* was ____"); write the item in your own words, avoiding taking the language directly from a textbook (although textbook statements are correct, they typically are not specific enough for a short answer item); when possible, ask a question (e.g., "Who wrote *Common Sense*?") rather than use blank spaces, but if blank spaces are used, do not allow the lengths of the blanks to cue the lengths of the answers and make sure there is enough information to identify the correct answer (e.g., the item "____ was written by ____" is clearly faulty); and specify the units and degree of precision needed for numeric answers.

Essay items are more flexible than all the types discussed thus far. With that flexibility comes the opportunity to assess combinations of thinking skills that are involved in broader thinking processes, such as problem solving and scientific reasoning, as well as to assess a student's ability to choose what material to use and to evaluate, integrate, organize, and express it. With these advantages come some drawbacks. Because they allow great latitude to students in responding and produce extended material, scoring is both more time consuming and less consistent than the other types. And, because fewer items are possible on a test, the scope of content that may be covered in a given time period is restricted. Since the educational outcomes they measure are considered important, essays are valuable item forms for teachers to use, but their inefficiencies argue for the use of other formats when appropriate. The use of essays is not an end in itself. Recommendations about essays are separated here between constructing the items and scoring the responses.

The most important suggestion for writing an essay item is to understand what elements should be present in a desired response. Actually writing, or at least outlining, a model answer is a useful way to do that. Another way is to construct a scoring key consisting of the desired elements along with descriptions of how student responses will be evaluated on each of them (see the later section on performance assessment). The task of writing a good item will then be easier, since the item should be written to elicit the desired elements. The item should tell students what types of thinking are required. For *recall*, students could be asked to define or describe; for *analysis*, students could be asked to subdivide or organize; for *comparison*, students could be asked to classify or differentiate; for *inference*, students could be asked to predict or speculate; and for *evaluation*, students could be asked to critique or describe strengths and weaknesses and to offer explanations.

It is also desirable to indicate how the response will be scored (e.g., for an item involving evaluation, "your answer will be judged in terms of your explanations of the criteria you use and the defensibility of your application of them"). To do all this, an essay item may be rather long. That is appropriate if the length enhances the clarity of the task. The model answer is the target, and the essay item should be phrased to point the student's thinking toward it. Of course, students should have been taught directly, using the content of the domain being tested, how to engage in the type of thinking they are asked to demonstrate; otherwise there will be a mismatch between instruction and assessment.

It is helpful to indicate an approximate time frame or length for the response to each item and enough time should be available for all the students to finish all the items. Finally, the use of optional questions should be discouraged. Students would then be evaluated using different tests, covering different portions of the domain, and students who anticipate optional questions may focus their study accordingly. Further, student choice of questions to answer introduces an invalid element into the assessment; a student who chooses a harder question is at a disadvantage. If in-depth study and assessment of portions of the domain are appropriate, it is generally better to use even more flexible assessment methods such as papers or projects (see the section on performance assessment).

The primary goal in scoring essays is to reduce subjectivity and bias. The model answer or outline that should have been prepared when the item was written is helpful. How the elements of the model translate into judgment (e.g., points) should be made explicit and augmented by describing how inaccuracies are reflected in scoring. Taken together, these so-called rubrics can be written down for reference while scoring. Consistency can be enhanced by scoring all student responses for each item together, since the scoring rubrics for one item can more easily be remembered and applied at any one time than can those for multiple items.

Several types of bias in scoring have been identified. Among these are the halo effect, in which attitude toward a student, positive or negative, affects the judgment; logical error, in which prior expectations that a student will do well (or poorly) influence the scoring; and location bias, in which a given rater tends to score either generously, severely, or near the middle of the rating scale. Biases are difficult to eliminate but can be reduced if a scoring key is carefully followed, if it is possible to rate each item response without knowing which student wrote it, and if elements of answers that are important but may be irrelevant to the objectives of the assessment, like neatness, sentence and paragraph structure, and spelling, are handled separately, such as by noting them in a summary of comments about each response but not including them in scoring.

Just as a multiple-choice test-wise student can often obtain a higher score by using cues in the items, an essay test-wise student can often obtain a higher score by intelligent bluffing. Bluffing occurs in many ways. A student might explain that the question is important, try to anticipate the rater's value judgment about the topic, "write around" unknown facts, write about tangential topics or about material that would fit any topic, or simply restate the question. The best defenses against bluffing are the written scoring rules and a healthy tendency to score off-target responses, assuming the target has been well defined by the item, the same as nonresponses.

Scoring essays may be either analytic or holistic. In analytic scoring, the characteristics of model answers are expressed as scales with point-assignment specifications (see the section on performance assessment for recommendations about developing such scales). Ratings and, usually, feedback to students are in terms of these elements. In holistic scoring, each essay response receives only an overall rating. Sorting the responses to each item into ordered piles of similar quality can help make such judgment. Feedback is usually global. Analytic scoring is more reliable and more valuable to the student, since it gives more detail about what the student should do to improve in the future.

Instructional Uses of Paper–Pencil Assessment

In general, assessment is the way teachers learn about the achievement of their students. But they are also the way the students learn about their own achievement. The power of assessment used formatively as well as summatively is strong. By giving students practice with paper–pencil forms of assessment like those they will eventually be asked to respond to at the end of instructional units, each student is able to engage in intelligent, formative self-assessment as instruction is progressing. The teacher can also identify problems that need to be addressed before instruction is complete. Homework and seatwork are useful ways to do this. When students know that they will be assessed summatively using the same formats they use instructionally, they understand what they can do to improve. When it eventually comes, the summative quiz or exam should not surprise the student. He or she should be familiar with the nature of the content domain and with the formats used to assess it and have had time to prepare for it.

Over time, teachers can generate numerous formative, paper–pencil assessments, perhaps adapting earlier summative assessments. Colleagues are a potential source of material for beginning teachers. At the school level or even beyond, a collection of assessments used by teachers who have taught specific instructional units can be generated and used instructionally. Such a collection could even help staff members define and understand the domain of objectives that should be educated toward in each unit. However, mindful of the tendency of teachers to assess primarily recall, past assessments should be evaluated critically to make sure they represent complex, higher-order thinking skills and processes adequately; this is also true of instruction-oriented and measurement-oriented assessments that accompany textbook series and other curriculum materials used in schools.

PERFORMANCE ASSESSMENTS

Many of the desired outcomes of education are in the form of complex tasks in which students are expected to be able to perform combinations of skills. Indeed, the life tasks adults engage in following schooling are qualitatively different in many ways than the types of assessment they completed while in school. Yet, their education is expected to enable successful graduates to perform their life tasks more effectively. Graduates are expected to be able to secure and advance in career-oriented jobs, participate in democratic self-government, and pursue avocations. While none of these can be measured directly during schooling, certain methods have been developed to rate how well students perform complex activities that are included in life tasks, such as doing research and writing reports, performing experiments, writing letters, presenting material orally, performing a particular skill like playing an instrument, working in groups, and operating or repairing machinery. These methods, called *performance assessment*, apply to outcomes that, because they are too complex, too time consuming, or require unusual settings or materials, do not lend themselves to paper–pencil forms of assessment. Performance assessment involves demonstration of knowledge or skills and often focuses on the process in which the student engages. For this reason, such forms are especially well suited to instructional applications. They are also key elements in many policy-driven testing programs, such as National Assessment of Educational Progress, and have been recommended for accountability as well as instructional purposes (Rudner & Boston, 1994).

Performance assessment may apply either to what a student does (an actual performance of some task) or to what a student produces (a product). Because the latter includes responses to essays, performance assessment methods may be effective for that form of paper–pencil assessment. Steps adapted from Stiggins (1987) for developing performance assessments are described here. They are time consuming, but the activity of designing a performance assessment almost invariably is useful to the teacher because it requires careful attention to instructional goals and it provides valuable instructional materials for use with students as a by-product. It is recommended that the outcomes of each step be written down.

Step 1. Identify the Content of the Assessment

What do you hope to be able to do with the performance assessment? What do you want to assess? These questions should be answered in a general way before proceeding. Writing down the content that the assessment will cover, even in terms as general as "this performance assessment will rate the speaking skills of high school students," helps focus attention on the nature of the process or product that is being evaluated.

Step 2. Identify the Decision(s) to Be Made

Since assessment supports decision making, the nature of the decision(s) that will be made based on the performance assessment should be clarified. Several possible decisions might be supported, including diagnosis of strengths and weaknesses, assigning grades, forming instructional groups, ranking students, evaluating progress, or determining mastery. Or, the performance assessment may be designed to support more than one decision, such as determining mastery and diagnosing strengths and weaknesses of those who have not reached mastery.

Step 3. Identify the Decision Maker(s)

The performance assessment should provide what the user of the information (the decision maker) needs. Therefore, who is making decisions should be specified. Again, there are several possibilities, such as the teacher, the student, parents, or school administrators.

One important potential use of performance assessment involves students, themselves, as decision makers. This deserves emphasis. As will be seen later, performance assessment includes defined criteria for successful performance. Students can use these criteria during instruction to learn how close they are to success and to understand how to improve. Student self-assessment can occur frequently during learning and can even involve students' peers in critiquing each others' work. The clarifying and motivating power of this formative use of performance assessment should not be overlooked.

Step 4. Identify the Nature of the Performance

The performance to be assessed may be either a process or a product. Is the best evidence of achievement found in observing what a student does (e.g., playing a piano or observing safe laboratory practices) or results of what a student does (e.g., a term paper or a drawing)? In some areas, both technique and outcome may be incorporated into the assessment (e.g., rating wood turning technique as well as qualities of completed wooden bowls). In general terms, the nature of the process or product should be specified.

Step 5. Specify the Performance Criteria

This is the heart of the performance assessment; it is the most time consuming and the most important step. The result should be one or more anchored rating scales, one for each dimension of quality that is to be observed.

An anchored rating scale is a continuum ranging from poor to excellent in defined increments. Each step on the scale should be described so clearly that different raters reach identical judgments about which step a particular example of the process or product falls into. For example, if we are rating student papers in an English class and one of the dimensions is mechanics, we might have four steps: (1) errors in word usage, spelling, punctuation, and sentence structure make the communication virtually impossible to understand; (2) errors in word usage, spelling, punctuation, and sentence structure force the reader to reread certain sections to understand the communication; (3) several errors in word usage, spelling, punctuation, and sentence structure are present but do not affect the ability of the reader to understand the communication; and (4) there are virtually no errors of word usage, spelling, punctuation, or sentence structure.

Taken together, the dimensions should include all facets of the process or product that are educationally important. The anchors (verbal descriptions of the steps) should be clear, mutually exclusive, and in an ordinal (greater than, less than) relationship with each other. It is also useful to have a general description of each dimension one is to rate.

Developing the performance criteria is a two-step task. First, the dimensions of quality need to be identified and described and second, the anchored scales need to be developed. It is helpful to involve colleagues in this process, since it usually is not obvious what the dimensions should be for complex outcomes. Several drafts are usually needed; if examples of processes or products are available they can be used as "test cases" to rate, refining the dimensions based on the results. Questions to ask are whether the scales are clear (do different raters give consistent ratings to the same processes or products?) and whether they seem to capture all the important features that differentiate the processes or products. Involving colleagues can also develop a shared vision of the important educational objectives.

It is valuable instructionally to involve the students, themselves, in developing the criteria. They will then not only understand them, but they will, through their own involvement, understand their importance. Student participation also develops a shared vision of quality that supports peer participation in providing feedback as instruction progresses.

It should be noted that some performance assessments take the form of checklists instead of rating scales. A checklist is a series of characteristics that are either present or absent. The rater then marks whether each appears or does not appear.

Step 6. Design the Assessment Conditions

One decision to make in designing the conditions of the assessment is to determine whether the students should be observed engaging in (or have produced products from) contrived behavior or naturally occurring behavior. Most performance assessments occur in contrived situations, such as when students are asked to write papers, give speeches, conduct experiments, and the like, and they are aware that they are being assessed (the assessment is obtrusive). However, say one is interested in rating laboratory safety. Students who are aware the rating is being conducted may alter their usual behavior to receive a higher score. This would invalidate the assessment if its purpose were to rate how well they normally practice safe habits rather than how well they can produce them. An unobtrusive assessment, on the other hand, would rate students' natural behavior since they would not be aware of the rating (one can muse on how safe roads might be if driving tests could be done unobtrusively).

If the decision is to use a contrived assessment, an exercise will be needed to elicit the process or product. The exercise should allow full expression of the quality criteria and collection of enough evidence to be consistent with the importance of the decision to be made. Many educators feel that the exercise should also be representative of ultimate objectives, such as those involved in real-life tasks; when it is, the performance assessment is considered authentic.

Herman, Aschbacher, and Winters (1992) describe several principles for designing conditions that are especially helpful for performance assessments used instructionally. Among these are allow multiple ways to approach the problem; relate information to personal experience and prior knowledge but apply it to a novel situation; encourage higher-order thinking at the same time that fundamental skills are developed; provide plenty of time to think, revise, and rethink; use concrete materials; provide examples of different levels of quality work; encourage student goal-setting and self-evaluation; use real-life tasks that connect to students' experience; help students see how results are related to effort; and encourage work in heterogeneous groups. Student awareness of the scoring methods (performance criteria) enhances the value of all these principles.

Step 7. Design Scoring Methods

The scoring method and what should be done with the scores depends in part on who makes decisions based on the results. If the assessment is to be used formatively, by the student or by the teacher to determine strengths and weaknesses, it may not be necessary to combine the ratings. If it is to be used for grading, then the ratings likely will need to be combined into an overall score and further, cutoffs may be needed for various levels of performance. See the section on setting standards for suggestions about determining cutoffs. The final issue to be addressed is whether and how the scores are to be recorded and who has access to them.

Criticism of Performance Assessment

Paper–pencil assessment instruments have received criticism because some feel their use encourages school professionals to concentrate on discrete skills in instruction. Many educators believe that performance assessment provides a solution to this problem since they are a closer match to the real-life tasks that schooling should be preparing students for. Yet concerns have been raised about reliance on performance assessment, mostly in summative contexts, and especially for high-stakes purposes in which students are denied a goal unless their performance is acceptable. Performance assessment has been shown to be less reliable than paper–pencil assessment and more time consuming to score. Because fewer tasks are used, they may not cover the achievement domain well and may vary greatly in difficulty. Performance assessment also involves more subjectivity in judgment. Nevertheless, performance assessment methods enjoy wide acceptance among educators and are a valuable asset to teachers.

INTERPERSONAL COMMUNICATION

Teachers make decisions at a rapid pace. Clark and Peterson (1986) found that teachers make interactive decisions, defined as deliberately choosing specific actions, at a rate of about one every two minutes. Shavelson (1973) has suggested that decision making may be the fundamental teaching skill, and among all professions, Stiggins, Conklin, and Bridgeford (1986) identified teaching as that with the most frequent need for information processing. While formal assessment methods play a role, most information a teacher processes comes from interpersonal communication, and most of that is informal. Airasian (1991) has differentiated informal assessment into three types: sizing-up assessment (getting to know students), assessment for instructional planning (relating the curriculum to student characteristics and instructional resources), and assessment during instruction (adjusting teaching as it occurs based on interactive feedback).

Sizing-up Assessment

Sizing-up assessment often occurs before teachers even meet their students. At the beginning of the year, a teacher is understandably interested in who his or her students are, what special problems he or she may face, and the strengths and weaknesses of individual students or the class as a whole. While some teachers prefer to learn about their students based on their own direct experience, many use several sources for sizing-up information before they begin to organize their classrooms. Among these sources are student records, formal procedures to alert teachers about students with special needs, comments from other teachers, and experience with older siblings.

Information for sizing-up continues to be developed intensively during the first few days of school. Based on such observations as clothing, posture, and interactions with other students and with the teacher, images are formed of each student and of the class as a whole that affect how the teacher approaches instruction, what he or she uses for motivation, and the establishment of classroom routine and handling exceptions to it. Indeed, without such images, the beginning-of-year task of organizing the classroom effectively would be very difficult. A teacher needs quickly to learn about his or her students so that they are no longer strangers.

These initial impressions can have long-term consequences because they influence teachers' expectations of and interactions with students. They also appear to be stable, even when teachers receive conflicting information later in the year. To improve their use of sizing-up assessments, Airasian (1991) recommends that teachers be aware that sizing-up is going on, that teachers view their initial impressions as hypotheses to be supported or rejected on the basis of later information, seek enough observations to be sure they are assessing students' typical behavior, emphasize inferences from observations of behavior that depend on few assumptions instead of those that are less directly related to the characteristic being assessed, and try to use information from multiple sources (this is an example of triangulation, which involves evaluating the consistency of findings arising from different assessment opportunities).

Assessment for Instructional Planning

To teach, teachers must translate curricula into unit, weekly, and daily lesson plans. Instructional planning thus occupies much of a teacher's professional time and assessments can enhance the planning process. Three elements are important: (1) the goals of the instruction, (2) the characteristics of the students, and (3) the resources available. While assessment for instructional planning is not interpersonal communication, strictly speaking, it is included here since its implementation is about and is eventually altered by later interactions with students.

Instructional planning is most effective if the goals of instruction are well articulated. The best way to do that is to identify the behavioral objectives desired as outcomes. As mentioned earlier, these are statements that indicate what students will be able to do with the content at the end of instruction. Because they are behavioral, they are stated in terms that lead to their assessment. Having them in front of him or her, a teacher can understand exactly what is being planned for by visualizing what successful students can do.

Student characteristics include aptitudes and skills that are prerequisite to the instruction being planned. If the sizing-up assessment has been done well, the teacher should have sufficiently accurate information about aptitudes for planning purposes. It may be necessary to use a more direct method to assess prerequisite skills. Other student characteristics that are useful to know about in planning are work habits, degrees of motivation, and social skills, along with any special needs that may exist; sizing-up assessment is useful for these insights.

Planning for instruction involves understandings about resources. These may be of four types: time, people, facilities, and materials. Materials include curriculum guides, textbooks, and other physical items the teacher has available. Aside from those in the classroom, facilities may include libraries and other school or community agencies. People such as aides and outside visitors may be utilized if available. Time must be allocated and organized. As professionals who understand the methods of their field, teachers should be critical users of available resources. The classroom teacher who has an understanding of the desired outcomes and knowledge about the particular students in his or her class is in the best position to plan effective and efficient instruction, choosing among or adapting the available resources to suit the unique educational situation and his or her own instructional strengths.

Airasian (1991) has cautioned against confusing means with ends in planning. Instruction is successful when students achieve the desired objectives. To accomplish this, a teacher develops several activities the students are to engage in, such as reading, writing, and discussing. Those activities need to be evaluated on the basis of whether they will lead to student attainment of the objectives. Interesting as they may be, they are not ends in their own right; they are processes, not outcomes. One of the values of having identified, assessment-oriented behavioral objectives is that they facilitate judging the value of possible instructional activities during planning.

Assessment during Instruction

Assessment that occurs during instruction is best thought of as providing information to support decisions about how to fine tune instructional plans. Teachers usually are aware of the effectiveness of their activities while these are ongoing and remain alert for potential problems, both instructional and behavioral. A teacher observes students' expressions and posture to gauge interest; he or she infers students' understanding during discussions and from the questions they ask. Observations are made of individual students and groups of students. Seatwork and homework are more formal ways teachers track developing knowledge and understanding. These forms of assessment are all ways of monitoring instruction to decide about whether to take corrective actions.

Three suggestions are given by Airasian (1991) to help improve assessment during instruction. First, remembering the distinction between processes and outcomes, a teacher should consciously try to assess the development of learning and not just how involved students are in the instruction. Second, information should be based on observations across the range of students in the class. Many teachers have a tendency to focus on a small group of students for decision making, but what is best for them may not be best for all. Third, remembering the need for triangulation, teachers should include formal types of assessment, such as homework and seatwork, to supplement their informal observations.

Formal Interpersonal Communication

Assessment using interpersonal communication may also take place in more formal ways. Examples include face-to-face meetings such as interviews and oral examinations as well as interchanges by telephone or mail (traditional or electronic). In these instances, the setting is usually overtly contrived for an assessment purpose. While there are general rules that are followed in most instances, virtually all such assessments quickly become unique as the participants interact. This capitalizes on one of the strengths of interpersonal communication. It is possible to follow up on issues raised and points made, probing for further evidence that may be needed to make eventual decisions. In such a flexible atmosphere, it is often tempting to stray from the function of collecting information pertinent to decision making as interest is sparked about topics that arise. The user of formal interpersonal communication for assessment should do so only when the resources (e.g., time) allow and should remember that the uniqueness of each assessment brings with it the possibility that irrelevant characteristics can affect the process. For example, the person being assessed may attempt to mask information he or she feels may lead to a negative interpretation (people differ in their abilities to do that). Persons who use such assessment differ in their abilities to elicit information with appropriate breadth and depth to be valid as well as to interpret the information they have learned. The principle of triangulation applies well for users of interpersonal communication; supplementing what has been learned with data from other sources enhances the validity of the basis for the decision to be made, particularly when the decision is important.

INTERPRETING ASSESSMENTS

Data arising from interpersonal communication are usually interpreted subjectively. However, additional methods are needed to translate numerical data, such as test scores, into judgment. Without these methods, they are just numbers. Two fundamentally different ways to infer meaning from numerical scores are criterion referencing and norm referencing. Measurement professionals disagree about which type of interpretation is best for classroom teachers to use and the voluminous literature around this topic has become quite confused (Mehrens & Lehmann, 1991).

Criterion and Norm Referencing

In criterion referencing, scores are compared with standards that have been previously defined. There may be a cutoff score necessary for a pass–fail judgment, there may be percentages of the maximum possible score that are needed for different letter grades, or the percentages themselves may be interpreted. In each case, rules for interpretation exist prior to administration of the assessment to the students being judged.

In norm referencing, scores are compared with other scores for judgment. A student who achieves the highest score in the class may be judged to be superior, a student who receives the lowest score to be inferior, and a student at the median to be average on the characteristic being assessed. Such judgment depends on the scores of others, which must be obtained before interpretations are developed.

If criterion referencing is used, then the achievement of any one student depends on what he or she does as opposed to how others do. It is also possible to explain to a student before the assessment how well he or she needs to do to achieve each degree of success and to interpret each score before collecting all the rest of them. Further, a student is not penalized by being in a superior class or advantaged by being in an inferior class. These are desirable features.

There are drawbacks to criterion referencing. While it makes sense to say that Jessica can add accurately two-digit numbers without carrying or spell words on a specific list correctly 80% of the time, it means less to say that she can add two-digit numbers or spell with 80% accuracy, even less to say that she has mastered 80% of what should be known about hurricanes, even less to say that she knows 80% of the Civil War, and even less to say that she has learned 80% of a topic such as United States history or written communication. The differences among these examples have to do with the nature of the domain being assessed.

When a domain can be defined explicitly, a degree of knowledge can be interpreted meaningfully, but as a domain becomes less precise, our understanding about what it contains becomes less clear and the tasks students can be asked to do to demonstrate proficiency become less comparable. Such notions as tests being hard or easy arise from this lack of comparability. If we are to believe that 80% is meaningful on a test, we need the assumption that different tests covering the same domain would yield similar scores, but writing even just two equivalent tests over the same domain is virtually impossible unless the domain is highly circumscribed.

Comparing proficiency among different content domains is even less justifiable. When we compare Ryan's 90% on an assessment of a science unit with his 80% on an assessment of an English unit to draw a conclusion that he is better at science, we must assume not only that the tests are equivalently difficult but that they represent their domains in equivalent ways. Further, an extraordinarily difficult test is subject to a "floor effect," in which students who differ in achievement nevertheless receive similar scores near the bottom of the possible range, while an extraordinarily easy test usually reflects a "ceiling effect," where students with high achievement receive similar scores near the maximum but actually differ.

Considerations such as these have led some professionals to recommend norm referencing. All norm-referenced interpretations are based on relative position in some group. Some methods to do that are

- Percentile ranks: A percentile rank is the percentage of the group that is below a given student's score; a related term is a percentile, which is the score a given percentage of the group is below.
- Scaled scores: These are derived to have a certain mean (average) and standard deviation (square root of the average squared deviation from the mean), such as a mean of 0 and a standard deviation of 1 (called standard scores or *z* scores), a mean of 50 and a standard deviation of 10 (called T scores), a mean of 500 and a standard deviation of 100 (used on the Scholastic Assessment Test), or a mean of 100 and a standard deviation of 15 (used on many IQ tests).
- Grade-equivalents: This is the grade, and months in that grade, at which other students are whose average on the test is the same as the student's score being interpreted.

There are also drawbacks to norm referencing. Whereas criterion-referenced interpretations require understanding about the domain that is often unrealistic, norm-referenced interpretations require similar understanding about the group. Great care is taken to ensure a representative sample of students in norming nationally standardized tests but in the classroom such a luxury is impossible. Even if a teacher feels confident that he or she can evaluate the abilities of a particular class accurately, justifying that understanding to others is difficult. It is also difficult to communicate the sometimes rather technical processes by which norm-referenced scores are derived and many people infer inaccurate meanings from them (percentile ranks are likely the easiest for unsophisticated audiences to understand). Finally, judging students with respect to each other can place them in competition with their classmates, with negative consequences for an atmosphere of student cooperation in learning many teachers desire.

Many measurement professionals feel that norms are implicit in criteria because criteria are expectations based on what students have been able to do in the past. In other words, to be realistic as an expectation for a student, a criterion must be achievable, but evidence for achievability comes from the achievement of other students. Derived scores based on norms often become criteria. For example, IQ score cutoffs are commonly used for special education placement, college admissions test cutoffs are used for eligibility decisions and course assignments, and standardized achievement test cutoffs are used for admission into special programs. This further confuses the distinction between criteria and norms.

Because neither approach seems implicitly superior, many teachers interpret tests using a combination of the two ways. Standards are developed, either using fixed percentages of total possible score or some other method, and then the scores students obtain are adjusted, sometimes called *curving*, based on the performance of the group.

Setting Standards

Although using fixed percentages for different grades is common, even mandated in many school districts, there are some serious drawbacks to them as a way to set standards. As previously mentioned, writing equivalent tests is unrealistic for most content domains. Writing tests that match specific grade-range interpretations is even harder. Further, interpreting computed percentages as percentages of achievement requires assuming that nothing learned is measured as zero points on the test and that complete proficiency is measured as the maximum score. These assumptions are virtually never justified. At the lower end, a score of zero is typically possible for a range of achievement levels or may be very unlikely (e.g., when guessing leads to nonzero scores, such as in multiple-choice tests), and at the upper end, achievement is almost always possible beyond the range being assessed. It is unreasonable to attempt to scale achievement on a continuum with a fixed minimum and a fixed maximum.

Various alternatives exist for setting criterion-related standards that do not require other students' scores. Since tests differ, judging the difficulty of each of the particular test items is usually suggested. Useful information may also be learned from how students perform on a test. An approach adapted from recommendations by Angoff (1971) and Hambleton (1978) that combines criterion referencing and norm referencing is described here. It is assumed that a teacher has developed a test and wants to establish a pass–fail cutoff score or cutoff scores for different grades. If there is more than one cutoff-score level, the procedure is the same for each one. First, the teacher mentally imagines a large group of students who are exactly at the border in achievement (e.g., if a cutoff between the grades of A and B is desired, the teacher should be thinking of a large group of people who minimally deserve As). Then, reviewing each item, he or she estimates what that group would average on the item (the average, of course, will be within the range of the lowest possible to the greatest possible item score). The item averages are added to arrive at the cutoff. If possible, a group of teachers can do this independently, and their item averages compared and discrepancies resolved. Finally, the actual performance of students on the test can be compared with the cutoffs and perhaps the cutoffs adjusted. Teachers and other professionals who apply this method seem often to feel they have erred on the side of making the cutoffs too high when they see actual test scores and react by lowering the cutoffs. If the test is to be used for more than one group of students, its agreement with the instruction each has received should be evaluated.

Curving

The practice of "curving" deserves some discussion. The term is used loosely here because in most instances there is no change in the score distribution's shape. Adjusting scores on a test is usually done to arrive at a more reasonable distribution of grades relative to existing cutoffs. It is fundamentally a norm-referenced process, depending on the actual scores students have earned on the test. One way this is often accomplished is to add enough points to each student's score so that the highest score actually achieved on the test becomes the maximum possible score (percentages are sometimes based on the adjusted scores, so the highest earned percentage becomes 100). This practice should be discouraged, since the most extreme observed score on any assessment is more a function of chance than virtually any other characteristic of the resulting distribution of scores (the mean, on the other hand, is one of those least affected by chance), and since earning high scores may have negative social consequences if others feel their own "curved" scores would otherwise have been higher. Another practice that should be discouraged is placing cutoffs at observed gaps in the distribution of test scores; these gaps would likely be in different places were an equivalent test given to the same students.

If curving is desired, it is best to use dependable characteristics of the distribution of scores as the basis. Two of the most stable statistics are the mean and the standard deviation, the first describing the general location of the scores and the second their variability. The mean is the arithmetic average and the standard deviation is the square root of the average of all the squared differences between each score and the mean. These statistics are readily available in almost all spreadsheet computer software. A standard score (z score) may be computed for each student by subtracting the mean from his or her score and dividing that difference by the standard deviation. These z scores will have a mean of 0 and a standard deviation of 1. Two further calculations often result in a reasonably satisfying outcome. First, each score is multiplied by 10 (this changes the standard deviation to 10, leaving the mean at 0, and is done because test scores may then be interpreted in 10-point ranges, such as 90–100 becomes an A. Second, the desired average score is added. If it is desired that about half the class receive As and Bs, and 80 is the cutoff for B, the teacher could add 80. Table 2 shows an example of this process. Since whatever is added at the last step becomes the average score, there is room for subjective judgment by the teacher about what the average score should be. Finally, these cutoffs should be judged on the basis of whether they are reasonable (e.g., result in appropriate grades) and further adjusted if they do not. It should be mentioned that curving is effective only in large classes since small classes produce unstable means and standard deviations. (Un)fortunately, most class sizes are large enough for curving to be reasonable.

GRADING

Grades are the currency of the classroom. As students learn, they earn grades as their basic extrinsic reward. The typical teacher, who as Hills (1991) has noted functions virtually without supervision in all areas of classroom assessment, has wide latitude in the ways grades are awarded, district policy notwithstanding. These grades have important consequences for judgment about students by others (e.g., parents, other teachers, counselors, employers) and by themselves (e.g., as they develop their academic self-concepts). Yet the procedures individual teachers use are mostly a function of their idiosyncratic value systems. Drawing primarily from work by Frisbie and Waltman (1992), this section describes some of the choices teachers make and suggests some steps that can be taken to develop a plan for assigning grades. Finally, some common grading practices that are likely to have negative effects are noted.

Value Choices in Grading

Grades are symbols that carry meaning and are used in communicating to others. But what meaning should they convey? Should they indicate levels

TABLE 2
Equal-Weighted Averages and Ranks of Seven Students' Scores on Three Quizzes

Quiz	Alan	Barb	Carl	Dawn	Eric	Fred	Gwen	Mean (M)	Standard Deviation (S)
			Student Raw Scores (X)						
1	36	32	16	24	20	28	12	24	8
2	26	23	28	25	27	24	29	26	2
3	16	20	26	22	24	18	28	22	4
Average	26	25	23.3	23.7	23.7	23.3	19.7		
Rank	1	2	5.5	3.5	3.5	5.5	7		
			Student Transformed Scores: $T = 10 [(X - M)/S] + 80$						
1	95	90	70	80	75	85	65		
2	80	65	90	75	85	70	95		
3	65	75	90	80	85	70	95		
Average	80	76.7	83.3	78.3	81.7	75	85		
Rank	4	6	2	5	3	7	1		

of understanding, amounts of effort, how much a student has gained, or the degree to which the student behaved appropriately? A single symbol cannot mean all these things, but different teachers' practices imply different beliefs about these issues, as well as those that follow.

The failing grade is of special significance. Students who fail are often forced into actions they would otherwise not be taking, such as repeating classes, grades, or attending special sessions. But what does failure mean? Is it no understanding, very low achievement, lack of effort, or an indication that the consequences of failure are in the best interest of the student?

Teachers have available to them a wealth of information on each student. This includes data from examples of assessment from different content domains within each area that a grade is given, from different assessment opportunities and methods, and of various characteristics that do not directly indicate achievement, such as work habits and participation. But availability does not imply relevance. Which of these should enter into grading decisions, what contribution should each have, and how can those contributions best be incorporated into the grade?

How much information is needed and of what types? What should be done about suspicious data such as tests that appear too hard or easy, work that appears not to have been done by the student, or pieces of information that conflict with each other?

Is it important that there be some desired distribution of the different grades? If so, what percentage of each is appropriate and how much latitude should there be around these percentages? Should the percentages change as the year progresses? Is it appropriate for an individual teacher to deviate markedly from the percentages typically given by other teachers?

What should be done about borderline cases? When a case is borderline, is it best to err on the side of leniency or severity? If additional data are used for borderline cases, what information is appropriate and how should it be obtained?

Throughout their schooling, most students have encountered teachers whose values about grading differ markedly from each other. Since grading is under almost total control of the teacher, students generally come to accept this variation as normal and try to determine early on what each individual teacher values. Whatever their beliefs, each teacher can give his or her students helpful direction by being explicit about how they will be rewarded.

Developing a Grading Plan

It is useful for each teacher to follow a process by which a careful grading plan can be developed in order to translate his or her values into a coherent system that can be used fairly and explained to others. Frisbie and Waltman (1992) have described a nine-step approach.

The First Step

Learn about district policies concerning grading. In most districts, not much is specified beyond some general statements often found on report cards or other documents approved formally by the district. They provide little in the way of answers to questions like those just raised. However, where explicit policy does exist, it is incumbent upon a teacher to apply it. The principal or other school-level administrator can help resolve conflicts between district policy and individual teacher values. If that fails, it is possible to consult with colleagues and perhaps question and attempt to change the district policy. In each of the remaining steps, then, it is assumed that district policy is silent on the issues raised.

The Second Step

Establish meaning for each available grading symbol. Three issues must be resolved: whether the symbols should have a criterion-referenced interpretation or a norm-referenced interpretation, whether they should reflect achievement or effort, and whether they should reflect status or growth over time.

Norm-referenced meanings are accomplished by comparisons with others. Terms such as "well above average" for a grade of A and "below average" for a grade of D are norm referenced. Criterion-referenced grades, on the other hand, are described in terms of amounts. For A, for example, a descriptor might be "strong command of subject" or "solid preparation for future learning." For D, such interpretations as "deficient in some basic areas" or "lacks many prerequisites for future learning" might be appropriate. Teachers who use a combination of criterion and norm referencing may provide both as alternate interpretations.

While effort, in general, leads to achievement, no one grade can reflect both. Although it is difficult for a teacher to give a low grade to a student who tries hard but does not succeed or a high grade to a student who succeeds with little effort, measurement professionals generally recommend that achievement be the basis for grading. The primary reason is that consumers of grades (parents, counselors, employers, etc.) will interpret them as reflecting what a student can do (mastery of material) as opposed to how hard he or she worked. A desirable feature of a grading system might be to give two grades in any area to indicate each of these. But when only one is possible, using criteria that will form the basis of eventual interpretations will communicate most effectively. Similar considerations lead most measurement professionals to recommend that status at the end of the grading period be used to assign grades instead of growth over time.

The Third Step

Compare the meanings for grades identified at the second step with the teacher's instructional approach. If the assessments a teacher uses are norm referenced, then norm-referenced interpretations of grades would be most consistent logically. If students in a given class work often in groups, then criterion referencing of grades would be more reasonable because they are more compatible with cooperative learning.

The Fourth Step

Differentiate between assessment that is used for grading and assessment that is used for other purposes. Sizing-up assessment, for example, should be used for purposes other than grading. Another example is formative assessment intended to further instruction but not to determine degree of attainment at the end of the unit.

The Fifth Step

Learn how other teachers of similar content areas tend to grade. Teachers whose grade distributions are markedly different from their colleagues probably attach different meanings to those grades. However, other people who receive and use the information will not understand those differences. Since a grade is fundamentally a means of communication, it should convey meaning within the frame of reference of the person who receives it. The best guide is the practices of others. Where students are tracked, it is also important to know whether the different tracks have produced different distributions in the past.

The Sixth Step

Determine how much and what sorts of information are needed for the grade. In general, the more the information (within practical limits), the greater is the reliability; and the more varied the information, the greater is the validity. Over the variety of assessment methods, different students are likely to be advantaged and disadvantaged differently. Some students excel at group work, others do well at oral communication, still others do best on essay examinations or perhaps term papers, for some physical manipulation or demonstrations may allow maximum performance, and others may do best on multiple-choice assessments. Further, information about each of the various units and components of outcomes within a grading period should be collected.

The Seventh Step

Decide, for each of the components, how much weight it should have in the grade. One way to do this is to assign percents to each separate item of information. A useful guideline is to weight according to the amount of instruction each piece represents, underweighting those that cover equivalent objectives and overweighting those that provide more reliable scores. These weights are used most easily if they sum to 1 (i.e., if they are proportions).

The Eighth Step

Decide how the components should be combined for a final composite to base grades on. A teacher using a criterion-referenced approach could find the percentages of maximum for each student on each component. When each component is expressed as a percentage, it is reasonable to multiply each percentage by the weight (a proportion) and add the products. The result is a weighted percentage composite.

If the teacher is using a norm-referenced approach, it is important to adjust the components so that their variabilities are equal before combining them. Table 2, which shows quiz scores earned by each of seven students, has been constructed to show that this can have a significant impact on the result. Say the teacher plans to weight each quiz equally. Finding the simple averages of the quiz scores originally earned by the seven students is shown first. Looking at these averages (and the class ranks based on them), some may feel uncomfortable with the outcome. In particular, Gwen earned the highest score on two out of the three quizzes but still had the lowest ranking. Notice that the quizzes' standard deviations are quite different. Gwen happened to score lowest on the quiz that had the largest variability. Since variability is mostly a function of the nature of the quiz (or other assessment), it seems unreasonable to penalize her for happening to exhibit poorer performance on the quiz with the greatest standard deviation. Indeed, her outstanding performance on the other two quizzes is swamped by the comparatively greater differences the first quiz produced.

When the procedure described earlier is used to transform all the scores to a scale with equal means and standard deviations, Gwen's average jumps from the lowest in the class to the highest, more accurately reflecting the equal weights the teacher intends. Had the teacher used the original scores to determine grades, the grades would mostly have been the result of the first quiz, and differences on the other two would have been relatively minor in comparison.

The Ninth Step

Establish a method to convert the composites to grades. Using prespecified cutoffs is usually best. Since grades are interpreted as representing achievement, it is appropriate that assessments of achievement status be used to determine them. Students whose composites are near the cutoffs, however, are about equally well represented by either of the adjacent grades that could be assigned. Perhaps a teacher might want to use growth, effort, or both to make the determination in these instances. Whatever the policy, it should be established and used consistently for all grades given.

Avoiding Poor Grading Practices

Unfortunately, most of this section will be familiar. The need teachers have to use grades, the autonomy they have in grading, and the inaccessibility of effective material for teachers to use in developing sound grading approaches, such as the recommendations of Frisbie and Waltman (1992) summarized earlier, have led many to apply their own idiosyncratic notions to grading. Many common practices, while seemingly sensible to some, actually interfere with student learning, accurate assessment, or both. Canady and Hotchkiss (1989) and Hills (1991) have identified several of these. The suggestions that follow are in response to the practices found in these sources.

Consistent meanings for letter grades should be used by different teachers and from school to school. An effort should be made to ensure that teachers in a given school are grading consistently. School-to-school variation is more difficult to eliminate but the advantages of being able to compare grades from different schools are obvious. Other grading policies should also be consistent, such as whether late work is accepted and whether test or quiz score are dropped in computing averages.

Different ranges should not be used for the different letter grades. This is particularly a problem for the grade of F. In some cases, an F is very close to a D, a poor but passing grade, but in others it is very far away. While this is also true for other grades, the larger range often allocated to F (e.g., 0 to 64%) emphasizes its uncertainty.

Atypical assessments should be de-emphasized. Unusual assessment results for a particular student often occur for nonacademic reasons. A disruptive event at home or at school can lead to a poor score. The validity of these "surprising" results should be questioned and their effects on grades de-emphasized. Perhaps a private discussion with the student about the cause of the unusual outcome would be helpful as a sizing-up assessment.

A score of 0 should not be used for missing or incomplete work. A 0 is so far from a passing grade on many teachers' grading scales that its effect on a student's average is devastating. As mentioned earlier, a 0 is not a meaningful indication of achievement; it is best viewed as just another arbitrary number. Furthermore, missing information provides no valid evidence for an inference about the student's learning. A grading system that incorporates zeros in this way is best regarded as punitive.

Grades should be based on summative assessments rather than formative assessments. Formative assessments (e.g., interim quizzes, homework or seatwork, first drafts of papers) are useful for instructional purposes while learning is ongoing. Grades, however, should be based on summative assessments of learning when instructional units have been completed.

The coverage of tests should not be biased toward recall as opposed to higher-order thinking. Higher-order outcomes are emphasized in most actual instruction. Therefore, summative (and formative) assessments are inconsistent with instruction if they focus heavily on recall.

Unannounced (pop) quizzes should not be given. Although they are used primarily to motivate students to study throughout an instructional unit, announced quizzes can do that more effectively. Further, unannounced quizzes assess only uncompleted learning, waste valuable instructional time, and introduce unnecessary anxiety in students.

Opportunity should exist to improve during a grading period. Some teachers give so much emphasis to assessments occurring early in a grading period that students are not able to increase their grades very much, if at all. Students may understandably lose motivation if they do not believe that their continuing efforts will be reflected in the grades they earn.

What will be covered on tests should be clear to students. Earlier, it was suggested that tests and other assessments should not surprise students. They should be aware of the objectives of the teacher and understand what they will be asked to do to provide evidence of their learning. Otherwise, they will be guessing about how to prepare; each student instead of the teacher will be determining what he or she should be studying.

Different standards should not be used to grade different levels of a course. Upper levels of a course are more demanding than lower levels. However, similar achievement should result in similar grades no matter what the level. But this is still a difficult issue since the objectives can differ for different levels. An approach some schools use is to increase the quality-points assigned to higher levels so teachers are able to use similar distributions of grades in different levels.

The importance and reliability of each assessment should be reflected in its weight. Many teachers simply weight all available assessments equally. Many also use ineffective procedures for combining them. Recommendations for factors to consider in weighting and ways to combine assessments appropriately were discussed already.

Grades should not be used to control student behavior. Since grades are the primary tangible reward teachers control, it is tempting to use them to maintain discipline. However, the grades then lose their meanings as indicators of achievement. It is better to show students that how they act affects what they learn and to use learning as the basis for their rewards.

Grades should not be based on improvement or effort. As discussed previously, grades will be misinterpreted if they are used to show either improvement or effort.

Assessment instruments of poor quality should not be used. Many teachers use instruments that have not been developed carefully, by either them or others such as authors of curriculum materials. Suggestions for improving assessments were given earlier.

Standardized test administration procedures should not be altered. Although standardized tests are not typically reflected in grades, they are also used for communicating achievement, usually to the same audiences (e.g., parents, administrators, other teachers). Indeed, they are commonly the only formal source of information parents and others have about student achievement that is independent of teacher judgment. An exception is examples of student work collected into portfolios; see Chapter 19. What makes a test standardized is its conditions of administration (not its item format, as popularly believed). Because a standardized test is given using consistent procedures, the scores students obtain may be compared with those of other students and with those of a norm group, if the test is normed. Altering the conditions compromises the consistency needed to make those comparisons. Teachers who deviate from the directions for administration therefore are invalidating the test for their students and reducing the value of what is often an expensive assessment opportunity.

Improving Understandings about Assessment

Classroom assessment is the topic of a full course in many (although too few) teacher education programs. This chapter is intended to cover many of the topics in a modern classroom assessment course, but space restrictions necessitate that numerous supporting details and some entire topics be omitted. Several excellent textbooks on classroom assessment exist for further reading, and the National Council on Measurement in Education has made available, through its publication *Educational Measurement: Issues and Practice*, several valuable instructional modules that may be copied freely for educational purposes. Many of these are included in the reference list. These sources may be consulted to learn more. Finally, the statement of Standards for Teacher Competence in Educational Assessment of Students, approved by the American Federation of Teachers, the National Council on Measurement in Education, and the National Education Association is available from all three organizations and provides a concise discussion of what classroom teachers should know about assessment. It may be used as a guide for choosing professional development activities that lead to deeper understanding about assessment and, consequently, to more effective teaching.

References

Airasian, P. W. (1991). *Classroom assessment*. New York: McGraw-Hill.

American Federation of Teachers, National Council on Measurement in Education, & National Education Association (1990). Standards for teacher competence in educational assessment of students. *Educational Measurement: Issues and Practice*, 9(4), 30–32.

Angoff, W. H. (1971). Scales, norms, and equivalent scores. In R. L. Thorndike (Ed.), *Educational measurement* (2nd ed., pp. 508–600). Washington, DC: American Council on Education.

Canady, R. L., & Hotchkiss, P. R. (1989). It's a good score! Just a bad grade. *Phi Delta Kappan*, 71, 68–71.

Clark, C. M., & Peterson, P. L. (1986). Teachers' thought processes. In M. C. Wittrock (Ed.), *Handbook of research on teaching* (3rd ed., pp. 255–296). New York: Macmillan.

Fleming, M., & Chambers, B. (1983). Teacher-made tests: Windows on the classroom. In W. E. Hathaway (Ed.), *Testing in the schools, new directions in testing and measurement* (Vol. 19, pp. 29–38). San Francisco: Jossey-Bass.

Frisbie, D. A., & Waltman, K. K. (1992). Developing a personal grading plan. *Educational Measurement: Issues and Practice*, 11(3), 35–42.

Hambleton, R. K. (1978). On the use of cut-off scores with criterion-referenced tests in instructional settings. *Journal of Educational Measurement*, 15, 277–290.

Herman, J. L., Aschbacher, P. R., & Winters, L. (1992). A *practical guide to alternative assessment*. Alexandria, VA: Association for Supervision and Curriculum Development.

Hills, J. R. (1991). Apathy concerning grading and testing. *Phi Delta Kappan*, 72, 540–545.

Mehrens, W. A., & Lehmann, I. J. (1991). *Measurement and evaluation in education and psychology* (4th ed.). Fort Worth, TX: Holt, Rinehart & Winston.

Messick, S. (1995). Validation of inferences from persons' responses and performances as scientific inquiry into score meaning. *American Psychologist*, 50, 741–749.

Newman, D. C., & Stallings, W. M. (1982, March). *Teacher competency in classroom testing, measurement preparation, and classroom teaching practices*. Paper presented at the annual meeting of the National Council on Measurement in Education, New York. (ERIC Document Reproduction Service No. ED 220 491)

Plake, B. S., Impara, J. C., & Fager, J. J. (1993). Assessment competencies of teachers: A national survey. *Educational Measurement: Issues and Practice*, 12(4), 10–12, 39.

Rudner, L. M., & Boston, C. (1994). Performance assessment. *Eric Review*, 3(1), 2–12.

Schafer, W. D., & Lissitz, R. W. (1987). Measurement training for school personnel: Recommendations and reality. *Journal of Teacher Education*, 38(3), 57–63.

Shavelson, R. J. (1973). *The basic teaching skill: Decision making* (R & D Memorandum No. 104). Stanford, CA: Stanford University, School of Education, Center for R & D in Teaching.

Stiggins, R. J. (1987). Design and development of performance assessments. *Educational Measurement: Issues and Practice*, 6(3), 33–42.

Stiggins, R. J. (1988). Revitalizing classroom assessment: The highest instructional priority. *Phi Delta Kappan*, 69, 363–368.

Stiggins, R. J. (1991). Relevant classroom assessment training for teachers. *Educational Measurement: Issues and Practice*, 10(1), 7–12.

Stiggins, R. J. (1992). High quality classroom assessment: What does it really mean? *Educational Measurement: Issues and Practice*, 11(2), 35–39.

Stiggins, R. J., Conklin, N. F., & Bridgeford, N. J. (1986). Classroom assessment: A key to educational excellence. *Educational Measurement: Issues and Practice*, 5(2), 5–17.

Wise, S. L., Lukin, L. E., & Roos, L. L. (1991). Teacher beliefs about training in testing and measurement. *Journal of Teacher Education*, 42(1), 37–42.

CHAPTER

18

Assessing Classroom Learning Potential

J. H. M. HAMERS
Utrecht University, The Netherlands

A. J. J. M. RUIJSSENAARS
Leiden University, The Netherlands

An essential part of learning potential assessment procedures is the identification of children with academic problems and the description of their strengths and weaknesses in such a way that remedial measures can be designed. A stimulus for using these procedures is the dissatisfaction with features of the standardized "static" intelligence and school achievement tests. In these tests children are asked to reproduce declarative knowledge, to combine known information, or to solve different types of problems without any kind of help. In general, learning potential assessment procedures aim to go beyond this method of testing by assessing the general and specific psychological processes needed to solve the test items. In the past, some children may not have acquired the knowledge or skills being assessed but are able to do so with help. The future learning of these children is presumed to be better than one would expect on the basis of their initial, unaided "static" test performance. To generate this additional learning and process-directed information, designers of learning potential tests use a variety of techniques, all of which involve the provision of some form of help or training to the child.

Learning potential assessment procedures not only can play a role in studying learning problems in general but also in the early identification of so-called learning disabilities. Learning disabled children usually are defined as being of average or above average intelligence but having specific problems in reading, spelling, or arithmetic. This definition can be operationalized as the discrepancy between an IQ test score and the actual reading, spelling, or arithmetic achievement. However, the validity of this discrepancy concept can be questioned (Hamers & Ruijssenaars, 1984).

The main purpose of this chapter is to address the role of learning potential assessment procedures in classroom teaching. Furthermore, we will clarify the role of IQ tests and school achievement tests in the definition and operationalization of the learning disability concept. As a guideline for this discussion, we refer to current insights and developments in learning potential assessment research. In this research, the attention has been shifted from test construction to assessing classroom learning and the early identification of learning problems.

LEARNING POTENTIAL ASSESSMENT

Learning potential assessment (e.g., Carlson, 1995; Feuerstein 1979; Guthke, 1977; Hamers, Sijtsma & Ruijssenaars, 1993; Haywood & Tzuriel, 1992; Ivanova, 1973; Kalmykova, 1975; Lidz, 1987) is a relatively new branch on the assessment tree. Much of its recent interest can be traced back to criticism of current intelligence tests. Some criticism concerns the use of IQ tests for selection and referral decisions in school practice, especially because of sources of unfairness in these tests: intelligence tests are unfair to sociocultural, economic, and racial–ethnic minority groups, and their outcomes can lead to social and economical injustices (e.g., Hessels & Hamers, 1993; Van de Vijver, 1993). It is also argued that intelligence test performance is influenced by a variety of irrelevant motivational and personality variables (e.g., Meijer, 1993). A main controversy, however, is rooted in the criticism that current IQ tests and school performance tests focus on end products of learning and ignore the relevant processes underlying test performance (Sternberg, 1982). The analysis of cognitive processes can enrich the understanding of what these tests measure and facilitate the identification of weak and strong aspects of cognitive functioning. As a result of this analysis, the diagnostic- and treatment-oriented value of tests will be enhanced.

Theoretically, learning potential testing starts with the principle that a test should not only measure previously acquired knowledge and skills, as is the case with conventional intelligence tests, but also *"the ability to learn"* (Lidz, 1987). Therefore, learning potential tests should measure the capacity to adapt to new situations, making use of past experiences. This description corresponds with Dearborn's (1921) definition of *intelligence*: "Intelligence is the capacity to learn or profit by experience." In much learning potential research this definition is accepted as the leading concept (Hamers et al., 1993). A learning potential test has the psychometric properties of a regular test but differs from it with respect to its administration procedure in that a conventional pretest is followed by a training phase and a post-test.

Vygotsky (1978) is generally regarded as the creator of the concept of learning potential, and his zone of potential development (ZPD) has become the cornerstone in learning potential research. Vygotsky (1978) described ZPD as "the distance between the actual developmental level as determined by independent problem solving and the level of potential development as determined through problem solving under adult guidance or in collaboration with more capable peers" (pp. 85–86). Luria (1961) transformed Vygotsky's qualitative developmental assessment procedure to a quantitative one, by translating the dynamic interaction between adult and child into a standardized training phase between the pre- and post-tests. By comparing pretest and post-test scores, Luria (1961) was able to differentiate between a child's actual (pretest) and potential (post-test) performance level and establish a rediagnosis for children whose initial intelligence test scores were low. Some of these children improved their performance substantially and were no longer considered to be mentally retarded despite their low initial test scores.

Studies in which Luria's interpretation of ZPD was used were also reported by Budoff and Friedman (1964). Using the Koh's learning potential task, these authors came to comparable findings with educable mentally retarded children. Fifteen years later, we find the same principles in the work of Brown and French (1979). They also make a distinction between a child's actual level of performance as measured with a standardized test and the potential level reflected by the degree of competence he or she can achieve with help. Help consists of providing progressive cues to facilitate problem solving. The number of cues needed reflects the "width" of the zone. Children who need a small number of cues show effective transfer (Brown & French, 1979, p. 260). In line with this, some researchers claim that learning potential tests are better predictors of school performance (Guthke, 1977; Hamers & Ruijssenaars, 1984, 1986; Hessels, 1993) or consider them as better suited for prescriptive purposes in education (e.g., Campione & Brown, 1987; Ruijssenaars & Oud, 1987).

In our own research thus far we have explored two themes. In initial studies (e.g., Hamers, Hessels & Van Luit, 1991; Hamers & Ruijssenaars, 1984, 1986) we examined the relation between general learning processes and overall academic ability. In more recent projects (Hamers, Pennings, & Guthke, 1994; Ruijssenaars, 1991), we gave more attention to the "dynamic" assessment of learning processes related to specific domains of the school curriculum in reading, spelling and arithmetic. An important aim of this last type of studies is to specify the processes in sufficient detail to serve as a basis for adapting classroom instruction. In an overview of studies on learning potential we will discuss the results of both the initial and recent projects in the next paragraphs.

INITIAL STUDIES

In the initial studies, the learning potential tests measured mostly domain-general processes like figural, reasoning concept formation, number series, and paired associate learning. These tasks are the same as in conventional intelligence tests and improvement of predictive validity was the main objective (Guthke, 1983; Hamers et al., 1991). To illustrate this we will describe learning potential tests for children of minority groups. First we discuss the problem of assessing minority groups.

An important research finding is that mean scores on psychological tests of children of dominant Western cultures are usually significantly higher than those of minority groups (e.g., Jensen, 1980). The cause of these differences is not obvious, but one possible explanation is that the tests are culturally biased. That is, minority children do not score lower on intelligence tests due to an inability but rather due to an inherent cultural bias of the tests. The (white) middle-class orientation of test constructors and their lack of relevant experience in taking tests are considered as the main causes of this bias. The cultural bias hypothesis has extensively been reviewed in literature (Jensen, 1980).

Teunissen and Golhof (1987) pointed out that the number of ethnic minority children in primary schools in the Netherlands has been increasing steadily since the immigration waves in the 1960s and 1970s. At first, this was not accompanied by a similar growth of the number of ethnic minority children in special education. In 1982, ethnic minority children were still underrepresented in special education. This is remarkable since the children who immigrated entered the educational system at an older age and lower academic achievement therefore could be expected. Apparently, at that time, their lower achievement was no reason for referral to special education. However, four years later, the percentage of ethnic minority children in special education was twice as much, resulting in an overrepresentation, especially in schools for the mentally retarded.

Three explanations are offered for this change (Theunissen & Golhof, 1987). The first is that the teacher's opinions about learning backwardness of ethnic minority children changed. They were more and more inclined to attribute learning deficiencies to differences in intelligence and less to cultural and linguistic differences or to an inhibitive environment. A second explanation is the diminution of extra facilities for schools with many ethnic minority pupils. As a result, teachers refer more children to schools for special education. A third explanation is the cultural bias of intelligence tests used in referral procedures.

For the assessment of ethnic minority group children, conventional intelligence tests or parts of these tests usually are administered. In general, school psychologists do not consider these tests adequate measures of the cognitive abilities of ethnic minority children. It appears, however, that selection and placement of minority children on the basis of IQ-scores still are common practice. The underlying assumption is that test results at least give some reliable indication of cognitive abilities.

LEARNING POTENTIAL TESTS FOR MINORITY GROUPS

In Europe, we know of three projects aiming at the construction of learning potential tests for ethnic minorities. We present them in this section. Although the studies are diverse in character, they give a representative impression of how learning potential procedures can be applied.

The Test of Children's Learning Ability

The Test of Children's Learning Ability (TCLA; Hegarty, 1979) measures what a child can learn and how easily new learning is acquired. The test is designed for the assessment of seven- to eight-year-old immigrant Pakistani and West Indian children in the United Kingdom. There are five subtests: concept formation, verbal learning of objects, number series, verbal learning of syllables, and analogies. The test procedure is based on the sequence teach, practice, test, teach, test. First, a simple task is demonstrated, followed by practice on analogous material until the instruction is understood. Then testing follows, with each test trial preceded by further practical teaching. The complete procedure can take place with nonverbal instructions, an important requirement when testing children who do not understand the standard language.

The reliability coefficients of the subtests vary from .55 (concept formation) to .80 (number series). The predictive validity is compared with that of a short form of the Wechler Intelligence Scale for Children (WISC) (similarities, vocabulary, block design, object assembly, coding). As criterion measures are administered a vocabulary test, a test for mathematics (with pictorial and computational subtests) and a reading test. The percentages of explained variance of the vocabulary criterion score by the TCLA and WISC were respectively 14.8 and 28.8%; of "pictorial" mathematics, 43.9 and 28.8%; of "computational" mathematics, 47.8 and 25.5%; and of reading, 40.8 and 24.5%. Therefore, except for vocabulary, the Test of Children's Learning Ability has a superior predictive validity.

The Learning Efficiency Battery

The Learning Efficiency Battery (LETB) (Coxhead & Gupta, 1988) was developed for Asian children ranging in age from 6 to 10 years and living in the

United Kingdom. The test battery consists of eight subtests, all falling into three categories: (1) tests based on Piaget's work (i.e., two seriation tasks, a serial correspondence task, and an ordinal correspondence task), (2) a visual sequential short-term memory task, and (3) three tests based on associative learning principles (i.e., an object picture association task, a word picture association task, and a symbol manipulation task). The LETB is based on the format demonstration, demonstration and practice, and testing. In the practice part, the child can show a capability of learning a new task with additional help. In the testing part, the responses of the child are scored according to the teaching effort that required to reach the criterion.

Factor analysis shows that the predefined three categories of subtests loaded on five distinct factors. The first factor comprises the Piagetian tests, the four remaining subtests retain their own identity. The reliability coefficients (Cronbach's alpha) vary from .77 (Piaget based tests) to .96 (symbol manipulation); retest coefficients vary from .46 (object picture association) to .98 (symbol manipulation). With respect to construct validity, the four Piagetian tasks seem to have much in common with two conventional IQ tests (i.e., Raven's Progressive Matrices and the Draw-a-Man test). The remaining subtests, though slightly correlated, are conceptually and empirically distinct. With respect to predictive validity, no substantial difference is found between the predictive value of the LETB subtests and the two conventional IQ tests. The average percentages of explained variance for mathematics as criterion variable are 41% by the LETB and 45% by the IQ tests. For reading, as a criterion variable, the percentages are 28 and 30%, respectively.

The Learning Potential Test for Ethnic Minorities

The Learning Potential Test for Ethnic Minorities (LEM; Hamers et al., 1991) is designed for Turkish and Moroccan children living in the Netherlands and for Dutch children, ranging in age from 5 years and 4 months to 7 years and 9 months. The test consists of six subtests: classification, word–object association recognition, word–object association naming, number series, syllable recall, and figurative analogies. The test has a train-within-test format. This means that training is an integral part of the test and consists of increasingly more help depending on the need of the child. The child is taught each task by demonstration and practice, until the instructions are understood completely. All instructions are nonverbal. During both practice and testing, gestures are used to instruct the child concerning what is expected.

Reliability coefficients (Cronbach's alpha) vary from .88 to .92. The test is equally reliable for Dutch, Turkish, and Moroccan children. In each of these three groups, factor analysis revealed two factors: a perceptual learning and reasoning factor and a verbal learning factor. The correlations between learning potential scores and IQ scores vary from .45 to .68. The correlations between learning potential scores and school achievement test scores used in grade 2, vary from .42 to .45 in the Turkish group and from .26 to .44 in the Moroccan group. In grade 3, the correlations between the LEM and reading comprehension, spelling, and arithmetic are .23 (not significant), .45 (significant at 1% level), and .50 (significant at 1% level), respectively.

Two statistical techniques were used to detect a cultural bias. First, factor analysis was used to determine whether the same factor structure accounts for test performance for different nationality groups. Second, rankings of item difficulties were compared between groups. It could be concluded that the two factors did not differ across ethnic groups, and in general, the rank correlations of the item *p* values between groups were above .90. But, despite a lack of bias, mean learning potential scores may differ across ethnic groups.

It was investigated therefore whether the LEM reduces differences between the various groups as compared with an IQ test. Mean learning potential scores of Dutch, Turkish, and Moroccan children were found to differ significantly. When children of the same social economical status (SES) were compared (the vast majority of Turkish and Moroccan children are of low SES), the differences between groups were markedly smaller. The differences in mean scores were reduced to 10.5 (Dutch vs. Turkish) and 9.2 (Dutch vs. Moroccan) in the youngest age group and to 7.5 (Dutch vs. Turkish) and 6.6 (Dutch vs. Moroccan) in the oldest age group. Although significant, these differences were small, especially when compared with IQ scores. It was found that the differences in IQ scores were 15.8 (Dutch vs. Turkish) and 14.0 (Dutch vs. Moroccan) in the youngest age group. In the oldest age groups the differences in IQ were 17.3 (Dutch vs. Turkish) and 17.4 (Dutch vs. Moroccan). The results thus showed that the LEM did indeed narrow the gap between Dutch and ethnic minority children. Possibly, differences stemming from cultural differences were partially reduced by including an extended practice phase and guiding the child during testing.

Further, a considerable shift in rank was found on the LEM in comparison with a conventional IQ test. Children who scored low on the IQ test either scored low, moderate, or high on the LEM. Using the conventional IQ scores, the percentage of Moroccan children that would be classified as mentally retarded was 73%, according to the LEM scores the percentage decreased to 44%. Of course, this finding has consequences for referral practice.

The aim of the studies described was to develop a test that could be used to determine the general cognitive abilities of ethnic minority children. The test therefore had to overcome the criticism of traditional intelligence tests. So, the main question was, "Do these tests meet the criticism mentioned?"

The tests appeared to be reliable instruments. Furthermore, they give a moderate prediction of school achievement, although not substantial better than traditional intelligence tests. Third, a test like the LEM appears to be nonbiased, resulting in smaller differences in scores between ethnic groups with the same SES. The LEM also strongly differentiated between children having low scores on the intelligence test. This finding may prevent children from being incorrectly labeled mentally retarded or from being unjustly referred to schools for the mentally retarded.

A second question is to what extent these tests lead to extra information that can be used in a prescriptive way to optimize further cognitive development. Although most authors argue that learning potential assessment techniques could bridge the gap between assessment and treatment, there still is a lack of a methodology enabling the translation of learning potential test results into prescriptive treatment programs for teachers. Although some serious attempts have been made (cf. Campione & Brown, 1987), it is still the beginning.

In general terms, the learning potential tests just described seem promising in tackling problems such as (1) inappropriate test content and test-wiseness by using familiarization and training, (2) inappropriate samples by providing specific norms, and (3) language bias by using nonverbal instruction. The main aim of these tests therefore is characterized as "providing a better estimate of the ability construct" (Embretson, 1987). Their theoretical basis, however, is derived from traditional psychometric theories of human intelligence. It therefore could be argued that these learning potential tests are "just" better IQ-tests.

NEW DEVELOPMENTS IN LEARNING POTENTIAL ASSESSMENT

At least two research findings in a study of Hamers and Ruijssenaars (1984, 1986) offer new perspectives in theory and practice of learning potential assessment: (1) the meaning of so-called prototypic learning tasks, and (2) the differences in learning curves, instructional need, and learning efficiency. In this section we will discuss these issues.

Prototypic Learning Tasks

Initially, in their learning potential research with first graders, Hamers and Ruijssenaars (1984, 1986) used four conventional tasks: visual discrimination, classification, figural inductive reasoning (matrices), and perceptual problem solving (block design). They based their choice on a survey of the psychological literature on cognitive tasks (e.g., Gagné & Briggs, 1974; Guilford, 1956) and learning potential research (e.g., Budoff, 1975; Guthke, 1977; Leyendecker, 1977; Roether, 1974). The tasks can be characterized as general and representative of basic tasks underlying academic learning. A result on the validity of these tasks was that their predictive power was not the same in the short term (two months) and the long term (nine months). For instance, the best predictors of long-term arithmetic achievement were inductive reasoning and problem-solving scores. The best predictors of short-term reading and spelling achievement were scores on visual discrimination. The results show that these predictors are not general in an absolute sense. Consequently, when assessing academic learning potential, it is fruitful to analyze the specific processes underlying school learning. By using such a process analysis, we came to a classification of different processes that are important in learning academic skills:

1. Learning on-task behavior.
2. Learning to discriminate and to apply discriminative characteristics.
3. Learning arbitrary visuoauditory associations.
4. Learning to apply rules and principles.
5. Learning to solve problems (simultaneous and successive processing).

A classification like this is helpful in identifying learning tasks that can be regarded as prototypical for specific curriculum-relevant learning processes. Learning arbitrary visuoauditory associations, for instance, is a crucial process in school learning. Children with learning disabilities usually show problems in learning arbitrary associations, such as the grapheme–phoneme correspondencies in reading and the declarative knowledge in arithmetic, and in the automatization of these associations. The choice for this type of tasks corresponds with the advice of Guthke (1977) to use learning tasks that are representative of the processes in school learning (Hamers & Ruijssenaars, 1984, p. 58). A maximal resemblance between learning potential task and actual school learning is achieved by using so-called simulation tasks or even real school tasks (Ruijssenaars & Oud, 1987; Spector, 1992; Swanson, 1992; Tissink, Hamers, & Van Luit, 1993; Tissink; cf. the research by Cuypers & Van de Weem, in Ruijssenaars & Hamers, 1986). In this way the prediction of future learning is very specific and can lead to prescriptions for the prevention of predicted learning problems.

In conclusion, it can be stated that, in learning potential research after a period of interest in general learning potential, attention on specific learning processes has been increasing. Later on we will discuss the usefulness of this idea in relation to principles of early detection of learning problems.

Learning Curves, Instructional Need, and Learning Efficiency

Hamers and Ruijssenaars (1984, 1986) found different types of learning curves characteristic of subgroups of children with and without learning difficulties. Pupils with high scores at the pretest remain high scorers in the intermittent tests and post-tests, whereas within the group of children with low pretest scores, a clear differentiation occurs between children with persistent low scores despite intensive help and children who benefit from direct instruction. Consistent with the philosophy of learning potential research, the amelioration of learning problems in the last group can be seen as a better indication of their cognitive potential than the pretest score.

But suppose a child's learning potential improvement is not reflected in his or her school achievement scores. In this case, we have simply created a new group of children with a discrepancy between ability and achievement. In checking for this possibility, the following analysis was performed. The results showed that on the learning task for inductive reasoning (matrices), 70% of the children with learning difficulties made substantial progress up to a normal level. On the learning task for perceptual problem solving (block design), 42% of these children made substantial progress up to a normal level.

Differences in progress is due to differences in help. Therefore, an analysis of the instruction process will further clarify this result. The instruction for giving help is standardized and prescribes when and how help gradually can be increased, resulting in a score that reflects the number of hints given. In conclusion, it can be stated that the concept of discrepancy does not reflect an absolute and stable phenomenon but needs to be specified in each case.

In line with the aforementioned results, the predictive validity of learning potential tests can be ameliorated by adding the help score to the regression analysis (Hamers & Ruijssenaars, 1984, pp. 191–193). At least some correspondence is found between learning more general tasks and the processes in school learning, despite the clear difference in task content. For that reason, it can be expected that, with a greater similarity between predictor and criterion tasks, the importance of help scores will be further extended. In addition, the same study also showed a further increase in predictive validity when there was a more precise correspondence between the instruction strategy used in the learning test and in actual school learning.

In conclusion, different learning curves seem to resemble different needs for help. Furthermore, a "help" score can be a good indicator of the amount of profit from help in other learning situations. Later on, when speaking about early detection of learning problems, we will connect this idea with insights in the automatization of learning processes.

In the foregoing paragraph we extended the learning test procedure to curriculum-related or domain-specific tasks. Perhaps this idea will lead to a more direct connection between assessment and intervention. In the following section, we will describe five studies on this type of tasks.

Association Learning Task

In two studies (Basten & Mestrom, 1987; Dierckx & Schalley, 1991) the Association Learning Task, developed for children in kindergarten, was used to

FIGURE 1
Example of items of the Association Learning Task (Ben . . . with the pen; Ann . . . with the can).

predict success in learning the system of grapheme–phoneme correspondencies in reading and spelling over a one-year interval. Of course, learning to read and spell is more complex than just knowing these correspondencies. Reading and spelling, for instance, also imply word identification strategies based on phonological processes (like sound blending and phonemic segmentation) as well as on recognition processes based on lexical knowledge. Still, it is expected that learning visual–auditory association significantly correlates with later reading processes. Further, the value for early detection and prevention could be extended by combining this task with learning tasks that represent the other aspects of the learning process.

The Association Learning Task consists of three test series of pictures in a changing order, every series representing the same 12 children. The administration procedure is as follows: the pictures of the 12 children are presented visually one at a time, together with an auditory presentation of their names. After the first and second series, it is measured with parallel sets of the same pictures how many associations can be remembered. In the third series, a memory strategy is offered by using the same pictures with a colored detail that rhymes with the verbal name of the child. For instance, "This is Ben . . . with the pen" (the pen is colored). Also, after this third series, the learning effect can be measured (association score 3). The whole procedure lasts less than 15 minutes. Figure 1 shows some of the pictures and the corresponding names.

TABLE 1
Correlations between the Two Predictors and the Reading and Spelling Tests One Year Later in First Grade (N = 61).

	EMT	Cito Technical Reading	Cito Words 1
Association 3	.50**	.44**	.53**
Learning names 2	.36**	.07	.26*

*Significant $p = .05$.
**Significant $p = .01$.

In the first study, a significant difference was found favoring children in regular kindergarten over children in special education kindergarten in using the rhyme strategy. The second study investigated the predictive validity of association score 3 for 61 children in regular kindergarten. The period of time between the administration of the learning test and the school achievement tests for reading and spelling was 12 months. At the time of the school achievement testing, the children had been in first grade for five months. Results can be compared with the subtest learning names, a subtest of a conventional intelligence test, and the Revision Amsterdam Child Intelligence Test (RAKIT) (Bleichrodt, Drenth, Zaal, & Resing, 1984). Table 1 shows the significant correlations between the two predictors (association score 3 and learning names, 2) and three school achievement tests: a word identification test with speed limit (one minute word reading, named EMT; Brus & Voeten, 1973), a word reading test without speed limit (CITO technical reading, 1; Verhoeven, 1980b) and a word spelling test (CITO words, 1; Verhoeven, 1980a).

Table 1 shows that the Association Learning Task turns out to be a reasonable predictor for reading and spelling achievement. Even though the task covers only a part of the reading and spelling process, long-term predictive validity is adequate. Further, the administration of the complete learning task takes only 15 minutes. These results justify the continued development of a psychometrically valid Association Learning Test that can be used in clinical practice.

Reading Simulation Task

Ruijssenaars and Oud (1987) addressed the question of whether or not two learning potential programs simulating the teaching of two different beginning reading methods would result in different learning. Furthermore, they examined whether measures of learning ability in the reading simulations would predict achievement on a formative reading test that was administered five months later.

The researchers analyzed two programs for initial reading that differed in content and instruction strategies. The learning outcome for both programs is automatic word recognition. The first program starts from a written whole word and its spoken equivalent. The relationship between graphemes and phonemes must be discovered by the child, supported by varied practice in matching symbols to sounds (cf. Perfetti & Lesgold, 1979). The second program starts with the spoken word. It first teaches the skills of phonemic segmentation and blending, supported by practice in auditory skills. Subsequently, the associations between sounds and letters are learned (cf. Elkonin, 1963).

In one study, researchers trained groups of kindergarten children, who had not yet learned to read, in one of two different reading simulations. One experimental group was trained to read in accordance with the principles of the first program (Training Form 1), the other group was trained in accordance with the principles of the second program (Training Form 2). In both simulations the materials consisted of six pairs of phonemes (*/k/*, */b/*, */t/*, */m/*, */o/*, */oo/*) and graphemes (letterlike symbols). With these sound–letter associations two instruction words (*boot*, *tom*, *bok*, *tok*, and *kook*) were constructed.

Training sessions given by a teacher consisted of 15 lessons of about 10 minutes each. Both experimental groups were administered a pretest, a test immediately after each lesson, and a retention test two weeks after training was completed. In every test, an unknown word (test item) had to be matched with one of four pictures. The criterion measure, a speed test for mechanical reading belonging to the first program, was readministered in the first grade after five months of reading instruction. The tests administered immediately after the lessons must be viewed as the operationalizations of learning ability.

An analysis of the series of daily measurements showed that most subjects demonstrate a rapid growth in reading achievements under both simulation conditions. However, the trends in both learning curves were different. The group of subjects trained with Training Form 1 showed steady, but significant, increases in performance from the fourth day on, whereas the group of subjects trained with Training Form 2 demonstrated rapid and significant performance increases from the 11th day. From the 11th day on, the groups did not differ significantly in meaning achievement.

For the group with Training Form 1, the correlations between the predictors (the tests of learning efficiency administered after 5, 10, and 15 lessons) and the reading speed test were .50, .62, and .70, respectively. For the group with Training Form 2, the correlations were .27, .29, and .44, respectively. The lower correlations might be because the latter group was also administered the reading speed test belonging to the first beginning reading program. It can be predicted that the pattern of correlations would be reversed for the group that would have been taught to read with the second program and tested with a formative test belonging to that program.

From the results of the first group, we can conclude that the measures of learning ability as assessed with the learning potential test are good predictors of reading achievement five months later. With respect to the variance in the last variable, 49% could be accounted for by the learning ability measures after the 15th lesson. The greater the similarity between the test situation and the actual reading situation in school, the higher is the predictive validity.

The Reading Simulation Task has some advantages and disadvantages. One of the disadvantages is that a whole series of lessons is needed before the learning to read process really starts. As a consequence, the whole procedure asks for a serious time investment from the teacher. On the other hand, the instruction is given in groups and offers an opportunity for real-life observation. The practical usefulness of the task could be further enhanced by constructing the test items in such a way that an analysis of the wrong answers would reveal problems with either the learning of correspondencies, the phonological process (sound blending), or auditory sequential memory. In addition, reaction time would give an indication of an individual's automatization capacity. It has to be questioned, however, whether it is realistic to attempt to get reliable and valid information on every aspect of a learning process with just one learning task.

In one of the research projects (Ruijssenaars & Coppens, 1991), the Reading and Simulation Task is used in a different way. The results of some pilot studies had showed that without exception all the children who, at the end of the simulation, succeeded in reading 8 or 9 out of 10 items could be qualified as good readers in first grade. Stated otherwise, are early detection and prevention of learning problems possible? Later on we will come back to this question.

Phonemic Segmentation Task

Spector (1992) developed a learning potential program to evaluate the ability of kindergarten children to perform a phonemic awareness task when given supportive prompts and cues. In each of the 12 items of her Dynamic Phoneme Segmentation Test (DPST), the examinee is asked to pronounce, in order, each of the sounds in a word. The test parallels a segmentation test of Yopp (1988) but provides increasingly supportive prompts and cues when the examinee is unable to segment a word correctly. The tester uses seven series of prompts each time an examinee is unable to segment a word: (1) pronouncing the target word slowly, (2) asking the examinee to identify the first sound of the word, (3) cueing the examinee with the first sound, (4) cueing the examinee with the number of sounds in the word, (5) modeling segmentation using pennies to represent the number of sounds in the word, (6) modeling segmentation as previously but working more and more with the examinee while pronouncing the segments, and (7) repeating prompt.

Each item is scored for the number of prompts, as follows: 6 = correct response with no prompts required; 5, 4, 3, 2, 1 for a correct response after prompt (1), (2), (3), (4), and (5), respectively; and 0 for no correct response. No credit is given after prompts (6) and (7).

The focus of the study was prediction. Spector hypothesized that the DPST would more accurately predict progress in word recognition from autumn to spring than would three segmentation tests of Yopp (1988). She also hypothesized that the DPST was a better predictor of phonemic awareness at the end of the kindergarten year than traditional tests of phonemic awareness. The DPST was administered to 38 English-speaking kindergarten subjects. In addition to the DPST, three other phoneme segmentation tests of Yopp, a verbal intelligence test, and a word recognition test were administered. All tests, except the DPST and the verbal intelligence test, were presented twice in the autumn and spring of the year when the subjects were in kindergarten.

The results of the study supported both hypotheses. The DPST as compared with other tests administered in the autumn showed the highest significant positive correlations with spring word recognition scores and spring phonemic awareness. Three stepwise multiple regression analyses with each of spring phonemic awareness tests as the dependent variable and the five tests administered in the autumn as the dependent variables, demonstrated that the DPST accounted for an additional 12 to 14% of the variance in the spring awareness measures. Furthermore, the dynamic assessment score accounted for an additional 21% of the spring word recognition scores. The results also demonstrate that examinees who showed the most growth in word recognition from autumn to spring tended to be those who were helped most by the prompts and cues provided in the DPST. From these results it can be concluded that different degrees of future success in reading can be predicted from measures in the DPST.

Phonemic Awareness Task

Hamers, Van Luit, and Tissink (1995) and Tissink (1993) developed the Phonemic Awareness Test (PAT). Based on a task analysis of initial reading, they determined what specific knowledge and which skills are the prerequisites of decoding and word recognition. Children who experience difficulties in this domain are often labeled as lacking reading readiness. Hamers *et al.* (1995) described the prerequisites for reading and spelling, and the nature of the tasks assessing these prerequisites in Table 2.

In constructing the PAT, each of these prerequisites was assessed in pretests and post-tests. The total procedure can be characterized as a standardized testing procedure with pretest, training, and post-test administered on consecutive days. There are four instructional modes, which are increasingly supportive in finding the correct answer on a practice item: repeated presentation of the item (mode 1), disclosure of the item structure (mode 2),

TABLE 2
Prerequisites of Initial Reading and Number of Items in the PAT

(a) Memory: repeating sentences of three to five words (2 items).
Example, "Repeat after me . . . Wim was ill" (these items are not trained or included in the results, because this part is considered to be a "warming up").

(b) Auditory segmentation 1 (identification of words): segmenting a sentence into words accompanied by clapping hands (5 items).
Example, "Clap once for each word . . . Hans (clap) runs (clap) away (clap)."

(c) Auditory segmentation 2 (identification of syllables): segmenting a word into syllables accompanied by clapping hands (5 items).
Example, "Repeat the word and clap it into parts . . . mu- (clap) sic (clap)."

(d) Objectivation of spoken meaningful words: pointing out which of two different words is longer (independent of their meaning) (5 items).
Example, "Which word is longer . . . cat or rabbit?"

(e) Objectivation 2: repeating a part of a compound (5 items).
Example, "Repeat . . . bedroom, leave out bed. What do you get?"

(f) Isolation of the first phoneme: repeating the first phoneme of a word (5 items).
Example, "What do you hear first in . . . dog?"

(g) Phonemic analysis: to segment a word into phonemes (15 items).
Example, "Say each part of . . . cat (*c/a/t*)."

presentation of a solution strategy (mode 3), and modeling (mode 4). Each time an examinee is unable to solve a particular practice item correctly, the item can be presented via modes 1 to 4, in that order. In the study, 115 kindergarten children, ranging in age from 5 years and 5 months to 6 years and 8 months, participated.

Cronbach's reliability coefficients for the pretest and post-test of the PAT were .91 and .92, respectively. To examine predictive validity, correlations were calculated between PAT pretest and post-test scores and reading and spelling scores from school achievement tests collected one year later. The correlations between PAT pretest and post-test scores and reading scores were .48 and .57, respectively, and between PAT pretest and post-test scores and spelling scores were .48 and .58, respectively.

To compare the PAT with other tests, we carried out two regression analyses. First, we compared the correlations of the PAT, the Revision Amsterdam Child Intelligence and the Learning Potential Test for Ethnic Minorities with school achievement. The analysis showed that domain-specific tests (subtests) are responsible for the predictive power. For the LEM, the number series and classification subtests contribute most to the predictive power and vocabulary and memory subtests for the RAKIT. Second, we studied what the PAT adds to the predictive power of the LEM and the RAKIT. In this multiple regression analysis, the RAKIT (eight subtests) was handled as the first predictor, the LEM (six subtests) as the second, and the PAT as the last predictor. It was found that the RAKIT predicts school achievement moderately to reasonably well, accounting for 17 (spelling) to 41% (arithmetic) of the variance in the scores. The RAKIT memory span and verbal comprehension subtests appear to contribute the most to this prediction. The LEM accounts for significant additional portions of the variance, in particular the classification subtest. The PAT causes a further significant increment in explained variance.

In this study, the analysis of test profiles provides the possibility of generating information for intervention. For instance, a child who initially achieves below average on the PAT, but shows progress after a training phase with instruction up to mode 2 (revealing the item structure) requires a different kind of intervention than a child who performs poorly on all tasks and continues to perform poorly despite extensive instruction (up to mode 4, modeling). In this way, the assessment procedure can also serve the practical aim of referral issues based on criterion-reference learning measures.

Working Memory Task

Working memory is a human information resource of limited capacity. Swanson (1992, 1993) addressed research questions concerning whether or not working memory performance can be modified and whether such performance would improve prediction of reading vocabulary development. Practice procedures in the working memory tasks were intended to reduce inefficient strategies for accessing previously presented information.

Swanson collected 11 working memory tests, which could be divided by factor analysis into two groups. The first group consisted of episodic memory tasks emphasizing temporal–sequential processing: recalling sounds in sequence (rhyming), sequencing dot patterns and pictures (visual matrix, mapping and directions, picture sequencing), sequentially coordinating episodes in a story (story recall), and remembering digits in sequence (auditory digit sequencing). The second group consisted of semantic memory tasks stressing organization processes (phrase sequencing, spatial organization, semantic association, semantic categorization, nonverbal sequencing). The testing procedures for all original tests were transformed into short-term learning tests. The new tests were sufficiently brief to be administered within a normal testing period (approximately five minutes per test). The intervention consisted of a series of four probes (hints), which was presented for each item not correctly reproduced.

All memory tests yielded four scores. An initial score was determined by summing the number of items recalled without assistance. A probe score was the number of hints necessary to achieve the highest level of items recalled. A gain score was determined by the highest level of items recalled correctly with assistance. A maintenance score was determined by presenting to the examinee the test item related to the gain score (items that produced the highest level of performance) but without the hints. If the examinee maintained the same level of performance, the maintenance score was the same as his or her gain score. If the examinee failed the item, he or she was assigned the same score as his or her initial score. Swanson administered the 11 learning potential tests to 129 participants (mean chronological age was 10.5 years; range 5–18 years). As a criterion measure, he also administered a reading achievement test to investigate predictive validity.

The results showed that the average gain and maintenance scores of all tasks were higher than the initial scores, revealing that the working memory performance increased. The effect size for each gain and maintenance score was calculated (effect sizes are interpreted in a manner similar to z scores). Gain scores had a mean effect size of .90 (range = 0.32 to 1.38), reflecting a performance change of about one standard deviation. The mean effect size for maintenance scores was .47 (range .05 to .99). The first effect can be interpreted as large, the second as medium. The difference in effect size between gain and maintenance performance demonstrated that many examinees were able to modify performance when assistance was offered under gain conditions but, when left alone under maintenance conditions, continued to apply an inadequate memorization strategy.

A change of procedure might influence the construct validity of the test (see Embretson, 1987, for a review). However, Swanson found that testing procedures did not substantially change factor loadings. The 11 working memory tests preserved the factor structure just mentioned. With regard to the prediction of reading achievement, the working memory model, which included initial score, total number of probes, gain score, and memory score, accounted for 32% of the variance in word recognition. A model, which included only the initial score and gain score, accounted for 31% of the variance in reading achievement, 26% of which came from the initial score. The increase of 5% in the extended model, which was explained by the gain score, was significant. This result suggests that enhanced working memory performance can improve prediction of reading.

In a previous section, we asked the question, "Is early detection of learning problems a possibility?" The aforementioned results indicate that this question can be answered positively. For the early detection of reading and spelling problems, tests that give an indication of the learning success in specific curriculum-related learning processes are useful. We mentioned recent studies of learning the system of grapheme–phoneme correspondencies or other arbitrary visual–auditory associations and of learning to handle the phonological structure of language.

The next question is whether this kind of information provides a basis for early intervention. For example, extra stimulation of specific learning processes before the start of the intentional reading and spelling curriculum to children "at risk" could possibly prevent the later emergence of (severe) problems. In one of our studies (Ruijssenaars & Coppens, 1991), we used this kind of specific learning potential test to detect children "at risk" in kindergarten. In the next months, their teachers stimulated the development of the phonological awareness of only these "at-risk" children with about 50, 15-minute lessons (see also Ruijssenaars, Haers, & Vandenbroucke, 1993). When compared with a matched control group of "at-risk" children, a significant effect on reading speed was observed in January of the first grade. The relevance of this result is that reading speed, as an indication of the rate of automatization, is seen as the core problem experienced by children with severe reading problems or dyslexia. Any effect on success in initial reading provides these "at-risk" children a better starting position for the next phase in reading and spelling development.

FURTHER EDUCATIONAL IMPLICATIONS

Learning potential assessment research has experienced a gradual shift from the assessment of general learning potential to assessment of specific learning processes that are good predictors for future school learning. In our opinion, this also means a shift from prediction to explanation and description, resulting in an optimal interrelation between assessment and intervention.

What, at last, is the meaning of this development for the discrepancy concept that we spoke about in the introduction? We suppose that a domain-general, as well as a curriculum-related learning potential assessment can play a role in the identification of learning disabilities, operationalized as an IQ–achievement discrepancy. In the first place, a domain-general learning potential test can demonstrate that a low IQ score is not based on a structural mental deficiency. In that case, the observed learning problem cannot be explained by low intelligence and probably should be regarded as a specific learning disability. In the second place, a domain-specific learning potential test can answer the question of whether or not a learning disability is based on specific deficit. If neither apply, the explanation of the learning problem cannot be found in the learning process itself. In such a case, examples of alternative explanatory hypotheses are a lack of stimulation at school, at home, or underlying emotional problems.

Most of the studies discussed support the expectation that learning potential measure can enhance predictive value. But, what (theoretically) explains the predictive superiority of these measures? Spector (1992) suggests that these measures are better predictors because they are "cleaner or truer" measures of school achievement. Analysis of the results of traditional measures suggest the possibility that task demands unrelated to school achievement (e.g., asking too much at once, unfamiliar with task demands, fear of failure) prevent many children from achieving greater success. A second explanation might be that learning potential assessment provides a measure of "responsiveness to instruction." Thus, a measure of responsiveness is better able to forecast future "growth" in school achievement.

Furthermore, in recent studies, the sole intention was not only the enhancement of predictive validity (even though this remains an important issue) but also to study learning processes. Specific processes at the core of academic skills can be observed in prototypic learning tasks. Thus, task and process analysis will become a major goal of learning potential assessment. To achieve this goal, it seems wise to invest more energy in the development of systematic observation procedures that can be used by teachers to get insight in relevant learning processes (cf. the aforementioned prototypic learning tasks). The core principles of these procedures are a systematic instruction by the teacher (as independent variable) and a systematic observation of the responses of the pupils (as dependent variable). In one of our projects (Ruijssenaars et al., 1993), we constructed 52 lessons of 15 minutes each for teachers in kindergarten. The lessons were directed mainly at the application of (auditory) discriminative characteristics and the awareness of arbitrary visuoauditory associations in known key words (like *school*) and (their own) names. The instruction and materials of each lesson were standardized but could be adapted if necessary. The teacher daily had to observe the reactions of the children during the morning lessons and write down the names of the children who seemed to have problems with the instruction. During a rehearsal lesson in the afternoon with these selected (mostly three to five) children, a second observation was made and registered in an observation booklet. The study revealed a significant correlation of −.44 (significant at 1% level) between the number of times children were registered as "at risk" and their reading achievement one year later. Of course, for clinical practice it would be important not to strive for such a prediction but to give more individualized help to prevent learning problems later on. In addition, for the reading teacher in grade 1, these observations can be a tool for more systematic instruction. In our opinion, the same way of working can be applied to the learning processes mentioned in the foregoing paragraphs. In this way, assessing classroom learning potential will be a natural and permanent part of classroom instruction.

In this chapter, we placed learning potential tests with domain-general and domain-specific tasks in the context of evaluation goals for schools. We emphasized domain-specific learning potential tests in the subject matter domains of reading and spelling. However, such testing procedures can also be found in arithmetic (Guthke, 1983; Tissink, 1993). The overall results in the reviewed studies indicate that these testing procedure can substantially modify initial scores and assess a child's responsiveness to intervention. In contrast with the longer tradition of traditional school achievement tests, learning potential assessment with domain-specific tasks research is only at the beginning of what will become a new research tradition accompanied by the development of new instruments for school practice.

References

Basten, M., & Mestrom, A. (1987). *Ontwikkeling van een associatietaak* [Development of an association task]. Nijmegen: Nijmegen University Press.

Bleichrodt, N., Drenth, P. D. J., Zaal, J. N., & Resing, W. C. M. (1984). *Revisie Amsterdamse Kinder Intelligentie Test* [Revision Amsterdam Children's Intelligence Test]. Lisse: Swets & Zeitlinger.

Brown, A. L., & French, L. A. (1979). The zone of potential development: Implications for testing in the year 2000. *Intelligence*, 3, 255–273.

Brus, B. Th., & Voeten, M. J. M. (1973). *Eén minuut test* [One minute test]. Nijmegen: Berkhout.

Budoff, M. (1975). Measuring learning potential. *Studies in learning potential*, 39, 3.

Budoff, M., & Friedman, M. (1964). 'Learning potential' as an assessment approach to the adolescent mentally retarded. *Journal of Consulting Psychology*, 28, 434–439.

Campione, J. C., & Brown, A. L. (1987). Linking dynamic assessment with school achievement. In C. S. Lidz (Ed.), *Dynamic assessment: An interactional approach to evaluating learning potential* (pp. 82–115). New York: Guilford.

Carlson, J. S. (1995). *Advances in cognition and educational practice: European contributions to dynamic assessment*. Greenwich, CT: JAI Press.

Coxhead, P., & Gupta, R. M. (1988). Construction of a test battery to measure learning potential. In R. M. Gupta & P. Coxhead (Eds.), *Cultural diversity and learning efficiency: Recent developments in assessment* (pp. 118–140). London: Macmillan.

Dearborn, W. F. (1921). Intelligence and its measurement. *Journal of Educational Psychology*, 12, 210–212.

Dierckx, C., & Schalley, C. (1991). *Een associatietaak als mogelijke voorspeller van het aanvankelijke lezen* [An association task as a predictor of early reading]. Leuven: Leuven University Press.

Elkonin, D. B. (1963). The psychology of mastering the elements of reading. In B. Simon & J. Simon (Eds.), *Educational psychology in the* U.S.S.R. (pp. 245–260). London: Routhledge & Kegan Paul.

Embretson, S. E. (1987). Toward development of a psychometric approach. In C. S. Lidz (Ed.), *Dynamic assessment: An interactional approach to evaluation learning potential* (pp. 141–170). New York: Guilford.

Feuerstein, R. (1979). *The dynamic assessment of retarded performers: The learning potential assessment device, theory, instruments and techniques*. Baltimore: University Park Press.

Gagné, R. M., & Briggs, L. J. (1974). *Principles of instructional design*. New York: Holt, Rinehart & Winston.

Guilford, J. P. (1956). The structure of intellect. *Psychological Bulletin*, 53, 267–293.

Guthke, J. (1977). *Zur Diagnostik der intellektuelle Lernfähigkeit* [The assessment of intellectual learning ability]. Stuttgart: Klett.

Guthke, J. (1983). *Der Mengenfolgentest* [The sequence of sets test]. Berlin: Psychodiagnostisches Zentrum der Humboldt-Universität zu Berlin.

Hamers, J. H. M., Hessels, M. G. P., & Van Luit, J. E. H. (1991). *Leertest voor Etnische Minderheden: Test en Handleiding* [Learning test for ethnic minorities: Test and manual]. Lisse: Swets & Zeitlinger.

Hamers, J. H. M., Pennings, A. H., & Guthke, J. (1994). Training-based assessment of school achievement. *Learning and Instruction*, 4, 347–360.

Hamers, J. H. M., & Ruijssenaars, A. J. J. M. (1984). *Leergeschiktheid en leertests* [Learning potential and learning potential tests]. Lisse: Swets & Zeitlinger.

Hamers, J. H. M., & Ruijssenaars, A. J. J. M. (1986). *Leergeschiktheid en leertests* [Learning potential and learning potential tests] (2nd ed.). Lisse: Swets & Zeitlinger.

Hamers, J. H. M., Sijtsma, K., & Ruijssenaars, A. J. J. M. (Eds.). (1993). *Learning potential assessment: Theoretical, methodological and practical issues*. Amsterdam: Swets & Zeitlinger.

Hamers, J. H. M., Van Luit, J. E. H., & Tissink, J. (1995). *Leertoetsen voor oudste kleuters* [Learning potential tests with domain-specific tasks]. Hilversum: OBD Hilversum.

Haywood, H. C., & Tzuriel, D. (Eds.). (1992). *Interactive assessment*. Berlin: Springer-Verlag.

Hegarty, S. (1979). *Test of children's learning ability (individual version): Test and manual*. Windsor: NFER Publishing Company.

Hessels, M. G. P. (1993). *Leertest voor etnische minderheden* [Learning potential test for ethnic minorities]. Rotterdam: Erasmus University Press.

Hessels, M. G. P., & Hamers, J. H. M. (1993). Learning potential test for ethnic minorities. In J. H. M. Hamers, K. Sijtsma, & A. J. J. M. Ruijssenaars (Eds.), *Learning potential assessment: Theoretical methodological and practical issues* (pp. 285–311). Amsterdam: Swets & Zeitlinger.

Ivanova, A. (1973). *Das Lernexperiment als Methode der Diagnostik der geistigen Entwicklung der Kinder* [The learning experiment as a method for assessment]. Moscow: Pedagogika.

Jensen, A. R. (1980). *Bias in mental testing*. New York: Free Press.

Kalmykova, S. J. (Ed.). (1975). *Problems of assessment of the mental development of children* (in Russian). Moscow: Pedagogika.

Leyendecker, C. (1977). *Lernverhalten behinderter Kinder* [Learning ability of learning disabled children]. Rheinstetten: Schindele Verlag.

Lidz, C. S. (Ed.). (1987). *Dynamic assessment: An interactional approach to evaluating learning potential*. New York: Guilford.

Luria, A. R. (1961). An objective approach to the study of the abnormal child. *American Journal of Orthopsychiatry*, 31, 1–16.

Meijer, J. (1993). Learning potential, personality characteristics and test performance. In J. H. M. Hamers, K. Sijtsma, & A. J. J. M. Ruijssenaars (Eds.), *Learning potential assessment: Theoretical, methodological and practical issues* (pp. 341–362). Amsterdam: Swets & Zeitlinger.

Perfetti, C. A., & Lesgold, A. M. (1979). Coding and comprehension in skilled reading and implications for reading instruction. In L. B. Resnick & P. A. Weaver (Eds.), *Theory and practice of early reading* (Vol. 1). Hillsdale, NJ: Erlbaum.

Roether, D. (1974). Der Lerntest von D. Roether. In W. Gutjahr (Ed.), *Verfahren zur Diagnostik der Schulfhigkeit* [Test for the assessment of school readiness] (pp. 39–121). Berlin: VEB Deutscher Verlag der Wissenschaften.

Ruijssenaars, A. J. J. M. (1991). Dyslexie: Diagnostiek en behandeling [Dyslexia: Assessment and treatment]. In L. Heylen & R. Elen (Eds.), *Omtrent logopedie* 8 [Logopedics 8] (pp. 31–62). Herenthals: VVL.

Ruijssenaars, A. J. J. M., & Coppens, V. (1991). Vroegtijdige interventie bij potentieel leeszwakke kinderen [Early intervention with backward readers]. In A. van der Leij & E. J. Kappers (Eds.), *Dyslexie* 1990 [Dyslexia 1990] (pp. 77–98). Lisse: Swets & Zeitlinger.

Ruijssenaars, A. J. J. M., Haers, M., & Vandenbroucke, A. (1993). *Vroegtijdige onderkenning van leesproblemen en de waarde van preventieve training van het fonologisch bewustzijn* [Early identification of reading problems and the advantage of phonemic awareness training]. Brussels: Ministerie van Onderwijs.

Ruijssenaars, A. J. J. M., & Hamers, J. H. M. (1986). Leertests in het toelatingsonderzoek [Learning potential test as a referral instrument]. *Tijdschrift voor Orthopedagogiek*, 25, 314–325.

Ruijssenaars, A. J. J. M., & Oud, J. H. L. (1987). Leesleertest via leessimulatie volgens twee didactische methoden [Reading simulation in accordance with two reading methods]. *Pedagogische Studiën*, 64, 97–103.

Spector, J. E. (1992). Predicting progress in beginning reading: Dynamic assessment of phonemic awareness. *Journal of Educational Psychology*, 84, 353–363.

Sternberg, R. J. (Ed.). (1982). *Handbook of human intelligence*. New York: Cambridge University Press.

Swanson, H. L. (1992). Generality and modifiability of working memory among skilled and less skilled readers. *Journal of Educational Psychology*, 84, 473–488.

Swanson, H. L. (1993). Individual differences in working memory: A model testing and subgroup analysis of learning disabled and skills readers. *Intelligence*, 17, 285–332.

Teunissen, J. M. F. B. G., & Golhof, A. (1987). Etnische minderheden en speciaal onderwijs [Ethnic minorities and special education]. In K. Doornbos & L. M. Stevens (Eds.), *De groei van het speciaal onderwijs* [The growth of special education] (pp. 113–148). 's Gravenhage: Staatsuitgeverij.

Tissink, J. (1993). *De constructie van leertests met curriculum (on) gebonden taken* [The construction of learning potential tests with domain-general and domain-specific tasks]. Utrecht: Utrecht University Press.

Tissink J., Hamers, J. H. M., & Van Luit, J. E. H. (1993). Learning potential tests with domain-general and domain-specific tasks. In J. H. M. Hamers, K. Sijtsma, & A. J. J. M. Ruijssenaars (Eds.), *Learning potential assessment: Theoretical, methodological and practical issues* (pp. 243–266). Amsterdam: Swets & Zeitlinger.

Van de Vijver, F. J. R. (1993). Learning potential assessment from a cross-cultural perspective. In J. H. M. Hamers, K. Sijtsma, & A. J. J. M. Ruijssenaars (Eds.), *Learning potential assessment: Theoretical, methodological and practical issues* (pp. 313–340). Amsterdam: Swets & Zeitlinger.

Verhoeven, L. Th. (1980a). *Handleiding voor de toets Woorddiktee* 1 [Manual for the word test 1]. Arnjem: CITO.

Verhoeven, L. Th. (1980b). *Handleiding voor de toets Technisch Lezen* 1 [Manual for the test technical reading 1]. Arnjem: CITO.

Vygotsky, L. S. (1978). *Mind in society: The development of higher psychological processes* (M. Cole, J. Steiner, S. Scribner, & E. Souberman, Eds. and Trans.). Cambridge, MA: Harvard University Press.

Yopp, H. K. (1988). The validity and reliability of phonemic awareness test. *Reading Research Quarterly*, 27, 159–177.

CHAPTER

19

Reflections on Portfolios

VICKI SPANDEL
Northwest Regional Educational Laboratory, Portland, Oregon

Setting up a portfolio system is a little like buying good shoes. One size does not fit all. The best choice depends on purpose. And a really good fit happens over time, with lots of use and the right give and take by the user. Portfolios come in all shapes and sizes, from an artist's case, ring binder, scrapbook, or journal to drawstring bag, or portable file, or humble manila folder. All this variety would seem to make it hard to define what a portfolio is, but in truth, the concept of "portfolio" has little to do with form and structure and everything to do with helping students become thoughtful, reflective managers of their own learning.

A WORKING DEFINITION

A *portfolio* can be defined as a purposeful collection of self-selected work that, together with personal reflection, tells the story of who a student is now and who she or he is becoming.

Purposeful collections tend to be small. That is good. Imagine a "portfolio" in which the student saved almost *every* piece of work completed during the year—every project, every homework assignment, every quiz, test, essay, worksheet. How would we make sense of it? How would we separate the significant from the trivial? The answer is that we could not. This must be the job of the student. In the process of choosing, sorting, separating, and distinguishing between the significant and the trivial, students learn to trace the path of their own learning. Pathfinding is what a portfolio is all about.

ASSESSMENT, INSTRUCTION—OR BOTH?

Perhaps nowhere are assessment and instruction so closely intertwined as in portfolios. Students learn about themselves as they collect, choose, create, and assemble. That is the instructional value of portfolios. We learn about students by reviewing their work, measuring their growth, meditating over their self-reflections. Such is the assessment potential of the portfolio.

Both assessment and instructional value are enhanced when the portfolio is driven by a strong sense of purpose. Random collections of unrelated work neither tell a coherent story nor help a student set goals. But when students understand the reason behind the portfolio (e.g., to show growth) and when they have criteria to help them select meaningful work, the stories their portfolios tell are clear and powerful. This does not make assessment via portfolios simple, however.

The concept of portfolio-based assessment, in fact, has remained annoyingly and bewilderingly fuzzy over the past few years, even as the portfolio concept itself has gained unprecedented popularity. It is not at all clear to many *what* exactly is being assessed or how the teacher (or other assessor) should go about this. Depending on how the portfolio is structured, there are several possibilities: first, we can simply assess individual pieces of work, using whatever method would be used if the portfolio did not even exist; second, we can base assessment on whether work within the portfolio shows attainment of specific goals, such as ability to write for a range of purposes and audiences or ability to apply algebraic concepts to real-life problem solving; third, we can base assessment on the amount or nature of growth demonstrated through comparison and analysis of work samples over time; or fourth, we can assess the portfolio itself as a kind of project in its own right, considering how well the student has chosen and presented work samples to tell a particular story and how much we learn about the student by reviewing the portfolio.

Successful—or effective or satisfying—portfolios have some qualities in common, including an order or structure to the presentation of materials; a clear sense of purpose (e.g., to show growth); textual clues such as a table of contents, letter of introduction, and dates on all entries that make it easy for a reader to "get inside" and make sense of the big picture; and thoughtful, expansive self-reflections that guide and enrich the reader's perspective on the work. Of course, these various assessment approaches can be combined; it is possible, for instance, to look at *both* growth and goal attainment or to consider either of these in combination with the effectiveness of the portfolio as a whole.

STATE AND DISTRICT GOALS

More and more, portfolios are being used to show student achievement relating to district or state standards and goals. Portfolio collections, with their emphasis on planning, self-assessment, and goal setting, are an ideal vehicle for showcasing hard-to-measure abilities, such as the ability to

- Apply mathematics and science in real-world situations.
- Think critically, creatively, and reflectively.
- Communicate effectively to various audiences.
- Plan and carry out complex projects.
- Use computers and other technology to process, synthesize, and summarize information.
- Communicate in a second language.

A list of goals like this one often looks intimidatingly ambitious, but remember, a single piece of work can often show competency relating to more than one educational goal. Consider the many different skills involved, for instance, in conducting community-based research, producing a video, preparing for and participating in a debate, planning and carrying out a science experiment, or writing, illustrating, and publishing a children's book. Projects that require complex planning, multiple steps, or presentation of results and conclusions to an audience will usually satisfy a range of performance goals because each offers so much significant, hard-to-get-at information and reveals so much about the person who created it.

It is also important to keep in mind that assessment is not an essential part of the portfolio picture. It is tempting, *inviting* even, to assess via portfolios because broad collections of work, especially those assembled over time, offer a potentially richer, more complete, and more authentic picture of student performance than we can hope to gather in any other way. Whenever students stop to reflect on their work and the learning process that produced it, whenever they set goals, compare early work to what they can produce now, or select work to show how goals have been met, they are learning and thinking. The instructional value of portfolios does not change, however, regardless of whether or not we take advantage of the assessment opportunities portfolios give us.

WORDS OF WISDOM

Through portfolios, students discover who they are as learners and reveal to themselves, their teachers, and their parents strengths and talents that might otherwise have gone unnoticed. Teachers document their students' growth in tangible ways that show clearly how far students have come and where they are headed. Parents see firsthand that learning does not stop with knowledge acquisition but only begins there.

For all its benefits, though, portfolio management is far from trouble free. In fact, some people find it downright stressful. Many teachers are quick to point out that they have yet to discover a truly easy, efficient way to store portfolios (sure, they will be electronic eventually, but not everyone is ready for that yet); manage portfolio conferences with 150 plus students; pass portfolios on year to year when students move, leave the district, or simply change schools; or even teach self-reflection. Of course, compromises are possible. Teachers can confer with students in groups or invite parents, siblings or friends to "walk through" portfolios occasionally. It may not be necessary to pass on the *whole* portfolio to next year's teacher (who may wonder where to find the time to read all those portfolios anyway); a single telling sample of work combined with a perceptive self-reflection or letter to next year's teacher may be sufficient, even preferable. Further, despite problems, an impressive number of teachers say it is all worth it. They credit portfolios with improving students' management and goal-setting skills, helping students think and solve problems, and making students more aware of their own learning. Many teachers maintain that portfolios have helped students grow in confidence because portfolios put students in charge of their own learning and help them see their growth in real examples (not just grades and numbers). And, they offer six suggestions for making it all work.

Simplify!

There is probably no way to bury an educational idea—even a very good one—faster than to allow it to overwhelm the very people it is meant to serve. Unfortunately, this has often happened with portfolios.

Consider Ellen, who teaches grade 6 in a self-contained classroom. It is May, and Ellen has been working on portfolios with her students since mid-September. She is exhausted. So are her students. A quick look through her students' portfolios shows why. Each week, they select for their portfolios one item from music, one from art, one from language arts, social studies, science, math, and so forth. They write a self-reflection on *every* piece (can anyone honestly reflect that much?), date it, then include it in their portfolios, which are now gigantic, bulging, and actually hard to lift. When someone from outside the classroom tries to make sense of the portfolios' contents, it is a little like trying to "read" the inside of an overloaded closet.

Ellen could cut down on how frequently her students put things into their portfolios. In most classrooms, it may be quite sufficient to pull one piece each three to four weeks. Ellen's students could also *focus* their portfolios on *one* content area or skill: growth in artistic self-expression *or* problem-solving skill in math *or* improved editing skills. What makes a portfolio readable and informative is not the quantity of work it contains, but the care with which that work was produced and chosen. A portfolio that contains six, eight, or even a dozen pieces of carefully chosen, significant work that captures who that student is and his or her goals for improvement is not only more inviting to a reviewer but more revealing as well.

Ellen's students could also keep a dual filing system: one working file to hold everything, a kind of cache for ideas, collectibles, and works in progress. Periodically, students could select from this working file one item to go into the smaller, more exclusive portfolio. At that time, they could reflect on why that item was selected, what growth it showed, or what problems it presented.

Make It Your Own

Portfolios from one class need not look like those of the teacher down the hall or in another school district or on that video featured at a conference some weeks ago. Over and over, teachers suggest that one important key to success is to ensure that portfolios reflect the spirit, philosophy, and special teaching style unique to a given classroom.

Define the Purpose Clearly

By nature, portfolios embody a virtually endless round of decisions: How do you begin? What do you put in? Who gets to decide what goes in? How, if at all, do you assess the results? Who has access to the portfolios? What happens to them at the end of the year? These and countless other decisions depend in turn on a more fundamental underlying decision, the importance of which cannot be overstated: What is the purpose of your portfolio? Possible answers to this question include these:

- To show growth or change over time.
- To create a collection of personally important work.
- To assemble a collection of work that demonstrates readiness to move to a new level.
- To document achievement for alternative credit.
- To celebrate best or favorite moments.
- To provide information for classroom or large-scale assessment.

While these purposes are by no means mutually exclusive, they do call for somewhat different kinds of portfolios, each with its own focus, flavor, and content. Once the purpose is crystal clear, every other question becomes easier to answer.

Let the Curriculum Drive the Portfolio

In Ellen's classroom, the portfolio had taken over, almost as if it had a life of its own. That is not how it should be. Ideally, the portfolio exists to reflect and capture the good things happening within the classroom; the classroom is not created for the sake of the portfolio. Portfolios are not an end in themselves. We need to begin with a clear vision of success, a clear vision of what we want from our students, then ask if the portfolio will serve that vision well. We need to ask, "What am I hoping my students will gain from their experience in this classroom?" That could be more confidence in math, skill in revising writing, ability to plan and carry out creative problem solving, understanding basic geometry, growth in reading skills, or virtually any academic, personal, or social goal significant in a given classroom. Once that vision is clear, we can ask, given that vision of success, "Can my students use a portfolio to show they have met the goal(s) important in this classroom?"

Put Students in Charge

The more involved students are in assembling the portfolio, choosing what goes in, reflecting on their work, assessing their progress, making predictions, and setting goals, the greater the instructional value of the portfolio. That is the number one reason to encourage student involvement.

But, if we need a second reason, all we have to do is get realistic for a moment. An elementary teacher responsible for, say, 30 plus students or a secondary teacher with 150 or even more students cannot possibly coordinate all those portfolios single-handedly. Who has that kind of time or would wish to make that many choices?

Of course, putting students in charge is not always simple. It means teaching them the criteria on which to base their decision making and goal setting, giving them time to look through their working files and compare pieces of work over time, and sometimes, living with choices that are not the same as those we would have made. If a student chooses as his or her "best" piece of writing something we find less than impressive, we can console ourselves with the realization that learning to self-evaluate (which takes time) is more important than having the perfect portfolio.

Think P*rocess*, Not P*roduct*

Portfolios have a most magical way of transforming the ordinary and the mundane into the elegant and eye catching. Daily assignments somehow take on a special aura when showcased in a decorated holder, dressed up with self-reflections, dates, introductory letters to reviewers, and a table of contents. This new packaging can make us see a student's work—and the student—in a whole new way.

The trouble with the razzle-dazzle side of portfolios is that it tempts us to focus on *products* when the real work of the portfolio lies in what goes on inside the students' heads as they dig through their work, analyze the ways they have changed, and think how best to order, display, or write about their work to make sure the portfolio tells the stories they want them to tell.

EVERYONE IS DOING IT; SHOULDN'T I?

Sometimes it seems as if everyone is either creating a portfolio or trying to get someone else to create one. Portfolios are the topic of choice at every conference and seminar, so it seems only natural to wonder whether they belong in *every* classroom. While portfolios offer remarkable potential for enhancing and enriching student learning, however, they are probably not for everyone. Asking students to create portfolios will not automatically enrich curriculum, improve teaching, or make students strong self-assessors. Portfolios tend to thrive in classrooms where

- Risk taking is encouraged.
- Conceptual understanding is valued more than getting the "right" answer.
- Teacher and students together form an interpretive community of learners who establish their own criteria for judging quality performance.
- Students are encouraged to think of learning less in terms of memorizing and more in terms of exploring possible solutions and identifying important questions.
- Self-assessment is taught, refined, and nurtured.
- Self-reflection is not just a portfolio activity, but a way of life.

WHAT KINDS OF PORTFOLIOS MAKE MOST SENSE IN MY CLASSROOM?

In Maggie's eighth grade algebra classroom, growth portfolios show student confidence blossoming as the weeks go by. In Sylvia's kindergarten–grade 1 combination classroom, celebrational portfolios reflect the joy of learning in two dozen different formats. The kind of portfolio that works best depends on what you and your students hope to learn as you put the portfolio together. Here are four possibilities.

THE CELEBRATIONAL PORTFOLIO

In a very real sense, all portfolios are celebrational. When we encourage students to keep a portfolio, we say to them in effect, "Your work is important enough to save and to showcase." Portfolios are a way of honoring and preserving work that might otherwise be lost. But "celebrational" can also signify a portfolio that is a personal collection of favorite works and treasured keepsakes. Like a scrapbook or photo album, the celebrational portfolio offers a way to gently revive memories of times or events we want to hold onto.

A celebrational portfolio is a good first portfolio. It is free spirited, undemanding, unbounded by rules or requirements. For this reason, celebrational portfolios are favorites among primary teachers, who use them to introduce the whole concept of portfolios to their students. This is not to say that celebrational portfolios are useful *only* at the primary level. They offer a good path to understanding portfolios for students of any age who are new to the process.

Virtually anything can find its way into the celebrational portfolio: photos, ticket stubs, notes or picture postcards, sketches, awards, bookmarks, book jackets, poems, drawings, thoughts preserved on paper or by some other means, scraps of this or that. One student may choose to include a poem written to a friend or a picture of the trip to the pumpkin patch, while to another, a photo history of a science or social studies project or a letter from someone who has visited the class holds the most significance.

Some teachers like their students, even the youngest students, to make purposeful choices, such as

- Work I am most proud of.
- Best work.
- Something I am good at.
- Something I would like to do over.

This somewhat more structured approach to decision making guides students' choices in a way that leads quite naturally into self-reflection:

> This was hard. We had to look at our plants grow ever day and make notes on them and keep track of things. I kept loosing stuff. We had to write abowt our plants and draw pichers of our plants. (Lisa, Grade 2)

Reflections help students recall later why a piece was important or valued. Taking time to reflect, even for a few seconds, reinforces for students the importance of doing work not just for the sake of completing it, but also because it is enjoyable, it teaches you something, and it shows you can do hard things.

Celebrational portfolios are personal collections, near and dear to the heart of the creator. They are not intended for assessment, except in the very broadest sense: they show participation in learning, participation in the portfolio process. The purpose of the celebrational portfolio is fulfilled if students rejoice in the portrayal of themselves as successful learners and capable people and take pride in discovering that they can create portfolios on their own.

Growth Portfolios

If all portfolios are celebrational, most are in some sense growth portfolios, too. It is the nature of portfolios to capture growth and change. Portfolios do this better than grades, better than test scores, better than report cards or narrative reports. In assessing change, nothing is more compelling than comparing samples of students' work, seeking the clues that speak directly to that change. But while most portfolios will show *some* evidence of growth, an actual growth portfolio—one created explicitly to show change over time—is a little different.

It begins with a sample of early work that may or may not be strong; it is simply representative of what the student can do at that point. The student may be tempted from time to time to replace that early sample with something stronger, but the whole point of a growth portfolio is to *document* change. Take out those early pieces and you lose the sense of contrast.

It is also important for the area of growth to be specifically targeted: the more specific, the better. A general target like "growth in writing" may be difficult for students to visualize. What does that look like anyway? To one person, it might be participation in all phases of the writing process, from prewriting through drafting and sharing to revising and editing. In another person's vision, it might be as simple as writing more pages. Someone else might see it as writing for a wide variety of purposes and audiences. It is critical (for good decision making by the student or sound assessment by the teacher) to define the area of growth as explicitly as possible.

How often should students make selections for a growth portfolio? That depends. The real question is, "How long does it take to spot growth?" A track runner may see herself improving almost daily. She might keep a log of running times and reflect on her progress every few days. By contrast, a poet may review his work after two weeks and see minimal change, then a week later write a heartfelt piece that, for him, is a breakthrough. That is the time to add to the portfolio and reflect on new skills or insights.

In building a growth portfolio, students learn first and foremost that they *are* making progress. Voila! This may be quite apparent to a teacher—and sometimes to a parent, too—but it is often a murky mystery to the student, who wonders, "Am I *ever* going to get it?"

When Mark, a tenth grader, looks at the simple half-assertion, half-guesswork summary of his physics experiment in October and compares it to an authoritative, well-documented, and well-illustrated piece on electrical circuits done in December, he can honestly say, "Wow—I've come farther than I thought."

A growth portfolio really invites assessment because it is set up to show improvement. But before you use it in this way, you must ask, "What is it I really want to assess?" Several options are possible, depending on what you feel is important, and it is critical to be very clear with students about whether assessment will be based on the quality of *individual pieces* of work, the amount or kinds of *growth*, student *self-assessment* of that growth, quality of performance achieved by the *end of the grading period*, or some combination of these factors.

Growth portfolios also have profound instructional value. In keeping a growth portfolio, a student becomes a learning manager, tracking every road bump and breakthrough, and plotting a course for achievement. In effect, the student takes over a portion of what is normally the teacher's role: assessing work, monitoring progress, and deciding how to deal with weaknesses. Watching themselves grow step by step, students discover *how* they learn and put their new knowledge to work in a thousand future contexts.

> I've grown in science this year. I like it, for one thing. Last year we didn't get to do any experiments. This year we are designing habitats for an animal. Our group's animal is the gorilla. They are very sensitive and intelligent. They are also shy and they need to hide sometimes. Did you know they are a lot like us in many ways? They talk to each other with their facial expressions and body language. They even use hand signals! They are very affectionate with their young, and carry them around and watch over them for a long time. I would like to be a scientist and study animals in the wild. To do that you have to have good record keeping skills. I am not that good at taking notes but I am working on it. (Grade 9 Science Student)

Selected Works Portfolios

A selected works portfolio is a place for students to showcase personally important work. What is personally important varies student to student, class to class. "It's the best I've done so far" is often the very first reason students think of for making a choice. Yet the work from which students learn most, about the curriculum and about themselves, is not necessarily their best. Some potentially more interesting questions, which might prompt students to think about their work and their learning in new ways, include these:

- What challenged you?
- What did you try that was new?
- What was the most important, or surprising, thing you learned?
- What did you feel proudest of? Why?
- What was *one* tricky problem you solved? How did you do it?

When students begin to think beyond "best," they find themselves digging into the process of learning, particularly the challenges, roadblocks, or surprises.

As its name implies, the selected works portfolio is a lot like an anthology: everything within the collection is included for an important reason and not everything will make the cut. Sometimes choices are based on a goal the student sets for himself or herself; sometimes they are based on one the teacher has determined is important.

In one social studies classroom, important learning goals included understanding of basic concepts, mastery of key knowledge, ability to communicate, and enjoyment of learning. All were revealed in one student's Medieval diary, in which she took on the role of a squire, a 13-year-old boy studying to become a knight. What mattered most to the student, however, was her personal selection of a unique project:

> I worked a long time on this diary and it is my favorite thing in my portfolio because I am the only person out of three social studies classes who chose to do a diary. I got the idea from my social studies teacher saying one day that if you could get inside a person's head you would know what it was like to live in the time he lived. I felt like I could make the Middle Ages more real by becoming a person who lived in that time. I chose to be a boy because boys had a lot more interesting lives in the Middle Ages than girls. One of the most interesting things I learned was how young people died. In those days, 40 was very old. Some knights were probably only 16 or 17, even though that is not how they show them in movies today. People were poor. Disease was everywhere. They ate things we would not think of eating (birds cooked with their feathers on) and washed in soap made of mutton fat. I tried to put in my diary what life was like in 1300. If I had more time, I would have put in more. I did not have a spell checker, and I am not the best speller. But I thought it might be more authentic the way it is. People in those days did not care that much about spelling.
>
> (Grade 7 Student)

Selected works portfolios are popular with students and teachers alike because, like celebrational portfolios, they encourage freedom of expression, exploration of self, and adventurous thinking. Yet, while variety is refreshing, a portfolio built around a theme is invariably more purposeful.

For instance, a student might construct a portfolio to show investigative skills, and that portfolio might include such items as a computer-based research project, a community research project, samples of videotaped interviews, and reflections on how he or she dug up little-known, tough-to-track-down information. "I'm good at uncovering facts and details" is the underlying theme of such a portfolio.

One of the greatest challenges in creating any portfolio is knowing where to stop. Students often have an easier time making good choices once they recognize that significant pieces of work often meet two or more academic goals or satisfy two, three, or more personal reasons for selection. By limiting the number of works selected for the portfolio, we challenge students to select carefully.

> Dear Reviewer—
>
> Welcome to my portfolio. It is meant to show my skill in writing for a lot of different purposes and audiences. I chose two of the eight total pieces because they were funny and I like that in my writing. You can really let your sense of humor go if you have a teacher who appreciates it. One of those also shows that I could do research or organize information well in a long report. The other three show particular skills: editing, use of dialogue, and ability to translate technical information into something a human being would read. This is only *part* of what I wrote. The rest is home in our kitchen cupboard where it will stay until my mom gets into one of her cleaning frenzies.
>
> (Grade 8 Student)

The selected works portfolio can include work from one year, several years, or an entire school career; it might contain samples from one subject area or from across several disciplines and learning contexts. This flexibility is ideal for secondary portfolios because we may wish to see students include work from several academic programs; say, social studies, language arts, dramatic arts, science, and mathematics (just to name a few possibilities). But what we do not want is a portfolio for *each* class. We cannot read them all, and students will say, as some are already saying, "No! Not *another* portfolio."

We can solve most of this problem by making cross-disciplinary goals the focus of the portfolio. Say one important goal is ability to communicate. A student could demonstrate skill relating to this broad academic goal by including a persuasive essay from a political science class, a mystery story written for language arts, a videotaped performance from Thornton Wilder's *Our Town*, a promotion for aerobic exercise created in a health class, a research project on DNA completed in science class, and an explanation—complete with drawings—of how to calculate the office floor space in a four-story building. Within such a collection we would see variety as well as communication for many purposes and many audiences; and we would not have to evaluate five separate portfolios to see those goals met.

Passportfolios

Passportfolios show a student's readiness to perform at a new level or take on a new challenge. College applicants are often given the opportunity to prepare a portfolio to complement other information, such as grades or test scores. In fact, some colleges and universities now require a portfolio as part of the application package. Institutions of higher education are expanding their use of the portfolio as well, often placing students in the appropriate courses based on knowledge and experience demonstrated through a portfolio.

Passportfolios, by nature, have an authenticity that resumes and letters of recommendation alone lack; they are the real thing. A person reviewing a well-constructed portfolio often comes to feel, by the end, that he or she knows the person behind the work.

A passportfolio may reflect the process of learning, but its primary purpose is to show *readiness for a new level* of work or education. A reviewer of such a portfolio is often more interested in the current quality of work than in the learning process the student went through to get there. In the reviewer's mind, the primary question is, "What kinds of work are you prepared to do now?"

Take, for example, a passportfolio used to apply for a job. Virtually all employers would probably want to have certain standard items included as a part of the application process: table of contents, resume, formal application and letter of introduction, vision statement, letters of recommendation, and so on.

Additional items however, which could potentially give a more accurate and complete picture of someone's value as a prospective employee, may give one applicant the edge over another:

- Explanations of why key pieces of work were chosen.
- Philosophy statement.
- A video of the applicant on the job.
- Personal writing.
- Reviews of one or two influential books.
- Biography on someone who has inspired the applicant in a significant way.

Traditional documents such as resumes tell only part of the story about what a prospective employee can do to enhance a company's productivity or image. Of even greater importance to many employers are creative samples of actual work and real-world problem solving in action.

Passportfolios play an important role in academic settings, too. Suppose a student wants to gain entrance to a specialized program, a program for the talented and gifted, say. Until now, the only way to get into this program may have been to achieve a specified minimum score on some relevant test. A passportfolio can enable a student who may not have the requisite test scores to show that he or she can, modest test scores notwithstanding, readily handle the more challenging work of an advanced curriculum. Such a passportfolio might include items such as a community-based research project, summaries of science experiments, a math proof with illustrations, a videotape of an oral presentation, an example of a journalistic report, an essay on a current political issue. This collection would enable the student to show that he or she could plan and coordinate research, use time effectively, conduct interviews, identify and track down critical information, package and present information to suit the needs and interests of an audience, and use a computer for research, data analysis, information retrieval, and production of high-quality text and graphics.

A carefully prepared portfolio can often tell much more about a student's capabilities, in fact, than all the scores from all the tests that student has ever taken. Completion of a strong passportfolio requires abilities and qualities hard to measure on tests, but critical to success in 21st century educational contexts: perseverance, creativity, risk taking, time management, foresight, flexibility, tolerance for stress, judgment, and talent for positive social interaction.

> I think the work included in this portfolio is some of the best I've done in the past two years. The projects I've included here show (I hope) that I am a creative person with good ideas. I see this as my main strength. Other things I'm pretty good at are organizing information and projects and planning my time. I'm also a good writer, although I do not enjoy reports as much as stories because the teachers will not let you put in enough voice. I am not sure why reports have to be dry. I want to be in

> accelerated classes because the discussions are on a different level. They don't talk down to kids. All classes should be like this. Then kids would like school more.
>
> (Grade 7 Student)

A passportfolio can take you where you want to go and sometimes even show you a road you never thought of. In creating the passportfolio, students travel simultaneously back through time and ahead to the future. Small wonder the journey holds a few surprises.

> All my life, since first grade, I wanted to be a teacher. I have done some volunteer teaching and tutoring after school and during summers at our district's elementary school, so I thought I would make a video of myself working with kids—just to include with my portfolio I'm sending to a state college. A friend offered to do some videotaping for me and show me how to edit it so I could just save the best parts. While we were working, I got really hooked on the video stuff. I couldn't get enough. Pretty soon, I was holding the camera, filming kids. I haven't given up on the teaching, but this gives me a new option. I'm not closing any doors yet, but it's nice knowing you can open a new one.
>
> (College Freshman)

SELF-REFLECTION

A self-reflection may introduce a portfolio, explain the significance of individual work samples, take us inside someone else's thinking, capture the best (and worst) moments of the learning process, or provide a powerful conclusion to the story told by the portfolio. Student self-reflection can underscore the significance of work that might otherwise have been overlooked. It can open our eyes to thoughts, feelings, impressions, reactions, hopes, fears, or concerns of which we might otherwise know nothing. Teachers maintain that from self-reflections they gain insights like these:

- "Students who seem to be enjoying my class are really struggling."
- "Students who look bored or lost are actually quite involved."
- "Students who seem to be doing fine are having trouble with tests/homework/keeping up."
- "A lesson I thought made perfect sense to everyone left a lot of kids in the dark."
- "I am often teaching something totally different from what I thought I was teaching."

Self-reflection is a way of bringing meaning to important work, and its personal, evaluative and revealing qualities expand our understanding of and enrich our response to that work.

Reflection sometimes focuses on what a student has done ("I really like this picture"), sometimes on the process of creation ("This was harder than anything I've ever done—the research took me nearly six weeks"), and sometimes on feelings, hopes, worries, or personal goals ("I'm not that good in math, and I worry that algebra will be too hard for me"). Through self-reflection, we discover a little more (sometimes a lot more) than we could by simply looking at the work alone.

Repeatedly, teachers remark that self-reflections are the single most meaningful and captivating part of any portfolio, that this is the part they read first and the part from which they learn the most. Further, the process of *writing* self-reflections

- Encourages students to think of themselves as writers, mathematicians, planners, readers, etc.
- Enables them to celebrate what is going well.
- Provides a vehicle for sharing how the world of school looks through students' eyes.
- Builds thinking skills, for self-evaluation takes time, thoughtful comparison, and in-depth analysis.
- Puts students in control of their learning, particularly as they set goals and evaluate their process.

From the teacher's point of view, the process of *reviewing* students' self-reflections

- Helps teachers discover strengths or gaps in instruction.
- Enables them to respond to each student as an individual and as a whole person, not just as a student.
- Provides a means of establishing a collegial dialogue with students.

In Matt's eighth grade algebra class, a primary goal is gaining confidence and skill in math. The work Matt displays in his portfolio shows that he is beginning to think like a mathematician. But there is a lot we do not learn about Matt from the work alone that his self-reflections do make clear. In September, his self-reflection looks like this:

> September 1992
> I think [algebra] will be hard. I worry that I am not good enough in math to do algebra. But I hope I am. Algebra is math that helps you find answers when you only have part of the information. I think algebra takes logic plus imagination. I think I have more imagination than logic.

This self-reflection adds another dimension to our picture of Matt: articulate and imaginative, yes, but also apprehensive. By the end of the second quarter, his fears, unfortunately, begin turning into reality:

> January 1993
> This quarter has been hard. I did not like exponents! Scientific notation makes no sense to me at all. I don't get why you put things in scientific notation or when anybody would ever use this. I have never seen numbers like 4.1 times 10 to the fifth power anywhere in real life. . . . Algebra is still better than writing research papers, but I hope it doesn't get too much harder. I had trouble keeping up with the homework. Thirty problems a night is too many for me.

This revealing self-reflection shows a student struggling to keep pace and to relate math to real-life applications. It is not the end of the story, though. Matt rebounds from his midyear low, and by the end of the school year, we see his confidence soar.

> June 1993
> I have learned a lot in my beginning algebra class. I think I have a lot more confidence now, for one thing. I am better at math than I thought. I have also learned that math isn't just homework and worksheets. It is solving problems and using what you know. I want to take more math, especially geometry. I think I could be pretty good at it if I pay more attention to little details. It was a good year for me mostly. I worked harder than I did in seventh grade. My grades do not show that, but I think my portfolio does.

How Does Self-Reflection Begin?

The very first self-reflections students write tend to be simple: "I chose this because it is my favorite piece of writing." But students who talk to one another about their work and how they solve problems, who keep learning logs, who take notes on processes and strategies (their own and others') and who use explicit criteria in choosing work for the portfolio, can learn to expand their reflective thinking.

> I chose this piece of writing because it has strong ideas and good details. I could really picture my grandma's kitchen when I wrote this. I could smell the caramel rolls baking in the oven. I wanted the reader to be right there, too. I think my paper makes it easy to see what I am talking about. (Grade 5 Student)

Students may also begin to offer comparisons between two pieces of work: "At the beginng of the yer I did not yuse descrptiv words in my storys but now i do. So now my storie has many many drescrptiv words" (Grade 1 Student). Or share personal perceptions that would otherwise not surface:

> What I've learned in the last three weeks is that I hate bats. It is not the teacher's fault I learned this. She meant for me to learn something else. We had a speaker come in to show us fruit bats and everyone kept talking about how cute they were. I am sorry to say but if something that ugly were clinging to my arm I would probably be screaming even if I did have gloves on. Fruit bats are called that because they eat fruit. Right. They don't look like they eat fruit. We were supposed to learn that bats will not hurt you and that they are helpful. How are they helpful? Do we have too much fruit to be eaten? I was glad when this lesson was over. (Grade 6 Student)

Getting Started

Self-reflection comes more easily to some people than to others. But few would call it simple or completely natural—at least on the very first try. For most people it takes both time and practice. Because it is often personal, it takes courage and honesty as well. One way to begin is by asking students to respond to specific questions, like these:

- From which activity did you learn most? What did you learn?
- What have you discovered about yourself you did not know before?
- Is there any piece of work you might do differently if you were to begin again? Why?
- What is it about the way you work that makes you successful?
- What is the most important way you have grown or changed in the last two months?

Some teachers share samples of other students' reflections. Better still, if you keep a portfolio yourself, you can share your own self-reflections as you create them.

Browse through literature for the reflective thoughts of writers and artists. Their ideas, uniquely revealing, often inspire students to take a closer look at their own work:

> Long before I wrote stories, I listened for stories. Listening for them is something more acute than listening to them. I suppose it's an early form of participation in what goes on. Listening children know stories are there. When their elders sit and begin, children are just waiting and hoping for one to come out, like a mouse from its hole. (Eudora Welty, *One Writer's Beginnings*, 1983)

Encourage students, before trying to *write* anything, to talk with one another about what they are learning and how—what is fun, what is frustrating or hard to get at. Picture student writers seated in a circle, taking time to dig through their working files, looking, browsing, exploring, comparing, and then thinking of how they have changed as writers over the last two or three weeks (since the last visit to the working file). Before writing their self-reflections, they share, one at a time, what each has learned since writing the last self-reflection:

- Think like a writer—never stop making notes in your head.
- Do not use too many exclamation points—they lose their power.
- Think of what your reader does not already know—then write that.
- It is better to make up a good detail than live with a boring fact.

As they listen to one another, students find their thinking about their own work expanding. They borrow from each other, each idea becoming a springboard for half a dozen others.

Encourage students to reflect on their work in whatever way feels comfortable. For one, it might work to write a poem; for another, to draw a picture or make a graph. Dictation is sometimes *essential* at the primary level, where students may have much more to say than their limited experience or comfort with writing will allow them to capture. Older or more experienced students might interview others, asking questions about learning process; that way, both learn something about self-reflection.

What Makes Self-Reflection Work?

It can be hard, even intimidating to assess your own work, share personal goals with someone else, or be pressured to identify personal strengths or write about needs and weaknesses in performance. It takes time not only to get comfortable with the process, but also to develop the analytical skills needed to do it well. Given practice and encouragement, students begin to create self-reflections that exhibit these critical strengths:

- Honesty and openness.
- Insight, awareness.
- Reference to actual pieces of work that illustrate strengths and problems.
- Skill in using performance criteria to assess growth, and to show the reviewer things she or he might otherwise overlook.
- Ability to see the "whole story."
- Ability to link self-reflection to both personal goals and academic goals.

Self-reflection is the heart and soul of any portfolio. Without it, we have only a collection of work—conveniently packaged, perhaps, even telling or impressive, but lacking in that magical wholeness that signifies a portfolio story.

> Fifth grade was a good year overall. We had read-ins where all we did was read all day. Ms. Foster said you could not really get into a book and make it your own if you only read for 15 minutes at a time, so she would let us read all day. And the things we read seemed important in real life, not just because they were printed in books. Of course we did tons of math and science. We visited about a hundred wetlands and I will never think of frogs or slugs or even spiders the same way again. Fortunately, not too much bad happened that year except the War in Iraq which was bad enough and my fourth grade teacher who I had loved forever died of cancer and I cried for about three days. I will remember fifth grade as a time of growing up and learning to think of others and not just myself. (Grade 5 Student)

HOW DO YOU KNOW IF IT IS WORKING?

The first year really is a time for exploring and experimenting. But after that, there are some signs of success many teachers feel signify that all is well, and that the decision to bring portfolios onto the scene was a good one:

1. You can hear the word *portfolio* without feeling stressed.
2. You feel you are learning more about your students than you could learn without reviewing portfolios.
3. Students are learning more about themselves than they could learn without creating portfolios.
4. Students find learning exciting, engaging, and sometimes surprising.

5. Students can manage their own portfolios, with appropriate coaching.

Best of all, when you open each portfolio and read the story within, you will see the best of what you have shared reflected there, you will hear the voice of a student coming to understand and appreciate his or her own capabilities, and you will say to yourself, "I'm glad I didn't miss that."

CHAPTER

20

Epilogue: Classroom Learning, Looking Ahead

GARY D. PHYE
Iowa State University

CONSTRUCTIVIST MOVEMENT

The German word *zeitgeist* means "spirit of the times." In this respect, the constructivist movement can be viewed as a political force within the education profession. This statement in itself does little to clarify the influence of the movement in terms of classroom practices. Being an educational psychologist rather than an educational philosopher, my concerns are pragmatic. What does this mean for individual teachers in specific classroom who have the responsibility of promoting the learning of real, live students? A tentative answer to this question posed can be approached from two levels of analysis or discourse, the macro-level or the micro-level.

At the macro-level of analysis, the standards movement is an example. Within the content areas (e.g., history, English, mathematics), an attempt has been made by subject matter experts to *construct* or redefine what is meant by a subject matter domain and how it is to be taught in the classroom. In this respect, we are talking about a restructuring of the K–12 curriculum as it is loosely defined in the United States. In some instances, this has involved a redefinition of the discipline (see history as an example). A second issue that is also a part of the constructivist movement at the macro-level of analysis is the question of standards of performance by students. Here, concern is for minimal standards, defined in terms of student competency. This issue is reflected in concern for how students in large urban centers stack up against the rest of the country and how our nation as a

Handbook of Academic Learning

whole compares with the other industrial countries of the world. For the individual classroom teacher, this may mean a modification in terms of curriculum goals and objectives at the school site.

At a micro-level of analysis, the focus is on individual teachers, interacting with individual students in a specific social setting (her or his classroom). This level of analysis traditionally has been the purview of educational psychology. At this level of analysis, most of us (teacher–educators) opt for the terminology and tenets of constructivism. Constructivism with its focus on "how" individual students (within social settings) construct personal meaning and understanding, has a strong tradition in education and psychology in the United States (see Chapter 1).

There is no single school of constructivism; as recently observed, there is the good, the bad, and the ugly (Phillips, 1995). Phillips is simply reminding us that, while differences exist among schools of thought, the differences can be plotted on a continuum. Not to be overlooked, however, are the beliefs that are common to the various schools. Common perspectives include the view that academic knowledge construction on the part of students is basically a learning process that involves change. Thus, knowledge is the desired outcome or effect of the process of learning. Since change in humans is the result of either maturation or learning, academic knowledge has always been viewed as resulting from classroom learning. Finally, teaching and instruction has commonly been viewed as fostering classroom learning. The manner in which teacher–educators go about fostering academic learning are the points of contention among the various schools of constructivism.

Two points of contention that serve to locate various schools of thought on a constructivism continuum are (1) the learning situation most appropriate for constructing academic knowledge and (2) the most critical tools for engaging in the construction process. A good classroom learning situation has two easily observed attributes. The first attribute involves the physical setting. Are students working cooperatively with fellow students and also interacting with the teacher when such learning activities are appropriate? There is also the recognition that students need some time to practice on their own (individual seatwork or homework). The second attribute involves the manner in which the learning episode is structured. When appropriate, is the learning task framed as a problem-solving activity that requires the development and use of higher-order thinking skills? The second point of contention involves the critical tools for learning. Most educators agree that literacy (verbal and written communication skills) are the critical tools for classroom learning. The disagreement comes in terms of "how" the tools should be developed.

For many classroom teachers, constructivism means modification of teaching practices rather than sweeping change. The modifications will likely take the form of changing the social structure of individual classrooms with less teacher-initiated instruction and more cooperative learning opportunities. This aspect of change in the classroom is relatively easy to introduce. However, the aforementioned changes involving (1) an emphasis on structuring learning activities so that a problem situation exists and (2) the re-emphasis on literacy development will be more difficult. As teachers however, we should not be discouraged by this prospect. Implicit in the constructivism perspective is the belief "a teacher is, and always has been, the most important agent of change in the classroom." The irony for teachers is that, while we encourage students to be coteachers, we must not forget that as teachers we are also students. To foster change in others, we must change ourselves.

THE LEARNING PROCESS

"Learning is obviously basic to the educative process, and it must also be considered as a fundamental process or characteristic of mind" (Melton, 1950, p. 668). Although this quote is certainly timely, it is taken from an article that appeared in the *Encyclopedia of Educational Research* in 1950. In some respects, this is a reminder of the recursive nature of change. This becomes more apparent on reading the remainder of the article, in which Melton laments the lack of agreed-on terminology employed in referring to the learning process. This problem could be addressed, according to Melton, by more experimental and theoretical studies that would provide more detailed information about the learning process.

Given the advantage of 45 years of hindsight, one might suggest that the proliferation of learning models has exacerbated the problem of a common terminology and understanding of the classroom learning process. Rather than delve into a lengthy discussion of the strengths and weaknesses of current models of the learning process, I suggest a simple description of the learning process as a first step in the development of a shared terminology of *classroom learning*.

A major problem in the literature today is a failure to distinguish between the learning process and the product of that learning process. The *product* that we have been describing in the previous chapters is what I have called *academic knowledge*. Elements of the learning process are described and discussed by various chapter authors as they seek to help us understand how academic knowledge develops.

The problem of communication, even at the level of analysis taken by individual chapter authors, is due in part to a lack of common terminology describing the classroom learning process. A conceptualization of the learning process is dynamic rather than static and must be addressed from the perspective of the learner. Consistent with the ideas expressed in many of the previous chapters is a view of a *classroom learning process as an adaptive function with reference to the prevailing motivation of the student*. Further, the concept of a "problem situation" is seen as basic to the conception of adaptive behavior (Gibson, 1994; Mayer, see Chapter 15; Melton, 1950; Phye, see Chapter 2). In the classroom, a problem situation exists when a motivated student engages an academic task, a solution is not provided, and a ready solution cannot be automatically retrieved from memory. Lack of an automatic solution is an obstacle to successfully adapting to the academic task. Therefore, a classroom learning process might be described in the following manner. A motivated student encounters a problem situation and (1) exhibits persistent goal-oriented activity involving (2) the construction of varied domain-specific strategies and procedures that (3) result in a problem solution. On again encountering the problem situation or a similar problem situation, the student demonstrates an adequate solution.

The description of a classroom learning process in this manner has functional utility for the teacher–educator and is consistent with a perspective of constructivism. Such a definition has the following implications for pedagogical practice. The classroom teacher must be in a position to (1) influence or create motivating conditions for students (see Chapters 3 and 4), (2) take responsibility for creating problem situations (see Part II), (3) foster acquisition and retrieval of prior knowledge (see Chapters 2 and 5), and (4) create a social environment that emphasizes the attitude of learning to learn (see Part III). As teacher–educators we must understand that the learning process *not* the product of learning is the primary focus of constructivism as a pedagogical perspective.

MEETING THE AUTHORS

This handbook of academic learning was developed with the thought that it would provide a basis for enhancing communication among professionals in the educational community. In this spirit, I am using the epilogue to introduce readers to the senior authors of each chapter. These are the people in the profession that contribute to the theory and research that affects daily classroom practice. However, many of us are also involved with the development of educational activities and techniques in addition to theory. This combination of endeavors characterize the chapter authors contributing to the handbook. Consequently, they are valuable resources to draw upon for professional development activities.

Having read the previous chapters, one has probably developed an impression of individual chapter authors based on theory and research they contributed. The following is a brief resume of professional activities that also reflects the interests and efforts of contributing authors in transforming theory into effective educational practices in the classroom.

Eric Bredo is a professor in the School of Education at the University of Virginia. He received his training in the sociology of education at Stanford

University. Eric is currently teaching courses on the sociology of education and the philosophy of education. As is evident in his chapter, he is greatly enamored with the pragmatists, especially James, Dewey, and Mead. Eric suggests that this attraction is due to the level of intellectual sophistication they brought to education as well as a kind of humanity: "They wrote about lives, not systems." Eric's empirical work has focused on teaching and school organization, including the study of ways in which teaching and learning go on in very diverse educational settings (e.g., a range of public and private elementary schools). He is currently on the governing board of a small progressive school. In addition to writing numerous journal articles, book chapters, and books, Eric currently serves on the editorial boards of several journals.

Myron H. Dembo is professor of educational psychology at the University of Southern California. He is author of *Applying Educational Psychology* (5th ed.), a widely used book in teacher education and has written and presented over 75 papers and articles in the area of teacher behavior, learning, and motivation. He recently developed an applied cognitive psychology course for the "at-risk" college students and is developing workshops to help junior high and senior high students become more successful learners. He also serves as a consultant with the Los Angeles Unified School District, working with staff members to develop learning environments to enhance student motivation. Myron received his Ph.D. in educational psychology from Indiana University and a B.A. in Mathematics and an M.A. in student personnel from the State University of New York at Buffalo. He taught junior high and high school mathematics before joining the USC faculty.

Barry J. Zimmerman is professor and director of the Doctoral Program in Educational Psychology at the City University of New York (CUNY). Barry was recently elected vice president and president-elect of Division 15 (educational psychology) of the American Psychological Association. Barry has written over 100 articles and chapters on learning and motivational processes of children and youth from a social cognitive perspective. He recently coedited two textbooks on the topic of self-regulatory processes in academic learning and motivation. Barry is currently principal investigator of a NIMH grant for instructing minority families to self-regulate their children's asthma. He has also served as a consultant to the Board of Education of New York City. Barry received his Ph.D. in educational psychology from the University of Arizona.

Paul D. Nichols received his Ph.D. in educational psychology from the University of Iowa and is currently an assistant professor of educational psychology at the University of Wisconsin—Milwaukee, where he teaches courses in classroom and alternative assessment. Paul's research interests include problem solving and the combination of psychological and psychometric theory. He has worked with a number of school districts to encourage and facilitate teachers' use of assessments and improve school site assessment systems.

Michael Pressley is chairperson of the Department of Educational Psychology and Statistics, School of Education at Albany, State University of New York. Mike earned his Ph.D. in 1977 from the Institute of Child Development, University of Minnesota. He has written extensively in the areas of children's and adult memory, strategy instruction, and reading comprehension. More than 200 articles, chapters, and books of his have been published. Mike is currently a member of 10 journal boards and incoming editor of the *Journal of Educational Psychology*. He is also a consulting author for the 1995 version of Open Court's new elementary literacy series, Collections for Young Scholars. In this role he has addressed educator groups across the nation about elementary literacy instruction and frequently is an invited speaker at conferences and universities in North America and Europe. Among Mike's proudest professional accomplishments are the successful graduate students he has mentored, many of whom now hold faculty positions in psychology and education at leading universities.

James M. Royer is professor of psychology at the University of Massachusetts. He received his Ph.D. in educational psychology from the University of Illinois—Champaign. In addition to writing numerous research articles, books, and book chapters, he is currently the editor of *Contemporary Educational Psychology*. Mike is currently being funded by the U.S. Agency for International Development for the evaluation of a distance learning project that involves the delivery of math and reading lessons to schools in Haiti. He is also working with a local school system in Amherst, Massachusetts, to identify the nature of learning problems in young children and design instructional interventions to remediate the problems. This involves screening in both reading and math at grade 8 and the screening in reading capabilities in grades 1–4. Mike also directs LATAS, a university based research–service laboratory that provides diagnostic and prescriptive services to children with learning disabilities.

Stephen L. Benton received his Ph.D. from the University of Nebraska—Lincoln in 1983 and is professor of educational psychology at Kansas State University. Steve is editor of *Educational Psychology Review* and past chair of the Counseling and Educational Psychology Department at KSU. He teaches graduate and undergraduate courses in educational psychology as well as research design and statistics courses. Steve has written over 40 articles and book chapters and has made more than 30 presentations at professional conferences. He is also heavily involved with public and private school activities, having served on advisory boards or consulted with a dozen school districts in the surrounding area.

Rebecca E. Burnett earned her Ph.D in Rhetoric from Carnegie Mellon University and is currently an associate professor of rhetoric and professional communication in the department of English at Iowa State University. Rebecca spends her professional time as a teacher, researcher, writer, and consultant. She teaches undergraduate and graduate courses in rhetoric and communications. Before teaching college full time, she spent 19 years teaching secondary school English. Rebecca conducts research about the ways in which writers create documents and readers interpret those documents. Recent research efforts have focused on the ways in which collaborative teams interact as they plan and develop documents. Rebecca has written numerous research articles, authored or co-authored six books, and co-edited two others. She has presented over 100 scholarly papers and workshops at regional, national, and international meetings. Rebecca regularly works as a consultant with secondary teachers interested in restructuring their curriculum to include courses that balance reading and writing, speaking and listening, viewing and designing. These consulting workshops encourage pedagogical approaches that enable students to see communication as constructing and interpreting information, rather than simply transmitting information.

Douglas Grouws is professor of mathematics education at the University of Iowa. He began his professional career as a mathematics teacher in Eau Clair, Wisconsin. On returning to the University of Wisconsin—Madison for graduate work, he received the Ph.D. in mathematics education in 1971. He is past president of the Missouri Council of Teachers of Mathematics and a recipient of the William T. Kemper Fellowship for outstanding teaching. His research interests include mathematics teaching, teacher beliefs and conceptions, the use of technology in teaching mathematics ideas, and mathematical problem solving. Douglas is editor of the *Journal for Research in Mathematics Education* monograph series. He has written numerous articles, chapters, and three books. These publications focused on the effects of teachers' organization and presentation of lessons, with particular attention to effects on student mathematics achievement, and how teachers' conceptualize mathematical problem solving and implement their beliefs in classroom settings. Recently, Douglas has been working with middle school teachers on using technology in teaching key ideas in mathematics.

Steven R. Williams is a professor in the Mathematics Department at Brigham Young University. He graduated from BYU with B.S. and M.S. degrees in mathematics. Steve obtained the Ph.D. in curriculum and instruction from the University of Wisconsin—Madison. In addition to writing numerous articles and book chapters, Steve has been involved with several large-scale mathematics projects. While at the University of Wisconsin—Madison, he worked on documentation efforts for the Urban Collaborative Project and assisted in the implementation of a nationwide survey of how mandated testing affects instructional practices. As a faculty member at Washington State University, he headed a two-year project on communication in middle mathematics classes. He recently served for four years as a documentation consultant for the QUASAR Project. These efforts reflect his current research interests in classroom discourse, the communication of beliefs about mathematics and mathematics learning, and the social creation of mathematical knowledge. Steve reports that he is currently struggling to bring his own teaching practice in line with what he preaches.

Kenneth Tobin is professor of science education at Florida State University. Prior to arriving at Florida State, Ken taught physics, chemistry, biology, mathematics, and general science in high schools in Australia for eight years and in England for one year. For the past 22 years, he has been a science teacher–educator in Australia and the United States. Ken has written numerous articles, chapters, and books and received many awards for his research from the national Association for Research in Science Teaching and the American Educational Research Association. His recent research has involved studies of the knowledge and beliefs of teachers in the context of teaching and learning science. Two recently edited books are *Windows in Science Classrooms* and *The Practice of Constructivism in Science*. He is the series editor for Kluwer's Science and Technology Education Series.

Joel J. Mintzes earned the B.S. and M.S. degrees in biological sciences at the University of Illinois at Chicago and a Ph.D. in science education at Northwestern University. He currently is a professor of biology at the University of North Carolina at Wilmington, adjunct professor of science education at North Carolina State University, and director of research at the Private Universe Project, Harvard–Smithsonian Center for Astrophysics. His research centers on conceptual development and cognitive processes in the natural sciences, an area in which he has written many articles and chapters. He has served on several editorial boards including the *Journal of Research in Science Teaching and Science Education*. Currently, he is collaborating on a six-part television miniseries that focuses on students "alternative conceptions" of natural science. The programs will air on the PBS and BBC broadcasting networks as an effort funded by the Annenberg Foundation and the CPB Math and Science Project.

Richard E. Mayer is a professor of psychology and education at the University of California, Santa Barbara. He is past president of the Division of Educational Psychology of the American Psychological Association, former editor of the *Educational Psychologist*, and a former coeditor of *Instructional Science*. He is the author or coauthor of over 200 publications, mainly in the area of educational psychology, including 14 books such as *Educational Psychology: A Cognitive Approach* and *Thinking, Problem Solving and Cognition*. Richard is serving his fourth term as an elected member of the Board of Trustees of the Goleta Union School District, a 10-school elementary district near Santa Barbara. His current research activities include studying the role of illustrations in science textbooks, how students learn to solve word problems, and the use of animation in multimedia instruction.

David R. Olson is a professor of applied cognitive science at the Ontario Institute for Studies in Education, where he has taught since graduating from the University of Alberta (1963). He has held fellowships at Harvard's Center for Cognitive Studies, The Netherlands Institute for Advanced Studies in the

Humanities and Social Sciences, and Stanford's Center for Advanced Studies in the Behavioral Sciences. He is a fellow of the Royal Society of Canada and holds an honorary doctorate from University of Gottenberg, Sweden. His research on relations between language, literacy, and the mind has resulted in some 200 research publications, two of which have become "citation classics" and 10 authored or edited books including *Cognitive Development* (1970), *Spatial Cognition* (1980), *Literacy, Language and Learning* (1985), *Developing Theories of Mind* (1986), *Literacy and Orality* (1990), and *Scripts and Literacy* (1995). A *Handbook of Human Development and Education* (1996), and an edited book, *Modes of Thought* (1996), are currently available. His latest authored book, *The World of Paper: The Conceptual and Cognitive Implications of Writing and Reading*, was published in 1994. David is a frequent participant in international conferences and workshops, most recently at the Einstein Forum in Berlin and the Colegia de Mexico in Mexico City.

William D. Schafer is a professor in the Department of Measurement, Statistics, and Evaluation at the University of Maryland—College Park. In addition to numerous research articles, Bill has recently been editor of a book on *Assessment in Counseling and Therapy* (1995). In addition to holding office in several national associations, he has served as journal editor of *Measurement and Evaluation in Counseling and Development*. Bill is extensively involved in training and development workshops dealing with various assessment topics. Much of his consulting work has been done for local school districts in Maryland and surrounding states. As one might expect, among other teaching activities, Bill teaches a graduate course in classroom assessment at College Park.

J. H. M. Hamers is a professor in the Department of Educational Sciences at Utrecht University in the Netherlands. Johan is a university teacher in special education. He teaches courses in general learning disabilities, dyslexia, plus intelligence testing and the alternatives. As a university researcher, he has written extensively in the areas of dyslexia, dysorthographia, and learning potential. He recently coauthored a book on the assessment of learning potential and developed two tests of learning potential that have been adopted on a nationwide scale in the Netherlands.

Vicki Spandel, coauthor (with Rick Stiggens) of *Creating Writers*, is a senior research associate at the Northwest Regional Educational Laboratory in Portland, Oregon. A former language arts teacher and journalist, Vicki is author or coauthor of 17 textbooks and has been a scoring director for over 60 district, county, and state writing assessments. Vicki currently spends her time designing and presenting national training institutes for teachers on writing, writing assessment, and the use of portfolios. The research on which these institutes are based comes from many hours spent in classrooms working with students K–12. Areas of special interest include writing portfolios, student self-assessment and reflection, the teaching of revision, and the development and use of friendly criteria. During the past year, she also designed her own portfolio as part of NWREL's new procedures for employee performance review. Vicki reports that "it was a uniquely rewarding experience—but much more fatiguing and time consuming than you could ever imagine without having actually done it. If it's truly successful, it will turn out a little differently from how you'd planned it."

References

Gibson, E. J. (1994). Has psychology a future? *Psychological Science*, 5(2), 69–76.

Melton, A. W. (1950). Learning. In W. S. Monroe (Ed.), *Encyclopedia of Educational Research* (pp. 668–690). New York: Macmillan.

Phillips, D. C. (1995). The good, the bad, and the ugly: The many faces of constructivism. *Educational Researcher*, 24(7), 5–12.

Index